COMPLETE MANUAL FOR RECRUITING, HIRING, AND RETAINING QUALITY EMPLOYEES

- **Job Analysis and Descriptions**
- **Recruiting and Advertising**
- **Screening, Testing, and Interviewing**
- **Orientation and Integration**
- **Initial Training and Evaluation**

- **Personnel Policies**
- **Legal Compliance**
- **Forms and Letters**
- **Recordkeeping**

Joseph D. Levesque, SPHR

PRENTICE HALL
Englewood Cliffs, New Jersey 07632

Library of Congress Cataloging-in-Publication Data
Levesque, Joseph D.
   Complete manual for recruiting, hiring, and retaining quality
employees / Joseph D. Levesque.
      p.   cm.
   Includes bibliographical references and index.
   ISBN 0-13-573445-2 (cloth)
   1. Personnel management.   I. Title.
HF5549.L4625   1996
658.3—dc20   96-35132
                                                    CIP

"This publication is designed to provide accurate and authoritative information in regard to the subject matter covered. It is sold with the understanding that the publisher is not engaged in rendering legal, accounting, or other professional service. If legal advice or other expert assistance is required, the services of a competent professional person should be sought."

—From the Declaration of Principles jointly adopted by a Committee of the American Bar Association and a Committee of Publishers and Associations.

Printed in the United States of America

10 9 8 7 6 5 4 3 2 1

ISBN 0-13-573445-2

9 780135 734452   90000

ATTENTION: CORPORATIONS AND SCHOOLS

Prentice Hall books are available at quantity discounts with bulk purchase for educational, business, or sales promotional use. For information, please write to: Prentice Hall Career & Personal Development Special Sales, 113 Sylvan Avenue, Englewood Cliffs, NJ 07632. Please supply: title of book, ISBN number, quantity, how the book will be used, date needed.

PRENTICE HALL
Career & Personal Development
Englewood Cliffs, NJ 07632
A Simon & Schuster Company

On the World Wide Web at http://www.phdirect.com

Prentice Hall International, Inc., *London*
Prentice Hall of Australia, Pty. Ltd., *Sydney*
Prentice Hall Canada, Inc., *Toronto*
Prentice Hall of India Private Ltd., *New Delhi*
Prentice Hall of Japan, Inc., *Tokyo*
Prentice Hall of Southeast Asia Pte. Ltd., *Singapore*
Whitehall Books, Ltd., *Wellington, New Zealand*
Editora Prentice Hall do Brasil Ltda., *Rio de Janeiro*
Prentice Hall Hispanoamericana, S. A., *Mexico*

This book is dedicated to Jean Hyner without whose support and encouragement this book would have been a considerably more difficult effort, and to the memory of Paul Hyner and Tom Winn whose contributions live on through those they touched in life.

ABOUT THE AUTHOR

Joseph D. Levesque (B.A., M.A., M.P.A.) is the founder and managing director of HR & Management Systems Consultants, a human resource and organizational management consulting firm established in 1983 and now located in Sacramento, California. He is the author of such nationally sold books on human resource management as:

A Model Personnel Policies Handbook—and Employers Guide—For Smaller Businesses in California (Employment Law & Practices Institute, 1992)

The Human Resource Problem-Solver's Handbook (McGraw-Hill, 1992)

Manual of Personnel Policies, Procedures and Operations (Prentice Hall, 2nd ed. 1993)

He has authored numerous published articles on employment law, human resource management, and organizational development.

Prior to entering private practice in 1983, Mr. Levesque worked as a personnel director and management practitioner for eleven years where he was responsible for the development and operations of comprehensive human resource departments including recruitment, selection testing, policy and program design, compensation and benefits administration, information systems, performance programs, training, organizational analysis, forecasting, and labor relations. As a visiting lecturer, Mr. Levesque has also designed and taught courses and workshops at the Universities of California (Davis), Nevada (Reno), and Hawaii. As a frequently sought trainer and speaker, he has conducted numerous workshops for the California Chamber of Commerce, national business associations, in-company training programs, and for the Society for Human Resource Management.

Mr. Levesque is accredited as a Senior Professional in Human Resources (SPHR) by the Society for Human Resource Management, and spoke at the 1989 and 1991 SHRM national conventions. He served as the 1990 President of the Sacramento Human Resource Management Association and as a member of the California Human Resource Management Council from 1988 to 1992.

The author offers a unique blend of experience in a wide range of human resource management operations based on his work as a personnel director, professional consultant, university instructor, and trainer. This blend of experience has resulted in books that are practical, thorough, and best of all, usable tools to guide employers toward more effective human resource management practices.

HOW THIS MANUAL WILL HELP YOU ACHIEVE BETTER HIRING RESULTS

The Complete Manual for Recruiting, Hiring, and Retaining Quality Employees has been written for the person responsible for any or all aspects of the hiring process. It provides you with a comprehensive, concise, and easily understood approach to carrying out all hiring activities in a successive fashion, from job descriptions to initial employment training and performance monitoring. Therefore, this *Manual* represents a complete hiring *system* since it provides you with all of the steps that should be followed during each phase of the hiring process (the "how-to's"), detailed guidance and samples of job descriptions, policies, forms, job ads, testing aids, hiring letters, and training plans, and it will enable you to better understand the laws that apply to various aspects of the hiring process and learn how to comply with them and thereby avoid potential complications.

This "systems" method to the hiring process is depicted in the following flow chart. Staffing should also be viewed as a critical strategic function of your organization since the results of any hiring process reflect on the organization's mission, goals, products and/or services, and effectiveness of work results. As you can see from this chart, the hiring process begins with an initial identification of an increased demand for work output or the performance of new job functions. The next step should be the exploration of any feasible and appropriate alternatives to adding new staff to meet the demand since payroll, operating, and support costs run high for each new position, adding to organizational budgets. However, if the decision is made to add staff, the hiring process begins—in two concurrent phases. You will need to go through each of the progressive phases of the Programmatic Approach in order to classify, attract, screen, select, orient, train, and evaluate your new hire. Simultaneously, you will need to put in place all of the Administrative Approach components to ensure that your process, action and decision will be well documented, legal, and thorough.

By using this *Manual* as a complete reference and guidance source to your hiring efforts, you will be able to install a reliable, consistent, practical, and lawful process that gets the desired results—finding, hiring, and retaining quality employees. Likewise, this *Manual* is aimed at helping you avoid many of the problems and inefficiencies that often accompany hiring activities and decision making by pointing out such conditions as how to evaluate the need for new positions, how to plan an effective recruitment strategy, what recruitment sources are most beneficial, what tests should be used, what to look for when evaluating job applicants, how to properly integrate them into your organization, and much, much more. You will gain a decided advantage over your competitors for quality employees by having available to you a *Manual* that is complete in every pertinent detail concerning the hiring process, including such helpful and ready-to-use aides as

- The step-by-step procedures to develop useful job descriptions, including the forms and policies needed for improved recruitment and selection testing;
- An entire chapter on all of the personnel and employment policies you will need to support the types of decisions that accompany hiring matters;
- An Appendix (D) that provides you with all of the forms you will want to use for hiring and support documentation, including guidance on what records are needed and how to set up a practical yet simple records system;
- Numerous checklists to keep track of what needs to be done in each phase of the hiring process, and source listings that can save you hours of work trying to locate tests, advertising agencies, and other reference sources;

THE FLOW OF STRATEGIC STAFFING ACTIVITIES
*Identification of Need for Increased
Work Output/New Functions*

↓

ALTERNATIVES
- Redesign existing jobs/staff assignments
- Use overtime to distribute added work
- Use contingent workers
- Use leased or contract workers

↓

*Decision to Add Staff/
Concurrent HR Activities*

↓

| PROGRAMMATIC APPROACH | ←→ | ADMINISTRATIVE APPROACH |

↓ (each column)

Job Characteristics
- Job Requisition/Justification
- Job Analysis & ADA Conditions
- Job Description
- Classify Job & Set Compensation

Personnel Policies
- General Administration & EEO/AA
- Internal Hires & Testing
- New Hires & Records
- Conduct & Performance

↓

Recruiting & Advertising
- Designing & Placing Advertisements
- Use of Correspondence/Announcements
- Placement & Search Firms
- Use of Special Recruiting Sources

Laws & Legal Compliance
- EEO & AA
- Wage, Hour, & Work. Condit.
- Privacy Rights
- Negligence

↓

Screening & Pre-Employment Testing
- Application & Resume Screening
- Written, Performance, & Interview Tests
- Medical Examinations
- Reference, Credit, & Character Checks

Letters & Forms
- Testing Notices
- Offer of Employment
- In-Processing & Orientation
- Training & Perform. Evaluat.

↓

Hiring & Orientation
- Negotiating/Making the Offer
- Employment Letter/Agreement
- Employment Orientation
- Employment Integration

Records & HRIS
- Application/Resume
- Pre-Employment Tests
- In-Processing Documents
- Orientation Information

↓

Initial Training & Evaluation
- Initial Employment Training Plan
- Selection/Use of a Trainer
- Job Knowledge & Skills Training
- Evaluation of Initial Training & Adaptation

= SUCCESSFUL ACQUISITION,
HIRING, PLACEMENT, &
INTEGRATION

- Program approaches to setting up recruitment activities, where to put emphasis in getting the best applicants for different types of jobs, testing for different jobs, and getting background information on applicants;

- An entire chapter devoted to that most important hiring test—the personal interview—including how to set it up, what to look for, how to rate applicants, what types of questions to avoid, and how to get more reliable results by using advanced questioning techniques;

- How you should handle the final stages of hiring such as dealing with employment offers, using letters and agreements, arranging meaningful new employee orientations, integrating new employees into your organization, enhancing their productive adjustment through solid training, and monitoring their initial performance; and,

- A complete compendium of Appendix information on the laws affecting hiring activities and decisions, with suggestions on how to avoid legal pitfalls.

If your goal is to achieve better, more reliable, cost-efficient, thorough, and legally sound hiring results, then this is the book you have been waiting for, and the only one you will need.

The Complete Manual for Recruiting, Hiring, and Retaining Quality Employees should be considered a guidebook and reference source for each and every phase of the hiring process. This *Manual* starts with four chapters on the important administrative functions necessary to set up and support an effective hiring program. These chapters consist of evaluating options and alternatives to adding more staff, developing suitable job descriptions, implementing the needed policies and practices, using proper forms, and establishing a records system to satisfy both operational demands for processing information and legal recordkeeping requirements.

The second stage of hiring involves *direct* hiring activities. The following chapters will guide you through the processes of recruiting, advertising job vacancies, screening applicants, selection testing, and interviewing applicants. These chapters represent the "nuts and bolts," so to speak, of the work that needs to be accomplished in order to attract and select just the right employee for the job. However, it is important that employers—small and large alike—learn to follow the suggestions and advice contained in these chapters since countless wasted hours and many erroneous hiring decisions are often the result of cutting corners on these phases of the hiring process.

The third stage of the hiring process is the one that makes the difference between ensuring a new hire's success and leaving it to chance. These chapters contain those *indirect* but equally consequential activities of the initial employment experience that are frequently overlooked, and undervalued, in a company's approach to the hiring process. Finding and selecting people to work is only part of the solution to a company's work force problems. The true test of a company's hiring program is whether quality new hires can learn and accept all of the company's employment-related conditions, become quickly productive, acquire the particular kinds of skills and behaviors needed, be desirous of making more than a casual contribution to the organization's goals, and in other respects adapt to *all* operational conditions in an embracing way.

Therefore, these chapters deal with the types of processes necessary to professionalize your employment operations by treating new hires to a full complement of support services. The first chapter in this segment deals with making or negotiating the employment offer in a way that conveys your company's individual interest in each new employee. The next chapter tells you how to develop a worthwhile orientation and integration process for new employees, and how these two processes are different yet complementary—and vital to each employee's ability to adapt to unique conditions within your organizational setting. The last chapter provides you with information, suggestions, and guidelines on how to conduct initial employment training, and how to monitor and evaluate their results in a manner that is fitting to new employees.

The last part of the book contains a comprehensive Appendix for your easy reference. Depending on your experience, interest, and needs pertaining to hiring process matters, you're likely to find a great deal of valuable information contained in these reference sources.

Appendices A–C provide you with vital background information on the most pertinent laws concerning the hiring of employees, as well as very specific steps that can be taken to avoid the proverbial minefield of liability for unlawful acts that have cost other companies thousands of dollars. Every concerned professional responsible for any part of a company's hiring process should be intimately familiar with the contents of these appendices.

Appendix A provides information and problem-solving suggestions on each characteristic of employment discrimination, including how discrimination laws affect such hiring matters as recruitment ads, employment applications, applicant screening, testing, and interviewing. Appendix B provides the reader with detailed information about the privacy rights of applicants and employees, and how to avoid the most vulnerable hiring practices that violate these legal rights, such as testing for drugs, alcohol, and AIDS, or conducting investigative checks on new hires. Appendix C introduces the reader to one of the newest legal threats faced by employers, and that is the costly liability for negligent hiring. Here, you will learn not only about the laws and legal theories used by many courts to determine an employer's liability, but also what steps should be taken by cautious employers to lessen the potential of these very costly law suits. Finally, Appendix D provides you with all of the forms you'll need to carry out the hiring, orientation, and initial training and evaluation functions.

This *Manual* will only be as valuable as the manner in which you follow its advice, and the effort you apply to each stage of the process. It is intended to be used as a successive process so that final results are based on the totality of the hiring effort rather than achieving partial results from partial use of the book. Once you have implemented each phase of the hiring process provided for you in this *Manual*, or in your own company's way made each phase more unique to your conditions, then and only then should this book be used as a reference source to revamp separate portions of your hiring approach.

Hiring is a progressive process, so let's start by taking one step at a time—but let's keep the destination in mind each step along the journey.

CONTENTS

CHAPTER 5.   PLANNING AND SOURCING YOUR RECRUITING EFFORTS

CHAPTER 6.   SELECTING THE BEST RECRUITING METHODS AND DESIGNING ADS TO ATTRACT QUALITY APPLICANTS

CHAPTER 7.   USING PREEMPLOYMENT SELECTION TESTS TO EVALUATE APPLICANTS

CHAPTER 8.   SCREENING APPLICANTS AND CONDUCTING INTERVIEWS

12.5 How to Calculate Your Turnover Rate 296

12.6 Turnover Prevention: Some Practices to Evaluate, Monitor, and/or Implement 297

12.7 Some Final Suggestions about Retaining Quality Employees 299

APPENDIX A.   WHAT EMPLOYERS SHOULD KNOW ABOUT EMPLOYMENT
              LAWS AND HOW TO AVOID HIRING PROCESS VIOLATIONS

    A.1 Equal Employment Opportunity and Affirmative Action Laws 301

        • State and Federal Fair Employment Laws 301
            + State Fair Employment Laws 302
            + Federal Fair Employment Laws 303
        • Federal Affirmative Action Requirements 304
            + Executive Order 11246 304
            + Executive Order 11375 306
            + Executive Order 11478 306
        • Uniform Guidelines on Employee Selection Procedures 307

    A.2 Wages, Hours, and Working Conditions Laws 308

        • Fair Labor Standards Act 308
            + Who Does the Act Cover? 310
        • National Labor Relations Act 310
            + General Background 311
            + Is My Company's Industry Covered by the NLRA? 312
            + Which Employees Are Excluded from the Act? 313
        • Drug-Free Workplace Act 313
        • Workplace Health and Safety Laws 314
            + Occupational Safety and Health Act 315
        • Workers' Compensation Laws 316

    A.3 Avoiding Hiring Process Violations 317

        • Recruitment Advertisements 318
        • Employment Applications 318
        • Employment Verification Form 318
        • Job Descriptions 319
        • Written Tests 319
        • Interview Questions 319
        • Medical Evaluations 320
        • Background Evaluations 320

    A.4 Avoiding Age Discrimination Violations 321

        • What Are Age Discrimination Violations? 321
        • How to Avoid Age-Related Violations 323
            + Applicant Screening 323
            + Applicant Testing 323
            + Initial Employment Periods 324

    A.5 Avoiding Race, Color, and National Origin Violations 324

        • What Are Hiring Practice Violations? 325
            + Civil Rights Act of 1964 325
            + Immigration Reform and Control Act of 1986 326

APPENDIX C.   A NEW THREAT: EMPLOYER LIABILITY FOR NEGLIGENT HIRING

APPENDIX D.   WHAT FORMS ARE REQUIRED TO SUPPORT A SMOOTH AND ORDERLY HIRING PROCESS

1 Prehire Issues You Should Consider Before Getting Started

1.1 What's Creating Your Need to Hire?

The hiring of employees is an inevitable business transaction for employers of all sizes and types of enterprise. Yet, it is also one of the least understood and most damaging to business operations when it is mishandled. Clearly, the ability to find, select, and retain the right employees is essential to the success of any organization, and this is no less true for small employers than it is for the largest corporation. The latter merely possesses a greater ability to absorb its mistakes, but even absorption of misfits can create problems in the way of turnover of those employees who are unwilling to pick up the slack.

When we speak of the need to hire, we are usually talking about the acquisition of what we might call direct employees. Employees, regardless of their work schedules or how they're classified, are generally those individuals we put on our payrolls who obligate us to treat them in a legally correct manner, as opposed to individuals who work in our businesses under other legal arrangements that do not create an ongoing employment relationship. We can therefore have direct employees, indirect workers such as those acquired from temporary agencies or under contract conditions, or both, depending on the purpose of getting a job done and our needs concerning a particular job.

Vacancy of an Existing Job

The vacancy of an existing job is, of course, the most usual and therefore the most frequent reason to hire an employee. However, it isn't quite that simple or clear cut. There are several factors you should consider before making "replacement" hiring decisions. First and foremost among these considerations is whether or not the vacancy occurred as a result of the former employee's permanent departure from the company. If so, then you are free to proceed with your decision to acquire a replacement regardless of whether your decision is to fill the position with a direct or indirect employee. If, on the other hand, the job is vacated by an employee who intends to return to work and has the legal right to do so, then your decision is more limited. In cases where job vacancies occur by the temporary absence of a direct employee, and where such absence is either allowable by the employer's policies with return rights or these rights are inherent in applicable labor laws, then the employer may acquire a temporary replacement only for the duration of the rightful employee's absence.

1.2 Do You Really Need to Hire: Exploring the Options

Before anyone becomes immersed in the time-consuming hiring process, careful thought should be given to several options that might be available to the employer as another means of alleviating the labor shortage problem. You should understand from the beginning that there are pros and cons to nearly all employment decisions, and the hiring of full-time permanent or other kinds of workers is no exception.

Some of the Pros and Cons of Hiring Permanent Employees

Permanent employees are not only essential to the operation and success of business, but they also represent the particular mix of reliable skill and creative talent that distinguishes the market share of business by one company compared to its competitors. Therefore, a "permanent" workforce is needed to provide stability and continuity in business operations, and its retention and development is desirable if long-term goals are to be achieved. The employer with a skilled, stable, and goal-oriented workforce has a decided advantage over competitors. Therein lies the greatest problem: finding, developing, and keeping such a workforce in times when these assets are in short supply.

Permanent employees can likewise be disadvantageous to employers. There is of course the problem of constant turnover which keeps most companies routinely involved in the recruiting, hiring, and records processing function that is considered by most employers as a wasted (non-revenue-producing) cost of doing business. There are other administrative functions to be considered as well, such as processing payrolls, administering insurance and leave programs, conducting safety and training programs, processing workers' compensation and unemployment insurance claims, tracking performance, handling disciplinary matters, and a host of other situations that make up the personnel management operation for your company. Adding to this array of increasingly complex tasks are those members of the permanent workforce who see the world slightly, or vastly, differently from the views of management. These are the employees who make other employees look marvelous. They represent the poor hiring decisions, and instead of being the ones who turnover, they cause so much grief that valuable employees begin to leave.

So, permanent employees can be the salvation of energetic, growing, or highly competitive companies, or they can be some supervisor's Achilles heel. In either case, a permanent work force should make up the vast majority of employees in a business organization regardless of size or type even when their presence creates an inherent draw on human resource management functions. However, not all decisions to fill various operating needs should automatically turn to the acquisition of additional permanent employees. Here are some options you should consider before making the decision to hire, and perhaps help you find comfort in knowing you made the right decision.

Option 1: Evaluate Productivity, Work Distribution, and Overtime Among Current Employees

Employers are susceptible to both underreacting and overreacting to work force supply needs, be it new hires or replacement personnel. Business operations are a very dynamic set of conditions that require good judgment, timing, and use of resources. While increases in business activities and business growth is the desired goal of most companies, managing it is often a reactionary state that can quickly turn into impulsive decision making, crisis handling, or worse yet, avoidance—not seeing or acting on an apparent need. As this relates to a workforce supply, we sometimes underestimate the need to concurrently bring more resources to accommodate work increases and therefore stifle operations; or, we sometimes move too quickly in hiring more employees when other, more flexible options could have produced the same or better results. The trick is in knowing when and how to apply the right resources to any given set of changes in operational circumstance. These answers will only come when you evaluate both the operational situation in the short and long run, and the options available to you.

Evaluating Employee Productivity

Before unnecessarily hiring more employees, you should give at least some thought to whether your present operational group of employees is putting forth the amount and kind of productivity for which your company is already paying! If you're convinced they are, then proceed on to considering other options. If, however, you're uncertain about the amount and/or efficiency of your present employees, you should give the issue closer examination by taking these steps to see if you can find some ways of better utilizing existing staff rather than hiring more.

1. Examine the written performance appraisals on employees in the affected operations unit for the last two to three years to see if any of them received low ratings in their amount of work produced, efficient use of time, or ability to get the job done in the prescribed manner.

2. Talk to the unit supervisor and the known productive employee(s) about any ideas they have concerning ways in which productivity can be stepped up. Don't be reluctant, you may be pleasantly surprised!

3. Counsel weak or marginal performers, set specific productivity objectives, and monitor their results with routine interest to assure compliance.

4. Create a challenge among unit employees to pick up the productivity pace for a given period of time with incentives for the added work produced.

Evaluating Work Distribution

Another option that may be available to you is the potential redistribution of work assigned to existing employees. By examining whether or not the reassignment of particular tasks among present employees is a practical solution to increased work demands, you might be able to avoid the hiring of additional staff. Or, if such need remains, you may find that the position you first thought was needed is different after considering how work should be redistributed by better use of existing employee skills and strengths. Here are the steps to ascertain whether work redistribution should alter your need to hire additional staff, or change the position you initially thought was needed.

1. Write down what you believe to be the most important, difficult, and frequently performed tasks that are the basis of need for the prospective new position.

2. Write down each existing employee's name and list tasks, and the amount of time each is performed, that could and probably should be performed by lower level positions or better yet, eliminated as nonessential.

3. Make a list of the tasks or job functions that have the greatest importance, priority, difficulty, and consumption of time. Consider which job functions require the talent of which existing employees. If each of these employees is not already performing those tasks, then redistribute these assignments on paper.

4. Now ask yourself if the workload is balanced and more properly assigned to the correct employees based on their skills and abilities. If so, do you still need additional staff to get the increased work done as originally thought, and have the tasks required of the new position changed as a result of this redistribution?

Evaluating Overtime Work Assignments

While most employers cringe at the thought of paying overtime wages due to the apparent effect it has on sharply increasing payroll costs, a certain amount of well-planned overtime can be a significantly less costly means of achieving short-term, peak workload, or project demands by using existing employees rather than hiring additional staff. Not only are existing employees already trained for most of the work that is likely to occur in conjunction with increased operating needs, but they are familiar with company operations and can therefore get the job done faster and more efficiently than someone who is new to the work setting and operational conditions. New employees require a considerable amount of start up time in a variety of aspects of the employment relationship, work procedures, and coworker relations.

An equivalent cost factor is the greater payroll expense of hiring new employees as opposed to paying existing staff for overtime work. With the national average cost of employee benefits at 41 percent of base payroll, this means that employers are adding nearly time-and-one-half costs to their payroll for each new employee hired. Conversely, when existing employees are paid overtime wages, there is no additional cost for their benefits—just an additional half-time pay cost. Further, you may be providing a morale boost to existing employees by allowing them to earn additional income which can help satisfy some personal need they may have, or monetary goals being pursued.

Finally, we should not overlook the fact that overtime pay is a cost factor confined to nonexempt employees, not exempt employees. So if your need for additional staff is for a legally defined exempt position, then you may wish to take a closer look at the number of hours being worked by those exempt employees in the area of need before hiring more exempt employees. You may find that existing exempt employees should put in more hours to accommodate the increased operational workload, or that a redistribution of responsibilities upward is appropriate so that new employees can be hired at the lowest possible level in the company and thereby keep added payroll expenses at a minimum.

Option 2: Consider the Use of Contingent Workers

Contingent workers may well be the workforce lifeline for employers of all sizes and types during the coming years and beyond. What are contingent workers and why are they likely to play such an important role in the hiring and staffing functions? First, contingent workers represent a very sizeable labor supply that in the past has been viewed, and used, as necessary "seconds"—to merely augment an employer's cadre of permanent workers during their prolonged absence or urgent peak workloads. But this heretofore second-class status of replacement workers is changing rapidly due to the aging composition of the workforce and the declining number of permanent replacements.

The true impact of contingent workers began to develop in the 1980s as our more socially conscious society (workforce) made new demands on their employers for reforms in the employment relationship. Accompanying this movement were the many talented employees who decided to disengage from the traditional employment relationship and pursue options of their own. Some went into business for themselves while others changed careers, employers, went back to school, started families, retired, or merely decided to work full time but under temporary arrangements. In other words, the control over labor supply employment decisions began to shift from employers to the available market of skilled workers who were exercising their own decisions. As the Bureau of Labor Statistics reports on the 1980 to 1987 period, the number of employees working as temporaries increased by 125 percent, part-time workers by 20 percent, self-employed by 13 percent, and "business service workers" (contractors) by a whopping 55 percent. Moreover, the BLS noted that this mix of contingent workers is growing at a faster rate than the overall labor force which, by 1987, represented one-fourth of the labor force, and that one-third to one-half of all new jobs during this period went to contingent workers.

Indeed, contingent workers represent a significant option to employers who depend on a stable number of employees, and employees who offer special skills that may at times be unavailable (or inadequately available) in the permanent workforce. Contingent workers consist of skilled and available workers who, for one reason or another, choose not to engage in long-term, direct commitments to a particular employer. In essence, they place a slightly greater value on their own flexibility in deciding when, where, and for whom they will work than their regular workforce counterparts. They represent the hundreds of thousands available in the labor supply more commonly known to us as part-time, part-year (seasonal), temporary, and contract employees.

Contingent workers, as they are more favorably known, can provide a more flexible option to hiring permanent workers for employers of all sizes. In many respects contingent workers offer the flexibility employers need in the control over payroll costs, particularly among those industries vulnerable to the highs and lows of customary business cycles. This is not intended to imply that contingent workers should be used without restraint. There are some disadvantages in the use of contingent workers, and the most common of these are more personnel processing due to the higher turnover rates, less attachment to the employer's goals, policies, and teamwork, potentially higher unemployment insurance costs, and less continuity in work assignments for short-term workers. However, where contingent workers are managed as a well-designed part of a company's workforce, they can be the option that will give many employers the competitive edge in maintaining desired production levels.

Temporary Employees

More than 500,000 companies in the United States use an estimated 2.5 million temporary employees, or "temps" as they're commonly called, and most of these companies report that temps make up about 10 percent of their workforce. With a 36 percent growth rate in the brief 1992 to 1994 period, the Bureau of Labor Statistics cites temporary employees as one of the fastest growing industries of the decade.

Typically, temps are used as limited-term replacements for absent regular employees or to supplement peak workloads being experienced by regular employees. When used to absorb the highs and lows of business cycles, they can be an extremely effective resource. During the highs, they are there to take on the additional work while allowing your regular employees to handle their normal work routines. During the lows, they can be let go without the grief and disruptions that usually accompany layoffs, or some can be retained to absorb the work of regulars taking vacation or leaves.

There is a big difference between hiring temps yourself and hiring them through a temporary employment agency. If you hire them yourself, you haven't accomplished much in terms of eliminating the formal employment relationship (liability), paperwork, and additions to your legally required benefit plans. The only difference between a regular employee and a temp you hire is that the temp is on notice from the beginning that their employment is for a fixed term. Alternatively, you can acquire a temp employee by contracting with a local temporary employment agency. Temp agencies are private businesses just like yours, so they exist with varying degrees of operators who are truly knowledgeable and qualified in matters of personnel management. Therefore, great care must be exercised in your selection of an agency.

The service offered by temp agencies—not to be confused with permanent placement agencies—usually consists of a limited service personnel office. They interview applicants to acquire a resource pool of various workers, place them with contracting employers, handle the payroll and benefits administration, remove them from assignments when requested by a contracting employer, and in some cases will provide such other services to their employees as training, coaching, and counseling. In other words, these temps are employees of the temp agency, not of the employer providing the work opportunity. In exchange for this outside employment service, the company pays the temp agency a monthly amount representing the temp's prearranged wage rate and hours worked plus the agency's fee. The total cost for using temps approximates one-and-one-half to two times the hourly rate of a similar regular employee on your payroll, which is frequently a large savings given all the extra costs associated with each new employee placed on your payroll.

In selecting a temporary employment agency that is right for your company and the kinds of temp workers you would require, you should consider following these few steps.

1. Call a few of your counterparts in other, same kind or similar companies to see if they use temps. If they do, ask what jobs they are used for, what success they have had, what agency they use, and whether they would recommend the agency.

2. You can supplement this information by using the yellow page listing of temp agencies in the phone book. Jot down the names and telephone numbers of those that appeal to you in terms of providing the kinds of services you seek and their professional appearance.

3. Make appointments to meet with the owner or person in charge of the office nearest your business. This will allow you to get first-hand knowledge of their business setting and their style of doing business.

4. During your meeting, ask enough pointed questions to determine whether or not you will be comfortable with them, their staff, and their services. Consider asking questions like

   - How long have you (or this company) been in business?
   - How many people do you have working for you, and what are their qualifications?
   - How do you select your temporary employees?
   - Do you give them tests; if so, what kind?
   - Do you require your temporaries to undergo medical exams, drug/alcohol tests, or reference checks as to their attendance, performance, and honesty? (Most prior employers won't give this information.)
   - As the legal employer of these employees, what laws and regulations are you required to abide by, and what paperwork are you required to file with governmental agencies?
   - What benefits do you provide your temps? (The more benefits you provide beyond those required by law, the more you can expect to pay. On the other hand, better benefits may equate to better temps.)
   - What qualities do you look for in a temp applicant?
   - How do you deal with a temp that doesn't perform very well, is late in arriving for work, has irregular attendance, makes frequent personal phone calls, or has to be told how to do things repeatedly?
   - How many temps do you have available who possess the type of qualifications I will need? (Name the job types.)

If you're satisfied with their answers to these kinds of questions, the next thing to do is request a copy of their service brochure, list of clients, and a copy of their contract. You will want your company's legal counsel to look over and approve the contract before signing it, and your evaluation of their service capabilities would be more complete if you checked out a few of their references.

Part-Time/Part-Year Employees

This group of contingent workers, like temps, is a rapidly growing segment of the American, Canadian, and Western European workforces. Unlike temps, however, these prospective employees desire a direct employment relationship with an organization; they seek more involvement in the operations and goals of the employing company; and they desire more permanent employment features such as commensurate pay, a somewhat regular work schedule, and at least one or two fringe benefits. Now, to some of you that may sound rather demanding for mere part-time or part-year employees—after all, who do they think they are; they should be grateful for the work, right? Think again, this time with more objectivity toward the flexible use and payroll control of your company's workforce.

Where you seek the consistency and continuity of work, close and informal work relationships, and employees who work with a sense of belonging as well as attachment to the company, but you don't need or want more full-time employees, then this group of contingent workers is probably the answer to your hiring needs. Yes, it does require the customary routine of recruiting, testing, hiring, and handling all the other administrative details that direct employments necessitate. But this option offers less payroll cost than a full-time employee, and will ultimately give the company greater staffing, workflow, and work assignment flexibility in response to the ebb and flow of normal business operation cycles.

Who are these contingent workers that make up the rather consistent supply of usually skilled and enthusiastic part-time/part-year employees? The majority of them are composed of these limited availability people:

1. Previously employed women who now care for their school age children. Most tend to desire half-time to full-time work during the week with major segments of time off, such as during the summer months and holiday seasons when their children are out of school.

2. Active, and perhaps premature, retirees who possess a wealth of employment experience and refined skills. Their motivation to work is twofold: to keep busy by doing meaningful work on a limited basis, and/or to offset the decline in their income resulting from progressive inflation. Bearing in mind that retirees under Social Security have a limit on the amount of income that can be earned before their benefit income declines, they tend to prefer either part-time or part-year work to the extent their work hours for any year do not exceed the allowable earnings limit. Interestingly enough, in warmer climates they often prefer to work during the summer months in order to work in your air conditioned facility rather than pay the high expense of cooling their homes—a rather practical lot they are!

3. Full-time college students, many of whom have prior employment experience in a variety of jobs, who either want the diversion and additional experience that employment offers, and/or need the income to help support them while attending school. Their first choice is, of course, jobs that relate in some way to their educational goal and a work schedule that can flexibly coincide with changing class schedules. Therefore, they typically seek part-time work during the school year and (preferably but not necessarily) full-time during the summer months.

As you can see, these groups of people mix nicely in terms of their diversity of work experience, potential skills, motivation, and availability for different work schedules. A well-designed mix of these contingent workers would likely result in the best acquisition and use of supplemental employees, as well as a more interesting workplace.

Where job and workforce consistency are important to your company, it is highly advisable to develop a "program approach" for the hiring of part-time and/or part-year employees. Doing so will make it clear to them and your full-time employees that they are a meaningful, respected, and regular component of the company's workforce. At a minimum, your program should commit the company to providing these contingent workers adequate and regular training, regularity and advance notice of work schedules, the opportunity for pay increases and possibly promotions, and at least some limited forms of fringe benefits (even if it consists of a few days paid sick leave and vacation on an accrual basis of hours worked). Yet another program option would be to hire a pool of part-time/part-year employees, provide them thorough orientation and training, pay them at a straight *premium* hourly rate, and use them on an as-needed basis much like schools use substitute teachers.

There is one very important thing to remember about limiting the employment of part-time/part-year employees. Unless you want them to be eligible for participation in your company's pension or welfare plans, you must not allow any of them to work 1,000 or more hours in a plan year. To do so would place your company in noncompliance with the Employee Retirement and Income Security Act (ERISA). Further, you may wish to make note of the fact that your company can establish special personnel policy provisions for the employment of part-time/part-year employees, so long as their different terms and conditions of employment do not conflict with prevailing federal and state labor laws.

Contract Workers

Independent contractors are yet another contingent worker option that may be an appropriate alternative to your hiring need. Contract workers are best utilized when their exists a definable project of limited scope and duration, or where specialized skills and/or composite experience are required to get the job done with particular results, and such skills do not exist among your staff. Common examples of independent contractors are consultants, trainers, engineers and architects, computer experts, trade professionals, security companies, and janitorial services.

Although the cost can be high to retain contract workers—because in essence you're hiring a company be it one or more people—there are some real advantages. First, these workers are not on your payroll so you don't have to be concerned with the usual employment processing and ongoing personnel transactions. Second, when their work is done there are no attendant problems with their departure or out-processing and replacement. Third, the job gets done properly or you don't pay for it—wouldn't you like to have that option with your regular employees!

Because contract workers are either independently (self) employed or they are the employees of another company, your cost in retaining them to provide services to your company is likely to be higher than most other nonemployee options of getting some type of work accomplished. Not only are you having to pay for the workers' time, which may be premium rates due to their specialization, but their fee will also have to cover the cost of the workers' benefits, operating overhead, and some amount of profit. The issue thus becomes the value you place on time, specialized skills, and convenience in getting a particular job done. If you find that using an independent contract worker is right for this purpose, it is suggested you follow these few steps.

1. Prepare a written definition of the work to be accomplished with particular emphasis on the nature and scope of the project, duration, requisite skills or experience, results to be achieved (finished product), and cost.

2. This information then becomes the basis of a Request For Proposal (RFP), or Bid Specification, that you attach to a cover letter and send out to sources who provide this type of contract work. In your letter, you should specify a submission deadline and ask for a response in simple letter format unless you are dealing with a very large or complex project.

3. After receiving written responses, interview the most appealing ones, check out the references of your favorite one, and either get a copy of their contract or have one prepared by your legal counsel. Legal review of the contractual relationship is important since you want assurances that your company will not be held liable in any way for acts or events relating to the contract worker. In other words, that this is *not* an employment relationship.

4. Determine who in your company will oversee the contractor's work and approve payments, and assign that person to the project. Make sure this person understands that they are dealing with a contractor, not an employee, therefore their responsibility is limited to seeing that the job gets done, not how it gets done or otherwise exercising the customary supervision of an employee.

5. If you find disapproval with any part of the contractor's work during the project, get the problem corrected through the worker's superiors or, if self-employed, you can terminate the contract if need be.

As a final word of caution if you decide to enter into a contractual agreement with an independent contractor to provide one or more workers for your company, be sure that you have taken proper steps to avoid the "borrowed servant" rule of law or violation of the IRS 20–rules for determining if the contractor is really an *employee* (see below). That is, you may incur legal or payable liability for various damages caused by an independent contractor worker if such worker is treated like your employee in the course of performing work for your company. Therefore, you should carefully consider the following rules when you intend to use a contract worker.

1. **Instructions.** One who is required to comply with others' instructions about when, where, and how to work is ordinarily an employee.

2. **Training.** Training a worker by requiring an experienced employee to work with him, by requiring him to attend meetings, or by using other methods, indicates that the employer wants the services performed in a particular way.

3. **Integration.** Integration of the worker's services into the business operations generally shows that the worker is subject to direction and control.

4. **Personal services.** If the services must be rendered personally, presumably the employer is interested in the methods used to accomplish the work as well as in the results.

5. **Hiring, supervising, and paying assistants.** If the employer hires, supervises, and pays assistants, that factor generally shows control over the worker on the job. However, the following indicates independent contractor status: One person hires, supervises, and pays the other assistants according to a contract under which the worker agrees to provide materials and labor and under which the worker is responsible only for the attainment of a result.

*6. **Continuing relationship.** A continuing relationship between the worker and the employer indicates that the person is an employee. A continuing relationship may exist where work is performed at frequently recurring, although irregular, intervals.

*7. **Set hours of work.** The establishment of set hours of work by the employer indicates control.

*8. **Full time required.** If the person must devote substantially full time to the employer's business, then it has control over the amount of time the worker spends working and impliedly restricts the worker from doing other gainful work. An independent contractor, on the other hand, is free to work when and for whom he chooses.

*9. **Doing work on the employer's premises.** If the work is performed on the employer's premises, that factor suggests control over the worker, especially if the work could be done elsewhere. Work done off the employer's premises by a contract person is less likely to be considered within the employer's control.

* These factors are the most crucial.

10. **Set order or sequence.** If a person must perform services in the order or sequence set by the employer, that factor shows that the person is not free to follow his own pattern of work but must follow the established routines and schedules of the employer. Often, because of the nature of an occupation, the employer does not set the order of the services or sets the order infrequently. It is sufficient to show control, however, if the employer retains the right to do so.

11. **Reports.** A requirement that the worker submit regular oral or written reports to the employer indicates a degree of control.

12. **Method of paying wages.** Payment by the hour, week, or month generally points to an employer-employee relationship, provided that this method of payment is not just a convenient way of paying a lump sum agreed upon as the cost of a job. Payment made by the job or on a straight commission generally indicates that the worker is an independent contractor.

*13. **Payment of expenses.** If the employer ordinarily pays the worker's business and/or travel expenses, the worker is ordinarily an employee. An employer, to be able to control expenses, generally retains the right to regulate and direct the worker's business activities.

*14. **Furnishing tools and materials.** The fact that the employer furnishes significant tools, materials, and other equipment tends to show the existence of an employer/employee relationship.

*15. **Significant investment.** If the individual invests in facilities that he uses to perform services and that are not typically maintained by employees (such as having one's own office), that factor tends to indicate that the person is an independent contractor. On the other hand, lack of investment in facilities indicates dependence on the employer and that the person is an employee. The IRS will give special scrutiny to certain types of facilities, such as home offices.

*16. **Realization of profit or loss.** One who can make a profit or suffer a loss as a result of his work (aside from profit or loss ordinarily incurred by employees) is generally an independent contractor. The person who does not make or lose money as a result of his efforts, however, is an employee. For example, if the person is subject to a real risk of economic loss as a consequence of significant investments or a bona fide liability for expenses such as salary payments to unrelated employees, that factor indicates independent contractor status. The risk that a person will not be paid for his services, however, is common to both independent contractors and employees and thus does not constitute a sufficient economic risk to support treatment as an independent contractor.

*17. **Working for more than one firm at a time.** If a person performs more than *de minimis* services for a multiple of unrelated persons or firms at the same time, that factor generally indicates that he is an independent contractor. However, a person who performs services for more than one person may be an employee of each of them, especially where they are part of the same service arrangement.

*18. **Making services available to the general public.** The fact that a person makes his services available to the general public on a regular and consistent basis indicates an independent contractor relationship.

19. **Right to discharge.** The right to discharge a worker is a factor indicating that the worker is an employee and the person possessing the right is an employer. An employer exercises control through the threat of dismissal, which causes the worker to obey the employer's instructions. An independent contractor, on the other hand, cannot be fired so long as he produces a result that meets the contract specifications.

*These factors are the most crucial.

20. Right to terminate. If the worker has the right to end his relationship with the employer at any time he wishes without incurring liability, that factor indicates an employer-employee relationship.

In considering the borrowed servant liability issue, the courts will usually note that these questions carry varying degrees of weight and that liability is not normally determined on a singular question (*Alday v. Patterson Truck Line, Inc.*, 5th Cir., 1985; and *Hebron v. Union Oil Company of California*, 5th Cir., 1981). It is further advisable to ensure that your contract with the independent contractor spells out the fact that the contractor shall possess liability over its own employees used in performance of the contract work, and then make sure your company abides by the terms of the contract clause. Here is an example of such a contract clause.

> It is agreed and understood that any work requested by COMPANY and agreed to be performed by CONTRACTOR shall be performed under the terms of this agreement and that CONTRACTOR shall be and is an independent contractor, COMPANY being interested only in the results obtained, and having the general right of inspection and supervision in order to secure the satisfactory completion of any such work. Under no circumstances shall an employee of CONTRACTOR be deemed an employee of COMPANY; neither shall CONTRACTOR act as an agent or employee of COMPANY.
>
> Any person who is on CONTRACTOR'S payroll and receives, has received or is entitled to receive payment from CONTRACTOR in connection with any work performed or to be performed hereunder shall be the employee of CONTRACTOR even though COMPANY reimburses CONTRACTOR for the amount paid such employee.
>
> CONTRACTOR shall furnish at its own expense and risk all labor, materials, equipment, tools, transportation and other items necessary in the performance of the work or services covered hereby, except such of said items as COMPANY specifically agrees in writing to furnish.

Option 3: Employee Leasing as a Hiring Alternative

Employee leasing became a fashionable new industry, an option to obtain employees for very small businesses, in 1982 with the passage of the Tax Equity and Fiscal Responsibility Act (TEFRA). Among other effects, TEFRA established certain Internal Revenue Services (IRS) codes that allow a company to deduct various payroll-related payments made to a leasing firm that provides the company with its employees. For example, Section 414(n) of the IRS code requires companies that use the services of leasing firms to cover employees under the company's pension, welfare, and insurance benefit plans. Leased employees are defined under this section as workers who are not employees of the contracting company, but whose work for the company satisfies these three conditions:

1. The leased employee's services are provided to the contracting company pursuant to a written agreement between the company and the leasing firm.
2. The leased employee has previously worked for the company on a full-time basis (at least 1500 hours per year) for a minimum of one year.
3. The work that will be performed by the leased employee is the kind typically performed in the company's business.

In essence, employee leasing would require you to fire your employees then have them hired by the leasing firm under contract with your company to provide workers. However, for purposes of qualified pension and insurance benefit plans, you must treat leased employees like your own while all other aspects of the legal employment relationship and liability are that of the leasing firm. This is no doubt why the target market of employee leasing firms are the 4.4 million very small (under 35 employees) businesses in the United States.

The potential advantage in considering the use of leased employees for very small companies is the avoidance or elimination of dealing with such personnel matters as hiring, payroll and legally required benefits administration, processing the customary personnel transactions, and general management of the personnel function. A more hazy area of liability for both the employing company and leasing firm is in cases where employees are (were) unionized, and how the continuing relationship with the union is maintained. Clearly, the statutes that established the legality of leasing employees did not intend to provide employers the opportunity to nullify their union-affiliated obligations by passing their employees on to another employer under leaseback arrangements. In fact, both the former employer and leasing firm can be held accountable for unfair labor practices against unionized employees as defined under Section 8(a)(s) of the National Labor Relations Act.

Despite these apparent obstacles and limitations, by 1988 there were 275 such leasing firms in the United States employing some 75,000 employees. Largely as a result of the legal complexities, staffing requirements, and general administrative tasks associated with the internal operation of a personnel management program, some sources are speculating that leasing firms may well employ about 10 million workers by the year 2000. Those sources have perhaps underestimated the value most employers, even very small ones, place on internal control and the benefit of guiding your own destiny! However, if this option appeals to you and conditions within your company, by all means you should investigate whether it is right for you as an alternative to hiring and maintaining your own cadre of employees. In approaching this arrangement, you should consider taking these steps:

1. Locate as many leasing firms in reasonable proximity to your business location as possible and arrange a meeting with the owner/manager and the service representative who would handle your account.

2. Get a detailed listing of the services they offer and make sure it includes the services that comply with law and relieve you of the majority of administrative details.

3. Find out how long the firm has been in business, what the reputation of the firm is, and the credentials of its owner/manager and all staff.

4. Acquire and check out *all* of their client references.

5. Find out what the client load (number of employees) is for each of their service representatives, and ask to interview the representative who would be assigned to your account. Conduct a very thorough interview with this person to ascertain the depth of their knowledge and breadth of their personnel management skills.

6. Determine what knowledge, or better yet, experience they have with your industry, special laws, unique employment conditions, and handling union or employee relations matters.

7. Find out how they handle such matters as workplace safety (OSHA compliance), equal employment opportunity, affirmative action recruitment, workers' compensation and unemployment insurance claims, and other legal aspects of employment in your business.

8. How frequently will the service representative meet with the company representative, what is their response time to inquiries and requests, and how frequently will they produce service reports? (quarterly is standard)

9. What is their service fee? (5 to 10 percent of the leased employee payroll is standard)

Naturally, you will want to obtain legal counsel approval of a contract with the leasing firm, and this contract should be airtight concerning the limited nature of your company's legal liability related to the employment of leased employees.

2 How to Develop and Use Job Descriptions to Achieve Quality Hiring Results

There are some well established reasons why companies fail to get the results they want and need from the process of hiring new employees. One reason is the failure to provide adequate time, effort, and funds to develop a proper hiring program. Another major shortcoming of many companies, small and large, is that employers tend to overlook the importance of developing thorough job descriptions as the first component of a well organized hiring program. Job descriptions should be designed to serve as the catalyst to numerous human resource management, operational, and organizational activities. The first and most important of these activities is the hiring process—the selection of one particular person to fit your company's needs in each of its jobs.

Some of the fundamental functions of the hiring process are the use of various recruiting tools, screening applicants, developing and conducting preemployment tests, performing background investigations, making employment offers, deciding pay and benefit entitlements, preparing new employee orientations, processing new hires into the company, ensuring that they are adequately trained, and evaluating their ability to adapt properly during the probationary period. *Each of these functions relies on the accuracy, thoroughness, and depth of job descriptions.* Without a quality job description, you have no road map to chart your course. Moreover, in the absence of a quality job description, your company remains vulnerable to allegations of discrimination, arbitrary decision making in employment matters, and outright violations of statutory and regulatory labor laws. However, for the purposes of putting quality into your hiring and subsequent employment programs, it is of little value to merely throw something together that looks like a job description—that's precisely why they have failed to serve each of the hiring functions as a quality tool in the past.

2.1 Quality Job Descriptions Begin with Reliable Job Analysis

If job descriptions are to be developed properly, they must rely on meaningful job analysis. Job analysis that gathers and organizes thorough information about each job in a company's employ has many important purposes. Fundamentally, this job content information is used for developing precise job descriptions, determining rates of pay, establishing selection testing elements, and identifying job valid performance appraisal dimensions. Thorough job analysis also serves important operational purposes such as educating employees about the company's expectations concerning their job content, skills needed for job performance and promotions, training necessary to maintain high levels of performance, and the nature of supervision in differing job assignments. Given the importance of those purposes, it should be apparent that the need exists for every employer to place emphasis on using proper job analysis methods to gather job content information.

Job Analysis Definitions

To understand the process of analyzing and classifying job information, you should first become familiar with a few terms that will help you distinguish the relationship of these activities.

Job Analysis: through the use of one or more designed methods, job analysis involves the activity of gathering, organizing, and analyzing information about what people do in the performance of work and their associated work requirements.

Job Description: a written document that captures the essential definition of a particular job by describing the most pertinent duties, responsibilities, authorities, performance conditions, and employment requirements.

Job Evaluation: through the use of a designed method, job evaluation is the process of identifying particular job content factors within each separate job that have differential (weighted) compensable value to the company. This process enables the setting of wage scales for all jobs.

Job Classification: the distribution (listing) of jobs into salary and occupational groupings in order to establish a sequential, equitable, and meaningful ordering of jobs within the company.

Job Reclassification: the change in a job's title, content, and/or wage assignment that results from a significant change in the job's duties or required skills brought about by operational need, technological changes, or staffing restructures.

Position Control: a listing of all job titles, specific positions, and incumbents (employee names) that have been authorized by the company's budget as staffing, and by which vacancies, promotions, prolonged leaves, and other status of positions can be controlled.

Position Requisition: a form used in conjunction with position control to document and authorize the filling of position vacancies, and to provide written justification for new or reclassified positions.

Job Analysis Methods

The designed method of job analysis to be used by a company depends on how the information is to be used. Each method has slightly differing values for applications related to preparing job descriptions, setting wage scales, and identifying performance dimensions. The most frequently used methods are

1. *Functional Job Analysis* collects detailed *task* statements and rates them on the basis of functions related to the way a worker interacts with data, people, and things, including the time spent in each task area. Each task is analyzed and rated to determine the skills needed to perform the task. The method provides information about both the nature of work and the worker traits needed for successful performance of the job.

2. *Skills Inventory Analysis* uses subject matter experts such as the supervisor, employee, and others to compile a set of the more important job tasks within a particular job, and then to prepare a list of associated skills, knowledge, and abilities (SKAs) necessary for successful performance of each task statement. This method also identifies work and worker information.

3. *Position Analysis Questionnaire* uses 194 predetermined, standardized work activities applicable to numerous jobs. The results are scored by computer based on each job's profile of job dimension information.

4. *Critical Incident Analysis* uses subject matter experts to identify those tasks and behavioral traits of workers that are critical to either successful or unsuccessful performance of the job. These statements are then compiled into organized job dimension statements (that is, major realms of job responsibilities) that describe the more critical activities of work and associated work behaviors.

5. *Job Element Analysis* provides information mostly about workers since this method uses incumbent employees to identify the skills, knowledge, abilities, and personal traits necessary to perform specified job activities. Each job element is rated by the employee using four scales to identify its level of importance. The ratings are used to determine minimum entry qualifications as opposed to those that can be acquired through training new employees.

6. *Structured Interview of Job Incumbent* is a method often used to informally gather standardized information about each employee's job content, or to verify and supplement information gathered in connection with one of the more formal methods mentioned above. It has the advantage of directly involving employees who are performing actual job activities, and it provides the analyst an opportunity to obtain clarifying information that may otherwise be overlooked about some important aspects of the job.

7. *Observational Note Taking* is another method used by analysts to gather information about work activities and worker traits. Here, the analyst goes to the job site to observe incumbent employees during the performance of their work, and takes notes that describe both the nature of work activities being performed and the characteristics of workers who perform the job well. On site observation may also be an important step for the analyst to take in order to better understand what is necessary to carry out a particular kind of work that is unfamiliar to the analyst.

There are, of course, other methods of conducting formal and informal job analyses, but these represent the more prominent ones used to obtain work content and worker characteristics information. The method that has been selected and provided for your use in this book is a combination method based on the need to gather information that can be used for multiple purposes. The process described later in this section uses a custom designed combination of the first six methods, and the corresponding forms have been provided for you in Appendix D.

Job Analysis Weaknesses Requiring Correction

Over the course of time during which job analysis methods have been developed and refined, there have emerged certain weaknesses which stem from improper method, poor process design, and a lack of technical skills needed to accomplish the effort in a truly meaningful way. You should be aware of these shortcomings so that they can be corrected before undertaking serious job analysis. The eight most common weaknesses in the use of job analysis methods are

1. Not involving incumbent employees directly in the identification and writing of work content and worker characteristics statements, and not providing them proper training to do so.

2. Gathering and attempting to use information about a job that is insufficient in detail, unclear, inaccurate or inappropriate, and sometimes redundant.

3. Not allowing sufficient on-the-job time for participants to dedicate to the effort (for example, thinking about their job activities, how to describe them, how to prioritize them, getting in touch with associated skills, knowledge, and the like).

4. Using only one informational source to gather job analysis information, and then writing the job description.

5. Using a poorly designed job analysis method, process, or form (format of information) to gather work content information, making analysis difficult to impossible.

6. Using poorly trained and/or inexperienced job analysts to do the work or handle the project.

7. Trying to perform job analysis without making it a part of an entire job classification system that includes updating job descriptions, reclassifications, new classifications, and position control.

8. Lacking upper management support and adequate funding as either a project or ongoing administrative activity essential to quality human resource decision making.

If these weaknesses can be overcome in the early stages of a job analysis effort, the process will operate much more smoothly and results are more likely to be seen by others as useful and practical.

2.2 The Formal Job Analysis Process

Formal job analysis begins with selecting a suitable method, corresponding forms, assigning staff (analysts) to work on the effort, establishing work schedules, organizing all participants, obtaining the support and cooperation of management, and allocating sufficient funds and time to get the work done properly. The method that has been prepared for your use in this book, and the procedures that follow, takes care of the first two items mentioned. If you feel comfortable with your own analytical skills, you can act as the job analyst/project leader and, using other staff resources as defined in the following process, you can accomplish the effort alone. Better yet, try to obtain the assistance of another administrative person to help with the compiling and typing of information received from incumbent employees. This will make the process faster and easier.

Step 1

First, make a list of the jobs to be analyzed. Next to each job title, list the name of each incumbent employee who is to participate in the job analysis. If there is only one employee who occupies a job title (referred to as a single position class), every such employee should be included. Where you have several employees occupying different positions under the same job title, select a small but representative group of these employees (who are also your better performers) to participate as a sample group.

This list will tell you how many jobs are to be analyzed and how many incumbent employees should participate. Next, get management approval to use these employees as participants in the job analysis effort, and give advance notice to participating employees and their immediate supervisors as mentioned in Step 2.

Now, locate the first set of job analysis forms in Appendix D and either photocopy a sufficient number of them for use by each participating employee whose position is being analyzed, or modify the contents of the form to meet the unique conditions of jobs in your organization.

Step 2

Plan a work schedule for the entire job analysis effort, then meet with the supervisors of participating employees to go over it with them. Make any necessary modifications to the schedule, but keep the effort moving steadily toward a timely completion. Your schedule should include such milestone dates as this sample illustrates:

Sample Job Analysis Work Schedule

March 12	Distribute memo to participating employees and supervisors informing them of the job description project, the importance of their participation, and the project schedule.
March 26	Distribute Job Analysis Questionnaire and Supervisor's Review forms to participating employees.
April 1	Conduct training session for participating employees and supervisors on how to complete the forms, and give them initial assistance in filling them out properly—writing thorough task and other job content statements.
April 15	Job Analysis Questionnaires should be completed by participating employees and submitted to their supervisors for review.
April 22	Supervisor's Review forms should be completed and all forms returned to the Human Resources Department (or reviewed by division managers before return to Human Resources).
April 27–30	Conduct job analysis interviews of participating incumbent employees.
June 6	Preliminary draft job descriptions prepared by Human Resources staff and distributed to all job incumbents and affected supervisors for review and final comment.
June 20	Comments on preliminary draft job descriptions due in Human Resources.
July 14	Final draft job descriptions prepared by Human Resources and distributed to affected employees, supervisors, managers, and files.

Your schedule may have to be modified further if the project includes such additional efforts as gathering external salary data and performing job evaluation work, or designing a new performance appraisal method in conjunction with the job analysis project. In any event, it is imperative to develop a working schedule in advance, get agreement from those who will play an important role in the process, and keep everyone informed of the time expectations and their commitments to its completion.

Step 3

Review the Job Analysis Questionnaire in Appendix D completely so that you are familiar with the contents of each page before conducting training sessions for your participating employees and supervisors. The form is designed to be self-instructive, but it is best to provide a three-hour session for up to twenty people per session. Group together those employees who occupy the same job title where possible so they can collaborate during the training. The training should cover

1. Why it is important to have them help in the preparation of job analysis information, and how this information will be used.

2. The importance of providing thorough detail and accurate descriptive information about their jobs so quality job descriptions can be developed (and perhaps more equitable wage rates and performance dimensions established).

3. The process and schedule that will be used to complete the project, including the fact that they will have an opportunity to review the preliminary draft job description and receive a copy of the final version.

4. A step-by-step instructional demonstration of how to complete the Job Analysis Questionnaire—and for supervisors, how to complete the Supervisor's Review form. Also, let them know that you will stop after each section of the form to give them a little time to complete a small amount of each section so they will better understand how to do it when working on it alone later.

To enhance the learning experience, you should have a writing easel available to jot down examples of major *job domains* and *sample task statements* as employees begin to ask for your help in identifying these characteristics about their jobs. Also, it's helpful to have a sample form partially completed in each section for illustrative use on an overhead projector (transparency copies). In this way, you can explain and show each page of the form and how it is to be completed. A partially completed sample form has been provided with the step-by-step instructions that follow.

Step 4

Begin explaining the form by identifying each item and allowing a little time for participants to fill it out. As they work on each section, walk around and check their work to ensure that they are writing the type of information needed—particularly when they begin writing task statements (Domains A through H). Follow this procedure (see sample):

GENERAL INFORMATION	
Name: **Robert Wingate**	Position Title: **Telephone Installer**
Work Unit (Dept./Divis.) **Plant Installation**	Work Location: **St. Louis/So.**
Supervisor's Name: **Paul Garrett**	Title: **Supervising Crew Chief**
Time in Present Job: **3 yrs., 4 mos.**	In Occupation: **Same**
SUPERVISION: Routine supervisory activities performed on a regular basis:	
❑ Interviews/Hiring recommendations ❑ Pay increase recommendations ❑ Disciplinary recommendations ❑ Termination recommendations	❑ Assigning and reviewing work ❑ Coaching and counseling ❑ Training subordinate employees ❑ Evaluating employee performance

EMPLOYEES YOU SUPERVISE: D=Directly   I=Indirectly

Name	Title	D or I
_____	_____	____
_____	_____	____
_____	_____	____
_____	_____	____
_____	_____	____

General Information: Identify each item in the top section and allow them time to fill in the information.

    If any of them perform in a supervisory capacity, ask them to place a check mark next to any of the designated functions they perform as a matter of routine responsibilities assigned to their job. They should then write in the names and job titles of any employees they supervise directly or indirectly (that is, through subordinate supervisors).

Major Domains of Job Responsibilities: Read the instructions and examples at the top of the page to the group, and give them a few minutes to think about (and jot on scratch paper) how their job would be divided into four to eight major domains. You will probably need to give additional illustrations after they have had a chance to think about their job in this manner, and the best illustrations are those you can identify from among the group present. You might wish to select the job of a participant who seems to be struggling with the concept of breaking the job into major domains, and use the group for a moment to identify that person's domains. The exercise will help others see domains in their own jobs.

MAJOR DOMAINS OF JOB RESPONSIBILITIES

List below the four (4) to eight (8) major domains of your job. Domains are the general areas in which you have major and significant duties, responsibilities, authorities, and which are carried out by performing a variety of specific tasks. Examples of domains are:

Processing Billing/Insurance Data   Filing
Repairing Electrical Tools   Scheduling Conferences
Preparing Technical Reports   Building Finished Cabinets
Designing & Teaching Training Programs

	Percentage Weight
DOMAIN A: **Install Residential Telephone Service**	60
DOMAIN B: **Maintenance Service—Residential**	10
DOMAIN C: **Residential & Light Comm'l. Repair Service**	20
DOMAIN D: **Vehicle Stock & Inventory**	5
DOMAIN E: **Training & Staff Meetings**	5
DOMAIN F:	
DOMAIN G:	
DOMAIN H:	
Total:	100%

    All domains should be identified before moving on to subsequent sections. Once participants have identified all pertinent domains representing the entirety of their jobs, give them about 10 minutes to assign a percentage weight to each domain, rounded to the nearest 5 percent. The weight assigned to each domain should represent the participant's general impression of the combined factors of time, importance, and difficulty, and the total weight of all domains should always equal 100 percent.

Writing Task Statements: You should emphasize the need to begin each task statement with an active verb that clarifies what activity the employee is engaged in. Also, give participants examples of some task statements that apply to their jobs, and show how such statements describe three things about the activity: the details of *what* is being done during the performance of the task; *how* the task should be performed; and what *results* should be expected.

Using these three task statement elements, the first example on the form "Writing Task Statements" in Appendix D would be restated something similar to, "Receive, open, time stamp, and route incoming mail in a timely and accurate manner to ensure that recipients receive correspondence within one hour of its arrival."

Domains A–E (see samples): Starting with Domain A, ask participants to begin writing task statements. Allow 30 minutes for them to write three or four statements, and use this time to walk around to give assistance where needed. Also, tell them to disregard the four rating blocks for the time being.

Rating Task Statements: After completing a few task statements, tell the participants to turn to "Rating Task Statements" and to follow your reading of the instructions. Then, give them 15 minutes to go back to Domain A to enter the scales in the blocks. Let them know that when they're working on the form alone, they are to follow these same procedures—to finish all Domains and related task statements before entering the scales.

Minimum Requirements and Physical Characteristics: By reading the instructions and showing an illustration to participants, the information needed from these pages can be conveyed easily and quickly. However, you should emphasize to participants that the information they provide is that required for *minimal* qualifications of the job, not what they personally possess. Likewise, participants should be encouraged to write thorough statements concerning the knowledge and skills necessary for successful performance—these are important elements needed to construct and validate preemployment tests.

Physical Characteristics and Other Performance Characteristics: Read the instructions and show an illustration to participants concerning Physical Characteristics and Other Performance Characteristics. The questions are reasonably self-explanatory, so after reviewing them briefly, ask if participants have any questions.

Before releasing nonsupervisory participants from the training session, you should restate the time schedule to complete the form, and ask if they have questions concerning any part of the form or process.

DOMAIN A: Install Residential Telephone Service   **WEIGHT:** 60 %

Provide task statements that are descriptive of what and how significant duties and responsibilities are performed when work is done effectively and efficiently.

	R/L	F	I	D
1. Evaluate work order to determine materials needed for daily installation workload, complexity of jobs, sequencing and priority of work orders, and special instructions.	L	5	3	2
2. Confer with supervisor and coworkers on operational directives, special problems, hazards, and coworkers needing assistance on particular jobs and/or work projects.	L	5	3	2
3. Stock vehicle with required supplies and materials, travel to various job sites throughout district, check area terminals to ensure presence of "hot" lines for active job orders.	L	5	4	3
4. Connect telephone circuit to dwelling protection device, install telephone instrument, and verify line number and quality of transmission.	L	5	5	2
5. Install "drop" and/or dwelling cable when install is not prewired, where such cabling is damaged, or where extension phone locations necessitate external wiring to primary line.	L	4	3	3
6. Determine source and type of line problems, call to receive new line assignments and test for quality, and determine/correct instrument problems when discovered.	L	4	4	4
7. Drive equipped van several miles in varying types of inclement weather (heat, cold, rain, ice, and snow); park and maneuver van in congested traffic; and follow safe driving procedures.	L	5	5	3
8.				

DOMAIN B: Residential Maintenance Service   **WEIGHT:** __10__ %

Provide task statements that are descriptive of what and how significant duties and responsibilities are performed when work is done effectively and efficiently.

	R/L	F	I	D
1. **Conduct field tests at area terminals using Ohm meter to determine quality of active line transmission.**	L	3	2	2
2. **Request new line assignments where active lines show test problems such as "shorts," "grounds," or "crosses." Transfer troubled lines to new assignments, and prepare construction repair order.**	L	3	3	2
3. **Clean area terminals of external debris and internal dust, moisture, or other foreign objects.**	L	3	3	2
4. **Review Maintenance Service Orders to determine the need for repair/replacement of working but damaged drop lines, terminal covers, protective devices, and loose wiring.**	L	2	2	2
5. **Perform field repairs and/or replacements based on the priority of existing Maintenance Service Orders.**	L	3	3	3
6.				
7.				
8.				

DOMAIN C: <u>Resident. and Lt. Comm'l. Repair Service</u>   **WEIGHT:** __20__ %

Provide task statements that are descriptive of what and how significant duties and responsibilities are performed when work is done effectively and efficiently.

	R/L	F	I	D
1. **As assigned routinely or periodically, perform troubleshooting tests on repair service orders, determine type and origin of line transmission problem, repair or replace same.**	L	3	4	3
2. **Use test set, Ohm meter, and other test devices to determine nature of line or "house" cabling trouble.**	L	5	4	3
3. **Repair or replace drop and/or dwelling cables as necessary, including protective devices and telephone instruments.**	L	2	4	3
4. **Periodically required to climb telephone poles (stepped or with "hooks"), use extension ladder to access cable terminals, and crawl into confined spaces such as attics and subflooring.**	L	3	4	4
5.				
6.				
7.				
8.				

DOMAIN D: Vehicle Stock and Inventory   **WEIGHT:** __5__ %

Provide task statements that are descriptive of what and how significant duties and responsibilities are performed when work is done effectively and efficiently.

	R/L	F	I	D
1. **Check vehicle inventory to ensure adequate stock of supplies/materials; requisition needed supplies and acquire from stock; and arrange vehicle inventory in neat, orderly, and safe manner.**	L	5	3	2
2. **Complete inventory reports on supplies requisitioned in vehicle stock, and used on job orders. Submit reports to Supplies Supervisor.**	L	3	2	2
3.				
4.				
5.				
6.				
7.				
8.				

DOMAIN E: Training, Meetings, and Safety _____   **WEIGHT:** ___5___ %

Provide task statements that are descriptive of what and how significant duties and responsibilities are performed when work is done effectively and efficiently.

	R/L	F	I	D
1. **Attend, learn, and maintain increasingly more complex knowledge of telephonics circuitry, electrical systems, and installation/repair methods.**	R	1	4	3
2. **Attend work unit meetings and participate in discussions, identification of operational problems, and methods of resolution.**	R	4	3	2
3. **Attend, participate, and learn new information and skills in training sessions on a variety of work-related subjects.**	R	2	3	3
4. **Carefully inspect assigned vehicle for existing or potential hazardous conditions; abate vehicle hazards before use; and park/operate vehicle using proper safety procedures.**	L	5	5	2
5. **Keep tools, equipment, and materials in safe operating condition; use proper safety precautions when climbing, crawling, and otherwise working to install/repair residential service.**	L	4	5	3
6.				
7.				
8.				

Step 5

MINIMUM REQUIREMENTS

In order to successfully perform the position you occupy, what entry-level skills, knowledge, and abilities must a minimally qualified person possess? NOTE: Also indicate any courses, training programs, and previous experience that have been particularly important to the successful performance of your position.

Education: What do you feel is the minimal level of formal education, or its equivalent, to perform your job satisfactorily?

- ❑ No formal education required
- ❑ Eighth grade education
- ❑ High school diploma
- ☑ 2-year college degree (or equivalent)
- ❑ 4-year college degree (or equivalent)
- ❑ Graduate work and/or advanced degree (specify):
- ❑ Professional license (specify): _____

Experience:

Amount

- ❑ None
- ❑ Less than 6 months
- ☑ 6 months to one year
- ❑ 2–4 years
- ❑ 5–7 years
- ❑ 8–10 years
- ❑ 10+ years

Kind: **Employment where basic mechanical skills and abilities were learned and performed with proficiency such as use of hand tools and small electrical tools**

Skills/Abilities: State the skills and abilities needed to adequately perform the more essential aspects of your work. Example: type accurately at 60 wpm; ability to read blueprints; perform mathematical calculations accurately; administer and interpret vocational tests; ability to analyze situations accurately and pursue an effective course of action.

1. **Skills at use of hand tools, small electrical tools, hand dexterity to work on small and intricate objects.**

2. **Ability to learn, understand, and apply installation work procedures and methods.**

3. **Skill at reading and writing reports, work orders, electrical diagrams, technical manuals, and warning notices.**

4. **Skill at dealing with people; following written/oral directions; working cooperatively with others; and being courteous to customers.**

Knowledge: Indicate whether a qualified person would need general, working, or technical knowledge, followed by a description of the area of knowledge that should be possessed by the individual. Example: General knowledge of local hiring trends: working knowledge of standard office procedures; technical knowledge of the laws, rules, and regulations governing employment law.

1. **Basics of electrical and mechanical functions; basic reading, writing, and math.**

2. **Driving laws and defensive driving practices.**

3. **General knowledge of customer service and working knowledge of employee relations.**

PHYSICAL CHARACTERISTICS

Physical characteristics are the physical demands and requirements placed on you by the nature of your work activities. Think about how often, or for how long, various physical activities must be performed in your job. For example, a job requiring prolonged standing requires more physical effort than a job requiring periodic standing.

1. Physical strength and mobility is needed in my job to **Drive, lift and carry heavy (50 lbs.) objects, climb poles, and crawl in confined spaces.**

   Examples: lift and carry heavy (or large) objects; move furniture; crawl in confined spaces; stoop to lower file drawers; frequently climb three flights of stairs; climb extension ladders.

2. My job requires that I have the stamina to **stand on pole or ladder in uncomfortable position for up to 2 hrs., sit/squat in confined space, and climb stairs frequently** for a considerable number of my work hours.

   Examples: stand for 8 consecutive hours, except for breaks and lunch; walk rapidly for prolonged periods of time; concentrate on precise and critical information for repetitive 2-hour intervals.

3. The environmental exposures connected to my job are **congested traffic, working in inclement weather, exposure to odors, dust, and fumes, and "unusual" living conditions of customers.**

   Examples: high-level noise; fumes; obnoxious odors; dust; extremes of temperature; rain; confined working space; poor lighting.

4. Other (list): **Deal effectively with angry/peculiar behavior of customers.**

OTHER PERFORMANCE CHARACTERISTICS

People are required to perform a variety of other functions and activities related to their jobs, and are often evaluated, rewarded, or disciplined based on how they handle these situations or comply with conditions. Please complete the statements that apply to your job, or enter N/A for not applicable.

1. **Judgment/Decision Making:** What tasks do you perform that require you to take action on your own, or to make recommendations? <u>**Work order priorities, job site conditions, and work methods on my own; hazard abatement recommend.**</u>

   For what type of work do you make final decisions? <u>**None**</u>

2. **Independent Solutions:** Describe those parts of your job that require you to interpret and think through in order to develop a solution to a problem. <u>**Troubleshooting installation and repair (technical) problems.**</u>

3. **Special Requirements:** These include such conditions as the necessary possession of technical/trade certificates, driver's licenses, being available for 24-hour on-call duty or overtime/weekend work, travel within a prescribed distance, speak effectively before large groups, attend evening meetings; fluently speak and read a particular foreign language.

   A. <u>**Must have valid driver's license.**</u>

   B. <u>**Must have color vision (distinguish wire color coding).**</u>

   C. <u>**Be available for overtime and work on weekends, holidays, and emergency work schedules.**</u>

   D. <u>**Must not have "space" phobia problems.**</u>

4. I routinely have to deal with people who are <u>**uneducated, ill, angry, scared, and hostile.**</u> Example: assertive; complaining about problems; rude; fearful; uneducated.

5. I work under such adverse conditions as <u>**Changeable priorities and sometimes obnoxious environmental conditions.**</u>

   Examples: changing priorities; short deadlines; more than one supervisor; conflicting expectations and standards; uncooperative coworkers.

Spend an additional 15 minutes with supervisory personnel to explain how the Supervisory Review form (attached to each Job Analysis Questionnaire) is to be completed (pp. 29–30). You should point out that the most important part of the form is items two through four where they are to note particular task statements that have been poorly or incorrectly stated, scales rated too high or low, important tasks and scales that were overlooked by the employee, and any other information about the job that may have been omitted by the employee.

Supervisors should be reminded to allow sufficient on-the-job time for participants to complete the form. Also remind them of the date it is due to be submitted to supervisors, and the date completed forms are due back to you.

Step 6 (Optional)

Included in Set One of the job analysis forms is a Performance Accountabilities form that can be used in conjunction with the Job Analysis Questionnaire. By having participating employees complete this form, you can acquire job valid performance dimensions that correspond to each of the job's task domain, statement, and the relative weighting to be placed on them for purposes of establishing weighted performance measures. Add this page to the Job Analysis Questionnaire and ask participants to follow the instructions.

Step 7

During the time participants are working on their Job Analysis Questionnaires, you should prepare copies of the last form in Set One of the job analysis forms—the Job Analysis Interview form. Also, use this time to establish and send out your interview schedule.

The job analysis interview is an integral part of the job analysis process. It allows you, or whoever is to conduct the interview, to verify, clarify, and elaborate on very specific aspects of each participant's job. It will additionally provide new information about the job since it is usually difficult for most people to adequately describe their job in writing as opposed to just talking about the different things they do. Allow 30 to 45 minutes for each interview, and feel free to modify the questions on this form to suit your own needs and conditions.

SUPERVISORY REVIEW FORM
(Please Print or Type)

Supervisor's Name **Paul Garrett**   Title **Supv. Crew Chief**

Employee Being Reviewed **Robert Winfield**   Title **Install./Repair**

Dept. **Plant**   Divis./Unit **Installation**   Location **St. L./So.**

---

1. How long have you provided direct supervision of the review position? **14 yrs.**

---

2. After a thorough review of this employee's job analysis questionnaire, please identify the domain, task statement number, and specific comments or concerns you have with statements made. Please pay particular attention to the accuracy of reported statements made, domain titles and weights, and the ratings on task statement scales.

Domain	Task#	Comments
B	All	**Although rating scales are low, these tasks are important enough to keep in the job description.**
C	3	**F.I.D. ratings should be 3 4 4**

---

3. Please list any additional tasks and related rating scales that may have been overlooked by the employee, but are important enough to be listed.

Domain	Task Statement	R/L	F	I	D
A	**Make technical decisions on laying out jobs requiring wiring work to achieve most efficient, safe, and practical work methods and materials.**	L	5	4	4

4. Please provide any other comments or amplifications concerning the characteristics or qualifications of this position that you feel would be helpful in describing and/or classifying the job.

   A. Installers must be very patient and diplomatic with customers who come from diverse walks of life.

   B. Technical aspects of work require strong orientation toward common sense and practical judgement.

   C. Recommend testing for mechanical aptitudes, drug/alcohol dependencies, and character references.

Certification: I have reviewed the referenced employee's job analysis questionnaire and find it to be an accurate representation of the position to the best of my knowledge, except as otherwise noted by my comments herein.

Supervisor's Signature	Date

❑　I would like to discuss this employee's position in greater detail with the Job Analyst.

Step 8

Keep all completed forms together that belong to each participant, then group participants by job title. You are now ready to begin the process of analyzing job content information and preparing your preliminary draft of the job description for each job title as outlined in Sections 2.3 and 2.4.

2.3 Selecting a Suitable Job Description Format

Job description formats vary based more on the information they contain than on style. Generally, the more information they contain, the more useful, understandable, and appealing the job description will be. Proper and detailed formatting also increases the richness and quality of job content information, thereby enhancing its application to a number of human resource and operational decisions.

The format most suitable to your organization depends largely on such factors as the number, nature, and type of jobs in your employ; the type of business operations you conduct; and the level of detail you wish to use to define various jobs. Minimally, you should identify major categories and subcategories of information and activities about the job in such a way that it is clear how the information is used for employment decisions. Here are the basic and recommended categories of information that should be formatted on job descriptions.

Basic Format Information

1. Job Title: the payroll title, not the position or "working" title.

2. General or Summary Description of the job: a generalized synthesis of the more important functions of the job including who incumbents report to or receive work from.

3. Examples of Duties: a detailed description of duties, responsibilities, and authorities that clearly illustrate the most frequent, important, and difficult tasks of the job written to convey the desired manner of performing work and results expected. This category should consume the bulk of the job description and be representative of at least 80 percent of all responsibilities. Duty descriptions can also be formatted by

   • Functional areas of responsibilities (task domains).

   • Frequencies of task performance.

   • Levels of importance the task is rated.

   • Type of task activity (all the tasks where the incumbent "assists" or "prepares").

   • Individual versus group activities.

4. Employment Qualification Standards: a descriptive listing of the *entry* or *minimum* qualifications acceptable for competitive acceptance including such subcategories as the *type* (not amount) of education, type and amount of related job experience, possession of specific kinds of skills and knowledge, licenses and certificates required, and any other special requirements a person must or should (preferred) have to be considered qualified. Examples might include language skills, possession of own tools, ability to travel frequently, and the like.

Recommended Format Information

1. Date Approved and Date Revised

2. Former Job Title (to track reclassified jobs)

3. Pay Classification (exempt or nonexempt status)

4. Pay Rate or Range

5. Division/Department (location of assigned positions)

6. Reports to (immediate supervisor)

7. Totality of Work Disclaimer: "This job description should not be construed to imply that these requirements are the only duties, responsibilities, and qualifications for this job. Incumbents may be required to follow any additional related instructions, acquire related job skills, and perform other related work as required."

On pages 32–35, you will find three sample formats and one blank format that you can use as models to develop your own preferred job description format. Simply photocopy the blank format on the fourth page and enter the format details you wish to use on all of your job descriptions. Whatever format detail you choose, be consistent in its use for the sake of a professional looking appearance and ease of use.

Job Description Format: Sample 1*

Title

Date Approved: _____   **Status:** _____ (exempt/nonexempt)

Revised: _____ (dates) _____   **Rate:** _____ $ (salary or hourly)

General Description

Describes under what level of supervision and control the general functions of the job are performed.

Illustrative Essential Duties/Responsibilities

Describes by functional categories of the job those tasks and realms of responsibilities that are frequent, important, and difficult to perform.

Qualification Requirements

Describes the minimum requirements a person must have to be considered eligible, and characteristics a successful employee would possess.

Education:

Experience:

Skill at:

Knowledge of:

Licenses:

Special Requirements:

*SOURCE: Joseph D. Levesque, *Manual of Personnel Policies, Procedures and Operations* 2/E, (Englewood Cliffs, NJ: Prentice-Hall, Inc., 1993), p. 472.

Job Description Format: Sample 2*

Title

Summary Description

Illustrative Essential Duties/Responsibilities

Employment Standards

Education/Experience:

Skill at:

Knowledge of:

Statement of nonlimitation of requirement to perform other related duties.

Date Approved: _____   Dept./Division: _____

Revised: _____   Status: _____

Reports to: _____   Pay Grade: _____

*SOURCE: Joseph D. Levesque, *Manual of Personnel Policies, Procedures and Operations* 2/E, (Englewood Cliffs, NJ: Prentice-Hall, Inc., 1993), p. 473.

Job Description Format: Sample 3

Title

Summary Description

| | Activity Index (1–10) |
| Illustrative Essential Functions | Frequency Importance Difficulty |

Minimum Qualifications

(Statement of nonlimitation of requirement to perform other related duties.)

Date Approved: _____ Pay Class: _____

Date Revised: _____ Pay Rate: _____

Former Title: _____ Status: _____

Your Stylized
Business Name/Logo
Here

Job Description

2.4 How to Write Job Descriptions for Multiple Uses

One of the most common problems with job descriptions in use today is that they are written so poorly that their use becomes extremely limited, if usable at all. Job descriptions began as an instrument of managing the productivity of a business's operations, basic hiring information, and other personnel decisions in an era when the skills of employees were less diversified and specialized, and their involvement in the organization was not the prominent factor for successful job performance that it is in this era. Employees were merely *told* what tasks had to be performed if they wanted to receive their pay, and they did the prescribed work whether it was in their job description or not.

Other Common Weaknesses of Job Descriptions

Today, employees are much more educated, enlightened, skilled, demanding of their expectations to be involved in operational decisions, and desirous of meaningful explanations about their work. If we ever hope to make job descriptions the meaningful instruments they are intended to be, we need to begin revising them in a manner that: 1) provides considerably more explanatory and relevant detail about the nature of significant responsibilities; 2) provides descriptive wording that conveys the manner in which work is expected to be performed; and, 3) states what results are needed.

The problem with task-only descriptive statements about job duties is that they often lack clarity about *how* the task is to be performed with respect to such matters as methods, behaviors, and desired results. For example, a task-only statement might say, "Repairs damaged or inoperative small electrical motors," where it is possible to have the task done (repair the motor) without accomplishing the intended results (the motor resumes operation for optimal and prolonged use). Rather, the motor can be repaired without it operating well or for very long, but that level of job performance or work quality was not what we wanted—we merely overlooked stating so in the job description and/or in defining performance standards.

Other common weaknesses that create major deficiencies in the way job descriptions are written and used are

1. They are written with short, unclear, and weakly defined statements, providing insufficient detail about the more frequent, important, and difficult tasks or activities to be performed.

2. They do not provide management with enough information about performance or compensatory factors.

3. They fail to explain why the work is needed and its relationship to the work performed by other employees.

4. They do not provide enough, nor the right kind of information about job skills, knowledge, and abilities to develop effective recruitment and selection testing devices.

5. There is no distinction between individual versus shared work activities, nor are any job functions given weighted dimensions.

6. They often fail to describe key relationships with other employees who perform work that relates to, or relies on, the job incumbent.

7. Important work environment factors are often omitted.

8. Necessary physical and mental demands are either omitted or understated.

9. Working conditions such as hazards, confinement, noise, inclement weather exposure, and the like are omitted.

10. They are not reviewed for necessary revisions on a three-to-five year schedule, therefore they easily become obsolete and employees get understandably disgruntled.

The goal, then, of preparing more effective and reliable job descriptions lies in eliminating as many of the weaknesses as possible. The additional time to do so will be well spent since the effort becomes easier after completing a few of them. Also, subsequent revisions are quickly done, and their use increases greatly when making a host of employment decisions. Now, let's examine some of the ways you can create more useful descriptions.

How to Use Job Analysis Information in Preparing Job Descriptions

Now that you have received, grouped, and reviewed the job analysis forms used to gather job content information, you're ready to begin the job analysis that will allow you to prepare quality job descriptions. Additionally, the information provided in your job analysis documents can be used for developing logical pay rate or range structures and job-specific performance dimensions to be used during annual appraisals. Here are the step-by-step procedures you should follow to analyze and extract relevant job content from your job analysis documents for these purposes.

Compiling Job Content Information from the Formal Job Analysis Method

If you used Set One of the job analysis forms, then you should have groupings of these completed forms: Job Analysis Questionnaire, Supervisor's Review, and Job Analysis Interview. To begin the preparation of job descriptions, you should focus your attention on one job at a time. The easiest way to begin is to start with those jobs that have only one incumbent employee occupying the job—this limits the number of forms you have to analyze until you get comfortable with the process. Select one such job and begin your analysis of the applicable forms as follows.

Step 1 Read through the Job Analysis Questionnaire to become familiar with the domains, weightings, task statements, qualifications, and working conditions. Try to develop a mental image of what this job would look like during the performance of the work, or perhaps you might even want to spend a little time observing the incumbents perform their work. During the initial review, make note on the form of anything that strikes you as a domain that could be combined with another domain, an unclear statement, or unreasonable/invalid job qualifications.

Review the Supervisor's Review form information carefully to see if the incumbent's supervisor has provided additional information about the job. Any such information should be transferred on to the Job Analysis Questionnaire.

Review the Job Analysis Interview form in conjunction with the Job Analysis Questionnaire. Information obtained on the Interview form that provides more enlightening, amplifying, or new information about the job should be transferred on to the Questionnaire form, thus leaving you with all the pertinent information from the Supervisor's Review and the Interview forms transferred to the singular Questionnaire form.

Step 2 Once you've verified any information you felt was unclear, weakly stated, or inappropriate, you're ready to begin analysis and compilation of the job's information. Start this process by using the edited Questionnaire form and begin with a review of domain task statements rated in the "Frequency," "Importance," and "Difficulty" (F.I.D.) columns. Task statements on the F.I.D. scale rated below 3 in any column should be made a part of an associated, higher rated task statement, or eliminated if the statement is not sufficiently associated with another task statement. A below 3 rating level suggests that the task is either inconsequential overall, or that the task can reasonably be learned and performed with nominal effort and time.

Task statements that have been rated three on the F.I.D. scales should be treated in the same way if they also marked under the "L" (learned) column, since this notation and rating *may* mean that the task can be learned and performed well in a relatively short period of time. According to the Uniform Guidelines on Employee Selection Procedures, any job activity that can be learned in eight or less hours cannot be subject to preemployment testing, and such tasks are therefore considered of minimal consequence. If you or the incumbent's supervisor feels that such a task is significant, then it may have been underrated, so merely attach this task statement to an associated, higher rated task statement. The remaining task statements should be used to form the basis of preparing the "Duties and Responsibilities" illustrations section on the job description.

Step 3 Review the Minimum Requirements section of the Questionnaire form with particular care. Many courts hearing discrimination cases have found that the minimum (entry) requirements for numerous jobs are overstated or do not relate directly to the actual performance of the job, and are therefore invalid. Care should be given to making sure that any requirements for *entry* into the position are legitimate standards of the job—not a case of the incumbent employee having higher levels of education, experience, or SKAs, and not wanting the job viewed as requiring less.

Another reason to ensure that you have detailed information about the job's requirements, particularly the SKAs, is that this information should be used as the basis of developing preemployment qualification tests. Such tests must bear a *direct* relationship to the job tasks, or the test will likely be considered legally invalid. You should therefore insist that the information concerning skills, knowledge, and abilities requirements is stated in clear and thoroughly descriptive detail so that its relationship to job tasks is legitimate in all respects.

Step 4 The section addressing Other Performance Characteristics in the Questionnaire form also has a great deal to do with preemployment testing since these items take into account special mental, personal, environmental, and unique working conditions of particular jobs. These conditions should be reflected on the job description in two ways: first, items 1, 2, and 4 should be written into the "Duties and Responsibilities" section when describing associated tasks; and, second, items 3 and 5 should be noted on the job description under the category or subcategory of "Special Conditions."

Make sure that you can distinguish between those characteristics and conditions that are *required* in order for a person to apply for the job, as opposed to those that are *desired*. If a characteristic or condition is desired but not required at the time of application for the job, then it should be listed on the job description under the category or subcategory of "Desired Condition," and may not be a primary consideration of preemployment testing.

Step 5 The information contained in Physical Characteristics in the Questionnaire form should be treated and used in the same fashion as Step 4. It should be explained on the job description in summary form under a category or subcategory of "Physical Conditions," and made a part of preemployment testing. Related physical activities required by the job such as lifting, climbing, walking, bending, standing, reaching, holding, color vision, and hearing—that cannot be accommodated by the employer for those with physical limitations—should also be listed on the job description and definitely incorporated into the testing process.

How to Write Job Duty Statements from Formal Analysis

Having completed the analysis and editing functions under Steps 1 and 2 of the formal method, you're ready to compile a preliminary draft of the job's "Illustrative Duties and Responsibilities" and "Job Summary" sections of the job description. First, select one of the recommended job description formats, or your own combination of features, from those in Section 2.3. If you have a computer or word processor, prepare the job description format on a style sheet so that it can be easily repeated when you're compiling categorical information on each separate description. Then, follow these steps to write your job duty and summary statements from your edited Questionnaire form.

Step 1 Decide on whether you're going to group the job's task statements by such features as functions, type of work activity, importance and frequency of work activities, or other common traits of the job. Then, begin extracting edited task statements from the Questionnaire to fit your grouping style.

Step 2 Each task statement should begin with an action verb that conveys a clear picture of what the person does to perform the work. For example, the word "conducts" is not as clear in describing the actual activity as the word "prepares." If you choose to group task statements by the type of work activity performed, then select all the work activities within all domains that require the incumbent to "prepare," followed by such other common activities as "schedules," "repairs," or "reviews."

Once you have completed the normal realm of job duties and responsibilities, give some thought to either adding or incorporating tasks that would describe

- unforeseen and/or unassigned work that is within the scope of the job;
- nominal routine work that is within the scope of the job; and,
- work outside the normal scope of responsibility that is connected to training the incumbent for higher level job skills.

A nonlimitation disclaimer such as that previously suggested, or the similar one used at the end of the sample job descriptions provided in Section 2.5 can also be used to address these "and other related duties" aspects of a job.

Step 3 Review your compiled task statements to see if they are orderly, make sense, and depict a clearly defined illustration of at least 80 percent of the most frequently performed, important, and difficult duties and responsibilities of the job. If so, you've done a good job with this section. If not, then go back to the Questionnaire domains to see if you overlooked or eliminated some task statements that fill notable voids, or seek further information on the area of void from the incumbent's supervisor.

Step 4 Now write the Job Summary based on your viewing of the general nature and scope of the job as reflected in the Duties and Responsibilities section. Job Summary statements normally begin with who the incumbent reports to, and receives assignments from, such as

- Under the immediate supervision of (title of supervisor),
- Under the general supervision of _____ ,
- Under the immediate direction of _____ ,
- Under the general direction of _____ ,

Job Summary statements should be a succinct way of conveying the most generally significant things the incumbent does, why such work is important, and what kinds of results should be achieved by performing the work.

How to Prepare Qualification Statements from Formal Analysis

The Minimum Employment Qualifications, Other Performance Characteristics, and Physical Characteristics are highly important hiring considerations with regard to preparing recruitment ads, developing selection tests, and providing initial training and performance monitoring of new hires. However, the minimum qualifications and characteristics one must have to be considered eligible for employment can also be very deceptive. First, you should recognize that these features of a job are vulnerable to strict evaluations of their validity by fair employment compliance agencies and the courts. Each and every qualification and condition associated with the job *must* bear a direct relationship to actual requirements of the job, not merely what you feel such requirements should be, or what they are customarily.

Second, there is an inherent tendency for job incumbents to overrate the minimum qualifications and other work characteristics for two reasons: 1) incumbents typically possess more than minimum qualifications and feel their level of qualifications should be used as the standard rather than something less; and, 2) incumbents psychologically resist the idea that their job can be done, or at least qualified for, by someone having lesser qualifications than themselves. It is for these reasons that you need to approach the analysis of minimum qualifications and *required* characteristics and conditions of the job with great caution, if not skepticism.

For example, with unskilled and semiskilled jobs, most employers require a high school diploma as the minimum educational level to qualify for these lower-level jobs. However, when functioning job duties and conditions are examined carefully, you are likely to discover that the actual reading, writing, math, and comprehension skills required for successful performance of the job are at an eighth grade (newspaper print) level. In other words, it is the *type* of education and experience that matters, not merely the amount.

The Questionnaire form should serve as your guide to the job's minimum employment qualifications. These qualifications should be divided into two categories on the job description. The first category is Employment Standards or Minimum Qualifications, whichever you prefer. Under this category, you will list

1. The *type* of education required.
2. The *type* and *amount* of experience required.
3. The *kind* of skills, knowledge, and abilities required.

Since qualified job seekers can possess different variations of these requirements, you should state on the job description that you will consider any combination of illustrative qualifications if they represent equivalencies of stated requirements. This allows the applicant who has considerably more prior job experience and less of the educational requirement to qualify for consideration. You would not want to eliminate someone who has a demonstrated history of performing the type of job you're trying to fill. Rejecting an applicant with "equivalent" qualifications could be considered discriminatory on the basis of establishing artificial standards for the job.

The second category on the job description that deals with job requirements is simply listed as either Other Required Conditions or Other Conditions and Desirable Qualifications. The choice of which to use depends on whether there are fixed and unavoidable conditions, and/or some special qualifications that you would *prefer*, but not require, an applicant to possess in order to qualify for consideration. Most of these conditions and special qualifications would be found in the Questionnaire form under the headings of Other Performance Characteristics and Physical Characteristics. Here, you might list such special conditions on the job description as the job *requires* possession and maintenance of a valid driver's license; that registration as a Professional Engineer is *desirable;* that work is frequently performed in inclement weather; or that the job *requires* the physical ability to walk, climb stairs, and carry objects weighing up to 45 pounds occasionally.

Any qualification requirements or special conditions given to you as imperatives should be carefully checked out if you doubt their validity. Do this by personal observation of actual job performance of incumbents, as well as discussion with the applicable supervisor(s). Both incumbents and supervisors may have to be reminded that required qualifications and special conditions are to be confined to the *minimums* on the job description for purposes of determining the lowest threshold of qualifications eligibility.

Keep Job Descriptions Current

Many of the problems associated with poor-to-weak job descriptions are related to their obsolescence, writing quality, detail, accuracy of the more significant work responsibilities, and completeness of required qualifications. The problem of job description obsolescence is a common one in most organizations due to the constantly changing nature of work and worker attributes. An easy way of keeping job descriptions current is to require that all supervisors perform a job description review with each of their employees as part of the annual performance evaluation process.

Minor changes that improve the quality and maintain the accuracy of job descriptions can be noted on a copy of the employee's job description, sent through operational channels for approval, and given to you for review and amendment. Major changes, on the other hand, should not await this annual event. Rather, they should be described in detail on a form like the Personnel Requisition form (sample in Appendix D), and amendments or reclassification made at the time significantly new responsibilities have stabilized within the job. Remember, by keeping quality in your job descriptions you are also maintaining the accuracy of your entire hiring process, since each phase of the hiring process relies on the thoroughness of job description detail—as you will see in the chapters that follow.

2.5 Sample Job Descriptions

In order to provide you with a few illustrations of how job descriptions should appear in detail and finished format, a few samples have been provided on the following pages. These samples are illustrations of different job classes, showing the formatting of duties and responsibilities, performance dimensions, and compensable factors. The samples consist of descriptions covering the jobs of

Executive Director: exempt status, functional area duty description format, a list of (yet to be defined) performance dimensions, and a list of compensable factors.

Secretary I/II: nonexempt status, sample of "series" job description to illustrate how different levels of the same occupation are defined.

Customer Service Representative (Teller) I/II: nonexempt status, and a second sample of a "series" description.

Building Maintenance Helper/Worker: nonexempt status, and a third sample of a "series" description, but includes a listing of the compensable factors.

Your business
name/logo
here

Job Description*

Executive Director

Summary Description

Under policy direction of the Board of Directors, performs a wide range of difficult-to-complex administrative activities related to finances and accounting, marketing and promotion of services, staffing and personnel operations, and discretionary activities that serve to support effective business operations. Uses considerable independent judgment in decisions that influence operations. Advises and assists the Board of Directors in planning, policy, and operations matters.

Illustrative Essential Duties/Responsibilities

Directs and participates in the development and implementation of goals, objectives, policies, and procedures; directs and ensures proper coordination of all administrative affairs; prepares and submits to the Board of Directors reports of finances, staffing, programs, and other administrative activities; prepares agenda and documents, attends and participates in Board of Director meetings to receive general direction.

General administration: Develops and implements organizational and program plans; researches applicable laws, legislation, and regulations; prepares reports, correspondence, memos, records, and forms; evaluates activities and interacts with representatives of comparable firms; develops and prepares forms, records, charts, and other operational materials, and implements operations systems to achieve effective workloads and workflow.

Prepares and delivers formal presentations before various public and private concerns; attends meetings, conferences, and seminars requiring periodic to frequent travel.

Secures the services and products of outside sources such as business insurance, security systems, vehicles and equipment, office supplies and furnishings, and legal or other advisory/support services.

Performs immediate supervision of department heads and key support staff, and maintains official records.

Financial administration: Prepares the annual budget and approves subsequent modifications and transfers; monitors and evaluates accounting systems, audits of accounts, and internal control methods; establishes the method and means of determining fiscal accountability; reviews and approves accounts payable, payroll, and other financial warrants, requisitions, purchase orders, receipts, and records or reports.

Personnel administration: Develops and revises personnel policies, rules, procedures and directives, job specifications, performance evaluation methods, and all personnel forms

*SOURCE: Joseph D. Levesque, *Manual of Personnel Policies, Procedures and Operations* 2/E, (Englewood Cliffs, NJ: Prentice-Hall, Inc., 1993), p. 475.

and records; ensures compliance with applicable federal and state employment laws and regulations; makes hiring, performance, and disciplinary determinations; conducts staff meetings and wage surveys, and initiates wage increases based on meritorious performance; hears and resolves complaints, problems, grievances; and maintains employee personnel files and other confidential records.

Employment Standards

Education/Experience: Any combination of education and experience providing the required skill and knowledge for successful performance would be qualifying. Typical qualifications would be equivalent to

1. possession of a Bachelor's degree from an accredited college or university with major course work in business or public administration, political science, sociology, or closely related field; *and*
2. three (3) years' experience performing responsible general administrative work.

Knowledge: Principles and practices of business administration including personnel practices and employment laws, program budgeting, general accounting, and fiscal management practices; office procedures and business operating systems; and the appropriate methods and means of dealing with human behavior situations in a variety of business circumstances.

Skills: Communicating effectively, verbally and in writing, in a diverse range of audiences and settings; persuasion and negotiation of conflicts and problems; assessing operational, program, staffing, and fiscal needs; interpreting legal documents and government regulations; evaluating fiscal and financial reports, forms, and data; analyzing complex written documents; identifying and resolving administrative problems; working long and irregular hours, and under pressure conditions; delegating responsibility and achieving results through subordinates; and maintaining order in an environment of changing priorities.

Licenses: Possession of a valid _____ motor vehicle operator's license, and willingness to use personal vehicle in the course of employment.

This job specification should not be construed to imply that these requirements are the exclusive standards of the position. Incumbents will follow any other instructions, and perform any other related duties, as may be required.

Executive Director Performance Dimensions

Performance Dimension	Percentage Weight
1. Assistance to the Board of Directors (insert definition detail)	15
2. Policy Development & Implementation	10
3. Program Planning & Organizational Development	15
4. Budgeting & Fiscal Management	10
5. Personnel Operations	15
6. Supervision	10
7. Regulatory Compliance	10
8. Agency & Public Liaison	15

Executive Director Compensable Factors

Compensable Factors	Factor Level 1	2	3	4	5
1. Scope of duties, responsibilities, and decision making authorities				X	
2. Criticality of judgments and decisions				X	
3. Span of control over program and budgetary matters				X	
4. Consequence of errors			X		
5. Supervision of staff				X	
6. Operations management					X
7. Education and experience requirements				X	
8. Skill, knowledge, and abilities requirements				X	
9. Mental demands					X

Job Description*

Secretary I/II

Summary Description

Under general supervision, performs a variety of complex, responsible, and confidential secretarial and administrative duties; and performs related work as required.

Distinguishing Characteristics

Secretary I: Positions in this class perform varied secretarial and clerical work under general supervision within a framework of standard policies and procedures. Assigned tasks require initiative, organization, and independent judgment in solving routine problems. There may be leadership responsibilities.

Secretary II: Positions in this class are normally filled by advancement from the lower grade of Secretary I, or when filled from outside, require prior secretarial and administrative experience. Appointment to the higher class requires that the employee be performing substantially the full range of duties for the class and meet the qualifications standards for the class. A Secretary II performs varied complex, responsible, and confidential secretarial and clerical duties under limited supervision requiring a thorough knowledge of policies, procedures, and precedents. Reports, documents, and records prepared and maintained by employees in this class are often of a confidential nature. Assigned tasks require tact, independent judgment, initiative, and organization in solving a variety of problems. There may be leadership or supervisory responsibilities.

Illustrative Essential Duties/Responsibilities

Reviews logs, determines priority of, and routes, correspondence; composes routine correspondence and independently prepares correspondence not requiring supervisor's personal attention; acts as receptionist, screens calls, visitors, and refers inquiries as appropriate; responds to complaints and requests for information in relation to the intent, coverage, and content of instructions, guides, precedents, and regulations; gathers, organizes, and prepares information for comprehensive reports; supervises, initiates, and maintains a variety of files and records of information such as payroll, attendance, budget, production, and cost records; recommends organizational or procedural changes affecting administrative clerical activities.

Takes and transcribes dictation from rough draft, shorthand notes, or taped recordings; takes, edits, and types minutes and distributes copies; researches, compiles, and analyzes data for special projects; supervises, trains, and evaluates subordinates.

*SOURCE: Joseph D. Levesque, *Manual of Personnel Policies, Procedures and Operations* 2/E, (Englewood Cliffs, NJ: Prentice-Hall, Inc., 1993), p. 483.

Employment Standards

Secretary I

Education/experience: Any combination of education and experience providing the required skill and knowledge for successful performance would be qualifying. Typical qualifications would be equivalent to

1. completion of the twelfth (12) grade, supplemented by specialized secretarial courses; and
2. one (1) year of responsible secretarial and clerical experience.

Knowledge: Correct English usage, grammar, spelling, punctuation, and arithmetic; modern office methods, procedures and equipment, and business letter and report writing; fundamental record-keeping principles and procedures; receptionist and telephone techniques, and filing systems.

Skill: Following oral and written directions; working effectively with others; learning rapidly, interpreting and applying laws, rules, and office policies and procedures; typing accurately from clear copy at a speed of 60 words per minute; taking dictation at a rate of 100 words per minute; operating modern office equipment, including word processors, memory typewriters, and data entry equipment; communicating tactfully and effectively in both oral and written form; working independently in the absence of supervision; analyzing situations carefully and adopting effective courses of action; compiling and maintaining complex and extensive records and files; preparing reports; composing correspondence independently.

Secretary II

In addition to the qualifications for Secretary I:

Experience: Four (4) years' increasingly responsible secretarial and clerical experience; or three (3) years' experience performing duties comparable to those of Secretary I.

Knowledge: Principles of supervision, training, and performance evaluation.

Skill: Supervising and prioritizing the work of subordinates; training and evaluating subordinates; compiling and maintaining complex, extensive, and confidential records and files; preparing extensive and confidential reports.

This job specification should not be construed to imply that these requirements are the exclusive standards of the position. Incumbents will follow any other instructions, and perform any other related duties, as may be required by their supervisor.

> Your business
> name/logo
> here

Job Description*

Customer Service Representative (Teller) I/II

Summary Description

Under general supervision, performs a variety of clerical, record-keeping, and consumer-service duties concerned with receiving and disbursing money and recording transactions; answers customer's inquiries; and performs related work as required.

Distinguishing Characteristics

Customer Service Representative I: This is the entrance level for clerical teller employees requiring basic business mathematic computation skills and little or no previous experience. Employees in this class work under close supervision performing a group of repetitive or closely related duties according to established procedures. While a variety of tasks may be assigned, each step usually fits a pattern that has been established and explained before work is started. Any changes in procedure or exceptions to rules are explained as they arise. Generally, work is observed and reviewed both during its performance and upon completion.

Under this training concept, as the difficulty and variety of work increases, positions may be assigned to the higher class of Customer Service Representative II as vacancies occur. Positions may remain in the Customer Service Representative I class if assignments remain limited, work continues to be closely supervised, or the difficulty of the work does not increase.

Customer Service Representative II: Positions in this class are normally filled by advancement from the lower class of Customer Service Representative I, or when filled from the outside, require prior teller experience. A Customer Service Representative II is expected to perform a wide variety of moderate-to-difficult clerical, record-keeping, and customer-service duties with only occasional instruction or assistance. Employees in this class are expected to solve routine problems by working within a framework of established procedures and by choosing among the number of limited alternatives. Judgment and initiative are required in making decisions in accordance with approved procedures and precedents. A Customer Service Representative II is expected to work productively in the absence of supervision and may have leadership responsibilities over others. Work is normally reviewed only upon completion and for overall results.

Illustrative Essential Duties/Responsibilities

Receives and pays out money, and keeps records of money and negotiable instruments involved in transactions. Receives checks and cash for deposits, verifies amounts, and examines checks for endorsements; enters deposits in depositers' passbooks; issues receipts; cashes checks and pays out money upon verification of signature and customer balances; computes service charges, interest, and discounts; explains and sells additional services to customers; prepares and posts data to pertinent documents, logs, and forms; answers customer inquiries

*SOURCE: Joseph D. Levesque, *Manual of Personnel Policies, Procedures and Operations* 2/E, (Englewood Cliffs, NJ: Prentice-Hall, Inc., 1993), p. 487.

or services customer's requests in person, by telephone, or through correspondence; operates office machines, such as typewriter, calculator, bookkeeping, and check-writing machines; balances daily monies.

Employment Standards

Customer Service Representative I

Education/experience: Any combination of education and experience providing the required skill and knowledge for successful performance would be qualifying. Typical qualifications would be completion of the twelfth (12) grade or its equivalent, with course work in business math, business practices, and English usage. No experience necessary.

Knowledge: Correct English usage; basic business mathematical computations; modern office equipment and practices.

Skills: Following oral and written instructions; reading, writing, and performing mathematical calculations at the level required for successful job performance; operating calculating machine quickly and accurately; typing 40 words per minute from clear copy; learning rules, methods, policies and procedures of the work place; communicating effectively, orally or in writing; working cooperatively with others; paying attention to detail.

Customer Service Representative II

In addition to the qualification for Customer Service Representative I:

Experience: Any combination equivalent to the experience providing the required knowledge and skills. Typical qualifications equivalent to

1. one (1) year's experience performing duties comparable to Customer Service Representative I; *or*
2. two (2) years' increasingly responsible record-keeping and customer-service duties.

Knowledge: Working independently in absence of direct supervision; analyzing situations accurately and taking effective action; performing teller work of average difficulty; compiling statistical data for documents and reports.

Special consideration: Both Customer Service Representatives I and II will be working in a nonsmoking area.

Licenses: Possession of a valid _____ motor vehicle operator's license and willingness to use personal vehicle in the course of employment.

This job specification should not be construed to imply that these requirements are the exclusive standards of the position. Incumbents will follow any other instructions, and perform any other related duties, as may be required by their supervisor.

Your business name/logo here

Job Description*

Building Maintenance Helper/Worker

Summary Description

Under general supervision, performs skilled and semiskilled building maintenance and repair requiring a working knowledge of carpentry, plumbing, and minor electrical work; and performs related work as required.

Distinguishing Characteristics

Building Maintenance Helper: This is the entry level class in the maintenance worker series. Positions in this class normally perform a variety of unskilled or semiskilled physical tasks in construction and maintenance activities. Work is usually closely supervised and fits a pattern that has been established and explained before work is started. Work is observed and reviewed both during its performance and upon completion. Building maintenance helpers are normally considered to be on a training status. Under this training concept, the difficulty and variety of work increases, positions may be assigned to the class of Building Maintenance Worker should a position become vacant. There is no supervision over others.

Building Maintenance Worker: Positions in this class are normally filled by advancement form the lower grade of Building Maintenance Helper, or when filled from the outside, require prior construction, carpentry, or electrical experience. A Building Maintenance Worker works under general direction within a framework of established procedures, is expected to perform a wide variety of skilled and semiskilled building maintenance and repair work. Judgment and initiative are required in making decisions in accordance with established guides. There may be supervision and training responsibilities over others.

Illustrative Essential Duties/Responsibilities

Repairs and maintains machinery, plumbing, physical structure, grounds and electrical wiring and fixtures in accordance with blueprints, manuals, and building codes, using hand tools and carpenter's, electrician's, and plumber's tools; performs routine maintenance on machines; replaces or repairs machine belts; removes dust, dirt, grease, and waste materials from machines; and paints machines or equipment to prevent corrosion.

Installs electrical equipment and repairs or replaces wiring, fixtures, and bulbs; repairs or replaces brick and plaster walls; paints walls, floors, ceilings, or fixtures; repairs and replaces gauges, valves, pressure regulators, and other plumbing equipment, and opens clogged drains; repairs various types of furniture, doors, windows, floors, lockers, gates, roofs, and ceilings; builds sheds and other outbuildings; digs ditches, trenches, and post holes; patches and repairs sidewalks and streets; and maintains grounds.

*SOURCE: Joseph D. Levesque, *Manual of Personnel Policies, Procedures and Operations* 2/E, (Englewood Cliffs, NJ: Prentice-Hall, Inc., 1993), p. 508.

Employment Standards

Building Maintenance Helper

Education/experience: Any combination of education and experience providing the required knowledge is qualifying. A typical way to obtain the knowledge and skills would be sufficient formal or informal education to ensure the ability to read, write, and perform mathematical computations at a level required for successful job performance. No experience is necessary.

Knowledge: Use and care of construction hand and power tools; and safe work practices.

Skills: Following oral and written instructions; performing unskilled and semiskilled tasks in a variety of construction and maintenance activities; learning to perform skilled carpentry, plumbing, and electrical work; performing heavy physical labor; working at a height of fifteen (15) to twenty (20) feet above the ground; establishing and maintaining cooperative relationship with those contacted in the course of work.

Building Maintenance Worker

In addition to the qualifications for Building Maintenance Helper:

Education/experience: One (1) year of experience performing building maintenance and repair work.

Knowledge: Standard tools, materials, methods, and practices involved in building, maintenance, and repair, including carpentry, plumbing, electrical, and painting; safe work practices; estimating materials and labor need; and supervising and training others.

Building Maintenance Helper/Worker Compensable Factors

Factor Level	Helper					Worker				
Compensable Factors	1	2	3	4	5	1	2	3	4	5
1. Scope of duties, responsibilities, and authorities	X							X		
2. Education and experience required		X					X			
3. Skills, knowledge, and abilities required			X							X
4. Exposure to environmental conditions	X									X
5. Mental demands		X								X

3 Using Human Resource Policies to Shape Effective Hiring Practices

In order to launch a hiring program, and keep its related procedures and decisions on course, you will need sound personnel policies to act as the guidance system. As a guidance system, policies serve the essential functions of providing information to those inside the organization involved in hiring (as well as to new hires), and they guide decision making so that it remains consistent, fair, lawful and understandable. Since no two organizations are alike in their needs, approach to employment matters, or operating philosophy, there is a certain amount of "inventive creativity" that must be brought to the writing of policies in order to assure that they guide the organization toward appropriate practices.

Conversely, there are numerous legal issues that must be observed and addressed in personnel policies that stem from the laws discussed in Appendices A–C. Likewise, we should heed the warning of the courts concerning those policies we adopt—abide by them or risk potential damages! In other words, care must be given to the task of writing policies so that the wording matches what we meant to say, and what we want to be able to do in differing circumstances. The following sections of this chapter, then, are intended to provide you with the framework of those personnel policies you will need, and should have, to establish an effective hiring program. Feel free to modify the wording of sample policies to better suit the conditions in your company but, as you should with the adoption of any new personnel policy, have them reviewed by competent advisors before implementing.

Finally, if your company employs individuals represented by a union, you should keep in mind that personnel policies are required to be the subject of collective bargaining. So, if you're changing existing personnel policies, or creating them anew, they cannot be implemented unilaterally in a unionized employment environment. You must present such policies as any other proposal of management, and make reasonable attempts to achieve union agreement on each new and/or changed policy prior to implementation.

3.1 Administrative Policies Related to Hiring

Administrative policies are those that define the nature or condition of operational concerns. With respect to employment matters, personnel policy manuals often have an initial section dedicated to various administrative matters such as who is responsible for policy issues, revision rights, which employees are covered by policy, policy definitions, categories of employment, at-will employment statement, and the like.

While "at-will" employment policy statements have become a frequently advised type of personnel policy disclaimer by labor attorneys, you may want to give some thought to what psychological impact such statements will have on existing employees. If you decide to use at-will statements, use plain language, avoid harsh wording, and place this type of disclaimer language 1) at the beginning of your manual/handbook, and 2) in policies dealing with performance appraisal, promotion, salary increases, discipline, and employment separation.

At-Will Employment

Policy Sample 1

All employees who do not have a written individual employment contract, signed by the President of the Company, for a specific, fixed term of employment are "at-will" employees. This means that these employees may resign at any time, and the Company may terminate their employment at any time with or without notice for any or no reason. This policy may be modified only in a written document signed by the President of the Company. This Manual [handbook] does not constitute, and should not be read to create, any promise by the Company that the policies set forth will be followed in every case. Nothing in this Manual [handbook] alters an employee's at-will status.[1]

Policy Sample 2: Large Company

Employment at (*Company name*) is for no definite period and may, regardless of the time and manner of payment of wages and salary, be terminated at any time by the Company or by an employee, with or without cause, and without any previous notice.

Further, no organization manager or representative of (*Company name*), other than the President and Chief Executive Officer or the Executive Vice President of Human Resources, has the authority to enter into an agreement for employment for any specified period of time or to make any agreement contrary to the foregoing. This lack of guarantee or employment contract also applies to other benefits, working conditions, and privileges of employment at (*Company name*).[2]

Policy Sample 3: Small Company

This handbook does not represent an employment contract between (*Company name*) and its employees. The guidelines herein are for information purposes only and may be changed by the Company at its sole discretion. The Company is also not bound by any oral promises concerning an employee's length of employment. The policies and procedures set forth in this handbook, then, are for the purpose of providing employees general information about Company operating policies and guidelines concerning employment matters.

Employees and the Company are engaged in an "at-will" employment relationship, meaning that either are free to terminate the relationship at any time, with or without reason, and with or without notice. Employment contracts, on the other hand, are only authorized in writing by the President of the Company.

Employment Agreements

Policy Sample

The Company may from time to time enter into written employment agreements with certain employees. Normally, the Company will make such agreements only with executives, managers, and professional employees. Employment agreements are binding on the Company only if in writing and signed by the President of the Company. Employees who do not have a written employment agreement meeting these criteria are at-will employees.[3]

Personnel policies that define the "types of employment" hired or employed by a company are important distinctions, since they usually regulate different employment conditions. Some of the more common employment conditions that vary depending on the type of employment one holds are; the number of hours worked in a workweek, qualification for fringe benefits, and whether the employment is temporary or regular status.

Types of Employment

Policy Sample 1

It is the policy of (*Company name*) to categorize the types of employment with the Company in order to clarify the distinctions in benefits and conditions of employment among employees, and to aid in a better understanding of employment relationships with the Company.

Probationary Employees: New, rehired, or promoted employees who serve a prescribed period of close training, supervision, and evaluation to assess their abilities and adaptation to the job.

Regular Full-Time Employees: Employees who regularly work a minimum of forty hours per week on a continuous basis following satisfactory completion of a probationary period, and who are entitled to all privileges and benefits of employment as defined in other policies of the Company.

Regular Part-Time Employees: Employees who regularly work more than twenty but less than forty hours per week on a continuous basis following satisfactory completion of a probationary period, and who are entitled to many of the privileges and benefits of employment on a pro-rata basis as defined in other policies of the Company.

Temporary Employees: Employees holding jobs of limited or specified duration arising out of special projects, vacancies pending appointment, the absence of a regular employee, peak work loads, emergencies, or other reasons established by the Company. Temporary employees may work either full- or part-time schedules, but are not eligible to receive fringe benefits, accrue any form of service credit, or file internal complaints except in matters pertaining to alleged discrimination.

Nonexempt Employees: Employees who are eligible for overtime pay and other defined employment treatment pursuant to the Fair Labor Standards Act or applicable state laws. Employees classified as nonexempt are entitled to overtime pay for work *required* to be performed by authority of Company supervisors or managers in excess of forty hours per payroll week.

[Note: many state laws require that overtime be paid over eight hours worked in a twenty-four-hour period]

Exempt Employees: Employees who are ineligible for overtime pay, but who are paid on a predetermined salary at least once each month, pursuant to their defined job responsibilities as contained in the Fair Labor Standards Act and applicable state laws. Generally, exempt employees are those occupying executive, administrative, professional, and outside sales jobs.

Unless provided with a written contract at the time of hire or promotion, all employees are employed conditionally on the basis of continuing fitness, need, and desire. None of the types of employment defined above, nor anything contained in Company policies and procedures, guarantee employment for any length of time. Rather, employment is at the mutual consent of each employee and the Company, and can be terminated at will by the employee or Company.

Policy Sample 2

It is the policy of (*Company name*) to classify employees according to their responsibilities, working conditions, pay and benefit entitlements, and other provisions of their employment. Employees hired by the Company will be classified in one or more of the following categories, and informed of their type of employment at the time of hire or promotion.

Management Employees: Employees who are given the responsibility and authority to render policy, program, financial, operational and personnel decisions. Management positions are classified as exempt from the overtime provisions of the Fair Labor Standards Act and applicable state laws, and are therefore paid a predetermined monthly salary for all hours worked.

Supervisory Employees: Employees who are given the responsibility and authority to train, assign work, and oversee the performance of other employees; to make recommendations concerning operational and personnel matters; and to carry out assigned and self-directed work in their designated work unit in a manner that ensures efficient and effective results. Supervisory employees who are predominantly engaged in these activities will be classified as exempt.

Confidential Employees: Employees who, in the course and scope of their employment, are given access to confidential information, data, and documents including, but not limited to, financial records, personnel files and documents, customer lists and information, collective bargaining information, trade secrets, and strategic business plans of the Company. Depending on other aspects of the employee's assigned work, confidential employees may be classified as exempt or nonexempt.

General Hiring

It is also advisable for employers to adopt a "general hiring policy." Such a policy has the advantage of informing concerned individuals that your company hires and promotes employees on the basis of their fitness and qualifications. In the absence of this kind of a policy, you are leaving the issue open to speculation and doubt by those who may choose to challenge the arbitrariness of a hiring decision. With the policy, you create a perceived atmosphere of objectivity in your hiring process and resultant decisions.

Policy Sample

The Company's basic hiring policy is to ensure that reasonable efforts are made to recruit, test, and select job applicants on the basis of predetermined qualifications that do not arbitrarily discriminate against any qualified person. It is the Company's intent under this policy to hire and promote individuals who demonstrate the greatest and most desirable level of skills, knowledge, abilities, adaptations, fitness, and other qualifications appropriate to the position.

It shall be the responsibility of the (*Human Resource Manager*) to develop the most suitable methods of recruitment, selection tests, and related hiring programs and procedures to ensure that this policy is carried out in the most efficient, timely, and lawful manner reasonable in each case of a hiring decision. The (*Human Resource Manager*) will therefore review applications, conduct preemployment tests and investigations, select and refer the most qualified applicants to the hiring department for interview, and perform related activities in support of the hiring function. Department managers are responsible for making the hiring decision after consultation with the (*Human Resource Manager*).

3.2 Equal Employment Opportunity, Affirmative Action, and Nepotism Policies

Policies that address a company's stance on fair employment practices are a valuable source of information. New hires should be able to read such a statement on the employer's application form. Employees should be able to learn of the company's position from observing how the company handles its employment decisions in an unbiased, non-discriminatory manner as stated in the personnel manual or employee handbook. Additionally, such outsiders as attorneys and compliance agency representatives may find the need and opportunity to review the company's policies on this matter to determine whether or not the organization has taken an interest in making fair employment decisions. If your company has not already adopted equal employment opportunity policy statements, you may wish to consider the use of one of the following samples for small-to-medium size employers. (Similar policy samples for large size companies are too extensive for the purpose of demonstrating reasonably succinct policy provisions.)

Equal Employment Opportunity

Policy Sample 1: Small Company

The Company supports and has a strong commitment to the principles of equal employment opportunity. The Company recruits, hires, trains, transfers, promotes and compensates individuals and makes all personnel decisions without regard to race, color, religion, age, sex, national origin or ancestry, marital status, veteran status, or physical or mental disability unrelated to an individual's ability to perform the job, in accordance with applicable law.[4]

Policy Sample 2: Small Company

The Company is committed to abide by all the laws pertaining to fair employment practices. All persons having the authority to hire, discharge, transfer, or promote employees shall support, without reservation, a nondiscrimination policy in hiring any applicant or otherwise deciding employment matters of any employee. This policy shall apply without regard to race, color, religion, national origin, ancestry, marital status, pregnancy, childbirth or related medical condition, age, sex, handicap, or veteran status, except where such individual characteristic represents an essential bona fide occupational (dis)qualification.

Policy Sample 3: Medium Company

A. It is the Company's policy to employ, retain, promote, terminate, and otherwise treat any and all employees and job applicants on the basis of merit, qualifications, and competence. This policy shall be applied without regard to any individual's sex, race, color, national origin, religion, marital status, pregnancy, age, or physical handicap.

In establishing this policy, (*Company name*) recognizes the need to initiate and maintain affirmative personnel measures to ensure the achievement of equal employment opportunities in all aspects of our workplace settings, conditions, and decisions. It shall be the responsibility of all employees to abide by and carry out the letter, spirit, and intent of the Company's equal employment commitment.

B. It is prohibited for any employee of the Company to refuse to hire, train, promote, or provide equitable employment conditions to any employee or applicant, or to discipline or dismiss any employee solely on the basis of such person's race, color, national origin, age (over 40), sex, marital status, religious beliefs, or physical handicap; except where the doctrine of business necessity or a bona fide occupational qualification can reasonably be established.

It shall further be prohibited for any employee, contractor, or other agent of the Company to engage in the following types of discriminatory conduct:

1. *Race, Color, National Origin, and Religion*
   Making statements or jokes, or committing acts regarding a particular race, ancestry, or religion that are regarded as derogatory, offensive, prejudicial, or harassing.

2. *Sex, Sexual Harassment, and Marital Status*
   Intimidating or interfering with an employee's work or work environment through unwelcome, offensive, or harassing sexual comments, questions, or acts, implicitly or explicitly, including prejudicial statements or acts regarding pregnancy or marital status.
   Employees who believe they have been harassed by a coworker, supervisor, or agent of the Company should promptly report the facts of the incident or incidents and the names of the individuals involved to their supervisor or to the (*Human Resource Manager*). Supervisors should immediately report any incidents of sexual harassment to the (*Human Resource Manager*). The (*Human Resource Manager, or designee*) will investigate all such claims and take appropriate corrective action. If you have any questions concerning this policy, please feel free to contact the (*Human Resource Manager*) at your convenience.[5]

Affirmative Action

Affirmative action policies are another important way to show that fair employment principles and practices are used to make hiring decisions. While equal employment opportunity is a conceptual condition that all employers should choose to create, it is a company's affirmative action measures that become the vehicle for the actual creation of an EEO environment.

There is an important distinction between having affirmative action policies and adopting a formal Affirmative Action Plan (AAP). Due to a few U.S. Supreme Court cases in the late 1980s, it has become inadvisable for private sector employers to adopt *voluntary* AAPs since you can be held liable for violating them in any way. However, employers need not be unduly wary of practicing sound affirmative action practices that are spelled out in policy. Typically, such policies merely state that your company makes specific kinds of attempts to ensure that all sectors of the available labor market have access to employment, and that you take steps to remove artificial barriers to employment. Here is a sample policy you may wish to add to your EEO policy.

Policy Sample

In furtherance of the Company's policy on equal employment opportunity, the Company additionally adopts this policy on affirmative action measures that may be taken from time-to-time as a means of ensuring that all people have a reasonable access and consideration with (*Company name*). In adopting this policy, the Company gives recognition to the potential of all individuals who wish to participate in or seek entrance into the active work force.

In carrying out its affirmative action efforts, the Company shall periodically take the following steps as a means of making jobs known to the greater pool of human resources who might be qualified for employment, and to continuously improve upon any practice that is found or tends to be discriminatory in any known respect.

1. Develop and recommend any policies, procedures, practices, or programs that are in the Company's best interest to consider as a means of strengthening equal employment opportunities and the validity of employment decisions.

2. Develop and use recruitment sources that would provide information about Company job opportunities to all sectors of the available labor market.

3. Develop and use contemporary selection testing methods and standards that are determined appropriate for differing employment conditions.

4. Monitor hiring results to evaluate the effectiveness of nondiscriminatory employment practices, and attempts to achieve and maintain a representative work force.

5. Review and update job descriptions to ensure that they are relevant in all respects to actual job duties, requirements, and qualifications.

6. Investigate internal complaints or reports of discrimination and take the appropriate corrective action where warranted.

Management and supervisory personnel are expected to become aware of, and all employees are expected to abide by, the Company's policies and efforts concerning equal employment and affirmative action. Specifically, supervisors are expected to cooperate with the development of valid job descriptions and selection tests; to be responsible for making objective employment decisions; and to report any condition that has the appearance or effect of discrimination solely on the basis on an individual's race, color, national origin, religion, age (over 40), sex, marital status, pregnancy, or physical handicap.

Nepotism

Finally, employers should clarify their position on nepotism—the hiring of spouses and other relatives of employees—since these policies and/or practices have been found to be an illegal form of discrimination in many instances. Although the very nature of this type of policy may be particularly sensitive for smaller companies, many of which may be family owned and operated, it is important to recognize that the company is a business entity and will be expected by the courts to function with business objectivity and nondiscriminatory employment practices. Consequently, you may wish to formulate a policy on the subject that neither absolutely prohibits nor gives undue preference to spouses and relatives, particularly those having authority for making hiring decisions.

Policy Sample 1

A. *Employment of Spouse*

It is the policy of the Company not to discriminate in its employment and personnel actions with respect to its employees, prospective employees, and applicants on the basis of marital status. No employee, prospective employee, or applicant will be denied employment or benefits of employment solely on the basis of marital status. This policy also applies to the selection of persons for a training program leading to employment or promotion.

Notwithstanding the above provision, the Company retains the right

1. To refuse to place one spouse under the direct supervision of the other spouse where such has the potential for creating an adverse effect on supervision, safety, security, or morale.

2. To refuse to place both spouses in the same department, division, or facility where such has the potential for creating an adverse effect on supervision, safety, security, or morale, or involves potential conflicts of interest.

B. *Employment of Other Relatives*

1. Relatives within the third degree of kinship by blood or marriage of the Company's senior management or administrative employees, or any person exercising hiring, promotion, and termination authority, may not be hired into the Company service without written approval of the President.

2. Relatives within the third degree of kinship by blood or marriage of any Company employee, regardless of status, will not be hired in the same department, division, or facility where such has the potential for creating an adverse effect on supervision, safety, security, or morale, or involves potential conflicts of interest, without the written approval of the President.[6]

Policy Sample 2

Nothing in the Company's equal employment opportunity policy is intended to be interpreted as preventing the Company from reasonably regulating nepotism for reasons of supervision, safety, security, or morale. Generally, employee's relatives will be eligible for employment with the Company as long as no conflicts in supervision, safety, security, or morale, or potential conflicts of interest exist. Relatives include an employee's parent, child, spouse, brother, sister, in-laws and step relationships. If two employees marry or become related, and a conflict arises, only one of the employees will be permitted to stay with the Company unless reasonable accommodations can be made to eliminate the (potential) problems. The decision as to which relative will remain with the Company must be made either by the two employees within _____ calendar days, or by the Company on the basis of service value.[7]

3.3 Internal Hiring Policies

Hiring decisions and processes are not merely confined to external job applicants. There are many jobs in an organization that will be filled on the basis of internal placement activities such as transfers (lateral job moves) and promotions. Although not strictly an internal placement activity, rehires have been included here since these individuals were once employees of the organization and the hiring process for them is more akin to internal hiring practices than the more elaborate screening of unfamiliar applicants.

Job Posting

Policy Sample 1

For many positions, the best candidates are current employees. Thus, the Human Resources Department will post many open positions to advise current employees of openings. The Company encourages employees to apply for any posted position for which they are qualified.[8]

Policy Sample 2

It is the policy of the Company to keep employees informed of job vacancies that occur periodically in order to provide opportunities for transfers within the same job, new vocations, promotions, or referral of qualified applicants by employees. When job vacancies occur that are deemed appropriate and desirable by the (*Human Resource Manager*) for posting, the details of the vacant job will be listed along with the filing deadline date. Interested employees who occupy the same job may submit a Transfer Request form to the (*Human Resources Office*) not later than the filing deadline. All other interested employees are to submit a completed Employment Application form to the (*Human Resources Office*) by the filing deadline.

Employees should understand that the posting of job vacancies does not mean that the selection process will be confined to existing employees. Rather, employees who make application for transfer, job change, or promotion to a posted job vacancy should be aware that they may be subject to competition for the job from among a larger group of applicants, unless noted otherwise on the posted job announcement.

Job Transfer

Job transfer policies that permit employees to file such requests whether or not applicable vacancies exist have advantages and disadvantages. The advantages are that an otherwise unhappy employee may become revitalized, the job gets filled quickly, and there is a minimum amount of paperwork involved. Disadvantages include having to fill more than one position, transfers do not always provide the best employee for the vacant position, and the request forms can be difficult to store, keep current, and track. Smaller companies tend to find this internal placement practice easier and more advantageous than larger companies. Here is a sample transfer policy for your possible use.

Policy Sample

Employees who wish to transfer to the same job in another part of the Company, or to a substantially similar job having equivalent responsibilities and qualifications, may file a Transfer Request form with the (*Human Resources Office*) at any time during normal business hours.

As job vacancies occur, the (*Human Resource Manager*) may consider transfer requests on file as of that date. Requests considered to be appropriate to the vacancy may be considered subject to the following conditions

1. Only full-time regular status employees will be eligible to file transfer requests;

2. Requesting employees must have completed a minimum of six months of active, continuous employment in their present job;

3. The requesting employee's job performance must be rated satisfactory or better in all performance categories on the most recent appraisal. A written reprimand or more serious disciplinary action against an employee within the six month period preceding a transfer request will constitute unsatisfactory job performance for purposes of this policy; and,

4. The requesting employee must possess at least the minimum qualifications for the position to which transfer is requested.

Transfer Request forms shall be kept on file in the (*Human Resources Office*) for a period not to exceed six months from the date submitted. Employees may, however, submit a subsequent Transfer Request form in order to keep their request active.

Job Promotion

Job promotion policies (or "promotion from within") are similar to transfer policies inasmuch as they have both advantages and disadvantages. On the advantage side, promotion policies give first opportunities for higher level jobs to existing employees, thereby creating a heightened sense of morale and employment benefit for employees. Additionally, the company often benefits by placing a person whose talents and attributes are familiar into a more consequential position rather than risking chance on an outsider.

Some of the disadvantages include the fact that not all employees who have been promoted, under policy pressure to do so, have turned out to be good performers in the higher position. A classic example of the Peter Principle—promoting employees to a level of their incompetence—is the all-too-common practice of promoting otherwise good employees into supervisory jobs without adequate assessment or pretraining. Also, when higher level job vacancies are filled by internal promotion, the lower level job must then be filled, amounting to two hiring decisions and processes rather than one. Each company must weigh the respective advantages and disadvantages of promotion policies. If you choose to adopt such a policy, it is advisable to write it in a flexible manner leaving the company some discretion to ensure that all hiring decisions are made on the basis of the best qualified person for the job.

Policy Sample 1

Depending on conditions within the Company or work unit location when a promotional job vacancy occurs, the Company may announce the vacancy and consider existing employees before recruiting applicants from the outside. If no employees apply, or if the Company deems internal applicants to be disqualified in some respect, external recruitment for applicants to the vacancy shall commence. However, the Company may alternatively determine the need or desire to recruit from outside the Company concurrent with internal considerations.

Policy Sample 2

Generally, it is the Company's policy to give promotional consideration to existing employees working within the occupational path of higher level job vacancies before testing outside applicants. The Company will give such notice and consideration when it is determined to be in the best interests of the Company to do so, and when it is known that qualified or potentially qualified employees exist.

This policy is by no means intended to create a promise to employees, nor an obligation on the part of the Company, that every job vacancy constituting a promotion will be subject to selection from within the Company. Rather, it is the Company's way of exercising discretionary judgment in each case of a job vacancy, yet giving due consideration to the merits of promoting qualified and deserving employees into opportunities where they can acquire greater responsibilities, skills, occupational challenge, and pay.

Employees interested in promotional job opportunities may learn of such job vacancies when announcements are posted (on employee bulletin boards, at the Human Resources Office, in memos to supervisors, etc.). Those interested employees who meet the prescribed qualifications of the promotional job will be required to file a completed Employment Application form with the (*Human Resources Office*) no later than the filing deadline. Thereafter, applying employees will be notified by the (*Human Resources Office*) regarding their acceptance or denial of further consideration for the job. Employees should remember that denial does not mean that you do not possess qualifications; rather, it means that other applicants possessed qualifications deemed more suitable to the job or related conditions.

Employment Rehire

Rehires can occur from two different conditions; *reemployment* of a former employee who resigned in good standing within a prescribed period, or *reinstatement* of a former employee who was laid off by the Company within a prescribed period. Under either of these conditions, many companies will rehire former employees into jobs where they previously held regular status without retesting their job skills if the rehire occurs within one or two years of the employment separation date. It is advisable to have rehire policies in place so that you can approach each situation based on predetermined policy standards. Here is a sample of such a policy.

Policy Sample

Former employees may be considered for rehire by the Company without taking competitive tests, provided the rehire is being made to a position in which the former employee held regular status with the Company in the same or substantially similar position as determined by the (*Human Resource Manager*) in accordance with the following.

A. *Reemployment:*

Employees who resign from the Company in good standing may be eligible for reemployment consideration within twelve months of the date of their employment separation. To determine eligibility, the former employee must file an Employment Application form with the (*Human Resources Office*) and await notice as to the existence of an available position within this time period.

If a former employee is reemployed under these conditions, no credit will be given for former service with respect to benefit accruals or other forms of longevity entitlements that are normally associated with an employee's continuous service. Each reemployment will be assigned a new probationary period and accrue benefits as would any other new employee, except that reemployments may be assigned a pay rate commensurate with the rate received at the time of their separation.

B. *Reinstatement:*

Employees who are laid off from their jobs with the Company, and who had at least a rating of satisfactory performance in each category on their last formal appraisal, may be eligible for rehire within twenty-four months from the date of their employment separation. To determine eligibility, the former employee must file an Employment Application form with the (*Human Resources Office*) and await notice as to the existence of an available position within this time period. Since Employment Application forms are kept active for a period of twelve months, those who file for reinstatement may have to renew their application to keep it active.

If a former employee is reinstated under these conditions, credit will be given for former service with respect to vacation and other longevity-related accruals that would have occurred had the employee not had a break in service. Additionally, each reinstatement will be assigned a pay rate commensurate with the rate received at the time of separation. However, a new anniversary date will be established on the basis of the date of reinstatement even though a probationary period of employment will not be required.

3.4 Preemployment Testing Policies

This section deals with those policies that describe how the hiring process works, explain procedures that are required to be followed, and define the realm of hiring tests. The importance of having such policies is attached to the need for employers to communicate this information to company supervisors and managers to let them know the company's expectations of their role in the hiring process. Another reason is to inform outsiders that your company knows what it's doing when it comes to the procedural formalities associated with the hiring process, including those policy statements that reaffirm your company's knowledge of applicable laws and management principles. It is suggested that you choose from among the following policy samples in order to enhance the internal and external clarity of your hiring program.

Employment Applications

Policy Sample

Applications for initial or promotional employment with the Company will be made on forms provided by the Company, and shall be completed and submitted to the (*Human Resources Office*) in sufficient detail, clarity, and timeliness to be considered for job vacancies and/or filed for future reference. Employment Application forms will minimally require information concerning the applicant's training, experience, and other pertinent employment history, and may provide additional information on certificates, licenses, educational records, employment reference, and similar supporting evidence of suitability for the position for which application is being made.

All Employment Applications must be dated and signed by the applicant to attest to the truthfulness of information provided and to acknowledge any notices placed upon the application form.

Employment Applications will be kept on file in the (*Human Resources Office*) for a period of twelve months unless otherwise disqualified.

Disqualification of Applications and Applicants

Policy Sample

The (*Human Resource Manager*) shall be responsible and have the authority to disqualify Employment Applications and individual applicants on the basis of the following conditions.

A. *Disqualification of Applications*

1. The application has not been completed in adequate detail or sufficient legibility to determine suitability for employment;

2. The application has not been submitted to the (*Human Resources Office);*

3. The application has not been submitted in a timely fashion as prescribed; or,

4. There exists other evidence on the application that the (*Human Resource Manager*) deems to be of a disqualifying nature.

B. *Disqualification of Applicants*

1. The applicant is found to lack basic qualification requirements for the position based on the application form or through selection testing;

2. The applicant is not lawfully eligible for employment in the United States;

3. The applicant is determined to be physically unfit to perform the necessary duties reasonably associated with the position based on legitimate business or operational conditions;

4. The applicant has willfully made false statements of a material fact, or omissions thereof, or has practiced or attempted to practice deception or fraud in the application or selection testing process;

5. The applicant's personal history, character, reputation, or other characteristic or condition is determined to be in contravention to the interests of the Company; or,

6. There exists other legitimate evidence about the applicant's suitability or qualifications for employment as determined appropriate for disqualification by the (*Human Resource Manager*).

Applicant Limitations

Policy Sample

Employment selection testing may periodically result in an unusually large number of applicants who meet the prescribed minimum qualifications. When such circumstances arise, the (*Human Resource Manager*) may limit the number of applicants selected to advance through the testing process based on such considerations as

A. Length, type, and level of prior work experience related to the position being tested;

B. Applicability of prior work experience to the Company's business, facilities, operational practices, special needs, and problems encountered in the course of performing the job being tested; and,

C. Type, amount, and recency of job preparation for prescribed responsibilities, including the possession of applicable certificates, specialized training or course work, and educational achievement.[9]

Types and Methods of Selection Tests

Policy Sample

The selection techniques used in the testing of prospective new or promotional employees are intended to be impartial and of a practical nature based on the conditions associated with each separate position in the Company's employ. To the degree possible, selection tests will relate directly to the actual duties and conditions of the job in a way that fairly and accurately measures the applicant's capability to perform its essential duties. Consequently, selection tests may include, but shall not be limited to, written examinations of the applicant's job knowledge, abilities, and actions; performance and achievement tests; personal interviews; work samples; medical and/or medically related tests; or any combination of these tests or other requirements that may be deemed suitable by the (*Human Resource Manager*)—except that such tests will not be intentionally discriminatory in nature or result.

It will be the responsibility of the (*Human Resource Manager*) to determine the manner and methods of selection tests, and make arrangements for the use of facilities and Company resources necessary for the conduct of such examinations. No applicant taking a selection test will be treated in any preferential way to any other applicant participating in the same selection test to the extent that such treatment would compromise the impartiality of the testing process. Applicants participating in selection tests who are found to cheat, falsify information, or be disruptive to others will be subject to immediate disqualification from further consideration and, if such applicants are current employees of the Company, they may have their employment terminated.[10]

Medical Examinations

Policy Sample 1

Those positions in the Company's employ that require particular physical conditions in order to properly carry out or endure prescribed duties of the position may be subject to successful evaluation by a medical practitioner (selected and paid by the Company) prior to an offer of employment. Such medical examinations will be based on bona fide occupational standards reasonably related to the position in question, with consideration given by the Company to accommodating the physical disabilities and limitations of otherwise qualified applicants. Applicants who fail to appear for Company arranged medical examinations without good cause will be automatically disqualified from further selection consideration.[11]

Policy Sample 2

It is the Company's policy to employ applicants whose physical and mental health is consistent with the bona fide requirements and conditions of the position they are to occupy, and to assure that all employees maintain a standard of health that will contribute to safe, healthy, and efficient performance of work. It is likewise the Company's policy not to discriminate against qualified applicants due to the existence of physical disabilities where such disabilities can be reasonably accommodated. In order to achieve these goals, the Company may provide medical and/or medically related examinations as follows.

All new hires may be subject to certification of physical and related medical qualifications for employment based on testing by medical practitioners selected and paid by the Company. If certification of suitability is issued by the medical practitioner to the (*Human Resource Manager*), the applicant may be hired any time thereafter. If no certification is issued, or is issued conditionally, the applicant may not be hired until and unless the medical practitioner

1. Issues a revised certification;

2. Revises conditions of the certification such that the condition does not present undue complications, liability, or economic hardship for the Company; or,

3. Advises that a remedial program has been initiated that will permit unconditional employment consistent with job requirements and Company needs.

The (*Human Resource Manager*) will be responsible for arranging medical examinations and coordinating results thereof with the person supervising the position under consideration. Failure on the part of an applicant to appear for a scheduled medical examination may result in disqualification from further consideration of the position being tested.[12]

Drug and Alcohol Program

Policy Sample 1

A. *General Policy*

The Company is committed to maintaining a safe and healthy work environment free from the influence of alcohol and drugs. To that end, the Company has adopted a drug and alcohol abuse policy. Compliance with the Company's drug policy is a condition of employment. The Company intends to take severe disciplinary action, up to and including termination, against an employee who violates the Company's drug and alcohol abuse policy.

B. *Prevention and Treatment*

The Human Resources Department has developed a Drug-Free Awareness Program to educate employees and their families about the dangers of drug and alcohol abuse and the Company's drug and alcohol abuse policy.

The Company encourages any employee with a drug or alcohol abuse problem to voluntarily seek treatment. The Company has established an employee assistance program to provide counseling and referral services for employees with drug or alcohol abuse problems who voluntarily seek help.

C. *Prohibited Activity*

The Company strictly prohibits unauthorized use, possession (including storage in a desk, locker, car or other repository), manufacture, distribution, dispensation or sale of illegal drugs, drug paraphernalia, controlled substances, or alcohol on Company premises or Company business, in Company supplied vehicles or during working hours; any activity that compromises the integrity or accuracy of the Company's drug and alcohol testing program; and failure or refusal to abide by the Company's alcohol and drug abuse policy; or an employee's conviction under any criminal drug statute will be a prohibited activity under this policy and therefore subject to disciplinary action by the Company.

D. *Testing*

The Company may require employees and applicants to be tested for drugs or alcohol upon hiring (all offers of employment are conditional on passing a drug or alcohol test); when the Company suspects that the employee's work performance or on-the-job behavior may have been affected in any way by drugs or alcohol; when Company policy requires an employee to undergo a physical examination; or when the Company determines that an employee may have contributed to an accident involving fatality, serious bodily injury, or substantial damage to property. Any positive drug or alcohol test is a violation of the Company's drug and alcohol abuse policy.

Supervisors are trained to identify job performance and on-the-job behavior that may reflect drug or alcohol abuse. When a supervisor concludes that declining job performance or erratic on-the-job behavior may be the product of personal problems, the supervisor will refer the employee [to the Medical Department] for a breath, saliva, urine and/or blood test for alcohol or drug abuse.

Any test for drug or alcohol abuse will be conducted using reasonable procedural safeguards.

E. *Searches*

Where the employee's performance or on-the-job behavior may have been affected in any way by drugs or alcohol, the Company may search

1. the employee;

2. a locker, desk, or other Company property under the employee's control; and

3. the employee's personal effects or automobile on Company property.[13]

Policy Sample 2: Federal Contractor's Policy, Drug-Free Workplace Act of 1988

Illegal drugs in the workplace are a danger to us all. They impair safety and health, promote crime, lower productivity and quality, and undermine public confidence in the work we do. We will not tolerate the use of illegal drugs here—and now, by law, we cannot. Under the federal Drug-Free Workplace

Act, in order for this company to be considered a "responsible source" for the award of federal contracts, we have developed the following policy.

Effective immediately, any location at which company business is conducted, whether at this or any other site, is declared to be a **drug-free workplace.** This means

1. All employees are **absolutely prohibited** from unlawfully manufacturing, distributing, dispensing, possessing, or using controlled substances in the workplace. . . . Any employee violating the above policy is subject to discipline, up to and including termination, for the first offense.

2. Employees have the right to know the dangers of drug abuse in the workplace, the company's policy about them, and what help is available to combat drug problems. We will institute an education program for all employees on the dangers of drug abuse in the workplace. To assist employees in overcoming drug-abuse problems, the company may offer the following rehabilitative help:

   • Medical benefits for substance-abuse treatment.

   • Information about community resources for assessment and treatment.

   • Counseling program.

   • Employee assistance program.

   In addition, the company will provide supervisory training to assist in identifying and addressing illegal drug use by employees.

3. Any employee convicted of violating a criminal drug statute in this workplace must inform the company of such conviction (including pleas of guilty and nolo contendre) within **five days of the conviction occurring.** Failure to so inform the company subjects the employee of disciplinary action, up to and including **termination for the first offense.** By law, the company will notify the federal contracting officer within 10 days of receiving such notice from an employee or otherwise receiving notice of such a conviction.

4. The company reserves the right to offer employees convicted of violating a criminal drug statute in the workplace participation in an approved rehabilitation or drug abuse assistance program as an alternative to discipline. If such a program is offered, and accepted by the employee, then the employee must satisfactorily participate in the program as a condition of continued employment.

ALL EMPLOYEES ARE ASKED TO ACKNOWLEDGE THAT THEY HAVE READ THE ABOVE POLICY AND AGREE TO ABIDE BY IT IN ALL RESPECTS. BY LAW, THIS ACKNOWLEDGEMENT AND AGREEMENT ARE REQUIRED OF YOU AS A CONDITION OF CONTINUED EMPLOYMENT.

Please refer any questions on the above policy to your supervisor or the personnel department.[14]

Employment References

Policy Sample

In keeping with the Company's policy on taking reasonable measures to determine the overall suitability of new hires, and to provide the Company with greater assurance of a new employee's successful adaptation to employment conditions, the Company reserves the right to investigate and obtain prior employment, educational, credit, character, and other pertinent information about any prospective applicant under consideration for hire. While most reference investigations are conducted at the time of hire, the Company may additionally determine the propriety of gathering similar information on existing employees when doing so is deemed suitable and in the best interests of the Company.

Reference information may be obtained by (*designated management personnel, or the Human Resource Manager*), however all such information shall be treated in strictest confidence and kept on file in the (*Human Resources Office*). Conversely, reference information may be given to inquiring and verified employers *only* by the (*Human Resource Manager, President, and/or Department Heads*), including letters of reference, only when a written request and authorization has been obtained by the respective employee.

3.5 Employment Selection and Records Policies

Policies that address employment selection, the initial employment period, and hiring-related records are fundamental sources of information that support the organization's hiring program. Typically, these policies serve as a guide concerning the procedural and processing actions of decision makers involved in hiring. When you use policies that define and guide hiring actions in advance, you stand a better chance of developing an orderly hiring program, getting a better understanding of the hiring process and human resource management principles from those supervisors and managers involved in hiring decisions, and maintaining better decision making continuity. Here are a few of the more important types of policies that should be adopted to achieve those results.

Employment Offers

Policy Sample 1

Neither supervisors nor department heads have the authority to offer employment to any applicant; only the Human Resources Department [or President] does. All offers of employment are conditional, subject to satisfactory results of a background investigation, reference check, preemployment alcohol and drug tests, and production of documents sufficient to demonstrate identity and authorization to work in the United States, as required by the Immigration Reform and Control Act.[15]

Policy Sample 2

It is the Company's policy to confirm all offers and acceptance of offers of employment in writing. Upon notice from the hiring authority to the (*Human Resource Manager*), a letter will be prepared by the (*Human Resources Office*) to the selected applicant making an offer of employment and providing such information as the new employee's start date and time, job title, rate of pay, and employment orientation instructions. It also will state that acceptance of the employment offer must be made in writing by a specified date. Only the (*President, General Manager, Human Resource Manager*) will be authorized to sign employment offer letters.

An employment offer may not be made until the selected applicant has satisfactorily demonstrated suitable job abilities, background, physical condition, and legal requirements that are a customary part of the hiring process. When this process is completed, and results are satisfactory, the (*Human Resource Manager*) shall promptly notify the hiring authority who may then request that an employment offer letter be presented to the applicant. Upon acceptance of the offer by the applicant, the (*Human Resource Manager*) shall notify the hiring authority of the applicant's report date and request that preparations be made to orient the new employee.

It should be understood by all employees and selected applicants that employment offers are not a contract for employment, and that the employment relationship can be terminated by either the Company or employee at any time, for any reason, with or without written notice.

Introductory Employment Periods

Policy Sample 1

A. *Purpose*

The introductory employment period is an intrinsic part and extension of the employee selection process during which the employee will be considered in training and under careful observation and evaluation by supervisory personnel. Generally, this period will be utilized to train and evaluate the employee's effective adjustment to work tasks, conduct, observance of rules, attendance and job responsibilities, and to provide for the release of any introductory employee whose performance does not meet required standards of job progress or adaptation.

B. *Duration*

The (*Human Resource Manager*) will establish introductory employment periods for each job in the Company on the basis of such factors as the complexity of job tasks, unique or difficult nature of work operations, the importance of work activities and decisions, and the time involved to reasonably accomplish an evaluation of full job adaptation. Generally, nonexempt employees will serve an (*60, 90, 120-day, 6 months—see note*) introductory employment period during which their job progress will be formally evaluated at least once based on the standards established for the job. Part-time employees will serve introductory employment periods commensurate to the number of hours served to that of full-time employees.[16]

Policy Sample 2

A. All non-exempt employees, whether new, rehired or promoted, are required to serve an (*60, 90, 120-day, 6 months—see note*) introductory employment period. New and rehired employees will not be eligible to accrue or use paid sick leave, vacation, or any other form of paid absence excluding designate holidays. Additionally, introductory employment workers will be limited to filing complaints or grievances on matters related only to alleged discrimination and harassment pursuant to Company policies.

B. Introductory employment periods may be extended by the (*Human Resource Manager*) for a limited additional period where it is determined that such an extension is necessary to thoroughly evaluate the employee's ability to perform the full scope of assigned duties. Introductory employment periods may also be extended by the number of days a probationer is absent from scheduled work for any reason. In these cases, the employee will be advised of the introductory employment period extension prior to the conclusion of the initial introductory employment period.

C. Introductory employment employees are not eligible for some benefits paid for or sponsored by the Company. However, upon successful completion of the introductory employment period, they are considered regular employees of the Company and thereupon become eligible for these benefits, provided they satisfy the terms and conditions of the various benefit programs.

D. Notwithstanding the provisions of the Company's introductory employment period policies, the Company reserves the right to terminate any employment relationship at will.[17]

NOTE

While it is common practice for employers to use only one introductory employment period—90-days being the most frequently used—it is advisable for employers to use at least two distinctive periods, say for exempt nonmanagerial employees and a lesser period for nonexempt employees. Remember, the theory behind introductory employment periods is to provide new hires with initial training and to evaluate such performance characteristics as adaptation, skills development and productivity progress as a matter of the final *selection* process. Therefore, it does not logically follow that a company could reasonably assess these selection characteristics during the same amount of time for a newly hired file clerk and an engineer. Consequently, the length of introductory employment periods should be determined by the amount of time needed for full assessment of the essential duties of various types and levels of positions in the company.

Employee Orientations

Policy Sample 1

During each new employee's first workweek, the designated supervisor will conduct a thorough orientation for the employee on such matters as the Company's organization and functions; the employee's role in helping to achieve operating objectives; the employee's job content and scope; training, performance and evaluation standards, and promotional opportunities; job safety; and any other matters of operational importance. Work unit and departmental orientations are to be recorded on the prescribed orientation form, signed and dated by both the new employee and person administering the orientation, and placed in the employee's personnel file as a permanent record.

Within the new employee's first workweek, the (*Human Resources Office staff*) will provide an additional orientation consisting of the completion of employment forms and records; an explanation of the Company's compensation and benefit program, and personnel policies; and any other information as determined appropriate to orient and integrate the employee into Company service.[18]

Policy Sample 2

The Company believes that a smooth and thorough orientation of new employees results in a positive integration into the Company's operations, and will lead to a more productive and satisfying employment relationship. For this reason, new employees are to be scheduled for a thorough orientation promptly following their report date whereupon they are to receive information about the Company's employment benefits and to complete related documents.

The employee's supervisor is to provide such information as the Company's background, organization and function of each department, personnel policies, the employee's role in helping to achieve Company goals, the employee's job content, performance and safety standards, promotional opportunities, and any other information deemed pertinent to establish employee familiarity with operations. New employees should also be introduced to their coworkers, and other supervisors and managers with whom they will be working or should know.

The topics covered by a supervisor in a new employee orientation shall be documented on a form prescribed by the (*Human Resources Office*), who will receive the completed, signed form for placement in the employee's personnel file. Following initial orientation, supervisors and managers should regularly check with employees concerning questions they may have, their working conditions, any problems or difficulties they may have encountered, and feedback concerning their performance or job progress.[19]

Confidentiality and Security of Company Property

Policy Sample 1

It is the policy of (*Company name*) to maintain strict control over entrance to the premises, access to work locations and records, computer information, and cash or other items of monetary value. Employees who are assigned keys, given special access, or assigned job responsibilities in connection with the safety, security, or confidentiality of such records, material, equipment, or items of monetary or business value will be required to use sound judgment and discretion in carrying out their duties, and will be held accountable for any wrongdoing or acts of indiscretion.

Information about (*Company name*), its (*customers, clients, suppliers*), or employees should not be divulged to anyone other than persons who have a right to know, or are authorized to receive such information. When in doubt as to whether certain information is or is not confidential, prudence dictates that no disclosure be provided without first clearly establishing that such disclosure has been authorized by appropriate supervisory or management personnel.

This basic policy of caution and discretion in the handling of confidential information extends to both external and internal disclosure. Confidential information obtained as a result of employment with (*Company name*) is not to be used by an employee for the purpose of furthering any private interest, or as a means of making personal gains. Use or disclosure of such information can result in civil or criminal penalties, both for individuals involved and for the Company.[20]

Policy Sample 2

All employees are expected to protect Company property, which includes information and the expertise of our employees, at all times. Accordingly, visitors are not to be permitted on Company premises without an employee escort. When visitors arrive, they will be asked to wait in the lobby area until an employee can accompany them to meeting or working locations. In addition, certain employees with access to proprietary information may be required to sign agreements regarding the use of such information as a condition of employment.[21]

Personnel Records Access and Disclosure

Policy Sample 1

Personnel files are kept on all employees. They contain the employees' employment application, salary and employment histories, performance appraisals, emergency contact data, signed acknowledgement forms, orientation form, and other documents as required by law or regarded as necessary by the Company. (*As permitted by state law*), secondary files are kept on employees that contain medical history, employment reference, and investigative information, the contents of which are not subject to access or review by the employee. However, employees wishing to review their primary personnel file may do so during normal business hours, at convenient times, and with advance notice to the (*Human Resource Manager*). Such records may not be reproduced, removed, or altered without the consent of the (*Human Resource Manager*).

To ensure employees' rights to privacy, personnel files are considered confidential. The Company limits information disclosed to third parties to only lawful access and disclosure, unless an employee signs a release authorizing the Company to provide file information. Reference information on employees, including letters of employment reference, will be provided when appropriate only by the (*Human Resource Manager*).

It is each employee's responsibility to keep information, such as address, marital status, birth of children, emergency notification and other important personal information current in their file by notifying the (*Human Resources Office*) promptly when these events occur. Many status changes affect benefit and insurance plans, so it is essential that employees let the Company know when these changes occur.

Policy Sample 2

A. *General Policy*

The Company keeps certain records on each employee in a personnel file kept in the Human Resources Department.

B. *The Personnel File*

The Company's policy is to keep only the most essential documents such as applications, payroll information, performance reviews, and disciplinary records in the personnel file. The Human Resources Department has ultimate discretion to determine what documents should go in each employee's personnel file.

C. *Employee Inspection of File*

An employee may inspect his or her personnel file and copy documents in it. To do so, the employee must make an appointment with the Director of Human Resources or [his] designee to inspect the file at a time that is both convenient for the Human Resources Department and outside of the employee's normal working hours.

D. *Information Employees Are to Provide Human Resources*

Employees are expected to notify Human Resources of any changes in name, address, phone number, marital status, names or number of dependents, and persons to be notified in case of an emergency.

E. *Requests for Information about Employees*

All requests for information about current or former employees are to be forwarded to the Director of Human Resources. No information will be released in response to oral requests. The Director of Human Resources will normally release only the dates of employment, last position held, and final salary.[22]

Checklist of Hiring and Initial Employment Policies

Administrative Policies Related to Hiring

- ❑ At-Will Employment Policy
- ❑ Types Of Employment Policy
- ❑ General Hiring Policy

Equal Employment Opportunity, Affirmative Action, and Nepotism Policies

- ❑ Equal Employment Opportunity Policy
- ❑ Affirmative Action Policy (optional)
- ❑ Nepotism Policy

Internal Hiring Policies

- ❑ Job Posting Policy
- ❑ Job Transfer Policy
- ❑ Job Promotion Policy
- ❑ Employment Rehire Policy

Applicants and Preemployment Testing Policies

- ❑ Employment Applications Policy
- ❑ Disqualification of Applications and Applicants Policy
- ❑ Applicant Limitations Policy
- ❑ Types and Methods of Selection Tests Policy
- ❑ Medical Examinations Policy
- ❑ Drug and Alcohol Program Policy, or
- ❑ Drug-Free Workplace Policy
- ❑ Employment Reference Policy

Employment Selection and Records Policies

- ❑ Employment Offers Policy
- ❑ Introductory Employment Periods Policy
- ❑ Employee Orientations Policy
- ❑ Confidentiality and Security of Company Property Policy
- ❑ Personnel Records Access and Disclosure Policy

Endnotes (See References for Full Citations)

[1] Copus, David A. (ed.); *Modern Human Resource Policies*, p. 4.

[2] Levesque, Joseph D.; *People In Organizations: A Guide To Solving Critical Human Resource Problems*, pp. III.3.107–108.

[3] Copus, p. 5.

[4] Copus, p. 3.

[5] Levesque, Joseph D.; *Manual of Personnel Policies, Procedures and Operations* 2/E, pp. 21–23.

[6] Levesque, *People In Organizations*, p. I.3.94–95.

[7] Levesque, *Manual of Personnel Policies* 2/E, p. 84.

[8] Copus, p. 6.

[9] Adapted from Levesque, *Manual of Personnel Policies* 2/E, pp. 27–28.

[10] Ibid., p. 26.

[11] Ibid., p. 27.

[12] Ibid., pp. 27–28.

[13] Copus, pp. 42–43.

[14] _____; "How to Comply with The Drug-Free Workplace Act." *Legal Reporter*, July 1989, pp. 5–6.

[15] Copus, pp. 6–7.

[16] Adapted from Levesque, *Manual of Personnel Policies* 2/E, pp. 31–32.

[17] Ibid., p. 32.

[18] Ibid., p. 31.

[19] Ibid., pp. 30–31.

[20] Ibid., p. 84.

[21] Copus, p. 52.

[22] Copus, p. 54.

4 Maintaining Proper Hiring and Employment Records

In today's ever increasing legal environment, many demands are being made on every type organization to establish and maintain accurate records of business accountability. To many business people, records seem like a waste of time—usually meaning they either do not know, understand, or agree with the reason some records are being made and kept. Indeed, there is probably much that can and should be done to reduce the amount of paperwork that each of us have to contend with in transacting our business responsibilities. This is equally true with the morass of forms and other documents related to hiring employees.

However, we must also give due recognition to the three controlling elements of hiring and subsequent employment records:

1. those records *required* by law for reporting or prospective inspection purposes;
2. those records that are likely to have legal implication should certain events arise with any employee which may prove or disprove the company's liability for wrongdoing; and,
3. those records that a company desires to have on its employees for various decision-making purposes, and that is legal to collect on employees (that is, in the context of employment).

If you follow the suggestions and procedures provided in this chapter, and use the forms provided in the preceding chapter, you are most likely to establish both a quality recordkeeping program and one that satisfies the three controlling elements.

4.1 How to Set Up Personnel Files

Personnel records of any type are confidential and therefore demand a high degree of security. To satisfy the requirement of security and control over personnel records, file storage should be located in the private office of the person who has the designated "custodian of personnel records" responsibility. This responsibility is a legal one, meaning this person can be subpoenaed to testify as to the keeping and contents of these records. Further, it is advisable that official personnel records be placed in a locking, fireproof file cabinet to which only a few designated people can gain access. In those personnel operations where there is additional clerical and professional staff, it is most common to place the personnel file cabinets in the main personnel office work area so the staff who need most frequent use of the files can have easy access to them.

Using a Simple Personnel Records System[1]

One of the best and most widely used methods of setting up personnel files is the use of heavy-duty legal size file folders with Acco fasteners at the top of both covers. An excellent folder is available from Universal Paper Goods in Los Angeles. The product (#253F26) is called a pressboard folder, has a two-inch expansion spine, and can be ordered from most office supply stores. Regular legal file folders are normally not strong enough to withstand the amount of handling, duration of use, and general treatment given to personnel files over an extended period of time. Heavy-duty folders also have the advantage of expandable spines to accommodate the inherent growth of documents that typically occurs with prolonged employment. They can be used as stand-alone files, or placed in individually labeled Pendaflex® folders so that when the file is removed it is easy to locate its place in the file drawer. The employee's name should be on both the file folder and the Pendaflex® folder.

Personnel files can be arranged in alphabetical order of employees' last names with full-time employee tabs on the left of the Pendaflex® folder edge, and part-time employee tabs on the right. Another method is to use color-coded tabs, or symbols on the tabs (for example, self-adhesive colored dots), for easy visual identification of a certain group or class of workers such as exempt/nonexempt, management, plant, or shift employees. The easier you can make the order and visual location of each employee's file folder, the faster and more reliable will be the task under the heavy and frequent use conditions you may encounter with personnel files.

It is suggested that the left inside cover be used to compile the following hiring and benefits records, leaving the right inside cover for other chronological employment records, both covers of which should be filed in inverse order (most current on top).

1. Employment Application form and/or resume
2. Preemployment tests, excluding those that may contain sensitive information which should be stored in a separate file
3. Letter of Employment confirmation to the employee
4. Employee Orientation Checklist form
5. W-4 form (declaration of income tax withholding)
6. Benefit plan (insurance) enrollment forms
7. Employee Information Log form

These documents represent the items most often referred to on a routine basis. Using the left cover makes them easy to find and less cumbersome when seeking routine information. With the Employee Information Log on top, initial hire and ongoing summary information can be logged on one form that contains several different types of personnel transactions such as leaves, pay and benefit changes, job classification and promotional changes, training, and performance report information. The right side cover, on the other hand, can be used to store forms, letters, and other records that serve as supporting documentation of data and events entered on the Employee Information Log, as well as any other type of personnel record generated during the employee's tenure with your company.

The initial compilation of an employee's personnel file typically starts with such hiring documents as the individual's employment application form and/or resume, reference letters and reports, and various other reports related to medical examination, credit and/or bonding information, citizenship status, driving history, and educational verification documents that support the hiring decision. This and other *personal* information can only be obtained once the employer has extended at least a tentative offer of employment to an individual applicant.

Once the employee is hired and reports to work, other sensitive records are developed in which the employee is required to divulge a great deal of personal information relating to payroll, benefits, beneficiaries, and emergency notification. Thereafter, other documents emanating from the personnel office, the employee's superiors, the employee, or interested third parties (for example, insurance and pension plan representatives, agents of the employer, and unions) begin to collect in the employee's file. Each of these documents should be reviewed carefully by one person designated as the company's personnel records custodian to ensure that they are being recorded and filed properly.

Two issues that are very important for employers to bear in mind are:

1. employee personnel files are the property of the employer, but that in itself does not make them inaccessible to the employee or others who may have the legal right to see its contents; and,

2. each and every document in the file should be considered confidential even though they may have varying degrees of sensitivity.

The documents having greatest sensitivity, and which most state laws will allow exclusion from even the respective employee's knowledge and access, include

- Medical and workers' compensation reports
- Employment reference reports and information
- Security, credit, and bonding reports
- Surveillance and investigative reports relating to an employee's or applicant's criminal activities, drug activities, discrimination complaints, and industrial injury investigations

Many state laws permit employers to establish secondary official personnel files for the storage of this kind of sensitive information so long as it is nonaccessible to the employee and others who do not have the need or right to know its contents. You should investigate whether this or a similar practice is permitted in your state before arranging files in this manner and establishing corresponding access policies.

A few other personnel files you will need to establish in relation to hiring records are:

1. employment forms,
2. completed applications and resumes submitted,
3. job descriptions, and
4. hiring process forms.

Assuring Confidentiality of Personnel Records

Virtually all hiring and employment records should be regarded as confidential documents since they bear personal and private information about individual applicants and employees. Some records, however, are more sensitive than others because the information on these documents is of a particularly private nature. As such, they must be treated with more than usual care in their preparation, handling, filing, and disclosure. A few of the previously named records that would qualify as sensitive documents include background investigative reports, preemployment reference information, medical examination reports, and internal investigation and legal action reports. Given the liability employers now have in regard to applicant and employee privacy rights, there are a couple of points you should keep in mind when dealing with sensitive employment records.

Negligent Maintenance of File Records and Failure to Use Due Care

This legal theory of privacy law has been postulated by several courts hearing cases involving informational damage to an employee that arose out of poor recordkeeping and/or mishandling of employment records by company officials. The more common occurrences that tend to give rise to this type of employer liability are

- Providing false or misleading employment reference information believed to be from the employee's file.

- Determining what constitutes relevant information in a file in conjunction with a disclosure process (that is, only giving information that is pertinent and applicable to the need).
- Placing, or allowing the placement of, false information in a file.
- Providing others with false information about an applicant or employee, even if the information is not particularly damaging to the applicant/employee.
- Failure to keep records accurate and current, and failure to keep consistent records among employees.
- Providing information to any person who does not have a legitimate right to know the information.

NOTICE

This does not mean that you should react with unwarranted alarm about your personnel files. Rather, it is intended to point out the need for you to assume the role of an official personnel records custodian and to ensure that your hiring program is processing, handling, and filing both confidential and sensitive record information with due care using the above as guidelines.

Two Approaches to Filing Sensitive Hiring Records

By law, employers are required to establish and maintain at least one *official* personnel file in which prescribed and other lawful employment information is to be stored for each active employee. Some state laws permit the keeping of a second employee file in which certain sensitive records can be stored that are nonaccessible to the respective employee. All other records being kept on employees, such as a supervisor's "desk file," are generally considered unofficial records until their contents find their way into the official personnel file—which happens from time-to-time when employees continue to be late to work or experience disciplinary actions as a cumulative result of the supervisor's recordkeeping.

When it comes to hiring records, most employers encounter the problem of what to do with sensitive records that come into their possession as part of the preemployment testing and background checking processes. There are two approaches to overcoming this problem. The difference in these approaches lies in whether the keeping of a second official file is permitted or prohibited by state law. Your first step is to determine which position your state law takes.

1. If Second Official File Permitted:
   Set up a separate file drawer exclusively for sensitive employment records and classify these documents *not* by applicant or employee name, but by the type of records (for example, I-9 forms, Drug-Alcohol Tests, Preemployment Medical Exams, Background Reference Checks, etc.). Be sure that everyone understands that these records are nonaccessible to the individuals they concern, and disclosure of their contents is only available to a few designated company officials—or to others only by advice of legal counsel.

2. If Second Official File Prohibited:
   Place sensitive records and documents at the rear of the left inside cover of the employee's file in a sealed envelope, and mark the envelope "Confidential Document—To Be Opened Only By (title of designated company official[s])." The inherent problem with having sealed sensitive documents in the employee's file is that it adds awkward bulk to the file and arouses unnecessary curiosity and skepticism when observed by the employee during review of the file—which is a requirement in most states.

Four Privacy Rights Elements of Personnel Records

It would be worth your time to acquaint yourself with the contents of Appendix B on employee privacy rights before attempting to acquire and process hiring and other employment records. If you are already familiar with these legal issues, then you may wish to make note of four elements relating to the special handling of employment records, including those acquired and processed during the hiring effort, that are essential in order to protect both the applicant's/employee's privacy rights as well as your company's interests in having such information.

1. *Collection*

   Information recorded about employees should be obtained only by those who possess proper authority relative to the employee and nature of information being collected. This usually consists of the Human Resource Manager, the employee's supervisor, or management personnel in *direct* line of the employee's organizational department. Where collection involves an investigation, it may also include an external agent of the employer. In any case, the information must be factual, objective, and made available only to those who have a need and right to know.

2. *Documentation*

   The written word is a powerful influence upon an employee's privacy rights with regard to potential defamation, slander, false impression, and negligence. For this reason, considerable care should be exercised by the person responsible for gathering and verifying employment information to assure that the information is accurate and relevant to employment prior to its decision-making use or placement in a personnel file.

3. *Processing*

   This consists of the typing, delivery, and storage of employment information. Routine employment documents should be prepared by appropriate human resource, payroll, and similar specialty clerical staff. Sensitive documents such as investigative, medical, and background reports should be prepared *only* by clerical staff designated as "confidential" employees, and only when it is absolutely necessary for them to see or process this information. Any deliveries of either routine or sensitive documents should be made personally to the employee or mailed "registered receipt" to the employee's last known address. Access to file storage should be limited to those who have proper authority to view file contents.

4. *Use*

   The use of employment records should be confined to legitimate business purposes, meaning that only authorized personnel may access, view, and consider the contents of employment documents in order to render necessary decisions about the employee. Care must be exercised to ensure that information is not deceitfully purged, altered, or added without the employee's knowledge. However, obsolete information in a personnel file that has the potential of creating an adverse employment decision should be given consideration for removal from the file (for example, a written reprimand two years ago for a nonrepetitive behavioral problem).

Setting Up the Employment Forms File

Employment forms consist of all of those forms used for the hiring and subsequent employment processing of employee information. It is best to dedicate an entire file drawer for these forms and to have a good supply of each. Each different form should be arranged in a separate folder, tabbed at the top with the name of the form or document, in order of their customary use. That is, start with those forms that are likely to be the first used for recruitment, testing, hiring, initial employment, during employment, and employment separation. Some of the forms and documents that will be needed in this file in support of the hiring program are

1. Personnel Requisition form
2. Job Analysis forms
3. Recruitment and Test Planning form
4. Recruitment Ad form
5. Employment Application and Employment Interest form
6. Equal Employment Opportunity (voluntary self-identification) form
7. Employment Interview and other testing forms
8. Medical Examination form/referral
9. Employment Reference/Educational Records Authorization form
10. I-9 (Immigration and Naturalization Service) form
11. Employee Information Log form
12. W-4 (declaration of income tax withholding) form
13. Payroll Processing (entering employee on payroll) form
14. Insurance and pension benefit plan booklets and enrollment forms
15. Employee Orientation form
16. Employee Issuance of Company Property form
17. Employee Acknowledgement of Personnel Handbook Receipt form

Filing Applications and Resumes

There are two circumstances under which an employer deals with employment applications and resumes: 1) when job vacancies exist and the employer is collecting them until a set deadline, at which time they will be screened for further consideration; and, 2) when applications or resumes are submitted "blindly" (without solicitation from the employer or reference to a particular job). So, one of your hiring program decisions needs to be whether you will accept or discard unsolicited applications and resumes. Some employers accept them by placing them in a general applications file. Other employers give or mail an Employment Interest form to inquiring job seekers which, when returned, is kept on file by job category or occupational grouping for a prescribed period in the event such a job becomes vacant—at which time they mail an employment application form and job announcement to the interested person. Yet other employers merely discard any application materials, or refuse to accept them unless a job for which they might qualify is currently open.

The more practical need you will have in dealing with applications and resumes concerns those arriving in the mail and over-the-counter from job seekers responding to your recruitment efforts. Here, the need is to have an effective way of receiving and filing them until they are no longer needed. To accomplish this task, it is suggested that you follow these steps:

1. At the time you begin recruiting for a job vacancy, set up an empty file folder in the front portion of the file drawer used to store applications and transfer requests. Tab the folder with the name of the job being recruited and let those who handle mail and do filing know about the existence of this file folder.
2. Sort through any files being kept on current employees requesting transfer to see if there is a match with the vacant position. If so, place their request forms in the active applications file for consideration after the filing deadline.

3. Sort through the files of unsolicited applications, resumes, or Job Interest forms. Place those applications and resumes that look like they may qualify in the active applications file. If you're using the Job Interest form, now is the time to send an application form and job announcement with the filing deadline.

4. At the close of the recruitment deadline, pull the file and begin the process of selecting a suitable number of the most qualified individuals to be considered for preemployment testing. Send letters thanking the remaining applicants and letting them know that others are being considered at this time, but that you will keep their applications on file for an additional (90-day) period.

5. Applications or resumes that arrive after the application filing deadline should be dealt with by a letter that politely rejects their application on the basis of late arrival, unless of course there exists a reasonably legitimate excuse for its delay.

6. Merely because you rejected other applications from this file doesn't mean the forms can now be discarded. Rather, *all* applications and resumes in the file, whether considered further or not, must be retained for up to two years from the date of a hiring decision in case one or more applicants files a discrimination complaint within that period.

Establishing a File for Job Descriptions

Each employer should additionally maintain a file of all current and past job descriptions covering every job in the company's employ. These documents are frequently used in employment decision making, and they are being subpoenaed with increasing frequency in connection with matters of employment law. Job descriptions should be included in every new employee orientation packet since the new employee's pay, classification status, performance standards, and other employment conditions are theoretically predicated on the job description as pointed out in Chapter 2.

Depending on the number of separate job titles representing all the different positions in your company's employ, you will need anywhere from a partial file drawer to as many as two drawers. The first couple of file drawers should contain a supply of the Job Analysis Questionnaires and/or Job Description Review forms you use for this purpose, the Job Analysis Interview form, and a historical file bearing copies of your Position Control lists— annual listings of job titles and the number of authorized (budgeted) positions. Next, you should have a separate file folder for each job description that bears a different job title. Typically, these are filed in alphabetical order in smaller organizations where there are a limited number of total jobs. In organizations having fifty or more different job titles, they are sometimes filed according to major subdivisions of jobs such as

- Operating Subdivisions
- Office, Plant, Transportation, and Field
- Locational Subdivisions
- Headquarters Office, Branches, Warehouse
- Classification Subdivisions
- Management, Professional-Technical, Clerical

It is advisable to keep at least a small supply of each job description in each file folder so that you or others do not have to keep photocopying them every time one is needed. You may also want to place a colored sheet of paper behind the original copy, or otherwise mark the original so that it does not inadvertently get removed. Another point to remember is that when a job title is changed, the revised job description should note the job's former title, and should be refiled under the new job title. At the same time, you will want to note the former job title in parentheses next to the new job title on the master listing of all your authorized positions (Position Control List) for reference purposes.

4.2 Records to Be Completed at the Time of Hire

The forms, records, and reports that you will want and need to have completed *before* making a hiring offer, and arranging for the new employee to report to work, are divided here into two categories: 1) legally required records, and 2) recommended hiring records.

CAUTION

A major mistake routinely made by employers of all sizes, but particularly by smaller sized companies—due to greater operational impact from vacant jobs—is the practice of hiring people and putting them on the job before all the facts are in. As mentioned in Appendix C concerning negligent hiring, bringing people into the employ of an organization before all appropriate sources of information concerning their qualifications and personal traits are found to be in all respects suitable is a very risky practice at best.

Countless employers have been surprised to learn *after the hiring fact* that a new hire—including highly placed managers—had some otherwise disqualifying element that emerged when all records were completed. This leaves the employer with an awkward decision concerning the employee's retention. Quite simply, it is not uncommon for *any* applicant to

1. falsify some information on their application or resume;
2. attempt to conceal an unpleasant prior employment event;
3. omit some embarrassing encounter with the law; or,
4. have a history of bad credit, precocious behavior, or physical disorder that would likely preclude their employment with your company.

It is for these collective reasons that you should attempt to gain the cooperation of other managers in completing the entire hiring process before placing new hires on your payroll. It will take a little more time and patience for those awaiting the arrival of new hires, but in the long run the small amount of extra time to handle the process correctly will be worth it. The following, then, are the two categories of records that should be completed before or at the time of in-processing of new hires.

(1) Legally Required Records

In compliance with the Fair Labor Standards Act, Equal Employment Opportunity laws, and various state laws that regulate mandatory recordkeeping by employers, you should gather and record the following information on new and rehired employees.

1. A completed, verified, and legally acceptable I-9 form that attests to the individual's lawful right to be in the United States and obtain employment.
2. File all applications and selection testing records applicable to the hiring process that resulted in the employment of the person you hired. Do not store these in the employee's individual personnel file.
3. Employers with 100 or more employees must record the personal characteristics of each employee by designated equal employment opportunity categories in order to

prepare and submit the annual EEO-1 report to the Equal Employment Opportunity Commission.

4. Compile and maintain a record of the employee's general personal information to include

   - Name, address, phone number, and emergency notification information.
   - Date of birth, social security number, and driver's license number.
   - Marital status, and dependent and beneficiary information.
   - Job title, classification status, and pay rate.

5. Completed W-4 form (declaration of income tax withholding) and payroll processing information.

6. Complete the applicable forms and records that would add the new or rehired employee to your workers' compensation plan and unemployment insurance account.

(2) Recommended Hiring Records

These records represent information at the employer's discretion to compile, record, and keep in each employee's personnel file. While each employer may establish differing kinds of discretionary records depending on the unique nature of its business, this employment information should be recorded for future reference to protect company interests. When developing special purpose forms and other records to be placed in an employee's file, keep in mind that the information must relate directly to employment, and the employer should be prepared to argue the need of having such information. The kinds of discretionary records that are generally recommended for employers to prepare and keep in employee files include

1. The employee's application form and/or resume, and copies of any information the employee submitted as testimony to qualifications and/or abilities.
2. The employee's acknowledgement form showing receipt of, and agreement to comply with, the personnel policy (employee) handbook.
3. The employee's acknowledgement form proving the employer's issuance and employee's receipt of particular items of company property for use in the employee's job.
4. Notices from the company's insurance carriers certifying acceptance of the employee with regard to bonding, driving company vehicles, workers' compensation coverage, and similar notices that are not sensitive in nature.
5. Health care, pension, and other fringe benefit plan enrollment forms provided by plan administrators that have been completed by the employee.
6. A completed Employee Orientation Checklist form that has been signed and dated by the employee.
7. A copy of the employee's job description and employment offer letter.

4.3 How to Control Access and Disclosure

While employment records and personnel files are the private property of the company that prepares them for their own purposes, the contents are not necessarily the sole domain of authorized company officials and representatives. *All* employment records pertaining to specific employees are discoverable through the acquisition powers of a subpoena. Also, the courts have determined that certain third parties such as governmental representatives (law enforcement and compliance agency personnel), union business agents, and the courts themselves can obtain certain kinds of employment records. Moreover, many states have adopted laws enabling employees to inspect their personnel files at convenient times and locations within a reasonable distance of their work location.

So, on the one hand, there are individuals who have the need and right to access employment records and personnel file information, while on the other hand, there are individuals who may not gain access or knowledge of this information because of the employer's obligation to protect each employee's privacy rights. Here are some guidelines that should help you better understand and formulate your operating practice to control the inappropriate access and disclosure of employment records.

Internal Access and Disclosure

First, you should recognize the obvious fact that particular individuals in your organization do have legitimate need-to-know right to access, review, and modify file documents during the normal course of processing a variety of employment matters. These internal company representatives usually consist of

1. The Human Resource Manager who has ultimate internal responsibility for establishing and maintaining employment records and personnel files.
2. Human Resource office staff whose jobs require access to files for storage and processing actions.
3. The employee's supervisor, department manager, or senior management personnel, each of whom must have some relevant and stated purpose for accessing these files.
4. Company advisors such as attorneys, consultants, and insurance company representatives whose work necessitates access and review of these files in order to acquire the information needed for some legitimate company interest.

Second, you should avoid making many of the mistakes commonly associated with employment records access and disclosure. One such mistake is to allow a file to leave the area (Human Resources Office) in which it is stored. To accommodate internal access by those who have the right to these records and files, you should have available a desk or table where those individuals can review this material—but within eyeshot of the person responsible for monitoring those allowed access (yours would not be the first company to have an employee or supervisor conceal their removal of a file document).

Another common mistake is to allow supervisors to use an employee's personnel file as a repository for assorted handwritten notes. Rather, every supervisor should make use of a "supervisor's desk log" to record casual employment events until such time as the information is acted on in a more official fashion, and thereupon made a formal part of the employee's file. And finally, you should never allow coworkers or indirect managers access to employment records or personnel files—even if the coworker is a union steward attempting to represent the employee's (grievance) interest. In each of these cases, access to the file should be denied and disclosure protected.

Third Party Access and Disclosure

Access to employment records and improper disclosure of their contents is where most privacy rights problems arise, largely because third parties are taking immediate, visible, and often damaging action on the basis of information they receive. Consequently, access and disclosure should be severely controlled under advice of qualified legal counsel. Third party representatives that are generally entitled to *limited* access to employment records are as follows:

1. Those representing the employee's interests and who present proper identification, purpose, and/or authority:

   - Union business agent with identification, legitimate purpose, and the employee's written authorization to view records applicable to the nature of representation.

   - Private attorney representing a stated employment matter that *directly* concerns an employee, and who has proper subpoena authority to access those records applicable to the cause of representation.

2. Those representing employment compliance agencies who present proper identification, purpose, and authority:

   - Labor Standards Enforcement personnel conducting routine audits or investigating records in relation to a claim made by an employee.

   - Occupational Safety and Health Administration (OSHA) or National Institute for Occupational Safety and Health (NIOSH) personnel conducting audits or investigations.

   - Equal Employment Opportunity Commission (EEOC) personnel conducting audits or investigations.

   - Similar state compliance agency personnel performing the same functions.

3. Those representing law enforcement activities who present proper identification, documented proof of reasonable purpose, and advice from your company's legal counsel to cooperate:

   - Federal Bureau of Investigation (FBI) or the Department of Justice (DOJ).

   - State or local law enforcement representatives.

   - Court order having authoritative jurisdiction.

It should be understood that not all of these representatives have an automatic right to access any employment record or personnel file document they wish. One of the first things that you should establish is what document(s) are pertinent to their purpose, and whether they possess proper authority to access, view, and/or photocopy certain documents. Second, if access and disclosure is given, you or your company's authorized records custodian should participate in the examination and disclosure process with the external person acquiring information *after* reviewing the file to mark pertinent documents, and thereby prevent sensitive or inapplicable documents from being viewed out of context.

Developing an Access and Disclosure Policy

For those employers who truly desire a forthright yet controlled approach to matters of the confidentiality, security, access, and disclosure of employment records (rather than leaving these issues subject to quizzical or suspicious minds), it can prove worthwhile to publish and disseminate a company policy that addresses each of these major concerns—see Section 3.5 sample policies. Prior to adoption and release of such a policy, you should enlist the help of qualified legal and human resource advisors, as well as internal key managers, to identify various components and conditions related to employment documents, their access, use, and disclosure. It is important for you to consult with these individuals in order to consider all the prospective scenarios of records access and disclosure; to obtain current and clear information about applicable state laws and legal decisions; and to consider that company policies are adopted to deal with a variety of situations, not to control a particular outcome.

Each employer's development of an employment records and personnel files access and disclosure policy may differ because of unique conditions within the company or the nature of its business, state laws, or the philosophical approach management takes to regulating this practice. As a means of at least starting the deliberation of what components and conditions might be included in your access and disclosure policy, the following are some preliminary items for you to consider.

1. What employment, personnel, and personal information does the company obtain in the course of its hiring and employment processes? Make a list of the types of information either required or acquired during the hiring process, and note which information should be designated "sensitive." Your list should include those employment records and personnel file documents mentioned earlier in this chapter.

2. Describe and list the personnel file information that employees can have access to for the purpose of reviewing the contents of their own files. How often, where, and under what conditions can employees review their personnel files? Are employees prohibited from reviewing their files any time after employment separation, or will they be given a short period thereafter to do so?

3. Determine whether employees can have copies of the contents of their files. A recommended approach is to *insist* that employees be given copies of documents placed in their personnel file at the time such documents are produced, then charge them a small fee for preparing copies from their file.

4. Determine whether employees have the right to rebut or challenge statements made in file documents; if so, when and how?

5. Determine whether state law allows the keeping of two official personnel files, the second of which can be used for the (employee or others) nonaccessible storage of sensitive information. If so, consider including the fact that these records exist but are nonaccessible, except to company representatives who have a need and right to know.

6. Consider identifying in your policy what other individuals, such as third parties, may have access to employment records and under what conditions.

7. Determine what information will be disclosed to a verified, prospective future employer upon a reference inquiry, and if this information is to be given with or without the employee's signed authorization and release to do so.

4.4 How Long Should Employment Records Be Retained?

Retention requirements of employment records are controlled by both federal and state laws. Because state laws vary considerably, no attempt is being made here to identify the records retention requirements of the various states, but generally they follow similar periods as corresponding federal law. Nevertheless, it is advisable to conduct a little research or consult with qualified labor counsel in your state to determine specific record retention requirements applicable to state laws dealing with employment matters.

There are, however, six federal laws that have particular recordkeeping requirements in the absence of more stringent, corresponding state requirements that you should incorporate into your hiring records management program. Bear in mind that these laws focus primarily on general hiring and employment records rather than those kinds of documents typically stored in individual personnel files. The federal law sources, records types, and specific retention periods you should use as a starting point in your employment records management system are as follows.[2]

Verification of Right to Work in the U.S. (Immigration Reform and Control Act)

The Immigration Reform and Control Act (IRCA) requires that employers complete the I-9 form for each employee hired to verify and determine whether the person is a lawful resident of the United States and has the legal right to obtain employment

Three years, or one year after employment separation

Basic Employee Data, Pay Records, Work Hours, and Training (Fair Labor Standards Act)

1. Basic records containing employee information, work schedules including overtime and premium rate hours, payrolls, individual contracts or collective bargaining agreements, and sales and purchase records (if any employee is paid by commission)

   Three years

2. Supplementary basic records including basic employment and earnings records and wage rate tables. Also work time schedules including order, shipping, and billing records, records of additions to or deductions from wages paid, and documentation of basis for payment of any wage differential to employees of the opposite sex in the same establishment (Equal Pay Act)

   Two years

3. Certificates of age

   Until termination of employment

4. Written training agreements

   Duration of training program

Discriminatory Practices or Actions (1964 Civil Rights Act, Title VII, and 1990 Americans with Disabilities Act)

1. Any personnel or employment record made or kept by the employer, including application forms and records having to do with hiring, promotion, demotion, transfer, layoff, or termination; rates of pay or other terms of compensation; and selection for training or apprenticeship

   Eighteen months from date of making the record or taking the personnel action involved— whichever is later

2. Personnel records relevant to charge of discrimination or action brought by the Attorney General against an employer, including, for example, records relating to charging party and to all other employees holding similar positions, application forms or test papers completed by unsuccessful applicant and by all other candidates for the same position

   Three years from date of final disposition of charge or action

3. For apprenticeship programs: (A) a chronological list of names and addresses of all applicants, sex, and minority group identification or file of written applications containing same information; and other records pertaining to apprenticeship applicants (for example, test

   (A) Two years or period of successful applicant's apprenticeship—whichever is later

papers and interview records); and, (B) any other record made solely for completing the EEO-2 report or similar document	(B) One year from due date of report
4. Copy of EEO-1 (Employer Information Report) for employers with 100-plus employees	Three years from date of preparation

Age Discrimination (Age Discrimination in Employment Act)

1. Payroll records containing each employee's name, address, date of birth, occupation, rate of pay, and compensation earned per week	Duration of employment
2. Personnel records relating to (A) job applications, resumes, or other replies to job advertisements including records pertaining to failure or refusal to hire; (B) promotion, demotion, transfer, selection for training, layoff, recall, or discharge; (C) job orders submitted to employment agency or union; (D) test papers in connection with employer-administered employment tests; (E) physical examination results considered in connection with personnel action; and (F) job advertisements or notices to the public or employees regarding openings, promotions, training programs, or opportunities for overtime work	One year from date of personnel action to which record relates, except ninety days for application forms and other preemployment records of applicants
3. Employee benefit plans and written seniority or merit rating systems	Duration the plan or system is effective plus one year
4. Personnel records, including the above, relevant to an enforcement action commencement against the employer	Until final disposition of the action

Workplace Safety and Health (Occupational Safety and Health Act)

1. Log and Summary of Occupational Injuries and Illnesses briefly describing recordable cases of industrial injury and illness, the extent and outcome of each incident, and summary totals for the calendar year	Five years following the end of the year to which they relate
2. Supplementary Record containing more detailed information for each occurrence of injury or illness	Same as above

4.5 Automated Recordkeeping

The arduous hiring process and related employment transactions have become overly consumed with repetitive paperwork and tasks that absorb valuable time—if the job is being done correctly. In fact, largely due to the time required to perform quality hiring processes, many employers have progressively created shortcuts that damage the quality of end results, rather than look for more efficient ways of *adding* qualitative and creative measures to improve results while actually decreasing the amount of time it takes to hire the best people. This requires one thing—automation of the entire hiring program including recruitment, applicant flow, selection testing, and most if not all of the records-processing function.

Using Micro-Computer Systems in Smaller Organizations

Smaller organizations who do not need a large "mainframe" computer system to accommodate other aspects of their operations will want to consider starting out with a micro (personal) computer. Since most available software programs are designed for IBM or compatibles, you will want to acquire one with a large memory capacity to handle the hiring and employment software programs and information that is placed in those programs. One advantage of the micro-computer is that security of file data can be easily maintained by merely isolating the computer from use by others and storing informational software in a secured place. Mainframes, on the other hand, require a password to access programs but private employment information is nevertheless available through the mainframe's information storage bank.

Use of computers for the storage, retrieval, and manipulation of employment data and records has been refined considerably. It now presents smaller organizations with an easy alternative to manual recordkeeping by simply modifying standardized software programs to fit the organization's special needs. Acquiring a computer to handle the hiring, employment, and personnel functions is an investment that will have enduring returns. The initial investment will include the time it takes to select a suitable computer, software programs, vendor support, staff training, work with a consultant to carefully think through needed customizing of standardized programs, and initial transforming of existing records into computer memory. Clearly, micro-computers have made it possible for smaller organizations to operate with the same efficiency as their larger competitors, and the success of any business requires efficiency where the element of time is involved.

Initially, you will want to use your computer system to handle the recordkeeping aspects of employment transactions and personnel file documents, even though hard-copies of many personnel file contents must be maintained as well. Once these records become a matter of routine computer handling, you should begin to develop a computerized method of dealing with all hiring process activities to simplify and streamline these tasks. For example, organizations required to (or interested in) tracking applicant characteristics for compilation of EEO and affirmative action reports will want to acquire software programs available for this purpose, and similar to the information contained on the Applicant Flow Data form in Appendix E. Additionally, computers can be very effective devices for preparing job announcements from stored job description information; for planning and layout of recruitment and testing activities; for the design of recruitment advertisements; for the development of specific, job related selection tests including interview rating forms and sample questions; and payroll processing.

There is almost no limit to the type of information that can be created, stored, and used more wisely by organizations of all sizes to enhance the cost effectiveness of employment information. After all, for most organizations, employees represent the single largest cost of doing business, and computers are the answer to managing those cost factors more precisely.

Ultimately, however, the decision to acquire and use a computer system to manage the hiring and employment functions must be based on overall efficiency versus the costs to initiate and operate the system. It should be remembered that efficiency is a long-range measure, while cost is generally measured as a short-range investment. As a fundamental rule, automated hiring, employment, and personnel records systems may not be efficient for employers with fewer than twenty-five to fifty employees unless

1. the nature of employment in the organization requires an extraordinary amount of data to be dealt with (for example, high turnover, diverse jobs, etc.);

2. the organization has other business applications that necessitates the acquisition of computers, and the added costs associated with employment related software programs would be nominal; or,

3. the organization anticipates growth beyond the current number of employees and desires to convert to computerized recordkeeping in advance of the growth.

Selecting a Human Resource Management System for Medium and Large Organizations

As you are probably painfully aware, computer technology and automation of manual work processes seems to change at the speed of light. Thus, yesterday's innovation becomes tomorrow's obsolescence. The good news for human resource professionals is that the availability of more useful, flexible, and comprehensive software for human resource management systems (HRMS) continues to expand, creating more affordable pricing through competition among vendors. The bad news for those exploring initial implementation of an HRMS is that the conversion process is cumbersome, exceedingly time consuming, and still very expensive. Thus, the acquisition and complete implementation of an HRMS should be viewed as a long term investment whose primary advantages are quicker and more reliable processing of massive data, decreased reliance on manual records and information accessibility, reduced labor costs as company growth continues, and an abundance of previously unavailable data from which more informed human resource cost decisions can be made.

As desirable—and no doubt suitable—as it would be to provide you with detailed information about how you should proceed in the rather complex journey of selecting and implementing an HRMS, the subject is regrettably too voluminous to present here. You will need to do some research on this subject before deciding how to proceed within your organization given its structure, existing computer system(s), types of human resource functions, and available resources. You may find it a worthwhile initial investment to hire a broadly experienced HRMS consultant to conduct a preliminary evaluation of your needs and resources, followed by assistance with the planning, bid acquisition, selection, training, conversion, and subsequent support processes necessary to keep the project moving toward a timely and effective completion.

To help you get started, it is suggested that you examine the following book which was written with the intent to provide a practical guide for human resource professionals seeking computerization of the HR function.

Vincent R. Ceriello; *Human Resource Management Systems: Strategies, Tactics, and Techniques.* New York: Lexington Books, 1991 (796 pp.).

Additionally, you might wish to contact these organizations for further reading and resource information:

Society for Human Resource Management (SHRM)
606 N. Washington Street
Alexandria, VA 22314
(703) 548-3440

and

Association of Human Resource Systems Professionals, Inc.
P.O. Box 801646
Dallas, TX 75380-1646
(214) 661-3727

Checklist of Hiring, Employment, and Personnel File Records

Setting Up Employment and Personnel File Records

- ❏ Review state laws to determine the need to establish, file, and/or report different employment records than required by federal law.
- ❏ Place file cabinets in a private location, but where their use can be observed.
- ❏ Assure that file cabinets are fireproof and equipped with locks to which only designated staff have keys.
- ❏ Officially designate a management level person as the "employment records custodian."
- ❏ Designate staff who are to prepare hiring, employment, and personnel file documents as "confidential" employees.
- ❏ Acquire file folders, fasteners, and tabs to set up personnel records, employment forms, and job description files.
- ❏ Determine if state law permits the keeping of secondary personnel files for sensitive documents; if so, set up these file folders.
- ❏ Gather and place employment forms in file folders.
- ❏ Prepare a policy on the handling, access, use, and disclosure of hiring, employment, and personnel file documents.
- ❏ Set up file folders for the storage of completed application forms, submitted resumes, and (if used) job interest and transfer request forms.

Completing and Filing Hiring Records

- ❏ Keep a separate file on all completed applications and test materials for each job subjected to a hiring process.
- ❏ Have new employees complete the I-9 form and file these in a single folder with other employment records.
- ❏ Complete the EEO identification characteristics of each new hire on a compiled log of all employees, and file in a separate folder with other employment records.
- ❏ Complete the Employee Information Log (or facsimile) form, or record basic personal, job, and payroll information about the new employee and place it in the employee's personnel file.
- ❏ Complete the W-4 form, forward a copy to the person handling payroll, and place the original copy in the employee's personnel file.
- ❏ Complete the appropriate forms and records to add the new employee to payroll, benefit plans, workers' compensation, and unemployment insurance policies.
- ❏ Complete and place in the employee's personnel file:
  - Application/resume and qualifications documents
  - Testing records
  - Background and medical examination reports and information (store in secondary file if permitted by state law)
  - Employee's acknowledgement forms verifying receipt of company property and employment handbook
  - Notices from the company's insurance carriers applicable to the employee
  - Orientation Checklist form

- Job description
- Employment (hiring) confirmation letters

❑ Prepare a master list of what hiring, employment, and personnel records need to be retained for designated periods of time and use this list as a guide to your company's records retention practices.

Endnotes

[1] Adapted from Levesque, Joseph D.; *Manual of Personnel Policies, Procedures and Operations* 2/E, (Englewood Cliffs, NJ: Prentice-Hall, Inc., 1993), pp. 138–139.

[2] Adapted in part from Levesque, Ibid. pp. 160–162.

5 Planning and Sourcing Your Recruiting Efforts

Most employers hire someone from among the group of applicants they receive regardless of whether or not that someone meets all of the specifications and expectations for the position in question. Hiring is therefore regarded as competitive in nature, with the job going to the person who is most suitable from among the lot. While few employers get exactly what they want in the way of employee characteristics (expectations rarely match the nuances of human diversity), those employers who get the best results are those who put forth the maximum recruitment effort. Consequently, recruitment is the key to maximizing your prospects of getting the closest match between job and applicant.

The more applicants you have to draw from, the better your chances are of getting the person you desire. Those chances are proportional to the time, effort, creativity, and to some extent money that your company is willing to put into its recruitment program—not just for the more critical jobs, but for all jobs. Remember, the more critical jobs in an organization rely on the quality of less critical employees, so all jobs are important. Also, experience has shown that the difference between quality employees and those mediocre ones hired out of an impulsive response to an unexpected vacancy is found in a company's

- quality of output
- quality of work
- reliability of results

- ability to learn and improve
- initiative and self-direction
- cooperation and team work

When designing a recruitment plan, you should realize at the outset that passive recruitment is no longer going to work effectively. Employment has become big business and the competition for skilled, quality employees is becoming fierce. This means that smaller organizations are going to have to become better acquainted with, and skilled at, the use of more creative recruitment efforts—and do a better job at selling the benefits of employment in their business settings. This is precisely what this chapter sets out to do—to acquaint you with the recruitment planning and execution process, and to provide you with the resource skills needed to get the best recruiting results for your company.

5.1 Planning Your Recruitment Strategy

There are three important factors that make up the planning of any recruitment strategy and ensuing activities: resource factors, cost factors, and location factors. Each of these factors should be given careful thought prior to launching any type of recruitment effort aimed at attracting a select group of talented people. Since recruiting is a time and cost-intensive hiring function, energy should not be misappropriated to the wrong use of these resources out of a lack of preparation. That preparation is best accomplished by devising a simple plan that accounts for each of the recruiting factors.

Resource Factors

Resource factors are those that allow the job of recruiting to get done in a timely, efficient, and accurate way. Regardless of job type, each recruitment will require the identification of such resource factors as various elements of the job being recruited, recruiting methods and sources, budgeted funds, staffing availability, and scheduling activities.

Elements of the Job

The planning of each recruitment should begin by careful evaluation of the job to be filled. Here, you should identify the important elements of the job, such as

1. Degree of skills required
2. Physical location of the position
3. Nature of supervision and management overseeing the position
4. Realm and type of job responsibilities involved
5. Work schedule and nature of coworkers
6. Environmental conditions and physical demands of the work
7. Personal attributes of incumbents of this job that have performed successfully in the past
8. Where similar workers have been recruited in the past, and what methods, time, and cost were involved

These elements should provide you with a clearer picture of the important job characteristics, and these will, in turn, enable you to become more focused with respect to preparing job announcements and ads, identifying features and benefits of the job, and providing some preliminary recruiting sources.

Identifying Recruitment Methods

How you are going to recruit job applicants is another major consideration to be included in your plan. Given the nature of the job and available supply of labor meeting requirements of the position, you will want to select from among the following methods.

1. Newspaper advertisements
2. Trade publications
3. Job posting and bidding
4. "Point-of purchase" (posting Help Wanted) notice
5. Employee referrals
6. Employment agencies
7. Professional recruitment firms
8. Executive search firms
9. Advertising firms
10. Temporary help firms
11. State employment office
12. Community employment organizations
13. Job fairs, college recruiting, and open house events
14. Labor unions

As you can see, there are many methods to choose from and each one tends to produce slightly different results depending on the kinds of jobs being recruited and the nature of your organization. Each method also carries with it a slightly different set of activities required by company staff, the time involved to complete recruitment, and cost of the effort. Smaller companies tend to do best when their time, energy, and funds are concentrated in recruiting areas that have proven to be beneficial in the past, but to improve their approach with these sources as suggested in the next section. Most reliable for smaller businesses are newspaper ads, employee referrals, trade publications, temporary placement firms and State employment offices, walk-in and unsolicited applications, and community organizations.

Recruitment Budgeting

A survey conducted by the Employment Management Association determined that the 1990 cost-per-hire was about $6,600 for exempt employees, and $1,500 for nonexempt workers. Another study by the California-based Saratoga Institute found the cost for higher calibre professional, technical, and managerial employees ranged between $15,000 and $27,000 per hire. These figures include the kinds of costs associated with recruiting that should be budgeted by either the human resources office or each operating department in a company. They include

- Advertising
- Clerical support
- Recruiting literature
- Professional service fees
- Relocation expenses

- Telephone calls
- Travel expenses
- Staff time
- Employee referral awards
- Sign-on bonuses

If you're not prepared to analyze past turnover or project next year's growth to ascertain the amount needed to budget for recruiting activities, then at least pick some average figure (say $6,000 to $10,000) and multiply that figure times the average number of turnover positions during the last three years as the starting point for a recruiting budget. These amounts should be distributed among the categories noted above and against which funds will be drawn. Then, as you encounter these expenses, payment should be coded back to the fund account in such a manner that your year-end budget statement will give you a more accurate indicator of how much is likely to be needed for next year's recruiting for average turnover—plus any forecasted growth in jobs that will have to be recruited. A sample forecast budget is provided below to illustrate the case of a small electronics company. Further explanations on the nature of these types of costs are provided on the pages that follow.

Sample Recruiting Forecast Budget *Small Electronics Company*						
	Prospective Turnover				Budgeted	Actual
Budget Code/Item	1-Mgr.	2-Profess.	4-Tech.	2-Office	Expenses	Expenses
3.01 Advertising	$1,500	$2,000	$3,000	$600	$7,100	
3.02 Printing	$150	$300	$800	$100	$1,350	
3.03 Clerical	$700	$1,600	$3,500	$2,800	$8,600	
3.04 Telephone	$100	$75	$150	$50	$375	
3.05 Staff Hours	$2,500	$4,000	$5,500	$2,000	$14,000	
3.06 Prof. Serv.s	$5,000	$1,000	$3,000	—	$8,000	
3.07 Travel	$1,500	$500	$1,500	—	$3,500	
3.08 Refer. Awards	$2,000	$1,000	$4,000	$1,000	$8,000	
3.09 Relocation	$3,000	$2,500	$6,000	—	$11,500	
3.10 Bonuses	$5,000	—	$8,000	—	$13,000	
TOTALS	$20,450	$12,975	$35,450	$6,550	$75,425	

As you can see in this example, the cost of recruiting and hiring certain types and levels of new or replacement jobs can be very expensive for some industries. Some expenses can be avoided depending on your recruitment strategy and methods, types of selection tests, and the particular expenses associated with acceptance of an employment offer. For example, if you use an Employee Referral Program to recruit technical applicants, you can save considerably on advertising, printing, staff hours, and possibly sign-on bonuses. Likewise, if you handle your own recruitment for the manager vacancy, you could save on the professional services expenses. Ultimately, each company must consider what kinds of expenses should be allocated to a recruiting and hiring budget based on the nature of its jobs, industry type, and expected or known level of hiring activity each year. With experience, you can begin to project these expenses with reasonable reliability.

Staff Availability

Regrettably, very small companies have little choice in the matter of who takes responsibility for the recruiting task; it inherently goes to one person who is a generalist over personnel matters, does not have the time or inclination to become a specialist in the vast assortment of personnel functions, and may well be responsible for a few other administrative functions completely outside the realm of personnel matters. If this describes your situation, you can do a good thorough job of recruiting if you handle not more than a couple of vacancies at the same time and use this book as your guide.

Beyond a couple of concurrent recruitments, you will need additional help if you are expected to get your other work done—it's a matter of someone determining what your priorities are to be during periods of needed recruitment. Outside help can be obtained by hiring temporary clerical help or temporary staff that has recruiting experience. The latter can be quickly obtained by contacting your local professional human resource association which is likely to have members recently relocated to the area and other possible sources of experienced help. If you're uncertain how to find them, contact the Society for Human Resource Management (SHRM) in Alexandria, Virginia.

For those of you fortunate enough to have human resource staff, this portion of your recruitment plan should identify which staff member(s) will be assigned to the recruiting of which jobs. This is a workload and skills distribution function, and your choice should depend on the time and talent available for each recruiting effort, given the nature of vacant jobs and existing workloads of staff.

Scheduling Activities

Whether the handling of recruiting efforts to fill job vacancies and new positions will be your responsibility or that of other staff, it is helpful to the planning process if each of the recruiting activities are scheduled in an identifiable manner. Doing so has the added advantage of establishing something of a road map for the recruiter to follow when embarking on and tracking his or her efforts. The first step is to prepare a list of the recruiting methods for each different recruitment effort, along with identifying the sources that will be used, such as the names of newspapers, trade publications, and professional services. Second, next to each recruitment source, enter the publication or listing deadlines, publication dates, and contact person. When identifying and scheduling recruitment methods, it is advisable to collaborate with the hiring manager and/or immediate supervisor to get their ideas on sources they feel might be effective based on their past experience.

The last item to identify on your recruitment schedule is the date to be established as the closing of recruitment, beyond which applications will not be considered for the vacant or new position—and the reason for rejection (or holding in abeyance) of further applications.

Sample Recruiting and Selection Schedule		
	SECRETARY	**SR. ACCOUNTANT**
Recruiting Methods:		
Newspapers	June 18–25	July 3 & 10
Job Referral Agencies	—	—
Commun. Refer. Agencies	June 15–29	June 28–July 13
Professional Recruiters	—	—
Professional Journals	—	—
Trade Publications	June 21 (local)	July 10
Other: _____	Employee Referrals	—
RECRUITMENT DEADLINE:	June 30	July 15
Screening & Testing:		
Applications/Resumes	July 2	July 18–20
Written Exam(s)	July 8	—
Performance Exam(s)	July 8	August 3
Interviews	July 19	August 3
Background Check	July 20–27	August 4–14
Medical Exam	—	—
Hiring Offer & Start:		
Employment Offer	July 27	August 14
Written Agreement	July 27 (letter)	August 23 (contract)
START DATE	August 12	September 16

Cost Factors

Recruiting costs can vary considerably. Each recruiting effort tends to be somewhat different based on the methods and sources used, as well as the availability of internal staff to handle many of the activities that might otherwise be relegated to outside service firms. Smaller organizations should spend their time wisely; that is, if there is only one generalist available to handle the recruiting of applicants, then that person should focus on the more routine tasks of designing job announcements, ads and simple literature, and developing a mailing list of employment-oriented community organizations to send announcements to. Very specialized jobs may have to be turned over to employment agencies or recruiting firms who have more time and expertise to locate and solicit qualified applicants. Given the probable mix of internal and external resources that are brought to bear on different recruitment efforts, here are some of the costs that should be incorporated into your recruitment plan and made a part of your strategy determination.

Staff Costs

While many companies absorb staff salaries and benefit costs related to recruiting activities as part of their overall job function, it should be recognized that recruiting may be a minor activity that takes up a considerable amount of time for the small business generalist. In cases where recruiting begins to consume a good deal of time, other duties get neglected and this added strain on workloads affects the quality of that person's work. This may be the time to add (temporary) help to alleviate workload strain and thereby improve recruiting efficiency. Staff activities dedicated to recruiting and selection of new hires, including temporary staff expenses, should be anticipated and budgeted as shown in the Sample Recruiting Forecast Budget previously illustrated.

In addition to the possible supplement of temporary or part-time staff to help with some of the more tedious chores that accompany recruiting activities, the need may also arise to fill the vacant position on a temporary or other interim basis due to operational demands. This can usually be accomplished quickly by contacting a temporary help agency, but the cost for the temporary employee thereby becomes a staffing cost while the agency's fee becomes an indirect recruiting cost. Likewise, you may find other hidden costs attributable to the recruiting function. These costs include such expenses as printing of literature and forms, postage, travel, and long distance telephone calls that can easily mount up with only one recruitment effort.

Each of these items should be identified and tracked to some extent to assure that the organization knows what it is spending on each recruitment, and that sufficient funds and resources are being made available to carry out appropriate types of recruiting activities.

Service Costs

Too often smaller companies tend to overuse outside service firms for recruiting and end up paying a large amount of money each year for these services. Again, depending on the level of recruiting activity and type of jobs being recruited, the use of service firms may be either a good and necessary use of company funds, or it may be an unnecessary waste of money merely to avoid some of the "mystique" attached to recruiting by the inexperienced person. What you should examine more carefully is which parts of the recruiting effort you and others have reasonable time for—and collective knowledge of—to get some or all of the job done. You are likely to find that, with the advice and help of one or two supervisors, you can do a completely adequate job of preparing advertisements and job announcements, and making contacts with good sources of available applicants. When the task becomes specialized, or the vacant job is a hard-to-find set of conditions, it may be time to use the services of various employment firms.

Some of the more common types of service firms that will add costs to your recruiting plan are

1. Recruiting firms who usually provide a range of services such as advertising your position, conducting applicant searches from among their files, interviewing responding applicants, qualifications testing, referrals to the contracting employer, and background investigations. Recruiting firms are also retained by some companies to handle their ongoing recruiting programs like job fairs and college recruiting events. Fees are typically flat rated for a definable project, or they may be on a per-hour basis which is common where the exact type and extent of services are to be progressively determined by the client employer.

2. Advertising firms who prepare recruitment advertisements, company image design, copy and layout of recruitment literature, and company information packets. Fees are normally based on a per-hour rate of firm staff assigned to different parts of the project, or a flat fee for the entire project if defined in sufficient detail.

3. Executive search firms who, like recruiter firms, usually take on the entire recruiting of a particular job but with more emphasis on the search function of finding a small number of pre-screened applicants that fit the client company's specifications. Executive search firms also tend to specialize in executive and higher level managerial positions. Fees are customarily fixed at 30 to 35 percent of the hired person's first year annual salary (sometimes including bonuses and other "perks").

Similar costs that should be included in your recruitment plan are the cost for advertisement publications, typesetting if ads are prepared by you but professionally produced, and fees for ancillary services such as the word processing of correspondence and promotional literature directed at those who respond to your recruiting efforts.

Locational Factors

The location of your prospective recruits is a third factor in your recruitment plan, and one which will affect the strategy by which you approach the recruiting effort. Here, consideration should be given to the geographic region to be covered as the most likely location of your applicant pool, the effect that larger-scale recruiting may have on your budget and time schedule, and travel by applicants vying for the job. Depending on your methods and approach to conducting larger-scale recruitment, the cost and time factors may not be much different than conducting local recruitment. For example, smaller companies wishing to recruit an executive, key manager, or very specialized professional may find multi-state or even national recruiting relatively inexpensive by placing attractive advertisements in such print media as *The Wall Street Journal* or *USA Today*. Also, national association and trade publications (monthly magazines) can be effective sources of larger-scale recruiting along with the use of select newsletters.

Location of Recruiting Effort

Your recruitment plan should identify the location of each recruitment effort based on such information about the job as its degree of specialized skills and conditions, the availability of qualified applicants in different locales, and where past incumbents have been found with the greatest ease and reliability. Using this information, decide on one or more of the following locations where your recruitment efforts are the most likely to produce positive results. You will also want to consider, and identify, what sources of advertising are available to suitably cover the selected location, and whether a combination approach, such as using two or three metropolitan newspapers, one or two regional newsletters, and one national magazine, is best.

- Immediate labor market defined as the city or county in which the company is located.
- Extended labor market defined as the three- to five-county locale from which a wider and more diverse group of qualified applicants are likely to be found.
- Regional labor market within reasonable access and travel to the company might be available, including the entire state or neighboring states.
- National labor market consisting of national media advertising to a targeted group of qualified applicants.

Your recruitment appeal should be directed at both the employed and unemployed audience. Your ultimate goal is to hire the person who meets all of the various needs of the job, so don't make the mistake of selecting recruiting methods that target only the most available—the unemployed.

Locational Effects on Cost and Time

Working to recruit applicants for many jobs under an unreasonably tight time schedule is another common problem that plagues the recruitment process. Too often vacancies occur with short notice and the absence of any employee places pressure on others who must accommodate the loss. However, hasty recruitment efforts and hiring decisions cause even greater problems, particularly for small companies who feel the impact of a wrong decision faster and greater than larger companies.

If the demand to fill a vacant job is great, it may be necessary to eliminate the use of monthly publications, but it is no more time consuming to place newspaper ads in a wider range of locales than in your home town newspaper. You can also use weekly business newspapers that are available in many parts of the country. If, however, your limitation is the cost rather than time of conducting more elaborate recruiting, you should attempt to perform all of your own recruiting efforts and concentrate on such methods as listing your job with regional or statewide metropolitan newspapers (ads), community service organizations with access to the kinds of applicants you seek (job announcements), and State Employment Offices (job listings).

In other words, it may not be necessary to automatically eliminate larger-scale recruiting merely because you have limited time or funds. It may be simply a matter of selecting the right mix of recruiting methods, sources, and availability of people within the company to help do small chores.

Travel Considerations

When conducting regional, statewide, multiple state, or national recruiting, the company should give advance thought to a few travel-related considerations. Specifically, some early decisions should be made concerning what day of the week (or weekend) travel will be easiest on out-of-town applicants and their likely mode of travel. Additionally, if applicants are recruited from beyond a distance of 50 to 100 miles from the employment location, it is generally assumed that the company will pay for the round-trip travel of persons selected for interviews or other selection tests. If that is not the desire or intent of your company, then you should either confine your recruiting to a more localized area or so inform prospective applicants when they are contacted for selection arrangements.

Some applicants may be willing to absorb the expense, but usually only when they know that the number of applicants being invited is very small. In general, however, asking applicants to pay for their travel expenses beyond a reasonable driving distance establishes a poor image of the company, creates negative feelings toward the company by otherwise interested applicants, and can have the effect of discriminating against economically disadvantaged applicants who cannot afford the expense of travel. For these reasons, you may want to select ten to twelve of the best applicants, conduct a preliminary telephone interview to screen down to five or six applicants, and pay for the travel of those select applicants to come to your location for further evaluation of their employability.

5.2 Using Traditional Recruiting to Find Qualified Applicants

There is nothing particularly mysterious about recruiting; it merely takes some imaginative thought, getting ideas from other people, a little creativity, and methodical work. It is a matching process that requires communication on the widest possible scale to let interested individuals know about the existence of the job, and some alluring reason for the quality applicant to take part in the screening process. Yes, it is relatively easy to get large numbers of people to apply for many semiskilled jobs, but even those jobs are important to fill with quality people so your effort should be in that vein—attracting the *quality* applicants. You are also likely to find that getting any number of applications for skilled managers, supervisors, professionals, and technical employees is going to get progressively more difficult as the labor supply diminishes during the 1990s and beyond. This is all the more reason to begin preparing more alluring means to create attraction—to your organization, to your location, and to the job's vast set of conditions that must now be used to provide what today's employees are looking for in their employment—even by use of traditional methods.

Internal Recruiting Methods

Job Posting

Posting job announcements of vacancies or new positions that exist in the company is one of the more popular methods used to fill positions that become available, particularly promotional opportunities such as higher grade jobs and supervisory positions—although the latter is not always the best hiring practice. You should realize that if jobs are filled from within the company, you will have another job to fill thereafter, thus creating a second recruitment cycle. This alone should not deter you from posting job vacancies since doing so can add a material boost to morale inasmuch as it communicates to employees that the company takes an interest in providing opportunities for job changes.

When posting job announcements, there are a few things to keep in mind. First, they should be posted in a conspicuous place where employees congregate such as the break room, locker room, or employee lounge area. Second, the announcement should be noticeable, so you may wish to use a consistent, attention-getting color of paper or large heading of "JOB ANNOUNCEMENT." Third, specify a deadline date that applications must be submitted, to whom, and who to contact for more information about the job. A sample job announcement that can be used for job postings as well as external recruitment is provided in Section 6.3 for your reference and use as a model.

If your company has no interest in starting up an Employee Referral Program, job announcements can be an effective source of indirect advertisement for those employees who are not interested in the job for themselves, but may tell a friend or other associate outside the company about the job opening. Don't underestimate the value of employee referrals from job announcements; in fact, you might even consider inviting referrals.

Employee Referral Programs

Employee referral programs are one of the best, least-costly, and most underutilized recruiting methods available to all size employers. Naturally, the best results come *if* you have done a good job of recruiting quality employees in the first place. They, in turn, refer other quality friends, relatives, and associates based on their belief that the company is a good place to work and operates with respected employment practices. A few of the more apparent advantages of using employee referrals as a primary recruitment method are:

- The company does not have to pay external service firm fees, travel or relocation costs, or payment for sign-on bonuses—unless of course the job is very unique and hard to fill;
- The recruitment process can be accomplished very easily and quickly; and,
- Referring employees have a natural tendency to pre-screen their referrals because they don't want their own reputation with the company tarnished by being responsible for referring a problem employee.

While employee referral programs vary in the amount of awards for each hired referral based on the size of a company, the average monetary award is about $100 for a nonexempt hire, $250 for an exempt hire, and progressively larger amounts for each successive hired referral in a specified period of time. Typically, one-half of the award is paid to the referring employee at the time their referral is hired, another one-fourth after three to six months, and the final one-fourth payment at the conclusion of the new hire's six-month-to-one-year initial employment. The idea is to make the award high enough or attractive enough to get employees interested and active in the effort; small or meaningless awards will not arouse interest and are likely to be scoffed at by employees.

Some employers have found that employees become interested in referral programs where awards vary with each recruitment effort made as part of the referral program. Items like dinner for two at an above-average restaurant can attract attention, along with cash awards. Or consider using a paid vacation for two to some enticing location like the Caribbean—which is cheaper than you might expect and less expensive than paying professional service firms—as the grand prize or reward after an employee has referred a certain number of hires.

For example, Apple Computer offered its employees a drawing for a trip to Carnival in Rio de Janeiro for each referred new hire. They concluded this particular referral program with 85 referred hires at an average cost-per-hire of $694.11, representing a fraction of what was previously spent for large-scale advertising and search firms. Likewise, Home Federal Savings & Loan Association in San Diego offered its statewide employees a drawing for a trip to Maui or Puerto Vallerta for each hired referral. They concluded this recruitment drive after hiring 162 out of the 264 referrals. An idea for the smaller size company might be to offer referring employees the $100–250 award for each new hire, but then add a longevity incentive for both by adding a $100 bonus to the employee and referred hire after the completion of two years of continuous service.

Success of an employee referral program depends, first, on having employees whose morale, loyalty, and sense of company pride are high. Second, you should focus the referral program on those specialized, hard-to-fill, or costly to recruit jobs rather than every job vacancy. You want your program to be new and challenging with rewards each time it is offered. Third, you will need a few rules to guide the program such as who is ineligible (for example, hiring managers, human resource staff, and senior management), when it starts and ends, what job(s) it applies to, and how referrals are to be made. Fourth, you will need some attention-getting bulletins to announce the program (with mention in your employee newsletter), awards, rules, and perhaps a tear-off coupon to have the referral attach to their employment application to reveal the referring employee. A few samples of such an announcement are illustrated in Section 6.3 along with design and format suggestions.

External Recruiting Methods

There are several choices among the methods of recruiting by external means for the small-to-medium employer. The first four methods are those where the employer takes on the most active recruiting role, while the last three methods inherently limit the employer's involvement since selection of a service firm is deliberately intended to relieve the employer of those tasks.

Newspaper and Trade Publication Advertisements

Advertising in the classified section of a local or metropolitan newspaper has been one of the most steadfast and reliable sources of recruiting job applicants, particularly the Sunday edition when people have more time to browse through the morass of ads. Yet this form of advertising job openings has had mixed results. On the one hand they have tended to generally produce a reasonable—sometimes alarming—number of responses, but on the other hand they frequently fail to produce high quality applicants. In response to this dilemma, many employers have developed the poor practice of concealing information; for example, using post office box response addresses or requiring that responses be mailed to the newspaper, not giving the company's name or phone number, and omitting salary and other information of vital interest to job seekers. In turn, only desperately unemployed individuals have tended to respond to such uninviting job ads.

If your true goal is to attract and invite quality applicants to your job openings, it simply cannot be accomplished by less than quality ads. It's a matter of getting only that which you project. Improving job ads to attract quality people will cost more and take a little more time to design the proper image and message you *need* to convey, but your chances of getting better results are likely to improve proportionately. To demonstrate the difference between poorly constructed and well designed ads, Section 6.2 contains a few examples of contrasting job ads along with suggestions on how to design more appealing ads using the features that attract quality applicants.

Trade publications such as magazines, journals, and even newsletters are excellent sources of recruiting quality applicants. Some reasons are:

1. those who subscribe to these publications are inherently interested in their field;
2. they tend to take a professional approach to the industry and/or their occupation;
3. they want to keep abreast of new information; and,
4. they are likely to be employed but always interested in a promotion, relocation, or new challenges.

Trade publication ads are not much different from newspaper ads; the latter can be easily redesigned where necessary to emphasize the particular technology, industry, or orientation of the publication or its audience. Advertising your specialized job opening in a trade publication is often less expensive and longer lasting than newspaper ads, but the major disadvantage is the lag time between placement, publication, and response of trade ads. While newspaper ads can be published in about three days after placement, trade ads take three to eight weeks from placement to publication.

Community Organizations

Another direct involvement recruitment source, but one that is often overlooked by smaller employers, is advertising job openings to local community organizations that have access to people looking for job opportunities. Community organizations consist of public and nonprofit agencies whose clientele possess various kinds and levels of job skills, but who have been out of the employment world for differing reasons and periods of time while using the services of the community organization. Examples include people who have been undergoing physical rehabilitation, developmentally disabled, sight and/or hearing impaired, welfare recipients, economically disadvantaged, abused women, or the homeless.

Once employers begin to set aside the stigma often attached to individuals whose life conditions necessitate using these kinds of services, it is likely they will learn that many—not all—of these human resources make very loyal, dependable, and skilled employees. The best way to conduct recruitment among community organizations is to develop a listing of prospective sources providing these and similar services. The list should contain a contact person to whom you can convey information about your hiring needs, the nature of jobs and your industry, and what skills and other employee attributes you seek from time to time. Next, use this list to mail job announcements to your contact person and request that referrals be made directly to you.

College Recruiting and Job Fairs

College recruiting and job fairs are traditional sources of job applicants for employers seeking either entry-level professionals or those with specialized skills. While these recruiting sources are traditional among medium-to-large employers, they are less so for smaller employers who have fewer vacancies, less staff to get involved in these events, and who cannot often justify the expense associated with recruiting in this fashion (costs estimated at $1,500–$6,000 per hire).

Even with these obstacles, college recruiting and job fairs can be productive sources of quality applicants for the smaller employer—perhaps more from scaled down college recruiting than job fairs. Most job fairs are sponsored by industry associations where, generally, the emphasis tends to be placed on jobs having very specialized, higher-level kinds of skills. They can be quite costly since they typically require display booths, airline travel, lodging and meals, staffing, video promotions, and expensive literature. College recruiting, on the other hand, accounts for as much as 50 percent of all college educated talent hired each year. It is also one of the few sources where a pool of younger workers are available with a dedicated interest in acquiring skills that lead to employment. The process can be elaborate or simple depending on your needs, budget, and expectations.

Larger companies have recruited numerous managers from entry-level to middle-management, professional, and technical people right out of college into their organizations for many years. They have become heavily involved with those colleges and universities that produce the kinds of skills they need in their industries, and they put a great deal of money, effort, and time into this recruiting source by providing scholarships, equipment, speakers, tours, liaison staff, library donations, technical literature, and other visible ways of keeping their image present on campus, including making instant job offers during annual recruiting drives.

Smaller companies should not be intimidated by the larger, flashier college recruiting companies. If your smaller company experiences regular demand for people with occupational skills (vocational schools), mid-level skills such as might be required of supervisors, entry managers, and entry careerists (two- and four-year colleges), or highly specialized and more sophisticated talent (universities with specialized graduate programs), then college recruiting may be a very beneficial source of quality applicants.

Here is a suggested plan of action for smaller companies to conduct college recruiting on a more achievable, competitive level with larger companies:

1. Make personal contact with the instructors of classes that relate to your business and let them know of your jobs and needs.

2. Arrange speaking engagements to appropriate classes by you or others in your organization.

3. Offer intern jobs to students through faculty and the college placement office.

4. Advertise job opportunities in the college newspaper.

5. Provide the college placement office with descriptive brochures about your organization, the kinds of employment opportunities, and various types of appealing benefits about the company.

6. Arrange for interviews in the college's placement office when particular jobs become available. Have students post the job announcement and interview process around campus and in the college newspaper. Coordinate the event with the placement office staff, provide a skilled and image-oriented interviewer, and make your acceptance or rejection decision in one to two weeks after interviews.

Recruiting the Experienced Older Worker

Older workers should not escape the attention of a fully developed recruitment program. These individuals represent a talented and readily available group of applicants who possess strong work ethic, loyalty, and productivity not always shared by others in the workforce. For example, in 1992 a study of recruitment and retention of older workers (over age fifty) conducted by the Society for Human Resource Management and the American Association of Retired Persons found that older workers offered their employers the advantages of:

- Overall workplace skill
- Low absenteeism
- Flexibility in scheduling
- High motivation
- Strong loyalty
- Mentoring abilities for younger workers

Yet most of the organizations surveyed admitted to a lack of retention practices and inadequate retraining programs that might otherwise ensure the maintenance and/or adaptation to new technological changes for older workers. Many such workers have thus been lost or squeezed out during the massive trend in downsizings and acquisitions/mergers during the 1990s, thereby falling victim to the search by American business to curtail operating costs and maximize profits. Further, it is a false assumption to believe that the hiring of older workers equates to higher payroll costs merely because these individuals bring more experience and skill to employers. While it is generally true you get what you pay for, remember that older workers can provide an important balance of work values, work methods, and teamwork processes. Many older workers are willing, and often desirous, of scaling back to part-time work hours, assuming a less demanding or strenuous position, working for a smaller or less complex organization, or working as a consultant or temporary worker.

To recruit this vast pool of talented workers, you can contact and place ads with the local chapter of the American Association of Retired Persons, contact your local senior citizens center (usually sponsored by city or county governments), or contact your local state employment office for details on how your employment opportunities can best reach this segment of the workforce.

State Employment Services

Every state is mandated to provide cost-free employment referral services to any legitimate and law abiding employer. As a source of recruiting job applicants, state employment services represent a vast reservoir of unemployed people with a wide range of job skills, many of whom have merely been displaced from their jobs or have relocated from another locale. Using this recruitment source has been made simple for employers in most states. The employer merely needs to call the local employment service office and give the job information over the telephone to a representative. Typical information desired by employment service offices to prepare job listings and applicant searches are:

- Job title
- Salary or wage rate
- Brief description of job duties and qualification requirements
- Application filing deadline and process
- Days and hours of work
- Employer's name, address, telephone number, and contact person

For smaller employers to get higher than normal quality applicant referrals from an employment service office, it is advisable for you to additionally:

- Try to find time to visit your local employment service office, meet the manager, and have a representative explain their services and processes to get people placed in jobs. Normally, the office staff is very receptive to prearranged visits by employers, and this orientation will be helpful to your knowledge of how best to use their services.
- Get the name of a representative you found to be understanding and professional. This is the person with whom you should place future job orders on a more personalized level.

- Express and emphasize important job standards to your representative when you list each job opening, including some of the more personalized and candid information about the company's expectation of job performance, proper attire and grooming, work values, and personality characteristics—not their preferred race, color, national origin, sex, age, or other "protected" discriminatory characteristics.

- Follow up with your employment service representative after each listed job is filled to discuss what you liked and disliked about particular applicants referred by him or her to give the representative a clearer idea of the kind of attributes your company values so future referrals are more in keeping with your company's expectations of applicant qualifications.

Employment, Recruiting, and Placement Firms

These traditional recruiting sources may operate by any of these trade names but they usually represent essentially the same type of services for all size companies who do not have the time, experience, or interest in undertaking an entire recruitment process for one particular job. Private employment firms offer an easy, quick, but somewhat expensive alternative for the smaller employer who prefers that other, perhaps more experienced professionals, handle recruiting and referral of prescreened applicants.

WARNING

Be cautious in your selection of an employment firm since not all of them are operated by seasoned human resource management professionals, and this weakness could severely influence their evaluation of applicants and compliance with anti-discrimination employment laws, particularly if you request that they perform preemployment tests.

The customary services offered by most employment recruiting and placement firms include advertising job openings (yours may be among many others the firm is publicizing), receiving applications and resumes, interviewing applicants to make a preliminary determination of their qualifications, matching applicants to their client's job specifications, and referring the more qualified respondents (or those already on file) to the client employer for hiring consideration. Some firms will additionally conduct limited preemployment tests and background checks.

Some employment firms specialize in the occupations they recruit and provide to their clients such as sales, accounting, management, clerical, production, or scientific. Others may specialize in certain types of industries such as legal, medical, or transportation. The third group are the generalists who provide searches for nearly any occupation or industry. Further, some firms are one office, sole proprietor owned and operated, while others are either franchise or local offices of a national network who can offer the client potential access to a larger geographic distribution of prospective applicants.

Fees for the services of employment firms can likewise vary. The more common methods are: 1) the contingency fee (usually 30 percent of the hired person's first year salary) plus expenses like long-distance calls; 2) the flat-rate-per-hire fee based on prescribed services that often amount to merely referring applicants from among the firm's existing file of applicants; and, 3) the sliding-scale per hour fee based on the type and level of services desired by the client, such as interviewing, testing, and background checking. The hourly fee arrangement is probably the most appropriate and equitable for both the firm and client employer, since this arrangement provides the firm with fair compensation for services rendered and the client employer has some say in the work that is performed and results produced. Some of the variables that should be considered by the employer in negotiating an employment firm's fee, and determining costs for their services, are:

- The degree of recruiting difficulty and cost-oriented measures the firm will likely have to take to acquire qualified applicants.
- The location from which applicants will have to be recruited (number of advertisements, phone calls, correspondence, etc.).
- Time and operating costs involved in the search process and duration.
- Level and type of services desired by the client employer (advertising, receiving and screening applications, conducting preliminary interviews, testing, and conducting background checks).

It is advisable for most companies to select two employment firms (for both permanent and temporary jobs) that can be called upon when the need arises. When considering the selection of an employment firm, you should evaluate such factors as:

- Their reputation of successful, long-lasting placements and thoroughness of screening to assure proper client "fit" with the types of jobs you hire.
- How long they have been in business and the degree of satisfaction by other clients (contact several of their references, particularly those who have hired the types of applicants you hire).
- Visit their business to observe their operation and procedures, and to evaluate the firm's overall professionalism.
- Determine what fee arrangement they use and, if acceptable to you, ask for a copy of their contract to have your attorney look over. In particular, see if they offer at least a thirty-day guarantee on each placement; that is, that they will replace at no cost any referred hire who resigns or terminates within thirty calendar days of his or her hire date.

Executive Search Firms

Executive search firms specialize in locating mid- to high-level managers and executives on the basis of a client's detailed specifications of desired qualifications, background, and unique business conditions and personal attributes. Similar to employment firms, some executive search firms specialize by the industries or types of positions they serve, while other firms may provide either general industry or upper level executive search services. Also, some are localized firms whereas others are located in several metropolitan cities offering access to a national pool of qualified applicants.

The degree of work involved in an executive search and referral can range from simple to very difficult depending on the firm's existing repository of interested applicants. Since most executive searches frequently span the continent to assure the client of optimal "fit," it is not uncommon for the search firm to encounter large expenses in conjunction with telephone calls and travel to conduct qualifying interviews, reference checks, and leads to other prospective candidates—some of whom become part of the firm's repository for other client referrals. Given the high visibility and degree of professional polish that must be brought to the business of executive search firms, it should not be surprising to know that most of these firms charge their clients 30 to 35 percent of the referred hire's first year salary plus bonuses and expenses (typically billed one-half in advance).

The selection of an executive search firm should be conducted with the same level of professionalism that you want brought to your search effort. Start by locating at least three such firms and mailing them a "Request for Proposal" (RFP) that specifies the search position, dates of vacancy and desired hire, job specifications, reporting relationships, desired business background and qualifications, personal attributes deemed part of job success, environmental conditions, financial stability of the company, contact person, and submission deadline. After receiving proposals, assemble an interview panel and evaluate each firm on the basis of such factors as:

1. Their experience and soundness of methods used to recruit the type of position you seek.

2. Their knowledge of your business, its practices, and modes of operating.

3. Their success in conducting searches for the position you are trying to fill.

4. Their staff and other firm resources that will be used to conduct the search, and what specific services will be provided. Services should include a thorough search and referral of eight to twelve preliminary profiles from which you can select four to six for serious consideration. Also, the search firm should conduct a thorough check of references on up to three finalists.

5. Their search and referral schedule, as well as the value received for the fee.

6. The professionalism of their presentation, enthusiasm, and confidence in achieving the desired results.

7. An admirable list of client references, most of which should be called for verification of their satisfaction.

Once you enter into a written agreement with an executive search firm, you should also make it clear to your contact person that you would like frequent status reports, even if they are verbally delivered. Additionally, it is advisable that the written agreement contain a clause requiring the search firm to obtain your advance approval for any major expenses such as air travel or lodging.

Recruitment Advertising Firms

Advertising job openings is no longer a simple matter of placing a written ad containing five or six small lines of print in the local newspaper. Smaller companies in particular must begin to learn from the lessons of their larger competitors that a short labor supply and decline in the number of quality employees demands more. Some of the added touches that are producing desired results are coming from advertising firms. These firms apply their creative skills to the recruitment process by conducting job market research, designing ads that attract attention and create appeal (such as those examples shown in Section 6.2), developing employee referral programs, designing copy for a company's promotional and recruitment literature, and experimenting with new methods such as tele-recruiting and direct mail campaigns.

While not all of these services may be of interest or cost effective for some smaller companies, advertising firms may be of immense help to the company who has been experiencing difficulty recruiting quality applicants for some jobs. When this occurs, you may find it well worth the cost to use an advertising firm to design a suitable ad that would attract attention and convey those job or company conditions that would create appeal for the kinds of applicants the company seeks. You may also want to use your selected firm to consult with you on the best sources of media to place your ad, what response techniques should be used, and what major "selling" points the company can use to get quality applicants to accept employment offers.

5.3 Using Innovative Recruiting to Combat Labor Shortages

Innovative recruiting consists of those methods that use either communications technology or more flexible management practices to find quality employees in an effort to meet the growing demand for a labor supply. Simply because these methods and sources are being classified as innovative (at present) does not mean that they are necessarily more risky or experimental than traditional methods. Rather, you should recognize the tremendous diversity that exists in the business community and, as a result, be aware that truly effective recruiting is likely to depend on each different business selecting a workable mix of both traditional and innovative methods. The following, then, are a few of the more successfully used innovative methods, sources, and practices you may wish to consider as you plan your recruitment strategy.

Innovative Internal Recruiting Methods

As pointed out in Chapter 1, there are other ways of filling jobs or work demands such as job-sharing, job-enhancement, job-enlargement, and working existing employees overtime. While these methods of getting work done are not recruitment oriented (with the object being to add new employees), they are nevertheless rather innovative practices of meeting workload demands in a difficult labor market. However, in terms of internal recruiting innovations, most of these efforts focus on more flexible use of retirees, student relatives of employees, and creating a pool of temporary/on-call employees.

Recruiting Retirees

It is estimated that two out of three retirees return to some form of paid employment during their first year of retirement. The reasons for their interest in returning to some type and level of employment involvement are many, but most center on boredom and financial need to supplement their retirement income. Given the vast number of highly capable, skilled, and stable workers, retirees represent a source of labor supply that should not be overlooked by employers seeking quality talent.

Recruiting one's own retirees to fill various jobs that might not be as demanding as career positions (many retirees don't want career-oriented job responsibilities or full-time work hours), can be as simple as making a few calls to your retirees to determine their interest in reemployment in their former or another capacity. Conversely, several companies have begun to actively recruit from among the general retiree community in their locales with a great deal of success. For example, as an incentive for retirees to consider employment with Wendy's (hamburgers) and Day's Inn (motels), these employers offer a program of tuition reimbursement for the grandchildren of retiree employees. What Wendy's and Day's Inn have successfully recognized is that retirees can be very reliable, capable workers who want part-time supplemental pay and occupation of their time. But these working retirees don't want to lose their social security income by earning more than the allowable amount of income, so the idea of contributing toward a grandchild's education becomes very appealing.

WARNING

Make sure that before you begin any advertising for retirees that you read Section 6.5, as well as the Appendix B relative to age discrimination to avoid unintentional, unlawful wording of your recruitment ad.

In addition to contacting your own retirees, or recruiting other retirees through advertisements, you may also want to locate community organizations in your locale where retirees are likely to be found such as the local chapter of the AARP, "adult" housing complexes, volunteer organizations, senior citizen centers, and churches.

Student Relatives of Employees

Another internal innovative method of recruiting both part-time and full-time employees is capitalizing on the skills being developed by student relatives of existing employees who are attending vocational and academic educations. While some employers may find the need to add an element of nepotism control within a program of recruiting the student relatives of employees, such internal recruiting can prove to be a quick and effective way of adding needed staff to fill full-time, seasonal, peak workload, regular part-time, or on-call positions. Not only does this method advantage the company in filling its staffing needs, but it also works to enhance employee morale when managed properly—and it can materially ease the cost burden for the family trying to support attendance at local educational institutions.

Recruiting student relatives of employees can be done as simply as posting notices of those job vacancies suitable to flexible scheduling with respect to the number of hours (20 to 30 or 25 to 35 hours per week) and days of the week work can be performed. You might even put the heading on the posted job announcement as "Student Job Opening," noting that student relatives of employees can be given first consideration (by a specified deadline) before the company recruits other applicants.

Temporary/On-Call Pool

In recognition of the vast and growing cadre of skilled workers who have major life interest or preoccupations other than employment, many small- to medium-size companies have successfully recruited people with a wide range of talent to fill various types of job vacancies. Usually, these "pooled" employees provide only on-call or as-needed staffing, but some businesses need them with frequent regularity to fill in vacations, leaves, resignations, peak workloads, and the like.

The sources for recruiting an on-call pool of temporary employees runs a gamut of people in your community. They often consist of retirees, students, former employees who are engaged in domestic or educational pursuits, professionally trained people who simply do not want nor need full-time work, physically handicapped persons, and others you might think of who offer the skills needed by your company but have limited availability due to other life demands. Such individuals can be recruited by using the traditional methods, but their use in the form of an on-call pool makes them something of a non-traditional source of labor when the demand is present.

Innovative External Recruiting Methods

Since recruitment is largely a communications process using available and new sources of media, the realm of recruiting has become limited only by one's imagination in today's technological environment of nearly instant information processing around the globe. Indeed, many of those recruiting methods considered innovative during the 1980s have taken on traditional proportions in the 1990s with the advances in the applications of computers. No doubt the use of computers for recruiting and screening job applicants will revolutionize the speed and improve the efficiency by which employers will recruit new employees during the 2000s. In the meantime, and in particular for smaller employers awaiting the lead of pioneering larger companies, there are other innovative recruiting methods that are worthy of consideration and use. The methods that follow are suggested approaches that the small- to medium-size company should give thought to when devising each recruitment plan.

Allied Industry Cooperative Recruiting

This method should be particularly attractive to smaller companies engaged in allied, or even competitive, industries in the same geographic region of a distinguishable labor market. The method is innovative because historically the same or similar industry employers have competed both for customers and employees, but this method sets aside the competitive factor in recognition of a mutual interest in recruiting similar employees from a common labor market. Considering the redundancy of ads, time, effort, cost, and administration of hiring chores, it truly makes little sense for smaller companies who are seeking essentially the same kinds of workers to compete and thereby waste their valuable individual resources doing so.

Cooperative recruiting among allied or same industries in a specific locale requires that one of them makes the first move—by contacting other owners to solicit their interest in discussing it and investigating the most workable approach. For example, in most urban and suburban areas there are a number of dental offices, office supply stores, auto dealerships, lumber and hardware stores, fast-food stores, dry cleaners, and countless other examples of the same or allied businesses regularly experiencing turnover and searching for similarly skilled replacement employees in a limited labor market. In fact, some of the turnover experienced by many smaller businesses is ironically attributable to employees being hired by a competitor! So, rather than competing with redundant results, why not work with your competitors on a cooperative basis to commonly recruit and hire from a joint effort using whatever methods of attracting quality applicants your co-op committee deems most suitable? Your ad, for example, could read, "The Dental Services Group of Icon Valley Seeks Interesting People for These Challenging Careers."

Direct Mail Recruiting

This method is another innovative means of soliciting job applicants for smaller size companies or for highly specialized, hard to fill jobs. Direct mail typically employs two steps; preparing an appealing and thorough job announcement, and compiling a mailing list that is most likely to reach the type of workers you seek. The job announcement should be comparable to that provided in Section 6.3, and enclosed with an invitational cover letter signed by your organization's top-ranking executive. Targeted audience mailing lists can be acquired through reliable direct mail list brokers, as well as by direct purchase of mailing lists or labels from sources of which you may already be aware.

Examples include trade publication subscribers, people who buy certain types of books, and those who purchase particular kinds of products. Three of the most common ways of getting interested persons to respond are:

1. offer them a toll-free telephone number to call for more information about the company, the job, or how to apply;

2. encourage the recipient to call collect during specified hours (after normal business hours and on Saturdays is effective for those already working); and,

3. enclose a postage-paid response card on which the recipient can complete brief information about their job interests and specify the best day, time, and telephone number for you to contact them about discussion of job opportunities or arranging an interview.

To conserve on the cost of recruiting by large volumes of direct mail, you should try to get mailing lists that are arranged by order of zip codes so that your postage can be set at the presort bulk rate. If, on the other hand, your volume is not excessive, you should mail this material first-class, which is more likely to get opened and read than bulk rate mail. Further, bulk rate mail is not returned to the sender if there is a problem with delivery whereas first-class mail is returned, and this return is the only way you have of knowing the "deliverability" of the list. It is also advisable to turn the mailing over to a direct mail marketing business to handle the tedious chore of folding, inserting, labeling, posting, and mailing your material.

Some of the advantages of direct mail recruiting are:

1. its low cost per solicitation if the list is carefully selected for the kinds of applicants sought;

2. its directness toward a particular skills audience;

3. it is one of the more reliable ways of reaching already employed people who might not look for or read other types of job ads, and who might refer others to your job(s) if they themselves were not interested in changing jobs; and

4. hiring results can be achieved relatively fast once you're accustomed to assembling direct mail efforts since the more interested people usually respond quickly.

Tele-Recruiting

Tele-recruiting is gaining popularity among some of the larger companies who have a fairly consistent need to fill new and replacement jobs, and it may eventually become a more feasible device for smaller companies to use to recruit new employees. This method takes essentially two forms: tele-marketing calls to prospective applicants with experience in the jobs being recruited, since most of the calls are placed to those already working; and tele-computer access by interested job seekers to a company's listing of available job opportunities.

Tele-marketing prospective job applicants involves:

1. assigning a staff member or outside service the task of contacting people employed in jobs similar to the one you are trying to fill as a means of "selling" them on coming to work for your company;

2. acquiring a list of names and telephone numbers of such individuals from various sources such as the telephone book (and asking for the "sales manager," "controller," "fleet supervisor," etc.) or a list of subscribers to a particular trade publication in a selected geographic area;

3. preparing a calling "script" to use on those called that quickly gets their interest and allows the caller to move into a descriptive conversation about the job, the company, and other appealing qualities of employment in the position; and,

4. closing the call by making arrangements to get the contact into the predetermined selection process (mail promotional material and an application form, application form returned, followed by contact for an interview).

Tele-computer recruiting is one of the newer methods of expediting the search, screening, and hiring of qualified applicants. This method currently takes two forms:

1. Applicants responding to job ads can call a telephone number where a staff member responds to questions and inputs applicant data (equivalent to application/resume information) into a computer, the results of which are used by the company to screen the more desirable applicants and invite them for interviews; and,

2. Applicants and those interested in promotions, job changes, and the like can use a modem to computer-access a company's job opportunities and promotional profiles of

the company, then input prescribed information about their qualifications if they wish to be contacted by the company for employment consideration.

Apple Computer is an example of one company using this technology to receive and screen job ad respondents, thus enabling them to interview the better qualified applicants within three days and hiring within three weeks. Another example of computer technology applied to recruiting has been developed by Resumix, Inc. in Santa Clara, California, who has developed a scanner system that can not only read hard copy resumes, but also has the artificial intelligence capabilities of extracting and analyzing resume information into specific informational formats. This system is said to allow the screening of numerous resumes by quick reference to such categories as work history, skill and experience, education, and job titles.

Cinema Billboards

For those companies who experience high or regular amounts of turnover among nonexempt jobs that require minimal training, the use of cinema "billboards" has been an effective means of making job advertisements known to a large and wide variety of potential applicants. Many movie theaters are now selling momentary showings of products, services, and other types of advertised announcements on their screens prior to the start of featured films. The billboard viewing is done on either a placard or slide which can be projected on the screen from the control room.

Information on how to prepare your job ad can be obtained from theaters selling this form of advertisement, but like other methods of using media marketing, the ad should give appealing information about the job, work hours, benefits of employment, the employing company, who to contact, and how to apply. This is also one of the few methods of recruiting where color advertisement can be used at low cost to enhance the attractiveness, appearance, and general appeal of a job ad.

Network Recruiting

As a process, this method requires that those in your company who have direct involvement with people in the occupation of the vacant job collaborate on known sources of business contacts. These may be professional associations to which they belong, meetings they regularly attend outside the company, or peers and their subordinates who can be contacted directly to investigate their interest in your job opportunity. Collectively, those in your company who are asked to help with network recruiting can often produce at least a few qualified and quality applicants interested in considering your job vacancy.

When network applicants are successfully recruited, it is advisable to communicate their interest quickly to the person handling the hiring process, and to conduct thorough follow up so that there is a welcoming feeling among those who become interested. Also, it is advantageous to invite network recruits to meet with your top managers, tour your facility, and create a personalized opportunity to promote the benefits of employment with your company. Taking these personalized steps may require after-hours receptions of potential new hires, but this approach usually hastens the screening and qualifying time to consider and hire network recruits.

Checklist of Recruitment Methods and Sources

Advertisements

- ❏ Newspaper ads, particularly display ads
- ❏ Local or regional business newspapers or news journals
- ❏ Trade magazines
- ❏ Trade newsletters
- ❏ Professional association newsletters
- ❏ College newspapers and placement offices

Announcements

- ❏ Posting on employee bulletin boards
- ❏ Employee Referral Programs
- ❏ Direct mail marketing to targeted mailing lists
- ❏ Mailings to community organizations, state employment offices, and former or retired employees
- ❏ Mailings to trade, technical, and business schools

Other Sources

- ❏ Unsolicited applications and resumes (file search)
- ❏ Transfers and employees on layoff
- ❏ Use of employment and/or executive search firms
- ❏ Use of advertising firms with job recruiting experience
- ❏ College recruiting and participation in job fairs
- ❏ Cooperative recruiting with competitors

6 Selecting the Best Recruiting Methods and Designing Ads to Attract Quality Applicants

During the late 1980s, labor shortages for skilled workers began to occur in nearly every major city across the United States. It was at this time that companies of all sizes started to reexamine their recruiting methods and budgets. While no major changes in recruiting methods have yet evolved to new prominence, employers have begun to either diversify their use of recruiting methods or to put more emphasis on the use of those methods that seem to be the most promising of getting the result desired.

6.1 Recruiting Methods That Work Best for Different Jobs

To get the best results from your recruitment investment means two things: 1) that the cost-per-qualified applicant is within an acceptable range as discussed in the previous chapter; and, 2) that you're getting a sufficient number of *quality* applicants in a timely manner so that operational disruption is minimized and hiring decision satisfaction is high. To achieve these objectives when recruiting for particular jobs, it is suggested that you focus your efforts on the methods and sources that follow.

Executive and High Level Management Jobs

The recruitment process used to attract executives and highly placed managers should be as sophisticated as the quality of applicants you desire. This is a case of "what you give is what you get." Therefore, when considering a recruitment for any of these jobs, you will need to make some early determinations on the following factors.

1. Is the financial condition of the company solid enough to attract quality applicants, and is the company positioned in a mode of challenge, growth, or opportunity that would appeal to a highly talented individual's desire to either change jobs or seek promotion?

2. Is the company's image and the nature of the business or industry such that appeal can be created for those who seek recognition, challenge, creativity, and new opportunities?

3. What condition is the company in with respect to its organizational structure, staffing size and talent, operational efficiency, and other factors that might serve to either distract or present a convincing challenge to prospective recruits?

4. How much time and funds are available to put into the recruiting effort, and what internal and external resources are available?

5. Is the job well established and defined within the organization, and what are the intended geographic boundaries to be covered by the recruiting effort?

Once these and other questions that may arise are answered about the job with respect to recruitment factors, you can begin to plan your recruiting campaign. The approach you take may be by internal means, use of external resources, or a combination of the two. Whichever approach is taken, the effort will require your close involvement and supervision.

Internal Resource Approach

If the need exists for you to handle the recruiting of an executive or high level manager, be prepared to spend a considerable amount of time and energy on the effort. The best methods and sources for recruiting these applicants are

1. Prepare well designed ads that appeal to the specific audience you're trying to attract with respect to the job, its challenges and opportunities, the skills needed, and a personalized yet confidential way for interested persons to apply or get further information.

2. Place your advertisement in such publications as *The Wall Street Journal, USA Today,* and in major metropolitan newspapers where you are most likely to find a concentration of skilled prospects.

3. Place particular emphasis on placing your ad in those specialized publications that prospective recruits are most likely to read, such as trade journals, association and industry newsletters, and the like.

4. Conduct your own executive search by asking other executives in your company for help and ideas on who to contact for referrals; acquire the membership directory of local or regional professional associations and begin contacting each member to determine their qualifications and interest; and contact similar executives and managers in the job you seek to fill who are presently employed in competitive companies.

5. Prepare attractive and descriptive promotional literature—preferably a packet of information—that can be sent to interested individuals to look over, and personalize each contact with a member of your company who can answer questions and project the proper image needed to "market" the job.

The best methods and sources when using the internal approach are appealing advertisements in the right publications, referrals from internal and external executives, your own search from among competitors of those already employed, and using attractive and marketing-oriented resources to gain the interest of those who respond to your efforts.

External Resource Approach

The two most effective external resources for recruiting executives and high level managers are professional executive search firms and advertising firms with experience in providing a full range of recruiting services. Given the importance of managerial and executive jobs to the successful operation of any company, you should budget (see Sample Recruiting Budget in Section 5.1) and use a combination approach. That is, retain an advertising firm to prepare ads and promotional literature on the job and company (which can be used for other recruitments and promotional purposes), and retain an executive search firm to use this material in conjunction with their own search, qualifying, and background checking methodologies.

Work closely with these firms to assure that their efforts are well coordinated early in the process, and that together they make a spirited team. You will also want to make sure that all of the bases are covered through the use of these resources such as meeting schedules, what geographic area(s) are to be included in ads and search, who has responsibility for selecting ad placement, who will respond to inquiries, how many finalists should be referred to whom, what profile information is to be provided on those referred, and similar details of the entire process so that confusion is avoided later. Whether your choice is an ad firm, search firm, or a combination of the two, your selection of the retained firm(s) should begin with the steps previously outlined for preparing a Request for Proposal (see Section 5.2, page 103, Executive Search Firms).

Combined Approach

Small- to medium-sized organizations with limited budgets but available staff to put in some creative time on an executive recruiting effort have been very successful at retaining advertising and search firms on a limited service basis. The first step in this approach is to identify the organization's abilities and interests in assuming specific aspects of the recruiting process. Second is the task of locating the right kind of expertise among advertising and/or executive search firms to meet the needs of your intended recruiting plan. Third, you will want to go through an interviewing and selection process among competitive firms who are willing and able to accommodate your desired configuration of services. And finally, you will need to negotiate the service costs and prepare a written agreement—which can be a simple engagement letter that defines service specifications, schedules, and cost. Following is an example of a combination approach:

1. You or someone in your company handles placement of ads, screens an initial group of prequalified applicants, makes all arrangements for the interviewing of finalist applicants, conducts reference and background checks, arranges any other testing or candidate "orientations" to the company, and negotiates employment offers and agreements with the hire choice.

2. The advertising firm prepares recruitment and company promotional literature to ensure and enhance maximum professional appeal of the job, and provides expert advice on the best source of ad placement.

3. The executive search firm uses their expertise and resources to seek out the most highly qualified persons for the job, sells interest in the job to prospects but carefully screens out those who do not meet all of the specifications of the job, conducts follow-up with those who respond to ads placed by the company, and provides comprehensive profiles of both initial and finalist candidates referred to the company.

Mid-Managers and Supervisors

While promote-from-within remains the most frequently used recruiting method to fill mid-level managerial and supervisory jobs, there are two things you should do to ensure that these jobs are filled with truly quality people: 1) conduct comprehensive internal training and development of your most talented employees to assess their actual skills and abilities (or limitations), and thereby prepare them for higher level responsibilities; and/or, 2) open recruitment of these jobs to external applicants and let interested employees compete with outsiders. Given the fact that internal employees almost always have the edge against outsider competition, open recruitments should pose little threat to the well prepared and confident employee.

The second most frequently used method of recruiting mid-level managers and supervisors is media ads. The two best sources are newspapers and trade publications but, depending on the particular job, other targeted media may prove even more fruitful—such as newsletter notices and direct mailing of job announcements to members of an appropriate professional association in your locale.

The third best method is employee referrals and the use of professional employment (recruiting) firms. If you are recruiting the job for both internal and external applicants, don't expect large numbers of referrals from nonexempt level employees since they may resent your outside search if they feel there is sufficient internal talent. Referrals should therefore be solicited among existing managers and supervisors along with any other ideas they may have concerning where to place ads or notices of the job vacancy.

When using an employment firm to either help with your recruitment or handle it exclusively, make sure you select a suitable firm and that they fully understand both the job and your company. It is suggested that you invite them to visit your company to get a first-hand idea of the company's operations and how the vacant job fits into the scheme of the business. In cases where the mid-level managerial job is especially crucial to the success of company operations, you may want to consider the use of an executive search firm rather than an employment firm (unless they specialize in the job you are trying to fill). Executive search firms can often be more effective at recruiting specialized mid-level managers, given their more sophisticated, professional, and expansive resources.

Medium- to large-sized companies should also develop some recruiting involvement with those universities that offer undergraduate and graduate programs in the disciplines used by the company, even if confined to a local or regional zone. Smaller companies, on the other hand, will likely find this method of limited value and considerable (relative) cost. Most small companies need to fill only a few managerial and supervisory job vacancies as they occur, not usually on a planned or projected basis. Nevertheless, smaller companies may find it useful to mail job announcements to college and university placement offices, and place ads or notices in collegiate newspapers to tap this valuable pool of aspirants.

Professional and Technical Employees

With the rate of increasing specialization and technological change in virtually every business enterprise, professional and technical jobs have become the most difficult to recruit. This problem is more likely to worsen than improve over the two decade period of the 1990s and 2000s. In fact, it is highly probable that the cost-per-hire for the more highly skilled professional or technical employee could rise above the cost to recruit managerial and executive jobs purely as the result of supply and demand for these jobs.

The best methods to attract and recruit applicants for professional and technical jobs are well designed newspaper ads, job posting (promotion from within), employee referrals, and college/university recruiting—with each method given about equal weight and effort in your recruitment plan.

Employees in general, and professional and technical employees in particular, have grown to desire and seek employment conditions that are different than in years past, and more in keeping with their *quality of work life* values. This means that very specific efforts must be directed at making changes within the company that will appeal to, and accommodate, the values of this "new breed" of worker. Particular emphasis to create the desired types of employment appeal should be placed on

1. Making changes in the philosophy, behavior, and practices of management to achieve participative, collaborative, and dignified treatment of employees.
2. Improving the work environment to maximize its pleasantness, spaciousness, and attractiveness to increase comfort and pride among employees.
3. Installing attractive and innovative policies on compensation, insurance and pension plans, promotional training, leaves, flexible work hours, opportunities for home work

during disabilities, assistance with child care and educational expenses, counseling and other employee assistance services, performance contests and incentives, and similar employment program innovations that catch the attention, interest, and pride of employees.

4. Designing jobs so that sufficient challenge exists to warrant a job seeker's attention, and holds the attention of quality employees. Keep expanding the jobs of those who show talent for more responsibility, but pay and/or promote them accordingly; that is, develop frequent recognition of talented people.

5. Allocating sufficient funds to conduct proficient recruiting of professional and technical applicants, including the preparation of appealing advertisements, using multiple placement of ads, retaining advertising firms to help with recruiting and designing employee referral contest programs, and in other ways giving some polish to the recruiting effort. The Sample Recruiting Budget in Section 5.1 may be of some guidance in formulating how much of a budget you will need to conduct proper recruiting of professional and technical applicants.

6. Training your people to "promote the company" so that when applicants call or visit your company they get the immediate impression that it is an ideal place to work. Carry this promotional theme through by staffing a job line where interested people can call in to inquire about job ads or referrals. This staff should be pleasant, skilled in arousing interest in the company and getting people to apply, and sufficiently knowledgeable about each job opening to answer most questions.

7. Preparing a well planned recruiting program for each job vacancy so that the entire process operates smoothly and in a timely fashion. You might begin by developing a plan similar to the Sample Recruiting & Selection Schedule in Section 5.1, and the Job Testing Plan Profile in Section 7.2. Be prepared to screen, test, and make hiring decisions quickly, followed by public relations letters to those not selected.

Office Occupations

Office occupations consist of clerical workers, bookkeepers, administrative assistants, order processors, inside sales representatives, account representatives, operations officers, and other similar positions. These nonexempt jobs require a range of semiskilled to skilled qualifications. The best methods of recruiting this general group of applicants are newspaper advertising, job posting (promote-from-within where applicable to the job level), employee referrals, placement offices of vocational schools, and unsolicited applications.

This, and the next group of recruits, provides good reason for a company to accept unsolicited applications and resumes from walk-ins, call-ins, and mail-ins that are not in conjunction with current job vacancies or ads. While this source of applicants can consume large amounts of time to receive, identify proper job grouping, and file in a manner that yields reliable retrieval at a later time, these applicants can produce a quality source of new hires at a very low recruiting cost. By filing an application or resume, they have already demonstrated diligence and interest in working from their effort to make contact with your company.

Unless a particular job is very specialized, you should not need the services of external firms other than perhaps the assistance of an advertising firm to help design and place targeted recruitment ads and notices. For skilled secretarial jobs where quality applicants are already in short supply, you should consider direct mail recruiting to such sources as larger companies in your locale where employment might have become too bureaucratic, impersonal, or lacking individual recognition of its employees, or the members of the nearest chapter of Professional Secretaries International (PSI). A potentially valuable and low cost source for office occupations is the placement office of local and regional vocational schools whose reputations often rely on the ability to find employment opportunities for their graduates. This source also has the advantage of offering employers those individuals who have made a special effort at acquiring usable office skills and better orientation to the demands and expectations of employers than many of the "open market" applicants for office jobs.

Newspaper ads for this group of job seekers should appeal to the challenging nature of work, the energy and enthusiasm of the company toward its business and employees, benefits of employment, and other reasons they should either apply or consider a job change. Attention-getting design should be used to make your ad noticeable among the vast and growing number of ads soliciting the same applicants. Equally important, clear information should be given on how to get more information about the job, and how to apply (perhaps for a preliminary eligibility determination) including during lunch hour and after normal business hours. In other words, address your ad to both those currently available and those considering a job change.

Trade, Production, and Service Workers

These jobs are made up of semiskilled and skilled workers who perform a relatively narrow set of job functions. Because many of these occupations either provide direct service to customers or produce the goods purchased, there is the need to place particular emphasis on improving the quality of applicants as well as the quality with which they are hired and trained. Quality applicants can only be obtained by quality recruiting, and that means putting from $5,000 to $15,000 per year into image-building display ads in newspapers and other print media, as well as the development of attractive promotional literature.

What quality applicants are looking for in trade, production, and service employment are such conditions as an employer who takes pride in the company, competitive pay and benefits, training opportunities, and some prospect of eventual promotion. For the smaller organization with limited promotional choices, this may mean using a new advertising twist like, "Start your career in automobile repair with us," or "Learn from us what it means to serve the best hamburgers in town." Many employers are beginning to realize that not all quality employees come with highly refined skills, rather they are quality *people* to begin with who have enough drive, confidence, and self-motivation to learn. Given those qualities, most people can learn trade, production, and service jobs rather quickly.

The best methods to recruit trade, production, and service applicants are newspaper ads, employee referrals, unsolicited applications, vocational and trade schools, state employment offices, community organizations, and "point-of-purchase" notices (well designed posters or placards, not "help wanted—inquire within" signs). One means of attracting quality people is to direct your advertising theme toward people who view themselves as having desirable qualities, and thereby allow others to self-screen themselves out of applying. For example, Taco Bell, Inc. uses the recruiting slogan, "We're looking for a few friendly people." The message here is that Taco Bell wants people who are oriented toward customer service and like working with the public. The implied message is that others need not apply.

Laborers and Other Unskilled Workers

Even during periods of serious labor shortages, there seems to be a plentiful supply of unskilled workers. The problem here is more with the shortage of jobs where this labor supply can obtain productive employment in light of an industry base that continues to move toward specialization of job skills. Further, for many available workers in this occupational group, the problem of illiteracy plagues their chances for learning new skills or even coping with the most fundamental employment conditions, such as being able to read employment applications, write legibly, and read and comprehend simple written instructions or warnings.

What employers of unskilled labor should be doing to improve the quality of their work force, and therefore the quality of their product or service, is to recruit those with the desire, ambition, and fortitude to put extra effort into learning first the job and second new or improved skills. This may require that these employers should have available such employment conditions as

- Well trained supervisors who are fluent in a second language (or for whom English is their second language).
- One-on-one employment and training assistance using supervisors and better trained employees to help new recruits during the hiring process, initial employment training, and after-hours literacy education.
- Solicitation of local educational institutions such as high schools, vocational schools, retired school teachers, or the nationally advertised Project Literacy Program to create a company-sponsored opportunity for employees to obtain the literacy skills needed for more reliable employment. Place emphasis on reading, comprehension and writing English, basic math, and cultural education.
- Preparation of innovative training programs that provide quality people with specific job skills. The cost of doing so will come back from what these employees will subsequently produce for you in the way of production, efficiency, accuracy, quality, and loyalty.

The best recruitment methods to acquire quality applicants for unskilled labor jobs are employee referrals, community organizations, unsolicited applications, state employment offices, county welfare offices, and "point-of-purchase" notices. Newspaper ads should be used very carefully to avoid excessive numbers of poor quality applicants who are difficult to screen because of the sheer volume and absence of strict job skill standards. If ads are used, they should require a short deadline to file applications, and perhaps even emphasize that those hired should be willing to participate voluntarily in after-hours, company-sponsored literacy skills programs.

6.2 Designing Your Own Job Ads

Designing job ads and announcements is a process of using your communication skills and creativity—or imagination. You should keep in mind that recruitment advertising is intended to serve two purposes: 1) to attract attention and interest of the reader; and, 2) to convey enough information about the job and application process to get the reader to apply for the position. Given those two purposes, it should be clear that small, non-graphic ads with vague details, weak incentives, and obscure application instructions won't get quality responses, so those employers should either save their advertising money or resign themselves to hiring your rejects.

To attract attention and interest of the reader, your ad or announcement must be noticeable by its design, size, layout, typestyle, catchy headline, and professional appearance. These features will become more apparent as you examine the samples included in this section which illustrate attention-getting features like the use of shading, photos and company logos, use of unique and bold typestyles, the ease of reading larger size print, use of "white space" to unclutter a lot of print, and appealing header phrases. Display ads such as the samples shown in this section may cost the employer a bit more, but they have the decided advantage of conveying the implied message to the reader that the employer operates on a professional level, and obviously views employees as important enough to warrant the cost of a noticeable ad.

To provide the right kind of information about the job and application process in ads and announcements, you should select the pertinent job requirements, duties, challenges, and interesting components to include in your ad. Be as clear, concise, and succinct as possible, but say enough to create a visual picture of the job. To enhance the reader's ability to "visualize" the job, use descriptive action words about the work, the people, and the environment. Finally, how you want interested and qualified persons to apply should be clearly stated. Provide a telephone number and the contact person's name to call or write for more information about the job and company. Remember, the idea is to sell rather than merely announce. Given five to ten good responses, you can be selective about who you invite for hiring consideration. If you try to be selective first by using ill-conceived ads and difficult application processes, you may not get the chance to be selective later about who to invite for hiring consideration.

What Gets Attention in Recruitment Advertising

The unavoidable truth about recruitment advertising is that small to medium employers are competing head on with larger, more capital-flexible employers in search of the best job applicants in a limited labor market. The winners get the better qualified, skilled, and productive employees—it's that simple. What sells to quality applicants, and what do they look for in an employer? Here are a few features that you should consider including in your recruitment advertising to get attention and sell the reader on advantages of employment with your company.

1. *The Job*
   - Full range of responsibilities
   - Challenging work content and learning opportunities
   - Creativity and autonomy (degree of independence)
   - Ability to broaden skills
   - Have decision making authority in areas of job responsibilities
   - Work closely with other highly skilled people

2. *The Company*
   - Interest in and concern for the welfare of its employees
   - Good image, reputation, and goal oriented
   - Progressive in its industry and state-of-art technology, practices, facilities, etc.
   - Diversity of jobs and career opportunities
   - Competitiveness of pay and benefits
   - Attractiveness of employment programs such as training, child care, educational assistance, and performance incentives

3. *The Employment Environment*
   - The "quality of life" appeal of the employment location (proximity of quality housing, shopping, schools, entertainment, and recreation)
   - Pleasantness of environmental features at the employment location
   - Informality and social context of interaction with others
   - Ease of transportation and travel to the employment location, and commute time

Recruitment advertising is human resource marketing in its purest form. Consequently, effective advertising should follow the general principles of marketing. First, you must identify your market (applicants), the key characteristics of your product (qualities and responsibilities of the job), and how the customer goes about buying your product (application process). Second, your ad or announcement must attract attention, be unique in some fashion, and demonstrate the benefits your product has over the competition (company and job image, challenge, progressiveness, location, economics, incentives, industry, etc.). Third, you must get your message to the right market (applicants) meaning the proper use of targeted methods and sources of your advertising.

How to Design Your Own Job Advertisements

Designing job ads is a combined process of using creative design to capture the reader's attention and interest, and communicating the right kind of information to sell the reader on either applying for the job or seeking more information. Since the amount of information you choose to provide has the greatest influence on the size and design features of an ad, you should start first by preparing the information and layout of your ad. When this is done, you can experiment with other design features such as shading, borders, company name and logo, typestyles, and headers that are thought-provoking, humorous, or in other ways appealing and eye-catching. You might want to think of it in this way: ad design is intended to capture attention, while ad information is intended to capture interest in applying.

Job ads are used in two primary sources of recruitment advertising: newspapers, and trade publications such as professional magazines and newsletters. As a general rule, the more targeted and exclusive the publication, the higher the cost for placement of an ad. Therefore, you can expect that trade publication advertising space will cost considerably more but this cost should be offset by the fact that you are publicizing your job vacancy to an audience whose qualifications are known. As a means of reducing the cost of trade ads, many employers will often edit their normal ads or in other ways reduce their size. However, care must be taken not to compromise the ad's appearance, content, and attraction—or its purpose will be defeated.

If you happen to have a personal computer with a desktop publishing or graphics design software program, the task of creating job ads can be made simple, quick, and professional enough to avoid the added cost of having your ad prepared in final form by a typesetter.

Preparing Informational Content

The primary source of information for job ads and announcements will be obtained from the applicable job description—if it was prepared properly in the first place. If your job descriptions are weakly or vaguely detailed, this will present a problem when trying to reconstruct job content information for your marketing piece, and it draws attention to the fact that you should use Chapter 2 as a guide to preparing better job descriptions at some future date. A valuable source of supplemental information about the job are those supervisors who oversee the work of employees in these job positions, and who are most familiar with descriptive features of the work, employment conditions, skills required, and personal traits that have proven to be tantamount to successful job performance.

The information that should be conveyed in the job ad should minimally consist of such features as

- Job title (use titles that create a commonly known and/or visual picture of what the job is, such as Accountant, Auto Detailer, Cashier)
- Brief description of the more important, frequent, challenging, and interesting job duties, responsibilities and authorities
- Qualification requirements, preferred (nondiscriminatory) traits, and desired characteristics such as advanced college degree, licenses, and industry experience
- If the job is a new one or due to the company's growth
- The nature of the work environment, work schedules, and interpersonal contact

Other informational content that should be considered for your job ad is anything about the company of which you are particularly proud, believe to be unique, or regard as attractively different from competitors. Such information might include one or more of these features:

- The company's attractive pay, benefits, and incentive programs
- The nature of the company's business, industry, goals, management style, state-of-the-art equipment, innovativeness, high regard for talented people, and/or the spirited energy of its employees
- The close and informal contact employees have with each other, customers, and managers
- The desirability of the employment location with regard to the quality of life, affordable housing, ease of travel, and the like
- The diversity of jobs, people, and career (promotional) opportunities

Having created an appealing description of the job, the company, and the employment environment, the last portion of your informational content should address the application/inquiry process. In marketing vernacular, this represents closing the sale by telling your audience how to apply for the job or get more information if the reader is not yet convinced. Features that should be included in job ads about the application/inquiry process are:

- Where and to whom resumes should be sent
- Where to complete an employment application or to call to have one mailed (or FAXed?)
- What is the application deadline
- Who can be contacted for more information about the job, company, and related employment information
- When calls can be made (after normal business hours, on weekends, or by toll-free means)
- Is salary history necessary (inadvisable)

Using Attention-Getting Design

Even if your job ad contains all the right information and alluring details of employment with your organization, it may not get the attention it deserves unless some specific design features are added to draw the reader's eye to it. This is best accomplished by the use of design techniques known to capture attention, create curiosity or intrigue, make the information easy to read, and generate confidence in the company by its implied professionalism. The techniques used to capture the reader's attention and convey these visual messages are

1. *Graphics*
   The use of company name in its normal typestyle, company logo, background shading, borders, half-tones, bullets or check boxes, and coupons or information request forms.
2. *Size and Layout*
   While the size of a quality ad is determined in large part by the amount of informational content and extent of graphics used, other considerations include the amount of "white space" allowed and the shape or configuration of the layout. Most ads, you will notice, are laid out vertically. If the information is arranged in a narrow space, reading becomes difficult and fatiguing. Wide ads and those arranged horizontally catch the eye more

quickly because they stand out from the others, and they are easier to read—we're trained to read left to right, so the less eye movement required, the easier it is to read, and thus the more likely it becomes that the reader will read the entire ad. Good layout should also consider the orderliness of information and design features.

3. *Typestyles*

The style, size, and boldness of print should tastefully get attention rather than be so dramatic or flamboyant that it becomes difficult to read. These three features—print style, size, and boldness—should therefore be sparingly used to draw attention to an interesting, attention-getting phrase (header), the job being recruited (job title), the employing company (name and logo), and important application information (deadline, address, phone number, and name of contact person). The style of design print should be appealing while informational print should be large and clear enough to read easily. You may also want to consider the use of "reverse" print—black background with white print.

4. *Headlines*

Headlines are intended to draw the eye to the top of the ad; create interest in reading more by the use of short phrases that appeal to the reader's sense of humor, thought-provoking values, and general ideals of employment; and create a sense of uniqueness about the employer. Headlines can be the added touch to job ads that gets more attention than those ads that do not have this form of reader appeal.

The four easiest ways to add design features to your job ads are: 1) use your personal computer graphics software program; 2) purchase press-on lettering and graphics available at art and stationery stores; 3) use cut-and-paste design features from other available materials the company may have already printed; or, 4) send your layout ad to a graphic artist or creative typesetter.

Sample Job Ads That Get Results

On the next few pages are samples of small, medium, and large job ads that contain variations of recruitment advertising features to be used to attract quality applicants. It would serve little purpose to provide you with samples of ads that, by contrast and comparison, are ineffective. Rather, emphasis has been alternatively placed on the relative strengths and shortcomings of the more well-written and designed ads, and where resultant success is most likely to be achieved in the recruitment of quality applicants.

SAMPLE 1

ACCOUNTANT

Doctor's Medical Center, a 298-bed acute care hospital located in Modesto, is seeking qualified applicants for the position of Staff Accountant for our Finance Department. This position requires a BS/BA Accounting degree and a minimum 2 years full-time experience.

Modesto, in the heart of the San Joaquin Valley, is located 1½ hours from the ocean, the mountains and San Francisco. The climate is mild and the cost of housing is very affordable. If these advantages interest you, then mail resume to: **Personnel Department, Doctors Medical Center, P.O. Box 4138, Modesto, CA 95352.** EOE M/F/H. A subsidiary of National Medical Enterprises.

Doctors Medical Center

Reprinted with permission of Doctors Medical Center, Modesto, CA, 1990.

SAMPLE 2

SAMPLE 3

EDP
Instruction

Technical Education Specialists

Don't miss this opportunity to learn about NCR. You'll discover the high corporate priority we place on the education of our customer service representatives. NCR knows where it's going in field engineering training, as we develop the very finest training programs ever created for field service engineers.

Now you can help lead the way. Your development efforts will include Self-Paced Computer-Based Training and instructor-taught courses for both hardware and software. The programs you generate here will not only be comprehensive, but will redefine the state-of-the-art in EDP instruction.

And your career will be backed by our $3.7 billion enterprise, highly successful in every segment of information processing. With a host of new product innovations, keen marketing insight and a new spirit of enthusiasm, NCR looks forward to a high growth future ahead for us and for you.

Right now, we have immediate openings in our expanding Technical Education Organization for instructors and course developers experienced in the training of field engineers. You must have a Bachelor's Degree, or equivalent, comprehensive knowledge of the design and implementation of Criterion Referenced Instruction, and the willingness to relocate to Dayton, Ohio. Involves some travel assignments.

We offer excellent compensation, extensive benefits, advancement potential and the opportunity to contribute significantly to our dynamic organization.

Our doors are open. Send your resume with salary history to Mr. Keith Jenkins, NCR Corporation, U.S. Data Processing Group, Dept. L-339, Dayton, Ohio 45479.

NCR
1884-1984
Celebrating the future

An equal opportunity employer

SAMPLE 4

Mechanics

FORKLIFT MECHANICS

VALLEY FORKLIFT, an established Komatsu major Dealership in Modesto, is expanding into the Sacramento area.

We are currently seeking 3 mechanics to start up this new facility. Two for field work and one for the shop.

As a mechanic you will receive:

* Top wages
* Excellent benefits including retirement
* Participative team environment
* Work where quality and service come first

If you are a top mechanic, please call Darryl Kielich at (916) 387-8000

Or send resume to:
VALLEY FORKLIFT COMPANY
P.O. Box 577440
Modesto, CA 95357

An Equal Opportunity Employer

SAMPLE 5

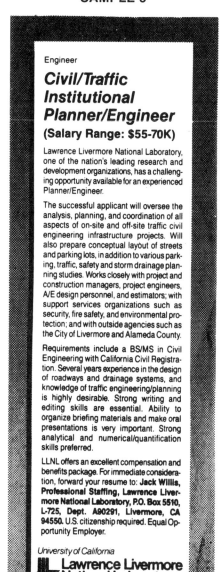

Engineer

Civil/Traffic Institutional Planner/Engineer
(Salary Range: $55-70K)

Lawrence Livermore National Laboratory, one of the nation's leading research and development organizations, has a challenging opportunity available for an experienced Planner/Engineer.

The successful applicant will oversee the analysis, planning, and coordination of all aspects of on-site and off-site traffic civil engineering infrastructure projects. Will also prepare conceptual layout of streets and parking lots, in addition to various parking, traffic, safety and storm drainage planning studies. Works closely with project and construction managers, project engineers, A/E design personnel, and estimators; with support services organizations such as security, fire safety, and environmental protection; and with outside agencies such as the City of Livermore and Alameda County.

Requirements include a BS/MS in Civil Engineering with California Civil Registration. Several years experience in the design of roadways and drainage systems, and knowledge of traffic engineering/planning is highly desirable. Strong writing and editing skills are essential. Ability to organize briefing materials and make oral presentations is very important. Strong analytical and numerical/quantification skills preferred.

LLNL offers an excellent compensation and benefits package. For immediate consideration, forward your resume to: **Jack Willis, Professional Staffing, Lawrence Livermore National Laboratory, P.O. Box 5510, L-725, Dept. A90291, Livermore, CA 94550.** U.S. citizenship required. Equal Opportunity Employer.

University of California

Lawrence Livermore National Laboratory

Reprinted with permission of Lawrence Livermore National Laboratory, Livermore, CA, 1990.

SAMPLE 6

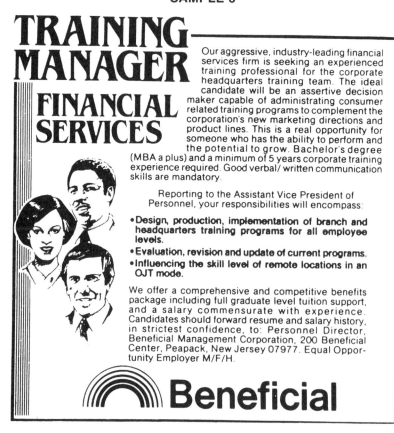

TRAINING MANAGER
FINANCIAL SERVICES

Our aggressive, industry-leading financial services firm is seeking an experienced training professional for the corporate headquarters training team. The ideal candidate will be an assertive decision maker capable of administrating consumer related training programs to complement the corporation's new marketing directions and product lines. This is a real opportunity for someone who has the ability to perform and the potential to grow. Bachelor's degree (MBA a plus) and a minimum of 5 years corporate training experience required. Good verbal/ written communication skills are mandatory.

Reporting to the Assistant Vice President of Personnel, your responsibilities will encompass:

• **Design, production, implementation of branch and headquarters training programs for all employee levels.**
• **Evaluation, revision and update of current programs.**
• **Influencing the skill level of remote locations in an OJT mode.**

We offer a comprehensive and competitive benefits package including full graduate level tuition support, and a salary commensurate with experience. Candidates should forward resume and salary history, in strictest confidence, to: Personnel Director, Beneficial Management Corporation, 200 Beneficial Center, Peapack, New Jersey 07977. Equal Opportunity Employer M/F/H.

Beneficial

SAMPLE 7

Fresh Air, Pine Trees, and Opportunity To Be Creative !!!

Director of Human Resources

SIERRA TAHOE BANCORP (dba, Truckee River Bank), located in the beautiful and bountiful Lake Tahoe region, is pleased to invite applications for this newly created senior management position. With administrative offices located in Truckee, California, Truckee River Bank has progressively grown to 185 employees and 16 area offices since it foundation in 1981. Through successful management of the company's assets, the Bank continues to expand its opertions and opportunities for continued investments and service to the community. To ensure an equally leading role in the administration of its human resources, we now seek highly skilled, motivated, and opportunistic applicants to fill this new position with a staff of three and reporting directly to the Chief Executive Officer. The successful applicant will receive attractive compensation ($45,000-$60,000 d.o.q.), benefit package, a leadership role in the management team, and a most favorable living environment.

Responsibilities: With a hands-on, direct involvement approach, the Director of Human Resources will be responsible for the planning, development, and implementation of a comprehensive human resources department serving all employees and working with other management staff in such areas as classification, hiring, training, compensation and benefits administration, performance monitoring, employee relations, legal compliance, employment policies, and operations planning.

Requirements: Bachelor's degree in Business Admin., Human Resources, or directly related field and ten (10) years exempt professional experience, of which at least five years were involved in technical generalist work in a human resources department. **Desirable qualifications consist of a Master's degree and experience in a bank or similar financial institution at a responsible management level in human resources.**

How To Apply: Send resume of qualifications and accomplishments to Mr. Joseph D. Levesque, HR & Management Systems Consultants, 3450 Palmer Drive, Ste. 7-290, Cameron Park, CA 95682 by April 19, 1991.

Truckee River Bank

EEO/MFHV

Reprinted by permission of Truckee River Bank, California, 1991.

SAMPLE 8

Medical

Better Way of Life in Another California

Away from crowded schools, cities, freeways and a higher cost of living is a better way of life. One of breath-taking scenery, great outdoor living and a friendly affordable life-style, perfect for raising families. The place is Redding, California.

The Redding Medical Center serves the community with progressive and personal health care. Known as the "Hospital with Heart", we also provide a comprehensive Rehab Center and opportunities for rewarding medical careers in the following areas:

Physical Therapists
Occupational Therapists
Respiratory Therapists
Cardiovascular Technologist
R.N.'s
- —O.R.
- —P.C.U.
- —Recovery Room
- —Cath. Lab

We value medical personnel in our California. They expect and receive supportive educational assistance, **$3,000 hire on bonus for selected positions,** advancement options, relocation assistance program available and competitive compensation. Affiliation with National Medical Enterprises ensures that our benefits are extensive. Explore a better way of life in our California by calling or sending your resume to: **Personnel, Redding Medical Center, P.O. Box 2458, Redding, CA 96099-2458, (916) 244-5150.** An equal opportunity employer.

REDDING MEDICAL CENTER

Reprinted by permission of Redding Medical Center, Redding, CA.

SAMPLE 9

▶ SR. PRODUCT SPECIALIST

Responsibilities:

- Assist in the development of next generation printers from concept through market introduction
- Conduct market analysis, forecasting and product Beta testing for use in the development of Marketing plans
- Provide technical interface between product development and field sales groups regarding design, specification, and applications issues

Qualifications:

- 3-5 years of direct experience in a Computer Marketing/Product Management or Applications Engineering role
- Printer Marketing experience desired; preferably in laser or page printers
- BS degree in a technical discipline preferred
- Excellent oral and written communication skills

NEC Technologies, Inc.

NEC Technologies, Inc., is a subsidiary of a Fortune 50 world leader in the computer and communications markets. Our consistent growth has been well planned. We offer the marketplace exciting, state-of-the-art products and we offer our employees competitive salaries, outstanding benefits programs, 100% educational reimbursement, and an excellent opportunity for personal advancement.

For immediate consideration, please send your resume to: Al McCarthy, Human Resources Department, NEC Technologies, Inc., 1414 Massachusetts Ave., Boxborough, MA 01719.
This position is available immediately.
Principals please.

A Committed Equal Opportunity Employer M/F/H/V.

Reprinted by permission, NEC Technologies, Inc., Boxborough, MA.

SAMPLE 10

Do for nursing what Steve Wozniak did for computers.

Steve Wozniak and his talented associates used their vast technical knowledge and understanding of society's changing needs to help extend the role and benefits of computer technology in everyday life.

Della Leavitt, Staff RN, was chosen to chair the Education Committee at Kaiser Permanente's Bellflower medical center because of her insightful suggestions on broadening the role of RNs in patient care delivery. She and her colleagues devised a program to educate RNs on new standardized, comprehensive methods for using Nursing Care Plans. The response from Staff RNs has been overwhelmingly positive. Improved communication and expanded participation in patient care have reinforced their vital role in providing quality health care throughout the medical center.

We're looking for Staff RNs who share Steve's and Della's innovative spirit and dedication to their profession.

Call our toll-free Career Opportunity Hotline at 1-800-553-1060, 24 hours a day, 7 days a week, for detailed information on our benefits — which include 100% health care coverage for you and your family — and current RN openings. Or submit your resume, in confidence, to: Kaiser Permanente, Regional RN Recruitment/Retention, Dept. PRO 10, 393 E. Walnut St., 7th Floor, Pasadena, CA 91188-8701. Equal Opportunity Employer.

KAISER PERMANENTE
Good People. Good Medicine.
Southern California

Reprinted by permission, MDK USA Knoth & Meads, San Diego, CA, 1990.

Recruitment Advertising Effectiveness Ratings of Ad Information and Design Features											
Ad Features	**Small Ads**				**Medium Ads**					**Large Ad**	
	1	2	3	4	5	6	7	8	9	10	
Meaningful Job Title(s)	+	+	+	+	+	+	+	+	+	+	
Interesting Job/Employment Content Info.	−	+	+	−	+	+	+	+	+	+	
Attractive Employment Benefits/Conditions	−	+	−	+	−	+	+	+	+	+	
Company or Environmental Attractions	+	+	+	−	+	+	+	+	+	−	
Clear and Easy Application Information	+	+	+	+	+	+	+	+	+	+	
Attention-Getting Use of Graphics	+	+	−	+	+	+	+	+	+	+	
Size and Layout of Ad	−	+	−	+	+	+	+	+	+	+	
Typestyle Techniques	+	+	+	+	+	+	+	+	+	+	
Alluring Use of Header Phrase	−	−	−	−	−	−	+	+	−	+	

+ = Moderate to very effective   − = Ineffective or absent

6.3 Designing Your Own Job Announcements

Job announcements are very similar to job ads in content and design, but they are usually prepared on a larger format and used for different methods of recruitment advertising. The primary uses of job announcements are for posting job vacancies within the company, mailings to community organizations and other business sources who are likely to know of qualified people and refer them, direct mail campaigns to potential applicants, and for college recruiting, job fairs, open houses and other public relations activities used for recruiting. Since there is more space to work with in preparing job announcements, you may want to start your recruiting effort with the construction of a job announcement, then edit or photographically reduce it for use in display ads. With the available technology of personal computers that provides a choice of type fonts and printers that produce high quality (300+ d.p.i) print, the task of preparing your own job announcements can be a quick, simple, and effective process.

Designing and writing your own job announcement is easier than you might think if you simply follow the suggestions and steps provided on the following pages. Also, samples have been provided to give you a more visual idea of how announcements should look when a little creative thought is applied.

Formatting Layout and Design Features

Unlike job ads that typically begin with informational content of the job, announcements have more space flexibility so it is advisable to start with formatting the layout and design features first. The format and design features will, in turn, guide you to the placement and amount of information that can be used in the announcements. Don't worry, there is almost always more than sufficient space for as much information as you wish to present. Your first decision is whether to use invoice (generally too small), letter or legal size paper. You will absolutely need to use a legal size page if: 1) your job descriptions contain a great deal of information; 2) there is a lengthy explanation for qualifications or the application process; or, 3) the announcement covers more than one position vacancy. Since it's easier to cut a page from legal to letter than it is to reformat from letter to legal, you may want to start each announcement on a legal size until experience tells you otherwise.

You want your job announcements to be just as attention-getting as your job ads, so your second formatting step is to select the layout (placement) of design features. Keep in mind where you will want to place job information so that the announcement's overall appearance is orderly and blends well with design features. For example, many companies use a standardized format for their job announcements. This has the advantage of making them easily recognized by those who see them with any frequency. This standardization of format might be the color of paper used, the way the information is displayed, or uniform design elements such as using a large, bold type repetitive heading of JOB ANNOUNCEMENT.

Company Name

Logo

JOB OPPORTUNITY ANNOUNCEMENT

JOB TITLE (salary range or rate)

About The Job

Place description of job responsibilities, conditions, challenges, and interesting features here.

Illustrative Qualifications

Explain and list the education, experience, training, skills, knowledge, abilities, and other qualification requirements of the job here. Be sure to distinguish between required and preferred/desirable qualifications.

Why You Should Apply For This Job

Describe "selling" features of the job, the company and its industry, and/or employment benefits such as attractive insurance and pension plans, flexible schedules, the community in which employment is located, etc.

How To Apply & Who To Contact

Give a person's name, title, address, and telephone number where applications can be obtained, where they should be mailed, and how to get further information. Use a toll-free number, if available, for out-of-area applicants.

Company Logo

CAREER ADVANCEMENT OPPORTUNITIES

What Career Advancement Offers You

Describe the various benefits of the Company, the nature of the jobs being recruited, and advantages of working in poitions of higher responsibility.

Job Vacancies That Offer Challenge and Growth

Job Title: *Describe major responsibilities, authorities, challenges, and qualifications*

Job Title:

Job Title:

How to Apply for Immediate Consideration

Stylized Company Name, Address, Telephone and FAX numbers

Company
Logo

Company
Name

JOB
ANNOUNCEMENT

Job Title

Opportunities & Challenges

Description of the job's responsibilities, performance measures, and tasks stated in terms of the more significant opportunities and challenges.

-

-

-

Typical Qualifications

Describe and list the education, training, experience, skills, knowledge, and abilities applicants should possess to be qualified for consideration.

How And Where To Apply

State the application process, including whether resumes can be substituted for application forms, where to acquire and mail/submit applications, and any other pertinent information.

FILING DEADLINE: Enter Date

At this point, you may want to experiment with other design features like shading, shadow boxes, borders, company logo, bullets, lines, and the use of different typestyles, sizes, and boldness of lettering as attention-getting devices. However, don't use more than three variations of typestyle, and use them sparingly only to emphasize important details of your announcement. Remember, you want your job announcement to create a professional image, so try to keep it uncluttered by using good design techniques to provide attention, order, interest, ease, and information. A few sample formats showing different design features are provided on the following pages to give you some ideas of what job announcements should look like, and to stimulate your creative ideas for designing your own.

Selecting and Placing Job Information

In 1989 the Army launched a recruiting campaign by televising various action scenes in which enlistees were engaged in a variety of interesting activities. Their theme was, "It's not just a job, it's an adventure." What the Army's advertisement captures is the idea that every employment of a person's time and energy should be viewed as an opportunity, a challenge, and a chance to succeed at doing something more than one is currently doing. This is precisely the orientation that job announcements should take; that the job vacancy is an opportunity, a new life experience, and an interesting set of activities that offers challenge and the chance for success. Far too often, job announcements (and job ads for that matter) are written with dry and boring details about duties rather than *interesting descriptions* of the work involved. So what you need to do when selecting and placing information about the job in the announcement is to turn on your creative, inspirational mind in order to convert dry details into interesting descriptions.

Start with a quick review of the applicable job description. Underline or highlight phrases that strike you as the more important, frequent, and challenging activities of the job. Also mark any other information that you feel might appeal to ambitious people as inspiring aspects of the job such as interpersonal contacts, to whom the incumbent will be reporting or working with, the existence of independence, opportunity to make one's own decisions, and similar attractions. Next, arrange to meet with the person(s) who supervises this job, and take notes on their responses to such questions as

- What are the most challenging aspects of this job?
- What are the most interesting aspects of this job?
- What are some of the more rewarding results that can be produced by an effective performer?
- What are the personal characteristics and qualities of people who have excelled in this job?
- Is there anything unique about this job in terms of the nature of work, people contacts, decision making, services provided, risks, or independence of actions?

From this information, you should be ready to prepare brief, representative, and interesting descriptions of the job responsibilities, conditions, and qualifications for presentation on your job announcement. If written in a marketing context, the result should provide information about the job that is appealing, suggests challenge, implies satisfaction derived from successful performance, and is sufficiently representative of the major functions of the entire job. Using a combination of full sentence structures and bullet listings (of descriptive responsibilities and illustrative qualifications), begin to place your job information on the remaining format of your announcement.

Some editing and/or reformatting of this information may be necessary to blend well with your selected design features. This is easily accomplished by using cut-and-paste sections

JOB
OPPORTUNITY
ANNOUNCEMENT

SENIOR STAFF ANALYST ($2850-3625 per month, exempt)

About The Job

This position reports directly to the Consulting Practices Director yet is independently responsible for the handling of major projects with direct client involvement. The job is one of diverse conditions relating to working with clients, staff, innovative applications of management practices, analysis of data and situational information, and periodic travel. The incumbent will be expected to be effective in these performance areas:

- Coordinate and oversee major and minor client projects, and perform the more difficult lead responsibilities and analytical tasks.

- Compile information and data into meaningful report formats, including the preparation of tables, charts, and other illustrative materials.

- Assist in the hiring, training, and general supervision of staff working on team projects.

- Travel to client locations and make professional presentations of project proposals, reports, findings, and recommendations.

Illustrative Qualifications

Eligibility for consideration will be based on equivalency of the following illustration of minimum qualifications, although the company reserves the right to hire above this level.

- Education: B.A. degree in business or related field

- Experience: Three years in Staff Analyst or similar position

- Skills & Abilities: Demonstrated evidence of possessing those required by the job through selection testing

How To Apply & Who To Contact

Applications, resumes, or inquiries may be made confidentially to I.B. Richfellow, Consulting Practices Director, 5530 Birdcage St. #110, Citrus Heights, CA 95610 (916) 961-7900, **not later than May 9, 1997.** EEO/M,F,H,V of your information to move around the page before deciding on where to paste them in. Finally, you will want to add a description of the application and further inquiry process selected for this recruitment. You will recall from the earlier discussion on job ads that the application/inquiry process should be clear, succinct, and made easy in order to encourage interested people to follow up. Place this information at the end of your job announcement in a way that stands out. You may also want to consider the use of a closing phrase at the very end or bottom of the announcement such as *"Apply Now, Or Spend The Rest Of Your Life Wondering About What Your Career Might Have Been."*

On page 134 you will find a sample of a completed job announcement to give you an idea of how the final product might look. Since the author lays no claim to expertise in writing marketing literature, there is no doubt room for improvement in the "appeal" that selected phrases could possess with the help of such experts.

6.4 Designing Your Own Employee Referral Program Announcements

Employee referral programs tend to be of two different types: 1) periodic programs with specified deadlines and targeted jobs that have been difficult for the company to recruit by customary means in which an award (usually a predetermined cash amount) is paid to each eligible employee who refers a new hire; and, 2) ongoing programs of referral for all job vacancies in which the referring employee receives a cash award per referred hire and a chance for a major prize drawing (say at the end of each year). In the latter case, cash awards to referring employees are often paid in increments; part upon hire, and part at predetermined lengths of service of the new hire. Yet another variation of ongoing programs is to award "threshold" prizes for specified numbers of hired referrals such as $1500 cash for five referred hires, a paid trip for two to the Caribbean for ten, a paid trip to Australia for fifteen, and a new car for twenty.

To be effective, employee referral programs must be well publicized, kept alive by a certain amount of marketing, and worthy in its rewards. So, one of your first decisions when considering the design of an announcement is to determine whether your need is for a program of periodic targeted jobs or an ongoing program to assist with the recruitment of all job vacancies. Next, decide on what rewards will be most alluring based on what you know about the perceived values, needs, and desires of your employees. Money is always a strong incentive if it is provided in alluring denominations—usually starting at a minimum of $100 for entry-level positions, $250 for skilled positions, $500 for professional and technical positions, and $750 for supervisory and entry management positions. The disadvantage of cash awards is that some better paid (and therefore higher skilled) employees will see the tax implications of cash, so you might want to offer alternatives such as additional vacation days, award money placed in a scholarship trust for the employee's children or grandchildren, dinners for two to expensive restaurants, and other nontaxable rewards.

Once you've selected the type of program and awards, you can begin to design your marketing campaign and program announcement. The marketing campaign can range from simple in smaller companies due to their less formal environment and more direct communication channels, to multiple communication mechanisms in medium-to-large companies. In any case, a certain amount of advertising flair and enthusiasm must be brought to this recruiting method if it is to attract the attention and interest of employees. Try to get your organization's highest level managers involved by talking up the program, encouraging employees, and explaining how the program works.

Keep the program simple and make the referral process easy. Your announcement should use color and attention-getting design (themes are very popular such as palm trees to illustrate a trip to the Caribbean), as well as a brief description of the program, jobs and awards involved, deadlines, and how your referral process works. Interested employees should be given tear-off coupons or some other means of giving referrals a way to signify that they were referred by a named employee so that you can track referrals.

You should also consider the referral; it's far more effective if your employees have something to hand their referrals about the company and specifications on job openings. One way of doing this is to make available a supply of job announcements in conjunction with the posting of employee referral announcements. Or, provide a plentiful supply of employee referral program announcements that include specifications of the jobs being recruited under the program. As you can see, referral program announcements can be designed to provide either brief or lengthy detail, or brief program detail supplemented with separate job announcements which is probably the more preferred way of keeping the recruiting effort as clear and simple as possible.

On pages 137–139 are a few sample illustrations of how employee referral programs can be designed. You will note that each of these do an effective job of getting attention and minimizing complexity. The simplest and least costly to design and administer is the coupon offering cash awards for hired referrals to specified job openings. This is also an easy way to test the success of a referral program in your company. If simple programs work well for you, it will likely prove worthwhile to develop something more enticing and challenging the next time around.

6.5 Keeping Your Recruitment Advertising Nondiscriminatory

The single most important precaution that should be taken with recruitment advertising in any form is to ensure that all recruiting material is devoid of express or implied employment discrimination. In this regard, you're strongly urged to read Appendix A at the end of this book. Appendix A deals with the legal liabilities your company may face if an error in judgment is made concerning discrimination based on an individual's race, color, national origin, sex, age (over forty), religion, physical handicaps, and in some states ancestry, marital status, and sexual orientation.

There are many ways in which even unintentional discrimination can occur in recruitment advertising. When it occurs, particularly if printed in some form, it can serve as a form of *prima facie* (implied or having the appearance) evidence of guilt. Applicants and compliance agencies can and will use this type of evidence to establish a case of discrimination against the employer, which must then be defended at considerable cost whether or not discrimination actually took place. The following, then, are some of the more vulnerable types of discrimination that tend to appear in recruitment advertising, and suggestions on how to keep your recruiting process free of this costly liability.

Age Discrimination

Discrimination law primarily protects those who are age forty and older from various forms of employment bias, however there are other legal requirements such as "job validity" standards that have the effect of prohibiting employers from discriminating against those under the age of forty. For example, an employer cannot specify in job advertisements that applicants be at least twenty-one years of age unless the job involves serving liquor, carrying a firearm, or some other valid job *requirement* controlled by federal or state law. Thus, those employers who merely want or prefer that applicants be over the age of twenty-one (usually based on the employer's perception of the likely maturity of applicants) can be held as discriminating unlawfully on the basis of an invalid job requirement. Some of the more common and obvious forms of *prima facie* age discrimination are the use of such terms as

- "Youthful and energetic"
- "Appealing to a younger clientele"

THE HEAT IS ON

DURING THE COOL CASH NWL EMPLOYEE REFERRAL PROGRAM

nwl Control Systems

NWL RESERVES THE RIGHT TO DECIDE WHICH REFERRALS TO PURSUE, AND TO CHANGE OR DISCONTINUE THIS PROGRAM AS REQUIRED AT ANY TIME AT THE COMPANY'S SOLE DISCRETION.

THE COOLCASH

NWL EMPLOYEE REFERRAL PROGRAM

Employee Referral Applicant Form

Log # _____
(for Human Resources Division use only)

CANDIDATE INFORMATION:

Name: _____

Address: _____

Home Phone: _____ Work: _____

Position Applied for: _____

EMPLOYEE INFORMATION:

Name: _____

Title: _____

Department: _____

Work Phone: _____

Relationship to referral: _____

Date/Employee Signature: _____

• ATTACH CANDIDATE'S RESUME/APPLICATION •

CLAIM AS MUCH AS A COOL THOUSAND DOLLARS!

If NWL hires a qualified professional that you refer under this program, you get $250 to $1,000.

SEE THE LIGHT!

Get a multi-function fluorescent/incandescent lantern for submitting a qualified referral.

WHY AN EMPLOYEE REFERRAL PROGRAM?

It's good for NWL because it helps us find qualified people for certain hard-to-fill positions. We believe that the friends you refer are more likely to have the right qualifications for the job . . . plus a high level of interest in joining NWL. Narrowing our search for good people saves us time and money.

It's good for you because we pass along to you money that we save in recruitment costs.

APPLICANT (CANDIDATE) ELIGIBILITY

To be considered as a referral under this program, candidates must have the experience and qualifications listed on posted job openings which are clearly designated "eligible for employee referral program." Referral prizes will range from $250 to $1,000 depending on the position filled! Current or former employees of NWL, persons whose application/resume we already have on file, and those who have been referred by employment agencies are not counted as referrals under this program. Qualified referral applications remain active for 12 months, as does your eligibility for a cash referral bonus.

We subscribe to the principle and practice of equal opportunity employment and encourage you to refer qualified individuals without regard to race, creed, color, sex, age, or physical handicap.

EMPLOYEE ELIGIBILITY

All full-time regular employees of NWL are eligible to participate except Vice Presidents and those in the Human Resources Division. Individuals who would subsequently be supervising their employee referral are also ineligible. To qualify for awards or prizes, you must be actively employed by NWL on: a) the day your candidate is determined qualified; b) the day the new employee starts work.

GET THE FEVER

If you know someone who is qualified for an eligible opening, submit his/her up-to-date resume along with an employee referral form (herewith) to the Human Resources Division and request that it be logged under the employee referral program. Submit as many referrals as you wish. More referral forms are available through the Human Resources Division. If more than one employee refers the same candidate, any awards or prizes will belong to the employee making the earlier referral (based upon time and date it was received by the Human Resources Division).

The Human Resources Division evaluates all referrals and determines the eligibility of applicants and employees.

PLAY FOR COOL CASH

You'll get a free multi-function lantern for referring a qualified candidate. This is true whether or not NWL interviews your candidate. If your referral is hired, we will pay you from $250 to $1,000 upon his/her completion of 30 days employment with NWL. Cash prizes are subject to applicable tax withholding.

ANY QUESTIONS?

If you have any questions about the rules, regulations and administration of the COOL CASH NWL Employee Referral Program, ask the Human Resources Division staff. Their word is final. They decide whether or not your candidate meets the posted qualifications, whom to interview and whom to hire.

WE'LL KEEP YOU INFORMED

As the COOL CASH NWL Employee Referral Program progresses, we'll publish names of award recipients and new hires. At the close of the campaign, we'll publish a wrap up.

Reprinted by permission, Nationwide Advertising Service, Cleveland, Ohio, 1990.

TO: ALL RALEY'S EMPLOYEES

Your friends are worth a lot!

At Raley's, we're proud of the talented, dedicated people we employ. Some of our most valued pharmacists were once referrals. If you refer registered pharmacists for current full-time job openings, we'll reward you with $250 upon hire, and $250 after the pharmacist has worked for Raley's for six months.

Raley's is an Equal Opportunity Employer

Reprinted by permission, Nationwide Advertising Service, Cleveland, Ohio, 1990.

- "Represent the youth in our field"
- "Retirees and those nearing retirement need not apply"
- "We want people who will fit into our corporate image of contemporary fashion"
- "If you are young at heart and want to move up in your career over the next several years . . ."
- "Must be twenty-one or older to apply"

Gender (Sex) Discrimination

Sex discrimination, whether directed at males or females, can take many forms in recruitment advertising and in particular in the use of job titles. Those preparing job descriptions, ads, announcements, and other written material that defines job responsibilities, requirements, and conditions should take extra care in the use of terms or phrases that might result in a discriminatory effect when applied toward job applicants. Keep in mind the inherent difficulty of defending alleged discrimination when evidence that is introduced was prepared and published by your company. Here are a few of the more flagrant gender discrimination violations that tend to occur in recruitment advertising, and suggestions on how they can be changed to eliminate the potential threat.

1. *Job Titles*

Change	To
Warehouseman	Warehouse Attendant
Waitress	Food Server
Repairman	Repair Technician
Girl Friday	General Office Assistant
Draftsman	Drafting Specialist
Stewardess	Flight Attendant

2. *Job Ads and Announcements*

   - "Must wear/provide own (dress, gown, cocktail uniform)"
   - "Be able to fit in as one of the guys"
   - "Military experience is particularly desirable"
   - "Should have a strong voice and be as assertive as a football quarterback"
   - "The ideal applicant would be a woman who can . . ."

In addition to these direct forms of gender discrimination, you should also be aware of potential forms of indirect sex-related discrimination. These consist of using ad design features that would be more likely to get the attention of one or the other sex such as pastel colors and flowers to attract women, or fishing poles and climbing hooks to get the attention of men.

National Origin Discrimination

Federal law prohibits employers from discriminating against applicants and employees on the basis of their (name or physical appearance) national origin, including those who are legal aliens. Recruitment advertising should therefore avoid such terms and phrases as:

- "Clean-cut, all-American look"
- "Citizenship required"

- "Must be Spanish speaking" (potential reverse discrimination)
- "Chinese Bank Seeks Asian Tellers"
- "Must be willing to work long hours for low pay"

The lawful exceptions to national origin are few and narrow. The two most prevalent defenses for an employer advertising these types of requirements are: 1) that a constitutionally valid state or federal law exists that requires the employer to establish the condition of employment (for example, national security employers may lawfully require citizenship); or, 2) that a legitimate compelling interest exists within the nature of the employer's business to condition employment on a "bona-fide occupational qualification" (BFOQ). An example of the compelling interest BFOQ is a Mexican restaurant whose business identity is "authentic Mexican food and atmosphere" where, to accomplish the desired identity, the employer would have to hire Mexican employees (whether or not they speak Spanish is another matter).

Use of Equal Employment Notations

Unless you work for one of the few employers in the business community who cares little about, or deliberately disregards, employment discrimination laws and resultant liabilities, it is advisable for you to place an equal employment notice on each separate recruiting notice used. This should include employment application forms, job ads, job announcements, the company's promotional literature, and employee referral program announcements. The customary shorthand designation used on ads and announcements is either "EEO Employer" or "EEO/M,F,H,V." The latter designation means that the company is an equal employment opportunity employer and invites applications from males, females, handicapped, and veterans.

Place equal employment notations only if your company actually practices conscious and *conscientious* recruiting, hiring, and employment of all suitably qualified people. It is intended to signify more than just appearances.

Checklist 1: Considerations in Placing an Employment Ad*

NOTE: The following checklist is geared primarily to prepare an employment ad for placement in the classified section of a newspaper or magazine.

1. *Decide where to place the ad.*
   - ❑ Consider geographic area desired.
   - ❑ Consider type of employment (e.g., technical, professional, or other).
   - ❑ Decide among the following media:
     - Newspapers
     - Magazines (new production techniques allow national magazines to target ads to appear in local markets at a fraction of the cost of national advertising)
     - Business magazines
     - Professional journals
     - Technical publications

*SOURCE: Richard J. Melluci, *Modern Personnel Checklists*, Warren, Gorham & Lamont, Inc. (1982), pp. S7-6 to S7-8. Copyright, Warren, Gorham & Lamont, Inc., 1982.

❑ Decide on placement within newspaper (Sunday edition purchased by more jobseekers). Note that you should consider which of two or more competing newspapers has a reputation for carrying more employment ads for the type of employment offered.

❑ Decide on placement within magazine (which section would be most appropriate).

2. *Choose the wording of the ad.*

❑ Position title

❑ Industry

❑ Basic job specification
- Let unqualified applicants know right away, to prevent their wasting their time and your own
- Convey specifications in a few well-chosen words, such as "MBA," "experienced [job title]," "with three years management experience," "familiar with XYZ equipment"
- Do not include specifications that suggest discrimination on grounds such as age, sex, race, religion, or national origin, unless such discrimination reflects a bona fide occupational qualification. Avoid discriminatory specifications such as college grad "RECENT" and "GAL Friday"

❑ Decide whether to include the name of the employer in the ad, or as an alternative, to place a blind ad giving
- Telephone contact (name, number)
- Newspaper box number [author's note: this is not an advisable practice—conveys concealment on the part of the advertising company]
- Address
- Post office number. Note that under federal law the post office is required to reveal the name of the person or business renting a post office box in exchange for an inquiry fee.

❑ Decide whether to include salary information
- On the "weeding-out-to-save-time" principle, include this if the amount is fixed or rigid
- If salary is dependent on credentials or experience, the ad should say so

3. *Design the ad's format.*

❑ The newspaper or magazine staff may provide help with simple graphics (e.g., including employer logo, setting ad off in a black box).

❑ If you want a large ad with a complex graphic presentation, you will require the services of a graphic artist. The services of an ad agency specializing in recruitment advertising may also be appropriate here.

4. *Decide on the time of the ad.*

❑ Consider the availability of staff to review applications and interview candidates.

❑ If a large part of the recruiting pool consists of recent graduates, concentrate advertising at the middle or even the beginning of the term to attract top-rank, highly motivated students to positions with highly competitive compensation and development opportunities; advertise toward the end of the school year for positions with only average or below-average salary and opportunities or for positions open to high school graduates.

❑ Decide how many times classified ads should run.

5. *Establish an ad evaluation file.*
   - ❑ Clip ads if practicable.
   - ❑ Note date(s) run.
   - ❑ Indicate number of applications received.
   - ❑ Compute number and percentage of applicants found qualified.
   - ❑ Record general impressions of ad campaign, noting whether
      - • Advertising medium was a plus for affirmative action planning (relevant only if company is making an affirmative action effort)
      - • Applications were received all at once or in a steady stream
      - • Unrealistic salary expectations were a persistent problem with the applicants
   - ❑ Note the cost of the ad.
   - ❑ Note the name of the contact person at the publication.

Checklist 2: Key Elements to Be Covered in Recruiting Ads

NOTE: The following checklist* is intended to be comprehensive. Some considerations guiding which facts you use in the advertisement include: the media you are using, the size of the target audience—are you aiming at a large group via television or a small, special group through a trade magazine; the length, size, or any special typographical effects you need to reach your target group; price or budgetary restrictions on the recruiting effort; the location of the job if relocation is required.

Generally, it is unnecessary to include all of the items in the checklist. If, for example, you are placing an advertisement in a local newspaper it might not be necessary to give the size of the company.

- ❑ Job title
- ❑ Statement of major job responsibility
- ❑ Statement of whether the job is permanent, temporary, full-time, or part-time
- ❑ Working hours or shift
- ❑ Experience required
- ❑ Special skills required
- ❑ Opportunity for advancement
- ❑ Major work or product
- ❑ Size and type of company
- ❑ Location of company
- ❑ Special working conditions
- ❑ Salary or rate of pay
- ❑ Benefits
- ❑ Telephone number or address for receipt of applications
- ❑ Hours recruiting office is open

*Ibid, pp. 7–9 & 10.

Checklist 3: Checklist for a Recruiting Brochure

NOTE: The following checklist* for a recruiting brochure covers a maximum of topics; it is likely that some firms will find not all of these topics to be pertinent. However, it's a good idea to use this checklist to make sure that you include all those matters which you would like to present to potential employees.

It is likely that your company would be willing to expend the funds to prepare and print such a brochure for use in recruitment for professional or executive positions or for new talent that might choose a career with your company and then rise to middle or upper-level management.

For purposes of this checklist, an account firm is preparing the recruiting brochure.

1. *Some suggested titles for the brochure*

   "Professional Careers With XYZ & Company"
   "Your Professional Opportunity With XYZ & Company"
   "Everything You Wanted to Know About XYZ & Company But Were Afraid To Ask"

2. *Outline of the brochure.* Most brochures begin with a brief summary of perhaps 200 words explaining why your firm is a good place to begin a successful career.

   ❑ The firm's identity:
   - Reputation in the business community
   - Growth potential of the firm
   - Associations in the profession and in the business community
   - Type of clientele and the opportunity for diversified experience (specific clients not mentioned)
   - Record as a firm in which many successful CPAs have begun their careers
   - Professional development program

   ❑ Opportunities for advancement:
   - Responsibilities at ascending levels of practice:
     a. As staff accountant
     b. As senior accountant
     c. As manager
     d. As partner
   - Synopses of careers of firm's members
   - Qualities the firm looks at when advancing personnel

   ❑ Professional development:
   - Training programs
   - Getting the CPA certificate
   - On-the-job training
   - Continuing education activities (paid for by the firm)
     a. Firm meetings
     b. Tax institutes
     c. Executive development programs

---

*Ibid, pp. 7–10 & 7–12.

      d. Society professional development programs

      e. University courses

❑ Salary and benefits:

- Compensation:

      a. Direct

      b. Overtime [author's note: unless exempt position]

      c. Other compensation

      d. Where the recruit may expect to be in five years

- Insurance:

      a. Life

      b. Medical

      c. Accident and travel

      d. Other

- Military obligation
- Jury duty
- Pensions
- Vacations
- Transfers
- Travel
- Sick pay
- Hours

❑ Services the firm performs:

- Auditing—value to clients, shareholders, and other parties
- Variety of tax services rendered
- Description of management services; the list should be aimed at pointing out the diversity of services ordered by the firm. Some items that might be included are: analysis of operating and financial policies, mergers and acquisitions, preparation of budgets, special costs analyses, government contract costs, inventory control, quality control, work measurement, organization planning, information systems including data processing applications, market research, sales forecasts, estate planning, operations research, and analysis of insurance coverage.

❑ Types and size of clients serviced in terms of sales or assets. If there are public clients, this should be mentioned; however, it is not proper to mention specific client names. The discussion should be aimed at informing the potential recruit about the kind of experience he or she will be getting.

❑ Discussion about how the firm has been involved in some of the most significant economic activities in the business community:

- Founding
- Historically significant engagements
- Growth in kinds of services rendered—tax, SEC registration, etc.
- Data processing and its effect on practice
- Number and location of offices
- Number of employees and growth in recent years

❑ Summary of the firm's future plans and how new member of the firm will fit in.

7 Using Preemployment Selection Tests to Evaluate Applicants

Assembling the proper set of selection tests can ensure that your choice of a new employee is the right one. Selection testing also represents something of a paradox for most employers. On the one hand, testing applicants to verify the adequacy of their abilities and distinguish their characteristics is essential for gaining confidence in the probable success of new employees, as well as to protect your company's potential negligence liability.

On the other hand, preemployment testing has caused much consternation among employers who have been challenged over the validity of such tests on a given job. Without job-specific validity, the test is likely to have a disparate impact on one or another protected group of applicants, with the result being alleged discrimination.

Selection testing in the 1990s and beyond will require more precision and common sense on the part of employers preparing tests that truly measure job-specific traits—not because the law demands it, but because it is the only way to distinguish the *quality* applicants from among a larger group of seemingly *qualified* applicants.

In fact, a 1991 survey of 600 companies revealed that 57% of the companies were satisfied with the results of their new hires when their testing programs consisted of multiple selection processes. The testing methods most often cited as used for a good and reliable program were application forms, work samples review, interviews, background checks, and drug/alcohol testing. These results are illustrated in the chart on page 148 which shows a significant difference in satisfaction by worker group of those companies who use multiple selection methods versus those who have no formal procedures.

Let's face one fact as you begin to consider how to use preemployment selection testing to make the right hiring choice; there is risk in nearly every employment process and decision. With selection testing, there is the risk of discriminating against protected groups of applicants due to some disparate impact feature of a particular test or, even more operationally important, the test fails to identify the most meaningful skills and traits of applicants given the responsibilities of the job and its impact on the organizations. Conversely, with the use of proper selection tests, the organization gains a higher degree of confidence in each hiring decision, and a higher probability of lower turnover, improved employee relations and morale, and greater operational efficiency.

7.1 The Law and Preemployment Selection Testing

Perhaps nowhere more than with preemployment selection testing is an employer as vulnerable in its employment practices in running afoul of the morass of state and federal employment laws. It is therefore critical for every person involved in the process of testing job

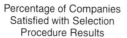

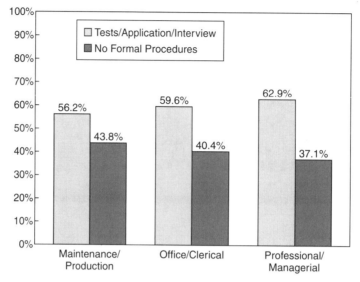

Source of data: HR Strategies, Grosse Point, Michigan

applicants to understand these ever-present conditions as well as the nature of hiring-related laws, while at the same time never losing sight of the goal. Selection testing thus becomes a simultaneous process of protecting your organization's liability for legal error (real or perceived), and putting forth the time and effort to construct meaningful tests that get the results you need. If the latter is done thoroughly and professionally, the likelihood of legal error will inherently diminish.

The Laws That Control Selection Testing

The three areas of employment law that impose various kinds of controls on selection testing are state and federal discrimination laws, privacy right laws, and negligence laws. Whether such laws emanate from statutes, regulations by authoritative compliance agencies, or court decisions, they should never be taken lightly by the prudent employer, nor overdramatized. Rather, they should be well understood and complied with by incorporating their intent into pertinent aspects of your employment practices.

As these laws relate to selection testing, particular care should be applied to your recruitment advertising, application forms, documents handling and recordkeeping, screening of applicants, and every aspect of your selection testing to avoid creating a discriminatory effect, privacy deprivation, or negligent hiring decision (or omission) on any individual applicant. While the brief discussions that follow are aimed at providing you with summary information about these three areas of law concerning selection testing, you are urged to read the corresponding discussions in Appendix A–C of this book for a more complete understanding of these laws as they apply to the entire hiring process.

Discrimination Law

Both state and federal discrimination laws have one primary purpose—the eradication of employment practices, decisions, and actions of those in the organization having the effect of barring or otherwise interfering with a person's right to equal opportunity because of the individual's race, color, national origin, sex, age, or physical handicap. With regard to selection testing, discrimination law prohibits any preemployment practice having the result, whether intentional or not, of creating a *disparate treatment* or *disparate impact* on any one of these "protected" groups of applicants.

Disparate treatment is where a selection device serves to discriminate by virtue of an employer's differential treatment of one or a protected group of applicants from the treatment of other applicants (e.g., screening out a disproportionate number of female applicants due to a bias that favors male applicants). Disparate impact results from a selection device causing discrimination when the device adversely effects the selection rate of a protected group (e.g., nonwhite applicants always achieve lower scores on a particular test). Moreover, under disparate impact analysis, a plaintiff does not have to prove discriminatory *intent* of an employer's facially neutral test, merely that the test has had a discriminatory *effect* on a protected group.

To be considered nondiscriminatory, the Equal Employment Opportunity Commission (EEOC) and the courts have rather consistently held that preemployment selection tests must be valid for the particular job being tested. To be valid, selection tests are supposed to be structured in accordance with the standards contained in the *Uniform Guidelines on Employee Selection Procedures* as interpreted and enforced by the EEOC. Test developers should become acquainted with these standards, deferring some of the complexities to outside experts when and where necessary, in order to gain a better understanding of what test construction conditions should be present to produce valid tests. Generally, selection tests should be developed on the basis of a sequential process consisting of:

- Job Analysis
- Test Item Development
- Test Construction
- Preliminary Testing among Job Incumbents
- Item Analysis of Failed Test Elements
- Revision and Use with Job Applicants

Selection tests purporting to have "general" validity are not satisfactory for compliance with discrimination laws. For example, in *EEOC v. Atlas Paper Box Company* (1989), the Sixth Circuit Court of Appeals determined that the company's use of a Wonderlic Personnel Test for the preemployment testing of numerous *different* jobs had a disparate impact on minorities, and that the test was not valid for any one of these *specific* jobs. The same conclusions were reached by the U.S. Supreme Court in *Griggs v. Duke Power Company* (1971) and in *Albemarle Paper Co. v. Moody* (1974). Furthermore, the validity of selection tests apply to both "objective" (standardized) tests and "subjective" (interviews and performance reviews) tests. The U.S. Supreme Court's decision in *Watson v. Fort Worth Bank & Trust* (1988) concluded that the disparate impact theory of preemployment testing could be applied to subjective as well as objective tests.

Privacy Rights Law

Individual protections and employer prohibitions concerning the privacy rights of applicants and employees vary among state laws. Yet, the common thread that exists between present state and federal laws in this more recent realm of employment law is to guard against the unreasonable intrusion into the private domain of individuals merely because an employment relationship raises other interests. For the employer, the task becomes one of balancing the rights of individual privacy against the rights and interests of the organization's *legitimate* business concerns.

The dilemma raised by privacy right laws for employers is that the protection they afford applicants frequently runs contrary to the acquisition of desirable preemployment information concerning the individual's suitability for the job or employment setting. While these laws may be somewhat of an obstacle during selection testing, they should not be viewed as a barrier. It is important for employers to recognize the law and either abide by its prohibitions (and find another way to acquire needed information in a manner not prohibited), or to take precautionary steps when delving into allowable but vulnerable privacy right areas. For example, it is now prohibited for employers to use polygraph (lie detector or deceptograph) tests to ascertain such information as an applicant's truthfulness or history of theft, drug use, and other undesirable proclivities. Such information, if reasonably germane to the job or nature of the employer's business, can and probably should be learned by other means.

Similarly, employers may find the need to make inquiries into an applicant's past employment history, medical evidence of present freedom from drug use, credit and character reputation, the absence of any deviant behavior, honesty, prior job injuries, and/or a history of driving violations or criminal experiences. While some or all of these types of inquiries may be perceived as reasonable interests by employers, one or more of them may not be justifiably legitimate nor performed by the employer under proper testing methods. Caution must therefore be exercised by every employer with respect to:

1. establishing a reasonable job or business purpose for the particular type of inquiry;
2. making only those inquiries that relate specifically to the job and/or nature of the business' operating interests; and
3. using proper methods and (confidential) controls to gather, handle, disclose, and use for employment decision making purposes.

The privacy right laws of which employers should gain a clear understanding pertain to these preemployment selection testing practices:

- Personal Interviews (see also Chapter 8)
- Drug and/or Alcohol Testing
- Honesty Tests
- Psychological or Personality Tests
- Prior Employment Reference Inquiries
- Workers' Compensation Records Inquiries
- Driving or Criminal Records Inquiries
- Credit and/or Character Investigations
- Surveillance of Applicant
- Interviewing Personal Acquaintances of Applicant

Negligence Law

Negligence law was resurrected during the 1980s from its original turn-of-the-century intent to be an economic remedy in the absence of workers' compensation protections for employees seriously injured or disabled as the result of their employer's negligence. In more recent years, negligence law has been applied by several courts to cases involving injury of some kind to third parties at the hand of an employee. Here, the courts have theorized that such an injury would not have occurred had the employer either:

1. conducted more thorough selection testing and background inquiry of the employee, or
2. acted properly on information the employer gained during the course of employment about the employee's risks (e.g., drinking problem, quick temper, threats made, delusional behavior, or propensity toward violence).

Negligent hiring, as this employer liability has become known, represents a very strong justification and need for employers to take a comprehensive approach to selection testing. Yet is also presents another dimension of the aforementioned dilemma—running afoul of both discrimination and privacy right laws in the course of conducting selection tests and inquiries. To guard against violating discrimination laws, employers must ensure that preemployment inquiries are made equally of all finalist applicants whose jobs have conditions or responsibilities that reasonably warrant more than casual investigative information. To guard against violating privacy right laws, employers must exercise due diligence in seeking relevant (job related) information acquired by proper methods, and exercise due care once the information is received in its confidentiality, handling, disclosure, manner it is applied to employment decision making, and its storage.

Negligence law presents a potential liability to be avoided by every employer whose business has exposure to external risks of injury to other persons. Organizations having such risks should carefully consider the types of preemployment tests, inquiries, and investigations that are justified by virtue of the job's conditions and responsibilities for the acquisition of pertinent information about *any* person who is a serious contender for the job, and before an employment offer is made. Depending on the specific nature of a job's external risk factors, the general types of information an employer should consider acquiring about prospective new hires are their

- History and presence of drugs or alcohol use/abuse
- Record of criminal or violent behavior, particularly sexual assault, battery, and murder
- Record of driving violations, particularly speeding, reckless driving, driving under the influence of controlled substances, or failing to stop at controlled intersections
- Information from past employers, work associates, or personal sources about the individual's temper, violence, or acute behavioral peculiarities
- History or presence of proclivities toward stealing or robbery

For a more detailed discussion of negligent hiring, see Appendix C.

Complying with the Laws

As suggested repeatedly throughout this book, the first step in legal compliance is to become acquainted with those employment laws that control or influence hiring practices. Second, every employer should conduct regular—at least annual—audits of their hiring and other employment policies, practices, forms, and procedures to ensure that they remain both legal and operationally practical. Third, employers should follow the suggestions and guidelines provided in Chapters 2 and 3 to ensure that job descriptions are prepared by some structured method of job analysis, and that policies designed to frame hiring practices and procedures are congruent with prevailing law. Other specific steps that should be taken to assure legal compliance when selection testing is involved are:

1. *Discrimination Liability Avoidance*
   - Recruit from among the widest practical group of available job applicants in your community to establish solicitation of all categories of job seekers who might be interested and qualified for your job openings.
   - Use your job analysis worksheets, questionnaires, interview forms, and any other related documentation as the basis of constructing test types, testing areas, and test elements (questions and exercises).

- Eliminate sexist job titles, insignificant job duties, and any qualification requirements that are insufficiently justified by actual performance of the job.

- Make sure that each test type used in the hiring process, and each test element is directly correlated to actual job duties and work conditions (i.e., has "content" validity) based on measurable success factors.

- Train and use only those people in your organization who are free from discriminatory bias to participate in the screening, testing, interviewing, and final decision making (subjective testing) of applicants.

2. *Privacy Rights Liability Avoidance*

- Determine what types and sources of inquiry of an applicant's personal lifestyle, background, and other history are relevant to the job and/or nature of the business, and therefore defensibly necessary to obtain.

- Limit inquiries only to those applicants who are being considered for hire.

- Obtain the applicant's written authorization to acquire each separate (or a blanket) inquiry, including a statement releasing the holder of the information from liability for its disclosure.

- Use a professional and well trained person (preferably management level but not the hiring authority) to make inquiries, conduct investigations, and be the recipient of these sources of confidential information.

- Disclose only general information about adverse information that is received, and then only to those who have a need and right to know for purpose of employment decision making.

- Treat all personal information as confidential with respect to its receipt, handling, access, and storage.

3. *Negligent Hiring Liability Avoidance*

- Identify any position having risk potential (external exposure to third parties) inherent in the nature of job responsibilities and/or working conditions, and identify the specific types of tests or background inquiries most likely to resolve questions concerning employment suitability.

- Make reasonable efforts to acquire relevant background information on applicants to these risk positions, and document the results of each effort.

- Conduct background checks on any applicant where you have reasonable suspicion that some particular unacceptable condition exists.

- Conduct diligent prior employment reference inquiries on *every* applicant under serious consideration, and document the results.

- Don't make employment offers until all of the facts are in concerning relevant aspects of an applicant's suitability for the job or other employment conditions that may prevail in the organization's business.

7.2 Determining Which Tests Are Right for Different Jobs

The first aspect of selection testing to recognize, is that it can be done poorly or with professional accuracy—even by novices. Poorly conceived testing will get you poor results; people who do not have the right skills, become performance problems, and who don't last in the job. Professionally conceived testing will get you more accurate results and a higher probability of quality hires—it's that simple! To begin the development of more professional and reliable preemployment tests, you should follow the suggestions that are presented in the remainder of this section before implementing the kinds of specific tests discussed in subsequent sections of this chapter.

Identifying Pertinent Job and Employment Conditions

Developing a reliable testing plan for any job begins with at least a brief evaluation of the more pertinent features of the job being filled and those significant employment conditions related to the job.

Job Features as Test Elements

To identify what features of a job should become the primary elements of one or more selection tests, first give careful and *thorough* thought to two different aspects of the job itself:

1. what are the most frequently performed, important, and difficult responsibilities of the job exclusive of a person?
2. what are the personal traits and characteristics of past incumbents who have demonstrated successful performance?

Identify these aspects by preparing two lists from information contained in the job description *and* the job analysis information you compiled (from Chapter 2) when the job description was initially prepared. Supplement this information freely with your own knowledge of the job.

The first list should contain one-sentence descriptions of *what* specific tasks, responsibilities, decisions, skills, knowledge, and abilities are most significant about the job (meaning all lesser job functions could be easily performed). The second list would also use one-sentence statements to describe *how* the work would be performed by a successful employee in terms of methods, personal traits and qualities, behavioral characteristics, and work styles. After compiling these two lists, review each statement to begin visualizing whether it is measurable by some method of testing; if not, rewrite or eliminate the item. Each item that can be measured should be given a preliminary notation as to the type of test that would produce distinguishing results among differing applicants.

Employment Conditions as Test Elements

Employment conditions are perhaps one of the most overlooked yet important features of successful job performance. These conditions tend to be characterized by *adaptive* features in the organizational setting that relate directly to overall job performance, but many companies overlook the importance of including these features in their testing of applicants. When this happens, a company may hire someone who possesses good job skills (they can get the job done in isolation of all other employment conditions), but who is later assessed as being somewhat of a problem. The problem, more often than not, is the new hire's inability or unwillingness to *adapt* to one or more employment conditions connected to the job—which might have been foreseen or eliminated by including such related job conditions in the initial testing process.

Examples of employment conditions that should be identified and considered for inclusion in preemployment testing are

- Nature of the company's business, products and/or services, customers, philosophy, values, and attitudes toward its work force
- Nature of people in the organizational setting, the diversity of jobs and people, quality of interpersonal relationships, leadership styles, structural and role relationships within various operating units, staffing levels, and the demands placed on people

- Nature of the company's policies, procedures, practices, fairness, ways of getting work done, emphasis on quality versus quantity, degree of expansiveness and challenge within jobs, and consistency within the organization
- Nature of changes that occur in technology, work routines, work relationships, task functions, management and supervision, and operating practices

Each of these are adaptive conditions that exist concurrently with the performance of every job. However, each organization is different in the way these generalized employment conditions carry over meaning to each job in the employment setting. For that reason, you should make your own list of *specific* employment conditions related to the job being filled to identify those adaptive features most pertinent to an individual who would perform successfully under those conditions. When you have completed this third list consisting of adaptive employment conditions, you will have a composite profile of the test elements most likely to lead you to selection tests that will produce distinguishing results from among a divergent group of applicants.

Gaining Input from the Experts

While you may possess a certain amount of knowledge and familiarity with various jobs in your organization, it would not be wise to set yourself up as the definitive source of information about proper test elements that are tantamount to the measurement of successful job performers. So, your next step is to refine your three lists with the help of "subject matter" experts—incumbent employees and supervisors. In selecting these individuals, if you have a choice, it is important to choose those who are the better performers and possess the mental ability to remove themselves from the job in order to view its requirements and conditions from an objective perspective.

Begin by explaining to your subject matter experts what you are trying to accomplish—the identification of significant job and employment condition features to use in testing applicants. Let them know that you need them to think very carefully about the job, what tasks and other features are important to success, related employment conditions (environmental and operational) that have a significant impact on the job, and personal traits of people that are most likely to do well in the job. Give each of them a copy of your three lists, and ask that they take the next day or so to add, delete, or modify any of the statements you have prepared. Finally, let them know that it is important that they be specific and detailed in their proposed changes.

At the conclusion of your agreed completion time, collect the modified lists from your subject matter experts and make one composite set of the three lists. Then, meet with them again to review each statement on each list, discuss clarifying details of the statement to ensure that you have a clear picture of it, ask again if anything important has been omitted (and enter any new significant offerings), and conclude your meeting by asking their opinions on how each element on the lists could best be tested from among these methods, or others you may have used in the past with success:

1. Written test of job knowledge
2. Written test of personal traits
3. Performance (demonstration) test of job skills and abilities
4. Interpersonal test such as role play, group exercise, or individual interview
5. Medical examination for such conditions as physical requirements, freedom from certain vulnerabilities, or dexterity (body movement)
6. Prior employment and character reference inquiries
7. Driving, credit, or law enforcement investigative reports

You are now ready to prepare a testing plan and assemble the contents of each test to be used in the preemployment selection sequence for your vacant job.

Matching Test Elements to Testing Methods

The statements you have identified in your three lists now become your test elements. They are the focal points of the entire preemployment testing process, and the results of testing on these elements become the basis of a hiring decision. The first step in planning which testing methods to use is to match each test element (descriptive statement) to one or more of the seven testing methods. Hopefully your subject matter experts have given you some ideas on the best testing methods for each test element, but ultimately it should be up to you to choose the method(s). In making this determination, you should consider such factors as

1. Which method(s) will yield the most measurable and reliable results?
2. Which method(s) are the most practical to test the type of job or employment feature (for example, interviews are not practical test methods to measure an applicant's job skills)?
3. Which methods are prone to subjective evaluation and therefore vulnerable to being found invalid on the basis of disparate impact analysis? If the method is useful, can the test be easily validated thus eliminating uncertainty about its discriminatory effect?
4. Which methods are the easiest and least costly to prepare and conduct given the demands on time and available funds to complete this hiring process?

After giving consideration to each of these factors, go back to your list of test elements and enter beside each one the method you intend to use to measure the element among those applicants being invited for testing. To complete your test planning process, prepare new lists for each testing method to be used. Do this by extracting each test element from your former three lists and write them in on the corresponding "test method" list. This will give you a list of the test elements to be included in each different testing method you have determined to be most suitable for the vacant job. It should look like the following partial sample.

Sample Testing Method/Test Element List
Written Proficiency Test
Secretary II

1. Understanding of Office Methods and Procedures
   - Possess advanced level of working knowledge about office operations, practices, and procedures in the insurance industry or similar field.
   - Familiar with the terms, applications, and methods of using office equipment, and prioritizing work to achieve maximum efficiency.
   - Knowledgeable about proper format and style of correspondence used in the insurance industry or similar field.
   - Can distinguish what type of office work should be delegated to lower level positions, and knows what procedures to use to accomplish proper delegation.

2. Knowledge of Records Management
   - Can properly identify and distinguish between the three types of filing methods—alpha, numeric, and cross-reference.
   - Demonstrates advanced knowledge of what method is most suitable for the records retention and retrieval of commercial, personal, and product lines of insurance.
   - Can identify proper techniques for purging file documents, recall schedules, and cross-referencing master file lists.

Preparing a Profile of Testing Methods for Different Jobs

Your last task in deciding on a course of selection testing is to chart which testing methods are deemed the most reliable, practical, and best possible means of measuring the composite features of various jobs. The effort should be a simple one if you followed the previous steps suggested in this section. Those steps, and the resultant set of test elements, should make it clear as to which of the seven—or combination thereof—testing methods are the best for your vacant job.

If you are going through this exercise because of one job for which you wish to develop a testing strategy, it is not much more difficult or time consuming to include a few other jobs in the same or similar occupational field once you gather their test elements. The following sample of a testing methods profile is intended to illustrate how you might prepare such a test planning document. Remember, once you put the time and effort into the identification of job and employment condition features, test element list, a testing methods profile, and develop the tests themselves, it takes very little time to make the kinds of minor modifications needed as jobs change over time. Look at it as a one-time investment of effort that will have enduring and monumental value to your organization.

Job Testing Plan Profile				
Test Method	**Secret. I**	**Secret. II**	**Acct. Rep.**	**Acct. Mgr.**
Written Job Knowledge	X	X	X	X
Written Personal Traits Honesty & Integrity			X	X
Behavioral Charact.			X	
Psychological				X
Leadership Styles				X
Performance Tests of *Job Skills & Abilities*	X	X		
Interpersonal Tests Interview	X	X	X	X
Role Play			X	X
Group Exercise			X	X
Medical Evaluation			X	X
Reference Checks Prior Employment	X	X	X	X
Personal/Profess.			X	X
Investigative Reports Credit			X	X
Driving			X	X
Law Enforcement			X	X

7.3 Evaluating the Applicant's Job Skills, Knowledge, and Abilities

There is an interesting phenomenon about the relationship of the thoroughness, preciseness, and completeness of preemployment selection testing to the respect and value new hires adopt toward their employment. The preemployment interaction between applicant and employer is a function of human nature in the context of perceived values. If a job is easily acquired, it is more likely to be perceived as less valuable than one having rigorous standards, thorough and practical testing, and a professionally administered hiring process. Therefore, human nature suggests that people will value and respect an employer more when their acquired job is perceived as valuable enough by the employer to be thorough and selective in their choice of an applicant.

To produce quality results from your selection tests, you need to place emphasis on

1. Diligent effort to identify accurate and meaningful test elements (job content);
2. Time to give careful thought to assembling a professionally run testing process, and in some cases constructing your own tests; and,
3. Making any singular testing process sufficiently diverse in methods used to compile an adequate profile of each applicant in order to render an informed, confident hiring decision.

Assuming that you use the customary initial screening method of reviewing applications and/or resumes to determine who to invite to your testing process, the general purpose of using job knowledge tests is two-fold: 1) to verify that each of the "paper qualified" applicants possesses at least essential types of job-specific knowledge; and, 2) to make preliminary distinctions among a larger test group of applicants before moving a smaller number of applicants into more complex, costly, and time-consuming test processes. Your goal, after all, is to achieve one quality hire (sometimes more) from a larger group of applicants produced from a single recruitment and testing process, which is why testing is often referred to as a "process of elimination."

Therefore, it is common for employers to first screen applications to find those with the most suitable background and likely skills to undergo sequentially eliminating testing. Second, applicants are usually tested to determine which ones have the greater amount and type of job knowledge required by the job and desired by the employer. Third, remaining applicants may then be subjected to testing for personal traits and conditions essential for success in the job, and so on until the applicant with overall quality prevails victorious.

Written Job Knowledge (Aptitude) Tests

Written tests, or "paper-and-pencil" tests as they are sometimes called, fell into disfavor during the 1970s when they became the subject of tremendous controversy as courts hearing discrimination cases found many such tests invalid. However, with increased attention by employers to match actual job features to written and other types of selection tests, the threat of disparate impact from written tests and resultant discrimination litigation has lessened.

Written tests that measure an applicant's level of specific job knowledge remains one of the most reliable methods of preemployment testing. They are used most often for office, production, service, skilled trade, professional, and technical jobs. Job knowledge can also be evaluated by means of personal interviews and work sample exercises, but these methods are usually reserved for a small group of finalist applicants, while written tests are effective at screening down to a select number of applicants from among a larger group of those seemingly qualified after an initial review of applications.

Written job knowledge tests have the advantage of producing quick and effective early distinctions about the type and level of knowledge various applicants have about performing a particular job. Results can become known quickly on the basis of predetermined pass-fail or pass-point scores with the use of scanning or other electronic devices. The major disadvantage is the time and expense to produce a single test. However, this deterrent can be lessened by preparing your own job knowledge tests rather than purchasing standardized tests that (at best) measure general knowledge within certain job categories such as office clerk, teller, welder, electronic technician, and the like.

If you have compiled the job and employment condition features (testing elements) lists previously suggested, then the construction of a content valid written test on job knowledge should not prove to be too difficult. To do so, you need to prepare anywhere from 20 to 100 questions that directly correspond to specific knowledge a suitably qualified applicant should know in order to pass the test. Test questions can be either true-false, multiple-choice, fill-in-the-blanks, essay, or some combination of these, but remember that written answers take longer to score and tend to be more subjective in the correctness of answers than prescribed choice answers.

Generally, written job knowledge tests start with relatively easy questions and become progressively more difficult. You want a range of difficulty in your questions in order to get distinctions in scores and level of knowledge, but also remember that each question should be at the level of the job being filled—not a measurement of promotional prospects into higher level jobs requiring advanced knowledge. In terms of wording test questions, keep in mind that the words, terms, and phrases you use should be at the reading and comprehension level of the job. Here are examples of how you might construct written job knowledge test questions.

True-False Questions

1. The primary function of a truss brace is to strengthen the support of converging cross-member beams.
   ❑ True   ❑ False

2. The proper method for supervisors to use when dealing with a chronic tardy employee is to issue a written reprimand after the third incident.
   ❑ True   ❑ False

Multiple-Choice Questions

1. Which of the following is the best method to build trust between employees and their supervisors?
   A. Hire participative supervisors
   B. Hire participative employees
   C. Train supervisors on employee relation skills
   D. Train employees on supervisory relation skills

2. If you had three strips of wood molding, each 72 inches in length, to go around a doorway eight feet tall and three feet wide, what lengths would you use to get the job done?
   A. 2 @ six feet, 2 @ two feet, 1 @ three feet
   B. 2 @ eight feet, 1 @ three feet
   C. 2 @ seven feet, 2 @ one foot, 2 @ One and one-half feet
   D. 4 @ four feet, 2 @ One and one-half feet

Fill-In-the-Blanks Questions

1. The most accurate device to use when calculating the precise angles on an architectural drawing is a _____, and to draw that angle you would use a _____.

2. A two and one-half inch hose will produce a water supply of _____ G.P.M., whereas a four inch hose will produce _____ G.P.M.

Essay Questions

1. Explain the three steps of verifying customer account records when "discrepancy reconciliation requests" are filed, and why banks use these three steps.

2. If modifying the undesirable behavior or performance of an employee is the principle of discipline, what is the principle behind the practice of a company conducting annual performance appraisals?

As you can see, these are job-specific examples of test question types. To measure more general cognitive and psychomotor skills of applicants, the General Aptitude Test Battery (GATB) is one of the best known tests. This test can be purchased from available test sources listed at the end of this chapter and administered by following instructions, or you can use the services of a trained examiner from among testing sources such as private vendors or your local Employment Service office. Cognitive tests measure such abilities as:

1. Verbal
   - Verbal comprehension
   - Reading comprehension
   - Analogical reasoning
   - Word fluency

2. Analytical
   - Word problems
   - Inductive reasoning: concept formation
   - Deductive logic
   - Investigative interests
   - Figural reasoning

3. Quantitative
   - Numerical computation
   - Use of formulas in number problems

4. Attentional
   - Perceptual speed and accuracy
   - Processing efficiency
   - Selective attention
   - Time sharing
   - Rote memory
   - Following directions

Psychomotor test questions measure such abilities as:

- Control precision
- Rate control
- Arm-hand steadiness
- Aiming
- Multi-limb coordination
- Speed of arm movement
- Manual dexterity
- Finger dexterity
- Wrist-finger speed

If you prefer to purchase and use standardized tests, or consider their application to particular jobs in your organization, rather than preparing your own job knowledge tests, a few sources you may wish to investigate are listed at the end of this chapter. You may also wish to inquire about other sources of standardized preemployment tests from trained examiners at your local Employment Service office.

Skills and Abilities Performance Tests

Performance tests are demonstration activities used for the purpose of having applicants carry out one or more sets of actual job tasks in order to show the examiner that they possess the type of requisite skills and abilities for the job.

To be considered a valid measure of the applicant's skills and/or abilities, performance tests must seek to *replicate* the actual job environment and conditions as closely as possible, and *simulate* the actual tasks of some major function of the job. The object of performance tests is to have examiners observe relative skills possessed by applicants as they conduct the activity and evaluate them based on preestablished rating factors. With typing and stenographic tests, the skill rating factors are speed and accuracy while the ability rating factor is use of the equipment. Physical agility performance tests measure such applicant skills and abilities as climbing technique, endurance, timeliness in executing strenuous activities, strength, manipulating objects, and completion.

Yet another example of a performance test is work samples. This type of a performance test typically requires that a select group of applicants individually complete some prescribed task that also simulates a realistic job function. Many professional jobs, for example, involve a considerable amount of time performing such tasks as reading particular kinds of information or data, interpreting and/or analyzing it, and writing reports, policies, instructions, and memos. A common work sample test for applicants for such jobs consists of using a (moderately difficult) sample of the kind of information (e.g., budget, vendor contract, equipment specifications, written identification of a problem) a job incumbent would have to deal with in the actual job, and asking the applicant to follow written instructions. What is measured in written or interpretive work sample performance tests are such factors as understanding of the test material, depth of comprehension, analytical ability, writing skills, orderliness and thoroughness of dealing with the test issue, practicality of application or solution to the problem presented, and completion.

Performance tests can be a very effective method of differentiating particular skills and abilities among a group of applicants that are requisite to successful job performance, because they replicate and simulate—rather than postulate—the actual job. Upon careful examination of your list of test elements, you may find that one or more important job functions do not lend themselves well to other testing methods. If these functions involve some observable or measurable *activity*, then you may find it advantageous to develop a performance test to distinguish the skill and ability differences among your applicants before making a hiring decision.

Assessment Center Tests

The assessment center testing method was a technique originally developed by the military during World War II to evaluate potential combat officers. Later, the method was adopted by a few large corporations to assess potential skills and traits of entry-level management employees as a means of determining which managers would be the most likely candidates for advanced training (fast-tracking) into executive positions. Since the method worked extremely well for this purpose, it quickly became one of the most popular, reliable, and valid methods used by all employment sectors to evaluate applicants for executive, management, supervisory, and more recently, professional jobs.

Assessment center tests (or labs as they are sometimes called) consist of having a small group of select applicants perform a variety of simulated exercises at the same time, with some of the exercises being performed in a direct competitive fashion with other aspirants. Test exercises are designed on the basis of: 1) the types of situations and work tasks that would be required in the job; and, 2) the nature of requisite skills, knowledge, and abilities to perform the job in a successful manner. The types of exercise activities most often used in assessment centers are a combination of written job knowledge, performance, and interactive tests such as:

1. In-Basket Tasks Exercise
2. Group Problem Solving Discussion Exercise
3. Group Planning or Evaluation Discussion Exercise
4. Written Assignment Exercise
5. Role Play Exercise
6. Personal Interview

While assessment center exercises and other test components normally have at least one event to measure the job knowledge of applicants, most emphasis in evaluating candidates is placed upon their interactive and process skills and abilities since these are the more important measures of success probability in jobs requiring leadership, creativity, and interactive prowess. The particular measures commonly used to rate applicant results are:

- Verbal Communication Skills
- Written Communication Skills
- Analysis and Problem Solving
- Judgment and Decision Making
- Practicality and Initiative
- Leadership Qualities
- Planning and Organization
- Technical Knowledge
- Professional Development
- Clarity and Control
- Thoroughness/Completion
- Interpersonal Skills

Those who observe, evaluate, and rate the test group of applicants are referred to as "assessors," and their role is different from that of examiners or interviewers who interact directly and individually with applicants. Assessors undergo prior training and orientation on each assessment center test for familiarity with logistic, exercise content, evaluation, and administrative issues associated with the test. Their role is mostly that of observer rather than participant, thus allowing them to concentrate on what is taking place throughout the day's sequence of different simulated job activities.

Assessment Center Test—Association Manager
Examination Schedule

8:30–8:45 A.M.	Candidate Orientation to the Assessment Center Process
8:45–9:30 A.M.	Exercise #1 (Written): Association Policy Development
9:30–10:00 A.M.	Candidate and Assessor Introductions
10:00–10:20 A.M.	BREAK
10:20–12:00 A.M.	Exercise #2 (Written/Discussion): Dealing With Administrative Problems and Issues
12:00–12:45 P.M.	LUNCH
12:45–2:45 P.M.	Concurrent Exercises
	Exercise #3 (Written): Publications and Editorial Evaluations
	Exercise #4: Personal Interview
	Exercise #5: Conference Meeting
2:45–3:30 P.M.	Discussion of Exercise #3 Issues and Approaches
3:30–4:00 P.M.	Candidate Debriefing
3:30–4:30 P.M.	Assessor Scoring and Evaluations

Assessment Center Examination for the Position of
Association Manager

Exercise Scoring & Weighting Profile

	Exer. #1 Intro.s/ Policies	Exer. #2 Admin. Issues	Exer. #3 Organiz. Prob. Solv.	Exer. #4 Personal Interview	Exer. #5 Handling Meeting
Written Communication Skills					
Verbal Communication Skills					
Decision Making Abilities					
Analyzing and Problem Solving					
Planning and Organization					
Leadership and Control					
Flexibility					
Interpersonal Skills					
Professional Development					
TOTAL POINTS					

CANDIDATE RATING FORM					
Assessor		CANDIDATES			
		1	2	3	4
CANDIDATE INTRODUCTIONS					
Oral Communication Skills	10				
Planning and Organization	20				
Control	10				
Professional Development	10				
EXERCISE #1: WRITTEN					
Written Communication Skills	20				
Planning and Organization	10				
Analyze & Problem Solving	20				
Professional Development	10				
EXERCISE #2: WRITTEN/DISCUSSION					
Oral Communication Skills	10				
Planning and Organization	10				
Leadership Skills	20				
Interpersonal Sensitivity	20				
Flexibility	10				
Written Communication Skills	20				
EXERCISE #3: WRITTEN					
Written Communication Skills	10				
Planning and Organization	10				
Decision Making Skills	20				
Analyze & Problem Solving	20				
EXERCISE #4: PERSONAL INTERVIEW					
Professional Development	20				
Control	10				
Interpersonal Sensitivity	10				
Flexibility	10				
Leadership	20				
EXERCISE #5: CONFERENCE MEETING					
Oral Communication Skills	10				
Planning and Organization	10				
Leadership	20				
Control	10				
TOTALS					

Scoring Values—10 Point Scale

0-3 pts (substandard)	Demonstrates poor or uncertain knowledge and/or skills; low proficiency and development; need for considerable training and supervision.
4-6 pts (average)	Demonstrates moderate knowledge and skills, development, and desired proficiency in necessary attributes.
7-10 pts (superior)	Well above average demonstration of the skills, talent, development, and attributes determined essential for job success.

Assessors are selected for their knowledge about all aspects of the job being tested; their particular sense of objectivity, observational skills, and ability to interpret interactive behavior; and ability to be keenly analytical in the sense of evaluating differential levels of applicant traits. It is therefore normal to have a somewhat diverse group of assessors such as a senior executive, human resource director, technical expert, psychologist, or some similar combination of professionals at or above the level of the job being tested. Due to the increased focus between applicants and evaluators in the assessment center method, the customary ratio is one assessor for every two applicants.

Assessment center tests can vary in the number, length, and type of exercises used for evaluation of applicants. They can also vary in the duration of the testing process, but one to two full days—and sometimes extending into evening hours—is most common. To help you further visualize how an assessment center test can be developed, the samples on pages 162 and 163 illustrate a typical test schedule, exercise rating summary, and rating form for the job of Association Manager.

Personal Interviews

Personal interviews are the single most prevalent preemployment selection testing method, and for that reason the entire next chapter has been dedicated to that subject. However, it should be pointed out here that personal interviews serve as another testing device to evaluate the job knowledge and some of the basic interpersonal skills of applicants for jobs where those elements are performance imperatives. Conversely, interviews are *not* effective testing methods for evaluating other required job skills or abilities. Employers would therefore do well to discontinue making hiring decisions solely on the basis of applicant interviews—particularly in light of the fact that few people are truly skilled in the more refined and advanced techniques that will be introduced in the next chapter.

Personal interviews should be used as a preemployment selection method with every new hire, but as a supplement to other testing methods deemed more reliable in the measurement of a wide range of job skills, knowledge, and abilities. In fact, one of the better uses of personal interviews is as a screening device among a group of say ten to twelve applicants who have successfully completed other tests. Initial interviews can thus be used to screen down to three applicants for further testing, or referred to the hiring authority for selection of one applicant to be subjected to background and reference inquiries prior to an employment offer.

Prior Employment References

Much controversy exists about the getting and giving of employment reference information on prior employees due to the rash of costly litigation over defamation and other privacy right violations. Yet, what better way of determining an applicant's ability to perform in a similar job is there than finding out their strengths and weaknesses in past employment? Clearly, prior employment experience is a legitimate measurement of how individuals are likely to perform in a similar job with respect to their skills, knowledge, and abilities in their execution of job responsibilities. Without such information, we can only rely on our own preemployment testing methods and a brief, speculative trial employment period.

Isolating Job-Related Information

If you hope to obtain more than the usual "name, rank, and payroll number" verification from wary former employers, then you should know what specific information is important to the job in your organization. Generally, there are two types of information that are useful to employers considering a new hire:

1. Information about Applicant's Job Skills, Knowledge, and Abilities such as

   - Job duties performed, training received, and ability to apply knowledge to responsibilities
   - Application of skills and abilities to job situations
   - Particular performance strengths and areas of difficulty

2. Information about Applicant's Personal Traits Related to Job Performance such as

   - Attendance record
   - Interpersonal relationships and ability to work well with others
   - Behavioral idiosyncrasies that affected their performance positively or negatively
   - The existence of any serious disciplinary actions including acts of misconduct, or personal problems having a performance manifestation

As you can see from these two areas of information, the focus is—and should remain—on job and employment characteristics that are *directly* related to the job being considered and/or the nature of the employer's business. Keep in mind that the most frequent cause of legal action is defamation—the giving of false and injurious information—and most employers have been taught to overprotect this potential liability by giving little useful or no information about former employees. Therefore, one of your initial obstacles to overcome is isolating the type of information you seek (questions asked of the former employer) and communicating it in a manner that yields disclosure.

Getting Disclosure from Former Employers

The two methods of obtaining employment reference information disclosure from former employers are telephone contacts and the use of a written form. Since both methods should be fully documented, forms have been provided in Appendix D for this purpose. Telephone contact between you (or another confidential source for your company) and a representative of the applicant's former employer is the quickest means of handling the information gathering process, but may meet with resistance because of the contact's preoccupation with other work or skepticism about who you are. To alleviate both of these barriers to a comfortable conversation, you may wish to say something along the line of:

> "Hello Mr./Mrs. _____, my name is _____ and I am the (your job title) for (company name). We are considering the employment of (name of applicant) for the position of _____ with our company. He/she has given us your name as a reference source, and permission to ask you a few questions about their employment with your company that relates to their employment here. Do you have a few minutes available to discuss this with me now, or would you like to call me back sometime today?"

Generally, the best source of information—and the one usually given by applicants—is their former supervisor or department manager rather than the human resources office. Supervisors and managers who worked directly with the applicant are in the best position to give you precise and insightful details about the individual's work abilities, limitations, habits, and personal characteristics. That is exactly the type of information you want and need in order to make an evaluative assessment of the applicant's suitability to your job vacancy and related employment conditions. Should you receive negative information, try to verify its accuracy with another source merely because not all supervisors and managers are as objective and emotionally detached from people they have worked with as they should be.

Written forms are slower to process, but they present a more professional appearance and allow you to structure the kind of information you wish to obtain. Additionally, a form like the one provided in Appendix D gives the former employer more information about the job under consideration (attach the job description) and includes a signed release and waiver of liability by the former employee. Therefore, an employment reference form tends to impart greater confidence to the former employer of your company's thoroughness, professionalism, knowledge of the concern over legal risks, and assurances of keeping their response confidential. When sending an employment reference form to a prior employment source, it is a good idea to call the source to advise them of the mailing and request a response date. A personal contact of this type can also open more informal opportunities for information about your applicant that the source may be reluctant to document.

Another important aspect about getting employment reference disclosures is that other employers may not know as much as you do about privacy right laws, particularly if you read Appendix B. Rather, ask yourself what would make a skeptical, conservative employer comfortable enough to give you the information you seek. Chances are it would be one or all of three things:

1. A written authorization and release of liability signed by the former employee giving the employer permission to release records and information;

2. Telling the former employer what questions you have about the applicant's prior employment, that these questions only relate to issues pertinent to employment with your company, and that all information given is held in the strictest confidence (i.e., is privileged information between the two employers—see, *Circus Hotels v. Witherspoon*, Nev. 1983 and other case ref.s); and/or,

3. Informing an uncooperative employer that they could be sued for unnecessary withholding of reasonable reference information by the former employee if rejected from this job due to your inability to obtain this information, and that your company *would* name them as a co-defendent should the company hire this applicant and subsequently get sued for negligent hiring. While this latter method is obviously threatening and should only be used in cases where obtaining information from a difficult source is vital, it can be an effective means of educating staunch employers about the risks of reciprocal liability.

Are Reference Letters Really Useful?

Reference letters should be taken at face value, rather than as a major or particularly validated source of selection testing, and evaluated accordingly in the context of all other information about the applicant. At a minimum, reference letters may provide evidence that the applicant takes their career and/or your job opportunity seriously enough to seek out those who would give testimony about their attributes. Doing so can be a measure of motivation, ambition, sincerity, pride about their work record and relationships, eagerness to succeed, or—in a few regrettable cases—deceitfulness in hopes of creating false confidence in lieu of a reference check. Some of the features of reference letters that should be considered by employers are

1. Is the applicant offering an original copy of a reference letter, or does it look like a tenth generation photocopy?

2. Is there a date on the letter to indicate when it was prepared? You might legitimately question a letter dated recently from a source describing the applicant from a situation that occurred years ago—why didn't the applicant get the reference then?

3. What is the apparent credibility of the person giving the reference, and how likely is it they would be the best source for the circumstances being described?

4. Is the letter a "custom" reference addressed to you or your company, mentioning the job under consideration or relating reference information to the job responsibilities, or is it a generic "To Whom It May Concern" letter?

5. Is the letter on business, personal, or blank stationery? You can disregard the last two unless the letter makes it clear that their relationship with the applicant is based on personal familiarity and therefore a character reference.

Some of these reference letter features are necessarily subjective on your part. However, most human resource professionals prefer two-to-four custom and detailed references by highly credible sources over a greater number of poor quality generic letters. In other words, consider the source and consider the content of reference letters in light of other information you gather about the applicant.

Preemployment Medical Examinations

Prior to the onslaught of laws and legal scrutiny over discriminatory and privacy right effects of medical examinations, it was a common preemployment practice among nearly all employers to require that potential hires undergo a complete physical evaluation. If any medical problem or physical limitation was discovered, the applicant was automatically rejected for either being considered unsuitable to perform essential duties of the job, or because their state of health was viewed as having a potentially adverse cost impact on the employer's medical plan and/or workers' compensation rates.

During the 1970s, however, employment discrimination became a popular social concern and several states adopted prohibitive laws that paralleled the federal 1970 Occupational Safety and Health Act (OSHA) and the 1973 Vocational Rehabilitation Act. These state and federal laws had the effect of making it illegal for employers to discriminate against an applicant or employee on the basis of a physical or mental impairment so long as the individual was *otherwise qualified* to perform the essential functions of the job (even if doing so required reasonable accommodations). Similarly, the 1980s and early 1990s (ADA) witnessed the introduction of additional legal and economic concerns related to medical testing—the rise of drug and alcohol dependency among workers, the prevalence of cancer, the AIDS epidemic, smoking, and fetal protection on the one hand, and sharply rising medical plan and workers' compensation cost contributions on the other.

The net result of these conflicting liabilities caused many employers to discontinue their former practice of conducting preemployment medical examinations. The issues on both sides of the argument seemed to be evenly balanced, but legal liabilities almost always present a more threatening condition for employers; until yet another legal concern tipped the scales in the late 1980s—the threat of a negligent hiring lawsuit—that brought about renewed interest in evaluating the medical condition of applicants. The question for employers during the 1990s thus became one of how to protect the company's reasonable legal and economic interests, while at the same time conducting medical evaluations that were employment valid (free of discriminatory effect), nonintrusive (free from unreasonable privacy invasion), and sufficient in detail to get job-suitability results (due diligence in qualifying applicant traits).

Generally, preemployment medical testing for the presence of the AIDS virus remains a prohibited practice under discrimination laws enacted by numerous states—unless an employer can demonstrate that the job in question has a high risk of transmission exposure, or is in some abnormal respect susceptible to infectious transmission. Questions on what jobs might legitimately qualify for consideration of AIDS testing should be referred to an experienced labor attorney in the employer's state for a review of circumstantial details of the job and nature of the employment setting.

The evolving legalities of employers conducting preemployment testing for the presence of drug and alcohol use are only marginally different from those concerning AIDS testing. Here, the courts have generally held that applicants are less effected by employment rejection resulting from a positive drug and/or alcohol test than are employees who have a greater "vested" interest in their jobs, so prohibitions are not *as* strict for applicants as they are for employees. Furthermore, in 1989, the National Labor Relations Board (NLRB) ruled in

Minneapolis Star Tribune that unionized employers are *not* required to bargain over the employer's interests in requiring drug and/or alcohol testing of job applicants.

Yet another significant legal issue to keep in mind is the effect the Americans with Disabilities Act (ADA) has on preemployment medical exams. It is important to remember that the ADA prohibits employers from requiring applicants to undergo a medical exam prior to an actual (conditional) offer of employment. The ADA also limits the use of medical exams (types of medical tests and disclosure of results) employers have traditionally used to make hiring decisions.

Under the ADA, employers may require an applicant to pass a medical exam after an offer has been extended, provided: 1) the employer has adopted and maintains a practice of requiring the same exam for *all* similar prehire candidates in the same job category; 2) that *all* elements of the medical exam are relevant to realistic measures of the job's essential duties; *and,* 3) that all medical exam information is handled and maintained in a confidential manner. On the latter point, the ADA requires medical exam information to be on separate forms and in files separate from the employee's official personnel file, and that information about the employee's medical condition(s) may only be provided to:

- Managers and supervisors regarding necessary restrictions or accommodations;
- First-aid and safety personnel appropriate to handling a medical emergency; or,
- Government officials investigating a claim or compliance matter, including the company's workers' compensation representative who is handling a claim.

Therefore, the mere presence or applicant acknowledgment of the existence of a physical and/or mental impairment is not enough in itself to warrant requiring the applicant to pass a medical exam if the employer would not require such a test of any other applicant of the same occupational category. To aid employers in making new hire medical exam result decisions, the EEOC advises employers to consider:

1. The examining physician's opinion with respect to such factors as the duration of any risk, nature and severity of potential harm, likelihood of potential harm occurring, and the imminence of potential harm to self and others.
2. The opinion of any other doctor with experience pertaining to any revealed disability and/or limitation (may require a second opinion examination).
3. The advise of rehabilitation counselors and/or occupational therapists.
4. Consideration of the experience of the prospective employee in previous similar jobs and nonwork activities.

So where does all of this leave employers on the issue of whether or not to conduct preemployment medical examinations, and what aspects of an applicant's medical condition should be included in such tests? Regrettably, there is no easy answer to these questions; only guidelines and a few suggestions to help you avoid some of the more frequently encountered legal liabilities, and ways in which to satisfy your need to have legitimate medical facts about those you are considering for employment.

Baseline Medical Examinations

Baseline medical examinations are used for the purpose of establishing the existing state, or baseline, of various job related physical conditions of applicants so that the employer might be able to "prorate" possible workers' compensation injuries or illnesses that may accrue during subsequent employment. To be considered valid, the employer should be able to show that their business has more than casual job injury/illness risk exposures or experience; that claims payment represents a high cost of the employer's business; and that the employer has made reasonable attempts to identify particular medical conditions associated with each job to be tested, rather than general or blanket physical examinations of applicants for all jobs. While these three conditions do not assure a legal determination of validity, it does create a much greater likelihood of legal defense from such a challenge.

The best source of information that will help you identify physical and/or health related medical conditions of a job is the job analysis you performed in conjunction with developing your job descriptions as outlined in Chapter 2. By referring back to your job analysis documents, you should be able to identify very specific physical conditions, job task demands, and work environment situations that correspond to particular types of medical tests and evaluations—preferably administered and interpreted by a physician trained in industrial or occupational medicine. Depending on the realm of job functions and environmental conditions, you are likely to identify such medical examination elements as

- Lifting, carrying, and placing objects
- Standing, walking, or sitting for long periods
- Bending, stooping, and climbing
- Physical strength and/or endurance abilities of various types
- Dexterity and manipulation abilities associated with the use of fingers, hands, arms, and legs
- Sensory abilities that might be subject to impairment under job conditions such as sight, hearing, and odor detection
- The presence, absence, or susceptibility to cancer, heart disease, tuberculosis, and similar ailments that, if present, would (not could) materially affect or limit the person's *present* ability to perform the job

Baseline medical examinations can be conducted in one of two ways:

1. identifying and testing for specific physical conditions common to all jobs in the company's employ, and testing *all* applicants being considered for hire against those standards (thus eliminating discriminatory effect since all applicants are subject to testing, excluding possible physical handicap discrimination of rejected applicants who are otherwise qualified); and,

2. testing only those who are applicants for jobs in which there exists a clearly identifiable set of physical and/or health conditions, establishing what medical tests are to be performed on applicants for each of those jobs, and testing *all* applicants being considered for hire into those jobs.

The second method is the more practical of the two. Why? Because it is more reliable and valid as a predictive determination of hiring suitability, and because it is more practical in conserving hiring costs. Let's face it, not all jobs require the medical scrutiny that other jobs *should* be given, and medical examinations slow down the hiring process considerably, so why not exclude those jobs that are absent exposure risks? Whichever method is selected—and depending on the nature of the employer's business, type of jobs, and kinds of employees—it may be worthwhile to include drug and alcohol tests to avoid unsuspected surprises.

A sample preemployment medical examination form has been included in Appendix D for your prospective use, however it is advisable to review these types of forms with qualified legal and medical advisors. It is also advisable to provide your medical advisor with a copy of the applicable job description or other listing of job activity/environmental conditions with each applicant referral. Better yet, ask your examining physician to assist you in the identification of medical elements to be tested or evaluated for each job in advance of referrals.

Special Condition Medical Examinations

There are a vast number of jobs that possess special job functions or environmental conditions where applicants should be medically tested based especially on those elements. A good example is truck drivers who are required under federal law to pass medical standards prescribed by the Department of Transportation. Likewise, public safety employees, airline pilots, air traffic controllers, laborers, and those exposed to toxic substances are performing jobs in which special physical, mental, and/or emotional conditions exist that should be subjected to medical evaluation.

Naturally, such special medical tests are subject to the same validity scrutiny as any other medical criteria associated with preemployment selection determinations. Therefore, it is important that any job function or employment condition that requires a special medical test be precisely documented by the employer with respect to the legitimacy and business necessity of conducting applicable test(s). Special medical tests might include such elements as

- Respiratory (breathing) abilities due to such activities as running, use of breathing apparatus, or physical exertion that can cause stress to body organs
- Cardiovascular condition and endurance abilities
- Emotional stability to encounter, endure, and deal with particularly stressful conditions
- Back disorders and weaknesses that affect the individual's *present* ability, or create an undue limitation, to perform the job
- Contagious disease presence, the nature of which would absolutely endanger others, and where there is abnormal risk of transmission
- Addiction to the use of controlled substances (illegal drugs and alcohol) where the job is legitimately classified as sensitive, hazardous, or has direct effect on the public safety and welfare.

The results of both baseline and special condition medical tests should be reviewed carefully by the employer prior to making an acceptance or rejection decision. If medical terms are used in the examiner's report that are not understood, or there exists any degree of uncertainty about an applicant's present condition, these should be discussed at length with the examining physician, and possibly legal advisors, to ensure that hiring decisions are based on well understood facts and circumstances.

Introductory Employment Period

This category may surprise you as a testing method of measuring an applicant's job skills, knowledge, and abilities. More likely, it is a hiring practice that you (and many others) have overlooked in the context of being a "test," yet that is precisely the purpose of defined initial employment periods. Furthermore, the courts have generally recognized the legitimacy of an employer's need to test new hires under actual job conditions for a reasonable period of time prior to making a more formal (regular employment status) retention decision. After all, what could be more valid than placing an applicant in the actual job and assessing their job skills, knowledge, and abilities against performance standards deemed necessary for job success?

However, the major weakness of introductory employment periods as a testing method of a new hire's job skills, knowledge, and abilities is the subjectivity often found in evaluation techniques. To enhance the objectivity of performance appraisals, you should use only job related and reasonably measurable performance criteria that are defined in such a way as to narrow the opportunity for subjective opinion. (No performance appraisal technique will likely *eliminate* rater subjectivity.)

The other major weakness of initial employment as a final selection testing method has to do with the length of the assessment period. Contrary to the principle of needing enough time to train, observe, and evaluate new hires in a vast number of *different* types of jobs to ascertain suitability, nearly all employers still use a *common* period of time for the initial employment of new hires. The problem here is one of a contradiction of principles.

If, in fact, jobs are different and take varying amounts of time for new hires to train, receive various job assignments, be exposed to a range of job conditions, have their adaptive abilities observed and performance results evaluated sufficiently for a retention determination, *why* then would a court of law accept any rationale about the employer's practice of using a singular initial employment period common to all jobs? To eliminate this form of potential invalidity in the use of initial employment periods as a final selection testing method, you should separate the jobs in your organization into two or more categories of initial employment periods (test lengths).

The number of periods will depend on how difficult, complex, diverse, and risky each job is with respect to the time needed to learn job functions, adapt to working conditions, and demonstrate competence in the more essential responsibilities of the job. The most common periods from which to choose for your categories are 30, 60, 90, and 120 days, 6 months, 12 months, 18 months, and two years. Initial employment periods beyond two years may be difficult to justify let alone convince an applicant to work against, but employers should give more serious consideration to the range of six months to one year for professional, technical, supervisory, and definitely managerial jobs.

7.4 Evaluating Applicant Traits

Worker traits are characteristics of *how* they operate in life, behave toward others, and view themselves in light of their surroundings. It is what they do and how they do things in the normal course of living, including the carry over of their personal being into a work atmosphere and set of conditions. Traits consist of such personal characteristics as the individual's values, habits, behaviors, beliefs, perceptions, trustworthiness, emotional orientation toward people and conditions, attitudes, and sources of motivation.

These human traits have, of course, been the subject of scientific inquiry for decades and there remains much more to learn about their workplace application, including testing. In fact, it is because of the lingering uncertainty of how to accurately and reliably measure these types of applicant traits that employers refrain from, or severely restrict, their use as a preemployment selection tool. Likewise, employers fear the legality of such tests with respect to their validity in any given test situation. It may be difficult to prove their nondiscriminatory effect, as well as the prospective vulnerability of such tests on the privacy rights of applicants. Even with these deterrents, it is becoming increasingly recognized that trait testing methods are improving in their reliability to predict important job performance characteristics with intrusion controls, and that there are some jobs where these tests can be especially useful supplements to traditional qualifying test methods.

Undeniably, a well planned interview conducted by a highly skilled examiner (such as that described in the following chapter) can produce *prospective* insights about an applicant's job related traits, but interviews are no substitute for more objective tests to get at the truth about significant, job-impacting traits. For that reason, you may wish to consider the use of one or more of the trait testing methods that are described in the remainder of this section as a potential supplement to traditional testing methods in conjunction with those jobs considered more than casually reliant on such traits.

Honesty, Personality, and Behavior Tests

Of all the applicant traits, these three are the most difficult to measure with a high degree of accuracy and reliability in terms of job success propriety. These types of tests are also used in differing situations. For example, in the retail, finance, manufacturing, and other industries where employee theft and similar acts of dishonesty are having a major impact on the employer's losses, employers are taking a keen interest in finding ways to ascertain various types of honesty traits of applicants to jobs in which more than normal opportunity for dishonest acts exists. Therefore, written honesty tests have gained favor with these employers in spite of their potential weaknesses that can cause rejection of some honest applicants who try to "second-guess" test questions. They have also increased in usage due to the passage of the 1988 Polygraph Protection Act which makes the giving of employment related polygraph tests unlawful for most employers.

Similarly, other types of psychological tests that purport to measure various personality and behavioral traits deemed necessary, or in some respect correlated to job success, are being used with greater frequency. Jobs where these traits have significance are in sales, supervision, management, and certain types of professional jobs where there exist specific interactive qualities that determine the success of job results. Perhaps the greatest problem inherent in the use of personality and behavioral tests, aside from the academic arguments over what features are true measures of success in any one job, is that such tests are standardized for application to a broad range of jobs rather than customized for any one job. Customization of psychologically oriented tests is the only way to enhance the assurance that test results are reasonably reliable and valid for the job being tested, but having such tests customized can be cost prohibitive for many employers.

Written Honesty Tests

Written honesty tests are designed to measure either general traits of an applicant's honesty or specific traits such as integrity, trustworthiness, maintaining confidentiality, or propensities toward theft. Depending on the nature of particular jobs and the presence of any or all of these job related elements, you may find it beneficial to acquire and administer one of these tests that most closely corresponds to the type of information you seek about prospective new hires. These tests tend to be relatively inexpensive, ranging from $7 to $12 per applicant, they can be administered at the employer's site, and results can be produced quickly.

When contacting test vendors, you should consider taking these actions:

- Ask what honesty elements their test is aimed at measuring and, if it is the type you need, ask that a review copy be sent to you.

- Request documentation on how the test questions were arrived at (test construction method or basis), and on specific validation studies that have been performed on the test including which types of jobs were involved in the validation effort.

- Request written information about the credentials of the person or persons who designed the test questions to ensure that they have the proper background to design such a test and withstand a qualifications challenge should you experience legal review of your testing effort. The most suitable credentials are possession of a Ph.D. in psychology or psychiatry, preferably with specialized training in testing, statistics, or industrial psychology.

- Retain the services of a local psychologist experienced in industrial psychology and test interpretation to assist you in the review of the honesty test to gain additional insight as to its utility, potential accuracy with the job(s) in which you are considering its use, and perhaps as an independent source to administer the test to applicants for greater face validity.

Written honesty tests tend to be less intrusive than polygraph or even personal interview questions aimed at discerning an applicant's honesty because written tests are usually taken by the applicants as theoretical situations rather than implied accusations. Nevertheless, those who might take exception to honesty tests by making claims of disparate impact or intrusion will place the burden of validity on the employer—not the test vendor—who must then defend the test. Obviously, the employer will want to use the test vendor's validity studies and the qualifications of the test preparer as a part of its defense. For your convenience, ten sources of written honesty test publishers have been listed at the end of this chapter in the event you wish to investigate the availability of tests designed to measure honesty related traits in applicants.

Personality Tests

Written personality tests tend to be more invasive of an individual's privacy rights than honesty tests because they must delve into the person's psyche on matters of personal traits rather than mere values and past or projected actions. Personality tests are typically composed of true-false questions from an inventory of situations aimed at measuring how the individual thinks, behaves, perceives, and regards lifestyle events. They are also more costly than honesty tests, ranging from $50 to $250 per applicant, due largely to the need for professional interpretation of answers. Further, personality tests are more difficult to defend from a validity perspective since they have more speculative relationships between test questions, job functions and employment conditions, and the accuracy of questions as reliable predictors of job performance success—in particular the *necessity* to possess certain personality traits. Therefore, tests that include several personality trait measures are prone to be less valid and reliable than those measuring one or two special traits that can be more reasonably identified as significant to a particular job.

Due to present conditions of cost, vulnerability to legal challenge, and higher than usual degrees of subjectivity as a predictive device in measuring performance success traits, the use of personality tests should be confined to those jobs that are highly sensitive to an individual's judgment, decision making patterns, style of interaction with other people, and temperament. The two most common jobs where these conditions usually exist are supervisors and managers, but there may be many other specialized jobs where these traits are tantamount to quality performance. The personality tests that can be used in group or individual test settings, and scored by objective means, are the following:

- Minnesota Multiphasic Personality Inventory (See NOTE on page 174.)
- Bernreuter Personality Inventory
- Humm-Wadsworth Temperament Scale
- Guilford-Martin Personnel Inventory
- Myers-Briggs Type Indicator
- PDI Employment Inventory
- Employee Reliability Inventory
- Sixteen Personality Factor Questionnaire
- California Psychological Inventory

NOTE

A 1989 California Superior Court case was filed involving a class-action suit against an employer by those who refused to take this test, and were thus rejected for employment. In *Soroka v. Target Stores*, plaintiffs alleged that the test violated their State Constitutional (Article 1) rights to privacy, discrimination, and negligent misrepresentation on the basis of the test asking questions relating to religious and sexual beliefs. Consequently, personality tests from any source should be dealt with by using the steps outlined for honesty tests.

If you wish to investigate various personality tests available from test publishers, you can start by contacting any of the sources listed under this category at the end of this chapter. You would also be well advised to take great care in how you treat personality, honesty, and other trait related tests with respect to their handling, disclosure to company representatives, and how you go about informing applicants of their test results—particularly those you decide to reject. Keep in mind that those you reject do not know that their rejection may be based on other test results or your composite assessment of their suitability.

Written Psychological Tests

Psychological tests are not much different from personality or honesty tests. They typically consist of written questions or inventories answered by true-false or multiple choice response to situations, identifications, comparative statements, and interpretive questions. What psychological tests aim to measure are various attitudinal, behavioral, belief, perception, and reactive patterns in light of the requirements and conditions of the job for which the applicant is being tested. Measurements are based on the range of score patterns—not singular responses—of preestablished norms (normal behavior) to that of aberrant trait scores indicative of varying degrees of psychosis or pathological disorder.

Employers have been using psychological testing of particular job applicants for many years, and this method of evaluating personal traits has been increasing due to the illegality of polygraph testing and emergence of negligent hiring liabilities. However, psychological testing is less commercialized than other forms of trait testing and it *requires* the services of a licensed psychologist or psychiatrist to develop, administer, and evaluate these tests—there is no substitute! To be considered valid, the test must also pass the scrutiny of a validation study or otherwise be demonstrably shown that the test questions are accurate predictors of necessary job performance. Consequently, when considering psychological testing it is advisable to use a licensed psychologist or psychiatrist with an industrial specialization or clinical background dealing with occupational disorders.

Psychological tests have been applied to a broad range of jobs with varying degrees of success in predicting the traits most meaningful to employers. The types of jobs that tend to have the most easily justified kinds of responsibilities and conditions are those that

1. are essential to the operation and decision making of a company's welfare;
2. have a single job incumbent who is responsible for the success of an important part of the company's operation;
3. include job activities that are sensitive to judgment errors or abnormalities in the individual's behavior; or,
4. by nature of the job, provide exposure or an opportunity to cause injury to others resulting from an acute disorder which could not have been diagnosed by any other means.

The types of jobs that employers may wish to consider for psychological testing as a supplement to traditional preemployment selection tests are:

- High level executives and managers such as the company president or chief executive officer, or the manager of a major division
- Nuclear power plant personnel
- Law enforcement officers
- Engineers and scientists involved in the development of hazardous products
- Laboratory technicians where dangerous materials are available or handled
- Workers who are required to enter private property, a person's residence, or have access to public facilities
- Those who operate public transportation such as airline pilots, train engineers, bus and cab drivers, and trolley/mass transit operators

Prior to selecting a qualified psychologist or psychiatrist, it is advisable that you first examine your job analysis documentation to identify those job responsibilities and employment conditions where psychological factors have the greatest importance. You will want to list these test elements, along with any other traits you believe are significant indicators of psychological job necessity, as a reference point when you meet with your examiner. This list of job traits will also be useful to your examiner in terms of suggesting what kinds of tests should be applied to applicants of each particular job.

Credit and Character Investigations

Credit and character investigations represent yet another supplemental source of testing for an applicant's traits prior to the offer of employment. Credit checks, allowable in accordance with the Consumer Credit Reporting Act (CCRA), can include an investigation of the individual's general character and reputation (as a credit source), and is a valid type of employer inquiry where the job being applied for carries responsibility for financial transactions of the employer. The applicant being investigated is required to sign a consent form bearing a statement similar to the one provided on the sample form in Appendix D, whereby the applicant authorized such an inquiry and is put on notice that they have the right to request a copy of the report if prepared by an external consumer credit agency. In accordance with the CCRA, and the case of the Federal Trade Commission against *Electronic Data Systems Corp.* (1991), employers are required to provide prospective employees with a copy of any credit report acquired as a preemployment reference, and in particular where applicants are being rejected because of poor credit histories.

Credit reports can generally be received within one week from the date of the employer's request. To do so, you merely need to locate one or more such agencies in your locale and ascertain their services, costs, investigation procedures and sources, and reporting details provided. They can be easily found in the yellow pages of your telephone book or by making inquiries to local banks, savings and loan associations, or mortgage lenders.

Fees are usually modest, ranging from about $10 to $25 per report, but the potential grief they can save an otherwise unsuspecting employer can be great when considering the hiring of someone to handle money or monetary transactions who is in financial straits. Imagine the liability your company could have in conjunction with an employee's embezzlement of company assets, "misappropriation" of customer assets, or robbery of a customer's property with respect to insurance recovery or lawsuit when, in fact, the employee was never investigated for their financial stability. Conversely, employers should not become unduly alarmed or paranoid about employees in general. Rather, employers should require credit reports on any new hire having exposure to, and direct involvement in, these types of financial opportunities to create a *reasonable* and *foreseeable* liability risk.

Character references, on the other hand, should be checked out on every new hire prior to the offer of employment in the same manner as former employment references. While doing so may seem like a waste of time to some employers because only positive sources are likely to be given by the applicant, these conversations can provide insightful information if you handle the inquiry in a creative manner. For example, you might ask your prospective hire for two personal (non-relative) sources by name, occupation, address, telephone number, and length and type of acquaintance who know the applicant's character in a positive relationship, and two similar references where some sort of disharmony occurred.

Another approach is to ask for three personal references and, after a brief conversation with each, ask them for another reference. Then, spend more time using probing questions with the secondary references, since they may well be more objective and truthful about the idiosyncrasies of your applicant than original references. The types of questions you may wish to ask personal references, aside from verifying information given to you by the applicant and after assuring the reference that their comments are held in the strictest confidence, are

1. Based on your past dealings with _____, what can you tell me about his/her

    - Truthfulness
    - Honesty
    - Integrity

    - Temperament
    - Inability to get along with others
    - Dependability and reliability

2. How would you describe his/her orientation toward work; vocation; past employers?

3. Has he/she ever done anything to disappoint you; offend you; annoy you?

4. What is it about him/her that causes you potential concern?

5. Has he/she ever talked about taking anything from a past employer or using sick leave when it was not necessary?

6. What do you consider to be his/her strongest and weakest personal traits, and why?

7. If you were to hire him/her in a job like the one we are considering, what steps would you take to ensure proper performance?

Both credit and character reference results should be fully documented and stored in a properly secured location along with other sensitive and confidential personnel documents. Documentation of character reference information should include all questions asked and answers given, even if your notations are paraphrased comments. Keep in mind that credit and/or character references are supplemental preemployment information, so if any of these results present acute new information, they should be verified before a rejection decision is made.

Driving and Conviction Records

Clean driving and/or conviction records are considered either a required or an unrequired condition of employment depending on the particular job being filled, but they also represent a potentially important applicant trait evaluation. In the case of driving records, you should check at least the last five years of an applicant whose job will require some degree of driving a personal or company vehicle in the course of employment. Here, the goal is to ascertain two conditions: 1) the applicant is acceptable for insurance coverage under the company's policy; and, 2) the applicant's recent driving record does *not* imply a reasonable history of risk to the company.

What might constitute a reasonable history of risk are such incidents as:

1. A repetitive type of moving violation (speeding, reckless driving, failure to signal maneuvers, etc.),
2. A significant number (more than three in a year) of moving violations whether of the same or dissimilar types,
3. A history of collisions—particularly where caused by the applicant, or
4. Any incident of driving under the influence of a controlled substance.

Driving records can be obtained with relative ease by calling or mailing a request for record information to your local state department of motor vehicles. Most insurance companies providing service to employers will conduct these record searches for their client policy holders free of charge, and results can normally be received within a week of your request, although out-of-state drivers may take a little longer. If your insurance carrier does not provide this service in your behalf, you should ask the applicant to sign a consenting release of driving record information and mail it, along with your written request for the five-year record information, to the Records Clerk at your local department of motor vehicles. Be sure to give the applicant's name, address, date of birth, and driver's license number with expiration date.

Similarly, an employer's right to obtain and use conviction record information in the context of employment decision making is based on the nature of the job, employer's business, and the liability risks that may reasonably occur as a result of the relationship between job exposures and a person's criminal history. As a general rule, the courts consider *arrests* and most types of *misdemeanor* convictions as irrelevant to employment inquiries, and should therefore not be a factor of hiring determinations—unless there exists a very strong correlation between the type of job and the nature of one or more serious misdemeanor convictions. In the case of most jobs, however, this narrows inquiries down to convictions of felonies and criminal conduct, which is no minor consideration given the threat employers face concerning potential negligent hiring lawsuits. Such litigation may be infrequent, but you don't want your company unduly exposed to the damage that a negligent hiring lawsuit can cause.

Obtaining records information on the presence or absence of an applicant's felony or criminal history is not as difficult as it is time consuming. There are three levels of public agencies that are most likely to have such records: county clerk's office, state department of justice, and the Federal Bureau of Investigation (or in some cases, the Department of Justice). Additionally, state laws vary considerably in the control and availability of this type of information. The best, least time consuming, and perhaps most objective way to go about a conviction records check is to hire an investigative or security firm who has a reputation of being thorough and professional. They have the experience, sources of available information, methods of acquiring timely information, and neutral positioning in dealing with public record agencies. They can also provide you with advice in many instances concerning the relevance of information they uncover to the job under consideration.

If you wish to undertake a conviction records check yourself, you should first obtain the written authorization of the applicant on a form approved by legal counsel. Then, call your county clerk's office to ascertain the fee for a conviction records search and report, to whom such a request should be addressed, and the estimated response time. Next, make the same inquiries to the nearest office of your state's justice department, and F.B.I. field office (particularly if the job being considered includes sensitive security responsibilities). With this information you can now prepare formal letters to these individuals requesting a records check and report, attaching a copy of the applicant's authorization to release the information to you. Your letter should contain such information as:

- The applicant's name, address, date of birth, driver's license number (and state of issuance), social security number, and any other identifying information that may be germane to these agencies available to you (e.g., visa registration, prior addresses, etc.);

- The job title of the position for which the applicant is being considered; and,
- A brief description of the justification for needing information pertaining to the possible felony or criminal conviction of the applicant (i.e., what duties, responsibilities, employment conditions, or nature of the employer's business give rise to the need for this information).

To say that documents containing adverse incidents of an applicant's driving, felony, or criminal history should be treated with sensitive confidentiality is an understatement. They are probably the most sensitive employment documents an employer can have in its possession, and for that reason you should take special care in how such documents are processed. First, results of these reports should be narrowly disclosed to company representatives on a *need to know* basis only, and then by merely indicating to the interested person (hiring authority) whether or not the information favors or disfavors an offer of employment.

Second, and only upon specific inquiry, applicants should be informed that they are, or are not, being offered employment as a result of the overall testing process. If the applicant persists in this line of questioning, you may wish to further inform him or her that the company has decided to select another applicant whose qualifications were felt to be more suitable to the demands of the job, and end the conversation on a positive but final note. Finally, documents of this type should be placed in a sealed envelope, marked on the outside "Confidential Document—to be opened and viewed only by the (Human Resources Manager or Company President)," and stored in a locking file cabinet with other sensitive applicant records for up to three years, after which it can be (carefully) destroyed.

List of Written Test Publishers/Sources

Job Aptitude (Skill, Knowledge, and Abilities) Tests

1. Employers' Tests and Services Associates
   341 Garfield Street
   Chambersburg, PA 17201
   (717) 264-9509
   Written and performance tests used for employee selection and promotion including Office Arithmetic Test, General Clerical Ability Test, Stenographic Skills Test, Mechanical Familiarity, and Mechanical Knowledge.

2. National Business Education Association
   1914 Association Drive
   Reston, VA 22091
   (703) 860-8300
   Written and performance tests in business areas used for employee screening and evaluation including Accounting Procedures Test, Office Procedures Test, Secretarial Procedures Test, Typewriting Test, and Stenographic Test.

3. National Occupational Competency Testing Institute
   318 Johnson Hall
   Ferris State College
   Big Rapids, MI 49307
   Student Occupational Competency Achievement Tests, consisting of written and performance tests in these 26 vocational fields:

- accounting/bookkeeping
- agriculture

- auto body
- auto mechanics

- carpentry
- commercial foods
- computer programming
- construction electricity
- construction masonry
- drafting
- electronics
- general merchandising
- general office
- graphic arts
- heating/air conditioning
- home entertainment equipment repair
- horticulture
- industrial electricity
- industrial electronics
- machine trades
- mechanics
- plumbing
- practical nursing
- refrigeration
- sewn products
- small engine repair
- welding

4. Purdue University Bookstore
   360 State Street
   West Lafayette, IN 47906
   (317) 743-9618

   Written preemployment selection tests such as the Trade Information Tests used for such vocations as welding, carpentry, sheet metal working, and engine lathe operation.

5. National Computer Systems
   Professional Assessment Services
   P.O. Box 1416
   Minneapolis, MN 55440
   (800) 328-6759 or (612) 933-2800

   Clerical, customer contact, sales, and managerial tests.

6. Psychometrics, Inc.
   13245 Riverside Drive
   Sherman Oaks, CA 91423
   (818) 783-5731

   Programmer, systems analyst, computer operator, and word processor tests.

Written Honesty Tests

InterGram, Inc.
4854 Old National Highway
Atlanta, GA 30337
(800) 227-8783

London House, Inc.
1550 Northwest Highway
Park Ridge, IL 60068
(800) 221-8378

Lousig-Nont & Associates, Inc.
3740 S. Royal Crest Street
Las Vegas, NV 89119-7010
(800) 447-3211

PBC Systems, Inc.
12810 Hillcrest Road
Dallas, TX 75230
(800) 232-5844

P.O.S. Corporation
P.O. Box 48232
Chicago, IL 60648
(800) 621-4008

Psychological Surveys
900 Jorie Blvd.
Oak Brook, IL 60521
(312) 990-8000

Reid Psychological Systems
200 North Michigan Ave.
Chicago, IL 60604
(800) 922-7343

Safe, Inc.
141 Briarwood North
Oak Brook, IL 60521
(312) 522-7834

Stanton Corporation
5701 Executive Center Dr.
Charlotte, NC 28229
(800) 523-5745

Wilkerson & Associates, Ltd.
15710 Drummet Blvd.
Houston, TX 77032
(800) 422-8326

Written Personality Tests

Bay State Psychological Associates
62 Staniford Street
Boston, MA 02114
(800) 438-2772

PBC Systems, Inc.
12810 Hillcrest Road
Dallas, TX
(800) 232-5844

Caliper Management, Inc.
741 Mt. Lucas Road
Princeton, NJ 08540
(609) 924-3800

Personnel Decisions, Inc.
45 South Seventh Street
Minneapolis, MN 55402
(612) 339-0927

Consulting Psychologists Press
577 College Ave.
Palo Alto, CA 94306
(415) 857-1444

Praendex, Inc.
40 Washington Street
Wellesley Hills, MA 02181
(617) 235-8872

London House, Inc.
1550 Northwest Highway
Park Ridge, IL 60068
(800) 221-8378

Psychological Surveys
900 Jorie Blvd.
Oak Brook, IL 60521
(312) 990-8000

Lousig-Nont & Assoc.s, Inc.
3740 S. Royal Crest Street
Las Vegas, NV 89119
(800) 447-3211

Safe, Inc.
141 Briarwood North
Oak Brook, IL 60521
(312) 522-7834

National Computer Systems
10901 Bren Road East
Minnetonka, MN 55343
(612) 936-8614

Science Research Assoc.s
155 N. Wacker Drive
Chicago, IL 60606
(312) 984-7016

Checklist of What to Look for in Commercially Developed Tests*

❑   *Well developed test construction*
  • The questions should be checked to make sure that they relate to the tasks deemed necessary for performance of the job.
  • The distractors used must seem plausible.
  • The test must not be too difficult for candidates—a 25 to 75 percent correct range is an appropriate difficulty level (meaning that 25 to 75 percent of the testing population should be able to answer the questions correctly).
  • The test should have undergone a statistical item analysis that compares scores of high and low achievers.

*SOURCE: James A. Douglas, Daniel E. Feld, and Nancy Asquith, *Employment Testing Manual*, Warren, Gorham & Lamont, Inc., p. 6–23. Copyright 1989 by Warren, Gorham & Lamont, Inc.

❑ *Test security*

- The test maker should secure the test and answer key.
- The method of test shipment should be determined.
- The test's availability should be ascertained. (Is it available only to qualified test administrators?)

❑ *Utility, validity, and reliability*

- The test should be validated in accordance with the Uniform Guidelines and have a validity coefficient above +0.40.
- Test utility figures should be available.
- Reliability figures should be available.

Checklist for Administering Written Honesty Tests*

❑ What are the components of the test?
❑ Is the test reasonably reliable?
❑ What is the extent of research from a validity standpoint?
❑ Was the test validated in accordance with American Psychological Association guidelines?
❑ Can the validity studies withstand the scrutiny of the Equal Employment Opportunity Commission (EEOC)?
❑ Do the completed studies have applicability from one geographic area to another?
❑ What type of predictive studies have been completed?
❑ Who conducted the research?
❑ Does the publisher of the test provide legal counsel?
❑ Has the publisher of the test ever been sued?
❑ What are the prohibitions against using the test?
❑ What scoring procedures are used?
❑ How is the test implemented?
❑ What are the problems associated with implementation?
❑ How much time does it take to complete the test?
❑ Will the publisher of the test maintain a policy of confidentiality as to test results?
❑ Is the test available in languages other than English?
❑ Is the test designed only for selected individuals or groups?
❑ How large of a group can be tested at any one time?
❑ Which of the following services are available from the publisher of the test?

- Psychological (to discuss validity of the test)
- Retrospective studies
- Computerized analysis of test results
- Software availability
- Legal consultation
- Client service staff availability

*SOURCE: James A. Douglas, Daniel E. Feld, and Nancy Asquith, *Employment Testing Manual*, Warren, Gorham & Lamont, Inc., pp. 14–7 to 14–9. Copyright 1989 by Warren, Gorham & Lamont, Inc.

- Training programs for test implementation
- Specialized pre-programmed computer availability
- Validity studies (at what expense; will the publisher indemnify the employer for any loss that results from a challenge to the test's validity?)

❑   Does the test account for cultural differences, so that aliens are not wrongfully excluded?

❑   Can the test be given orally and, if so, does this alter its predictive capabilities?

❑   What level of education is required to understand the test? What methods are available to assure that applicants understand the questions being asked? One risk in any written test of this nature is that less intelligent applicants are excluded merely because they do not comprehend the questions asked.

❑   What checks exist in the test to assure that intelligent applicants cannot "fool" the examination by answering questions in the way that appears most honest?

Drug Testing Laboratories Certified by the National Institute on Drug Abuse

To be certified by the National Institute on Drug Abuse, a laboratory must succeed in each of the three rounds of performance testing and an on-site inspection. To maintain certification, a laboratory must participate in a performance testing program every other month and allow periodic on-site inspections. The following are some of the laboratories to receive the Institute's certification.

Aegis Analytical Laboratories, Inc.
624 Grassmere Park Rd.
Suite 21
Nashville, TN 37211
615-331-5300

Alabama Reference Laboratories, Inc.
543 South Hull St.
Montgomery, AL 36103
800-541-4931/205-263-5745

American Medical Laboratories, Inc.
14225 Newbrook Dr.
Chantilly, VA 22021
703-802-6900

Associated Pathologists Laboratories, Inc.
4230 South Burnham Ave.
Suite 250
Las Vegas, NV 89119-5412
702-733-7866

Associated Regional and University
   Pathologists, Inc. (ARUP)
500 Chipeta Way
Salt Lake City, UT 84108
801-583-2787

Baptist Medical Center—Toxicology
   Laboratory
9601 I-630, Exit 7
Little Rock, AR 72205-7299
501-227-2783
(formerly: Forensic Toxicology Laboratory
   Baptist Medical Center)

Bayshore Clinical Laboratory
4555 W. Schroeder Dr.
Brown Deer, WI 53223
414-355-4444/800-877-7016

Cedars Medical Center
Department of Pathology
1400 Northwest 12th Ave.
Miami, FL 33136
305-325-5810

Centinela Hospital Airport Toxicology
   Laboratory
9601 S. Sepulveda Blvd.
Los Angeles, CA 90045
310-215-6020

Clinical Reference Lab
11850 West 85th St.
Lenexa, KS 66214
800-445-6917

CompuChem Laboratories, Inc.
3308 Chapel Hill/Nelson Hwy.
Research Triangle Park, NC 27709
919-549-8263/800-833-3984
(formerly: CompuChem Laboratories, Inc.,
    A Subsidiary of Roche Biomedical
    Laboratory, Roche CompuChem
    Laboratories, Inc., A Member of the
    Roche Group)

CompuChem Laboratories, Inc.
Special Division
3308 Chapel Hill/Nelson Hwy.
Research Triangle Park, NC 27709
919-549-8263
(formerly: Roche CompuChem
    Laboratories, Inc., Special Division,
    A Member of the Roche Group,
    CompuChem Laboratories, Inc.—Special
    Division)

CORNING Clinical Laboratories
South Central Division
2320 Schuetz Rd.
St. Louis, MO 63146
800-288-7293
(formerly: Metropolitan Reference
    Laboratories, Inc.)

CORNING Clinical Laboratories
8300 Esters Blvd.
Suite 900
Irving, TX 75063
800-526-0947
(formerly: Damon Clinical Laboratories,
    Damon/MetPath)

CORNING Clinical Laboratories Inc.
1355 Mittel Blvd.
Wood Dale, IL 60191
708-595-3888
(formerly: MetPath, Inc., CORNING
    MetPath Clinical Laboratories)

CORNING MetPath Clinical Laboratories
One Malcolm Ave.
Teterboro, NJ 07608
201-393-5000
(formerly: MetPath, Inc.)

CORNING National Center for
    Forensic Science
1901 Sulphur Spring Rd.
Baltimore, MD 21227
410-536-1485
(formerly: Maryland Medical Laboratory,
    Inc., National Center for Forensic
    Science)

CORNING Nichols Institute
7470-A Mission Valley Rd.
San Diego, CA 92108-4406
800-446-4728/619-686-3200
(formerly: Nichols Institute, Nichols
    Institute Substance Abuse Testing
    (NISAT))

Cox Medical Centers
Department of Toxicology
1423 North Jefferson Ave.
Springfield, MO 65802
800-876-3652/417-836-3093

Dept. of the Navy
Navy Drug Screening Laboratory
Great Lakes, IL
Building 38-H
Great Lakes, IL 60088-5223
708-688-2045/708-688-4171

Diagnostic Services Inc., dba DSI
4048 Evans Ave.
Suite 301
Fort Myers, FL 33901
813-936-5446/800-735-5416

Doctors Laboratory, Inc.
P.O. Box 2658
2906 Julia Dr.
Valdosta, GA 31604
912-244-4468

Drug Labs of Texas
15201 I-10 East
Suite 125
Channelview, TX 77530
713-457-3784

DrugProof
Division of Dynacare/Laboratory of
    Pathology, LLC
1229 Madison St.
Suite 500
Nordstrom Medical Tower
Seattle, WA 98104
800-898-0180/206-386-2672
(formerly: Laboratory of Pathology of
    Seattle, Inc., DrugProof, Division of
    Laboratory of Pathology of Seattle, Inc.)

DrugScan, Inc.
P.O. Box 2969
1119 Mearns Rd.
Warminster, PA 18974
215-674-9310

ElSohly Laboratories, Inc.
5 Industrial Park Dr.
Oxford, MS 38655
601-236-2609

General Medical Laboratories
36 South Brooks St.
Madison, WI 53715
608-267-6267

Harrison Laboratories, Inc.
9930 W. Highway 80
Midland, TX 79706
800-725-3784/915-563-3300
(formerly: Harrison & Associates Forensic
    Laboratories)

HealthCare/MetPath
24451 Telegraph Rd.
Southfield, MI 48034
800-444-0106 ext 650
(formerly: HealthCare/Preferred
    Laboratories)

Holmes Regional Medical Center
    Toxicology Laboratory
5200 Babcock St., N.E.
Suite 107
Palm Bay, FL 32905
407-726-9920

Jewish Hospital of Cincinnati, Inc.
3200 Burnet Ave.
Cincinnati, OH 45229
513-569-2051

LabOne, Inc.
8915 Lenexa Dr.
Overland Park, Kansas 66214
913-888-3927
(formerly: Center for Laboratory Services, a
    Division of LabOne, Inc.)

Laboratory Corporation of America
13900 Park Center Rd.
Herndon, VA 22071
703-742-3100
(formerly: National Health Laboratories
    Incorporated)

Laboratory Corporation of America
d.b.a. LabCorp Reference Laboratory
Substance Abuse Division
1400 Donelson Pike
Suite A-15
Nashville, TN 37217
615-360-3992/800-800-4522
(formerly: National Health Laboratories
    Incorporated, d.b.a. National Reference
    Laboratory, Substance Abuse Division)

Laboratory Corporation of America
21903 68th Ave. South
Kent, WA 98032
206-395-4000
(formerly: Regional Toxicology Services)

Laboratory Corporation of America
2540 Empire Dr.
Winston-Salem, NC 27103-6710
Outside NC: 919-760-4620/800-334-8627
Inside NC: 800-642-0894
(formerly: National Health Laboratories
    Incorporated)

Laboratory Corporation of America
    Holdings
1120 Stateline Rd.
Southaven, MS 38671
601-342-1286
(formerly: Roche Biomedical Laboratories,
    Inc.)

Laboratory Corporation of America
    Holdings
69 First Ave.
Raritan, NJ 08869
800-437-4986
(formerly: Roche Biomedical Laboratories,
    Inc.)

Laboratory Specialists, Inc.
113 Jarrell Dr.
Belle Chasse, LA 70037
504-392-7961

Marshfield Laboratories
1000 North Oak Ave.
Marshfield, WI 54449
715-389-3734/800-222-5835

MedExpress/National Laboratory Center
4022 Willow Lake Blvd.
Memphis, TN 38175
901-795-1515

Medical College Hospitals Toxicology
    Laboratory
Department of Pathology
3000 Arlington Ave.
Toledo, OH 43699-0008
419-381-5213

Medlab Clinical Testing, Inc.
212 Cherry Lane
New Castle, DE 19720
302-655-5227

MedTox Laboratories, Inc.
402 W. County Rd. D
St. Paul, MN 55112
800-832-3244/612-636-7466

Methodist Hospital of Indiana, Inc.
Department of Pathology and Laboratory
    Medicine
1701 N. Senate Blvd.
Indianapolis, IN 46202
317-929-3587

Methodist Medical Center Toxicology
    Laboratory
221 N.E. Glen Oak Ave.
Peoria, IL 61636
800-752-1835/309-671-5199

MetPath Laboratories
875 Greentree Rd.
4 Parkway Ctr.
Pittsburgh, PA 15220-3610
412-931-7200
(formerly: Med-Chek Laboratories, Inc.,
    Med-Chek/Damon)

MetroLab-Legacy Laboratory Services
235 N. Graham St.
Portland, OR 97227
503-413-4512, 800-237-7808
(x4512)

National Psychopharmacology Laboratory,
    Inc.
9320 Park W. Blvd.
Knoxville, TN 37923
800-251-9492

National Toxicology Laboratories, Inc.
1100 California Ave.
Bakersfield, CA 93304
805-322-4250

Northwest Toxicology, Inc.
1141 E. 3900 South
Salt Lake City, UT 84124
800-322-3361

Oregon Medical Laboratories
P.O. Box 972
722 East 11th Ave.
Eugene, OR 97440-0972
503-687-2134

Pathology Associates Medical Laboratories
East 11604 Indiana
Spokane, WA 99206
509-926-2400

PDLA, Inc. (Princeton)
100 Corporate Court
So. Plainfield, NJ 07080
908-769-8500/800-237-7352

PharmChem Laboratories, Inc.
1505-A O'Brien Dr.
Menlo Park, CA 94025
415-328-6200/800-446-5177

PharmChem Laboratories, Inc.
Texas Division
7606 Pebble Dr.
Fort Worth, TX 76118
817-595-0294
(formerly: Harris Medical Laboratory)

Physicians Reference Laboratory
7800 West 110th St.
Overland Park, KS 66210
913-338-4070/800-821-3627
(formerly: Physicians Reference Laboratory
    Toxicology Laboratory)

Poisonlab, Inc.
7272 Clairemont Mesa Rd.
San Diego, CA 92111
619-279-2600/800-882-7272

Presbyterian Laboratory Services
1851 East Third Street
Charlotte, NC 28204
800-473-6640

Puckett Laboratory
4200 Mamie St.
Hattiesburgh, MS 39402
601-264-3856/800-844-8378

Scientific Testing Laboratories, Inc.
463 Southlake Blvd.
Richmond, VA 23236
804-378-9130

Scott & White Drug Testing Laboratory
600 S. 25th St.
Temple, TX 76504
800-749-3788

S.E.D. Medical Laboratories
500 Walter NE
Suite 500
Albuquerque, NM 87102
505-244-8800

Sierra Nevada Laboratories, Inc.
888 Willow St.
Reno, NV 89502
800-648-5472

SmithKline Beecham Clinical Laboratories
7600 Tyrone Ave.
Van Nuys, CA 91045
818-376-2520

SmithKline Beecham Clinical Laboratories
801 East Dixie Ave.
Leesburg, FL 34748
904-787-9006
(formerly: Doctors & Physicians
    Laboratory)

SmithKline Beecham Clinical Laboratories
3175 Presidential Dr.
Atlanta, GA 30340
404-934-9205
(formerly: SmithKline Bio-Science
    Laboratories)

SmithKline Beecham Clinical Laboratories
506 E. State Pkwy.
Schaumburg, IL 60173
708-885-2010
(formerly: International Toxicology
    Laboratories)

SmithKline Beecham Clinical Laboratories
400 Egypt Rd.
Norristown, PA 19403
800-523-5447
(formerly: SmithKline Bio-Science
    Laboratories)

SmithKline Beecham Clinical Laboratories
8000 Sovereign Row
Dallas, TX 75247
214-638-1301
(formerly: SmithKline Bio-Science
    Laboratories)

SmithKline Beecham Clinical Laboratories
1737 Airport Way South
Suite 200
Seattle, WA 98134
206-623-8100

South Bend Medical Foundation, Inc.
530 N. Lafayette Blvd.
South Bend, IN 46601
219-234-4176

Southwest Laboratories
2727 W. Baseline Rd.
Suite 6
Tempe, AZ 85283
602-438-8507

St. Anthony Hospital (Toxicology
    Laboratory)
P.O. Box 205
1000 N. Lee St.
Oklahoma City, OK 73102
405-272-7052

Toxicology & Drug Monitoring Laboratory
University of Missouri Hospital & Clinics
301 Business Loop 70 West
Suite 208
Columbia, MO 65203
314-882-1273

Toxicology Testing Service, Inc.
5426 N.W. 79th Ave.
Miami, FL 33166
305-593-2260

TOXWORX Laboratories, Inc.
6160 Variel Ave.
Woodland Hills, CA 91367
818-226-4373
(formerly: Laboratory Specialists, Inc.; Abused
    Drug Laboratories; MedTox Bio-Analytical, a
    Division of MedTox Laboratories, Inc.)

UNILAB
18408 Oxnard St.
Tarzana, CA 91356
800-492-0800/818-343-8191
(formerly: MetWest-BPL Toxicology
    Laboratory)

8 Screening Applicants and Conducting Interviews

Every job vacancy should be looked at as a new opportunity for management to hire someone who can respond fully to job responsibilities, as well as to contribute to the organization's goals as change occurs during the ensuing years. In so looking at each new hire, it should become apparent that employers must take a new approach to the selection testing process in terms of both the methods used and the underlying investment assumptions about hiring costs. As discussed in the preceding chapter, there are a number of improvements that can be made to the type and extent of format selection testing methods, and employers should use various combinations of these methods to ensure the accuracy of hiring decisions. Additionally, since hiring is a costly proposition in itself, the amount of money an organization puts into the hiring process should be allocated for each vacancy to be filled as an investment in the organization's future success. These costs should be distributed among the hiring processes according to the merit of each vacant job's impact on the organization.

What this chapter will show you is how to go about screening applications and/or resumes, how you can get better results from the interview test method in terms of its reliability as a predictor of job success and its validity as an accurate measurement of the real job, and how to reduce the cost of conducting interviews. It is also being suggested that you use personal interviews as a semifinal means of screening down from six to twelve applicants (who have succeeded in other formal tests) to one, two, or three finalists you wish to begin reference and background checks on before making an employment offer to one. Until you have your applicant pool reduced to a realistic number of the more highly qualified, there is little reason to consume the time and effort of applicants or internal managers with interviews.

8.1 How to Screen Applicants More Confidently

Nearly every business uses application and/or resume screening and personal interviews as two, if not the only, preemployment selection test methods. Oddly enough, these two methods are probably the most costly and subjective of all testing methods due to the amount of personal time dedicated, and degree of personal bias that enters into the process. Screening applicant material on the one hand is a provincial way of separating unqualified, marginally qualified, and prospectively qualified applicants solely on the basis of the applicant's "paper credentials." It is therefore a process of attempting to identify those applicants with the most likely qualifications purely from information they have provided, omitted, or being speculated upon by the reviewer (often based on nothing more than a feeling).

CAUTION

Employment application and/or resume information should *not* be taken entirely at face value. Studies have shown that about 40 percent of all applicants falsify or distort information in their application materials, and about 50 percent of those submitting resumes do the same. This should not cause you paranoia. Rather, it should raise your awareness about this fact as you begin the process each time, and it creates the need to develop a "trained eye" for details that may be suspect, and therefore verified at a later stage in the hiring process.

What to Look for When Screening Application Material

Cover Letters

Cover letters normally accompany resumes but they may also be used to transmit the application form to the employer. Good cover letters should be typed, grammatically correct, and written in clear, orderly statements without an overindulgence of "fluff" conversation that makes applicants sound phony in their sincerity. The letter should be no more than one page in length, on white or another neutral businesslike color stationery, with the person's name, address, phone number, and date at the top. The letter should contain such information as

- Position sought
- Reason for seeking the job
- Referral source
- Familiarity with the employer
- Career objectives that the job would satisfy
- Special qualifications not covered by the format of the application form or resume, that relate strongly to the job

Resumes

Most resumes are decided on in two minutes or less during screening, particularly where there are numerous applications to review. Resumes should be typed, grammatically correct, neat, and orderly. Ideally, they should be original copy or the product of offset printing. However, a 1988 study of 2000 companies found that 95 percent of all resumes submitted were photocopied. This suggests that these applicants were canvassing multiple employers for a job rather than being currently employed and submitting an original resume out of singular interest in the employer's job opening.

As a general rule, quality applicants will submit resumes that are no more than one page in length for nonexempt applicants, two pages in length for exempt applicants, and possibly a third page added for higher level managerial or professional applicants who use the third page for listings of accomplishments, professional affiliations and memberships, publications, teaching assignments, or special projects. The type of information that should be provided on resumes, and scanned easily for your determination of the person's qualifications are:

- Name, address, and telephone numbers (residence and work—if currently employed). If no work number is listed, this may be an indication that the applicant is not presently employed.

- Previous employment history related to the job being applied for, beginning with most recent experience listed first and indicating the company's name, location, title of position(s) held, duration of employment, and major responsibilities held. Quality applicants are likely to additionally list their accomplishments and/or contributions as a reflection of their pride in each of their jobs.
- Education and special training related to the job beginning with high school for nonexempt applicants and college (name, location, major, dates attended, and degree granted—if graduated) for exempt applicants. Some jobs also require certain types of licensure such as CPA, P.E. (Professional Engineer), and other certifications that connote specialized training or professional credentialing.
- Applicants to exempt jobs should also be able to demonstrate their professional involvement in professional associations, officer positions held, and special contributions made to their field through membership in professional affiliations. Additionally, some applicants may also list their involvement in community or civic activities which may or may not be germane to the job or employer under consideration.
- References should be the last item on well organized resumes either by listing three to four sources by name, occupational title, address, and telephone number, or by reference to "gladly furnished upon request" since some applicants are sensitive about the privacy of their reference sources.

Application Forms

The major advantage of screening application forms is that they are preformatted with information the employer has determined is needed for this purpose. So, when designing your own application form, or using the sample provided in Appendix D, be certain that the form contains both lawful inquiries and the type of detailed information you find necessary for screening purposes. Because most employers place emphasis on prior experience, education and training, and specific skills possessed, these categories on the application form should be formatted for detail with clear instructions to the applicant as to what information is sought. Requiring detail also is a way of screening applicants, since it allows you to see clearly who has or has not provided the required information.

Application forms should be completed in ink, preferably typed, but doing so is not easy due to irregular spacing and the fact that not everyone has access to, or skill in the use of a typewriter. Information should be easily read (printed or clearly legible), neat, clean, and each inquiry answered or noted as N/A (not applicable). You should pay particular attention to such details as

- The existence of convictions for felony or criminal acts, or pleas of "nolo contendere" (no contest) for serious misdemeanors.
- The existence of any physical limitation noted by the applicants with respect to performing the job for which application is being made.
- The chronology of dates and events (the concurrency or overlap of work, school, or other events portrayed in the application).
- The qualifying level and type of education and/or training completed.
- The qualifying level and type of prior work experience that clearly illustrates the probability of the applicant's possession of requisite skills, knowledge, and abilities for the job.
- The applicant's signature and date of application as testimony of their reading, acknowledging, and accepting the informational and/or disclaimer clauses at the end of

the application form (e.g., at-will employer, information provided is truthful, authorization and release of liability for reference checks, drug testing, etc.).

How to Spot Suspicious Application Information

As previously mentioned, over one-half of all applicants lie, distort, or fabricate information on their applications and resumes to the extent of misrepresenting one or more details about their history. The absence of caution and trained eye screening of applicants has caused serious consequences for scores of unsuspecting employers, as well as employees who become the victims of masquerading new hires.

What to Look For

In order to avoid these forms of fraud and misrepresentation, and to increase your prospects of screening out those who are not being entirely honest to begin with, here are a few suggestions about how to develop a trained eye toward identifying application and resume information that may present the likelihood of phony or suspicious detail.

1. Use of words that create uncertainty or ambiguity about the applicant's work responsibilities or achievements, such as

    - "attended" rather than *graduated* from a particular school or specialized course of training
    - "completed coursework toward M.B.A. degree" as a means of possibly implying that they possess the degree when, in fact, they merely took some courses
    - "graduated from W.D.S.U. at South Carolina" (initialized colleges should be suspect) without a date of graduation, degree type specified, or major course of study.

2. Omitted information should be considered suspect, or at least worthy of marking and checking out at a later date if the applicant otherwise seems to be one of the better qualified. Omissions are more difficult to spot on resumes because the applicants are more in command of what information they provide and what they choose to omit. Nevertheless, you should ask yourself questions about provided information with respect to its fullness, clarity, or ambiguity—noting any questionable concerns you would like to have answered should the individual be invited for further consideration.

3. Omitting dates on resumes of prior employment to conceal short term employment or short tenure in the applicant's last/current job. Similar misrepresentations are made on application forms in the way of "shifting" dates of employment—usually stretching—in order to give the illusion that their employment history is continuous rather than broken by periods of unemployment. One way to spot this type of *possible* misrepresentation is to look at the reason given for leaving the former job.

    If the reason is "promotion" and the next job is in a higher position with a concurrent date, it is probably legitimate. If, on the other hand, the reason is "personal," "laid off," or "no advancement opportunity," the likelihood of shifting the date of next employment to be concurrent may be considered suspect to conceal unemployment or a possible termination. These should be marked and verified both during interviews and subsequent reference checks.

4. The types of professional associations of which the applicant claims to be a member, and offices held in such affiliations are often used to inflate the individual's professional appearance. This may be disregarded as merely "fluff" by some employers, but

the discerning employer should take such possible distortions more seriously as a potential indicator of the person's propensity to fluff their way through work assignments.

Rather than casting aside more than three professional associations as a bit excessive, you should make pointed inquiries during the interview to ascertain such factors as the frequency of their attendance at these functions, the purpose and advantage of belonging to the organization, what responsibilities they had (if an officer position held) and similar questions that are better indicators of their truthfulness in general. You should ask yourself if an applicant is going to distort information of such secondary importance as professional affiliations, what might that person be inclined to distort or treat more dishonestly in the context of protecting his or her job?

5. Regressive work history should be questioned during the interview to ascertain the truthfulness, reasons, and conditions surrounding irregular progressions (regressions) of job level, including those applicants applying for a job that pays considerably less than former salaries. There may be many plausible reasons for either regressive work history or application to a job having a lower salary, and neither of these conditions should be the basis of an automatic rejection.

    However, since they are irregularities from the normal progression of people who tend to seek progressively higher level jobs and salaries, it should be regarded as an area of concern until you have justifiable clarification. You may well find a case or two where the explanation is neither justifiable nor corroborated by references, in which case you have done your organization and employees a great service by rejecting this applicant.

6. Frequency of job changes should also be checked carefully as a matter of considering the applicant's stability, reliability, realism about employment expectations, and the maturity with which they approach each employment as a career-building opportunity. Again, frequent job changes may be more plausible for younger applicants or those in nonexempt occupations, but these changes in jobs and the accompanying reasons should be carefully scrutinized during application screening and subsequent interviews and reference checks.

Additional Preventative Measures to Take

Other measures that you should consider taking to help prevent applicant misrepresentations, or give you an early indication of such prospective distortions include

- Requiring that *every* applicant complete an employment application form, including those that submit resumes, and sign their testimony that the facts, information, and statements made on the form are truthful to the best of their knowledge. For those who submitted earlier resumes, you might find it worthwhile to compare information on the application to that on the resume, but limit the task to those who become serious contenders for the job.

- Having the hiring authority and/or supervisor of the job conduct a review of the application material among finalist applicants to check for possible misrepresentations that the reviewer may have more knowledge or insight about than you do.

- Conducting thorough background checks on *all* new hires, regardless of their reputation or job level, minimally concerning the accuracy of their education, prior employment dates and qualifications, licenses and certifications, and character references.

- Giving meaningful, measurable, and suitably difficult preemployment tests that validate the applicant's possession of *all* necessary skills, knowledge, abilities, and personal traits to verify their competence for the job in question.

Selecting Your Applicant Test Group

Screening application material is done for the purpose of identifying those with the most likely qualifications to be given further selection testing consideration, and to reject—as harsh of a reality as the word is—all others. It is also a common practice to invite several more applicants than might otherwise be needed, or even desired, in order to assure yourself that you have an adequate cross-section of those purporting to possess differing kinds and levels of qualifications. Some of these may even be initially (on paper) viewed as marginally qualified but, through testing, prove to have greater or lesser qualifications than represented—some applicants have been known to understate their skills and experience. Additionally, the testing of several applicants is advantageous from the perspective of having a pretest "reserve" group of applicants should the job or a similar position become vacant within a short time after your hiring selection of another applicant from the test group.

(Company Stationery)

_____ (Date)
_____ (Name)
_____ (Address)
_____ (City, State, Zip)

Dear (Mr./Ms.) _____:

Thank you for your application for the position of _____. We were pleased to receive many excellent applicants for this job opportunity and, after careful review of all applications received, I am pleased to inform you that your application has been accepted for further employment consideration. The selection process established for this position is as follows:

- A written test will be given to a select group of applicants on (date).
- A personal interview will be scheduled during the week of (date) for those who pass the written test with the higher scores.
- A preliminary finalist may be selected from among those interviewed to undergo the last phase of our selection process before an employment offer is made, and such additional qualifications may consist of (prior employment and character reference checks, driving and credit reports, law enforcement records search, a medical evaluation), and/or any other type of job related verification that enables (Company name) to ascertain particular suitability for this position.

In order to complete our processing of those applicants being invited for further employment consideration, we need you to call (name and title of contact person) at (telephone number) NOT LATER THAN (day and date) to confirm your further interest in our selection process. We wish to assure you that we recognize how difficult it is for busy people to undergo an employment selection process such as ours, but we hope you will understand the need for us to do so and will respect the thoroughness with which (Company name) hires superior employees. We sincerely hope that you are the one that meets our special needs, and wish you well as you enter our select group of applicants to be considered for this position.

Cordially,
(Signature)

_____ (Name)
_____ (Title)

The actual size of any test group (number of applicants to be invited) will vary depending on such factors as the number of applicants prescreened as qualified, the number of positions to be filled through a singular testing process, and the desired number of applicants to be interviewed before a semifinalist is chosen for background checking. Selection testing, then, is a process of elimination with specific numerical goals in mind with respect to how many applicants you want to move on to the next selection stage. The ideal objective is to start with as many *qualified* applicants as possible and, using increasingly refined and diverse testing methods as needed for the nature of the job, to narrow the applicant group down to the number of suitably verified and "right fit" new hires needed. The final stages of a hiring process should therefore be the personal interview followed by background checks of those to be given final consideration before making an employment offer.

The sample letter (on page 194) inviting select applicants to participate in a preemployment testing process is provided as a format and content model. It can be easily modified to suit your needs in differing test situations.

Rejecting Other Applicants Gracefully

Rejection in any form is difficult for people to cope with, and it inherently tends to be damaging to a hopeful job seeker's psyche (self-esteem) when the rejection is about a job that appealed enough to make application on the basis of perceived qualifications. Also, it may be necessary at times to reject applicants who have varying degrees of exceptional qualifications, but who do not in other ways meet the criteria used to invite a *more* select testing group. Those applicants who are qualified but rejected may occasionally take enough offense at the rejection that they vent their anger through such retaliatory measures as calling you to lodge a hostile protest or even filing a discrimination complaint.

More often than not a polite, personalized, and well constructed rejection letter will be properly received. In fact, most applicants complain more bitterly about getting no response at all.

What should be remembered about this phase of the hiring process is that if recruitment efforts have worked properly, all applications are going to eventually be rejected except one—the person you hire! Given this perspective on the number of people to which your company will have exposure, it is worth your time to develop a few different prewritten, word-processed letters that are public relations oriented yet get the essential rejection message conveyed. In other words, you let successively disqualified applicants down easily and with dignity. Failure to respond to those who have taken the time, interest, and effort to apply is not a dignified way of treating people. They and others they know may well be potential customers of your products or users of your services. The contents of rejection letters should therefore contain these elements:

1. Use company stationery and address each letter to the individual applicant, not to "all applicants for the position of _____." The letter should also be opened by Dear Mr./Ms. _____ rather than "Dear Applicant."

2. Express your appreciation for their taking the time and interest to apply for the job, and that all applications were carefully reviewed based on the demands of the job.

3. Provide a statement about either the number of highly qualified applications received or the general nature of those applications that are being given further consideration at this time.

4. Provide a dignified rejection statement such as "we regret to inform you that your application was not among those selected for additional testing for this job vacancy, but we would like to encourage you to apply for other job openings as they occur and for which you feel qualified."

5. A statement that the company will keep your application material on file for twelve months (should a similar job opening occur).

6. A closing statement wishing them "good luck in your endeavors for a new career opportunity" and a personalized salutation.

As you can see, each of these elements should possess a friendly tone and use language that conveys respect for the human side of the applicant, even if your personal view of a few of them is less than admiring. Here is a sample rejection letter that you may wish to use, or customize for your company's use.

(Company Stationery)

_____ (Date)
_____ (Name)
_____ (Address)
_____ (City, State, Zip)

Dear (Mr. or Ms.) _____:
On behalf of (Company name), I would like to take this opportunity to thank you for your interest in applying for the position of _____. We were quite pleased with the results of this recruiting effort, and it gave us the chance to review many fine applications such as yours.

We did, however, receive a very impressive number of qualified applicants with divergent types of experience and other relevant background for the position. This, of course, makes the selection process a difficult choice for us, but on the basis of our initial rating system applied to each application relative to the special needs and conditions of this position, it is our intention to give further consideration to those applicants having the most direct kinds of qualifications. While your qualifications met some or many of the preliminary requirements for this position, there were other applicants whose qualifications exceeded our expectations and who more closely fit our particular needs.

If we have similar job openings in the near future, we would be happy to reconsider your application at that time, or you are welcome to apply for other positions with (company name) for which you feel qualified.

Once again, we appreciate your interest in employment with (company name), and we wish you success in your employment goals.

Sincerely,
(Signature)
_____ (Name)
_____ (Title)

8.2 How to Plan Applicant Interviews

Applicant interviews have been taken far too casually by most managers, even those operating large companies. What must be remembered about preemployment interviews is that they are legally defined as a selection test. Moreover, the intent of applicant interviews is to evaluate very specific job and employment related traits of each applicant, *not evaluated by other testing means*, that the company has identified as significant to successful employment. To accomplish this specialized evaluation purpose with any sort of meaningful results, the interview must be just as well thought out, structured, and conducted as any other selection test if it is to be

1) considered legally valid, and 2) accomplish its intended purpose of identifying further characteristics about each applicant that are germane to the job, and selecting a quality new hire.

By and large, interviews are considered to have the least reliable success rate as a predictability measure because they are frequently conducted by untrained/unskilled individuals who

- do little more than gather biographical information from applicants and make their decisions on the basis of personality matches between themselves and the applicant;
- are unprepared to conduct a formal, well thought out and designed interview that elicits pertinent information about measurable applicant characteristics;
- talk more than they listen;
- ask superfluous, obvious, and meaningless questions that fail to distinguish applicant qualifications and unique traits; and,
- fail to make a reasonable effort at the measurement of whole job characteristics.

These shortcomings are only part of the long list of deficiencies that have been identified for years by human resource professionals, the courts, and discerning applicants. These listed weaknesses do not include the often cited examples of ill-conceived interviews where blatantly illegal questions are still being asked of applicants, or where the interview has all of the grace of a brief conversation with some overly self-esteemed manager rather than a critical testing device that bears directly on the organization's operational success. Indeed, it take so little time to make a mistake, and so much time to correct it. For that reason alone, the use of personal interviews as a key preemployment selection method demands better control over the way they are being handled and used.

Additionally, personal interviews should chronologically follow other testing methods. This is so because interviews are most reliable when used to evaluate applicant traits as a final means of distinguishing between applicants with comparable or off-setting skills, knowledge, and abilities (task oriented aptitudes), and in particular with respect to which applicant is the most likely to succeed given other "human" conditions of the job.

Setting Up Interviews

The time to establish your date, times, and location of selection interviews is well in advance (two to four weeks) of the event. This assumes, of course, that your company is willing to stop using "down and dirty" fast-tracking hire processes such as running an ad in the Sunday edition, reviewing applications and resumes on Friday, conducting shallow twenty-minute interviews on Monday, and making a hiring decision the next morning so the person can report to work by the next Monday—and then left wondering why the new hire doesn't work out very well! Fast-tracking the hiring process has never worked, it never will, and nowhere is this more apparent than with the use of selection interviews—it's that simple. Your company needs to keep in mind that interviews are the most subjective and least reliable predictor of job success among all testing methods when they are conducted in this fashion. However, their reliability and usefulness can be improved upon immensely if more effort is applied to the process, and skill applied to its execution.

Which Days Are Best?

Interviews should be scheduled in accordance with applicant availability, not that of the people conducting the interview. After all, you've put a great deal of time and money into the recruiting process to get applicants, so why would you want to schedule interviews and other preemployment tests on days when those who are currently employed are least available? The best days to conduct interviews for the sake of applicants differs slightly based on the occupational level and type. As a general rule, applicants for nonexempt entry and lower level jobs would find it most convenient to be absent from work in the middle of the week; on Tuesdays, Wednesdays, or Thursdays. Absence for these applicants on Monday or Friday raises suspicion by employers, and work for these applicants tends to peak at the beginning and end of a workweek.

Applicants who are mid- to higher-level technical, professional, and administrative employees usually find it easier to be available for testing on Mondays, Wednesdays, and Fridays if it is absolutely necessary for weekday testing. However, the first preference of these applicants—and therefore it should be yours—is Saturday. Even though most people don't like giving up a weekend day, it is a preferred day by most of these applicants because they don't have to take time away from their present work obligations, and they can maintain more discretion about their search for other employment. Mondays, Wednesdays, and Fridays will otherwise work best for them since Mondays and Fridays are the least disruptive to the *flow* of work for which most of these people would be responsible, and Wednesday is an opportunity for a mid-week pause rather than complete disruption.

For applicants to management jobs, the best day to interview is Saturday. This group of applicants are understandably sensitive to keeping their job search confidential. Additionally, their presence at work during the week is more essential than other occupational groups. If it is imperative to conduct interviews during the workweek, then the next best day is Wednesday if they do not have to travel far to get to your location, or Friday if travel is involved; the former day is least disruptive to the flow of work activities, while the latter day provides them the opportunity to investigate your locale (housing, schools, local economy, and so forth) as a prospective place to work and live.

How Much Time Should Be Allowed?

Interviews are an information gathering process, not an opportunity for a mere "look see" conversation. Sufficient time needs to be built into the questioning, listening, and evaluation effort. Similar to the variables for setting days to conduct interviews, the time it should take to *adequately* carry out a meaningful interview will vary depending on the complexity of the job in question, and the diversity of applicant backgrounds. Consider, for example, the following model of an interviewing schedule.

Model Interviewing Schedule	
• Brief review of next applicant's resume or application form for familiarity with pertinent background.	2–5 minutes
• Greeting applicant and introductions.	2–4 minutes
• Introductory remarks about the interview and one or two casual questions to make the applicant comfortable.	3–7 minutes
• Interview questioning and information collection.	20–50 minutes
• Closing remarks by interviewer and applicant.	5–10 minutes
• Completion of evaluation notes and scoring/remarks on rating form.	5–8 minutes
TOTAL	37–84 minutes

As you can see, interviews should range from approximately forty-minute to ninety-minute intervals to account for all of the details required of thorough interviewing. To do less is cutting the needed process short somewhere, and this is sure to have a damaging effect in some aspect of the evaluation results. Good interviewing is—and should be—hard work that takes time and very specific kinds of skills.

In general, the less complex the job and the less diverse the range of applicant characteristics to perform the job, the less time is needed to conduct the interview. However, you are likely to get better results from interviews if you schedule fewer applicants and take an extended amount of time to interview each of them *thoroughly*. Most of the variation in time for interview of differing jobs is in two aspects of the interviewing process: 1) the amount of time needed for specific questioning and responses; and, 2) the amount of time needed or desired to add professional touches such as getting the applicant comfortable, explaining the process, sophistication of questions, and casual pleasantries at the beginning and end of the interview. While some may regard these aspects of interview timing as a waste of the interviewer's time, they frequently become the basis of a quality applicant's later decision to accept the job as a reflection of the organization's obvious professional approach to hiring—quality begets quality.

What Environment Is Needed?

The location and environmental setting of preemployment interviewing is crucial to the outcome, yet frequently underestimated by employers who continue to interview in public locations such as restaurants or unsuitable locations like the reception area, a shop, or in the production area. To elicit and acquire the type of information needed to evaluate applicant characteristics, the location *must* be private in order to establish enough comfort for applicants to speak freely and sometimes candidly about their feelings, values, and sensitive events relating to past employment situations. If you want a rigid interview, conduct it within sight and hearing range of others; but understand that this it clearly not the proper way of interviewing.

Professional interviews are always conducted in pleasant locations such as conference rooms or private offices. Other environmental features that are important to make applicant's feel mentally and physically comfortable, and where interviewers can concentrate on the dynamics of evaluating applicants, are the following. You should use this listing of features as a guide to finding one or more interviewing locations that have *all* of these features.

- Well lit room from either indirect natural light or direct artificial light
- Light colored walls in a clean, orderly room with furniture that reflects the image your company is trying to portray
- Freedom from direct or secondary noise, including ringing telephones and other sources that disrupt and distract from concentrated interviewing
- Comfortable seating and seating arrangements such as a desk with side or opposing chair, or a conference table where there is enough room for your paperwork without it being too close or used in a distracting fashion to the applicant
- As the interviewer, you should be facing any windows so that your applicants are not enticed to stare out the window as they think and talk during the interview.

If such environmental features are not readily available at your business location, then you may want to find one nearby rather than continuing a discrediting hiring practice. You may find that merely cleaning up a small office will suffice. However, if your business is one in which the above amenities simply do not exist, then consider using the conference room of a secretarial/office leasing service who may charge by the hour, or ask for the use of a business associate's conference room. Finalist applicants can always be invited back to see the exact work location at a later date.

Selecting Interview Evaluation Criteria

Preparing for selection interviews is perhaps the most technically critical of all steps. The detail and accuracy of what is established here will determine whether the interview is a probing evaluation test of essential job knowledge and traits, or merely a personality screening device based on an exchange of learned or innate social conversation highlighted with key phrases all interviewers are led to believe they want to hear. If you hope to use the personal interview as a means of identifying a particular applicant with the "right fit" qualities for your job vacancy, then care must be taken at this stage.

What Interviews Should Measure about Applicants

Hiring the wrong person for any job is a serious and agonizing experience for all managers and every company. The most common symptom of a mismatched hire is that the employee will be quick to try various ways of altering the intended job, company policies, operating procedures, or the nature of supervision to match his or her own personal preferences. Customarily, these symptoms begin to take shape *after* the conclusion of the initial (probationary) employment period by which time the new hire has gained a sense of security about the job and sufficient familiarity with employment conditions. By this time the employer overlooks that this is still a new hire, and therefore often fails to attribute these symptoms to a hiring process mismatch.

The most important place to determine applicant matching or mismatching with the job and company is through skilled interviews. It therefore becomes imperative that interviews are focused evaluations of applicant abilities and traits based on accurate, predetermined characteristics of both the job and employment conditions in which the company operates. To achieve proper matching evaluations, you should be aware of what interviews can reasonably measure about applicants.

First, you should recognize that interviews are not the best testing method to evaluate the *job* skills and abilities of applicants. These qualifications are best tested by performance tests, prior employment references, and initial (trial) employment periods. What interviews can measure, and what should be the subjects of your focus, and important aspects of the applicant's job knowledge and those *interpersonal* skills, abilities, and traits that are predetermined characteristics of performance success. These job knowledge and interpersonal attributes include

- Comprehension and use of information
- Ability to analyze information and skills to present information
- Ability to follow verbal instructions
- Reasoning abilities
- Attitudes about people, places, events, and things that occur in employment settings
- Personal poise, control, and general demeanor (e.g., attire, sociability, sincerity, etc.)
- Personal marketing skills
- Use of time and the ability to separate superfluous from important facts
- Reaction to controlled and/or changing conditions
- Determining priorities and distinguishing between events requiring independent action or team involvement
- Personal orientation to the organization's established "culture," practices, and procedures
- Personal accountability (willingness and ability to take responsibility for own actions)
- Personal determination and orientation toward own career goals

As you can see, these is much to consider about applicants from the interview testing method if it is used in a properly focused manner. In order to draw out the specific measures for any one job, you must identify suitably congruent evaluation criteria. Therefore, considerable thought must be put into developing meaningful criteria by which you are going to evaluate applicants, and related questions that will elicit distinguishing types of answers. The place to start is with your test element lists (job requirements and employment conditions lists) mentioned in Chapter 7.

NOTICE

Don't try to shortcut this step by using only the job description to indicate what types of questions should be posed. The job description alone will not give you enough information to prepare a skilled, probing interview; nor does a probing interview mean stressful or interrogative.

Reviewing Test Element Lists for Evaluation Criteria

For each category in which the interview is intended to evaluate and rate some characteristic of the applicant, there should be one or more questions that directly correspond to, and allow measurement of, the evaluation category. Once all of the most important *and relevant* evaluation categories have been identified, the task of developing associated questions should become easier. To identify the criteria, or categories, appropriate to the evaluation of applicants for a particular job, you should use the test element lists you developed in Chapter 7, the information for which came from your original job analysis documentation.

In reviewing your test element lists, you should be able to spot various skills, knowledge, ability, and personal trait features of the job that are both important for job success, and reasonably measurable in the interpersonal question/answer method of testing. Write each of these test elements on a separate sheet of paper so that you compile an interviewing test list with such statements as

1. *Skill at communicating verbally* with others in a pleasant, service-oriented manner in which conversation is comfortable, casual, orderly, clearly expressed, and without unusual mannerisms
2. *Ability to analyze information*, organize thoughts, follow instructions, and base response on a practical approach to the situation
3. *Knowledge of the fundamental principles* and practices of positive employee relations and methods used to correct problem behaviors
4. *Ability to separate superfluous information* in order to arrive at the more important aspects of a demanding situation
5. *Individual responsiveness* to situations involving group interactions suggests a positive, flexible orientation to both individual and team player roles
6. *Personal mannerisms* are absent characteristics that might suggest such job related problems as defensiveness, disrespect, acute biases, narrow mindedness, and quick temperedness

These, of course, are merely examples intended to illustrate how you might write up the more significant skill, knowledge, ability, and personal traits that can be evaluated by the interview method. As you can see from these few illustrations, they should be worded in sufficiently clear, detailed, and descriptive terms so that very specific job situations come to mind, and from which questions can be framed. Once you have completed your listing of these evaluation categories, you should review each one asking yourself, "Can this be evaluated realistically through interview questioning?" If the answer is yes, keep it—if the answer is no or it's uncertain, discard it and figure out another way to measure that category.

Preparing Interview Rating Factors

To conduct proper and professional interviews, each applicant should be evaluated and rated against preestablished standards. To avoid the common problem of rating one applicant against other applicants (comparative ratings), you should set your standards at the level of interview performance that would achieve the "ideal" applicant, then rate each applicant against the ideal standard for the job. While no one applicant may obtain a perfect score, this practice of rating applicants against an idealistic success model has the advantage of creating a neutral standard and is more likely to result in a distinguishing range of applicant scores. Additionally, using the "ideal employee" model of setting rating standards usually reduces much of the subjective judgment of different interviewers by giving them a common rating model to guide their evaluations. Reliability of the interview is thus increased.

The specific rating factors will be derived from your evaluation categories. For example, if you have a few statements intended to measure or verify an applicant's technical and other types of job knowledge, then one rating factor should be "Job Knowledge." Rating factors vary in number and from very specific to general. Also, the scoring weight or points assigned to any one rating factor should correspond to the importance of that factor as an indicator of job success. Here are a few general rating factors that you may wish to consider for use, or at least to give you some thought-provoking ideas of how to prepare rating factors that fit the job you're trying to test.

- Verbal Communication Skills
- Written Communication Skills (when work sample used)
- Analyzing Situational Factors
- Judgment and Decision Making
- Independence of Thoughts
- Leadership
- Cooperativeness
- Work Values and Attitudes

- Composure and Control
- Ability to Follow Direction
- Interpersonal Sensitivity
- Personal Mannerisms and Behaviors
- Demeanor
- Job Preparation
- Professional Development

The rating factors you use for selection interviews should not be merely listed by title, but rather listed with a fully descriptive definition. The definition of each rating factor should convey the ideal standard in all important respects so that it is distinctively clear to the interviewer how the applicant performed in the rating factor, and thus is likely to perform in the actual job. Taking the first rating factor of "Verbal Communication Skills"—you might come up with the following definition as an example for the job of Customer Service Representative.

Verbal Communication Skills: Demonstrates the ability to converse clearly, concisely, and at different levels based on use of divergent vocabulary; uses moderate tone and pleasant, relaxed conversational style; asks for clarification to assure understanding of situations; provides complete answers without undue disruption or distractive mannerisms; is easily understood; remains polite and patient during conversation; and is knowledgeable about use of methods to calm aggressive customers.

Preparing the Rating Form

There are innumerable types, formats, and contents of interview rating forms that employers use to evaluate applicant characteristics. In fact, there are entire books available that provide several different samples of interview rating and similar employment forms that can be used as models for employers to design their own preferred form(s). One sample that depicts the necessary features for evaluation as presented in this book is provided for your use or modification in Appendix D. At a minimum, rating forms should list these features:

- title of the job being interviewed
- date of the interview
- applicant's name
- interviewer's name and title
- rating factor name and definition
- qualitative and/or quantitative scoring method
- sufficient space for the interviewer's written remarks

Rating forms serve two very important purposes that should justify their use and the added time that may be required to prepare them: 1) they are an objective means of documenting job related measures of the applicant's performance (personal notes are viewed by legal authorities as less objective than a structured rating form); and, 2) they can distinguish and describe specific results that may be used at a later date (when memories fade) to hire another applicant from the same interview, or to verify reference information on the applicant selected immediately following the interview process. Furthermore, should your interview be challenged for alleged discrimination, the rating form may be the only reasonable basis of a solid defense—along with your written list of interview questions!

Preparing Basic Interview Questions

Interviewers usually like to create their own questions based on their knowledge (or perception) of the important aspects of either the job under consideration or what they regard as an ideal applicant. If interviewers are not *highly* skilled and trained in this test evaluation method, they will instinctively use their personal perceptions, values, beliefs, and biases to determine the course of the interview, rather than using the more objective role of test evaluator based on preestablished standards. To provide interviewers with the needed touch of objectivity, you should prepare several initial questions that are directly related to each rating factor, probing for different types and levels of applicant response, and legally appropriate to the job.

From your list of interviewing questions, interviewers can select the number and type of questions they will have time to ask each applicant as "basic" questions. Basic questions can be supplemented with more "applicant-specific" questions that allow the interviewer to probe into related areas of inquiry particular to the background of each different applicant. Also, you should keep in mind that interview time passes very quickly. Therefore, the time allotted for questioning should be regarded as extremely precious given the monumental goal of evaluating a diverse field of applicant characteristics. Because of this intense value that should be placed on the effective use of questioning time for evaluation purposes, the interview should move quickly from opening pleasantries to casual, friendly, but probing questions.

The following are a few basic questions often used to get the structured interview underway. Your basic questions should be tied to rating factors specific to the job under consideration. Further, basic questions should follow any questions or clarifications asked about each applicant's uncertain work history, chronology of events portrayed on their application form, or other items you may have marked as curious (or suspicious) on their application material.

Samples of Basic Interview Questions

1. What appeals to you most about this job?
2. What do you know about (Company name)?
3. What do you regard as the more important responsibilities and performance results of a (Job Title)?
4. In what ways do you feel your prior work experience, training, and education makes you particularly suitable for employment in this job?
5. What are your strongest skills and how were they developed?
6. What parts of this job do you feel the most knowledgeable about?
7. What skills, knowledge, and abilities do you feel you need to develop or improve to achieve full competence in this job?
8. Do you prefer working alone or with coworkers (small or large groups of coworkers)?
9. What part of this work gives you the most satisfaction and why? What is it you would tend to like least about this work?
10. Describe the characteristics of supervisors you liked least from your past experience, and what effect it had on you.

You will note from these few questions that they are all: 1) job or employment related (legally valid); 2) aimed at evaluating the applicant's job skills, knowledge, abilities or traits (reliable); and, 3) allow for a range of responses (measurable). Additionally, the questions are "open-ended" thus allowing the applicant to give a personalized answer, and they are short phrases so that most of the interview time is dedicated to applicant answers—not interviewer questions. Unless you are merely verifying facts, you should never use interview time with true-false questions, nor should you use leading questions or those that seek an obvious response.

For example, a *leading* question for our Customer Service Representative job might ask, "Do you like to work with people?" What applicant in their right mind would answer "no," thus the question leads the applicant to the desired response. Similarly, an *obvious* question for this same job might ask, "If a mildly angry customer used profanity would you hit him or try to disregard his rude behavior?" Such a question may be so obvious as to appear ridiculous, but you might be shocked at how many untrained interviewers ask these types of wasteful questions. To ensure that each interview is conducted properly, *all* interviewers *must* be adequately selected and trained for the role as indicated in the following section.

8.3 How to Conduct Professional Interviews

Even the most professionally prepared interview will fail if the person(s) conducting the interview is not equally prepared. It therefore is essential that you select individuals within your organization who possess the requisite skills, traits, and willingness to be trained as interviewers, or get an experienced source from outside the company.

What should be remembered about the selection and training of good interviewers is that the role demands very specific skills and personal qualities. These skills and qualities are essential ingredients for the accurate measurement of both human qualities and employment conditions associated with the job under consideration. Some of the more significant skills and qualities you should look for in selecting good interviewers are

- Objectivity and neutrality in their evaluation of other people and employment situations.

- Curiosity about information and the ability to formulate probing questions that lead to full, complete, and accurate accounting of details.

- Skilled in the observation of people's behavior, expressed values, and ability to draw out characterizations of the individual's attitudes, temperaments, beliefs, and true experiences.

- Highly skilled at listening and evaluating both what is being said and how it is expressed as a matter of identifying the need for further information, clarification, more probing questions, or the particular orientation the applicant takes to the subject.

- Professionally poised to the extent of instilling confidence in the person being interviewed.

- Casual and friendly to the extent of making the person being interviewed relaxed, comfortable, and conversationally open to talking freely.

- Strong intuitive abilities about the character of other people based on their demonstrated responses during brief encounters such as interviews.

- Knowledgeable about the job requirements, responsibilities, conditions, and organizational expectations.

What Interviewers Should Know about Legal Issues

The two most formidable areas of employment laws with which interviewers should be familiar are discrimination and privacy rights legal issues. Presuming that your recruitment effort attracted a diverse group of applicants, and your application screening advanced an equally representative group of applicants through your testing process, then it follows that your interviewers should be seeing a similar diversity of people during interviews. You should also be aware that preemployment interviews are one of the most common places where both overt and covert discrimination occur, as well as unreasonable intrusion into legally protected privacy of applicants.

To train otherwise good interviewers on legal issues, there are a couple of approaches you should consider. First, you or whoever is to provide training should be thoroughly familiar with state and federal laws, regulations, and significant court decisions that bear on discrimination and privacy right employment practices such as applicable discussions provided in Appendix A and B of this book—at a minimum. Second, you will need to convey this information to your interviewers. There are several ways to accomplish this, but the best approach is a combination of structured (classroom) instruction, briefly compiled written information, and a brief review of salient points just prior to the beginning of every interviewing day.

Structured instruction can easily be assembled from the material contained in Appendix A and B and supplemented by state laws appropriate to your locale. Alternatively, you may wish to retain a consultant-trainer who is qualified to provide the instruction to a larger group of managers and supervisors as part of a professional development program, but with emphasis on legal aspects of interviewing. Required reading material can also be easily prepared in the way of written guidelines for interviewers such as the sample provided at the end of this chapter. Such a condensed document can be an effective way of reminding interviewers about what questions and evaluation errors should be avoided during interviews. Finally, each interviewer or panel of interviewers should receive a fifteen to thirty minute verbal orientation before beginning an interview day to set the stage and focus on such matters as legal issues, essential responsibilities and qualifications of the job under consideration, and special features of the work setting that interviewers should give special attention to.

What interviewers need to know most about legal issues is what types of questions are disallowed because of their discriminatory inference or privacy rights intrusiveness.

Discriminatory Inference Questions

Discriminatory inference means that the question places particular focus on a personal characteristic of the applicant that is, or has the appearance of, being unrelated to the responsibilities or qualifications for the job. The inference, of course, is that the personal characteristic is being regarded as a potential disqualifier by the interviewer or person posing the question, such as contained in the question, "Do you have preschool aged children?" As a general rule, if any part of an interview question is not *directly* job related, or verbally qualified to the applicant as such, then the question has discriminatory potential. At the end of this chapter is a listing of illegal interview questions on the basis of their discriminatory inference. You may wish to copy the listing and use it during interviewer instruction and briefings.

Intrusive Privacy Rights Questions

There may be any number and type of questions that employers need to have answered about an applicant before making a hiring decision, but interviews are not the place nor interviewers the people to make such inquiries. Privacy topics that tend to occur most frequently, and where legal rights to their protection exist under federal or most state laws, consist of the following:

- Applicant's use of drugs or alcohol
- Applicant's acts of dishonesty (lying, stealing, concealing, falsifying, and misappropriation of company property or assets)
- Applicant's arrest or conviction history
- Applicant's sexual behavior, lifestyle, or proclivities
- Applicant's activities during personal time
- Applicant's family members' histories

Question areas such as these should quite simply be eliminated from the interview test method. If disclosure is *necessary* to the function of the job or legitimate interests of the employer's business, then such inquiries should be left to more suitable test methods as outlined in Chapter 7. By eliminating such sensitive and vulnerable inquiries from the interview, it will give your interviewers more time to delve into specific areas of job and employment conditions suitability of your applicants.

Maintaining Control of the Interview

If you have selected interviewers who possess the traits and skills previously recommended, training them about interview conduct and rating applicants should be easy. Doing so will also put an important final touch to the professionalism and quality of results you can expect from interviews. Instruction materials and discussions should focus on these three topics in order for interviewers to gain a deeper appreciation of the behavioral dynamics involved in preemployment interviews.

Applicant Physiology

Interviews are highly interactive in nature, and the character of these interactions are often valid measures of an applicant's predisposition toward such possible job factors as the right type and level of confidence, sensitivity toward others, eagerness, pride of accomplishment, and several other traits that stem from one's inner-self. Often these thought patterns, feelings, attitudes, and personality features will manifest themselves into observable physiological functions and mannerisms of the applicant during questioning. While interviewers should not go beyond the "layman" realm of evaluating applicant traits that are observable and reasonably measurable, there are some fairly reliable physiological conditions of applicants that can be useful sources of evaluation.

First, interviewers should be aware, and expect, that applicants are likely to display signs of nervousness, anxiety, and perhaps even fear during the first several minutes of an interview. Physiological response to such *subdued* thoughts and feelings is often displayed in the way of excessive perspiration, shaky hands, quick arm or leg movements, tight or quivering voice, and flushness of skin. At the other end of the physiological spectrum are the applicant's reactions to *assertive* or *dominant* thoughts and feelings that can be stimulated during interview questioning. These types of reactions take the form of bodily rigidity, defensive or sarcastic answers, voice intonation, becoming argumentative, and observable signs of controlled anger.

Applicant physiology that results from subdued thoughts and feelings should be accommodated by casual, friendly, and informally light conversation to give the applicant a chance to settle down and become comfortable. Only when this occurs is the applicant likely to feel confident enough to talk freely, which is the primary objective of interviewing—to listen and evaluate. Conversely, physiology that results from assertive or dominant thoughts and feelings should be allowed only to the extent of evaluating the applicant's suitability to job or employment conditions, and either controlled or cut off by the interviewer thereafter.

Second, interviewers should be trained to observe and evaluate the mannerisms and body language of applicants throughout the interview process. In particular, interviewers should make note of

- "non-conjunctive" expressions (e.g., saying "I like to work with people" in a disinterested or annoyed tone of voice, or facial expressions that are contrary to what is being said);
- evasive, vague, or distracting (changing the subject) answers accompanied by a notable change in eye contact with interviewers; and,
- other physical mannerisms that appear peculiar to "normal" behavior such as fidgeting, staring out a window for prolonged periods, taking an unusual amount of time to respond to questions, sitting slumped in the chair, rambling conversation, continuous handling of a pencil (or other object), and similar applicant activities.

Interviewers should not, however, make presumptive conclusions about mannerisms that are either within the normal and expected range of behavior considering dynamics inherent in interview situations, nor those associated with possible cultural differences. For example, many nervous mannerisms fade once rapport with the interviewer is established, and there are some cultures in which it is impolite to maintain eye contact or sit too close to another person.

Interviewer Behavior

Professional interviewers must also be aware of their own behavior, manner, and appearance since the interviewer is one of the more important "environmental" features that will influence the course and results of interview dynamics. Just as the physical environment of the interview location should evoke a pleasant and professional image of the company, so too should the attire and manner of the interviewer instill comfort and confidence in the applicant.

The interviewer should approach the interview process and each applicant subject to it in a positive, enthusiastic fashion. The interviewer should be well prepared for each applicant through familiarity with their application materials, and make this familiarity known to the applicant by framing at least some questions around specific background information. Each interview should start as if it is the first one of the day, meaning the interviewer should be fresh, attentive, friendly, casual, interested, and sincere. Further, they should remain this way throughout the interview, which is one of the reasons interviewing is hard work and requires especially talented people to conduct them.

CAUTION

Interviewers must also stay in control of the interview. This includes both themselves and the applicant, as well as how the interview proceeds during the course of questions and answers. Interviewers must be cautious of posing questions that are likely to arouse unintentional antagonism, insult, or defensiveness among applicants. Therefore, the interviewer needs to be trained in framing questions properly, use of voice tone and intonation, facial expressions that communicate what is intended, and similar mannerisms aimed at conveying particular messages or soliciting particular responses—except "poker faces" which are usually construed by applicants as boredom or callousness.

Interviewers must be prepared to control rather unexpected reactions and behaviors of applicants. These can range from mild forms of obvious discomfort such as anxiety, to uncontrolled perspiration or even vomiting (nervous stomach after consumption of a meal—a good reason not to conduct lunch interviews), to an occasional applicant who turns hostile or obnoxious. Likewise, the timing of interviews must be observed carefully so that they start and end on schedule, do not get distracted with elaborate, uninformative answers, and at least all basic questions get a chance for response and evaluation.

Evaluation Errors

Finally, interviewers should be trained on frequently encountered types of evaluative errors that stem from the interviewer's own set of biases and other predispositions that have the effect of "polluting" the rating of applicants during interviews. You will also recall that the absence of personal bias and similar predispositions is one of the selection traits of professional interviewers, but the fact remains that human nature predisposes everyone to some type of perceptive screening device.

One such perception screen that interviewers should be aware of, and therefore guard against, is the temptation to make a premature evaluation on the basis of a *first impression.* Research in this area has indicated that many interviewers tend to rely on the impression created by an applicant during the first two-to-six minutes of an interview. To counter such a fundamental predisposition of the first impression of an applicant, interviewers need to be reminded to keep an open mind so that changes in applicant characteristics can be more objectively evaluated as a result of the entire interview as it unfolds. Likewise, the interviewer's *general perception* of applicants who display certain types of attire, grooming, speech, and mannerisms should be controlled within the context of the job and employment setting, and evaluated accordingly after the conclusion of the interview to allow a more complete view of the individual.

Two other influential types of evaluation errors result from either singular statements by applicants in the course of an interview, or from an interviewer's lack of ability to make critical distinction judgments about other people. Singular statements of applicants that trigger a highly positive or negative response by interviewers to the extent that all other applicant statements become secondary are referred to as either *Halo Effect* or *Oppositional Effect*. Conversely, when an interviewer's own nature is to avoid making a distinctive range of judgments about other people, this poses a problem with compressed scoring of applicants referred to as *Leniency* (scoring all applicants higher than they should be for purposes of making critical distinctions), or *Central Tendency* (scoring all applicants in a closely clustered range of average to high-average scores).

8.4 How to Use Advanced Interviewing Techniques

Thus far, you have learned a great deal about how to select the right applicants for job testing, preparing the right kind of interview testing materials, and developing a professionally conducted interview to ensure that the right hiring decision is made. If you wish to add even more professional sophistication to your interview testing process, then there are a couple of further areas that you may wish to consider during the developmental and conduct stages of interviews. These include the use of advanced interviewing techniques such as panel interviews, supplementing basic questions with more advanced ones, rating applicants based on succinct distinctions, and collaborative selection decision making.

Replacing Individual Interviews with Panel Interviews

The singular advantage to using only one person to conduct interviews is saving time of other managers or supervisors. But, if in fact, other managers and supervisors are being used as successive interviewers, it would make much more sense to put them together as a panel to conduct one collective interview for a slightly longer interview period in a planned, structured setting. It is also more cost efficient to involve more than one interviewer in this way. For example, if three successive interviews are conducted by separate individuals, each for an interview period of forty-five minutes (thirty minutes interviewing and fifteen minutes for before and after tasks), then the process has taken two hours and fifteen minutes per applicant. It should be obvious that less time and better results would be achieved by scheduling fewer top contenders, say six to eight, for extended interviews of one to one and one-half hours per applicant.

Further, the cliche that "two (or three) heads are better than one" was probably derived from just such an example of group dynamics as the observations, evaluations, and resultant decision making that is intended to occur with employment interviews. Indeed, it is far more difficult for one person to ask questions, listen carefully to responses, take notes, and at the same time be a good observationalist. Panel interviews provide interviewers with more opportunity to listen, observe, and take notes while other questioning is taking place.

Consequently, panel interviewers are more conjunctive about what they ask, hear, and see in the same applicant with respect to important features of the job, rather than roaming about on different topics as they occur to them, as happens in individual, unplanned interviews. If you haven't used panel interviews before, arrange a few of them, then compare the difference in results to the former method of individual interviews and the confidence of hiring decision making.

Using Advanced Questioning Techniques

Until the late 1980s, preemployment selection interviews had been traditionally structured around the objective of acquiring job task information about the applicant. This was based on the theory that the applicant's job skills, knowledge, and abilities were the primary determinant of performance success. Interview questions and rating factors were therefore framed around the applicant's explanations of past work experience, education and training, and responses to questions about type and level of job abilities.

It was then recognized that these were task traits, and tasks measure only the "what" of job performance. What was missing was the "how" of job performance along with associated behavioral measures of "how" the applicant would be most inclined to adapt to environmental, operational, and organizational conditions that are unique to each employer.

Thus, emphasis shifted from task interviewing to behavioral interviewing. Behavioral interviewing incorporates tasks, but assumes that the better qualified applicant is the one who demonstrates those ability and trait characteristics that define *how* the job is to be performed successfully. Measurement of applicant distinctions in likely success factors is based on questions aimed at doing (task), thinking (cognitive reasoning and attitudes), and interacting (behavioral orientation). For example, the applicant response of, "I know how to operate all types of office equipment" is traditional task-only information. However, this information is not measurable to any reasonable extent nor does it convey more important traits like how the equipment is operated, what priorities or work methods are used before use of the equipment, nor how the applicant works with others using the same equipment.

To conduct this type of advanced interviewing, employers have to take a much closer look at each job to identify what specific task and trait characteristics are most important for job performance as well as employment success. Further, these factors have to be suitable for measurement in the interview setting. Once task and trait factors are identified, the next step is to frame questions that replicate actual job situations in a sufficiently probing, revealing, and distinguishing manner. To accomplish advanced interview results that lead to more accurate and reliable selection decisions, you should incorporate one or more of the following questioning techniques into the interview process.

Accomplishment Questions

The past accomplishments of applicants related directly or even indirectly to the job under consideration are good indicators of applicant-job *matching*. Accomplishments represent a preexisting demonstration of what the applicant has done, how and why it was done, and what the performance outcome was. What should be clarified when asking about accomplishments is whether the applicant initiated and handled them, or merely had partial or indirect involvement in them. By not making such clarifying inquiries, you can easily be deceived by an applicant who makes such inference remarks as, "I reduced the company's staffing budget by $458,000 in 1991 through a study of job realignments." It is not clear from this statement as to exactly what the applicant did in relation to the study or its resultant savings to the company.

In posing questions to applicants about their accomplishments in areas related to the job under consideration, applicants can additionally be led into associated questioning about work related attitudes and reactions to situations that arose in the course of past accomplishments. These responses then become measures of the applicant's prospective employment *fit*. It should be understood that fit does not mean cloning; rather, it means that the applicant

- Can lead and follow in the right situations
- Will work well in the type and variety of circumstances associated with the job and operational conditions

- Has a desirable, compatible orientation toward work, relationships, problem solving, creative expression, and the nature of the organization's business
- Is aligned with the organization's philosophy, culture, policies, and ways of conducting business

When interviews focus on job matching and employment conditions fit characteristics, applicant (scoring) distinctions become much more apparent and selection decisions more vivid.

Situational Questions

Situational questions can be effective measures of both task abilities and trait characteristics of differing applicants. They are more reliable and valid indicators of performance success than speculative task-only questions if they are properly framed to replicate actual job responsibilities and conditions. To be effective at bringing out distinctive applicant abilities and traits, questions should be selected on the basis of either actual or reasonable hypothetical situations; they should be moderately difficult in their situational complexity; and they should involve both task and trait elements. The following questions include both task and trait elements:

1. "What would you do if you were reconciling monthly customer records and discovered that another employee was making consistent errors?"
2. "If you were out on a job site working with a group of three other employees and two of them were 'horseplaying' by dueling with shovels, what steps would you take if one of them was seriously injured?"
3. "One of the five employees you supervise is regularly late to work, immaturely defiant toward your directions, and makes excuses to cover up work errors. Describe the actions you feel should be taken with this employee."

Because the range of desirable answers is not obvious, applicants are more likely to answer from their own perspective rather than speculating as to what the interviewer wants to hear. Situational questions of this type have the advantage of allowing you to evaluate the applicant's job knowledge, types of skills applied to differing situations, and reasoning, methods, values, and belief traits—all of which are more accurate measures of how well differing applicants are likely to perform since questions reflect actual job and employment conditions.

Three-Tiered Questions

Three-tiered questions are like a "rolling scenario" in that the question is framed in three progressively more difficult parts in order to measure distinctions of skill, knowledge, and/or trait characteristics among applicants. This technique is the most advanced and tell-tale about applicants because it allows interviewers to evaluate each applicant's *depth* of job and employment suitability. You can use either job knowledge, past accomplishments, or situational questions as the basis of framing three-tiered questions by merely breaking the type of question into three distinguishing levels of difficulty.

If the applicant is vague, inaccurate, or has difficulty with the first tier, you need not create an embarrassing interview situation by posing the second or third level of difficulty of the same question. Rather, you should evaluate the applicant according to his or her level of question performance. Consider, for example, the following two illustrations of three-tiered questions.

1. *Job Knowledge Question*

   First Tier (easy): "What are the five basic functions of management?"

   Second Tier (moderate): "What does 'controlling' mean with respect to a company's operating policies?"

   Third Tier (difficult): "What is the relationship between personnel policies and a company's need to control productivity of its employees?"

2. *Situational Question*

   First Tier (easy): "What would you do if your supervisor was absent for the day and you were uncertain about the priority of work given to you by three different people?"

   Second Tier (moderate): "Suppose that the last person to assign work to you was the company President. Would your decisions or actions change? If so, why?"

   Third Tier (difficult): "How would you be inclined to handle this work situation if one of them was the aggressive Sales Manager, another was your supervisor's boss—the compassionate Administrative Director—and the third was the company President known to be suspicious of the Administrative Director's productivity?"

In addition to evaluating the applicant's *level* of abilities and traits in handling three-tiered questions, you should also evaluate such related factors as decisiveness, justified changes in decisions or actions, methods and approaches, and similar characteristics that are by-products of the responses to increasingly more difficult job conditions.

Advanced Interview Rating Techniques

There is nothing mysterious or difficult about the use of advanced techniques to rate applicants based on their performance in the interview process. But, few employers even bother to take notes, let alone use a rating form, to guide their selection decisions from interview results. So the use of advanced rating techniques consists of just a few added steps that help to make distinctions among applicants clearer, better described and documented (legally defensible and useful for recall at later dates), and more precise measurements of those abilities and traits that are true predictors of performance success. If these attributes appeal to you, then you should consider using the advanced techniques that follow.

Advanced rating techniques must, at a minimum, identify the job's evaluation criteria and resultant rating factors previously discussed in this chapter. Second, a rating form must be used on which the rating factors are identified, defined, and preferably given some value of their relative weight to other rating factors, such as the point values indicated on the sample form in Appendix D. Third, interviewers must be skilled at taking notes during the interview. These notes must be succinct, objectively stated evaluations of applicant responses and characteristics based on preestablished and job related test elements. Other rating considerations you should use to achieve advanced and practical results of the interview process are as follows.

Using Quantitative and Qualitative Ratings

There remains much debate among human resource professionals about whether quantitative (numerical) or qualitative (descriptive) rating of applicant interviews are best. The argument is normally based on which technique is a more accurate or useful measure for selection decision making. Quantitative ratings have the advantage of displaying more precise distinctions among a group of applicants, but can be challenged as a mere attempt to appear scientific when, in fact, the degree of evaluative precision is not that sophisticated. Quantitative ratings, on the other hand, have the advantage of allowing more decisional room since rating descriptions can utilize any assortment of each applicant's abilities and traits that the rater deems beneficial or adverse, but this type of subjectivity and lack of controlling job standards is the basis for its challenge.

Both techniques have their advantages and challenges. To achieve more reliable, advanced use of interview ratings, you should first eliminate the source of their primary challenge, then use *both* techniques concurrently as illustrated on the sample form in Appendix D. To eliminate the challenge of quantitative ratings, each rating factor should be preassigned a score range that reflects the relative weight of that factor to others being evaluated (say using a 100% scale), and then define sub-range scores based on different types of applicant responses. If, for example, one rating factor carried a value of 0–10 points, then you should be able to break different applicant responses down into such sub-range scores as 0–3, 4–6, and 7–10 points. Quantitative rating thus leaves you with the advantage of displaying usable, decision making distinctions in each rating factor among competing applicants.

To eliminate the challenge of qualitative ratings, the descriptive statements that define each different level of the applicant's *overall* performance should be tied to the relative value of all rating factors, or at least distinguishing in terms of how each applicant is evaluated as likely to perform in the job. With this improvement to descriptive ratings each applicant can be seen in a clearer light with respect to their level of job abilities, responsiveness to supervision, training needed, and prospective adaptation to employment conditions.

Changing Scores When Justified

Applicant ratings should always be done initially in pencil. Why? Because pencils are equipped with erasers, and erasers are a clean way of correcting the frailties of human judgment. The desire or need to change scores at any point during an interview process will lessen if the interviewer uses "ideal" rather than "comparative" evaluations of applicant responses. Ideal evaluations allow the interviewer to rate each response against a preestablished standard, whereas comparative evaluations create confusion about standards because the interviewer is rating each applicant's response against the responses of other applicants. Consequently, "ideal" standards evaluations result in fewer score changes while "comparative" evaluations result in frequent score changes simply because each successive applicant can redefine the rating standard.

At the end of the interview day, when all applicants have been given initial scores, the interviewer should reexamine his or her notes and fully reflect on the performance of each applicant in order to gain a more complete perspective of the applicant group. Then, the interviewer should lay out each rating form in order of highest to lowest scores, and set aside those who received failing scores. It is at this time that the interviewer should consider whether or not the scoring order of applicants is proper, and if the score that separates each applicant is sufficiently accurate. If either of these conditions do not exist, the interviewer should change the scores in suitable rating factors to reflect a more accurate accounting of the day's interviewing results, followed by completing each form in ink including the interviewer's signature and title.

Disqualifying Deviant Ratings

Deviant ratings are those in which an interviewer either rated and/or remarked on the basis of unlawful discrimination, privacy rights violation, or similarly "polluting" kinds of inquiry or evaluative notations that lead to the applicant's rating. The effect of a deviant rating is that it serves to *destroy* the integrity of the interview process, and casts a doubtful shadow on other applicants rated by the same interviewer. Also, should a claim of discrimination or other unlawful acts result because deviant ratings were not disqualified, your company could then be exposed to a more comprehensive examination of all other employment practices and decisions associated with the alleged impropriety. Therefore, deviant ratings should be disqualified even if doing so means that all applicants have to be rescheduled for interview by a different interviewer. Correcting the error is a better decision than risking erroneous results, including the wrong hiring decision.

The best way to eliminate the occurrence of deviant ratings is to select skilled people to conduct interviews and train them thoroughly as suggested earlier in this chapter. If your company does not select and train interviewers to be professionals, it is advisable to have a qualified representative of your human resources department (if your company has such) sit in on each interview to monitor questions, verbal and written remarks, and score for their objectivity.

Selecting the New Hire by Collaborative Decision Making

A final advanced interviewing technique goes back to the previously stated concept that "two heads are better than one." The fact that hiring and other important decisions bearing a direct impact on a business' success is traditionally made by one person—"the hiring authority" as we like to refer to him or her—coupled with the fact that too many mismatched hiring decisions are being made, should suggest that Western civilization's emphasis on one-person responsibility has been taken to a compromising extreme. While it may be entirely reasonable for organizations to create a separation of powers through delegated responsibilities in *some* decisional circumstances, it should not necessarily follow that *other* decisions—like hiring—should likewise be relegated to just one person.

Quite simply, hiring decisions are too important to subordinate to the culture of one-person responsibility (along with termination decisions). The time has come for management practices in the Western Hemisphere to change their orientation toward how decisions are made, and what kinds of new methods are more beneficial, to the greater interests of the organization as a whole. With respect to such employment decisions as hiring, the answer lies in collaborative decision making.

Collaborative decisions on new hires involve direct participation of one or a few other key people in the organization whose operation will be influenced in some important way by the new hire. Representatives of the "home" work unit (formerly hiring authority) and "influence" work units would be included in the interviewing process, individually or better yet collectively, and thereafter collaborate on which applicant is regarded as being the quality hire sought by all. Consensus decision making is the ideal result, but disagreements can be resolved by either final decision resting with the "home" manager or a higher, neutral authority. At a minimum, collaborative hiring decisions inherently shed more light and a different perspective on the evaluation of applicant suitability when more than one manager who is influenced by the decision is allowed to get involved.

Checklist for Interview Preparation and Set Up

Selecting Interview Day, Times, and Location

Job Type	Day	Times
Nonexempt—Lower Level	❏ Tuesday-Thursday	❏ 40–50 min.
Professional, Technical, and Administrative	❏ Saturday preferred ❏ Mon., Wed., or Fri.	❏ 1–1½ hrs.
Managerial and Executive	❏ Saturday preferred, or ❏ Wednesday, or Friday if travel is required	❏ 1–2 hrs.

Location Features

- ❏ Private and quiet room without noise or distractions
- ❏ Well lit and nicely furnished room that represents the company's proper image
- ❏ Comfortable seating and desired seating arrangement
- ❏ Conference room or orderly office setting

Selecting Rating Factors, Form, and Basic Questions

- ❏ Review test element lists
- ❏ Review job description and/or job analysis documents
- ❏ Discuss important job requirements and working conditions with immediate supervisor
- ❏ Identify rating factors and write definitions
- ❏ Assign scoring weights or rating values to each rating factor
- ❏ Prepare rating form
- ❏ Prepare basic questions to be asked of all applicants

Selecting and Training Interviewers

Interviewers selected on their possession of such skills and traits as

- ❏ Objectivity and neutrality
- ❏ Job knowledge
- ❏ Casual friendliness
- ❏ Professional poise
- ❏ Interpersonal assessment ability
- ❏ Observation and listening skills
- ❏ Natural curiosity and ability to pose probing questions

Interviewers trained on such legal issues as

- ❏ Discriminatory inference questions
- ❏ Intrusive privacy rights questions
- ❏ Misrepresentation of the job or company

Interviewers trained on interviewing conduct and behavior issues

- ❏ Applicant physiological awareness
- ❏ Interviewer behavior and conduct
- ❏ Interviewer evaluation errors

Preparation and Use of Advanced Interviewing Techniques

- ❏ Use of panel interview rather than individual interviewer considered; if used, panel interviewers scheduled
- ❏ Advanced question techniques developed and reviewed with interviewers
  - ❏ Accomplishment questions
  - ❏ Situational questions
  - ❏ Three-tiered questions
- ❏ Interviewer(s) instructed to take notes and use for descriptive evaluations of each applicant
- ❏ Rating of applicants based on use of quantitative and qualitative scoring
- ❏ Collaborative decision making used for selection of the prospective new hire

Materials Needed for the Interview Day

- ❏ Copy of applicable job description
- ❏ Sufficient number of rating forms plus a few extras
- ❏ Application materials for each interviewer
- ❏ Writing pad, pencil, and pen for each interviewer
- ❏ Water or other refreshment and glasses

Illustration of Discriminatory Interview Questions

In an attempt to ensure that job applicants do not have reason to believe they have been discriminated against during employment selection processes, the following has been prepared for your reference. These samples of discriminatory, or potentially discriminatory, questions should be known by all supervisors and managers having hiring authority, interview involvement, or other types of participation in the company's hiring processes. Please read them carefully for complete familiarity. Should the company discover that you have posed such unlawful questions to job applicants, or employees, your involvement in the hiring process will be terminated and you may be subject to additional personnel action by the company.

Subject	Unacceptable Questions	Acceptable Questions
Age	Any question expressing or implying a preference for a specific age group, particularly those which identify applicants over 40 years of age.	Are you over 18 years of age? If hired, can you furnish proof of your age and date of birth?
Race/ National Origin	What is the origin of your surname? Asking certain applicants if they speak particular foreign languages based on their physical or surname appearances.	No reference to an applicant's color or race is acceptable. Asking all applicants about one particular foreign language skill required in the job. Are you a U.S. citizen or can you furnish proof of your legal right to be employed in the U.S.?
Arrests/Convictions	Any questions relating to the number and kinds of arrests of the applicant. Arrests do not necessarily mean guilt, and not all types of convictions are predictors of future job behavior.	Number and kinds of convictions for criminal offenses (applicant should be told that such information will not necessarily be disqualifying).
Sex	Why do you think a man/woman is best for this job? Do you think you can supervise men/women? How well do you work with men/women who don't like to work with other men/women?	What do you think are the abilities required for successful job performance? What has your supervisory experience been? How well have you worked with both men and women?
Marital Status/ Transportation	Marital status, family plans, ages of children, child care arrangements, or references to spouse. With whom do you reside? Do you live with your parents, husband/wife, children? Do any of your relatives work? Do you own a car? What make and year is your car?	Is there anything that would prevent you from meeting scheduled work days/hours? Do you have relatives working at this company? Do you have a reliable means of transportation to ensure regular work attendance?
Education/ Experience	Do you have a high school diploma/college degree? Are you willing to take courses on your own time and at your own expense if you get this job? How many years have you been performing this work?	What educational coursework or special training have you had that provided you with the knowledge and skills to perform this job? What type of experience have you had performing the work related to this job?
Religious/Political Affiliation	Any question that solicits information about the applicant's religious or political beliefs or practices.	Is there anything known to you that would interfere with your performing this job, working overtime or weekends (if required by the job), or complying with company policies?

(continued)

Subject	Unacceptable Questions	Acceptable Questions
Physical Condition	Do you have any physical disabilities? Have you ever had a job-related injury? Have you ever filed a workers' compensation claim? Any questions about physical handicaps that the applicant may have, or appears to have.	Do you have any physical conditions which may limit your ability to perform all of the physical demands of this job? Are you aware that employment may be contingent on passing a physical exam?
Financial/Credit	Do you have any overdue bills? Have you ever had a wage garnishment? Do you own or rent? Have you ever filed for bankruptcy?	If appropriate to the job, this information can only be ascertained by other means. How long have you resided in this area?
Birthplace and Residence	Any questions soliciting information about the applicant's or parent's birthplace, or requiring the applicant to submit birth, naturalization, or baptismal records.	Questions relating to the applicant's place of residence, length of residence in the region of the employer's locale, and/or the applicant's future locale plans.
Military Experience	Have you ever served with a military organization other than the U.S. armed forces? Are you an active member of the National Guard or any Reserve unit? Dates and conditions of discharge.	Questions relating to skills acquired through any branch of the U.S. armed forces. (If applicable), Was your separation from active duty for reasons other than an honorable discharge?
Organization(s)	Do you belong to, or participate in, the activities of any clubs, societies, lodges, or special interest groups? (where the answer may indicate the applicant's race, religion, etc.)	Are you an active member in any trade or professional organization and, if so, what roles have you assumed?
References	Would you be willing to provide us with the name of your pastor (or other religious leader). Any question asked of applicant's former employer or character references pertaining to the applicant's race, sex, religion, national origin, age, marital/family status, physical disabilities or medical condition, or sexual orientation.	Names, addresses, and phone numbers of persons willing to provide professional and/or character references for the applicant on job related conditions. Questions concerning the applicant's willingness to sign an authorization for the employer to obtain a narrative (written) job reference from former employers.

Interview Guidelines on How to Conduct Preemployment Interviews

Preemployment interviewing is one of the most critical steps in the testing process used to hire new employees. Since most people are not familiar with many of the technical aspects of interviewing, the company feels that the following information might serve to minimize any questions, or eliminate any misconceptions, you may have as an interviewer. Additionally, these guidelines are prepared with state and federal nondiscriminatory laws in mind, as well as the use of modern testing methods, techniques, and practices characteristic of professional human resource management operations.

The purpose of an interview is to give each applicant the opportunity to illustrate his or her possession of the personal qualities, characteristics, and capacities necessary to perform the job in a competent, desirable manner. The burden of proof rests with the applicant, but the responsibility for conducting and directing the interview, and inducing applicants to supply relevant information, rests with you—the interviewer. The questioning, observing, and evaluating process should be directed toward gathering information which is material to the job and distinguishing among applicants. Therefore, questions should be short, probing, and clarifying so that most of your time is used for listening, evaluating, and taking notes on applicant responses. Additional thought should be given by interviewers to the following types of preparation and conduct of interviews.

1. **Before the Interview,** please read the applicable job description so that you are completely familiar with the required duties, skills and knowledge requirements, and personal traits necessary for successful performance of the job. After studying these factors carefully, review the rating form and in particular rating definitions so that the relationship between the job and ratings are clear to you. You should consider how each rating factor relates to the job duties and requirements. As you do this, you should begin getting an impression of the "ideal" applicant for this job in terms of how they would respond to interview questions.

   While you have the job requirements and an image of the ideal applicant in mind, write down five to eight moderate to difficult questions (based on the rating factors) you feel will probe each applicant's job knowledge, abilities, or personal traits to do the job well. The interview results will be more effective if you phrase your questions in a manner that cannot be answered by a "yes" or "no," or equally obvious response. For example, you may wish to ask such open-ended questions as, "please give me your view on _____," or "can you explain how _____?" Generally, questions that ask how, what, who, or why tend to encourage the applicants to talk about their experience, reasoning, judgment, and abilities, thereby allowing you to observe and evaluate each applicant's performance. After developing your questions, put them to the following test.

   - Could this question unduly antagonize the applicant?
   - Does this question require or solicit an answer relating to the applicant's race, color, national origin, age, sex, marital status, religion, or physical handicap?
   - Is this question potentially intrusive upon an applicant's protected privacy rights such as their credit worthiness, sexual lifestyle, use of drugs or alcohol, arrest record, and the like?
   - Is there any aspect of this question that is not job related?
   - Can this question only be answered by advanced knowledge beyond the scope of the job?

   If your response was "yes" to *any* of these tests, you should either rephrase or eliminate the question.

2. **The Interview Process** begins with an individual review of each applicant's resume or application form before the applicant is called in. Once the applicant is introduced to the interviewer, questioning should commence promptly. An attempt should be made to make the applicant feel at ease, which will enable them to feel more expressive—thereby giving you more information to evaluate. Therefore, it is a good idea to open the interview by asking the applicant to summarize their preparation for this job (experience and qualifications). This is a familiar subject to the applicant and gives you the basis for posing your prepared questions.

   Questions to the applicant should then rotate among any other interviewers present so that each interviewer has the opportunity to pose questions which form the basis of evaluations. Please try to ask the same *basic* questions of all applicants in order to maintain fair continuity throughout the process. However, it is recognized that each applicant varies in their relative strengths and weaknesses. You are therefore encouraged to pursue additional questions based on information brought out by basic questions if doing so will enhance your ability to evaluate the applicant—so long as the questions remain job related. Also, you should not hesitate to ask probing, clarifying, or pressured (not aggressive) questions if you believe it will bring out an applicant's ability required in the job. This type of job simulation can often be presented best by asking the applicant to respond to a (realistic) hypothetical situation.

3. **In Concluding the Interview,** you should attempt to leave the applicant with a positive feeling toward the job and company, and avoid making misrepresentations of either. A moment of relaxation or a friendly comment at the close of the interview is appreciated by the applicant. Always try to remember to end the interview by asking the applicant, "Is there anything I (we) might have overlooked about your qualifications, or do you have any questions you would like to ask us?" Then, end the interview with a statement like, "Thank you for your time and interest in this job, it was a pleasure meeting you, and you should receive notice of the results within _____ (one to two weeks)."

   After the applicant has left the room, interviewers are welcome to discuss the relative merits of the applicant's performance. The purpose of such a discussion before scores are assigned is to allow interviewers to share their perspectives of the applicant's answers and various aspects of their performance. By no means should this discussion be used to sway an interviewer's opinions.

   Before rating the applicant by assigning a tentative score (in pencil), you should consider the following evaluation errors that are frequently made as a result of the personal interactions between applicants and interviewers:

   First Impression: Forming an opinion of the applicant throughout the interview based on the first thing demonstrated by the applicant; usually related to their personality or appearance.

   Halo Effect: Judging the applicant as a high performer from one very appealing answer or personal trait.

   Central Tendency: The desire to "play it safe" by assigning average or narrow range scores to all applicants in order to avoid the seeming harshness of using a fuller range of scores.

   In other words, it is best to maintain an open mind until the interview is over and all evidence is in.

4. **Rating the Applicant** is sometimes a difficult task at best, and consequently requires your most objective judgment and assessment. You should try to avoid judging them on the basis of being in line with your thinking (the "similar-to-me" cloning approach), for it is they—not you—who are being evaluated for their individual contributions to the company. You should consider the effectiveness and implications of their answers rather than whether or not the answer was the one you wanted. Keep in mind that frequently

there is more than one right answer to any given question or situation depending on one's perspective or experience. The applicant's reasoning, judgment, and decision making abilities may be more important than the rightness of the answer itself.

To make your assessments effective, do not hesitate to use the full rating scale. Only by assigning higher scores to better qualified applicants, lower scores to those less qualified, and disqualifying scores to those who fail to demonstrate suitability will you ensure that the interview has its properly intended weight in determining sequential ordering of applicants for hiring consideration. If you are not the person to make the hiring decision, put yourself in his or her position. That is, if this was *your* job vacancy and you were considering these applicants, how would you want them rated and arranged in rank order?

Specific written comments, whether positive or negative assessments of their suitability for the job or company employment, are extremely helpful to the hiring authority at the time of selection decisions. For applicants you rate as unacceptable (disqualified), it is imperative that you cite specific qualification or performance weaknesses related to the job which rendered them unacceptable. Please bear in mind that all written comments should be as objectively phrased as possible.

After completing your rating of designated job factors, and preparing your written assessments, you are to then assign one final score on the bottom of the evaluation form. This score need not be an absolute numerical average of the scores assigned to categorical rating factors since some rating factors are more or less important than others.

By following this guide, you should find the task of interviewing an easier, more pleasant, and reliable way of determining the prospective success of new hire decisions. Your participation and cooperation in this most important phase of the company's employment selection process is very much appreciated.

9 Making Employment Offers and Negotiating Employment Agreements

The decade of the 1990s has seen the start of a transformation from employers making simple offers of employment which were unconditionally accepted by job aspirants to an era of negotiating employment packages. Standardized pay plans became flexible compensation, company-defined benefits plans were converted to cafeteria or pretax employee benefit (IRS 125) accounts, fixed work hours and patterns changed to flexible schedules, family and health programs were added, paternalistic management gave way to worker involvement, performance became a measure of value added, and a host of similar changes began to take shape that would redefine the nature of the employer-employee relationship for years to come. This was a gradual shift by a work force who wanted more than a job, who disavowed being treated as a commodity, who valued the quality of life instead of worshiping the paycheck, and who saw employment as a long term investment in their occupational growth.

Further, as the demand for even more educated and talented workers continues to increase, and the need for an unskilled work force declines, employers will eventually be forced to revamp the entire realm of traditional employment operations to conform to the individual needs of this highly diverse work force. It will require vast changes in personnel policies, work relationships between management and employees, innovative programs to maintain attractive incentives for employees to stay, flexible everything, and perhaps even renegotiating individual employment agreements rather than merely deciding the employee's annual merit increase. To resist these kinds of changes may spell (competitive) doom for your company. The time has come for those who are responsible for employment operations in their organizations to begin thinking about converting traditional practices to more flexible ones that provide employees with choice, opportunity, and involvement.

Not all employers will be able or willing to change their approach to employment offers or operations at the same rate, or to the same extent. Your job thus becomes one of assessing the needs of your organization, its abilities and limitations, and becoming the instrument of progressive change—the type that guides your organization toward achieving its goals through the most effective use (acquisition and retention) of its valued employees. This will require above all else well-developed communication and negotiating skills, followed closely by creative design of employment programs and operations. You will need sharp negotiating skills to influence upper management to accept changes, and to deal with individual new hires by presenting offers and on-going incentives that will attract the quality of talent needed by your organization.

9.1 How to Initiate Offers of Employment

The process of making employment offers to those who pass through preemployment selection can range from simple to complex. Most semiskilled and entry level jobs tend to be fairly easy transactions where the employer representative simply offers a starting salary or pay rate, and whatever company-defined benefits are customary with the type and status of job being filled. The representative is usually the person responsible for the company's employment operations, rather than the hiring authority, to ensure that these programs are administered with consistency, thereby avoiding both illegal practices and demoralizing inequality within the work force.

Employment offers to more diversely talented and responsible employees will continue to become progressively individualized as their availability diminishes and their ability to demand personalized treatment increases. Thus, jobs that are defined as professional, technical, office, administrative, supervisory, and managerial—in other words, the majority of *all* jobs—will increasingly have their employment terms and conditions arranged by negotiated offers of employment "packages." Two of the greatest problems facing employers will therefore become: 1) how to arrange pay, benefits, and a host of other employment programs into an expanded, more flexible realm of use; and, 2) how to maintain relative equality among similarly employed personnel. The added cost of dealing with worker demands for more flexible employment treatment will be a lesser concern as employers realize that such costs will be returned in more reliable productivity, lower turnover, and higher retention of value-adding employees. The following, then, are suggestions intended to help you transact employment offers for different types and levels of new employees.

Unskilled and Semiskilled Employees

There are a wide variety and range of jobs categorized as unskilled or semiskilled. Employers will be able to retain control over the terms and conditions of employment for this group of employees because these workers will remain in plentiful supply for most types of jobs. They will not therefore command bargaining power unless, of course, their employment is represented by a recognized labor union.

Traditional employment offers consist of either verbal, written, or both forms of communication with the selected new hire. The transaction typically involves an offer of the job, a predetermined pay rate, the employer's choice of work schedule arrangements, starting date, and fixed benefits for all such employees established by company policy. The task of the employer representative is to merely convey what is being offered and ascertain whether the first choice new hire accepts or rejects the offer. If rejected, the employer representative may consider a modification requested by the first choice hire (an increase in the starting pay rate, for example), or merely take the offer to the second choice applicant, if he or she is deemed nearly as suitable by the employer.

Even though it's common for employers to give less attention to the details of hiring unskilled and semiskilled employees, employment offers should be documented after they're verbally accepted by the new hire. This can be easily accomplished by preparing one or more form letters containing the provisions you wish to communicate to various categories of new hires. Preparing these types of form letters on word processors makes the task simple and quick by inserting personalized information such as the new hire's name, address, job title, starting date, rate of pay, and the like. For your convenience, a sample of this basic employment offer letter has been provided in Section 9.4.

Professional, Technical, Office, and Supervisory Employees

This is the group of new and replacement hires that will be in greatest demand and least supply of the qualities needed by employers well beyond the year 2000. These are also the individual employees who contribute most directly to an employer's bottom line profitability and operational efficiency. Because of these two factors—short supply and revenue impact—they can leverage employers during employment offer negotiations, and they are quickly recognizing this fact!

The prudent employer will not view this as an adversarial situation. Rather, it is a give-and-take transaction similar to the negotiation process used to strike a deal for any desired resource. The best approach is to apply the information you have about the prospective new hire to start the negotiating transaction. Employers with fifty or more employees will likely see a fairly wide variety of people with respect to age, sex, family status, personal interests, job levels, and incomes. For example, younger applicants typically place emphasis on net income and maximum employer contributions toward insurance benefit plans, while older applicants tend to place emphasis on net income, retirement plans, and income deferral plans.

Employers will have to provide a solid array of "attractors" and "retainers" to create interest among a diverse work force. The person making employment offers should be able to negotiate particular packages of attractors to each separate employee in line with the individual's needs and desires at the new hire's present stage of work and personal life. This task can be simplified by computerized recordkeeping and payroll processing. Employment attractors and retainers span a wide range of appealing plans, programs, services, and policy provisions. Here are a few different types that you may wish to consider adding to your company's arsenal of attractors—they may determine whether or not your new hire choice accepts or rejects your job offer.

- Sign-on bonuses
- Choice of health plans
- Employer-paid healthcare plans
- Flexible compensation plans
- Flexible work scheduling
- Training programs by career tracks leading to promotions
- Performance pay plans
- Bonuses and awards
- Recognition programs
- Company sponsored socials
- Child care services
- Flexible family and educational leave policies

The only limit to the number, type, and variety of employment attractors that an employer can develop (or attach a cost to) is imagination. But whatever assortment of attractors are used by any employer, they should directly correlate to the interests and desires of the employer's work force. For this reason, medium to large employers would do well to periodically survey employee preferences concerning what current employment provisions are of greatest interest, and what new provisions might be worthy of consideration.

Interestingly enough, not all new employment attractors need to cost the employer a great deal of money. In fact, many employees may be interested in forgoing an annual salary increase in lieu of being able to place what would have been the same amount of money into a deferred income plan. This actually reduces the employer's cost of Social Security taxes (F.I.C.A.) and overtime rates since the employee's pay rate remains unchanged. Conversely, it may be more prudent for an employer to allow employees a periodic extended leave for family or educational reasons than to lose them altogether, and suffer the added cost of replacement.

Managerial and Executive Employees

This group of employees will likewise be in short supply—at least in terms of quality talent—as the aging of the work force pattern continues into the first decade following the year 2000. These employees carry with them an inherently higher price tag than other groups because the nature of their work involves more concentrated responsibility, authority, risk, and economic impact on their organizations. They tend to share a more direct relationship with the employer, be it a board of directors, sole owner, or the chief executive officer. Their primary sources of attraction are economics (money and future security), challenging nature of work and extensiveness of responsibilities, and opportunities afforded them through exposure to others in their field. Examples of attractors sought by higher level managers and executives are:

- Guaranteed minimum duration of initial employment
- Competitive base salary rate
- Fully paid healthcare benefit plans
- Liberal vacation provisions
- Profit sharing and/or performance bonus based on work results
- Paid relocation costs (including spousal placement services)
- Reasonable autonomy of decisions and independence of actions
- Severance pay provisions

The most common form of making employment offers to managers and executives is by negotiated, bilateral agreements between the individual and the employer representative. The contents of such agreements are then drafted into documents ranging from simple written agreements to lengthy employment contracts that elaborate on very specific details to define all of the terms and conditions of the employment relationship. Such agreements and contracts are enforceable in court or arbitration hearings, thus they are binding in every respect on both parties. For this reason, great care should be taken when negotiating and drafting these employment offers to assure mutual and complete understandings.

CAUTION

Employers should use a competent labor attorney for the drafting of these documents. An *illustrative* sample of an employment agreement and contract have been provided in Section 9.3 for your reference, but always use a legal advisor for review of categorical and legal content to ensure that your company's interests are protected.

9.2 How to Extend the Employment Offer

Up to this point in the hiring process, all efforts directed toward gaining a quality new hire have been controlled by the employer. The employer determines which applicants will be considered, which will be progressively tested, which go on to final interviews, and which will be selected as the right fit for the job. However, when it comes to extending the job offer, the tables may turn momentarily since filling the job is in the control of *one* applicant. While there may be a closely ranked second choice applicant available as a backup to fill the job, a thorough testing process will normally convince the employer that the first choice applicant is truly the one right person, and any second choice is just that.

Once the selection decision has been made, the employment offer process should commence immediately to "close the deal" and ensure that you don't lose the applicant by unnecessary delays. To a worthy applicant, delays signal an implied disinterest or disorganization on the part of the employer, either of which quickly become disillusioning. The hiring decision should therefore be made quickly along with internal clarity about what will be offered to the new hire. Given negotiations that may take place between the new hire and the employer representative before agreement is reached, company decision-makers should first explore what options are open for the offer, including outer limits that may have to be extended during negotiations to close the deal.

Selling the Employment Opportunity

Offers of employment no longer represent the values they once had for quality employees. Consequently, today's employees recognize the need to obtain the best *set* of employment conditions they can get for their own goals and long-term career progression. While employers used to manage the life-long careers of their employees, it is now the individual employee who is responsible for determining the course, timing, and duration of his or her career. The result of this shift has brought about more of an employment negotiation process rather than the former "take it or leave it" offer process. Employment opportunities, instead of mere jobs, must now be sold by those employers who truly want to capture the best talent available from among a limited pool.

Selling the employment opportunity is initiated during the employment offer. This is usually accomplished verbally, in person or by telephone, with the selected applicant. Selling, in the case of employment opportunities, does not mean making a high pressure or fancy pitch about the job, company, benefits, or expectations. Doing so would tend to offend most intelligent people and can lead to unintentional misrepresentations. What selling does mean is that you present positive features about the employment opportunity in an enthusiastic manner, and that you cordially overcome any objections that might be raised. Giving advance thought to both positive features and possible objections can help to ensure that these conversations run smoothly and conclude in a job sale. Any person who holds the "you should be grateful for the offer to work for us" attitude should not be given the task of initiating employment offers, period!

Presenting the Employment Offer

In contacting your selected applicant to present the employment offer, you should keep in mind that this individual

- has had some exposure to your organization,
- has likely formed some initial impressions and perhaps a few concerns or questions,
- has his or her own personal agenda of what is wanted from the employment opportunity, and
- probably knows relatively little about such things as fringe benefits, long-term goals of the company, or personalities of those they will work with.

A good employment offer presentation will take these issues into account by incorporating them into the opening conversation. Since your task is to close the hiring process by getting the applicant's agreement to accept the offer, you want to cover the more important points of interest at the outset of your conversation without overstating information. You should also attempt to create a full visual picture for the applicant in terms of the job itself, the company, and its people. A typical employment offer conversation might resemble the following illustration.

Good morning John, this is Mary Smith with Allied Technologies. I am calling you this morning to congratulate you on being selected as the company's choice to fill the position of Instrument Simulation Programmer. If you have a few minutes, I would like to tell you a little more about the job and company, and answer any questions you might have *(wait for affirmative response and note the applicant's "tone" of interest).*

First, you may be interested to know that Allied Technologies was founded in 1971 by three partners who recognized the growing demand for electronic simulation instruments. By 1980, the company had 300 employees, and by 1985 the company grew to over 800 employees and became publicly owned by over 200 shareholders. We presently have 1050 employees and are the exclusive company under contract with several public and private organizations involved in simulation analysis. Our five year plan includes expanding our products and field services into eight foreign countries and introducing two new areas of instrumentation analysis.

As a relatively new organization headed by some of the brightest minds in the field, Allied Technologies places a great deal of emphasis on employee involvement, training programs, team projects, and overall quality—which is why we selected you for this position. For example, we have an excellent benefit package for our employees consisting of such programs as *(describe highlights of various benefits)* to name a few. Also, you will have the opportunity to work with your supervisor, Brent Jones, who had over eight years of experience with NASA before joining us in 1983. He was promoted to his position as the Programming Division Manager in 1985, and like our other managers, he encourages people to use their own initiative and ideas in their work.

John, now that you have seen some aspects about how we operate, what we look like, and learned more about the job and company, I am curious to know what your impressions are of the company, our people, and this employment opportunity. *(Allow time for response, and overcome any stated objections.)* Thank for sharing that with me John, and by your comments it tells me that both you and the company will benefit from your employment. On that note, I wonder if you would also share what you would like to achieve from your employment with Allied Technologies, because we at Allied take a sincere interest in trying to meet the needs of all of our employees as best we can. *(Allow time for response, and reinforce any particular applicant interests accommodated by company programs, policies, or practices—but don't make implied promises.)*

John, at this time I'd like to offer you the position of Instrument Simulation Programmer. We would like to have you start on Monday, July 15, at which time you and other new employees would spend your first two days in the Company's orientation program to acquaint you more thoroughly with our organization, operations, and your division. Based on the established salary range for your position and your background, I am authorized to offer you a starting salary of *(state amount),* and as of August 1 you would be eligible for your choice of our healthcare plans. Would you like to accept this offer at this time?

Allow time for response, answer any questions posed, and give the applicant a day or two to consider the offer if there is hesitancy or an expressed desire to give thought to your conversation. This is the stage where further negotiations may be required to close the employment offer, including some prospective flexibility on your part to counter offer with a slightly higher starting salary, vacation accrual, paying a larger share of a desired healthcare plan, or other minor adjustments to the original offer. You may wish to indicate that you will need further authority to make such improvements, and that you will have to call the applicant back in a few hours. If and when the applicant accepts, you should proceed to close your conversation.

That's great John, welcome aboard! I'll be sending you a letter in tomorrow's mail confirming the details of our agreement. Are there any other questions you have at this time? *(Allow time for response.)* Then we'll look forward to seeing you on the 15th, and if you should think of any further questions before then, don't hesitate to give me a call at *(give telephone number).*

In this illustration, the presenter is selling the job, company, and advantages of employment without the customary "hype" of a sales pitch. This type of an employment offer conveys a clear message that the company is professional, takes pride in its accomplishments and direction, and takes an inviting approach to its prospective employees. In contrast, compare the appeal of this illustration to the traditional one in which the employer representative presents something as shallow as, "I am calling to offer you the job of Instrument Simulation Programmer starting at X dollars per month. We would want you to report for work on July 15. Do you accept the job?"

During your employment offer conversation, it's a good idea to have a writing pad handy. This will allow you to take notes of any questions asked by the applicant needing further investigation, or specific details of your employment offer. Consider how embarrassing it might be for you and the new hire if you were to forget the exact amount of the salary offer and misstate it in the confirming letter or contract. As soon as possible after your conversation concludes, you should have the written confirmation prepared and mailed. If there is a concern about receipt of your employment offer, you may want to mail the letter "registered receipt," or use overnight mail if a quick written acceptance is desired.

9.3 How to Prepare Employment Offer Letters and Employment Agreements

The most efficient way to prepare employment offer letters and agreements is to have two or more formatted samples stored in your word processor, subject to review by your labor attorney each time preformatted copies are prepared. These formatted letters and agreements that have been preapproved by your labor attorney should handle the majority of your employment offers. However, on a few isolated occasions you may have to prepare slightly different letters or unique agreement clauses to address special conditions. Even then, the remainder of your letter or agreement can be constructed from formatted language thus reducing the time and cost to process these hiring transactions.

As a general rule, letters are typically used to confirm offers to nonexempt and lower level exempt personnel, while agreements are normally used for mid-level and higher exempt personnel. This custom should not, however, dissuade you from the use of agreements to cover particular employment understandings for specialized employees, or the use of letters for less consequential exempt employees. Here, then, are a few of the more important points you will want to consider in preparing these documents.

Legal Issues to Consider

Since the early 1980s, employment letters and agreements have become the subject of sometimes intense scrutiny by the courts and arbitrators hearing employment cases. Such cases have been filed most often by employees (at virtually all levels) who feel they have been treated in contradiction to some expressed or implied written understandings conveyed in their employment letters, agreements, or company policies and practices, or they have been terminated wrongly under the terms of such document provisions. Regrettably, the notoriety of these cases caused some employers to abandon their practice of providing new employees with confirming letters or employment agreements, rather than merely reconstructing the language of these documents to conform to the (legitimate) principles being raised by legal authorities.

The central purpose of providing new employees with these documents is to communicate important employment information, and to confirm the employment transaction. However, given known legal vulnerabilities, they should be drafted with more than a casual state of consciousness about how information should be stated. Only by taking certain precautions can you feel more confident that

1. misrepresentations are not being made;
2. the entirety of the employment relationship is mutually understood and agreed upon;
3. agreements will be adhered to in a good faith manner; and,
4. there exists a mechanism to resolve disputes concerning employment agreements.

Misrepresentations of Employment

It is of little consequence to the courts or arbitrators whether employment misrepresentation was intentional or not. What tends to carry more weight is whether misrepresentation took place, the degree to which the information was relied on by the new employee, and the nature of damages suffered by the new employee in reliance of the information. Also, claims of misrepresentation tend to be easier to advance than fraud. Fraud exists when an employer *knows* the information being given is false with the *intention* to deceive the new employee, to induce the individual to accept the job. To establish a claim of (negligent) misrepresentation, on the other hand, it is not necessary for the new employee to prove that the employer falsified information or engaged in intentional deceit. Rather, the new employee merely has to establish that the information was, in fact, false, and that the provider knew or should have known it was false or misleading in a context critical to the new employee's acceptance decision (research *Harlan v. Intergy, Inc.* N.D. Ohio, 1989 in contrast to *Tipton v. Canadian Imperial Bank of Commerce*, 11th Cir., 1989).

Prospective misrepresentations about a job being offered, the company, or various employment conditions and practices can be made more easily than most might assume. They can occur during preemployment interviews, conversations with the prospective new hire during preoffer meetings, verbal offers, and written confirmation letters or employment agreements. What must be taken into account when discussing employment *related* information with prospective new hires are these two caveats:

1. That all information provided by you, or specifically requested by the prospective new hire, is factual and complete to ensure that information is not deceitful or misleading. If information is requested that would violate your company's reasonable standard of confidentiality, then you can simply state that the information cannot be disclosed due to its sensitive nature. If, however, you're dealing with a prospective high level manager who would otherwise learn of the confidential information (such as, the economic stability of the company) after hire, and who would have to leave another job and move a household to accept your job offer (damages), then you may be well advised to disclose otherwise confidential information.

   Information that is uncertain, speculative, or conditional beyond known facts should be qualified by such statements as, "It is my experience that . . . , Our practice has been to . . . but we cannot guarantee that . . . , If things continue as they have in the past, we should be able to expect that. . . ."

2. That any information about the job, company, or employment conditions reasonably germane to a new hire's reliance to act on accepting an employment offer be *volunteered* by the employer representative. Disclosing this type of information may not be very appealing to some organizations who have one or more skeletons they wish to keep under wraps, but if any of those skeletons represent a material influence on the new employee's reasonable expectations of employment or related conditions, then you should consider the propriety of volunteering factual information about the condition.

   For example, you may be hiring someone to help improve conditions in the products division of a plant which has experienced a high defective rate. If the defective rate continues much longer, the plant may be closed (reasonable expectation) by the corporate office. In this case, you should volunteer the fact that defect rates are high and that is precisely the reason you are making the employment offer to your new hire—to help reduce it or possibly lose the plant. Similarly, if the company is in financial trouble, if an acquisition or merger is pending, or there is talk of a salary freeze, this information should be considered for voluntary disclosure.

Some additional topics of potential misrepresentation where caution should be exercised during employment offer transactions are

- Stating a salary as an annual rather than monthly figure. Some state courts may interpret the annual salary as an implied promise for a minimal one year employment guarantee. For the same reason, you should avoid statements like, "Your performance will be evaluated at the end of each year (for purposes of determining a salary increase)."
- Statements, even innocent ones, implying the employer's intent to form a long-term employment contract, such as, "We look forward to having you with the company for many years."
- Statements giving the impression that present benefits or personnel policies would remain in force for the duration of the new hire's employment by saying something like, "During your employment you will enjoy the benefits of the company's insurance and retirement plans as well as the liberal provisions of our employment policies." This type of statement may be considered misrepresentation if later the company changes its policies or benefit programs from those in force at the time an employee was given a "promissory" offer.

When you are uncertain about a particular job or company conditions that may have an influence on hiring an applicant where damages could arise, it's best to consult with an experienced labor attorney. While these conditions arise most frequently with key professional, administrative, managerial, and executive jobs, you should enter the employment relationship with a full disclosure of pertinent information to all new hires. Doing so also instills needed trust and confidence between you and new employees to establish a common and clear understanding of relevant conditions.

At-Will Employment

According to common law or statutory provisions in each state, employment is said to be either at-will, bound by a fixed term, or otherwise defined by contractual agreement between the employer and employee. Most employers do not want to be bound by specified terms of employment for their employees since doing so restricts the employer's ability to terminate for any reason deemed suitable. Nor do most employers particularly like the notion of having to abide by the contractual terms of a collective bargaining or individual employment agreement for the same reason. Consequently, the type of employment favored by employers tends to be at-will, meaning either the employer or employee is free to terminate the employment relationship at any time, for any reason, and with or without notice to the other party.

Employees, quite understandably, do not favor at-will employment conditions. They fear its discretionary powers and feel that it creates an arbitrary and capricious ability for employers to threaten their job security. Likewise, under at-will employment, employees become concerned about damage to their careers and reputation at the whim of a single manager who may suddenly disfavor their presence. For this reason, employees prefer employment based on termination for *just cause* only, and arbitration of alleged unjust terminations. Labor unions and other employee rights groups have been actively lobbying in many states to alter at-will statutes with just cause and arbitration provisions, but these efforts have had only marginal success. Additionally, numerous state courts are becoming increasingly interested in reforms to at-will employment due to the surge in wrongful termination cases that began to appear in the early 1980s.

It should be clear from the foregoing that a lawful employment relationship is formed when an employer hires a new employee. The question then becomes what *type* of a relationship is created between the parties. The type of relationship formed—just cause or at-will—thus determines what obligations rest with both parties. So, the most common practice for employers hiring nonunion and noncontractual employees was to give them a confirming employment letter (the "Welcome Aboard" variety), and handing them an employment handbook during new employee orientations wherein they were told they had to abide by the company's policies. Wrongful termination litigation, however, began to cast doubt on whether implied at-will hires were sufficient for a legal defense. Following the publication of several court cases in which seemingly at-will employees were awarded damages because of their employer's own violation of expressed terms in their personnel policy manuals, handbooks, letters, or verbal promises, employers were quickly advised by labor counsel to inform new hires at the onset of employment that they were regarded as at-will employees.

Such notifications, by advice of legal counselors, were to be placed on employment application forms, in employment confirmation letters, in personnel policies, and (where appropriate) in employment agreements to ensure that each employee had advance notice of their mutual right to terminate the relationship freely. As you might suspect, both new and long-term employees took exception to their employer's mass publication of at-will employment notices. After all, there is a contradictory and demoralizing effect to say in one breath, "Welcome aboard and, by the way, we can terminate you any time we feel the need to do so."

In the final analysis, the question each employer must answer for itself is whether: 1) a *thorough* protective stance on the forming of an at-will employment relationship is desired by publishing several notices of this condition; 2) a *moderate* stance is suitable by publishing at-will notices in only one or two well distributed sources (e.g., application form and employee handbook); or, 3) a purely positive *employee relations* stance is taken by leaving at-will employment unpublished, but implied. Prudence would suggest that employers take at least the second stance by using such publicized disclaimer notifications as the following sample.

AT-WILL NOTICE DISCLAIMER

Employment at *(Company name)* is for no definite period and may, regardless of the time and manner of pay or other scheduled employment provisions, be terminated at any time by the Company or by an employee, with or without cause, and without advance notice. Further, no manager or representative of *(Company name),* other than the *(Title of authorized persons),* has the authority to enter into any agreement, verbal or written, for specified terms or other conditions of employment. The Company's at-will employment policy also applies to the right of the Company to alter employment benefits, working conditions, policies, and privileges of employment at its sole discretion.

PROGRESSIVE DISCIPLINE DISCLAIMER

Although employment with *(Company name)* is not for a fixed term or definite period, and may therefore be terminated by either the Company or employee at any time, the Company has established procedural guidelines for supervisors when dealing with discipline and/or termination matters. Depending on the nature and circumstances of one or more incidents, discipline and termination actions will normally be progressive and bear a reasonable relationship to the violation. This general procedure is not intended to form an employment contract, and therefore does not bind *(Company name)* to follow the procedure of progressive action in all cases.

If the foregoing at-will employment disclaimer notice, or facsimile, is used on the employer's application form, in employment agreements, and placed conspicuously in the employee handbook, then it should be unnecessary to taint the introduction of new employees into company service by using it in employment letters. However, the issue is important enough to cover during employee orientations and should therefore be an item placed on the new employee's orientation checklist to ensure their early understanding.

Breach of Contract

Employee claims of breach of contract by their employer are usually in relation to alleged wrongful termination of general employment violations specified in the employer's personnel policies. These potential violations of law are adjudicated by the courts or arbitrators, and represent very costly situations for employers due to legal expenses and possible damage awards to plaintiff employees. The primary sources that tend to give rise to a breach of contract action by an employee are

- Employment Letters
- Employment Agreements
- Personnel Manuals and Employee Handbooks
- Personnel Forms
- Verbal Statements Made By Company "Agents"

In each of these documents or sources of information about employment, the courts have frequently determined that an otherwise at-will relationship can be superseded by the subsequent forming of a contractual employment condition. For example, some courts have held that an employee can rely on the expectations formed from an employer's personnel policies where language conveys the essence of a promise (e.g., "Employees *will* be evaluated *annually* on their performance and *shall* be given *consideration* of a merit increase *at that time*"). Language such as this, many courts say, forms a contractual expectation that the employer will abide by its own policy, and this formation of a contractual obligation sets aside at least this aspect of at-will employment. Likewise, similar contractual expectations can be formed in employment letters and agreements.

When an employer publishes, or otherwise conveys, an expectation, promise, terms, or condition of employment by the use of compelling words such as "will," "shall," and "must," a lawful contract may be formed. If the provision of these types of statements are violated, then a breach of contract has formally taken place. To lessen the likelihood of misunderstandings and the potential for litigation over breach of contract in employment matters, employers should consider taking these precautionary steps:

1. *Employment Letters:*
   Only use compelling words where they are intended to oblige the company or employee in a particular way. You may also wish to use the short, but politely stated phrase, "Please understand that it is not the intent of this letter to form an employment contract. Rather, we merely wish to inform you of these initial understandings of your employment acceptance."

2. *Employment Agreements:*
   Use a clearly stated, easily understood at-will disclaimer, but make sure that the statement includes the fact that only the contents of the agreement and specific subsequent (written) agreements are subject to contractual obligations by the company.

3. *Arbitration and Forum Selection Clauses:*
   For those employees whose employment terms and conditions are covered by either an individual employment or collective bargaining agreement, you should consider the use of arbitration and forum selection clauses. Arbitration is generally a less costly method of resolving disputes over contract provisions than court actions, while forum selection clauses define what state court and laws shall be used (usually those where the business or headquarters office is located) if disagreements are litigated.

4. *Personnel Policy Manuals and Employee Handbooks:*
   Whether or not an employer elects to use an at-will disclaimer, a notice should be placed conspicuously in these documents conveying a notice that the provisions are not to be construed as obligatory or intending to form a contract.

5. *Review Personnel Forms and Train Supervisors:*
   All personnel transaction forms should be reviewed to ensure that no words, statements, or phrases convey *unintentional* promises or expectations that might be construed as contractual obligations by legal sources. In particular, forms that relate to pay increases, employment status, promotion, discipline, or performance evaluation should be given focal attention.

   Additionally, all managers and supervisors should be given periodic training on the subject of conversational powers that can create various forms of liability for the company (e.g., misrepresentation, creating a verbal contract through promissory statements, harassment, discrimination, and the like).

Employment Letter Topics to Cover

Despite the treachery that a handful of litigious employees have wrought on employment letters, they remain the most professional and dignified way for employers to confirm employment appointments and convey initial understandings. Quality new hires who are currently employed will want your written confirmation before giving up their present jobs, so the sooner you can get it in their hands, the sooner a commitment can take place by the new hire's resignation from his or her position.

Remember that this is a new person to your company, who has little knowledge of how the job or company functions. While employment letters should be brief, allowing deferral of countless details to a well-prepared orientation process, the letter should minimally convey the following topics.

Welcome and/or Congratulatory Statement

This statement should have a friendly, pleasing effect on the new hire that conveys the sentiment, "we're happy to have you join us"; or, you might state, "you can take pride in knowing you were our choice from among (thirty) applicants for this position."

Job Title and Date of Employment

The job title stated in your employment letter should be identical to the one you used in your recruiting advertisements and on the job description rather than casual working titles. If, for some inexplicable reason, you do not have a job description covering the position being filled, then your letter should include a reasonably thorough outline of the new employee's major job responsibilities, authorities, and performance expectations.

The date of employment should also be included in the letter. This date should be the new employee's report date, not the date the offer was made, and it should be used thereafter as the official hire date for purposes of calculating service length entitlements.

Pay/Salary Rate and Classification Status

Nonexempt employees should have their starting pay rate expressed in hourly amounts. If, however, you customarily express nonexempt rates in weekly, bi-weekly, or monthly amounts, you should also parenthetically note the approximate hourly equivalent. Why? Because expressing monthly amounts for a nonexempt employee may be misconstrued by a labor commissioner as an intent of the employer to treat the employee as an exempt employee, and thereby deny the employee his or her lawful right to overtime pay.

It is therefore advisable to notify new employees of their status (nonexempt or exempt) and starting rate of pay expressed in hourly amounts for nonexempt and monthly amounts (not annual for the reasons previously mentioned) for exempt positions.

Contingencies

Contingencies are unresolved conditions that must be satisfied either before the new employee's report date or during their initial (probationary) employment period. Ideally, all such conditions should be resolved even before an employment offer is made; however some hires need to be accomplished faster than others. In these cases it may be necessary to make part of the new hire's employment acceptability contingent on such conditions as

- The employee's passing a medical evaluation
- The employer's completion of a satisfactory background check
- The employee's submission of certain verifying documents
- Acceptance by the employer's insurance carrier of the employee's driving record
- Other requirements or determinations about the employee's suitability that are customarily carried out as a prehire decision by the employer

Special Information

Information that is unique to the nature of work to be performed in the job, or special conditions of employment, will vary depending on the type of job being filled and company operating conditions. Special information you may wish to convey in employment letters might consist of such items as: 1) joining the union that represents their job or having the option to not join (if covered in a collective bargaining agreement); 2) the required purchase of uniforms or specific items needed for employment (such as, safety shoes or tools); 3) designated employee parking spaces; or 4) having an identification badge prepared.

Orientation

It's always a good idea to inform new employees that they will be given an orientation to better acquaint them with such matters as their benefits, company operations and policies, and the people with whom they will be working. The preparation and conduct of orientation "in-processing" is provided for you in the next chapter, but at least telling new employees in their employment confirmation letters that such an event is planned for them usually sets them at ease about the many questions, concerns, and anxieties commonly associated with starting a new job.

Employment Agreement Topics to Cover

Employment agreements should be entered into *only* after both the employer representative and the new hire have reached complete accord on *all* issues to be covered in the written agreement. Merely discussing and reaching a mutual understanding is not the same as completing a negotiated agreement, nor is it advisable to negotiate the seemingly more important issues while leaving "administrative" items subject to the employer's drafting, followed by the new employee's approval. Doing so will only arouse discomfort with the new employee inasmuch as the process was not completed. Second, you may create possible feelings of deceit by the new employee if the contents of administrative matters were not discussed, but seem to favor the employer. Last, incomplete negotiations simply prolong the transaction because new language necessitates further discussion and perhaps review by the new employee's attorney (which you should encourage anyway—and openly).

Once a full, mutual, and agreeable understanding of the terms, conditions, and provisions of an employment agreement have been reached, they should be carefully drafted into a comprehensive document. You may wish to have this done by an experienced labor attorney, or you may wish to prepare your own draft and have it reviewed by a labor attorney. Since you're dealing with a lawfully binding contract instrument, it is imperative that you act under advice of legal counsel. Whether you or your selected attorney prepares the document, here are some of the topics you should include in nearly any employment agreement. You may also want to use this list to ensure that your negotiation with the new employee has likewise covered each of these topics.

Name of Parties to the Agreement

This should consist of the full legal name of the employee and the exact name of the employing entity. If the employing entity is a subsidiary company of a larger corporation, the subsidiary can be named so long as it has legally independent authority to enter into separate contracts.

Job Title, Responsibilities, and Authorities

See item 2 in the preceding subsection under Employment Letter Topics to Cover.

Reporting Relationships and Classification Status

It is advisable, not imperative, to specify what reporting relationship the new employee, covered by this agreement, will have with what other persons (by name of their job titles). In many instances where the employee is important enough to have his or her employment covered by a contractual agreement, that position usually fits into a definable part of the organization's structural hierarchy. To avoid confusion and possible disputes about working relationships, it may be worthwhile to spell out the positions and circumstances under which the covered employee will report to, or work equally with, others in their hierarchical sphere of organizational influence.

Also, as pointed out in the previous subsection, it is advisable to note the employee's status as either exempt or nonexempt for purposes of clarifying their wage and hours treatment under the Fair Labor Standards Act.

Employment Effective Date and Period

The employment effective date should be stated as the date the covered employee agrees to report to work. If that date changes between signing the agreement and the actual report date, the individual's employment records should be changed to reflect the actual report date.

The employment period, if a specified one is agreed upon (usually a minimum guaranteed period of one to three years is requested by the employee), should be expressed in terms of a beginning and ending date. However, you should be clearly aware that stating either an employment or contract period sets aside the company's ability to terminate the employee—and therefore the contract—at the company's at-will discretion. If your agreement is to include a specified employment period, then you should also include a mutual thirty-day written notice right to terminate the contract.

Regular Compensation

Regular compensation consists of base pay, predetermined bonuses, and any other form of fixed, direct compensation in relation to performance of the job. Base pay should be expressed in terms of a monthly salary for exempt employees, or hourly rate for nonexempt employees. However, if your preference is to specify the equivalent annual salary for an exempt employee, it is suggested that it be shown parenthetically after noting the monthly rate. This may lessen the likelihood of the employee making a case for an implied guarantee of at least one year of employment should you find the need to terminate the position earlier.

Additional Compensation and Benefits

Additional compensation may include such agreed upon items as a one-time reimbursement of relocation expenses, profit sharing, and deferred compensation.

Benefit entitlements should also be addressed in detail with respect to 1) what particular plans and programs are provided to the employee by the employer; 2) when they become effective and terminate (be sure to comply with COBRA and ERISA provisions); 3) who pays how much for their cost, including maintenance during any period of the employee's disability; and, 4) a statement that the company reserves the right to change plan carriers, administrators, and benefit provisions—either at its sole discretion, or that any such change will qualify for a renegotiation of the agreement provision should it result in a material effect upon the covered employee.

The types of benefits that should be covered in this part of the agreement are mandatory benefits (workers' compensation, unemployment insurance, and Social Security), healthcare insurance plans, stock option plans, retirement and pension plans, life insurance plans, expense accounts, vacation and holiday allowances, car allowances, sabbaticals, discretionary leaves (family emergency or death), and any similar cost or time related benefit your company may be offering as part of the hiring package.

Trade Secrets, Patents, and Copyrights

If the employee covered by an employment agreement will, or may, be involved during the course of employment in gaining information about company trade secrets, ideas or inventions that the company finds suitable enough to patent, or the publication of certain literature, then you should definitely consult a suitably qualified attorney to assist you in preparing contract language to protect the company's proprietary interests. With people being employed as engineers, scientists, researchers, authors, technical writers, and the like, there exists the possibility that they may produce some work to which the company wishes to proclaim title.

Employers should not make the mistake of assuming that matters such as these are automatically within their domain of ownership. For example, an employee is entitled to anything he or she *invents* unless such employment-related inventions are conveyed in writing to the employer at the time of employment or creation of the invention. An unassigned invention right remains with the employee even when the employee uses company property, time, and materials to create the invention.

Conversely, *copyright* law assigns the rights to any written, illustrative, or other type of information (including computer programs) to the company where such copyrightable material was created by an employee in the normal course and context of their employment. This fact alone, however, should not be cause for employers to disregard placing such a written clarification in employment agreements covering applicable employees.

If your company employs people in these types of capacities, but you do not provide them with employment agreement per se, you may still prepare and require the employee's signature on topic-specific agreements to protect such applicable conditions as trade secrets, inventions (patents), copyrights, and noncompetition.

Noncompetition

Noncompetition clauses in employment agreements are normally aimed at protecting the company's right to prohibit or limit an employee from engaging in direct competition with the company for a specified period of time after employment separation. Generally, such covenants will be upheld in court if 1) the employer has a legitimate business interest to protect; 2) the duration and location of an employee's noncompetition restraint is reasonable; and, 3) the restraint does not conflict with a public interest in the nature of commerce being restrained (*Paramount Termite Control Co., Inc. v. Rector*, Va. Sup. Ct., 1989).

The period of time that employees can be restrained from engaging in a competing business, including the taking of their knowledge learned from a former employer to a competitor, varies based on the nature of the business, but a two- or three-year period is typical in these agreements. Similarly, the location of restrained competition is best defined as the region in which the employer conducts business relative to the employee being restrained. This also should include restraint from soliciting, contacting, or using the employer's customers as sources of competitive business. On the other hand, it is not a reasonable restraint to impose noncompetition clauses on general employees—only those whose jobs expose them to trade secrets, unique business practices, customer information, product designs, and similar business conditions that give the employer a business edge in its enterprise.

Compliance with Company Policies

To avoid the uncertainty that can arise with employment agreements as to whether or not the provisions of the agreement are the sole source of employment matters with which the employee must comply, it's advisable to include a clause that clarifies this point. Most employers do not want to be restrained from imposing their personnel or other operating policies on employees covered by an employment agreement. However, in the absence of this condition, it could cast considerable doubt on whether such an employee had to abide by such policies if they are not mentioned or referenced.

Here is where you should exercise some clear thought about how you reference company policies. If, for example, the covered employee is a mid- to senior-level manager, but certain portions of company policy exclude or treat these employees differently from other employees, you may want to use such phrasing as, "Employee shall abide by all (applicable or named parts) Company policies relating to employment and operations except as otherwise modified herein."

At-Will Employment and Entirety of Agreement

If the employment agreement is not for a fixed term (is open-ended) as discussed previously in item 4 (Employment Date and Effective Period), then the employer should consider the use of an at-will employment statement. The absence of this statement will leave the question open to speculation, so it is best to clarify that either the employee or company may terminate the relationship and agreement at any time, for any reason, and with or without notice to the other party.

A similar statement should be made to clarify that the terms, conditions, and provisions of the employment agreement constitute the entirety of obligations between the parties, except as may be modified by mutual agreement from time to time. Caution should be exercised here to ensure that you have included *all* matters with which you want the employee and company committed to abide by and carry out. This will require some additional thought toward what likely, prospective, or even unlikely events and conditions might take place concerning this individual's employment.

Arbitration and/or Forum Selection

If an arbitration clause is omitted from an employment agreement, the implied assumption is that the parties intended to have disputes resolved by a court of authoritative jurisdiction. Litigation presents both the employee and employer with the prospect of very time consuming, costly, and formal legal proceedings in the event one or more aspects of the contractual relationship falls in dispute or is violated. For these reasons, arbitration may be a better remedy for the resolution of employment claims, complaints, or alleged violation of rights.

However, if the employer and employee agree to have such matters resolved through the courts, then it is advisable to clarify which state court and laws would apply in those cases where the employer's business is located in more than one state. The common practice is to select the (legal) forum of the employer's headquarters location or, alternatively, the state in which the employee conducts work for the company.

Severability

Severability clauses deal with the issue of validity of the employment agreement if one or more of its provisions are determined to be legally invalid. Generally, both parties share an interest in maintaining the validity of other contract provisions in order to preserve as much of the intended relationship as possible, but the absence of this clause may otherwise necessitate invalidation of the entire agreement—thereby necessitating renegotiations or reconstruction of the entire agreement.

To avoid invalidating portions of an employment agreement due to the illegality of any one provision, you may wish to use a severability clause like, "Should any part of this agreement be held unlawful by an arbitrator, court of competent jurisdiction, or other compelling legal entity, such a finding shall not have the effect of rendering any other part of this agreement invalid."

Statute of Limitations

The time period in which either the employer or employee can file formal action for resolution of a complaint or legal action is called a statute of limitations. Filing limitations are contained in various federal and state statutes, and they differ in length depending on the type of action or violation in dispute. For example, in discrimination matters, the statute of limitations for filing with compliance agencies is either 180 or 300 days from the date the act of alleged discrimination took place. For matters pertaining to employment rights protected by the National Labor Relations Act, filings must take place within six months of a violation, while tort or contract violations must be filed within one to three years of the actionable event.

Omitting a statute of limitations clause from an employment agreement infers that the parties intend to use those established by these various federal and state laws. However, you may be interested to know that parties to an agreement are not prohibited from establishing their own *singular* statute of limitations and, for the employer, it's a very good idea to do so. One of the greatest concerns many employers face upon the termination of an employee covered by contract is how long must we wait to see if this person is going to file a complaint or lawsuit challenging our termination action or employment treatment? To avoid this troublesome discomfort, you should consider negotiating a lesser, perhaps singular, period of time than that specified in contract law for your state.

NOTICE

The legality of doing so is more likely to be upheld upon review by a court if three conditions existed at the time the agreement was made.

1. The agreed statute of limitations was negotiated between the parties rather than offered by the employer as a "take it or leave it" proposition;

2. The period selected is not unreasonably short for the acting party to gather necessary facts, conduct an investigation, and prepare their case given the nature of the dispute in question. Here, it may be useful to know that one court accepted a singular six month self-imposed statute of limitations in an employment contract (*Myers v. Western-Southern Life Insurance Co.*, 6th Cir., 1988); and,

3. The employee is given a reasonable opportunity, and preferably encouraged, to consult with a legal advisor of his or her choice to give intelligent consideration to the acceptability of the limitation period.

A self-imposed statute of limitation might be worded like, "The parties hereto agree that no action or suit relating to employment or the provisions contained herein shall not commence later than six months after 1) the event that gave rise to such action or suit, or 2) the effective date of employment termination, and the parties in so agreeing do knowingly and willingly waive any other applicable statute of limitation contrary to this agreement."

As you can see from the foregoing list of topics to cover, employment agreements should clearly be negotiated in an open and bilateral manner. This requires that both parties have a good understanding of each topic raised, what they are getting or giving up (give and take), and how each provision is to be worded. The process requires honesty, integrity, fairness, and superior communication and persuasion (not intimidation) skills. What is accomplished during the negotiations of an employment agreement will set the stage for the ensuing employment relationship. If employees are made to feel that the transaction was too one-sided, and they were rendered powerless (compromised) in the process, you can probably guess what type of psychological predisposition they will bring to their employment.

9.4 Sample Employment Offer Letters and Employment Agreements

The sample of employment offer letters and agreements provided in this section do not necessarily contain all of the provisions mentioned in the previous section. Rather, they are intended to illustrate samples of wording and content you may wish to use as provided, or modify to suit the particular needs, desires, and circumstances of extending employment offers to different types of employees in your organization.

Sample 1
Employment Offer/Confirmation Letter

(Company Stationery)

____(Date)____

____(Name)____

____(Address)____

____(City, State, Zip)____

Dear (First name):

On behalf of (Company name), I am pleased to inform you that you have been selected for employment in the position of (Job Title) at a starting salary of approximately $2145 per month. Since your position is classified as nonexempt by the Company, your actual pay rate is $12.375 per hour and this is the amount used as the basis of calculating your regular overtime rate for such required work. As agreed during our telephone conversation on (Date), your employment will commence on (Date) when you report to (Specify location and title of person). Please make arrangements to report at 8:30 A.M. on that day. Your initial work schedule will be Monday through Friday, 8:00 A.M. to 5:00 P.M. (or other specified schedule), excluding holidays in which the office is closed.

As you know, your immediate supervisor will be (Name), who is the Processing Services Supervisor for your unit. I am confident you will enjoy your working relationship with Tom, and it may interest you to know that he has been with the Company for over five years. He also takes a great deal of pride in the abilities of his staff, most of whom you will meet during your first day with us.

(Insert any contingencies or special information about employment here.)

During your first (Day, Days, Week) of employment, you will be given an orientation to the Company, its people and their activities, our personnel and operating policies, and the benefits which you will be entitled to as a full-time employee. The orientation is also intended to allow you an opportunity to have any of your questions answered concerning employment matters with (Company name).

Once again, (Employee's name), we are delighted about your decision to accept employment with (Company name), and we hope that your experience here is a mutually gratifying one. If I can be of any further assistance to your employment interests, please do not hesitate to contact me.

Sincerely,

(Employer representative's name)
(Title)

Sample 2
Employment Offer/Confirmation Letter

(Company Stationery)

(Date)

(Name)

(Address)

(City, State, Zip)

Dear (First name):

This letter will confirm your employment with this company in the position of (Job Title) effective (Date) when you are to report for work. Please appear at 8:00 A.M. to this location in order to complete your initial in-processing of employment documents. Shortly thereafter, we will direct you to your supervisor, (Name and Title), who will provide you with an additional orientation to your job and other operational matters of mutual interest to you and the Company.

As agreed in our telephone conversation on (Date), your starting salary will be $2145 per month. Since your position is classified as nonexempt, you will be entitled to overtime pay for applicable hours worked at your equivalent hourly rate of regular pay. Additionally, advancement to regular employment status is contingent upon successful completion of a six-month initial employment period during which time both you and the Company can better evaluate the employment relationship. However, as noted on the Company's employment application form, (Company name) is an at-will employer, and therefore allows either employees or the Company the right to terminate employment whenever and for whatever reason is deemed suitable. Naturally, we hope that such an event will only arise in cases of a positive outcome.

Since we are anxious to receive your confirmation accepting this employment opportunity, we would appreciate learning of your decision by (Date). Please do so by signing below and returning the attached copy to me. Once again, we are pleased at the prospect of having you join our company, so do not hesitate to contact me if I can be of further assistance to you at this time or during your employment with us.

Sincerely,

(Employer representative's name)
(Title)

Sample
(Unilateral) Employment Agreement

As a condition of, and in consideration in, my employment with (Company name), I hereby represent, understand, and agree that said employment is subject to each of the following stipulations, including subsequent modification hereto:

1. Confidentiality: That I will observe the strictest confidentiality and secrecy over matters relating to the Company's accounts, customers, records, correspondence, processes, or business plans to which I may have access, possession, or knowledge in the course and scope of my employment. I promise not to divulge in any manner information of this type and nature to persons other than those to which it directly pertains, or those who I am informed have a right and need to know, and then only in the capacity of my position with the Company. I further promise not to solicit or use any information which may be available to me in the course of my employment for any purpose other than advancement of the Company's interests.

2. Honest and Faithful Service: That I will honestly and faithfully present and conduct myself, and represent the Company's interests, at all times during the performance of assigned duties. I pledge that the responsibilities and authorities associated with my position as determined by the Company shall be performed in a diligent, timely, and competent manner, and that I will truthfully and faithfully account for and deliver to the Company all (monies, materials, securities, etc.), and other property belonging to the Company which I may receive from or on account of the Company, and that upon my employment separation or Company demand I will immediately deliver to the Company all such property belonging to the Company.

3. Compliance with Company Directives: That I will adhere to, abide by, and comply with Company policies, rules, procedures, and practices now in force, or those brought to my attention as modifications thereto are made by the Company from time to time. I further agree and promise to comply with and carry out those verbal directives that may be given to me by persons to whom I am accountable or who possess superior organizational jurisdiction over my position.

4. Commencement of Employment: That my employment with (Company name) shall officially commence on the date I report to work, which has been determined to be (Date), and in accordance with those days and hours of scheduled work to be determined and possibly modified from time to time by the Company. I further understand and agree that my starting salary will be (Amount) per month, and that this period nor any other stated period relating to employment is not intended to imply that my employment is guaranteed for any such duration. I am aware and agree that the commencement of my employment with the Company shall additionally entitle me to those benefits established by policy and practice of the Company, or as otherwise specified herein, as may be associated with my position, and that the Company has the right to modify such benefits which shall be deemed acceptable to me by my election to continue employment thereafter.

5. At-Will Employment: That I understand and agree to the Company's policy of mutually terminable employment, such that either I or the Company may terminate our employment relationship at any time, for any reason we separately deem suitable, and with or without compulsory notice to the other party. Notwithstanding this agreement, either I or the Company may at our sole discretion give the other advance notice and cause for such termination, but doing so will not have the effect of altering our agreement that employment is to remain at-will for whatever duration of employment may take place.

6. Entirety of Agreement: That the terms, conditions, and provisions of this agreement constitute the entire agreement concerning my employment with (Company name), and that there are no other conditions or provisions of my employment, verbal or written, that apply unless subsequently modified in writing by mutual agreement between myself and the Company, and made a part hereto by attachment.

7. Arbitration: That in the event there arises a claim, violation, or other dispute during my employment, or within six months thereafter, concerning any employment matter, the Company and I agree to submit the matter to arbitration. However, prior to submitting an actionable event to arbitration, it is agreed that the parties will make reasonable attempts to resolve the matter internally by presentation of the issue(s) to the Company (President). Thereafter, if the matter has not been resolved to my satisfaction, I may initiate the arbitration process by submitting a written notice to the Company within thirty days from the date the actionable event occurred or not later than six months from the termination of employment, whichever is applicable to the actionable event. Notices made to the Company shall be submitted to the (Title of person). Selection of an arbitrator shall be made from a list three names submitted by the American Arbitration Association at the request of the moving party whereupon the moving party shall eliminate one such name by lining through it, followed by the elimination of a second such name by the other party. The remaining name shall be considered elected by both parties as the arbitrator to hear and render a binding decision on the matter based on their own rules, methods, and processes. It is further understood and agreed that the parties hereto waive any other statute of limitation that may otherwise apply under federal or state law pertaining to employment matters that is different than, or contrary to, the six month limitation imposed on both parties as referenced herein.

8. Approval by Authorities: By affixing signatures below, I and the duly authorized Company representative do hereby attest to understanding, agreement, and approval of the provisions contained in this employment agreement, and shall abide by and carry out its terms and conditions in a good faith manner.

EMPLOYEE:

_____

Name

_____

Signature

_____

Date

FOR THE COMPANY:

_____

Name

_____

Signature

_____

Title

_____

Date

Checklist of Contents for Employment Letters and Agreements

Employment Offer/Confirmation Letters

- ❏ Welcome and/or Congratulatory Statement
- ❏ Job Title and Date of Employment
- ❏ Pay or Salary Rate and Classification Status
- ❏ Contingencies Before Formal Acceptance
- ❏ Special Information about Employment
- ❏ Orientation Information

Employment Agreements

- ❏ Names of Parties to the Agreement
- ❏ Job Title, Responsibilities, and Authorities
- ❏ Reporting Relationships and Classification Status
- ❏ Employment Effective Date and Period
- ❏ Regular Compensation
- ❏ Additional Compensation and Benefits
- ❏ Trade Secrets, Patents, and/or Copyrights
- ❏ Noncompetition
- ❏ Compliance with Company Policies
- ❏ At-Will Employment and Entirety of Agreement
- ❏ Arbitration and/or Forum Selection
- ❏ Severability
- ❏ Statute of Limitation

Review of Legal Vulnerabilities

- ❏ Misrepresentation Issues
- ❏ At-Will Employment or Specified Term Issues
- ❏ Breach of Contract Issues

10 Assuring Successful Employment Adjustment Through Orientation and Integration

Hiring talented, quality people to work for your organization does not end the hiring process. Once a new employee has accepted an offer of employment, you must begin establishing the formal employer-employee relationship, and it is vital that this relationship be based on a mutual understanding of expectations. Orientation and integration is where the relationship starts, where the long-lasting values are established or missed, depending on the effort applied to creating a professionally conducted and thorough process, or a brief, ill-conceived, and disjointed one.

Orientation and integration are conceptually two distinct processes. However, they are connected as a singular, evolving series of events whose common goal is to maximize the opportunity for successful *adaptation* of new employees to the totality of their employment, not merely to their immediate jobs. The orientation phase should convey employment *information* vital to the new employee's complete understanding of important conditions. Conversely, the integration phase is aimed at *interactive* aspects of employment which will determine whether or not satisfactory adaptation to conditions and relationships can be achieved to the mutual satisfaction of *both* the employer and employee.

Conducting shallow orientation "programs" does not serve this purpose, and therein lies the reason why many new hires become maladjusted or *disoriented* during their first year with the organization. Likewise, a lack of understanding about the employee's need for integration into the dynamics of organizational life can be equally disastrous. Recognize at the onset of a new employee relationship that there is a vast difference between handling "in-processing" paperwork and a designed evolution of a human being into a prescribed set of employment conditions. Employees who are given little more than a paper in-processing view their employer and employment in a survivalist context. Survival is viewed as getting through their initial employment period, and then the first year, during which they will be exposed to enough trial-and-error experience to begin feeling more confident about how things work.

The approach concerned employers should be taking is that of creating a *transitional* process, not a list of isolated events. The transitional process should be focused on enabling new employees to make valuable, progressive contributions to the organization as rapidly as practical, and at the highest level of competence. Second, the process should involve the participation of a variety of company representatives in the educational experiences of new employees, and self-guided learning by each new employee. Third, the process should span the new employee's first year of employment rather than the first few days, weeks, or initial employment (probationary) period.

Fourth, the ideal learning method for employment adaptation is to alternate between structured (formal classroom) and personalized on-the-job experiences. Both structured and personalized learning should be guided by the use of such materials as employee handouts, employee handbooks, orientation packets, and supervisory checklists. Last, in order to identify the need for early changes and to measure the effectiveness of new employees, the organization should have some means of evaluating learning and adaptation results. There are any number of ways of accomplishing this, and they often involve such devices as giving new employees frequent but short written quizzes, close monitoring of work results, verbal guidance and evaluations by the supervisor, and frequent (quarterly during the first year) comprehensive written evaluations of progress in *all* pertinent aspects of employment adaptation.

10.1 How to Prepare an Effective Employee Orientation Process

One in three new hires fail (resign or are terminated) during their first year of employment. This represents a sizable turnover cost, let alone the sharp productivity drops associated with losing a *quality* employee who leaves out of dissatisfaction or disillusionment with the employer. So, what orientation of new employees should represent to the overall economic picture of employers is to

1. Promote a *company* orientation of the employee rather than a purely self-serving interest in employment.

2. Establish a greater, more comprehensive understanding of the company, its operations, and its people so that work has the dimension of importance in the context of the whole organization.

3. Develop effective interpersonal relationships to enhance each employee's ability and results at working with others in the organization.

4. Enable and empower new employees to learn important features about their job, the work setting, and operational conditions so their productivity is both quickened and reliable.

5. Avoid harmful early experiences that can occur when new employee adaptations are left to chance.

6. Avoid losing quality people during their first one to three years, and thereby retain the value of their hiring expense and progressive increase in productivity.

While new employees can fail to work out for any number of unanticipated reasons, the inadequacy of an employer's recruitment, selection testing, or orientation and integration should not be among the reasons for failure. These are *employer* failures, not that of new employees! Starting a new job represents a point and circumstance in time when people are highly susceptible to assimilating those values, beliefs, behaviors, styles, and conditions of their new environment. The degree to which employers take advantage of this limited opportunity to "mold" new employees into the established culture and conditions of employment will determine, in large part, whether or not the ensuing relationship is a mutually beneficial one.

Your emphasis should be on developing an orientation process that will instill respect for the quality of the organization within each new employee. To achieve this result, your orientation process should have the objectives of

- Fostering pride in belonging to an organization that values its employees and stresses the theme of quality throughout its employment operations;

- Creating a complete (big picture) awareness of the scope and nature of the organization's business, its values and goals, and its modes of operating;
- Decreasing the concerns commonly associated with new employment;
- Speeding the development and contributory worth of a new team member;
- Clarifying the quality of standards and expectations by which performance is to be measured; and,
- Establishing joint responsibility between the organization and its employees for individual growth and development of each employee.

The orientation of new employees should be developed as a process, not a program. Programs are distinguished by being singular events involving a prescribed set of repetitive conditions. A process, on the other hand, is an evolving set of events, some of which may be standardized to create partial uniformity and achieve prescribed objectives, but conditions may vary depending on uncertain variables—the nature of human beings in the case of employment processes.

Begin structuring the orientation process by considering the nature of your company. Do you have the enthusiasm and support of upper management, or merely acquiescence? Is upper management willing to show their interest in the development and use of a quality orientation process by agreeing to participate in it, as well as conveying these same sentiments to other managers and supervisors? If not, you're on your own until you develop a strategy that will accomplish this requisite condition. This part of your hiring process probably will not succeed if inadequately supported through involved participation at all levels of the organization. Why? Because effective orientations necessitate dedicated activities from others within your organization's structure. After all, these are their employees, not yours.

The components of orientation processes tend to vary in design by company size, philosophy about the desired quality of employee relations, the desire of the organization to empower its people through information sharing, and those conditions in the organization regarded as vital to the success of its employees. A brief examination of three different models may help you to determine which components would best meet your company's needs.

A Minimal Orientation Process

Minimal orientations infer that the organization has a higher regard for short-term productivity of new employees than for the duration of their employment. At least that's the message being sent to these employees as a result of being processed like some package that arrived too late. By and large, minimal orientations are geared toward minimizing the time of existing personnel. This is why employees exposed to such shallow welcoming ceremonies are frequently "underwhelmed" at incongruities between the employer's pre-hire hunt and post-hire haste. Obviously then, minimal orientations are not the model to be followed by organizations other than perhaps the family owned and operated business. However, to add contrast to differing approaches, here are the components of a minimal orientation process:

1. Have the new employee report the first morning to the person handling personnel matters for the company to fill out in-processing paperwork (payroll and benefit enrollment forms); or,

2. Have the new employee report to the personnel office, at which time they are taken to their supervisor for an unstructured "show-and-tell" walk around the work area, meet more people than they can remember, and spend not more than an hour in the supervisor's office talking about assorted operating issues—most of which will have no meaningful context to the new employee. Then, sometime during the employee's first week

or two—depending on the employer's pay cycle—the new employee is allowed to leave the work area long enough to sign in-processing forms.

3. With any luck, the new employee's work unit has some form of written procedures manual, or at least assorted memos, that the employee is handed and asked to read for familiarity. The unspoken expectation is that it should be learned quickly, completely, and forevermore become a second-nature body of gospel on how things are to be done.

4. Next, the new employee is given a few minor assignments in order to begin contributing some level of productivity, even though a sense of accomplishment is unlikely because the employee still isn't sure how to handle it, where to get materials, who can be trusted for help, or what to do next. Short of looking like an imbecile, the employee seeks out and poses countless questions to the supervisor. The supervisor, in turn, tolerates these inconveniences for a week or two, after which it becomes progressively more annoying.

This scenario has all the makings of a relationship doomed from the first day. Minimal orientations are quick at one thing—producing deep feelings of regret from new employees, particularly those who left another job where at least they had a sense of competence. If this description of minimal orientations is even close to what your company provides to new employees, you would be well advised to begin making upgrade changes toward a satisfactory orientation process.

A Satisfactory Orientation Process

The model presented here as a satisfactory orientation is best suited to an organization of 10 to 100 employees, and not more than two locations in the same area. These organizations are structured, but less formally than companies of over 100 employees, and the roles of staff are more generalist in nature. Access to and interaction with other company representatives is easier for purposes of arranging new employee orientations, thus making coordination of the process more simplified.

Two important distinctions between minimal and satisfactory orientation processes are that satisfactory orientations prearrange events, are organized, and are more systematically thorough in the information that is presented to new employees. Developing satisfactory orientations usually does not require an inordinate amount of time, merely the preparation of quality materials, getting others used to the routine (a little training helps), and learning to coordinate a few activities that require advance thought and planning. On the following page is a basic outline of the components of a satisfactory orientation process, but don't let this model impede your creative modification of it.

As you can see, satisfactory orientations are more of a gradual process than minimal orientations. They deliver informational and adaptive content from the standpoint of progressive knowledge, moving from general to specific aspects of employment that can more easily be absorbed by someone new to the complexities of a unique organizational setting. Also, emphasis is placed on just the right amount of structure to make the orientation orderly and professional, but not so much that it comes across as stuffy and impersonal. Supervisors and managers should make a special effort to be casual and make the new employee feel comfortable, thereby creating a friendly environment that allows the new employee to relax and become confident that accepting employment here was a good decision.

General Employment Orientation

1. Prepare new employee packets containing such materials as the company's Employee Handbook, job description, performance evaluation form, organization chart, information about the company, and payroll and benefit plan forms.

2. Personnel operations representative conducts a full-day orientation on the first day of employment (or one day during the first week, if necessary). The presentation should be informal but professionally structured through the use of handouts, overhead or slide illustrations during the presentation and reference to materials given to the new employee.

3. Morning topics that should be covered include:
   - Organizational structure, managers, goals, nature of operations, projects, clientele, and its people.
   - Organization's compensation and benefit programs.
   - Policies, practices, and procedures.
   - Performance expectations and problem solving procedures.

4. Lunch for new employees attended by a personnel representative, the employee's supervisor, and the highest ranking administrator.

5. Afternoon session consisting of:
   - Meeting and short presentations by the organization's managers covering their operations.
   - Tour of facilities, observation and explanation of work activities, and meeting key staff.
   - Completion of in-processing forms.
   - Informal period of questions and answers.
   - Supervisors brought in to spend one hour in "get acquainted" casual conversation with their new employees.

Work Unit Orientation

1. Supervisor and departmental manager meet with new employee to present information about departmental staffing, operations, goals, and expectations. Also, an effort is made to get acquainted with the employee's background, past employment experiences, work interests and goals, and what initial assignments should be undertaken.

2. Supervisor covers the new employee's job responsibilities, accountabilities, departmental rules and procedures, schedules and hours, and recordkeeping requirements.

3. Supervisor introduces new employee to departmental facilities, equipment and materials, coworkers, and makes initial job assignments aimed at getting the employee familiar with the type and nature of work rather than producing immediate results.

4. The first few weeks of the new employee's employment should be spent working directly and closely with the supervisor and, alternately, with one of the department's best performers who can show the new employee the "ropes."

A Well-Developed Orientation Process

Added sophistication should be brought to the orientation process of organizations with 100 or more employees. Organizations of this size tend to have more facility locations, diversity of jobs and people, complexity of management and operational structures, and specificity of work routines, policies, procedures, and programs that have to be absorbed before they can be assimilated into the individual's job context. For these reasons, care should be taken by those who develop, plan, and make arrangements for the orientation of new employees. Perhaps the greatest distinction between satisfactory and well-developed orientation processes is that the latter require more preparation of formal presentations, more people involved in orientation events, and a more gradual introduction of information to avoid overload and resultant confusion by new employees.

One of the better models of a well developed orientation process was designed by Corning Glass Works in the early 1980s after recognizing the cost and associated problems of turnover during the first one to three years of employment among the 200 to 300 professional employees hired each year. What Corning sought to accomplish was to reduce turnover rates during the first three years of employment; shorten the time for employees to learn their jobs and get involved in meaningful work; create an understanding of company objectives, principles, and strategies; and build a positive attitude about the company and community. Corning's education and training staff undertook extensive research on the subject of what was needed to produce a truly effective orientation process that would meet these goals. What was learned from their research was that

- Pre-arrival planning is part of the orientation
- Early impressions are lasting
- Day one is crucial
- New people have an interest in the total organization
- The basics should be taught first
- The learning process should be phased to avoid overload
- Key people from within the organization, especially supervisors, must be involved

As a result of its research effort, Corning designed a combined orientation and integration process spanning 15 months, the general contents of which consist of the following:

The First Day

On this important day, the new employee has breakfast with his or her supervisor, goes through processing in the personnel department, attends a *Corning and You* seminar, has lunch with the seminar leader, reads the workbook for new employees, is given a tour of the building, and is introduced to coworkers.

The First Week

During this week, the new employee (1) has one-to-one interviews with the supervisor, coworkers, and specialists; (2) learns the how-to's, wheres, and whys connected to the job; (3) answers questions in the workbook; (4) gets settled in the community; and (5) participates with the supervisor in firming up the Management By Objective (MBO) plan.

The Second Week

The new person begins regular assignments.

The Third and Fourth Weeks

The new person attends a community seminar and an employee benefit seminar (a spouse or guest may be invited).

The Second through the Fifth Months

During this period, assignments are intensified and the new person has biweekly progress reviews with his or her supervisor, attends six two-hour seminars at intervals (on quality and productivity, technology, performance management and salaried compensation plans, financial and strategic management, employee relations, and EEO and social change), answers workbook questions about each seminar, and reviews answers with the supervisor.

The Sixth Month

The new employee completes workbook questions, reviews the MBO list with the supervisor, participates in a performance review with the supervisor, receives a certificate of completion for Phase I orientation, and makes plans for Phase II orientation.

The Seventh through Fifteenth Months

This period features Phase II orientation: division orientation, function orientation, education programs, MBO reviews, performance reviews, and salary reviews.

Orientation processes of this magnitude require considerable planning, preparation, coordination, and involvement on the part of various company representatives. However, what Corning and other companies who have invested the time, money, and effort to prepare well-developed orientations have learned is that substantial savings can be realized in the way of reduced turnover from resignations, faster and more complete productivity, and improved morale among those who are allowed the opportunity to get more deeply involved with the company. Although you may not have the interest, need, or ability to undertake as extensive a process as Corning, you may wish to use the following modified model.

General Employment Orientation

Pre-Arrival Activities

- Prepare new employee orientation packets including handouts of first day's instructional materials and, if possible, mail packets to them for advanced review.
- Meet with applicable supervisors to coordinate scheduled events, and notify involved managers of the orientation schedule, pointing out those activities where their participation will be included.
- Arrange for the use of a conference or training room suitable to the number of new employees and presentation needs.

The First Day

1. Review material in orientation packets.

2. Present slide or other visual programs on the organization, its business, place in the industry, management and operations structure, mission and goals, and methods of operations.

3. Invite, introduce, and have presentations by key (division/department) managers.

4. Invite and arrange an extended lunch with applicable supervisors for casual conversation in a social setting.

5. Conduct a narrated tour of facilities.

6. Invite, introduce, and have a presentation made by the organization's highest administrative officer (president, chief executive officer, general manager).

7. Allow a one-hour period of open questions and answers, and networking/getting acquainted among new employees.

Departmental and Continuing Organizational Orientation

The First Week

1. Assign new employees to their respective supervisors on the second day. Make sure that supervisors have a copy of the New Employee Orientation Checklist, and that it's completed and returned promptly for deposit in the employee's personnel file.

2. The departmental orientation should be conducted by the employee's supervisor, including a meeting with the departmental manager, and topics covered by the supervisor should cover such general-to-specific details as
   - Job responsibilities and performance expectations.
   - Schedules, hours, overtime work, time records, vacations, and absences.
   - Work activities, procedures, rules, and forms.
   - Facilities, materials, equipment, breaks, and meals.
   - Other matters and points of information identified on the New Employee Orientation Checklist.

3. The supervisor's introduction of the new employee to coworkers, and scheduling the new employee's observation of coworker job activities.

4. Conduct a two-hour evening presentation for new employees and their spouse or guest on the organization's compensation and benefits programs. At the end of this presentation, new employees should be requested to submit their benefit enrollment forms to their supervisor by the beginning of the second week (or sooner if required for an impending payroll processing cycle).

The First Month

1. Conduct two- to four-hour presentations for new employees on such topics as
   - Company policies and operational procedures.
   - Workplace diversity issues (EEO, sexual harassment, employee relations, conflict resolution, etc.).
   - Service and general performance conditions.

2. Assign each new employee to a compatible coworker "sponsor" (a best performer model selected by the supervisor) who can show the new employee how things get done, provide information and advice, and help with new and unfamiliar conditions such as job details and assimilation into the informal work group.

The Second Through Sixth Months

1. Conduct private meetings with each new employee's supervisor to discuss various aspects of the employee's adaptation, problems, concerns, and needs.

2. Require that supervisors complete a written review of the new employee's progress in all aspects of employment adjustment, and discuss the results with the employee at the conclusion of every other month.

3. Make necessary minor adjustments that will better accommodate the specific skills and character of the new employee to the extent that doing so will benefit their adaptation, improve employee work relations in the unit, and maximize productive use of their talents.

10.2 How to Conduct Departmental Orientations

Departmental orientation is where new employees relate most to their job and the realities of their employment future. Assuming your organization has the desire to start every employee on the right track, it is imperative that the departmental orientation be a *designed* second stage of the overall orientation process.

Unlike general employment orientations where one person, usually a representative of the personnel office, has control over the process, departmental orientations are conducted by several different people. Most often, departmental orientations are handled by the new employee's immediate supervisor. Depending on the size and structure of an organization, then, departmental orientations can involve a considerable number of supervisors and their managers. This can be a potential problem in terms of the continuity of operational level orientations, the goals of which should be

- imparting and reinforcing more specific employment (performance) standards;
- providing detailed operations information;
- modeling expected role behavior; and,
- initiating job learning activities.

Achieving Orientation Continuity Among Departments

Too often, supervisors and departmental managers view new employee orientations as a one- or two-day process during which they are to cover those items on the orientation checklist provided to them by the personnel office. While doing so is a necessary means of assuring that each employee is provided the same *minimal* or standardized information, it is certainly not what is intended for a smooth and adaptive transition into the organizational setting. Rather, departmental managers and supervisors need to be made responsible for designing and implementing their own *transitional* orientation processes to conform to both the organization's employment standards and the department's operational demands.

This means that part of departmental orientations will have to be standardized to conform to what the organization wants to achieve as employment (performance) standards at all operation levels, and other parts of the departmental orientation will vary according to the special operation issues of each different department, or various operation units within the department. To accomplish this need for organizational continuity, you (or someone else) will have to spearhead a cooperative effort among departmental managers to design a checklist and related processes that will enable supervisors to orient new employees in the desired manner. The suggested steps for developing departmental orientations are

1. Get the approval of your highest ranking administrator to form a project committee of department managers, and communicate the need, purpose, and information of this committee to them in a management meeting or a memo from the administrator.

2. Schedule your first meeting by contacting each department manager to arrange a mutually suitable day, time, and location. At this meeting, you should thoroughly explain what needs to be accomplished, why it is important, and what you need from them. You should tell them that you need their help to identify uniform employment and performance standards, and to give thought to the unique or specialized kinds of operational adaptations that are most likely to ensure their employees' proper adaptation to their jobs.

3. Spend the remainder of your first meeting in an open discussion of what topics or aspects of uniform standards should be included in the departmental orientation. The results of this initial meeting should be a preliminary list of topics and scheduling a second meeting where topics will be refined in semifinal detail, including the proposed methods to achieve them.

4. Have your preliminary list typed and attach it to a memo reminding department managers of the next meeting, and that you need their continuing thought about additional items to be included, along with suggested methods.

5. During your second meeting with department managers, finalize the list of uniform employment and operations standards, then list consensus methods to be used to convey each one. Methods may consist of such things as a private meeting with the supervisor, breakfast or lunch discussion with department manager, small group meeting with select coworkers, or one-on-one activities between the new employee and the supervisor or coworkers.

6. Set up joint meetings with the supervisors of each separate department, and use the same procedure to develop a list of unique or special operation issues that should be addressed during the orientation process. Refine these lists during your second meeting with them.

7. Prepare a draft departmental orientation checklist containing both uniform employment and operations standards and special operation issues (separate page), along with written general guidelines for supervisors to use during the conduct of orientations.

8. Send your draft(s) back to department managers and request that they, and their supervisors, review it for accuracy, understanding, and thoroughness. Give them a date to return their comments, and then use their comments to make final changes.

9. Arrange a two- to four-hour training session for all department managers and supervisors (you may have to conduct split sessions) to introduce them to the new orientation form, supervisory guidelines, and the principles and techniques of conducting new employee orientations. Begin using the new departmental orientation form(s) with the next new employee hired. If you had other forms in use previously for departmental orientations, request their collection and return, then destroy them except for one file copy as a historical record.

How Supervisors Should Conduct Departmental Orientations

Since orientations are an infrequent responsibility of supervisors, much like conducting pre-employment interviews and performance appraisals, the process requires initial training, periodic follow-up discussion of results being achieved or problems being encountered, and advance planning each time the task is to be conducted. Orientations are therefore best characterized as a cyclical process; learning how to do them (training), preparing to conduct them (planning), reviewing results (evaluation and modification), and reviewing each stage when another one is to be undertaken (repetition).

The ideal way to begin the departmental orientation process is for you to meet briefly with the department manager and applicable supervisor prior to the arrival of each new employee. This meeting should take place at the time the applicant accepts the offer of employment and has agreed to a start date. In your meeting with the department manager and supervisor, help them plan for the employee's arrival and first few weeks on the job. Included here will be their involvement in the general orientation during the first few days, scheduling their own time to accommodate activities with the new employee, arranging work loads of staff who might be directly involved with the new employee for a few weeks, and providing staff with a little background on the new employee prior to his or her arrival. By meeting in advance of the new employee's arrival to discuss these orientation arrangements and measures, the department manager and the supervisor will be much better prepared to demonstrate a proper orientation process.

At this time, the supervisor should review written orientation guidelines and acquire a copy of the departmental orientation checklist. Also, the department manager and supervisor should agree on scheduling meetings with the new employee, reviewing methods of indoctrination, and assigning staff to help introduce the new employee to work activities. The following suggestions for the supervisor are based on the human nature and learning needs of new employees rather than the convenience desires of the department.

Meeting Managers, Supervisors, and Coworkers

All people have the ability to learn and perform a set of work activities based on varying degrees of these skills. However, skills alone usually do not carry much meaning until they are put into motion, and that motion normally means interacting with others in particular ways. Interactive abilities are frequently more important for job success than even job skills.

Interactive skills are learned traits based on long-established patterns of behavior, personality and attitudes, and are formed during the early part of new relationships. Employment is a very distinctive new relationship, and it is vital to a new employee's success that this new relationship be cultivated as early as possible. For this reason, orientation should place emphasis on creating the opportunity for new employees to establish a working familiarity with those they will be most directly involved with in the course of their work.

Although work relationships have, of course, an employment context, the process of establishing them are much the same as creating social bonds. Work is merely a social process with prescribed purpose and predetermined controls. Here are a few suggested ways in which you can begin establishing work relationships between new employees and others with whom they will have the greatest need to work interactively.

1. ***All Direct Involvement Staff***

   • Prior to the arrival of a new employee, prepare a short memo announcing the person's selection, start date, orientation schedule, and a brief statement on their background (without divulging confidential or privacy protected information). Ask staff to welcome the new employee and be prepared to answer questions or help him or her in any way they can.

   • Schedule orientation meetings ahead of time with management staff. Also, select and notify the key staff you intend to use for the new employee's initial orientation, sponsorship, or job training.

2. ***Meeting Management***
   Management is too often viewed in adversarial ways by lower level employees because management is perceived as having all the power, as well as dressing and thinking differently from others. This hierarchical myth and social distance should be dispelled early so that a more mutual understanding of each other's employment role can be undertaken with greater appreciation and respect for each other. Here are a few ideas for approaching the process differently.

   • Make advanced arrangements with all those managers directly or indirectly involved with the new employee's job to take one-half to a full hour to meet the new employee. This time should be dedicated to *sharing* both personal and operational background with the new employee, including an explanation of the manager's role, responsibilities, operational conditions, and needs to achieve their goals.

   • Or, arrange a ("brown bag" lunch) meeting with the new employee and all of these managers as a get-acquainted opportunity for all, and to provide the new employee with useable insights into the managers as people first, and operational officers second.

   • Managers should be known on a first-name basis by employees, except for perhaps the highest level executives, in order to make interactive work relations a comfortable, mutually empowering process. The new employee should be given some initial assignments that will provide working exposure to these managers rather than merely introductions.

3. ***Meeting Supervisors***
   Supervisors should be an extension of management. They should reflect a complementary—not contradictory—set of values, operational styles, and work behaviors. Proceed with creating bonds between your new employee and those from whom the individual will receive the most direction, learning, and guidance.

   • Assign new employees to their immediate supervisor during the first week of employment. This supervisor should spend dedicated time to establish a personal and operational familiarity with the new employee, and allow the new employee the opportunity to get to know the supervisor in both the personal and operations role context.

   • Next, schedule the new employee to spend a day with every other supervisor who is responsible for operations that relate directly or indirectly to the new employee's work. This process will not only strengthen the new employee's comfort with associate supervisors, but also establish greater familiarity with the operations of related parts of their assigned department. As previously pointed out, the more new employees know about how the organization and their department works, the more meaningful will be their work and its results.

4. *Meeting Coworkers*

   Coworkers form the immediate, most socially interactive work group. Relationships shaped here are very powerful in terms of teamwork success or behavioral dysfunctions. Drawing the parallel to a family setting, the interactive relationships between coworkers is much like that of siblings—they can be structured as positive and supporting, or they can be left to chance and hope that rivalries do not form. The best way of establishing good relations among coworkers is to create a nourishing work environment and the opportunity for them to get acquainted.

   - Avoid overwhelming new employees by the usual walk-around introductions giving coworkers' names and statements about their jobs. This only adds further confusion to an already nervous situation because new employees want to be liked and fit in, so they tend to feel pressured by the perceived need to remember people. Take this strain off by keeping the new employee focused on a relationship with you first, then progressively give the new employee one-on-one introductions to each coworker. Start introductions with those the new employee will be working most directly and closely.

   - Or, you can conduct the usual walk-around and let existing employees and the new employee know that there is no expectation of remembering names or what people do. Rather, the walk-around is for initial observation, and introductions will come later. Then, schedule small group meetings between the new employee and coworkers for about an hour. This time should be used as sort of a welcoming event in which existing employees are encouraged to tell the new employee about themselves, their jobs, and to show the new employee what they do.

   - Yet another approach is to develop what has been referred to as a "sponsorship" program with each work unit. Here, selected employees are given training on orienting and helping to integrate new employees hired into their work units. Each new hire is assigned to his or her (employee) sponsor during the general employment orientation much the same way some larger companies assign mentors to new, lower level managers. The sponsor is sort of a big brother/sister whose role is to get them comfortable in the work unit, show them how things work, introduce them to coworkers, take them to lunch, help them with questions or problems, provide advice, and sometimes provide initial training although the sponsor need not be a person who would have such background.

Getting Acquainted with Departmental Operations

Once the players become known to new employees, and comfortable relationships have begun to form to the extent the new employee can begin work interactions, the next step is to make the individual feel competent about how their department and work unit operate. At first glance, these concerns may seem obvious to you. But remember, they are not at all obvious to new employees, and the purpose of orientation is to achieve the highest possible level of successful adaptation.

The best way to orient new employees to departmental and work unit operations is to put yourself in their place: What would you want to know and what would be the easiest, most absorbing method of learning pertinent operational issues? Check to see if the thoughts you have are reflected on your departmental orientation checklist. If not, write them in or make notes to yourself so that you remember to cover those points. Ultimately, the following aspects of an operations orientation should be given careful time and attention.

1. *Operational Activities*
   New employees need to have a "feel" for the big picture of their department, and doing so creates a better context for the employee's understanding of the work being performed by them and others in their own work unit. So the emphasis here should be on what general functions the department serves in relation to the organization, what are department goals, how is it structured, how are the separate work units arranged to work together, and who are the players? Then, emphasis should be shifted to introduce the new employee to each work activity in his or her assigned work unit.

   • The departmental activities orientation should be scheduled with other orientation activities as part of one day. Other employees should be notified of your intended departmental orientation schedule so that the new employee can be greeted each step along the way by people who expected him or her, rather than reacting as a surprised interruption to their work. Preferably, as employees are introduced, they should stop their work, engage in two-way conversation about each other's jobs, and close by offering the new employee any help he or she may need.

   • On another day, and also mixed with other orientation activities, you should conduct the work unit orientation. Here, much more precise information should be divulged about the unit's objectives, functions, staffing, work flow, rules, procedures, facilities, materials and equipment, supervision, future plans, and how things tend to change (that is, is it a static or dynamic set of work conditions, and what does that mean in terms of what the employee can expect).

   • If the department and/or work unit has a written procedures manual or similar written documentation that would be helpful to new employees, this is the time to give them a copy, show them its contents and how to use it, and point out what sections to read first. Keep in mind that lengthy written material, such as procedural instructions and forms, are very boring to most people, so they should be made a part of the structured job learning (training) process. Structured learning means that the new employee is given direction on what to read, follow up discussion to assure absorption, and practice with its application—one piece at a time.

2. *Job Responsibilities and Performance Expectations*
   The last and most specific portion of the operations orientation is a detailed, open, and honest discussion with the new employee about his or her particular job responsibilities. This discussion should be not only detailed, but broadly stated as well, because responsibilities encompass individual and teamwork activities to get work done, the styles and methods used in work, what types of independent actions and authorities the employee may have or progressively work into, how problems are to be handled, and any other facet of the job and work conditions you can think of that may help prepare this person for situations that tend to arise in the course of work.

   Additionally, new employees should also have a complete understanding of what is expected of them by their departmental manager, immediate supervisor, and coworkers. Therefore, you should plan to orient new employees to these types of work expectations and how they are evaluated in terms of formal performance appraisals. During this discussion, use a blank copy of the formal performance appraisal form to point out how all aspects of their job, responsibilities, behavior, and work outcomes are measured. You should further let new employees know that your job is to not only help them, but to monitor and evaluate their performance as well.

3. *Learning the Job*
   While many new employees may come to your organization with existing job skills, that in itself does not necessarily mean they know exactly how to apply those skills in your

setting. Here are some ways in which you might approach helping new employees with job learning.

- Having completed all other aspects of the new employee's orientation, this is a good time to meet with the individual for the purpose of clarifying any questions or concerns. Specifically, you should ask them what they feel they need to know, be shown, have demonstrated, receive more explanation about, or have remaining uncertainty. You should attempt to verify if they feel comfortable with their knowledge about operations to the extent of starting a few assignments under the tutelage of a seasoned coworker and yourself, or if they would prefer a little more observation of the work details for which they will be responsible. Act on this conversation accordingly.

- Schedule one of your best performers who is also knowledgeable about the new employee's job to spend a few days, and periodically thereafter, with the new employee. Do this by shifting some of their work load to other employees so that they can spend dedicated time showing the new employee how to get started. This coworker should be instructed to start the new employee off with basics, let them practice each new task, and progressively introduce more responsible duties to assure a complete understanding of all duties.

- Assign new employees to their work station and see to it that they have all the necessary materials, supplies, tools, or whatever is needed to get started. If they are to perform at a desk, take them to wherever supplies are kept to requisition supplies, show them how to use the telephone system, give them a directory of personnel, and have their name plate ready so that they are made to feel they *belong* from the beginning. If the new employees' work is at some other type of a work location setting, use a similar approach to make sure they have all the provisions needed to get started in a comfortable manner.

- Make a special effort during the new employees' first week or two to observe them interacting with their assigned coworker, other coworkers, or working by themselves. See if they look comfortable or lost, are paying attention with interest or seem mildly disinterested, and if they are taking the initiative to mingle and fit in or isolate themselves. These can be important early signs that some additional attention and reorientation should be made before the new employee develops patterns of work behavior that become irreversible.

Employment Conduct Policies

If you want your new hires and other employees to be successful workers, then it's important to communicate two types of information: 1) what and how you *want* them to do their work and behave; and, 2) what things you *don't want* them to do. These are normally employment conduct issues that come into play for new employees during their orientation to the company and their probationary period of adjustment to its policies and customs. It is imperative that new employees learn early on what the company's expectations and "cultural" values are concerning employment-related conduct in order to properly shape the right kind of behavior.

Too often, employers leave this important behavior-shaping adjustment period to chance by either avoiding adoption of such policies, or failing to communicate them fully when a new person is brought into the organization—often out of concern that the new employee may get a negative impression of the company's interest in regulating conduct matters. Such concern is an unfounded myth. Most people are more likely to respond favorably to apparent and needed controls than to uncertain ones that they know should, and probably do, exist but are not being conveyed to employees.

Clearly, the orientation period is the single most important opportunity an employer has to shape the work behavior of new employees. Failure to take advantage of this opportunity by conveying and reinforcing your employment conduct policies is a major and frequently made mistake in the hiring process. If you are skeptical about this fact, ask yourself how many terminations are the result of the inadequacy of job skills versus the inadequacy of performance conduct.

Some examples of specific employment conduct policies that you should communicate and reinforce to new employees during the orientation process are

- Honest and Loyal Service Policy
- Conflict of Interests Policy
- Personal Appearance Standards Policy
- Employee Harassment Policy
- Romantic or Sexual Liaisons Policy
- No Smoking Policy
- Off-Duty Conduct and Outside Employment Policy
- Causes of Discipline Policy

10.3 Using Integration as a Planned Process of Employee Adjustment

Integrating new employees into the organization goes one very vital step beyond orientation; it provides them with a sense of *belonging* and gives them an opportunity to *participate* in the interests of the company. Integration is therefore a process of *immediate inclusion*. Underlying the integration process are such beliefs as

- Every new employee is a valuable asset to the organization, and we want them to contribute more than just work.
- With every new employee, we are given the opportunity to receive new ideas, new perceptions of our weaknesses, and new solutions to business or operational problems.
- The key to the success of any organization lies in the proper use of all talents possessed by their people.
- Nearly every person has talents that go beyond the immediate job, and the application of these talents should be both encouraged and used by prudent employers to maximize the potential for success.
- Employees perform best when they feel they belong, are allowed to be involved, and when their participation is recognized and used.

The patterns of employment change are beginning to suggest that quality employees will not stay long in a work environment that does not provide them with a solid sense of belonging, involvement beyond the narrow scope of their jobs, and the opportunity to participate in the larger affairs of the business. Conversely, those companies that foster employee belonging, involvement, and participation *from their first day of employment* are gaining the decided edge over their competition. They have learned that integration into the *company* is the vital link to successful adjustment of their employees, and that satisfied employees are retained for longer periods.

In the absence of a planned process to integrate employees into the company's business and its operations, new employees will be left to their own devices of employment adjustment. The process is taken for granted by an unconscious expectation after a short period of orientation that each new employee will assimilate by mere exposure to their job, work routines, and their coworkers. Instead of planning the integrated adjustment of new employees, we have developed the practice of watching them, evaluating them, and either adjusting to *them* or rejecting them.

A more effective way of assuring successful adjustment of new employees is to consciously plan a process of integration. The focus on an integration process should be, again, on instilling a meaningful sense of belonging, involvement, and participation—in other words, an identity with the organization itself. Given these focal areas, your integration process should attempt to address the following sub-elements.

1. *Sense of Belonging*

   - Creating an identity between the new employee's personal values and beliefs with those of the business, its culture, and its goals.

   - Creating an interpersonal bond between the new employee and his/her departmental manager, supervisors, and coworkers.

   - Creating opportunities for individual ideas, methods, experimentation, flexibility, and recognition among all employees, and that is celebrated by coworkers when one of them succeeds. Just as it is customary for all to celebrate a coworker's birthday, why not create other work related opportunities to celebrate notable events?

2. *Employee Involvement and Participation*

   - Creating involvement in the organization's business by every employee based on the level of interest, type of talent, and the kind of involvement desired by each individual.

   - Creating opportunities for employees to remain knowledgeable about the organization's current events, plans, industry standing, operational problems, and the like. Examples of such involvement might include asking employees to help with the company's newsletter by being a rotational "reporter" of events in their department or work unit, the chief administrator holding quarterly meetings of all employees to report on organization-wide events, or assigning employees to a task force charged with some organizational project.

   - Creating the opportunity for new employees to get involved immediately with coworkers on team projects, committees, or taking the lead on some work assignment with which they have particular (previous) experience.

Aside from the previously mentioned informal methods that can be used to integrate new employees (i.e., developing interpersonal relationships and providing opportunities to get involved with the company beyond their immediate jobs), there are two structured processes of integration that are gaining the favor of employers who have found the missing link that separates workers from contributory employees. The two processes are divided by the level and type of job held by the new employee, but both processes represent a form of mentoring.

Employee Sponsorship Programs

As mentioned earlier in this chapter, Employee Sponsorship Programs involve the training and assignment of the organization's best (rank-and-file) employee performers for the purpose of mentoring new employees. But rather than mentoring per se, sponsorship takes on more of a big brother/sister implication because the sponsor becomes the new employee's role model, advisor, confidante, trainer, and representative on any delicate matter that may arise during the new employee's first six months or so on the job.

Employee Sponsorship Programs work well in all types of business operations, and they are particularly suitable for rank-and-file jobs up to the higher levels of professional and administrative careerists. Beyond this level the company should use a Key Employee Mentoring Program for the further development of its people. Some of the major advantages of implementing an Employee Sponsorship Program are

- It involves and rewards your best performers by giving them special training and assignments to help new employees succeed.
- It demonstrates to new employees that the company truly works in a team spirit at all levels, and that the company is committed to the successful adaptation of their new hires.
- It provides the quickest possible productivity of new employees by having them trained by more seasoned coworkers who are most familiar with all aspects of the job and company, rather than a supervisor who is often too far removed from the actual job.
- It establishes early bonding with coworkers and the supervisor that accelerates the new employee's sense of belonging.
- It makes new employees feel they are a more active part of the organization because they are given a representative voice and "insider" information through their interaction with their sponsor.
- New employees are given the early opportunity to work in a team setting where their work adaptation is a clearly designed process being orchestrated between them, their sponsor, and the supervisor.

To begin the development of an Employee Sponsorship Program, start with a few preliminary steps. If there is some reluctance in your organization to implement this program in all operating departments, get approval to start with a pilot program and run it like a scientific test: select one or two departments as the control group (without new employee sponsors) and a test group (with sponsors). Compare the two groups over a year or two based on such factors as turnover rates, time to achieve productivity, promotions, and several characteristics of job satisfaction. Start your pilot program by taking these steps:

1. Select one or two departments (or operating units) you want to use for a sponsorship program, and confer with applicable managers on the nomination of employees to be asked to undergo sponsorship training and assignments. Enough sponsors should be nominated and selected to represent a cross-section of jobs in the department in which new employees are likely to be hired.

2. Design the training program to be given to sponsors consisting of at least these topics:
   - Detailed training on the organization's culture, goals, plans, structure, staffing, modes of operating, and policies and procedures.
   - Thorough "train-the-trainer" instruction.
   - Training on such topics as communications, employee relations, problem solving techniques, and acting as an advisor.

3. Participate in the training of sponsors so that you can assess their development and assure that each one is properly adapting to the role. Those who are not adapting should be counseled and, if necessary, gracefully removed from the training.

4. Have each sponsor prepare a checklist for integration and training activities they propose to use as a guide during their six-month direct involvement with new employees. However, similar to orientation checklists, some topics should be uniform among all

sponsors while some aspects of unit operations and job training will need to be tied to the nuances of differing conditions.

5. Begin assigning new employees to their sponsors during the orientation process, but give the applicable supervisor enough time to establish a solid working relationship with the new employee first. It is the supervisor who should introduce the sponsorship process to the new employee in order to establish the new employee's identity of the supervisor as the team leader.

Key Employee Mentorship Programs

Traditionally, mentorship programs have been associated with the training and development of new or lower level managers by higher level managers and usually then only those who are tagged for fast-tracking up the corporate ladder. Conceptually, however, the traditional approach is far too restrictive given the operational need for many *jobs* to be developed to high levels of proficiency, and the organizational advantage of developing more of a company's *people* at the excellence level of performance.

Clearly, management jobs are not the only ones that have a high impact on the contributory success of an organization, or where planned adaptation is essential to proper integration of a new employee. Therefore, key employees are typically identified from among the mid-to-higher ranks of technical, professional, administrative, and managerial jobs. Your planning process to implement a program of Key Employee Mentorship is very similar to that of employee sponsorship.

1. Develop a preliminary list of key jobs in your company where you feel new employees should be integrated by the process of mentorship based on the nature of their critical impact on the organization or departmental operations.

2. Confer with higher management on this list by first explaining the program, its advantages, factors used to select jobs, and their suggestions concerning jobs that should be added or deleted from the list. Remember, the focus should be on *jobs* at this point, not people or past experiences with job incumbents. Also, ask this management group for any suggestions they may have that might enhance the program's content or administration.

3. Train selected mentors in the same way as suggested for employee sponsors, but place more emphasis on role modeling, management practices, operational methods, marketing, and project leadership. Add any other specialized training topics that fit the nature of your company's business, keeping in mind that these are the organization's *key* people.

4. At the conclusion of training, have each mentor prepare an integration plan similar to the employee sponsor checklist. The mentor's plan should, however, be more descriptive in terms of phased learning over a one-year period with defined, measurable objectives, and representative of all aspects of employment in the respective job. Since the goal is complete and successful adaptation of new employees, the mentoring plan should include such measurable factors as transition into the company's "culture," depth and diversity of skills and knowledge acquired ranging from the job to company-wide matters, interpersonal skills development, use of methods and ideas, self-initiative, involvement and participation, and similar measures of a broad-based integration process.

5. Monthly meetings should be held between the new employee, the mentor, and the next higher level manager to review what has been accomplished from the mentoring plan, the next stage of the plan, an informal evaluation of performance to date, and an open discussion by the new employee and mentor about their experience in the mentoring process, and any adjustments that may be appropriate.

6. Conduct quarterly comprehensive evaluations on the new employee with specific detail given to any area in which the new employee is having difficulty or lags behind the plan. These formal evaluations should be prepared by the mentor and next higher level manager with informal input from other work associates above the level of the new employee who has had work exposure to the new employee. When completed, an informal conference should be held between the new employee, the mentor, and the next higher level manager to thoroughly discuss each and every evaluation factor, and to arrive at mutual agreements about how to proceed.

How to Select Sponsors and Mentors

Employee sponsors and key employee mentors are not easy roles to fill. The assignment requires a great deal of personal attention, thought, and consciously planned activities by a person who has an established record of demonstrating multi-dimensional talents. Therefore, when you and other high level managers in your organization begin the selection process for sponsors and mentors, your attention should be focused on people who possess *all* of the following characteristics:

- Senior level skills and knowledge pertaining to the new employee's job.
- A demonstrated record of excellence in achievement among a diverse range of operational challenges.
- Superior communication, motivation, and leadership skills.
- Knowledgeable about a broad range of company operations, policies, and practices.
- A good representative of the company's values and styles.
- A good teacher with strong interpersonal abilities to instill confidence, trustworthiness, alliance, and source of advice and guidance.
- One who does not have the authority to fire or promote their protege since these relationships should not be predicated on "heir-apparent," nor "fail and get fired" undertones.

10.4 How to Solve Special Integration Problems

The types of employees you hire will differ as greatly as the diversity of jobs, businesses, and employment conditions and practices that exist in the work world. It should not be surprising, then, to know that some types of employees can present unique or special problems when it comes to integrating them into the kinds of organizational life experiences that exist in your company.

Problems and unique issues should be anticipated, but not expected, so that you and others will know how to spot them and react favorably. The brief description of four employee types that follow are intended to illustrate some of the more common integration problems and recommended solutions.

College Graduates and Other First Employments

First employment new hires, whether college grads or others, can present some unique problems for many employers whose work setting is not suited to the idiosyncrasies of these individuals. One of the more notable—if not notorious—features of new entrants into the work force is the frequency of their job changes. These frequent job changes are caused by two very different reasons: 1) the noncollege workers are undergoing a process of discovery about available jobs, their skills, and skill-to-job values; and, 2) college grads are seeking idealistic career opportunities that match *their* sense of what employment should offer *them*. Both groups want employment on their terms, and both have incorrect preconceived notions about what employment means in real life terms. That should not be surprising since neither of these two first-employment groups have ever had personal exposure to the realities of work.

Both first-employment groups also hold firm beliefs that employment should offer them the same choices, options, challenge, diversity, and change they experienced in the developmental years of their youth. This characteristic, while others of us may view it as naive on their part, tends to make them less willing to adjust their established values and work styles to the usual company expectations and employment controls. Thus, if the company does not come through during their first year or two of employment with regular pay increases (they started lower than they thought they should), skills development training (they expect the company to provide their skills training), and promotions (they have an inflated sense of self-worth), then they are likely to move on if for no other reason than to see what else is out there. This presents another problem for employers; the youth work force of today is far more mobile than ever before.

College grads and those with some academic training are unique in some respects. As a work force resource, they are more interested in being generalists, making quick contributions rather than "paying their dues," having flexible opportunities to be creative, receiving meaningful and challenging work assignments, having independence and decision making abilities, getting the chance to take some risks, and being recognized for their achievements. The kinds of accommodation they seek in employment are primarily those involving independence and reward at an accelerated pace. If your company, or the job for which they are being considered, is not prepared to deal with their expectations, adaptation can be difficult for you and them.

To solve some of the obvious problems that can accompany both groups of first employment youth, here are some steps you should consider in advance of their hire:

1. Place additional emphasis during the orientation and integration processes on teaching the first-employment new hire about the company's values, expectations, policies, work routines, and what they can *realistically* expect from their employment. In other words, take a little extra time to provide them with the education about the work world that has thus far been overlooked during their development years. Try to create realistic expectations without dampening their determination to excel.

2. Use a sponsorship or mentor process to facilitate their transition into work life, relationships, and routines.

3. Get them involved as quickly as possible in meaningful and progressively challenging work where they can see short-term results.

4. Start work assignments using their existing knowledge and personal skills; determine where they need development of skills and knowledge; and begin providing on-the-job training followed by periodic attendance in structured training opportunities. Also, try to rotate their work assignments so that they get added exposure to the bigger picture of operations.

5. Keep them informed at short, regular intervals about their performance, and be honest—they need to learn that growth takes time.

6. If they demonstrate quick learning, applications of skills and knowledge, and the ability to assume greater responsibility, then try to promote them or at least advance their pay rate according to their development—not based on inflexible policies governing prescribed time sequences for advancement.

Shift and Variable-Schedule Employees

Problems can surface with the adjustment of employees who have been assigned to variable work schedules, particularly rotating shifts. Not only is their orientation, integration, supervision, and other customary forms of adaptation to employment more difficult, but they often regard themselves "out of the mainstream" of the real organization—what goes on during normal business hours.

Based on existing research, shift or variable schedule workers experience a number of personal and employment related difficulties. They are known to cope less well than day workers with family responsibilities, diet, health, leisure activities, and the meaningfulness of the employment contributions. Some of the factors most influenced by those working variable or rotating shift schedules are

- Work Behavior; job satisfaction, meaningfulness of work, organizational commitment, job performance and productivity, and high rates of absenteeism.

- Physical and Emotional Well Being; dietary adjustment, physical ailments and psychosomatic complaints, emotional stability, and mental health.

- Family Life; availability to spend time with family and friends, time spent alone, irregular time with spouse or other close relationship.

- Social Involvement; ability to participate in normal leisure activities, personal entertainment, and involvement in desired social or civic activities.

In order to properly orient, integrate, and retain new employees who will be working shift or variable schedules, their employment should begin first by creating a sense of belonging and involvement, followed by efforts to maximize their stability. To solve the kinds of problems associated with shift and variable schedule employees, you should consider these steps:

1. Start them on day work for at least one month or that period of time needed for thorough integration into the company and its operations.

2. Keep work routines, activities, and staffing (adequate employee levels and supervision) as close to that for day employees as possible.

3. Use bulletins or a newsletter, and shift supervisors as the source for keeping employees informed about company events. Have (day) managers periodically visit the work site during shifts to observe and interact with employees.

4. Avoid frequent changes in employee schedules, that of their peers, or their supervisors—they need more than usual stability in their work life since they don't have it in their personal life. Necessary changes should be made with advance notice of at least two weeks.

5. Simulate day employment practices such as providing them with training programs, meetings, work planning sessions, and the like.

6. Provide "home style" conveniences such as a microwave oven for hot meals, a television to watch during break or meal periods, and good lighting and music in their work area.

7. Provide economic incentives such as higher base pay rate (15 to 20 percent is common), premium time rate, bonuses, or accelerated longevity increases.

8. Rotate them back to days (if they are agreeable) for at least three consecutive months once a year to reestablish their ties with the company and its normal operations.

Handicapped Employees

Handicapped employees feel a greater need to prove themselves quickly in new employment. Part of this emotional predisposition is due to their need to prove their own worthiness and capability to themselves, and part is due to their need to be accepted by others as a normal contributor. These needs are more acute with handicapped employees, and serious adjustment problems can exist if these needs are not considered during their orientation and integration process. Yet another problem that can develop is the potential biases and predispositions of coworkers. They, too, should be considered if proper adjustment between the handicapped new hire and established workers is to be an open-minded, smooth adaptation for both. Here are a few steps you can take to effectuate an accommodating integration process:

1. Prior to the new employee's start date, ask the unit supervisor to meet with employees to provide them with a little background about the new employee. The supervisor should give employees information about the new employee's known skills and abilities as determined through preemployment testing, and be straightforward about the nature of the handicap, probable limitations, and the likelihood of the new employee's acute need for others to behave normally, help with initial adjustment, give him or her a chance to prove themselves, and be accepted as an equal member of the work unit.

2. Prepare the work place for the new employee's arrival such as by widening aisleways if the employee is wheelchair bound or uses crutches, acquire adaptive equipment at the new employee's work station if required by the nature of the handicap, take any other related measures that would convey a welcoming gesture to the new employee.

3. Plan and initiate a few beginning work assignments in which the new employee can quickly adapt and become productive.

4. Schedule the work of other employees to allow them time to get acquainted with the new employee on a personal level, and demonstrate the work they perform to the new employee.

5. Have the new employee observe, then participate, in work unit meetings during their first few weeks of employment.

6. Observe the work results and progress of these new employees closely so that you, or their supervisor, can expand their job responsibilities and development according to the timing and extent of their adaptation abilities.

Older Employees

Similar to handicapped workers, older employees represent a much overlooked employment resource. For many jobs, older workers have much to offer in the way of experience, maturity, and stability—features that are increasingly hard to find. Given the right attitude, motivation, and employee-to-job match, older employees can be just what the organization needs to fulfill operational demands and balance the diversity of employee talents. However, some of the issues that can surface with the employment of older workers are irregular or interrupted attendance due to health difficulties, disinterest in detail or repetitive work (unless previously burned out with having major responsibilities), impatience with others, coping with stringent company policies, and overcoming instilled behavior or work methods developed during their years of previous employment.

To overcome adjustment problems that can arise during the orientation and integration of older new employees, you may wish to consider taking these kinds of steps:

1. Make sure that your hiring decision is confident of the new employee having the right attitude, motivation (enthusiasm for the work), and in other ways a good match for the job.

2. Accelerate the orientation process given the fact that they have been there before, are more than casually familiar with employment conditions, and will easily adjust to preliminary in-processing.

3. Give them more than usual latitude with your integration process by asking *them* how they would like to get started—normally they will be more than willing to tell you, and probably hope you'll ask. However, make sure that the integration process begins with meeting people and an introduction to company goals, expectations, and the work of coworkers.

4. Use their strengths such as experience, maturity, and stability to the advantage of the company and employees in the work unit. Doing so will also make the older worker feel more valued. If they are inclined to work in groups, let them take a leadership role or take on a more advanced phase of a project. If they prefer more solitary work, give them work that is suitably interesting and worthy of their background.

5. Enforce your company's policy prohibiting any form of age discrimination to ensure that older employees are not subjected to age jokes, age-inferred remarks or naming, or any other form of discriminatory treatment.

Checklist 1: Orientation of New Employees[1]

NOTE: The first day of work can be hectic for a new employee, and often important orientation information is forgotten. Since a new employee who is not properly oriented will waste a good deal of time obtaining his own orientation, it makes sense to utilize second-and-third week follow-up procedures. These will also allow employers to tell whether the employee has been correctly placed. And feedback from the employee may lead to possible changes and improvements in new employee practices.

First Day

- ❑ Greet the new staff member, check your pronunciation of his name and ask him what he prefers to be called.
- ❑ Explain department function and organization briefly:
  - Purpose of department work
  - Relations to other departments
  - Organization of the department
  - Specific functions of new employee's section
- ❑ Review the new employee's particular job:
  - Go over the job description
  - Explain briefly the purpose of the job
  - Stress the confidential nature of work (where appropriate)
  - Give assurance that he will learn quickly
  - Stimulate job enthusiasm and satisfaction in doing work well
  - Briefly explain training period
- ❑ Spell the name of his supervisor, and give the company phone number and his supervisor's extension. Ask that these be written.
- ❑ Hours of work:
  - Starting and quitting time
- ❑ Lunch and break time:
  - Amount of time for each
  - Time scheduled
- ❑ Attendance records and reporting absences:
  - Where to put completed time cards and secure new ones
  - Importance of time cards being accurate
  - How and to whom to report absences
  - Importance of good attendance and punctuality
- ❑ Location of restroom and coat rack
- ❑ Smoking regulations
- ❑ Questions: Answer and indicate willingness to discuss questions at any point.

---

[1] SOURCE: Richard J. Mellucci, Modern Personnel Checklists, Warren, Gorham & Lamont, Inc. (1982), pp. S8-4 & 5. Copyright by Warren, Gorham & Lamont, Inc., 1982.

❑ Introduce to supervisor—supervisor will:
  • Show work area
  • Introduce to other employees
  • Arrange for someone to take new employee to lunch
  • Begin job instruction

Second Week

❑ Discuss progress—offer encouragement.
❑ Discuss strengths and weaknesses:
  • Go over positive aspects
  • Offer suggestions on weaknesses
❑ Ask that bond application be returned immediately if it has not already been returned (if applicable).
❑ Questions.

Third Week

❑ Review progress:
  • Point out areas where improvement is needed
  • Discuss details of job
  • Review job description
❑ Employee manual read?
  • Discuss importance of this
  • Go over any particular points in manual that need emphasis—for example, time cards
❑ Additional education benefits:
  • Suggest beginning courses
  • Explain registration and cost
  • Explain benefits of courses as related to job
❑ Discuss any problems and make suggestions.
❑ Questions.

Checklist 2: Involving Coworkers in the Orientation of New Employees[2]

NOTE: This checklist outlines steps the supervisor and the personnel department can take to encourage the new employee's sense of belonging by involving coworkers in the new employee's orientation.

❑ Tell other workers about the new employee before he arrives:
- His name
- When he will arrive and what he will be doing
- Where he has worked before and where he has studied

❑ Coworkers can be asked to meet together before the new employee arrives to plan ways to welcome the new employee:
- A letter of welcome on the first day
- A drink after work [*author's note:* this is not a recommended practice]
- A party—say, at the end of the first week, after the new worker has had the chance to learn a few names

  The meeting will serve its purpose if it makes coworkers conscious of the challenge of making the new employee feel comfortable and predisposes them to be welcoming.

❑ Introduce the new worker to the others when he arrives. To make the meetings with fellow employees more informal:
- Delegate the task of introducing the employee to one of his coworkers
- Point out which employees were recently hired and which are more experienced in the company, since each group has special insights to contribute to new employee orientation
- To avoid overwhelming the new employee, limit first-day introductions to those he will work with closely
- If available, provide a chart showing names, job titles, and other information such as physical location, reporting relationships, or job responsibilities to help the new employee keep track of the introductions

❑ Delegate various orientation tasks to the future coworkers:
- Have employees demonstrate job tasks, such as operation of machines or other work routines, which makes the new employee less self-conscious and provides an opportunity to praise employees for their grasp of these procedures
- An employee should be assigned to answer questions that arise when the supervisor is unavailable (of if the new employee is too embarrassed to approach the supervisor). This employee should be knowledgeable about procedures and act as a good role model
- The touring of such amenities as rest rooms, water coolers, lockers, coat closets, and coffee dispensers can be assigned to an employee
- Someone should "show the new person around the lunchroom," that is, provide him with company at lunch
- Someone can help the new employee with the sign-in procedure or with time cards, if these are used

[2] Ibid., pp. S8-6 & 7

❑ Follow through by delegating other orientation tasks as they arise later in the first week or month.

- Tour of the work units that work closely with the employee's new unit can be delegated
- Work assignments can sometimes be arranged to encourage positive relationships that spring up between the new worker and other employees

❑ A newsletter article or memo telling about the new employee's background and interests and including a picture, if possible, can help the new employee meet people who will facilitate his integration into the company.

11 Training New Employees to Meet Job Demands and Monitoring Their Performance

Training new employees to meet the demands of their jobs should not be confused with integrating the employee into your organization and work setting as discussed in the last chapter. Integration is a process of adapting each new employee to the organization, its activities, work procedures, and people. Training, on the other hand, is the task of providing each employee with the necessary knowledge, skills, and abilities to function adequately based on the level and type of current talents possessed by the new employee at the time of hire, and projected changes in the job. Consequently, training is a part of the integration process for most new employees, but training often extends well beyond the relatively short period of integration.

This chapter provides you with suggested approaches that will enable you to assess your organization's training needs, develop plans and programs to provide new employees with the type of training they will need to become valued performers, and how to evaluate the progressive adaptation of new employees.

11.1 What Types of Training Programs Are Best Suited to New Employees

Every manager would probably agree that it's important to start new employees on the right foot with regard to their ability to perform the job for which they were hired. If employees are hired with existing, high level, and easily adaptable skills, then further training may place them immediately in a pool with other job-seasoned employees where the emphasis will be more on *development* rather than training. However, most new employees are hired at the entry level of their occupations, so the need here is to provide them with training whose objective is to establish a predetermined level of job skills, knowledge, and interactive behavior conducive to organizational expectations and business demands. A brief examination of these types of training programs may help you plan better learning experiences for new employees.

Job Skills Training Programs

Job skills training has to do with the new employee's abilities to perform manual or process portions of the job. Normally, learning skills relate to some aspect of dexterity or physical abilities such as typing, use of hand tools, sorting, lifting, adjusting machines, and the like. However, some types of job skills training may also require preliminary informational learning before a particular skill can be used, as in the case of completing forms, repairing engines, or performing laboratory tests.

Depending on the nature of each job and what kinds of skills are essential for valued performance, the type of training necessary to ensure a new employee's proper learning and adaptation will target precisely those skills. Take, for example, the job of an Apprentice Carpenter. Upon examination of the job analysis information gathered about the *job*, it becomes clear that the essential skills necessary for successful performance are tools identification, use of tools, basic weights and measures, lifting, carrying and climbing, selection and use of proper materials, and basic mechanical aptitudes related to carpentry. Having administered some type of a preemployment examination that led you to the selection of a particular new hire, you should be able to ascertain what differences exist between requisite job skills and the skills possessed by the new employee. The difference between job and employee skills should form the basis of job skills training to be conducted at the time of hire, and progressively developed up to the most skilled level of carpentry.

Training programs whose objective is to provide job skills should therefore be individually tailored to each employee. The exception to this general rule is where the type of skill to be learned applies equally, or nearly equally, to more than one employee, as in the case of training employees to operate a new computer system. While job skill training programs such as this often begin with a group of employees, experience has shown that any given group will quickly deviate in their learning aptitudes and resultant proficiencies. Thus, as a group of trainees break into learning subgroups, it will become necessary to provide the less adaptive learners with more individualized instruction in order to reach the same level of proficiency as that achieved by more adaptive employees.

Job Knowledge Training Programs

These training programs are distinguished by the nature of the instructional material and type of learning methods. While training employees on job skills is best achieved on an individualized "show, tell, and try" basis, job knowledge is information-oriented and provided at two levels of learning: 1) informational knowledge of a very specific nature needed by individual employees in order to understand their respective job functions; and, 2) information that provides a body of knowledge that a number of employees must comprehend in order to use the information properly to carry out some aspect of their work common to the group being trained.

The first level of informational learning should occur during a new employee's integration process. This type of training is best provided by the employee's immediate supervisor or a select coworker who understands the need to give new employees thorough and systematic information and explanations about the work to be performed. Emphasis during this first level of knowledge training should be placed on job content detail in terms of *what* the new employee needs to know, *what* it is they are doing, *why* it's important, and *how* the work relates to the bigger picture of work unit activities.

The second level of informational learning provides employees with either individually advanced job knowledge (developmental training) or collectively obtained knowledge about new information related to their common occupational area. Individually advanced job knowledge can be provided by working with a senior level person, taking college classes or attending seminars. Here, the training tends to help the employee's promotional opportunities, or at least allow more advanced background about the job they perform. When job knowledge training is provided to a group of employees such as by internal programs, it is important that all participants share a common job interest in the information being provided, and clarity about how the information is to be used. A common example of job knowledge training provided to a "community of interest" group would be training supervisors about employment laws, company policies, or the fundamentals of management.

Interactive Abilities Training Programs

Training employees to use their existing interactive abilities, or learn new ones, places attention on the most common workplace need in a service-oriented society—people and behavior. While it is skills that teach employees *what* to do in their work, and information provides them with the *why* of their work, it is a person's interactive abilities that determine *how* work is performed. If an employee is both skilled and knowledgeable, but lacks the interactive abilities to perform well behaviorally, it is not likely the results of his or her performance will meet with an employer's desired expectations.

Interactive abilities are also the most difficult of the three requisite talents to teach people. Why? Because the behavioral characteristics of adults and their fundamental attitudes toward other people have been firmly shaped by impressionable past experiences. Until equal or more impressionable learning experiences nullify the attitudes from past experiences, the employee will remain entrenched in their behavior and predisposition toward people (certain types of people or certain types of events involving people). Regrettably, we often do not see adverse behavior or orientations toward people until the employee's actions have taken some acute form of performance. Then, our workplace method of nullifying the adverse behavior is to use counseling, discipline, and termination as the means of behavioral modification. These methods receive mixed results of changing the true orientation of employees simply because they *force* the employee to use controlled behavior in response to their "natural" tendencies to use adverse behavior—instead of reshaping the undesirable behavior.

There are probably few training programs whose sole topic and purpose is to teach interactive abilities. The closest and most commonly provided training programs are topics like Customer Service, Employee Relations, Communications, How to Deal with Problem Employees, Getting Along with People, Coping with the Difficult Customer, and similar workplace issues where the focus is on people situations and the nature of human behavior needed to deal with interactive problems. There are also countless other training programs where the subject matter will involve some amount of interactive conditions, yet these and the more directly interactive training topics often fail to create the right type of emphasis in order for *new* learning to occur. This is to say that the instructional approach to "what we want you to learn and why we want you to use this behavior on the job" is so soft that it is usually missed by participants, thus allowing them to read anything they want to from the instructional message.

For interactive training to be effective at reinforcing existing desirable behavior, and shaping new behavior from undesirable orientations that may exist within other trainees, the training must make a clear point of explaining

1. What the situation is and why it is important to the company's business;
2. What is undesirable interaction;
3. What problems and consequences result from undesirable interaction;
4. What is the desired and expected type of interactive abilities the company wants from its employees in these situations; and,
5. What benefits are derived from using desired versus undesirable interactive abilities.

The second condition that must exist with interactive training is the use of demonstration techniques in order to illustrate both undesirable and desirable models of interactions. In particular, demonstrations must involve the trainees in these exercises to allow them to practice and visualize proper methods in the controlled, and safe, conditions of a classroom setting. Instructor demonstrations followed by trainee role playing or group discussion exercises are much more effective than mere lecture.

Cross-Training Programs

New employees represent a key opportunity for employers to gain more flexible functioning of their operations. It is a well established fact that once employees become ingrained in the scope of their job responsibilities, and detail of their work, they will resist future change—especially the addition of new or expanded job tasks. New employees, on the other hand, are open to and expect training to occur with the commencement of any new job, even if they are already skilled in the occupation. Consequently, the circumstance of hiring new employees creates an unusual opportunity for the organization to implement what has been heralded as one of the most effective forms of operational efficiency, cross training employees to perform limited parts of another employee's job.

While many employees may, at first, feel resentment toward their employer for engaging in cross training, you should be aware that the resentment stems from a fear that they are being either replaced or made susceptible to easy replacement. Either may be partially true, but this form of resentment usually fades once cross training becomes a way of life in the organization, and employees begin to see its value for them. One such value is that there are fewer operational consequences that result from their (vacation, sick leave, or disability) absence, as long as the company establishes a record of integrity by reserving their jobs for a reasonable period of time awaiting their return.

Since cross training represents the acquisition of a larger application of the new employee's skills, knowledge, and abilities, it should be conducted on an individualized basis and concurrent with primary job function training. By using a concurrent training method, the new employee is better able to see the totality of their (primary and secondary) job in the perspective of one picture. Further, concurrent training allows the new employee to learn all job functions in a more conjunctive fashion than training first in primary tasks and then learning what feels like add-on tasks.

What must precede cross training is a critical evaluation of the new employee's primary job in light of these additional factors:

1. What tasks and responsibilities are being performed by coworkers that are essential to operations, and relate in some reasonable way to the primary work of the new employee?

2. Are there small but important functions of two or three coworkers that could reasonably be incorporated into the new employee's job as a matter of cross training?

3. Are the identified functions of cross training overly time consuming, burdensome in comparison to primary job functions, or too complex to undertake? If so, can one or more be eliminated or redefined in a way that resolves the conflict?

4. Are the cross-training functions within the reasonable scope of the employee's primary job to avoid working the employee beyond the general scope, nature, and pay of the job they were hired to perform?

5. How frequently will the new employee be called upon to perform secondary job functions? It should be no more frequently than as periodic "relief" work, otherwise you may be violating the underlying principles of the Equal Pay Act.

6. Does the new employee have the requisite skills, knowledge, and abilities to perform in an enlarged capacity, or have sufficient background to absorb this level of learning?

Once you have identified what coworker functions can be incorporated into the new employee's initial job training, you can begin preparing an individualized training plan. The training plan should place emphasis on primary duties but include concurrent training in secondary functions in such a way as to be a natural extension of the employee's primary job.

11.2 How to Plan Training Programs to Meet the Needs of New Employees

Too often, companies jump into training without much forethought, evaluation of needs, or planning. Conducting training of any type without these steps is a waste of time and money, and it causes the failure of each training effort. Training has therefore come to be viewed by many companies as lacking justifiable need, direction, business relatedness in terms that are meaningful to the company's goals, and the benefit of material results.

Before any company begins to study the question of its employee training programs or needs, the company should take stock of its goals, operational conditions, types of jobs employed, the type of training program desired, and what commitments the company is willing to make to support a well-designed program. Clearly, the first distinction to be made is the difference between initial employment training and ongoing programs whose aim is providing developmental learning. There are vast benefits to be derived by both types of training if these programs are designed with distinction, and sold to management and employees alike on the merits of separate purpose and objectives.

What Is Different About Initial Employment Training?

There are two features about initial employment training that differ from training conducted for other purposes. First, as was previously mentioned, new employees are normally fresh, eager, and willing to learn. That fact alone is perhaps the most important precondition to training than even the content of what is being taught to adults. If employees are predisposed to not having an interest in what the employer has to offer in the way of new learning, or they have only a mild interest in their employment conditions, or they already feel overloaded, then training will have very limited success.

Conversely, learning conditions that exist for new employees are much like that of newborn children through the age of four. It is a clinical fact that newborns enter the world with certain genetic blueprints and the first four years of life is the period in which most of their psychomotor, language, and reasoning skills are learned. The learning that takes place after age four is curiously a mere development and refinement of these basic human functions.

In a similar fashion, new employees come to you with a sort of genetic blueprint, obviously much more refined than an infant's, but nevertheless representing an indelible set of preexisting human learning traits. The manner in which these traits are *shaped* to the needs of their new job and employment conditions is dependent on whether or not the employer seizes the opportunity to provide a learning process. This initial employment learning process should be one that teaches the new employee how to *apply* what they know, and to *adapt* the information provided by new learning, in order to be employment successful.

The second feature about initial employment training is one that should be remembered when you are planning the training to be provided during the new employee's integration process. To be enduring and have productivity benefit, the training must be

1. Individualized for each new employee, and must therefore consider existing skills, knowledge, and interactive abilities compared to that required for fully successful performance.

2. Provided at the learning level and pace of each new employee so that each job function can be competently executed before moving on to progressively more difficult activities.

3. Job relevant with respect to the tasks for which the new employee was hired as well as employment conditions under which they will work. This latter issue is why external training seminars and workshops are not suitable for new employees since they lack a sufficient understanding of "home" conditions to which such training should apply.

4. Measurable in terms of whether or not, and to what level of performance proficiency, the training subjects have been learned as a matter of job execution. Here again, there exists a major deficiency in most company initial employment training efforts. The deficiency exists largely because of the lack of a suitable measurement method, including performance appraisal instruments where emphasis is placed upon *progressive learning* (i.e., job progress) and relevant characteristics of *employment adaptation*.

It is important to remember that initial employment training is different from other types of training programs. Generally, new employees are much more adaptive to learning than existing employees, while the contents of initial training also differs in that it must be formatted to individual learning, be progressive for each function taught, and be measurable to ascertain the results.

Assessing Employee-Job Match Traits

The first step in preparing a new employee's initial employment training plan is to conduct an assessment of the employee-job match traits. What you will be assessing is essentially the difference between traits possessed by the employee at the time of hire—presumably as determined through preemployment testing results—against known traits required by the job at a successful level of performance. The assessment process is therefore one of matching employee strengths against a list of requisite job traits, so that any remaining job traits not matched become areas of initial employment training.

If for some reason you have not administered the types of preemployment test that would provide you with employee trait (i.e., skills, knowledge, and interactive abilities) information, you may wish to give your new entry level employees either the Apticom System's Aptitude Test Battery or the Department of Labor's General Aptitude Test Battery as discussed in Chapter 7. The former test can be useful for measuring the nine primary aptitudes required in most entry level jobs, and claims to be validated for discriminatory impact. However, as a word of caution, tests used for the purpose of employee assessment should be examined carefully for the relevancy of each element to particular jobs in order to be useful in determining the training needs of employees.

The process of matching and assessing employee-job traits does not need to be time consuming nor scientific. It does however need to be thoughtful, and requires that sufficient objective information is obtained about employee and job traits in order to draw meaningful conclusions for the design of an initial employment training plan. On page 281 is a very basic sample of what a list should look like in order to assess the matching of employee-job traits for the illustrative job of Telephone Installer.

As you can see from this illustration of matching employee traits to those demanded by the job, there is a mismatch between the employee's knowledge of math compared to what will be required to learn the principles of electricity and perhaps make circuitry calculations. Additionally, there is no corresponding measurement of the employee's safety knowledge or ability to perform the work of an installer by use of applicable safety practices. Finally, it becomes apparent that the employee's ability to conduct work in a skilled customer service manner is at this time speculative.

Thus, these topics should be the areas of greatest focus during the employee's initial employment training. While a company's training program for entry level employees in occupations of this type may consist of providing a uniformly structured program of instruction for all such new hires to ensure consistency of skills, knowledge, and abilities, it should be clear from this illustration that each employee will differ in some respect concerning the strength of respective learning traits. Once again, these differences must be addressed in an individualized training format.

Sample Employee-Job Match Traits

Employee's Name _____   Title _(Telephone Installer)_____

Tests Used

1) _(General Aptitude Test Battery)_____   Hire Date _____

2) _(Technical Aptitude Test Battery)_____

3) _(Personal Interview)_____

Employee Traits

1. High proficiency in mechanical aptitudes.

2. Strong general mechanical aptitudes.

3. Moderate proficiency in reading and comprehension of technical literature.

4. Moderate proficiency in manual dexterity.

5. High proficiency in spatial relationship of objects.

6. Pleasant personality and easily understood conversationalist.

7.

8.

9.

10.

Job Trait Demands

1. Basic understanding of electricity.

2. Low proficiency in basic math.

3. Knowledge of and ability to use hand tools and power equipment.

4. Ability to read and interpret basic schematic drawings.

5. Knowledge of job safety as applied to the work of installers.

6. Ability to perform work in a safe manner, including the identification of hazards.

7. Ability to conduct work with a customer service approach.

8.

9.

10.

Preparing the Initial Employment Training Plan

To conduct thorough planning for the training of new employees you will need to do two things:

1. Be able to identify the nature, content, and objectives of general training subjects pertaining to common skills, knowledge, and abilities needed by new employees and known to lead to improved operational proficiency; and,

2. Be able to evaluate the traits of new employees and match them to those of their job in order to ascertain what individualized training the employee will need to establish job proficiency.

The reason for this two-level planning of training programs is that most new employees will need both general subject training and individualized instruction relative to their particular job and learning traits. The latter—individual training to achieve job proficiency—is normally a higher priority since the most immediate goal is to move the new employee toward productivity as quickly as possible. However, there are many jobs that will require concurrent general subject training, such as new supervisors, managers, administrators, and those hired into promotional jobs where certain general abilities are unfamiliar to them.

It is therefore important to distinguish which of the two types of training plans are needed for your intended audience. Preparing separate training plans will aid you in making sure that you have adequately prepared employees in the proper training program so that they will understand, value, and use the information in their job. Too often we include inadequately prepared employees in general training programs only to find out later that they did not comprehend the material nor understand its application to their jobs.

Preparing Training Plan Contents and Objectives

Training plans must have two essential components: 1) job or employment relevant contents developed for a suitable audience based on operational needs; and, 2) clearly defined and measurable objectives that can be best achieved by conducting the proposed training program. The first component should determine the justification for conducting the training, while the second component should establish the results and benefits to be derived. Armed with this information in a formatted, well thought out manner, such programs become much more saleable to higher management than merely preparing a speculative memo requesting approval (funding) for a generically described program that gives the impression of having vague operational consequence.

In Appendix D, you will find an Initial Employment Training Plan Form that provides you with the format, on which you should list specific skill, knowledge, and abilities objectives, and other pertinent details of a well-designed training program. The form can be used for either group or individualized training plans. When it is used for individualized training, you should find that it is easy to transfer information from your employee-job match traits listing to the identification of training content and objectives provided on the form. The form will further allow you and the trainer or supervisor to determine what priority each topic should have, at what level it should be taught, and when objectives should be evaluated.

Only by the use of such training plans are you likely to achieve the results you intend and need for your new employees. Absent this type of planning, it becomes far more probable that new employees will find themselves lacking direction, an adequate understanding of job context, and performance adaptation in the way the company prefers them to function. With planning, these problems can be overcome and the transition to new employment should be a successful experience.

Selecting the Right Trainer for the Program

Selecting a trainer for the individualized instruction of a new employee may or may not be a simple matter. Normally, an employee's immediate supervisor, or the coworker most familiar with the employee's job, is selected to conduct individualized job training for new employees. The fact that each employee has a supervisor, or that another employee may be familiar with the employee's job, does not necessarily make them suitable trainers. This is to say that your selection of a trainer who is suitable in all respects to the demands of training, whether group or individualized, should be based on their possession of the following characteristics:

- Knowledgeable about the work and scope of responsibilities of program participants.
- Knowledgeable about the organization, its culture, operations, and practices.
- Knowledgeable about the concepts of adult learning, and incorporates those concepts into the instructional process.
- An expert in the subject matter of the training program.

- Ability to communicate in an effective, clear, and understandable manner to a diverse audience, and impart information in several ways.

- Ability to establish rapport with participants, and engage them so that they are encouraged to participate in the learning process.

- Ability to use various instructional techniques, such as examples, illustrations, humor, voice modulation, visuals, and other learning aides.

- Ability to present information in an orderly manner, read whether or not participants are grasping the information, and make immediate adjustments in the instruction to ensure that learning continues.

As you can surmise from this partial list, conducting the training program is no easy task. Selecting a suitable trainer may likewise be no easy task given the standards that must be maintained by companies who expect satisfactory results from their training efforts. If you are conducting an individualized training program, you should select the person who meets the majority of these qualifications rather than on the basis of a person's status in the company. Group training programs, on the other hand, demand that you select a trainer who meets at least these qualifications simply because of the challenge presented by the inherent learning diversity of any given group.

11.3 Evaluating the New Employee's Job Performance and Employment Adaptation

Performance evaluation is the method used to validate the wisdom of a hiring decision. It is also the only means by which other hiring processes, such as orientation, integration, and initial training, can be measured for their effectiveness. However, for performance evaluations to be an *accurate* measure of the effectiveness of company hiring processes, the performance system must: 1) be assembled properly; 2) use relevant job and employment standards; and, 3) be conducted objectively by a well-trained supervisor who has been sufficiently involved in the new employee's transition. These three conditions are what separate the effectiveness of performance monitoring among employers.

First, to develop a properly assembled performance system, you must first view performance evaluation as a program rather than an annoying form. A cohesive performance system links company goals, operating objectives, performance policies, operating practices and standards, and job descriptions so that it *remains* clear to all employees what their job role is with respect to working toward company success. Second, the evaluation criteria and rating levels used to measure performance must be tied to exactly those things each employee does in his or her job. While rating levels may be a common measure for all employees, the evaluation criteria will differ from job to job. Further, to reflect the total performance impact of an employee's role in company operations, the performance measure must also account for general employment measures of effectiveness, not merely the narrow confines of their job as prescribed by their job description. Third, for any "test" or measurement method to be accurate, it must be conducted by a person who has gathered reasonably adequate performance data (documented observations and personal interaction), and who can objectify comparisons between performance standards and actual performance events.

Yet another important feature of performance systems is that they should differentiate between initial occupation of a new job as opposed to evaluating the performance of those who have reached "journey level" status within their jobs. Clearly, the performance standards and expectations between these two types of employees should be different, but many companies use the same evaluation criteria for both. Another mistake concerns those companies using a "probationary" employee evaluation form with the belief that these new employees should be given only cursory evaluation. These forms use an oversimplified check-box method for a generic list of (undefined) performance terms such as dependability, quality and quantity of work, enthusiasm, attendance, and similar report card indexes with little applicability to what is really going on with the new employee. The point is that those companies having a two-level evaluation process (probationers versus regular employees) are frequently using an inverse principle. The time to conduct thorough, concentrated, and detailed evaluations of an employee's performance is during their initial employment period, and less so thereafter once full competence has been achieved.

The issues that are paramount for accurate monitoring and accounting of a new employee's performance are:

- the role of the supervisor,
- how performance should be observed and documented,
- the use of meaningful measures, and
- communications with the employee.

A brief discussion of these issues should enable you to develop the type of performance program suitable to conditions in your organization, and provide you and the new employee with meaningful progress results.

The Supervisor's Role in Performance Monitoring

The job of supervision is a complex one with respect to new employees because, in most cases, supervisors must carry the role of trainer, mentor, and evaluator. The roles of trainer and mentor are often seen by supervisors as conflicting with the role of evaluator, and this is why supervisors (emotionally) resist their responsibility of conducting critical performance evaluations on their subordinates. What needs to be clarified for supervisors is that these roles are successive, not conflicting. In order to be practiced as successive roles, supervisors must be trained on how to carry out these roles in a complementary fashion, and how to orient their subordinates to the fact that their supervisory responsibilities—upon which supervisors are evaluated—consist of both sides of the performance coin.

The new employee's immediate supervisor should be responsible for conducting regular performance appraisals, even if this supervisor does not have the role of trainer or mentor. This is because only the immediate supervisor is familiar with what the employee's work entails, what abilities are necessary to perform the work, what conditions are associated with getting work done, what work has been assigned, and what types of performance events have occurred as a result of the supervisor's *direct* observation of those events. Evaluation of a new employee's performance should therefore never be made the responsibility of a person having less direct interaction with the employee.

The Supervisor's Vicarious Liability

The responsibility for conducting thorough, honest, and well communicated performance appraisals on employees should not be approached with casual abandon. As pointed out in Appendix C on the legal issues of negligent hiring, the legal theory of negligence can extend to "negligent supervision" as in the Michigan case where a judge threatened a supervisor with potential negligence concerning the supervisor's failure to be honest and communicative about an employee's performance deficiencies that eventually resulted in the employee's termination.

To avoid this type of potential liability with regard to evaluating the performance of employees, it is important for supervisors to understand that appraisals should be: 1) relevant to the employee's actual job duties (job related); 2) honest (critically fair); 3) communicated (discussed with the employee); and, 4) have consequence (be useful for employment decision making). In other words, what should *precede* a supervisor's responsibility for conducting performance appraisals is their training on how to carry out the obligation. Training supervisors should minimally consist of teaching them the principles, purposes, policies, methods, techniques, and instructions for conducting performance appraisals. With regard to new employees, supervisors should also understand the more salient distinctions between progressive and fully competent performance measures.

When New Employees Should Be Evaluated

This issue is somewhat of a judgment call depending on such conditions as the new employee's existing abilities and learning rate, the complexity of the job and/or company operations, the duration of the initial employment (integration) period, and the time required for the new employee to be exposed to a representative range of job responsibilities. However, as a general rule, effective performance evaluation programs for new employees typically require that they be formally evaluated at least three times during their initial employment period. If, for example, the job is such that initial employment is as brief as ninety days, then written appraisals would be conducted at the end of each thirty day period. Should the job require an initial employment period of more than six months, formal appraisals should be conducted at the end of every second or third month.

Informal appraisals should be a matter of daily and weekly occurrence. Informal appraisals consist of verbal evaluations made by the supervisor to the new employee in a casual manner as notable performance events occur. They range from complimentary comments to corrective meetings. Complimentary comments should be made on those occasions when the employee demonstrates the use of skills or information learned—positive performance feedback—which serves to reinforce and motivate the employee toward desired performance. Corrective meetings, at the other end of the performance feedback spectrum, should be conducted in private by the supervisor with the new employee. These meetings should be conducted for the purpose of discussing progress or problems regarding *specific* performance areas, or to agree on a corrective plan of action concerning a serious performance deficiency.

It is extremely important for these types of performance comments and discussions to be communicated at the time notable events take place, or otherwise materialize, rather than deferring them until the formal appraisal is prepared. People will be more responsive to the learning aspect of performance feedback, whether verbal or written, when it is communicated at the time of a notable event or pattern of performance, when it is done honestly and fairly, and when it is done with genuine interest.

Observing and Documenting Performance Events

To properly evaluate the performance of new employees, the supervisor must ensure that five preexisting conditions are met. These conditions are:

1. The supervisor should be confident that the employee is receiving adequate training and guidance on employment matters.
2. The supervisor should have provided the new employee with thorough details about the performance expectations, standards, and rating levels at the time of orientation, or soon thereafter.
3. The supervisor should be deliberate about assigning the new employee progressively more responsible, diverse, and representative tasks of the job in order to evaluate a sufficient cross-section of the employee's abilities and adaptations.

4. The supervisor should take the time and opportunity to interact frequently with new employees so that they have a solid basis of observation of the employee's performance results, and

5. The supervisor should have adequate documentation of notable performance events that support performance ratings and commentary.

Since the first three conditions should have been met by recommendations made earlier in this book, it is the last two conditions that should be the focus of attention at this stage in the new employee's relationship with the company.

What Is Reasonable Performance Observation?

Reasonable performance observation means that the evaluating supervisor has regular, frequent, and direct contact with the new employee concerning his or her work activities. This interaction between the supervisor and new employee should be such that the nature of contact provides the supervisor with sufficient opportunity to fully observe performance activities, behaviors, and results. To do so, the supervisor should be located in a place where routine visual observation can be made such as from the supervisor's office or by normal activities performed in the vicinity of the employee.

Supervisors also need to develop a trained eye concerning what aspects of a new employee's performance should be observed for purposes of evaluation. Most supervisors tend to watch for only performance ability characteristics, such as the nature of skills applied to the job, quality and amount of work produced, the extent of the employee's job knowledge, and other aspects of the job itself. While these are important observations to make, they are too narrow since they concentrate only on the job and omit other employment relevant characteristics of the employee's adaptation to conditions. In this regard, the supervisor should make a point of additionally observing such performance related concerns as:

1. Is the nature of the employee's interaction with coworkers pleasant, cooperative, supportive, caring, and in other respects team oriented?

2. Is the employee responsive to supervision and management?

3. Does the employee comply with policies, procedures, and established practices?

4. Does the employee demonstrate a sincere interest in the company, operating objectives, the work, and the people involved?

5. Is the employee self-motivated about seeking more work, taking greater responsibility, getting questions answered, and obtaining guidance?

6. Does the employee bring enthusiasm and contributory ideas to the work?

These are just a few thought-provoking questions that supervisors should be asking themselves when conducting performance appraisals that consider both performance results and employment adaptations of new employees. However, in order to evaluate these joint performance characteristics, supervisors must condition themselves to be observant, and then document them properly for future reference when conducting meetings or formal appraisals with the employee.

How Should Performance Events Be Documented?

Those performance events that are notable should be documented in a log-type fashion, commonly referred to as "supervisory desk notes." Notable performance events are those in which the new employee demonstrates the use of some skill or information learned, the handling of a job task or situation, and various adaptive characteristics to employment conditions. To be noteworthy, these types of demonstrated performance events are usually either positive or negative (or potentially negative if not corrected, such as each occurrence of being late to work).

Performance notes are the only valid way a supervisor has of collecting enough performance related information about new employees to make an intelligent, fair, and representative evaluation. These notes should be maintained in a confidential manner, since they pertain to individual employees, but at the same time they should not be kept secret from the respective employee. In fact, supervisors should be completely willing to show respective employees their notes during those occasions when formal evaluations are being made. Doing so should dispel any fear employees may have about the supervisor "keeping book" on them, particularly when employees learn that the notes are a customary practice of all supervisors for all of their employees. Keep in mind that supervisors who keep notes on only certain employees may be liable for engaging in unlawful discrimination.

To ensure that performance notations are kept objective, it is important for supervisors to learn how to prepare short statements that are based on observed or provable facts (not opinions), that are performance related, and that pertain to the employee's job and/or employment. This may sound more difficult than it actually is, so the following illustration is intended to demonstrate just how little time is required to prepare these statements, and that they can easily be prepared by any supervisor with a little training and practice.

Desk Notes on Mary Smith, Order Clerk

March 21	Arrived 15 minutes late to work, no discussion.
March 28	Voluntarily helped another employee log their orders at the end of the day.
April 9	Arrived 10 minutes late to work, no discussion.
April 10	Was abrupt and offensive to a customer placing a phone order on overdue supplies by tersely telling the customer "I told you once before that your supplies are on back order so there is no need for you to keep calling." Talked with Mary about the unacceptable way she handled the situation, and she agreed that she was out of line.
April 27	Late to work 25 minutes without mitigating conditions. Discussed the importance of punctuality with Mary, including her two previous late arrivals.
May 13	Another supervisor indicated that she observed Mary referring to her operations manual after telling a customer she would have to get clarification on special order procedures, and called the customer back within five minutes to convey what she learned.

As you can clearly see from these examples of performance notations, they are objective statements of actual performance events, factual in nature, absent personalized opinion, and relate directly to the employee's job and employment conditions. When the time comes to act on formal appraisals, performance discussions, or initiate corrective measures, they serve as essential reference sources of information to support resultant decisions.

Other Sources of Performance Information

Companies would do well to establish an operational culture of everyone in the work unit, and related work units, having a stake in the success of new employees. When such cultures operate, there is a greater likelihood of a new employee's integration success because there is more uniform support for the employee's achievement. The additional benefit is that it provides the new employee's supervisor with more direct linkage to other sources of performance evaluation information.

In those organizations who establish a culture of "shared ownership" in the success of a new employee, the supervisor can broaden their base of performance information to the new employee's coworkers, other supervisors and departmental managers having work exposure to the new employee, and even customers or clients having contact with the new employee.

To be as impartial as possible, and to obtain sufficient information for the purposes of rendering thorough evaluations, the supervisor should use these types of additional sources of constructive performance information. Experience has shown that when employees are evaluated from more than one source of perceptual judgment, they tend to give the results of the evaluation more credibility. This added credibility reinforces the concept that performance evaluations are intended to serve as a positive method to guide the employee's growth and success in the job. Consequently, the employee becomes more responsive to the findings rather than feeling pitted against the singular judgment of their supervisor. This also suggests to the employee that suitable performance must be displayed toward everyone, not merely when the supervisor is present.

Using Realistic Appraisal Forms

When evaluating the performance and adaptation of new employees, keep in mind that these employees are inherently different from those who have been in your employ, and their jobs, for an extended period of time. New employees should be subjected to progressive learning of their jobs, and progressive adaptation to employment conditions. It follows then, that their evaluations should be progressive and based on increasingly higher expectations of their performance and adaptation. To do this, you will need to develop a separate appraisal form that takes a more realistic approach to evaluating the progressive performance and adaptation of new employees. Realistic, in this case, means that the form should reflect only those performance and adaptive rating factors associated with the employee's job and employment conditions, and that these factors are rated on a scale consistent with progressive learning during the integration period.

You will find a sample performance appraisal form in Appendix D that may be suitable for use with new employees inasmuch as the rating factors and standards are applicable to a wide range of jobs, and uses a progressive scale rating method. However, the form is necessarily generic in nature so you may wish to use it only as a model in order to create more suitable rating factors and standards for the types of jobs in your organization. The rating factor categories that should be used for new employees are those discussed in the preceding section ("What Is Reasonable Performance Observation?"), along with any other factors that you find applicable to your organization and particular jobs.

Keeping the New Employee Informed

Most new employees are more than casually interested in how they are doing in their new job and fitting into the organization. Given the vulnerability of a person's self-confidence produced by new employment conditions, supervisors should be aware of each new employee's need for positive reinforcement of their performance abilities and adaptations. Positive reinforcement means complimentary comments as well as constructively worded criticisms. Both should be supportive in nature and convey the intent to provide guidance to the new employee. Because new employees will be inherently sensitive to any form of criticism, it should always be done in a positive fashion, followed by seeking opportunities to compliment the employee for their corrected action or behavior.

Reinforcing interaction with new employees should be a consciously planned part of the integration, training, and evaluation process—the period in which confidence can be created or broken. The key opportunities to build a new employee's confidence are when positive performance is observed by making brief comments that acknowledge and reinforce the performance, and during progress conferences with the new employee. These conferences should be conducted in conjunction with formal evaluations where the totality of the new employee's performance and adaptive progress is discussed openly and thoroughly. They should be conducted by either the employee's supervisor and department manager, or the employee's supervisor and another closely associated supervisor (or perhaps even a senior level employee familiar with the employee's work).

During the progress conference, emphasis should be placed on what has occurred since the employee's hire—or last appraisal—performance achievements, complimentary examples of performance events, and mention of the value such performance has on the operational unit. This discussion should be followed by any areas of performance or adaptation needing further development, concentration, or correction. Again, examples should be used to clarify the employee's understanding of these issues and reinforce further learning about where the company places value. The discussion should also encourage the new employee to participate in the conversation, and conclude with mutually agreed plans for work activities and further performance development during the next evaluation period. Keep in mind that progress conferences should *always* end on a positive note. Remember, your objective is to build confidence, self-esteem, and a successful employee who will want to share their success with others in the organization. If you can achieve this result, you have made the right hiring choice.

Checklist for Developing New Employee Training and Performance Appraisal Programs

General Conditions Required for Training Programs Conducive to the Needs of New Employees

- ❑   Do we have upper management support?
- ❑   Do we have adequate funding and staff support?
- ❑   Do managers participate in the development of training program content, objectives, and get involved by attending them?
- ❑   Are training programs offered at regular intervals and for a wide variety of employees?
- ❑   Are we developing training programs based on long-range goals to produce tangible benefits for the organization?
- ❑   Are a variety of instructional methods and techniques used in our training programs?

Planning and Structuring Training Programs

- ❑   Do we distinguish between group and individual employee needs in our training programs?
- ❑   Are individual training programs adequately geared toward the learning ability and pace of the individual?
- ❑   Do we prepare individual training plans for all new employees?
- ❑   Are new employee skills, knowledge, and interactive abilities measured sufficiently to assess areas needing initial employment training concentration?
- ❑   Do we take advantage of the opportunity to cross-train new employees?

❑ Do we structure training programs to ensure proper content and objectives for the intended audience?

❑ Are training objectives measurable and applied to our performance appraisal system for new employees?

❑ Are trainers selected on the basis of their expertise and demonstrated teaching abilities?

❑ Do we provide "train-the-trainer" instruction for supervisors and other internal trainers?

Monitoring and Evaluating the New Employee's Job Performance and Employment Adaptation

❑ Are new employees formally evaluated at least three times during their initial employment period?

❑ Do we use progressive rating factors and standards that are relevant to each employee's job?

❑ Does the performance appraisal form for new employees include both job performance and employment adaptation evaluation factors?

❑ Have supervisors been trained on the principles, policies, procedures, methods, and techniques of our performance appraisal system?

❑ Are all of our supervisors keeping proper "desk notes"?

❑ Are supervisors getting reasonable opportunity and time to interact, observe, and monitor the performance of new employees?

❑ Do we have a "shared ownership" culture in each operating unit that involves other supervisors and employees in supporting the success of new employees?

❑ Do supervisors seek input from other appropriate sources of performance information about the new employee's job abilities and adaptation?

❑ Do supervisors conduct regular progress conferences with new employees to discuss their performance and adaptation progress, and strive to build the new employee's confidence?

12 Reducing Costly Turnover of Quality Employees Through Retention Efforts

Turnover of employees represents more different worker and company characteristics than most managers realize. First, we should recognize that the true hiring and employment goal is to select then *retain* the very best employees in terms of the needs of our business operations and styles. When turnover becomes a problem is when we lose (i.e., fail to retain) our best employees or even those we might categorize as good workers. Rarely do managers complain of turnover when it is associated with the loss of marginal or poor performers. In fact, these situations are typically viewed as positive opportunities to acquire a better replacement, almost as if we were not in control of this employee's work habits and had no power or authority to alter his or her performance.

12.1 What Is Turnover and What Causes It?

The turnover of jobs, be they full-time or part-time positions, can be viewed in many different ways—which is often the basis of difficulty in calculating and comparing turnover rates. Some companies and sources of industrial research consider turnover to be any form of employment separation. However, most human resource professionals believe that a more accurate representation of turnover includes only those permanent full- and part-time employees who voluntarily quit, fail during their probationary period, or are discharged for individual reasons.

Other reasons employees leave their employment are generally beyond the employee's or company's control, or they are what is commonly considered "unavoidable" reasons. These kinds of departures can be due to retirement, disability, seasonal nature of the work, health problems, compelling relocations, and the like. So when it comes to determining the cause of turnover, and therefore the need to hire replacement employees, you should confine your attention to those employment separations that represent conditions which might be subject to preventing, reducing, or perhaps even eliminating. In so doing, it is entirely possible to save your company considerable time, money, and operational disruptions that accompany turnover and the need to hire replacements.

In considering the possible prevention or reduction of your turnovers, it may be instructive for you to be aware of some of the most common causes by each category of what is referred to as the True Turnover Rate. True turnover is, as you will recall, voluntary resignations, probationary failures, and discharges.

Voluntary Resignations

This form of turnover is usually associated with the employee's view or feelings about their job satisfaction. The most frequently cited causes of leaving employment by resigning employees are

1. Organizational influences such as inflexible company policies, authoritarian managers and supervisors, lack of organization and direction, lack of competitive pay and benefits, and lack of recognition and incentives.

2. Work environment and working conditions including safety, health, comfort, coworker relationships, amenities like employee lounges, and the quality (i.e., skill, training, and effectiveness) of managers and supervisors.

3. Job content such as the absence of challenge, responsibility, and interesting activities, the repetitiveness of unskilled or semiskilled tasks (meaning monotony), and the lack or infrequency of promotion and training opportunities.

4. Personal reasons such as child care, return to school, relocation with spouse, and change of career.

Probationary Failures

If the truth be known, there are probably fewer turnovers resulting from probationary failures than there should be. The truth of this notion rests in the fact that too many employers tend to feel somewhat guilty, and conceal the discovery that they made a wrong choice. In cases where the new employee is at least marginal, they tend to give employees the benefit of any visible evidence of doubt and keep them—at least until some later time when the employee's performance deteriorates even further, resulting in a termination, and therefore greater animosity toward the employer. On the other hand, probationary failures can and should be prevented since they do represent some weakness or failing of the recruitment, selection, orientation, training, and/or supervision function of the company. The most typical of these company-caused reasons for probationary failures are

1. Inadequate attention to screening applications, or screening done by inadequately trained staff.

2. Inappropriate preemployment testing such as giving general aptitude exams rather than those measuring the actual job skills, knowledge, and abilities, or use of interview questions that are insufficiently related to the particular job.

3. Absent or weak orientation and indoctrination of new hires including the absence of an employee handbook that provides guidance on policies to new hires.

4. Insufficient attention given to new hires by their supervisor, including concentrated training and work environment adaptation guidance provided by the supervisor.

Individual Discharges

The last cause of loss of employees who represent true turnover are those who are discharged from their jobs for reasons associated with their individual job performance, conduct, and either personal or work habits. Although there are numerous reasons employers find it necessary to discharge an employee, some of the more causal conditions related to *avoidable* turnover are the following:

1. Hiring and retaining employees that should not have been selected in the first place.

2. Having inadequate operating controls such as weaknesses in personnel policies, performance evaluations, job descriptions, supervisory monitoring, and performance correction methods.

3. Early detection of performance and behavioral problems, including notice, advice, and eventual intervention by upper management who should likewise take a keen, proactive interest in turnover avoidance.

12.2 Turnover Among Part-Time Employees

Workforce statistics have shown that the use of permanent part-time employees has been steadily increasing in recent years. The acceleration of this type of employment arrangement is believed to be characteristic of a society that has begun to place new emphasis on personal preferences and lifestyle conditions. This is the period in which women became major contributors to the workforce, sought employment in nontraditional occupations, moved into higher positions, and had to confront the personal challenge of balancing career and family. It was also a period of accelerated economic inflation causing the progressive devaluation of single salaries and retiree income.

As a consequence of these conditions, working women with dependent children and retirees have become significant additions to the permanent part-time workforce, joining the usual cadre of full-time students and others wishing to occupy their time in a productive fashion. What these individuals have in common is that their primary focus is upon personal interests external to their jobs or their employers, unlike their full-time counterparts who tend to hold a primary interest in their careers, getting along with coworkers and supervisors, getting promotions and wage increases, and working within the framework of company policies, goals, and operating structures. Rather, part-time workers tend to place greater value on family, personal time and interests, and maintaining a desirable or needed income level. While they need the money provided by part-time employment, they are not as likely to share in the same kinds of organizational attachments that full-time employees develop— they're not "vested" in these interests, so to speak.

So, it should not be surprising to learn that the causes of part-time employee turnover is quite different than for full-time employees. What is important to keep in mind while considering turnover causes among part timers is that the time, cost, and disruptions associated with replacing part-time workers can be even greater than for full-time workers, depending of course on how many part timers are employed and their rate of turnover. Here are a few of the more common avoidable and unavoidable causes of their turnover:

1. *Avoidable:* regarded by employer as "partial inclusion" to their workforce.

   • Treated with less status and given less attention.
   • Given the more menial, repetitive, and boring work.
   • Have less job security (subject to layoffs).
   • Tend to get paid less and receive fewer or no fringe benefits.
   • Assigned varying number of hours or irregular days.

2. *Unavoidable:* regard and act on their external personal interests, giving them greater priority over employment.

   • Increase or change their external involvements such as taking more classes, caring for an additional child, or pursuit of an avocation.

- Relocation.
- Another job offer more conducive to their personal interests.
- Return to full-time employment where such is not available or desired with the current employer.

As it was noted earlier, few if any of these conditions resulting in the turnover of part-time employees coincide with the causal conditions of the loss of full-time employees. What this result means is that the approach you need to take to reduce or prevent avoidable kinds of turnover is two-fold; one to address full-time employees, and one for part-time employees. It isn't as difficult as it may appear, and this section concludes with some recommended approaches to the prevention of avoidable turnover.

12.3 What Is the Effect of Turnover and How You Can Gather Data

The effects of turnover on any business can range from the devastation felt by the loss of an essential person to the mild inconvenience created by the departure of someone who was long overdue. Regardless of the emotional reaction that tends to accompany each turnover in personnel, there is the more practical aspect of how each employment separation affects company operations and the bottom line cost of doing business in a highly competitive marketplace of human resources. The effects that are characteristic with all forms of unplanned turnover are

1. Decreased productivity due to the loss of otherwise available manhours applied to a given work day.
2. Operational disruptions placed on other employees who are slowed by the loss of a person normally in their work flow system, or uncertainty about how their job will have to change in response to the loss of a coworker.
3. Increased stress on other employees due to their need to pick up the slack caused by the absent job, and required overtime that may be necessary to keep up operational deadlines or schedules.
4. Altered work relationships that tend to influence such performance factors as motivation, satisfaction, and productivity.
5. Administrative cost and effort that must be dedicated to finding and processing a replacement.
6. Training and adjustment time to bring the replacement into line with fully productive employees.

There are, of course, numerous subcategories within each of the above that represent substantial cost and nonproductive effects from job turnovers, but they are too detailed for the purpose intended here. However, for smaller companies it may be of some insight to know that the first three effects tend to be more pronounced in your settings simply because you have fewer resources to draw upon to absorb or overcome these conditions.

To begin gathering data on your turnover experiences and rates, you should first be aware that there are two components; why employees leave, and how many leave in each of those categories. If you confine your recordkeeping to just those who resign, fail probation, and are discharged, the task is a fairly simple one. For example, to gather information on why employees leave under these three conditions, you can

- Talk to past employees who resigned to identify their real reason(s) if unknown—resigning employees don't always give their sincere reason at the time they leave.

- Conduct thorough exit interviews with each employee who resigns.
- Keep a record of the reasons for all probationary failures and discharges by category (insufficient skills, inadequate adaptation, rules violation, etc.).

This information will give you the number of true turnovers as well as many of the reasons causing the turnover. If you want additional information that will help you reduce turnover among existing employees, then these supplemental measures should be taken.

- Conduct annual surveys of employee satisfaction and future plans, but be prepared to implement some changes based on negative information they provide you about the company or they won't answer honestly next year because they will distrust your reasons for asking the questions.
- Compare performance ratings, strengths, and weaknesses between your better employees and those who represent your turnover.
- Do the same kinds of comparison using personal traits and talents among valued employees with five or more years in the company versus those who were turnovers.
- Compare absence rates, position levels, and pay levels of existing employees to that of turnovers.

This kind of information can be invaluable to the company who is sincerely interested in reducing avoidable turnover, particularly among their more productive and beneficial employees. Why? Because it provides many answers about why employees are dissatisfied and perhaps contemplating departure, what they don't like about the company or their jobs, what personal traits and characteristics are the most likely for turnover/failures, and what kinds of weaknesses exist in the recruitment and selection process.

12.4 How Much Turnover Is Too Much?

Any turnover is too much turnover, you say. That's a bit unrealistic for one thing, and not true for another. As it was pointed out earlier, few employees or managers mourn the departure of a bad apple from the barrel. Too, we all know that it's healthy for a business to periodically get an infusion of new ideas, approaches, and opportunities that often accompanies the hiring of replacement personnel. While these changes in employees also represents another form of turnover, the effect on the company can be a much more positive one and therefore not as burdensome.

If you want to better understand and find ways to alter your turnover experience, there are a few decisions you have to make. First, you need to select the categories of employees you intend to use on a continuous basis. To track True Turnover Rates, you should keep data on only those regular full-time and part-time employees who resign, fail probation, or are discharged. Next, decide whether you're going to compare your turnover rates internal to your own organization, or to data compiled by research organizations about your industry or the whole of industry. Most human resource professionals find that internal comparisons are best, but when you need a yardstick to measure your experience with others, it is best to compare rates among those in your same industry and within your economic region—using the same method to derive the rate calculation of course.

If, however, your company is a multiple-state employer, then you might want to use available comparisons for your industry or major regions in which your company has facilities. For example, the Bureau of National Affairs (BNA) prepares a quarterly report on industry trends in absenteeism and turnover. Although their calculation method or the kinds of employee separations used to determine turnover in the companies responding to their research may be inconsistent with yours, these comparisons can be somewhat useful as a benchmark indicator of how well or poorly your company is doing.

When we consider the reasons full-time employees leave their employers, it should be of little surprise to discover that the companies with the greatest and most consistent pattern of turnover are firms with fewer than 500 employees (less job security, promotional opportunities, and organized structure); financial companies (low pay, management and policies that are too conservative, and inflexible decision making); and healthcare organizations (stressful jobs, working conditions and environment, and being subject to autocratic physicians who oversee their work). These facts are routinely confirmed by BNA and similar survey reports. To provide you with at least some general yardsticks to compare your turnover rates, here are some figures released by BNA:

- 18% annual turnover in companies with fewer than 500 employees.
- 19.2% annual turnover among financial and healthcare organizations.
- 16.8% annual turnover in nonmanufacturing companies.
- 13% national turnover for exempt employees.
- 17.5% national turnover for nonexempt employees
- 16.8% annual turnover in the Northeast U.S.
- 13.1% annual turnover in the Southern U.S.
- 10.8% annual turnover in the Central U.S.
- 15.6% annual turnover in the Western U.S.

Equally insightful in this BNA report was a survey conducted among 433 diverse companies throughout the United States concerning what activities their personnel operation performed. Of the eight activities that 99% of the companies reported as having, four of the activities (interviewing, recruitment, separation processing, and orientations) are the direct result of their turnover experiences. Now aren't you glad you're in the process of learning how to reduce your turnover problems?

12.5 How to Calculate Your Turnover Rate

There are three different types of turnover rates; *net* turnover which includes all forms of employment separations, *replacement* turnover which omits only retirements and permanent disabilities, and *true* turnover which measures departures resulting from resignations, probationary failures, and discharges. Most employers recognize the more realistic value of using True Turnover Rate since it is probably a better reflection of at least some conditions within their control and correction, and are more valid for calculating the correctable cost of turnover. The formula to calculate your true turnover rate is as shown and illustrated by example.

$$\frac{S + D - U}{Total\ Full\text{-}Time\ Jobs} \times 100 = TTR$$

Where   S = separations
         D = discharges
         U = unavoidables

If, in our example, your company employs 200 full-time employees (do not include temporaries or other casual workers), and during the last year or 12 month period experienced 27 separations of which 3 were retirements, 5 were medical disabilities, 5 were probationary failures, and 15 were discharges, your calculation would be:

$$\frac{27 + 20 - 7}{200} \times 100 = 20\% \text{ True Turnover Rate}$$

A major cost factor of turnover is the loss of production resulting from the absence of any employee who contributes to production measures within the company, and technically that should be everyone. So the following production loss formula can be used to calculate the cost of several different types of employee absences.

$$\frac{P \times T}{M} = L$$

Where P = production in dollars
               T = turnover
               M = man hours worked
               L = loss of production dollars

For our example, let's say your company employs 500 full-time employees all of whom work a 40-hour workweek. Over a 10-week period, a total of 154,000 hours were worked and production for this period is valued at $900,000. During the same 8-week period there were 65 employees who left your company, thereby creating the loss of 3590 hours of productivity. Your equation thus becomes:

$$\frac{\$900,000 \times 3590}{154,000} = \underline{\$20,981}$$

While this formula accounts for the loss of production resulting from employee turnover, it does not take into account the revenue value that could have been achieved had the turnover not occurred or been reduced. Nor does it take into consideration the following costs that you may wish to add to the cost of lost productivity:

- Increased unemployment insurance rates.
- Increased overtime rates to absorb some of the production loss.
- Increased accidents and accident insurance rates attributable to turnover.
- Added cost of recruiting, use of employment agencies, and activities of personnel and payroll staff.

One source has estimated the cost of turnover to be frequently in excess of $20,000 per employee, the amount of which represents production-related losses and full replacement costs. On a national scale, a 1987 estimate of total turnover costs among American businesses was set at $11 billion annually by Small Business Report. Given these alarming costs and their potentially destructive effects on the small to medium companies, you would be well advised to routinely collect turnover data, calculate and compare your turnover rates, evaluate employee feedback and employment condition within your company, and initiate preventative measures at every opportunity.

12.6 Turnover Prevention: Some Practices to Evaluate, Monitor, and/or Implement

As you have probably noticed from the foregoing discussion on the causes and conditions of turnover, there are indeed several contributors brought about by the company itself. If you take the small amount of time and effort to evaluate turnover causes using the method previously suggested, you should be able to easily identify specific conditions within your company that are contributing to your turnover experiences. You should additionally gain better insight into a few measures you can take to reduce a couple of the "unavoidable" and personal reasons employees are leaving your company. Ultimately, the best approach to prevent and/or reduce turnover will be determined by each employer's evaluation of the reasons and conditions under which employees are separating from their particular company. Nevertheless each employer doing so has the same goal: to eliminate those conditions within the company's control that tend to emerge as either causes or contributors of turnover. Here are a few thought provokers to get your started.

1. Place greater emphasis (time, money, and effort) on the development of a thorough, quality recruiting and selection testing program.
2. Meet with management and supervisory personnel to discuss the need for a reorientation of their attitude and behavior concerning employee relations.
3. Reexamine company policies and rules in light of their flexibility in handling employment conditions and the personal needs of employees.
4. Develop a strong, supportive orientation program for new hires including a check-off outline to be used as a skills training and development aid during their initial period of employment adjustment.
5. Design an improved ongoing training and performance evaluation program for all employees, including new skills development for supervisors.
6. Examine your company's pay and benefits program to see if any upgrades would improve your ability to attract and retain good employees (you might be better off by having fewer workers who are well paid and otherwise satisfied to realize maximum productivity).
7. Select supervisors on the basis of their technical knowledge and human management skills.
8. Require potential new hires to preview the job and company operations before making the hiring offer.
9. Start a company newsletter to keep employees better informed of things that affect their employment or their personal interests, even if your newsletter is a modest effort and issued quarterly.
10. Post job vacancies so that employees learn about available openings or promotional opportunities (or can refer others they know who might be interested and thereby reduce your recruiting costs).
11. Start an employee recognition and incentive award program.

A few other issues to consider in your attempts to reduce job dissatisfaction turnovers include those conditions that generally have high appeal to both full-time and part-time employees. For example, you might begin by identifying the ways your company can better accommodate desired changes in employee work schedules, the number of hours they're assigned to work (many full time employees like the four day-ten hour schedule), providing greater responsibility and variety within each job to improve job interest and challenge, considering which jobs can be subject to a flexible work schedule, carefully examining which job functions would be best served by part-time workers, and adding improvements to part-time worker benefits.

As a word of caution, don't go so far in your efforts to avoid turnover that you or others in your company end up compromising performance expectations and valued employees by tolerating unsatisfactory workers. Such poor performers and behavioral misfits often have a detrimental effect on your valuable employees causing their morale and work orientation to decline, perhaps leave the company because of unequal work distribution, and before you know it you have more marginal workers than good ones.

12.7 Some Final Suggestions about Retaining Quality Employees

This book has been written with one central focus—using the best available methods to ensure that each new hire will function as a quality employee for the company. The task is a formidable one, but it makes little sense for employers to put forth extensive time and resources to attract good people only to lose them later through demotivating, disruptive or disillusioning causes created by the company or its practices, policies, or people skills. Quality employees are indeed hard to come by, and when we acquire their talent we also need to put certain measures in place to heighten our chances of retaining them. If your boss wants a less esoteric reason than this, or the other countless pages in this book, you might point out to him or her that it costs American employers over $14 billion a year for turnover . . . and that there are even more significant impacts on each company's operations when a *quality* employee is lost. Just consider the dynamics and changed productivity habits/outputs of any work group where a central member you considered a quality employee subsequently left your employment.

Let's also keep in mind that quality employees won't put up with a lot of nonsense from any employer—they don't have to, because quality employees always have other employment choices, options and usually offers. I've stolen a few myself from other companies who were apparently practicing "bait-and-switch" employment practices. So, as you proceed through the recruiting, hiring, orientation and initial training phase of your new employee acquisition process, don't overlook training your supervisory, management and executive people to employ these simple reminders:

Our Company's Human Relations Role for Each Employee Is:

- To clear the obstacles that obstruct their productivity, efficiency, morale and professional growth.
- To gain an understanding of the needs, concerns and problems that face employees in the performance of their work.
- To provide humanistic leadership that guides employees to self-development and accomplishment through enhanced self-esteem.
- To establish goals with employees both by work projects and career objectives to enhance their chances to experience personal and vocational success.
- To be honest, fair, objective and direct at all times in the assessment of problems, solutions, and actions taken that effect employees.
- To be accessible, approachable and reliable in all dealings with employees regardless of personal feelings or bias.

What Your Managers and Supervisors Can Do to Keep Quality Employees

- Spend time getting to know your employees on a personal level.
- Spend time working directly with each of your employees.
- Catch employees doing something right, and acknowledge them.
- Be encouraging and supportive toward employees who show interest and potential for higher level jobs.
- Recommend better performers for higher pay, promotional jobs, and other forms of recognition.
- Train better performers for higher level job responsibilities.
- Be fair, honest, objective, consistent, and personable at all times.
- Deal swiftly with problem employees and job conditions.

What Your Company Can Do to Keep Quality Employees

- Start an Employee Recognition program with valued rewards.
- Provide regular training programs for line employees.
- Develop job "ladders" to create promotional opportunities.
- Use "promote-from-within" policies to fill higher level jobs by suitably prepared and deserving employees.
- Expand job responsibilities (not volume) and decision making in jobs to create more challenging duties.
- Adopt liberal pay, benefits, and time-off incentives for good job performance.
- Offer performance-related bonuses and incentives, including Suggestion Award program.
- Pay the cost of books for job-related educational courses.

Appendix A

What Employers Should Know About Employment Laws and How to Avoid Hiring Process Violations

Employment laws can be very complex and confusing for most employers whose primary mission is a straightforward one; to acquire the best employees available and get on with the nature of their business. Employment law can also be quite frustrating from the standpoint that there is so much of it. It seems to change constantly, and getting outside attorneys involved to help clarify or resolve some issue is a very expensive proposition. All of these points are regrettably true, but given the existing legal environment in which employment decisions must be made, we must proceed with a more knowledgeable level of caution than might have been desired or practiced in the past.

It is for these reasons that you should arm yourself with some basic understanding of laws relating to the hiring of employees, and give thoughtful consideration to the suggestions contained in this and other chapters where legal issues come into play in hiring decisions and practices. Remember, the easiest and least costly way to resolve employment-related problems is to prevent their occurrence. If you can prevent legal problems from the beginning, you will have mastered a major inefficiency in the hiring and subsequent employment of your employees.

A.1 Equal Employment Opportunity and Affirmative Action Laws

Equal employment opportunity, or fair employment laws as they are sometimes called, have as their primary purpose the eradication of employment discrimination. These laws are perhaps the most comprehensive in terms of their effect on nearly every employment practice since the 1938 adoption of the Fair Labor Standards Act. These laws now serve to protect such a wide range of individual characteristics of applicants and employees that it often becomes paradoxical for employers to initiate hiring and other personnel actions without having the apparent effect of discriminating against another interested person who possesses equally protected characteristics. Let's take a closer look at these laws and their meaning as they relate to the hiring of employees.

State and Federal Fair Employment Laws

The American population and its work force is the most diversified in the world, and the composition of our work force will continue this diversification into the foreseeable future.

Since the appearance of our society's diversity in the late 1950s when African Americans brought the issue to national prominence, there has evolved an onslaught of state and federal laws prohibiting discrimination against those historically disadvantaged by their age, sex, race, color, national origin, religion, and physical handicap. Due largely to the public demonstrations and work stoppages of minority groups in various states during this period, it was the separate states who acted first in the legislated attempt to halt the many forms of discrimination, including employment discrimination.

State Fair Employment Laws

Each state has the option to adopt their own fair employment laws or recognize and comply with federal laws. Since federal laws are in some respects limited to enforcement among public employers and those private entities receiving federal funds, most states have adopted their own laws to address more specific discrimination concerns within their respective territory. However, those states that have adopted their own laws must have equal or greater provisions than those contained in federal laws; and most do. Using California as an example, the population of this state is comprised of a large Hispanic (mostly Mexican) segment, so the California fair employment law additionally prohibits discrimination on the basis of *ancestry*, and they have a more stringent requirement concerning pregnancy discrimination, to name just a few differences with federal laws.

Employers should become acquainted with the fair employment laws in each state in which they do business, as well as the authorities and procedures by which that state agency operates. They can be found in the telephone book under "State Government," and they exist under various names such as fair employment, human rights, civil rights, and the like. If you are familiar with the provisions of federal laws, then your time might be well spent learning what is different about the state law in terms of protected conditions, their authorities and procedures, and precedent decisions—particularly those cases reviewed by state courts. Before a discrimination claim can be filed in court, it must first be filed with a compliance agency; either the state agency if the violation pertains to state discrimination law, or the EEOC if the violation is from federal law or the state has no equivalent compliance agency.

Most state fair employment agencies replicate the federal Equal Employment Opportunity Commission with respect to their procedures in receiving, investigating, and disposition of claims filed. To overcome the problem of claimants filing simultaneously with both the state agency and EEOC, those states having a fair employment agency usually maintain a coordination agreement with the EEOC so that one or the other agency (normally the state agency) handles the claim. In those states having a state compliance agency, the claimant has one year from the date of the incident that gave rise to an alleged act of discrimination to file a claim with the state agency. State agencies dealing with discrimination complaints have sixty days to investigate and act to resolve the matter before: 1) referring the case to the EEOC; 2) continuing their investigation which may take up to one year to dismiss the employer from wrongdoing, conciliate a settlement, or refer the case for an administrative hearing; or, 3) issue a "right-to-sue" letter to the claimant so that the matter can be pursued in court.

In states having no such state compliance agency, referred to as "deferral" states, the claimant has 300 days to file their complaint directly to the EEOC at the nearest regional office. Notice of the complaint filed is given to the employer within 10 days of the formal complaint. If the EEOC fails to act or resolve the matter to the claimant's satisfaction within 180 days of filing, the claimant may then request the EEOC to issue a "right-to-sue" letter. Thereupon, the administrative complaint is withdrawn, and the claimant may file the action in court. The exception to this general timing rule regards complaints of age discrimination. Here, the claimant may file in court 60 days after unsatisfactory results with the compliance agency, and such court actions must be filed within two years of the discriminatory event, or three years if the event was a willful violation.

Generally, fewer than five percent of all claims received ever go to a commission hearing or into the courts. The vast majority of claims are either dismissed due to insufficient evidence to support an alleged violation, or they are resolved through conciliation agreements negotiated by state agency case workers between the employer and claimant. Conciliation agreements can consist of such provisions as back pay awards up to a maximum of two years, agreements to hire or reinstate the claimant, fines for willful violations, and similar "make whole" provisions to overcome the effect of a discriminatory practice on the part of the employer.

If you receive a claim from a fair employment agency, your best approach is to respond quickly with the assistance of a competent advisor and legal counsel. After conferring with such advisors who can assist you in examining the merits of a discrimination complaint and determining a suitable strategy to defend your position, you should then gather all pertinent information and send it to the agency representative handling the claim. It is also advisable in most situations to enclose a cover letter with this material explaining the (nondiscriminatory) circumstances of the situation the claimant alleges a discriminatory effect upon. Take advantage of this opportunity to demonstrate your knowledge of the law, how your company has taken measures to comply with the law, and that you too are interested in having the matter come to an expeditious conclusion.

Not all of these state agency case workers are objective in their views toward the actions of employers, so be sure your position on the claim will support the contention of no wrongdoing. However, if you know your company erred in its actions and would not likely prevail under strict scrutiny, then you might be better off by working out an early (no fault) conciliation agreement rather than letting the state agency discover something they might like to take to an administrative hearing. In either situation, you should seek and consider the advice of professional counsel at the time a claim is received.

Federal Fair Employment Laws

Although not the first national antidiscrimination law, the 1964 Civil Rights Act was by far the most sweeping in terms of its application to employment practices, prohibited actions, cost of violations, and enforcement standards. The original Act prohibited employment discrimination on the basis of a person's race, color, creed, national origin, sex, and religion. Other protected characteristics such as age, sexual harassment, pregnancy-related condition, and physical handicap were added by amendment into either the 1964 Civil Rights Act, or its amended version—the 1972 Equal Employment Opportunity Act—which strengthened provisions and enforcement authority of the EEOC from the original Act. The federal fair employment laws you should have the greatest general familiarity with are as follows:

Law	Coverage
1. 1866 Civil Rights Act	National origin and race
2. 1871 Civil Rights Act	National origin and sex
3. 1963 Equal Pay Act	Equal pay for equal work and sex discrimination
4. 1964 Civil Rights Act, Title VII	Race, color, creed, national origin, sex, religion
5. 1967 Age Discrimination in Employment Act	40–60 age group
6. 1972 Equal Employment Opportunity Act	Strengthened 1964 Act and EEOC powers
7. 1973 Vocational Rehabilitation Act	Physical handicap for federal contractors
8. 1974 Veterans Readjustment Act	Physical handicap and vet hiring preference

Law	Coverage
9. 1975 Age Discrimination Act (amendment)	40–70 age group
10. 1978 Pregnancy Discrimination Act (amended 1964 Act)	Pregnancy-related disability and leaves
11. 1978 Consumer Credit Act	Marital status
12. 1986 Omnibus Budget Reconciliation Act	40+ age group (trailer provision)
13. 1986 Immigration Reform and Control Act	National origin and citizenship
14. 1990 Americans With Disabilities Act	Physical handicap (all employers)
15. 1991 Civil Rights Act	Race norming of selection tests and business necessity defense

The various state and federal courts, including the U.S. Supreme Court, have rendered decisions on literally thousands of discrimination cases since the early days of statutory and regulatory law. These decisions are far from consistent in terms of how these courts view both the law and attendant factual circumstances of each case, which has made discrimination law complex—even for attorneys specializing in this type of litigation! The jeopardy that exists for employers, however, is that the courts will not forgive *any* employer for ignorance of the law even though we all know there is a great deal more to our jobs than just being the vanguard to our organization's prospective discrimination problems. For most small to medium employers, the best and most realistic approach is to assign a management level officer to become the company's subject matter expert in the area of discrimination law, and thereby gain a working knowledge that can be applied to the more vulnerable aspects of your hiring and general employment operations.

In response to the practical approach, this Appendix has been prepared to give you just such a fundamental overview and background detail to develop the working knowledge you'll need to handle most discrimination concerns that are likely to arise in most employment settings (see sections A.3 through A.8). Particular emphasis has, of course, been placed on discrimination pertaining to the hiring process. For the time being, it should be noted that the collective effect of the aforementioned laws are to prohibit and create costly penalties for the employment exclusion of any qualified person as a result of their race, color, national origin, sex, pregnancy condition, age (40+), religion, and physical handicap.

Federal Affirmative Action Requirements

There are three primary sources requiring that certain employers adopt and carry out affirmative action plans. The types of employers required to do so include federal agencies, all public funded organizations, federal contractors and subcontractors, and recipients of federal funds, grants, and material endorsements. The three sources of "law" establishing the requirements and standards of affirmative action plans (AAPs) consist of Executive Orders 11246, 11375, and 11478.

Executive Order 11246

In September 1965 President Johnson signed this order. The central purpose was to advance the employment opportunities of minority group members. This was to be accomplished by requiring that employers take affirmative action to ensure that minorities were given equal opportunity to apply and compete for jobs within the federal government, and its contracting or grant agent employers. For employers with grants or contracts of $10,000 or more per year, the employer merely has to demonstrate that it was taking "affirmative" measures to provide employment to minority members. Contractors receiving $50,000 or more per year are additionally required to prepare and follow a written affirmative action plan in accordance with federal guidelines (41 CFR, Part 60-2). Employers covered by Executive Order 11246 must

1. Refrain from discrimination against any employee or job applicant because of race, color, religion, or national origin;
2. Take affirmative action to ensure that applicants are employed, and employees are treated, without regard to race, color, religion, national origin (the obligation extends to working conditions and facilities such as restrooms, as well as hiring, promotions, compensation, and firing/layoffs);
3. State in all solicitations and advertisements for employment and contracts that all qualified applicants will receive consideration without regard to race, color, religion, or national origin;
4. Advise each labor union with which the employer deals of their commitments under the order;
5. Include the obligations under the order in every subcontract or purchase order unless specifically exempted;
6. Comply with all provisions of the order, its rules, and regulations; furnish all information and required reports; permit access to books, records, and accounts for the purpose of investigations to ascertain compliance; and
7. File regular compliance reports describing hiring and employment practices.

Further, the mandatory starting point for affirmative action programs is analysis of areas in which the employers may be underutilizing "protected" group persons. Such employers must consider at least the following factors:

1. Minority population of the labor area surrounding the employer's work site;
2. Size of the minority unemployment force in the labor area;
3. Percentage of minority work force compared with the total work force in the immediate area;
4. General availability of minorities having requisite skills in the immediate labor area;
5. Availability of minorities having requisite skills in the area in which the employer can reasonably recruit;
6. Availability of promotable minority employees within the employer's labor force;
7. Anticipated expansion, contraction, and turnover in the labor force;
8. Existence of training institutions capable of training minorities in the requisite skills; and
9. Degree of training the employer is reasonably able to undertake to make all job classes available to minorities.

Unlike Title VII of the 1964 Civil Rights Act, executive orders relating to employment are the administrative responsibility of the federal Department of Labor, Office of Federal Contract Compliance Programs (OFCCP). In addition to enforcement of Executive Orders 11246 and others, the OFCCP also requires covered employers to prepare AAPs for veterans, disabled veterans, and handicapped persons under authority of Section 503 of the 1973 Vocational Rehabilitation Act and the 1974 Veteran's Readjustment Act. Since the legal standards of these two laws are different with respect to the protected groups under Executive Order 11246 (which merely requires *good faith* recruitment, hiring, and accommodation, but not quotas and timetables), many covered employers prepare a separate AAP for veterans and handicapped people.

Executive Order 11375

In 1967, Executive Order 11375 was issued having the singular effect of adding sex-based discrimination to the list of protected characteristics covered by Executive Order 11246. Therefore, in addition to making it unlawful to discriminate on the basis of an applicant's or employee's sex, the OFCCP also requires in its guidelines that covered employers take affirmative action to recruit women for jobs in which they had previously or traditionally been excluded. The guidelines also prohibit employers from

1. Making any distinction based on sex in employment opportunities, wages, hours, and other conditions;
2. Advertising for workers in newspaper columns headed "male" and "female" unless sex is a bona fide occupational qualification for the job;
3. Relying on state protective laws to justify denying a female employee the right to any job that she is qualified to perform; and
4. Denying employment to women with young children or making a distinction between married and unmarried persons, unless the distinctions are applied to both sexes.

Executive Order 11478

This order was issued in 1969 by President Nixon. Among other effects pertaining to the affirmative hiring of jobs in the federal government, it also prescribed that companies who advertise job openings must specify that they are an equal opportunity employer, and they must post antidiscrimination notices on company bulletin boards.

Employers are cautioned about the fact that there remains considerable debate among various courts, including changing positions on the part of the U.S. Supreme Court, concerning the manner in which affirmative action plans or similar agreements (e.g., collective bargaining) can or should be used in the making of hiring and other employment decisions. It is advisable for employers to consider precedent legal decisions in the area of their decision before development of AAP commitments or acting on the specific terms of AAP obligations. Simply stated, what many of the past U.S. Supreme Court cases have conveyed to employers concerning the use of their affirmative action plans is

1. That *voluntary* affirmative action developments are aimed at remedying present minority and other imbalances in the employer's work force.
2. That employment decisions made in light of the affirmative action plan goals do not infringe upon, or otherwise displace, non-minority employees.
3. That fixing of hiring quotas without an official determination (court decree) of present imbalance due to past discrimination under voluntary AAPs is unwarranted and unlawful.

    For reference to some of these precedent cases, see:

    Bakke v. Regents of the University of California, Davis (1978)

    Weber v. Steelworkers (1981)

    Stotts v. Fire Fighters Local 1984 (1984)

    Wygant v. Jackson Board of Education (1986)

    Martin v. Wilks (1989)

For employers who are not required to develop, implement, and use affirmative action plans to guide their employment decision making, these court cases imply that *voluntary*

AAPs are inadvisable if for no other reason than the courts will hold employers who use them accountable for their resultant decisions. While the courts have generally held that discriminatory *hiring* decisions or actions are less detrimental to the party discriminated against, as opposed to say the effect of a discriminatory layoff where the damaged employee holds a greater property interest in the job, the net result for employers remains the same—costly potential liability even if it was unintentional. For this reason, employers who are not compelled to use AAPs should probably refrain from doing so on a voluntary basis. If you are truly interested in remedying past or present (potential) effects of discriminatory hiring practices, you should consider an annual audit of your practices, work force composition characteristics, and other pertinent factors, then prepare an informal report that suggests proposed changes for the next year or so. For example, you may wish to make use of the Nondiscriminatory Personnel Practices Checklist provided at the end of this appendix.

For those employers who are required to prepare and use affirmative action plans, you may wish to obtain the reference manual entitled *How To Write An Affirmative Action Plan* published by Business & Legal Reports, Inc. (1989). Meanwhile, you can use the Affirmative Action Program Checklist provided at the end of this section to begin your evaluation of what parts of your programs will need attention or full development.

Uniform Guidelines on Employee Selection Procedures

Shortly following the U.S. Supreme Court's 1971 landmark decision in *Griggs v. Duke Power Company* in which the employer was held to have conducted a discriminatory preemployment written examination, the federal government required that several of its departments prepare regulations and guidelines for employers to follow in order to validate such preemployment "tests." By 1976, several federal departments had published and distributed various interpretations of what they regarded as reasonable regulations for public agencies and private companies having federal contracts, subcontracts, or receiving federal grants or financial assistance. However, considerable confusion ensued because the regulations from each department were notably different making compliance nearly impossible for employers having to deal with more than one such department. As a result of this disparity, the departments were ordered to collaborate and devise a singular set of regulations and guidelines on which employers could rely on for compliance. The result was the 1978 Uniform Guidelines On Employee Selection Procedures, and they are administered by the Department of Labor.

The Uniform Guidelines are aimed at controlling the use of any type of preemployment "test" that results in a discriminatory effect on those people having protected characteristics (i.e., women, minorities, handicapped, etc.). The regulatory portion of the Guidelines is the government's way of recognizing that employers have been using their own or purchased tests to determine who should be hired or promoted based on their test results, and that many of these tests were not valid for the job in question. Such was the case in *Griggs* wherein a black male applied for a maintenance job and was rejected for failing to pass a general aptitude test. The high court eventually determined that the test was illegal due to its discriminatory effect upon *Griggs* case because it was insufficiently related to the particular job for which the applicant was seeking employment.

In essence, the Uniform Guidelines require that all employers who use preemployment tests must determine that each test does not discriminate (does not have adverse effect or impact) against any group of people having protected characteristics. Test, as defined in the Guidelines, means any paper-and-pencil instrument or other measurement of a person's skill, knowledge, ability, or fitness. Given the scope of this definition, it is easy to see that virtually every conceivable type of preemployment test likely to be given by employers is covered as a regulated test under the Guidelines. In order for preemployment tests to be lawful, and therefore allowable, each element of the test must bear a direct relationship to the job (be valid), be administered equally for all taking the test, and otherwise not result in a discriminatory effect upon any protected group of people. The latter point means that, as a general rule, a test will be considered invalid if fewer than 80 percent of any protected group fails to pass the test—referred to as the 4/5ths or 80% rule.

Validating preemployment tests is a time-consuming, complex, and costly proposition for most employers, but that fact should not deter you from making some effort to take at least informal validation measures. Formal validation procedures require administering the test to a statistically significant cross-section of people, then analyzing the results using prescribed statistical formulas. If those results determine the test to be invalid, the problem questions (or components of other types of tests) must be changed and retested for validity. To avoid this elaborate procedure, yet demonstrate your interest in complying with the intent of this legal requirement, you should design each preemployment test based solely on the exact and more prevalent features of each separate job being tested.

Have your test reviewed by someone with adequate credentials, meaning someone who would represent a credible source to a court, before you administer it to applicants or employees. Also, you should keep a record of the characteristics of those who take your test and their respective test results as a means of determining possible bias within each test. You should compile these records on such tests as written examinations, performance tests, interviews, medicals, drug/alcohol tests, and any other selection device your company uses to make hiring decisions. If you purchase tests, you should request that the test developer provide you with proof of their validation effort and results pertaining to the test you are acquiring, and consider whether their information would hold up against the scrutiny of a court or compliance agency. Remember, *any* test you give is considered to be *your* test, and you will therefore be held liable for its results.

A.2 Wages, Hours, and Working Conditions Laws

The laws most applicable to employment wages, hours, and specific kinds of working conditions consist of four federal laws. They are:

1. Fair Labor Standards Act
2. National Labor Relations Act
3. Drug-Free Workplace Act
4. Occupational Safety and Health Act

The first and last laws are the ones most commonly duplicated by similar state laws, therefore you should likewise acquaint yourself with the basic provisions of those laws in your state relating to wages, hours of work, and health and safety requirements in order to comply with both federal and state regulations. Once again, state laws are required to conform in general to federal laws, so if you have some knowledge of federal law, you are more likely to adjust easily to the nuances of your state law differences. Also, try not to despair at the length or tedium of reading about these laws. Every attempt has been made to reduce them to only those conditions that bear a direct, common, and influential effect on the hiring of employees, and it is imperative to have a solid grasp of the basic provisions of these laws before making employment decisions. To do otherwise results in errors that are costly to correct and damaging to the organization's reputation.

Fair Labor Standards Act

The Fair Labor Standards Act (FLSA) was originally enacted by Congress in 1938 as a means of economic recovery from the Great Depression. Its basic intent was to ensure that the number of jobs paying a livable minimum wage made maximum use of the available labor force. To achieve this end, the Act sets forth legal standards concerning minimum wages, hours of work, overtime pay, equal pay, use of child labor, and recordkeeping that must be complied with by those employers covered by the Act. To create the needed incentive for employers to hire a maximum number of employees, Congress established an employer penalty for working employees more than the established forty-hour workweek by adding the requirement that an overtime premium rate must be paid above the forty hours worked in any week.

The Act has been amended several times to account for changes in law and other conditions of employment relating to coverage of the Act. For example, the Equal Pay Act of 1963 was incorporated into the Act to regulate unlawful differences in the pay rates between men and women performing the same, or substantially similar, jobs. With regard to minimum wage rates, the Act has been amended routinely to account for inflation and related economic conditions affecting the labor force. While most amendments to the Act are created by Congress, periodically the U.S. Supreme Court will render a decision having new interpretative meaning to the Act such as their 1985 decision in *Garcia v. San Antonio Metropolitan Transit Authority*. In this case, the U.S. Supreme Court overruled (by a 5 to 4 split decision) their own 1974 determination that state and local government employees were excluded from coverage of the Act. So, in 1986 the Act was significantly amended to account for coverage and special interpretive conditions of public employees previously subject only to state laws regulating their wages, hours, and general conditions of employment.

The FLSA is administered and enforced by the Department of Labor, Wage and Hour Division of the Employment Standards Administration through its ten regions. Each region has area offices in most metropolitan locations where claims are received, investigated, hearings conducted, and determinations made. Regional offices coordinate regulatory matters with the division concerning rules, regulations, and interpretations of the Act. Typically, it is the area office that conducts periodic audits of employer payroll records to determine compliance with the Act, and such audits can be either scheduled activities of a routine nature or in response to an industry or employer pattern of complaints by employees. Compliance should not be viewed as a tactical game by employers. Rather, the Wage and Hour Division is like any other enforcement agency charged with the responsibility to ensure compliance with applicable laws. Employers are therefore welcomed and encouraged to call the nearest area office for information and answers to questions, and you can do so without identifying your company should the nature of your inquiry have the prospect of casting unwanted light on your company's practices.

Complaints can be registered, and claims filed by employees within two years from the date an event covered by the Act occurred. This statute of limitation can be extended to three years in cases where it can be demonstrated that the employer's action was a willful violation of the Act, meaning that the employer knew about the law but chose to ignore it for the purpose of imposing a detrimental effect on the employee (such as refusal to pay overtime wages due the employee). Where the employer is found to have unwittingly violated or otherwise not complied with the provisions of the Act, a hearing or investigative officer will normally only require that the employer pay whatever is due the employee, and may additionally impose a small fine on the employer for the violation. However, wage claims that are lost by employers in court often carry the costs of back pay, liquidated damages (equal to the amount of back pay), and attorney fees.

While most of the focus of the FLSA is upon what *is* required by employers to be in compliance with its various provisions, there are a few employment conditions that are not required by the Act. Before taking them at face value, you should check to see if the laws in your state regulate the following conditions that are not required under the FLSA.

1. Extra pay for work performed on Saturdays, Sundays, or holidays where such days are part of the employee's scheduled workweek.

2. Pay for vacations, holidays, or severance.

3. Time off for vacations or holidays.

4. Limits on the number of hours worked in a workweek by persons over the age of 16 so long as overtime pay provisions are met.

5. Discharge notices (except as required by the Worker Adjustment and Retraining Notification Act of 1989).

Now let's move on to those basic provisions of the FLSA which are required by employers, and thus necessitate your familiarity. The few provisions addressed here are important for most employers since they represent the more common areas of mistakes made by the greatest number of employers.

Who Does the Act Cover?

The original Act was made to apply to private and nonprofit sector employers and their employees. However, amendments made in 1966 brought employees of hospitals, nursing homes, public schools, and local transit operations within the minimum wage and overtime provisions of the FLSA, and then in 1985 the U.S. Supreme Court decision brought all public employees under coverage of the Act. While some of these various employees have special conditions in their application to the FLSA, it has now become easier to designate who is *not* covered. Those who are not covered by the FLSA are:

- Boards of Directors
- Legal Advisors
- Independent Contractors
- Bona Fide Volunteers

- Elected Officials
- Officials' Staff Members
- Political Appointees
- Prison Laborers

Every other employed person is thus covered by the Act as either exempt or nonexempt, meaning they are ineligible for overtime pay if classified as exempt or eligible if nonexempt. A third category is those employees who have special conditions associated with their employment wages and hours. Fundamentally then, every covered employee should fall into one of these three categories:

Exempt Employees	Nonexempt Employees	Special Condition Employees
• Executive	• Hourly	• Law Enforcement
• Administrative	• Piecework	• Fire Fighters
• Professional		• School Personnel
• Outside Sales (Commissioned)		• Hospital and
• Seasonal Recreation Employees		• Nursing Home Staff

National Labor Relations Act

You may be somewhat curious as to why a book dealing with hiring matters would include the nation's dominant labor relations law, albeit in overview detail, as one of the basic federal laws with which employers should be familiar. The answer is quite simply that most employers fall under the coverage of this law regardless of whether or not their work force is currently unionized in whole or part. If your company is unionized, and the job you seek to fill is within a bargaining unit, then certain measures may have to be taken in accordance to the prevailing collective bargaining agreement relating to your methods of recruitment, selection, placement, wages, payroll deductions, benefits, and several other terms and conditions of employment.

Conversely, if your company is not unionized, or the job you seek to fill is not within a bargaining unit, then you should be prepared to classify the position in such a manner that future questions concerning the position can be easily determined should union representation become an issue. As you will see, certain types of jobs can be excluded from a bargaining unit if unionization takes place. For many employers, this topic is not a pleasant one given the internal strife that has accompanied the formalities of having to deal with third parties in such matters as wages, hours, and a vast assortment of working conditions formerly controlled by the employer. However, with some advance reading and thought to the ever present prospect of unionization, employers can minimize potential hardships and costly errors.

General Background

The principal law that governs labor-management relations for private sector employers is the National Labor Relations Act (NLRA), which was enacted in 1935 and commonly referred to as the Wagner Act. Public employees are subject to other similar laws: federal employees are covered by federal laws and Executive Orders, while state and local public employees are generally covered by state laws that fashion their labor-management relations on the federal employees law or the NLRA. State laws that deal with the same areas as NLRA provisions for private industries may be preempted by the federal law.

The NLRA is regulated and enforced by the National Labor Relations Board (NLRB) which promulgates, interprets, and makes rulings on regulations, conducts elections, hearings, and investigates complaints of unfair labor practices. The authority of the NLRB is contained in the Act itself including amendments made through subsequent laws and federal court decisions having the effect of rescinding some NLRB precedent rulings. The original (Wagner) Act was a post-Depression and historical labor unrest measure to formally recognize the right of employees to lawfully engage in collective representation and bargaining with their employer on matters of wages, hours, and working conditions. The goal was to restore labor peace and effectuate a balance of power in the labor-management relationship. The Act permitted employees to form, join or refuse to join, and participate in related concerted activities of a union without the threat of coercion, interference, or retaliation from their employer. The first amendment to the NLRA came in 1947 with adoption of the Taft-Hartley Act which, due to abuses of powers given to unions in the Wagner Act, added a number of unfair labor practice prohibitions for unions in order to reestablish the intended balance of power between employers and unions (known as Section 7 rights). The last amendment came in 1959 when the Landrum-Griffin Act was adopted as a means of correcting the problem of undemocratic administration within labor organizations.

The basic principles of the NLRA are divided into two components: 1) representation which allows employees to determine if they want to be represented by a union, and if so which union; and, 2) unfair labor practices which sets forth rules governing the relationship and actions among the parties—employees, the employer, and the union. Generally, the latter can be viewed as the ground rules for conduct between the parties as a means of preserving their respective rights, while the former has to do with forming the details of their relationship. The relationship is finalized by 1) formal recognition of the bargaining group and union, 2) collective bargaining to establish a labor agreement (contract), and 3) contract administration whereby each party must implement and abide by the terms and conditions of the agreement. Relative to hiring practices, it should also be noted that the NLRA contains a nondiscrimination provision that essentially precludes an employer from refusing to hire, disciplining, or terminating an employee solely/primarily on the basis of the employee's protected union-related activities, including concerted actions against the employer within the scope of lawful labor relations.

Is My Company's Industry Covered by the NLRA?

The NLRB has established detailed guidelines on which industries are covered by the NLRA, and they are usually responsive to the request of employers who contact them for such a determination. To do so does not necessarily mean that you will then be unionized or that a union will approach your employees. Rather, it is a way for you to ascertain whether or not your company falls within the jurisdiction of the Act's coverage. Even if your company is not covered by the NLRA, it may be subject to a state labor law relating to representation and collective bargaining that does not conflict with the NLRA.

In very general terms, the NLRA applies to employers who are engaged in a business that affects interstate commerce. Since the issue of potential obstructions to the free flow of interstate commerce was another major area of concern behind the Act, its principal application is to those industries which deal directly or indirectly with interstate movement of goods or services. In applying its discretionary authority to determine the coverage of an industry (company), the NLRB uses the following minimum dollar volume of business (in addition to other factors of the business operation that it may find appropriate):

1. *Nonretail Enterprises:* outflow or inflow of $50,000 of direct or indirect business.

   - Direct outflow refers to goods shipped or services furnished by the employer outside the state.

   - Indirect outflow includes sales with the state to users who themselves are engaged directly in interstate commerce.

   - Direct inflow refers to goods or services furnished directly to the employer from outside the state.

   - Indirect inflow refers to the purchase of goods or services that originate from outside the employer's state but are acquired from a seller within the state. Direct and indirect outflow may be combined to meet the $50,000 requirement; however, outflow and inflow may not be combined.

2. *Retail Enterprises:* $500,000 gross volume of business.

3. *Office Buildings:* $100,000 gross revenue of which at least $25,000 is derived from an entity that meets an established jurisdictional standard other than the $50,000 indirect outflow and inflow tests for nonretail businesses.

4. *Instrumentalities, Links, and Channels of Interstate Commerce:* $50,000 gross revenue from providing interstate transportation services, or serving as essential links to interstate transportation of passengers or commodities, or from services performed locally for employers within jurisdictional standards.

5. *Public Utilities:* $250,000 gross volume, or an amount that meets nonretail standards.

6. *Transit Systems:* $250,000 gross volume, except taxicabs which are determined by the retail standard.

7. *Communications Systems:* $100,000 gross volume for radio, television, telegraph, and telephone; $200,000 for newspapers in addition to interstate news service, nationally syndicated features, or national advertising.

8. *National Defense:* Substantial impact on national defense.

9. *Hotels and Motels:* $500,000 gross revenue, excluding residential hotels or motels that rent to guests remaining more than one month during an annual period (75 percent or more of their units or 75 percent or more of their rental income must come from these residents).

10. *Health Care Institutions:* $250,000 gross revenue for hospitals, $100,000 for nursing homes and visiting nurses associations, and $250,000 for other health care facilities and child care centers.

11. *Service Establishments:* Same as retail standard.

12. *Restaurants:* Same as retail standard.

13. *Entertainment Establishments:* Same as retail.

14. *Gambling Casinos:* $500,000 gross revenues.

15. *Country Clubs:* Same as retail standard.

16. *Colleges:* $1 million total annual revenue, excluding funds not available for operating costs.

17. *Symphony Orchestras:* $1 million gross revenue, excluding funds not available for operating costs.

18. *Professional Sports Enterprises:* Jurisdiction asserted regardless of revenue.

19. *Nonprofit Organizations:* Same as for-profit businesses.

Which Employees Are Excluded from the Act?

If your company is covered by the NLRA, then your next question might well be who is excluded from those rights and protections afforded by the Act? First, however, you should know that the Act defines an "employee" as regular full- and part-time workers, as well as seasonal and day-to-day workers including applicants to employment for positions that are covered by the Act. Second, those employees or positions excluded from the Act are students, including hospital residents and interns whose work is part of their training, and the following broad categories of individuals:

1. Supervisors
2. Managerial Employees
3. Confidential Employees
4. Independent Contractors
5. Agricultural Laborers
6. Domestic Servants
7. Employees of parents or spouses
8. Employees of employers not covered by the NLRA (for example, public or railway employees)

For more detailed definitions of these excluded workers, as well as more comprehensive information about the provisions of labor-management relations under the NLRA, you may wish to refer to *Personnel Director's Legal Guide* published by Warren, Gorham & Lamont. There are also numerous books dedicated to this and other labor relations laws and practices which you may wish to consult that are normally available in university, government, and business libraries.

Drug-Free Workplace Act

The Drug-Free Workplace Act of 1988 (P.L. 100-690) became effective in March 1989 for those employers who obtain contracts of $25,000 or more with the federal government, or receive federal grants in any amount. The requirements of the Act apply only to the principal contractor, and not to subcontractors. So, if a grant is made to a state agency who then sub-contracts by allocating all or a portion of the funds to other public agencies who are political subdivisions of the state, then it is the state that must comply with the provisions of the Act rather than its subcontractors.

The Act seeks to address the widespread problem of drug abuse plaguing the American work force that has cost employers virtually billions of dollars in lost productivity, avoidable industrial accidents, and health care costs. Although the Act is limited in its application to covered employers, and somewhat passive since it does not require drug testing or mandatory rehabilitation, it is nevertheless a beginning and a possible prescription for all employers who may wish to use the Act's provisions on a voluntary basis in order to establish company policies and practices in dealing with the problem. This is to say that even if your company is not technically covered by this law, you may wish to use at least some of its guidelines to prepare your own policies. Further, the issue of drug testing as it applies to applicant and employee privacy rights is discussed in Appendix B.

To be eligible for federal contracts and grants, applicable employers must agree to maintain a drug-free workplace by meeting these requirements:

1. Publish and distribute a policy to employees that prohibits the unlawful manufacture, distribution, dispensing, possession, or use of controlled substances in the workplace. Such a policy must specify the actions that will be taken against employees who violate the policy, including possible termination. Additionally, the policy should provide notice to employees that, as a condition of their continued employment under the contract, they must abide by the policy and notify their employer of any conviction of a criminal drug offense occurring in the workplace within five days after the conviction.

2. Establish an ongoing drug-free awareness program to inform employees of the employer's intent to maintain a drug-free workplace, the dangers of drug abuse, the availability of drug counseling, rehabilitation, and employee assistance programs, and the penalties that may be imposed on employees who abuse drugs.

3. Notify the federal contracting or grant agency of any criminal convictions of employees for illegal drug activity in the workplace within ten days of learning about the conviction.

4. Take reasonable and appropriate personnel actions against any employee convicted of a criminal drug offense including, but not limited to, satisfactory participation in a drug abuse assistance or rehabilitation program, or termination. Such employee sanctions must be initiated within thirty days of date the employer learns of the conviction.

5. Continue to demonstrate a good faith effort in complying with the intent and requirements of the Act to maintain a drug-free workplace. In making its determinations of compliance with the Act, the federal contracting or grant agency may consider the total number of employees reported by an employer as having been convicted of criminal violations of workplace drug laws.

Employers who fail to comply with these provisions risk the suspension or termination of their contract(s) or grant(s), and the possibility of debarment from participation in future contract or grant activities. Additionally, employers who do work under Department of Defense contracts are obligated by DOD regulations to conduct drug testing of employees performing work under the contract.

Workplace Health and Safety Laws

There are two kinds of workplace health and safety laws of which employers need to be aware: occupational health and safety laws regulated by federal law and those in most states; and workers' compensation law which is regulated for most employers solely by state law. The reason these two forms of health and safety law play an important role in each hiring decision is that each job contains various forms of health and safety risks, and each person hired will be subject to those risks. The outcome of that employment may depend on the employee's training, skills, awareness of such hazards, and common sense approaches to accident prevention. Employers, too, have a major role in assuring that job risks are minimized, if for no other reason than knowing that worker compensation and lost time injuries cost employers an estimated $50 to $75 billion each year. Given these considerations, it is advisable for you to be aware of a few of the legal requirements placed on employers by these laws, and then to account for them during the selection of each new employee.

Occupational Safety and Health Act

Adopted in 1970 as the nation's first comprehensive measure to deal with workplace accidents, the Occupational Health and Safety Act (OSHA) has as its primary goal the eradication of conditions in the workplace that cause or contribute to worker injury, illness, or death. The Act places responsibility on employers to maintain a hazard-free workplace in what is referred to as the "general duty clause," and this obligation is to be carried out by a series of measures to be performed regularly by each employer including the routine conduct of internal safety inspections and expeditious abatement of recognized hazards. Further, each job should be evaluated to determine those conditions considered to be risk exposures, and specific actions taken by the employer to eliminate or reduce the likelihood of injury or illness (for example, written procedures on the use of equipment, placement of guards on machines, exit signs, and fire extinguishers).

While certain industries such as mining, construction, longshore, and a few other specialized hazard operations have very specific safety orders, most employers will be subject to the General Industry Safety Orders. These set forth the guidelines and obligations for all other employers with regard to workplace safety procedures, evaluating risks, safety apparatus to be used in different kinds of operational situations, how to report work injuries and fatalities, and recordkeeping requirements. Compliance and enforcement of the Act is administered by the Department of Labor through its regional and area offices throughout the United States.

Investigations are normally triggered by three events: the complaint by an employee of a hazardous condition existing in their employer's workplace; an employer's (required) report of a work-related fatality; or a routine inspection scheduled by the OSHA office having jurisdiction over the employer. If hazards are discovered by OSHA, the employer is likely to receive a citation and required to clear the hazard by a specified date. The hazard may be taken out of service as in the case of equipment, or the work site may be shut down in serious cases until the hazard is abated.

Under the Act, employees have the right to file complaints and reports of hazards to OSHA, and to refuse to perform work that they believe presents a reasonable and imminent danger to them. These rights are protected by placing sanctions against any employer who obstructs, coerces, intimidates, discriminates, or retaliates against an employee who exercises these rights—even if an OSHA inspector subsequently determines the job condition to be safe for the performance in question. It is for these reasons that it would behoove every employer to take the following actions before hiring any new employee:

1. Review all applicable health and safety laws and regulations pertaining to the nature of your business.
2. Examine work procedures in the work unit to which the new employee will be assigned to ensure that adequate precautions are being taken and that hazards are well identified as part of the employee's orientation and initial training.

3. Ascertain what work knowledge, skills, procedures, and other conditions an employee working in this job should possess, so they are included in your preemployment testing.

4. Ascertain what physical and environmental conditions are associated with the job so they can be incorporated into your preemployment physical exam if you customarily administer medicals to new hires.

5. Train supervisors thoroughly on the important aspects of job safety and their responsibility to ensure safe and healthy working conditions, including the importance of training and closely monitoring the performance of their employees—particularly new hires who are not yet familiar with their new environment.

6. Keep thorough and accurate records on each and every job injury that occurs, regardless of its severity.

Workers' Compensation Laws

Only federal employees and certain conditionally employed kinds of workers (e.g., foreign service) are covered by federal workers' compensation law. Virtually all other employees are covered by state workers' compensation law, and *every* employee is required to be included in the employer's insurance coverage for workers' compensation. While there is no national law to provide guiding policies of workers' compensation to the separate states, each state is required to promulgate its own law, regulations, benefits, and administrative mechanism to ensure that each worker has rights, protections, and access to the services and income to sustain them during work-caused disabilities.

Consequently, state laws differ with regard to such matters as benefits levels, types of benefits available to disabled workers, the burden of proof to show the disability was related to employment, and other kinds of administrative conditions. Yet, the underlying principle of workers' compensation law is essentially the same among the separate states. Generally speaking, the laws regard work-related (industrial) disability as a "no fault" system (unless of course gross negligence can be shown). The primary goal is to make the disabled worker "whole" by providing all necessary medical care, rehabilitative treatment, temporary (or possibly permanent disability) income during recovery, and perhaps vocational retraining in cases where the injured worker's disability prevents a resumption of the job held at the time of injury. These costs are borne by the employer through their workers' compensation insurance policy, but naturally the higher these costs become, the higher the employer's subsequent insurance premiums will be. For this reason, many employers obtain insurance through larger groups of similar industry employers to share experience costs more evenly or they self-insure in the case of larger employers in those states allowing such indemnification risk.

In order to minimize the risks and high costs associated with the liability of every employer's workers' compensation obligations, you should take these simple steps concurrent with other preemployment selection considerations of new employees:

1. Gain familiarity with the laws, regulations, benefit provisions, and administrative procedures applicable in the state where your business(es) is located.

2. Develop a close working relationship with your workers' compensation insurance account representative, and in particular work out a mutual understanding of your needs to ensure proper control and administration of injury/disability claims.

3. Make job safety a visible and frequent priority with your company, and stress this priority to all new employees.

4. Provide new employees with detailed safety training in both general workplace safety and job-specific conditions in which safety is a particular factor.

5. Perform routine safety inspections, audits of safety records for accuracy of detail and prospective prevention measures, and conduct thorough investigations of disabling injuries with prompt followup to your workers' compensation account representative.

6. Prepare and disseminate thorough company policies on such workplace health and safety matters as:

   • Your company's expectations of employees about workplace health and safety, including every employee's obligation to abide by company policies and instructions given by supervision.

   • Employee rights pertaining to the filing of job safety complaints, workers' compensation claims, and the refusal to perform any job that presents an imminent personal hazard.

   • What procedures are to be followed in the event of a job injury, illness, or fatality, including the filing of job hazard, job injury, and workers' compensation reports.

A.3 Avoiding Hiring Process Violations

The laws that define discriminatory acts permeate not only every aspect of the hiring process, but nearly every employment-related decision and action thereafter. Further, business organizations have increasingly become the target of costly and time-consuming litigation by a less "company minded" labor force.

The hiring process is the first of three stages of legal liability for an employer's discriminatory actions—during employment actions are the second and termination of employment is the third. It is the hiring process that gives each employer initial exposure to causes for applicants to file discrimination complaints. The exposure arises out of two sources: first, today's labor force is keenly aware of employment laws such as discrimination and required employer actions; and, second, because each phase of the hiring process remains something of a subjective judgment call by employers who often are not aware of the nuances of how a particular hiring activity might be influenced by discrimination law. Given the fact that most employment related discrimination results from the *unintentional* acts of employers, the proper starting place for employers is to learn more about preventing the occurrence and/or likelihood of these liabilities taking place. The solution to the problems and dilemmas associated with hiring process discrimination begins with a basic understanding of what hiring activities and practices are most vulnerable to violations, what are considered violations by law, and what measures need to be taken to limit your company's exposure.

Hiring practices found to be discriminatory, or having a discriminatory effect upon an applicant, are considered invalid and therefore can nullify the entire hiring process. The reason for invalidity is that the discriminatory portion is deemed to have "polluted" the fair and objective rendering of a hiring selection. Discrimination law consequently views such invalidating practices as a barrier to the fair and equal opportunity for persons in the protected classes to obtain employment; that is, they have been subjected to some form of a bias that had the effect of giving preference to other applicants.

Some hiring practices are more vulnerable to bias errors than others. However, care must be taken with each practice since many of the commonly cited violations are due to unintentional mistakes, lack of attention to details, and the lack of exerting a reasonable amount of time, thought, and effort to ensure that each part of the hiring process is directly related to the job under consideration. Here are a few of the most vulnerable hiring practices that are either overtly discriminatory, or are perceived as discriminatory by applicants who then file complaints, claims, and legal actions.

Recruitment Advertisements

Newspaper and other written recruitment ads are a common source of error for making biased and outright discriminatory statements about an employer's hiring practices and employee preferences. For example, references to gender-bias job titles such as Warehouse*man* or General Office *Girl* are inherently discriminatory and suggest the employer is unaware of fundamental discrimination law. Likewise, references to age (mature person preferred), height and weight, foreign language requirements, physical standards, and even a desired educational *level* (high school graduate) can be a source of probable discriminatory hiring practices by the advertising employer. Such written ads are used by applicants to establish a *prima facie* (meritorious on surface evidence) case of discrimination against the employer if and when they don't get the job. These errors are also a red flag to some well-qualified job seekers who will not respond to the ad because the employer obviously uses poor personnel practices.

Employment Applications

Another discriminatory hiring practice is for the employer to give some applicants (referred or walk-ins) an employment application form to complete and turn in, while turning other applicants away—usually telling them that there are no openings at the present time. This practice may sound harmless enough, but it demonstrates irregularity in the employer's practice and, worse yet, it favors some applicants over others—one of whom is likely to view the rejection as an act of discriminatory treatment.

The employment application form itself frequently provides an indication that the employer is using information about the personal characteristics of applicants to make biased hiring decisions. If an employment application elicits personal information that divulges characteristics of an applicant that are protected by law, the employer may have to show that such information was not used in the hiring decision—and that won't be easy to do! It has therefore become common practice for employers to omit from their employment applications information relating to the applicant's age and date of birth, sex, ethnicity, physical handicap (limitations are okay), religious affiliation, dates of primary and secondary education attendance, and other conditions covered by state laws such as marital status, dependents, lifestyle conditions, and even social security numbers (can be a rough indicator of age).

There are, however, certain items that should be added to the employment application form as a result of recent laws and legal decisions that serve to protect an employer's interests against potential legal action by an employee. One such example—shown on the sample application form provided in this book—is the notice to applicants that they will have to provide the employer with documents establishing their legal right to be in the United States and their legal right to acquire employment. Further, should your company have a legitimate need to conduct preemployment medical examinations, background reports (driving, bonding, credit, criminal, etc.), prior employment reference checks, or any other special kinds of investigations/evaluations during its hiring process, these "tests" should also be mentioned as a condition of employment on the application form. Many employers also add statements reminding applicants that employment is "at-will" and the company's policy statement on nondiscriminatory employment.

Employment Verification Form

All employers are required to complete an employment verification form to comply with the Immigration Reform and Control Act (IRCA) which is enforced by the Immigration and Naturalization Service (INS). These verification forms can be obtained from the INS—referred to as the I-9 Form—or prepared by employers so long as the detail conforms to INS documentation and notice standards. A sample has been provided in Appendix D. If this form is not completed and on file for inspection by request of the INS, the employer may be found to be conducting a discriminatory (noncompliance) action; particularly where the reason for the absence of these completed forms is associated with the employer's predominant use of nonprotected group employees or illegal aliens. The documents required to be shown to the employer by applicants as proof of employment eligibility are prescribed by law, rather than at the employer's preference, are contained in the Appendix D instructions that follow the I-9 form.

Job Descriptions

Job descriptions are customarily used throughout the hiring process as a guide to recruitment ads, screening tests, interview questions, and job offers. They are also frequently requested by compliance agency representatives during complaint investigations. The most common elements of job descriptions that signal discriminatory effect upon applicants and employees are references to sex-bias job titles, height and weight requirements, foreign language skills, education and/or experience requirements not sufficiently associated with the actual job, and overstated physical requirements (lifting). The exception of these elements is where there exists a bona fide occupational qualification (BFOQ), or business necessity, requiring these conditions.

In other words, such conditions must 1) regularly exist within the job under consideration; 2) it must be carried out by the incumbent of this job; and, 3) performing this condition must be of a practical business interest to the employer, and it cannot be achieved under other reasonable circumstances. In the absence of any of these three conditions, a descriptive job requirement such as those mentioned is likely to be questioned as an invalid and/or discriminatory practice.

Written Tests

Written tests consist of any paper-and-pencil exercise aimed at measuring a job applicant's knowledge, ability, experience, honesty, or any other trait for the job. Many employers have shied away from the use of written preemployment qualifying examinations because of strict validation standards imposed by the Uniform Guidelines On Employee Selection Procedures. Employers who find value in the use of them run the risk of having such tests found to possess a discriminatory effect on one or more groups of protected applicants.

To be nondiscriminatory, written tests must be entirely job related. That means that each question must be a reasonable and representative part of the job under consideration; it must be stated in terms that can be understood by one who would normally qualify for the job; it should be representative of the kind of question or situation that a person successfully employed in the job would answer in the desired way; and it must be answered correctly by 80 percent of each protected group of applicants taking the test. If one part, or question, on a written test is determined to be invalid, then the employer stands a chance of having the entire test deemed invalid by a court (varying jurisdiction courts differ on this finding). Two landmark decisions on the job-relatedness, or validity, aspect of written tests were established by the U.S. Supreme Court in *Griggs v. Duke Power Co.* (1971) and in *Albermarle Paper Co. v. Moody* (1975)—and countless others since then by the U.S. and State Supreme Courts. Additionally, the practice of "race norming" of written or any other preemployment test for the purpose of ensuring that a greater number of minority applicants pass such tests is now prohibited under the 1991 Civil Rights Act. For these reasons, employers are well advised to have written tests prepared and/or evaluated by subject matter experts, and used under very controlled conditions.

Interview Questions

Interview questions top the list as the most consistent vulnerability employers have concerning discriminatory practice violations. Two principle offenders are 1) top level managers who still believe they're above the law and/or have not involved themselves in learning the proper techniques and laws associated with good interviewing practices; and 2) work unit supervisors who likewise have not been trained by their company to conduct legal interviews. It is typically mid-level managers and human resource professionals who attend training sessions on interviewing, but they frequently overlook others in the organization who have the same applicant interviewing task. Employers who make it a practice to *not* train those responsible for interviewing are operating at grave risk of overt violations that will most certainly be noted during an audit or investigation of a claim.

Regardless of who in the organization poses an illegal question during a selection interview, the employer is liable for the wrongdoing. Regrettably the wrongdoing goes undetected until it's too late; that is, until a discrimination claim or complaint has been filed and the employer is placed in the position of defending an erroneous practice. The obvious solution to this vulnerability is to prevent its occurrence by providing all personnel who conduct hiring interviews a thorough and regular training program that teaches and refreshes their knowledge of the law and how to use the most effective techniques to get the best results. For a further discussion of what constitutes illegal questions, how to get the information you need—legally during interviews—and how to conduct hiring interviews, you are encouraged to read Sections 8.2 through 8.4 in their entirety.

Medical Evaluations

The EEOC has been more actively engaged in scrutinizing the discriminatory effect medical examinations have on applicants in recent years, and it is likely they will eventually issue guideline regulations for employers to follow to assure validity of this practice. What holds true for other kinds of hiring tests also applies to preemployment medical examinations—each aspect of the medical evaluation must bear a clear and direct relationship to the job being considered. In terms of vulnerable practices, employers are frequently found to make arbitrary decisions as to which jobs (or which applicants) are to be subjected to "physicals" prior to an employment offer.

Irregularities in the determination of which jobs are subject to an employer's medical exam requirements point, again, to *prima facie* discrimination, as do medical exams whose test components do not bear a direct and reasonable relationship to the physical and environmental conditions associated with *differing* jobs. Yet another invalid practice pertaining to the use of medical exams is how results are evaluated and used by employers. Violations of (handicap) discrimination laws are commonly associated with an employer's rejection decision that was based on the applicant having some history of a physical condition (back injury, high blood pressure, diabetes, or drug addiction).

Typically, the employer rejects this applicant out of either fear that the condition will reappear and become a workers' compensation liability, or that the applicant cannot (presently) perform the job as well as another applicant absent the history of the condition—which may be true in some cases but not all. The fact that such hiring rejections are predicated on past or historical conditions, rather than conditions or limitations that *presently* preclude the applicant from performing the job requirements, is becoming more consistently recognized by compliance agencies and the courts as a discriminatory practice.

Background Evaluations

The last hiring practice vulnerable to discriminatory effects and allegations concerns the conducting of various kinds of background evaluations on applicants to determine their suitability for specific employment conditions. Some of the more frequently used background evaluations are credit reports, bonding, driving records, criminal records, security investigations, psychological tests, and prior employment reference checks. While each of these types of evaluations carry some element of legal risk for infringing on the rights of an applicant, it is credit reports, driving records, and arrest/conviction records that are of greatest vulnerability to an employer's practice of rejecting applicants based on negative results of such information.

For example, individuals who are or have been economically disadvantaged—which is often the case of minorities, women who are single parents, and many people in lower paying occupations—are the most likely to have a negative credit history. If they are rejected for a job solely on the basis of this information, particularly if consideration was not given to such relevant details as the nature, amount, and lapse of time since negative credit information, it should be easy to see that doing so can be construed as an act of discrimination instead of a way to protect the employer's reasonable interests. If, on the other hand, your company does have a predominant financial interest to protect in *this* job, then the rejection of a currently credit-unworthy applicant may be entirely defensible.

Driving records are an important source of information for employers who wish to protect their insurance cost liability, and certainly these should be obtained on any applicant for a job involving the operation of company vehicles *before* job offers are made. However, should an applicant be rejected for having a record of *past* "driving under the influence" arrests or convictions regardless of how long ago it (they) occurred, the applicant may be able to establish a good case for handicap discrimination. Under federal and many state's handicap discrimination laws, prior alcoholism and drug addiction are considered protected handicaps. So, care and consideration must be given to the nature of the job itself, the employer's business, and details of background reports before hiring rejection decisions are made. The liability for erroneous hiring decisions based on only superficial information obtained in a background evaluation must be balanced against the liability for hiring the wrong person. If background information is fully considered in an objective manner compared to the company's legitimate interests, then both rejection and acceptance decisions should be more reliable as well as defensible if challenged.

Similarly, the acquisition and use of an applicant's arrest/conviction history can result in discriminatory hiring practices, particularly where the nature of an arrest or conviction is insufficiently related to the job or general employment conditions. For this reason, many states prohibit employers from obtaining and/or using this information as part of their pre-employment decision making. In those states that do allow *reasonable* consideration of an applicant's criminal history, the employer is often confined to considering only *convictions* for offenses directly related to the nature of their employment. Here, particular emphasis should be placed on such offenses as violent acts, morality issues (child molestation), and serious acts of dishonesty and/or irresponsibility—see Appendix C concerning employer liability for negligent hiring.

A.4 Avoiding Age Discrimination Violations

Violations of age discrimination laws typically occur during the hiring process in two forms: one is during the screening and testing of applicants; the other is during their initial period of employment which, you should remember, is considered an extension of and final evaluation period of the hiring process. The first situation involves the company's antidiscrimination practices, while the second situation has more to do with how well the company has addressed and shaped attitudes of employees away from personal biases, prejudices, and preferences that result in discriminatory decisions and behavior.

What Are Age Discrimination Violations?

There are five sources of law that define violations of age and age-related discrimination. At the federal level, there is the Age Discrimination in Employment Act (ADEA) of 1967 found in 29 U.S. Code 621, et seq., the 1975 ADEA found in 42 U.S. Code 6101, et seq., and the

Omnibus Budget Reconciliation Act of 1986 which removed the previous upper age limit of seventy years of age from the protected age group over forty years of age. Second, is the EEOC Regulations on the Age Discrimination Act of 1975 found in 29 CFR, Part 1616. Third is the voluminous number and variety of decisional laws rendered by the federal courts and U.S. Supreme Court. Fourth, is state laws that may have more stringent and perhaps somewhat different conditions from federal law. Fifth is the regulatory law established by state compliance agencies charged with administration and enforcement of state age discrimination laws, and the precedent decisional laws established by state courts. While these sources may collectively sound complex, and certainly in many circumstances they can be, you should be aware that state laws generally conform to federal laws with regard to age discrimination violations. For this reason, it may be helpful to learn more about basic federal law.

Age discrimination became a prohibited employment activity in 1967 when the original ADEA was signed into law covering job applicants and employees in the forty to sixty age range. In 1975, the Act was extended to age sixty-five, and again in 1978 to age seventy. In 1979, administrative and enforcement responsibility was shifted from the Department of Labor to the EEOC who was given broad authority to receive, investigate, and either conciliate settlements, conduct administrative hearings, initiate court action, or abandon claims due to lack of sufficient evidence to support the allegation. Finally, in 1986, the ADEA was amended again to remove the upper age limit of seventy years so that now the protected age group is any applicant or employee age forty and above.

The ADEA is intended to protect the forty and above age group from arbitrary and age-biased discrimination in hiring and all other forms of employment treatment. It is applicable to private employers with twenty or more employees; all governmental employers and those who are contractors and recipients of governmental funds; employment agencies; and labor unions with twenty-five or more members. For most employers, the more pertinent sections of the ADEA are 623 (a) and (f) as follows.

¶ 623. Prohibition Of Age Discrimination.
(a) It shall be unlawful for an employer:
(1) To fail or refuse to hire or to discharge any individual or otherwise discriminate against any individual with respect to his compensation, terms, conditions or privileges of employment, because of such individual's age;
(2) To limit, segregate, or classify his employees in any way which would deprive or tend to deprive any individual of employment opportunities or otherwise adversely affect his status as an employee, because of such individual's age; or
(3) To reduce the wage rate of any employee in order to comply with this chapter.

(f) It shall not be unlawful for an employer, employment agency, or labor organization:
(1) To take any action otherwise prohibited under subsections (a), (b), (c), or (e) of this section where age is a bona fide occupational qualification reasonably necessary to the normal operation of the particular business, or where the differentiation is based on reasonable factors other than age;
(2) To observe the terms of a bona fide seniority system or any bona fide employee benefit plan such as a retirement, pension or insurance plan, which is not a benefit plan, shall excuse the failure to hire any individual, and no such seniority system or employee benefit plan shall require or permit the involuntary retirement of any individual specified by Section 61 (a) of this title because of the age of such individual; or
(3) To discharge or otherwise discipline an individual for good cause.

A further issue to keep in mind pertaining to a newly hired (and thereafter) employee is that, in 1987, the EEOC established policies with regard to "age harassment." The EEOC's position is that age harassment is to age discrimination what sex harassment is to sex discrimination. The essence of the policy, then, is to bring any form of age-related harassment into the fold of prohibited discriminatory conduct by employers, even where the harassment is being conducted between employees—but especially by managers and supervisors. For employers to avoid these violations, internal policies and monitoring should be adopted to prevent such conditions as:

- Age inferred remarks having derogatory connotation.
- Comments that attribute a person's health, attendance, performance, attitude, and the like to their age.
- Age jokes regardless of whether they are commonly viewed as not offensive.
- Use of age related terms such as "pops," the "old man," "goat," and the like.

How to Avoid Age-Related Violations

When considering applicants during the screening and testing process, there are some very specific measures that should be taken to ensure that the age of an applicant does not become a factor in which an age discrimination violation occurs. Here are some ways in which you can prevent, or at least reduce, the likelihood of making age related errors that result in violations of the laws that protect those age forty and above.

Applicant Screening

1. Remove entries on your employment application form that elicit, or are deductive, of the applicant's age. This includes a space provided for age, date of birth, and dates of primary and secondary education completion. Also, your form should not ask for the dates of employment going back to the applicant's first job, which is a date normally associated with the ages of eighteen to twenty-one. Finally, if employment in certain jobs in your business requires a *minimum* age, then your application form should state this qualification.

2. If your company solicits, receives, or generally accepts resumes from applicants, age-related information may be voluntarily placed on some resumes. However, volunteered age information does not make the employer immune from allegations of age discriminatory hiring decisions. Therefore, you should assign a confidential clerical employee the task of opening employment mail with instructions to black out any references to age, date of birth, date of first employment, and dates of K–12 education completion before placing them in your files awaiting review by someone having hiring authority.

3. Those involved in the review of applications and resumes to determine which applicants should be given further consideration (interviews or other testing), should be people who are familiar with all aspects of the job; they should be objective people who are absent age bias; and they should be of an authoritative managerial level to render hiring decisions—preferably representing different age groups themselves.

Applicant Testing

1. During interviews, avoid making any references to the age of the applicant including such indirect references as, "how long do you plan on working before considering retirement?" or "given the length of experience you have (interpreted as the number of years of employment), do you feel this position will continue to interest you?"

2. If you require applicants to pass a medical examination, make sure that physical limitations are established on actual, measured job conditions so the examining physician can compare these factors to the present physical condition of each applicant. Since physical deterioration accompanies the aging process, but at variable rates among people, it is

important that age enter into medical evaluations only in the case of an applicant who does not presently possess the physical ability to perform important job activities.

3. Guard against having any person in the company who has a part in the hiring decision use age as a *primary* factor in the rejection decision of any applicant age forty and above.

The second condition involved in the hiring process during which age discrimination violations occur is the new hire's initial (probationary) employment period. This period of adjustment and final evaluation is considered an extension of the original hiring process, therefore it is deemed to be an employment test subject to the same legal scrutiny as any other employment practice.

If a newly hired employee is subjected to any form of age discrimination during this period, including age harassment, then a violation of the law has occurred just the same as if it happened during the screening and testing process. The most typical kinds of age discrimination acts that occur during this initial employment period are age inferred remarks from coworkers or supervisors, age jokes, and decisions to release the employee before the conclusion of the trial period when the reason relates to their age but has no basis in the demonstration of their duties—that is, they can do the job but they just "don't fit in." Here are some suggested steps that can help avoid these kinds of age discrimination violations.

Initial Employment Periods

1. Adopt and communicate a philosophy in the company that makes age comments, jokes, and other forms of discriminatory conduct unacceptable and, if discovered, punishable. This type of a philosophy should be contained in the company's personnel policies, and included in every employee's initial orientation.

2. Company officials should remind the manager and supervisor in the hiring department to discount a new employee's age with regard to their treatment and initial training, and if the new hire is over forty, to monitor the conduct of other employees. Here, your objective is to avoid surprises and a common one is to find out after the fact that a supervisor was not paying attention to the comments and bias behavior of other employees in the work unit.

3. Establish a policy that openly and honestly encourages employees who feel they or other employees have been subjected to any form of employment discrimination (age discrimination or harassment in this case) to come forward and report the incident(s) without fear of reprisal. Such internal complaint mechanisms are frequently an effective way of resolving these kinds of problems that occasionally arise—and are often mere misunderstandings or misperceptions of a situation—rather than learning about an employee's discontent the legally difficult way.

A.5 Avoiding Race, Color, and National Origin Violations

The discriminatory rejection of applicants during the hiring process because of the physical characteristics of their race, color, or national origin continues to be a predominant violation of anti-discrimination laws. The EEOC reports that violations of prohibited forms of race, color, and national origin discrimination occur most frequently during the hiring process. More specifically, the greatest tendency to discriminate for these physical and language differences is during recruitment, defining job standards (physical qualifications such as height and weight or language skills in the job description, advertisements, and testing), and during the employment interview(s). These and other hiring process errors commonly lead to violations of law that can be avoided by taking a few simple affirmative steps.

The first step is gaining a better understanding of the laws and their prohibited employment practices.

What Are Hiring Practice Violations?

Like most forms of employment-related discrimination, there are usually two levels of law with which employers should gain a basic understanding, and they are federal law and state law. Since state law is normally fashioned after federal law, and each state enacting its own version of antidiscrimination laws makes these publications easily available to local employers, the focus here will be on federal laws. Among the federal laws covering race, color, and national origin discrimination, there are two federal statutes applicable to most employers and two Executive Orders applicable to federal contractors and financial recipients that provide at least fundamental guidance on what constitutes prohibited hiring practices and violations of these statutes.

Civil Rights Act of 1964 (42 U.S.C. 2000 et seq.)

This act contains several "titles" dealing with various types of discriminatory prohibitions in an effort to establish a national policy on the illegality of differential treatment of "protected group" members in our society. For employment purposes, it is Title VII, Section 703 (a) of the Act that makes it an unlawful practice for employers:

1. To fail or refuse to hire or to discharge any individual, or otherwise to discriminate against any individual with respect to his compensation, terms, conditions or privileges of employment, because of such individual's race, color, religion, sex including sexual harassment, or national origin; or

2. To limit, segregate, or classify his employees or applicants for employment in any way which would deprive or tend to deprive any individual of employment opportunities or otherwise adversely affect his status as an employee, because of such individual's race, color, religion, sex, or national origin.

As you can see from this definition of prohibited employment practices, Title VII deals with protecting most differentiation characteristics except age and physical handicap which are covered in separate federal statutes. In 1972, the Equal Employment Opportunity Act modified applicability of Title VII to public and private employers with fifteen or more employees. Further, Title VII is more pervasive than other titles in the Act inasmuch as Title VII affects virtually all employment practices, policies, and procedural decisions. Title VII is administered and enforced by the Equal Employment Opportunity Commission (EEOC) through its 59 regional and district offices.

Complaints may be resolved by the EEOC; they may find insufficient grounds to proceed but issue a "right to sue" letter to the complainant; or they may proceed against the employer on its own by filing a law suit in the respective federal district court—usually in cases where there is a controversial or significant issue they want judicially tested, or if they ascertain the existence of a pattern or practice of obvious discrimination on the employer's part. The few exceptions of Title VII are

1. It does not prohibit an employer from giving veterans' preference to qualified job seekers.

2. It does not prohibit discrimination when deemed necessary to protect the interests of national security.

3. It does not prohibit employers from using "bona fide occupational qualifications" (BFOQ) for jobs that are reasonably necessary to the operation of the business, such as black actors to portray a black person's role or Mexican food servers in a restaurant specializing in Mexican food. However, the employer bears the burden of proof of the "business necessity," and the courts have viewed these conditions narrowly. Mere preference to hire people with particular personal characteristics is irrelevant in the scope and intent of Title VII.

4. It does not prohibit seniority systems or intend to interfere with lawful collective bargaining agreements. Seniority and merit pay systems are lawful so long as they are not the result of an intention to discriminate. Therefore, seniority that accrues within a job or operating department of the company may be seen as perpetuating past practices of (unintentional) discrimination, while company-wide seniority would be less vulnerable to such a conclusion.

In summary then, as Title VII pertains to hiring practice violations, it is unlawful for employers to reject applicants or treat them any differently during the entire hiring process as a result of their race, color, or national origin—except in those rare jobs where there exists a BFOQ or business necessity to make some personal characteristic a job requirement, including foreign or English language skills. Care must not only be exercised with each phase of the hiring process (e.g., recruitment, screening, and testing), but also with the development, communications, enforcement, and adherence to the company's personnel policies and practices that guide hiring decisions.

Immigration Control and Reform Act of 1986 (P.L. 99-603)

President Reagan signed this law into effect placing regulatory authority with the Attorney General and administrative and enforcement authority with the Immigration and Naturalization Service (INS). The purpose of the Act is twofold: 1) to curb the economic incentive for illegal aliens to enter the United States to secure employment by making it unlawful to employ such persons; and 2) to provide a one-time opportunity for those unauthorized aliens working for American employers prior to enactment of the law to obtain legal employment status. Sanctions and penalties against noncomplying employers include civil fines for each illegal alien hired, but does not apply to simple, unintentional mistakes made in the hiring process. However, blatant disregard of the law, or repeated violations may result in criminal penalties including jail terms for up to six months.

This law dramatically strengthens the prohibition against national origin discrimination under Title VII, while simultaneously requiring that employers obtain preemployment (at the time of job offer) identification information concerning the applicant's eligibility for employment—if the applicant has the legal right to be in and remain in the United States, and whether that right includes employment. Under this Act, employers with four to fourteen employees are prohibited from engaging in *national origin discrimination*, while employers with three or more employees are prohibited from discriminating on the basis of *citizenship*, with one exception: a U.S. citizen may be preferentially hired over an alien if their qualifications are equal. The other important elements of national origin discrimination includes specific definitions and prohibitions.

National Origin Defined

National origin discrimination has been defined by the EEOC under Title VII to include but not be limited to the denial of equal employment opportunity because of an individual's, or their ancestors', place of origin or because such person possesses the physical, cultural, or linguistic characteristics of a national origin group. Examples of national origin associations include

- Marriage to, or association with, persons of a national origin group;
- Membership or association with an organization seeking to promote the interests of a national origin group;
- Attendance or participation in schools, churches, temples or mosques, generally used by persons of a national origin group; and
- The name of an individual, or spouse's name, that is associated with a national origin group.

Prohibitions

The Immigration Control and Reform Act specifies that it is unlawful for an employer to knowingly hire, recruit, or refer for a fee any alien not authorized to work in the United States, or to continue employing an alien once the employer knows that the alien is not authorized to work in the United States. Likewise, employers may not refuse to hire or discharge from employment an individual because of his or her national origin, or because of the individual's status as "citizen" or "intending citizen." Citizen is defined as a citizen or national of the United States, whereas an intending citizen is one who is a permanent resident alien, a newly legalized alien, a refugee, an alien who has been granted asylum, and who has completed a Declaration of Intention to Become A Citizen. The types of documentation acceptable to establish an applicant's employment eligibility are provided in Appendix D.

Executive Orders 11246 and 11375

These two laws are issued by the Executive branch of the federal government and their respective prohibitions as they relate to the hiring process and practices are detailed in the pages that follow. These laws are limited in scope to require specific prohibitions against race, color, and national origin discrimination in hiring and other employment conditions for contractors and subcontractors of the federal government, and those organizations who are the recipients of federal grants or funds. These laws also set forth particular requirements and standards by which such employers must adopt formal affirmative action plans and activities to assure that all possible measures are being taken to remedy any imbalances of minorities in their work force.

How to Avoid Race, Color, and National Origin Discrimination

Depending on the locale of your company, the particular ethnic mix of your available labor force will vary considerably from other geographic zones that determine the different population characteristics. You should remember that the underlying intent of anti-discrimination laws based on an individual's race, color, or national origin is not only to prohibit their unreasonable exclusion from employment opportunities, but also to mandate that each employer's work force should strive toward parity representation of their available labor force composition. Consequently, the closer an employer's work force is to the parity representation of their geographic region with regard to the race, color, and national origin mix of the available labor supply, the greater are the chances of defeating any allegations of discriminatory violations. By having and maintaining a balanced work force, this condition alone suggests that the company is using non-discriminatory measures to hire and otherwise treat employees in an impartial manner.

So, the first step to take in your efforts to avoid violations of race, color, or national origin discrimination laws is to assess those characteristics of your present work force and compare them to the available labor supply in your region. Where imbalance exists, you should then prepare an *informal* plan to correct the situation through such measures as more directed recruitment, reviewing job descriptions and personnel practices for potential forms of bias, and other conditions in your company that may be contributing to the underrepresentation of a particular group of people.

Here, you should give special attention to such details as reviewing how many applicants of this group you have had in the past and why they did not succeed in getting the job—precisely where did they fail in the hiring process, and who or what was involved in the process at that time. If you find that few individuals from this underrepresented group have applied for positions in the past, this fact alone suggests that the problem begins with insufficient recruitment of these individuals. If, however, a sufficient number of these individuals apply but are not hired, then something or someone involved in your testing process may be creating a discriminatory impact on these applicants. The source of this flaw will put your company in court, and perhaps the newspapers, sooner or later. Some other measures that can help you avoid race, color, and national origin discrimination violations are taken from this author's previous book, and they are

1. Make your organization color and racially blind by adopting firm philosophies that communicate the organization's commitment to employing any individual who demonstrates desired abilities.

2. Hire and promote into supervision and management jobs only those people whose inclinations toward others is positive and without strong proclivity toward adverse forms of discrimination.

3. Provide thorough and regular training of supervisors and managers on human relations, legal issues associated with employment discrimination, organizational policies, and how to handle discrimination problems.

4. Make it clear to supervisors and managers that it is their job to ensure a discrimination-free workplace, and that they are to confront and promptly resolve acts of discrimination including jokes, harassment (however mild), and investigate rumors and complaints.

5. Ensure that job descriptions, recruiting standards and selection examinations, and all job conditions do not arbitrarily create artificial barriers for minority employment.

6. Rather than develop a voluntary [formal] affirmative action plan (AAP), prepare an annual audit report reflecting the work force composition compared to the available labor market composition; where improvements in work force parity could be made and by what measures; and identify other efforts that ought to be taken to achieve the goal of meaningful equal employment opportunity.

7. Review personnel policies and operating standards periodically in light of the potential for discriminatory effect, particularly with regard to hiring . . . and other practices that often give rise to discriminatory events, however unintentional they may be.

8. Determine if English Only rules serve a legitimate business interest. Establish them only where they are valid and can be defended from a business necessity point of view, then communicate the policy to all employees but allow some forgiveness for minor infractions.

9. Require that all personnel actions are centrally reviewed and approved by a human resource professional or other knowledgeable person to ensure objectivity and consistency of decisions, particularly as they relate to new hires.

10. Use the human resource department as an internal consulting service, or external sources when qualified staff is not available, to obtain advice and assistance on vulnerable personnel actions *prior* to deciding or acting on them. Most human resource professionals prefer the service role over the control role, and they are trained in ways to make organizations run smoothly.

11. Establish an "administrative review" procedure that encourages employees to take complaints to higher management; requires them to bring forth any condition related

to discrimination including harassment; and you may want to add the required reporting of such conditions as malfeasance, dishonesty, and theft to this "whistle-blowing" type of policy.

12. Ensure that both federal and state antidiscrimination posters are displayed on bulletin boards at each work location in a prominent place.

Additional attention should be given to your applicant intake and flow recordkeeping to ensure a well-documented account of your company's selection process performance, and the thorough training of those who interview applicants and possess hiring authority to ensure they do not ask illegal kinds of questions nor use ethnic factors as a determinant in the hiring or rejection decision.

A.6 Avoiding Gender-Related Discrimination Violations

As it relates to employment discrimination, there exists a strong parallel between gender (primarily women) and ethnic discrimination. Both groups represent a type-specific class of people who have historically been a minority member of the predominantly white male work force. Similar to ethnic groups, employers are faced with the very real issue of women being subjected to various forms of inequitable and discriminatory employment treatment for decades. However, with women now representing one-half of the entire work force (and their participation is expected to continue this increasing trend into the foreseeable future) it becomes ever more important for gender-related discrimination to be eradicated—particularly from the hiring process.

Much of the discrimination that has disadvantaged women seeking employment and advancement opportunities has taken the form of exclusion from predominantly male jobs, or being cast into subordinant jobs based on stereotype values of employers and their preconceived notions about traditional life-patterns of women (i.e., second-income wage earner, temporary work force member, marriage, relocation for husband, and child rearing). These perceptive characterizations of the *majority* of women are simply no longer true, as evidenced by over a decade of demographic profiles of the American work force. Yet women as a group continue to be stereotyped by many employers, without notice of the dramatic changes that have occurred in our society, and hence our labor force. Despite how well-intended many of a company's decision makers are, blatant discrimination does exist in one form or another in just about every organization. This is a regrettable but true fact, and one that surpasses all other forms of discrimination according to the number of complaints filed with the EEOC.

When applied to the hiring process, blatant and overt sex discrimination is typically a conscious act done with the intent to exclude, or find reason to exclude, people for primarily gender-related reasons. For example, consider the Eighth Circuit Court of Appeals' 1984 case of *King v. Trans World Airlines, Inc.* in which a female applicant, who applied for the position of kitchen helper, was blatantly discriminated against during her employment interview. Her interview questions were directed at her relationship with an employee, how many children she had and were they legitimate, her child care arrangements, and future childbearing plans.

What Laws Prohibit Gender Discrimination?

In addition to state laws that may exceed the standards of federal authorities defining violations of gender (sex) discrimination, there are two primary sources of national law that are aimed at protecting one's sex as a source of employment discrimination: federal law, and EEOC regulations.

Equal Pay Act of 1963

As a result of increasing social emphasis on the issue of equality in the workplace, the rapidly growing number of wage claims filed by women with the Department of Labor, and the surge in women's participation in the work force during the 1960s, the Equal Pay Act (EPA) was adopted as an amendment to the Fair Labor Standards Act. In 1972, positions classified as exempt (executive, administrative, professional, and outside sales) were held *not* to be excluded from the provisions of the EPA. In 1979, enforcement of EPA violations was placed with the EEOC. The law itself essentially requires that employers provide all employees with "equal pay for equal work" doing the same or substantially similar work requiring equivalent skill, effort, and responsibility. As this provision relates to the hiring process, it means that employers should not reject an applicant on the basis of any former salary rate, and particularly that no applicant should be offered a job at a pay rate lower or higher than the rate(s) of pay established for the position. Potential evidence of sex discrimination exists when an employer pays different rates to two people of different sexes who are equally qualified, tenured, and performing essentially the same work.

Civil Rights Act of 1964, Title VII

Once again, Title VII of the comprehensive 1964 Civil Rights Act is the basis for prohibitions against gender (sex) related discrimination (Section 7.3 of the Act). As a result of amendments made to this Act by adoption of the 1972 Equal Employment Opportunity Act and case law interpretations, Title VII has evolved to prohibit gender induced employment decisions including those based on pregnancy and related conditions, and sexual harassment of employees (or applicants). Only state and local laws address marital status and sexual preference at the present time, but it would not be surprising to see a future amendment to Title VII for these voids in legal theory.

While hiring—interview questions in particular—and terminations top the list of the most frequent violations of Title VII prohibited sex-discrimination practices, other causes of legal infractions cited by compliance agencies are preemployment medical examinations, personnel transactions (promotion, demotion, and transfers), compensation and leave practices, performance appraisals and discipline, and behavioral conduct by others in the workplace that creates a sexually harassing and/or offensive work environment.

Pregnancy Discrimination in Employment Act of 1978

This law was a Congressional reaction to the displeasing U.S. Supreme Court's decision in *Gilbert v. General Electric Co.* wherein the high court determined that the company's policy of excluding pregnancy-related medical expenses from insurance benefit plans was *not* a form of sex discrimination. In response, the PDA was enacted as an amendment to Title VII (Section 701 (k)) thereby making pregnancy related discrimination a type-specific form of sex discrimination by providing in the Act that:

> The terms "because of sex" or "on the basis of sex" include, but are not limited to, because of or on the basis of pregnancy, childbirth, or related medical conditions; and women affected by pregnancy, childbirth, or related medical conditions shall be treated the same for all employment-related purposes, including receipt of benefits under fringe benefit programs, as other persons not so affected but similar in their ability or inability to work. . . .

Therefore, the Act not only requires equal treatment with respect to fringe benefits as other employees, but by bringing pregnancy within the definition of sex discrimination in Title VII, it makes it a prohibited employment practice to exclude pregnant women from jobs for which they apply either as a new hire or promotional opportunities. Interviewing applicants who are pregnant, or who let their pregnancy condition be known shortly after being hired, has always been a tough problem for employers since the condition requires a reasonably lengthy absence during the employee's first year of employment. Despite the employee's short work period before requiring a leave for this purpose, employers may wish to keep in mind that generally most employees will prove or disprove their worth during the first four to six months of employment, and that pregnant employees should be made to understand that they must serve a trial employment period like any other employee.

So, what the pregnancy of applicants and employees represent to employers is primarily that this protected group must be treated equally, yet be reasonably accommodated by the employer when their condition requires it. Accommodation, however, does not require an employer to hire a pregnant applicant if such pregnancy can reasonably be expected to disrupt a *formal* training program that any new hire for the position would normally have to undergo.

Federal Regulations

1. *1971 OFCCP Order No. 4*
   The Office of Federal Contract Compliance Program which oversees and audits private contractors of the federal government, grant recipients, and those organizations receiving federal financial assistance amended its Order No. 4 to require that applicable employers alter their affirmative action goals and timetables to include an effort at increasing the number and representation of women in their employ.

2. *1972 Guidelines on Discrimination Because of Sex*
   These routinely amended guidelines contain the EEOC's definitions, explanations of prohibited employment practices and activities, compliance requirements, and procedural matters relating to the handling of claims filed with the agency.

   Aside from explicitly prohibiting the rejection of any qualified applicant from employment solely or primarily because of the individual's sex, the 1972 amendments narrowed the BFOQ defense for employers to use as their reason for rejecting an applicant due to his or her sex.

3. *1980 Guidelines on Sexual Harassment*
   The issuance of these EEOC guidelines was in response to an alarming number of complaints filed by female employees who were being sexually harassed at work and threatened with termination or other retaliatory measures by male employees if their advances were rejected. This form of workplace conduct was brought within the meaning of sex discrimination under Title VII (Section 1604.11) in at least two 1978 precedent-setting court decisions. Specifically, the guidelines define sexual harassment as:
   Unwelcome sexual advances, requests for sexual favors, and other verbal or physical conduct of a sexual nature constitute sexual harassment when (1) submission to such conduct is made either explicitly or implicitly a term or condition of an individual's employment; (2) submission to or rejection of such conduct by an individual is used as the basis for employment decisions affecting such individual; or (3) such conduct has the purpose of effect of unreasonably interfering with an individual's work performance or creating an intimidating, hostile, or offensive working environment.

4. *1980 EEOC Guidelines on Pregnancy Discrimination*
   These regulatory guidelines provide information concerning various employment terms and conditions relating to the treatment of pregnant employees. Included are such topics as medical plan benefits, leave policies, fetal protection, and hiring matters. With regard to the latter, employers with fifteen or more employees cannot refuse to hire a woman because she is or may become pregnant, or because of pregnancy-related conditions and medical needs that may arise during employment. Mere preference for other

applicants who are not more qualified for the job is not considered a reasonable purpose for rejecting the pregnant applicant. However, a more legitimate reason (BFOQ) for refusing to hire a pregnant or fertile woman would be in cases of unavoidable exposure to substances in the workplace that are likely to create a reproductive hazard. Further, the guidelines make it unlawful to ask applicants such interview questions as

- Are you married?
- Do you intend to have children?
- Do you require child care services?
- Are your children illegitimate?
- Do you have children?
- Would you like to have children?
- If you had a child, would you return to work . . . how long would you be off work, etc.?

How to Avoid Gender-Related Discrimination

The first step in avoiding gender-related discrimination, including sexual harassment and pregnancy-related conditions, is for employment decision makers to begin realizing that all people represent a pool of human resources, and that it is the *performance abilities*—not disabilities or temporary conditions—that determine the success or weakness of a company's success. In other words, avoidance of violations begins with having unbiased attitudes and values toward the proper utilization of women, and the associated willingness to accommodate their needs as part of the "human condition." Other measures that should be taken to increase your chances of avoiding gender-related problems in hiring and employment practices are as follows.

Review Hiring Policies and Practices

Policies, practices, and actual hiring decisions should be reviewed periodically to assure that decision makers are complying with legal requirements, and that all efforts given the recruitment, testing, and selection of employees is done in an unbiased fashion; that records are properly kept on applicants and tests used to determine qualifications; that the organization has a clearly defined and well understood policy on nondiscrimination on the basis of gender, marital status, pregnancy, and sexual harassment; that employment decision makers are well trained in interviewing and employee relations skills; and that the company has both an informal and formal complaint procedure for resolving alleged acts of discriminatory treatment.

Review and Revise Job Descriptions

Regular evaluation should be done on the company's job descriptions covering all employees to assure that each job responsibility and requirement is both valid and reasonably measurable in terms of employment testing as well as performance monitoring; that any artificial barriers for female applicants are removed from descriptions (e.g., sexist job titles, height and weight requirements, and physical requirements such as lifting—without undue compromise of the job); and that equal pay practices are observed regardless of an employee's sex or marital status.

Train Supervisors and Managers

Regular and ongoing training should be provided to *every* supervisor and manager in the company on topics pertaining to discrimination avoidance, employee relations, company policies and practices, employment conditions requiring watchful attention, and why their role is important to the company's success at achieving a fair, harmonious workplace.

Advertise Your EEO Interests

Establish your company as an equal employment opportunity employer by advertising that fact in job advertisements, posted notices of job vacancies, on your application form, in vendor contracts, and by posting EEO placards on employee bulletin boards. Contact community organizations who have access to female job seekers and let them know of your interest in considering them for employment. Publicize special achievement stories of female employees working in nontraditional jobs, or men being the sole parent of their children.

Monitor Results

Each of the above efforts should be monitored to determine progress, effectiveness, and recognition of those who have made a difference or special efforts, and to define goals. Monitoring might include semiannual collection and analysis of such data as the composition of your work force by departmental and occupational gender representation, gender distribution of recent hires and separations, and promotions by gender. Monitoring should also include discussing gender-related employment matters in management meetings, or when conferring with another manager on a particular employment decision about to take place. Thorough monitoring should also entail reviewing performance appraisals for fairness and objectivity, pay increase recommendations to ensure that equitable factors are being consistently applied, and routinely talking to employees informally to get a sense of how they are feeling about their treatment by the company.

A.7 Avoiding Physical Handicap/Disabled Persons Discrimination Violations

The two most essential legal violations involving disabled applicants in the hiring process are 1) employer failures to consider reasonable accommodation needs of the handicapped, and 2) failure to recruit (or rejection of) handicapped applicants solely on the basis of preferring applicants without physical disabilities. Prohibitions against this type of discriminatory treatment now exist for nearly every employer, and these prohibitions have been established by law because the employment community has shown little willingness to set aside prejudicial exclusion of otherwise qualified workers from employment opportunities.

Able and eager to work disabled job seekers are undoubtedly one of the most frequently overlooked sources of valuable applicants in the labor force pool. The social stigma attached to people with various kinds of physical and mental impairments has been in existence for centuries, and it has created bias imprints into the minds and judgments of those who do not bear the burden of such impairments. Clearly, not all people with certain types of disabilities are capable of participation in the work force. However, studies have shown that as many as 60 percent of those with disabilities can easily adapt to normal working conditions; they are capable of being productive employees when given the opportunity to demonstrate their abilities; they are highly motivated to do a good job for those who provide meaningful employment opportunities; most require only nominal forms of accommodation (average cost is only $500); and they tend to have fewer accidents, less turnover, better attitudes, and create no impact on an employer's cost for workers' compensation insurance.

Like other forms of visible bias, the key to overcoming attitudinal barriers to accepting people with disabilities for consideration of employment opportunities is looking at the person's skills, abilities (rather than disabilities), and motives instead of mere appearances. A major shortcoming of employers is that their human resources planning, including recruitment of workers with particular skills, has not given much thought to ways in which those with physical, sensory, or mental impairments *can* be used in their employment settings. Rather, employers have been lulled into favoring applicants who are without any form of handicap based on a continuously sufficient supply of nonhandicapped workers. Not understanding how to evaluate the minor limitations of many job seekers, job requirements, and workplace conditions, most managers have felt inadequately equipped to accommodate the handicapped employee in an accepting, comfortable way from the perspective of workplace interaction or productivity measurement.

Given these kinds of "unconscious" considerations that accompany the thought of hiring a handicapped applicant, it has simply been easier for employment decision makers to give preference to the nondisabled applicant even if they possess lesser skills, abilities, and experience. As you have probably learned in your own career by now, the easiest is not always the most prudent course of action. Further, from the purely legal point of view, giving undue preference to one applicant over another who has some protected personal characteristic is referred to as *prima facie* evidence of prohibited discrimination. But, before we get into the legal aspects of rejecting disabled applicants in the hiring process, let's take a brief look at just a few of the evolutionary events that led up to the current type of legal protectionism applied to this group of job seekers aimed at the eradication of employment discrimination. Here are some of those events which may provide you with some additional insight into their struggle for recognition as able employees, and desire to regain independence and self-esteem.

1918 **Smith-Sears Veteran's Rehabilitation Act;** first law mandating rehabilitation for disabled veterans and providing vocational training.

1920– **Smith-Fees Act;** provided services for the physically handicapped, vocational train-
1965 ing, placement, and counseling.

1960s Social attitudes and national awareness began to transform from a parochial treatment (services and benefits) of the handicapped and disabled to that of providing rights and advocacy. During this period medical advances also surged in the areas of treatment methods, drugs, therapy, and prosthetic devices enabling more disabled persons to participate actively and fully in society.

1968 **Architectural Barriers Act;** required modifications to transportation and building facilities that would provide more accessible accommodation for the physically impaired.

1972 **Title XVI of the Social Security Act;** added disability benefits for disabled workers.

1973 **Vocational Rehabilitation Act;** required federal contractor, grant recipients, and those organizations receiving federal financial assistance to develop affirmative action plans to increase the utilization of disabled workers, and established prohibited hiring and employment practices that tended to disfavor disabled workers.

1978 **Developmental Disabilities Act;** provided at least partial funding of advocacy services in each state for persons with developmental disabilities which necessitated the assistance of trained professionals to help them deal with legal and administrative remedies for the protection of their rights and benefits.

Executive Order 12106; established the EEOC as the monitoring agency to ensure that the hiring, placement, and promotion of disabled workers in federal service met nondiscriminatory standards.

1982 Forty-five states had adopted physical disability nondiscrimination laws; among these states only five of them excluded private sector employers, and those states are Alabama, Arkansas, Idaho, Mississippi, and South Dakota. The five remaining states without laws equivalent to federal standards were Arizona, Delaware, North Dakota, South Carolina, and Wyoming.

1990 **Americans With Disabilities Act;** supplemented the 1973 Vocational Rehabilitation Act (which only applied to public sector employers and those contractors or financial recipients of federal funds) by requiring that all employers comply with nondiscrimination employment standards and practices concerning disabled, yet qualified, applicants and employees.

1991 **Civil Rights Act;** prohibited the practice of "race norming" (within group scoring of selection tests to ensure a larger group of minority passage of preemployment tests such as GATB Test) and tightened "business necessity" defense by employers involved in discrimination law suits.

What Are the Violations Resulting in Discrimination Against the Physically Disabled?

There are two primary sources of federal law that create the legal standards for determining what hiring and other employment practices constitute employer violations: the 1973 Vocational Rehabilitation Act and the 1990 Americans with Disabilities Act. An overview of these two laws should provide you with a better understanding of how to examine your company's present hiring efforts and practices, and thereby determine if there exists internal conditions that are likely to prompt violations. Similar state laws should also be fully considered with respect to legal requirements and prohibited employment practices.

1973 Vocational Rehabilitation Act

Within this law, there are two sections and three definitions with which you should gain familiarity.

Section 503 requires the development and pursuit of affirmative action hiring plans for contractors or subcontractors receiving federal funds in excess of $2,500 per year; it compels employer consideration of hiring and promoting "qualified handicapped individuals"; and such requirements are enforceable by the Office of Federal Contract Compliance Programs (OFCCP) within the Department of Labor. The courts have determined that legal suits cannot be brought against employers who violate provisions of the Act. However, the courts have upheld the right of DOL to discontinue funding if *any* part of a recipient employer's action violates this section, even if the violation involves employment outside the area of the program or project being funded.

Federal regulations further require that *any* federal contractor or subcontractor having a federal contract of $50,000 or more, and having 50 or more employees, must prepare and maintain an affirmative action plan (AAP) for the employment of handicapped persons at each of its work locations. Unlike AAP requirements under Executive Order 11246, applicable employers are not required to establish goals and timetables for hiring handicapped workers, but rather they must periodically review personnel procedures, examine the validity of physical and mental requirements of jobs, and to provide reasonable accommodations and workplace accessibility.

Section 504 applies to recipients of federal financial assistance (grants, loans, services, and property) and prohibits discrimination against qualified handicapped individuals in programs or activities supported by such federal assistance. The major objective of this section is to ensure accessibility for *qualified* handicapped persons, rather than all forms of handicaps or disabilities. This section is administered by the Department of Health, Education, and Welfare, and violations are enforceable in court when not resolved at the administrative level.

Handicapped Person is any person who:

- Has a physical or mental impairment that substantially limits one or more major life activities (e.g., caring for oneself, performing manual tasks, walking, seeing, hearing, speaking, learning, and working);

- Has a record of such an impairment (has a history of, or has been misclassified as having, a physical or mental impairment that substantially limits one or more major life activities); or

- Is regarded as having such an impairment, which may mean:

  +having a physical or mental impairment that does not substantially limit major life activities but is treated by an employer as constituting such a limitation;

  +having a physical or mental impairment that substantially limits major life activities only as a result of the attitudes of others toward such impairment; or

  +having no physical or mental impairment but is perceived or treated by an employer as having such an impairment.

Physical or Mental Impairment is defined as a condition that weakens, diminishes, restricts, or otherwise damages the individual's physical or mental ability to perform the requisite functions of a given job. Impairment need not affect the individual's general employability—only that it serves as a bar to employment—nor does it have to be a current condition (e.g., epilepsy, prior history of drug addiction, previous back ailments, etc.). Federal regulations define impairment as

- Any physiological disorder or condition, cosmetic disfiguration or anatomical loss affecting a body system.

- A mental or psychological disorder, including mental retardation and specific learning disabilities.

- Various disabling and debilitating diseases and conditions (e.g., tuberculosis, cancer, AIDs, etc.), and [current] drug addiction and alcoholism.

Qualified Handicapped Individual is the primary person for which legal protection applies, and consists of persons who can perform the essential functions of a job with reasonable accommodation. In this regard, employers are not expected to abandon legitimate job requirements or suffer burdensome sacrifices in their effort to provide the kind of accommodation that may be needed by some qualified handicapped workers. Rather, employers are expected to make reasonable changes in order to accommodate the otherwise qualified handicapped applicant. There is a three-part analysis employers should go through when considering handicapped applicants for employment.

1. Whether the applicant is capable of performing the job (possesses required skills, training, and experience).

2. If not, whether the applicant would be able to perform the job if the employer provides some type of reasonable accommodation.

3. Whether these circumstances would impose an undue economic hardship, unsafe working conditions for the applicant or other employees, or any other reason to reject the applicant on the basis of a sound bona fide occupational qualification (e.g., a blind person applying for the position of bus driver).

Reasonable Accommodation is not defined per se but rather requires some subjective judgment on the part of employers as to the kinds and costs of accommodation (devices or architectural changes) necessary for the employment of a particular qualified handicapped applicant. However, examples are provided in federal guidelines, and they include such actions as making facilities accessible to and usable by handicapped persons (a *prima facie* case could be made if a handicapped applicant cannot gain access to your employment office to fill out an application form), acquiring or modifying equipment or devices to be used by handicapped persons for job performance, redesigning job tasks, instituting part-time or modified work schedules, and similar methods that would allow these individuals to perform work in a normal fashion. Accommodation need not be provided if the employer can establish that doing so would present an undue economic or other significant employment hardship.

Consequently, the four reasons (defense) an employer may refuse to hire a handicapped applicant are

1. The handicap is such that the applicant is *unable to perform essential functions of the job*, and is therefore not protected by law since they are not an "otherwise qualified" individual.

2. The handicap would prove to be threatening or dangerous to the *health and safety* of the applicant and/or other employees in the work unit.

3. The necessary scope, nature, and responsibilities of the job itself creates a bona fide occupational qualification that prohibits the hiring of a person with certain types of impairments.

4. The applicant's accommodation would prove to create an *undue hardship* on the employer with respect to the type, cost, or delay in acquiring the kind of accommodation needed.

1990 Americans with Disabilities Act

For all practical purposes, this federal law is much the same as the 1973 Vocational Rehabilitation Act, but it expands coverage to *all* employers with twenty-five or more employees for the first two years of effectiveness, and employers with fifteen or more employees thereafter. Signed into law in July 1990, the provisions of the Act took full effect in July 1992 and essentially create a national policy governing public accommodation and employment treatment (by private sector employers) of disabled persons. Other material differences of this law are:

1. It is Title II of the Act that addresses employment discrimination, and the Act establishes the EEOC as the administrative and enforcement agency.

2. Section 202 expressly prohibits employers from discriminating against a qualified individual with a disability because of the disability with regard to job application procedures, hiring or discharge, compensation, promotion, training, and other terms and conditions of employment.

3. Section 205 provides that remedies to persons who believe they have been the victims of discrimination are the same as in Title VII action—"make whole" remedies such as back pay, front pay, injunctive relief, and fines for willful disregard of the law.

4. Inquiries pertaining to an applicant's disabilities such as by application form, interview questions, and preemployment medical examinations (unless job valid and given to any applicant under consideration for the job) are prohibited, whereas Section 503 of the 1973 Act allows employers to conduct preemployment physicals. Drug tests are not considered in the definition of medical tests and other inquiries.

5. The Act considers *current* applicants and employees who are users/abusers of controlled substances (drugs and alcohol) *not* to be "qualified individuals with a disability," and are therefore not protected by the provisions of this Act. Further, employers may:

   • Prohibit the use of alcohol or drugs or illegal drugs at the workplace;

   • Require that employees not be under the influence of alcohol or illegal drugs at the workplace;

   • Require that employees conform their behavior to the Drug-Free Workplace Act and other applicable federal regulations; and

- Require that a drug user or alcoholic employee be responsible for meeting the same performance and behavior standards as any other employee.

How to Avoid Physical Disability Violations

There are four principal hiring process areas in which employers tend to find it particularly difficult to refrain from discriminatory violations, and these are:

1. *Employment Office;* make sure that your personnel or employment office location where applications are filed is easily accessible to those with walking and climbing disabilities.

2. *Assistance;* identify employees or others who can provide assistance to applicants with sight, hearing, and writing impairments during the application, testing, and interviewing process.

3. *Interviewing;* refrain from asking questions about the existence of handicaps or disabilities, but rather focus on the distinguishing type and level of each applicant's ability to perform essential job functions.

4. *Physical Examinations;* do not require that an applicant undergo a preemployment medical examination merely because of a handicap or disability when you would not require the same examination of any other applicant. You may, however, wish to let all applicants know that an offer of employment is conditional on passing a job related physical exam and other preemployment considerations concerning their suitability to the job and your company (such as satisfactory results of driving records, prior employment, and the like).

If you have any doubt or concern about a disabled applicant's ability to perform the job being applied for, an alternative to having the applicant undergo a physical exam would be to contact prior employers to ascertain the existence of *significant* difficulties in performing a similar job.

A.8 Avoiding Religious Discrimination Violations

Religious discrimination in the hiring context is much the same as physical disability violations inasmuch as both require the employer to not only abandon prejudicial hiring practices, but also accommodate the applicant's personal needs. In the case of religious discrimination, accommodation means allowing religious followers to observe the customs of their religion on the applicable Sabbath.

What Are Religious Discrimination Violations?

Employer prohibitions against discrimination based on an individual's religious beliefs, observances, and practices are codified in Title VII of the 1964 Civil Rights Act. Although religious violations are the least litigated areas of discrimination law, it is nevertheless a potential vulnerability in the hiring process used by many employers that can carry formidable consequences.

The reason for much of the inattention given to religious discrimination violations is fairly straightforward. First, the law's primary focus is upon employer accommodation of religious observances; meaning the ability and willingness to arrange job assignments and work schedules to allow for Sabbath and other dates of religious observances. Typically, this does not present a major problem for those employers using the customary Monday through Friday work week, except for an occasional religious holiday that may be observed within a particular religion but not by the employer. For many other employers who operate under shift, weekend days, or seven day work schedules, their vulnerability to potential violations is ever-present. They are likely to encounter the accommodation condition eventually—which should not be skirted by merely refusing to hire a religious follower, or terminating one who makes such requests.

Second, complaints and litigation over religious discrimination are unusual because the two major prohibitions are easily complied with by discerning employers: namely, don't refuse to hire primarily due to the applicant's religion, or to avoid the prospect of religious accommodation unless there exists a very good business or job reason to do so; and don't arbitrarily deny an employee's request for taking a particular day off for a religious observance—the time of which does not have to be paid by the employer unless allowed by the employer's own policies. Typically, neither of these two conditions present major obstacles for management in the way of business disruption or economic hardship. Absent willful or negligent violation of the law, both the courts and EEOC have generally used back pay and reinstatement orders as the penalty for employer wrongdoing. The fact that litigation costs far exceed the remedy for alleged violations serves as sage advice to employers when confronted with the opportunity to conciliate, or even arbitrate, settlements where there exist some elements of wrongdoing in the hiring process.

In evaluating the sincerity of an applicant's religious attachments, there is a degree of judgment that must be exercised. Even compliance agencies and the courts have been skeptical of the sincerity of an individual's beliefs in cases where

1. The applicant had advance knowledge of the employer's required work schedule, but said nothing until after acceptance of the job.
2. The employee worked the assigned work schedule for some length of time without notice or objection to the employer.
3. The evidence suggests that the employee's religious belief is more "circumstantial convenience" than sincere since the employee's notice has been in conjunction with such employment changes as shift changes, reassignments, or unpleasant work assignments.

How to Avoid Discriminatory Hiring and Employment Practices

Based on prevailing federal law and those employment practices addressed by the courts during their most active decade (1978 to 1988) when religious discrimination became more clearly defined, the following are suggested approaches that should be taken by employers who wish to avoid the principal violations.

1. Do not avoid hiring an applicant merely because of the individual's religious beliefs, observances, or practices unless there exists a very practical business necessity associated with the job that would adversely reflect upon the company or the nature of its business, or unreasonably interfere with the rights of other employees.
2. Remove any reference concerning the identification of an applicant's religion on your employment applicant form.
3. Be careful about framing interview questions that elicit or indirectly prompt information about the applicant's religious affiliation or beliefs such as asking, "Are there any particular days during the year that your absence would be necessary?" or "Do you attend any organized activities with your family?"
4. If you reject an applicant on the grounds of a religious conflict with the nature or schedule of the job (assuming the applicant volunteered the information, of course), you should be certain that the reason your company cannot make an accommodation is because doing so would cause an *undue* (unreasonable) hardship such as the requiring of

considerable overtime costs, a significant operational disruption, or inconsistent with the legitimate business interests of the organization as in the partial exemption that exists for religious institutions and businesses.

5. Take employee requests for religious accommodation seriously, at least until evidence proves otherwise. Ask the employee to provide you with a written statement attesting to the specific name, requirements, and conditions of the religion; what, in particular, is the job or employment conflict; and what is the employee's requested or preferred accommodation.

   Before making a decision, consult with experienced advisors concerning the company's (policy) position and implications of a decision. If the request is determined to be legitimate, then you should try to identify and offer one or more ways of easily alleviating the conflict. If the employee rejects your offer of accommodation, your obligation is complete and you can notify the employee—in writing is best—of your offer, his or her rejection, and an order to perform the job under existing conditions or find other employment.

6. Deal with each religious accommodation request in a thorough and expeditious manner, and handle each one on an individual basis. Blanket policies and practices that openly disfavor any applicant or employee due to their religious observances and practices should be carefully reexamined for revision, or better yet abandoned.

Checklist for an Affirmative Action Program*

❑   Issue written equal employment policy and affirmative action commitment.

❑   Appoint a top official with responsibility and authority to direct and implement your program.

    1. Specify responsibilities of program manager.

    2. Specify responsibilities and accountability of all managers and supervisors.

❑   Publicize your policy and affirmative action commitment.

    1. Internally: To managers, supervisors, all employees and unions.

    2. Externally: To sources and potential sources of recruitment, potential minority and female applicants, to those with whom you do business, and to the community at large.

❑   Survey present minority and female employment by department and job classification.

    1. Identify present areas and levels of employment.

    2. Identify areas of concentration and underutilization.

    3. Determine extent of underutilization.

❑   Develop goals and timetables to improve utilization of minorities, males, and females in each area where underutilization has been identified.

❑   Develop and implement specific programs to achieve goals. *This is the heart of your program. Review your entire employment system to identify barriers to equal employment opportunity;* make needed changes to increase employment and advancement opportunities of minorities and females. These areas need review and action:

*SOURCE: Joseph D. Levesque, *Manual of Personnel Policies, Procedures and Operations* 2/E, (Englewood Cliffs, NJ: Prentice-Hall, Inc., 1993). Reprinted with permission. Copyright Prentice-Hall, Inc., 1993.

1. Recruitment: all personnel procedures.
2. Selection process: job requirements; job descriptions, standards and procedures.
3. Preemployment inquiries: application forms; testing; interviewing.
4. Upward mobility system: assignments, job progressions, transfers; seniority; promotions; training.
5. Wage and salary structure.
6. Benefits and conditions of employment.
7. Layoff: recall; termination; demotion; discharge; disciplinary action.
8. Union contract provisions affecting above procedures.

❑ Establish internal audit and reporting system to monitor and evaluate progress in each aspect of the program.

❑ Develop supportive in-house and community programs.

Self-Audit Checklist: Nondiscriminatory Personnel Practices*

This self-audit will help you conclude your review of elements in the employment process which may need attention and could have an effect on the acceptability of your affirmative action plans to a government investigator or reviewer.

Answer the following questions as best you can:

1. **Recruitment and Search Activity**

   What is the "recruitment area" for the following EEO–1 categories?
   —Officials and Managers
   —Supervisors
   —Professionals
   —Sales–exempt staff
   —Technicians
   —Clerical Staff
   —Craft Workers
   —Operatives
   —Laborers
   —Service Workers
   —Other classifications (identify)

2. **Have you developed a policy to define an "employment applicant" for your organization?**

3. **Recruitment Media**

   Do you use the phrase "EEO" in all ads?

   Do you use newspapers and other media which are read by minorities?

   Do you place ads by sex designation?

   Do you keep records of responses from ads?

If company photographs are used in employment advertising, do you picture minorities and women?

4. **Recruiting Agencies**

   What state employment office and or private agencies do you use?

   When and how often are they notified in writing of your policies?

   What agencies have been the most effective in making minority referrals?

   Have you kept records of this correspondence?

5. **Colleges and Schools**

   What schools do you use for recruiting purposes?

   What is the minority and female population of these schools?

   What jobs have you filled with referrals from these schools?

6. **"Word of Mouth" Recruiting**

   Which employees do you inform of job openings?

   Do you have a job posting program in existence?

   Do you use "friends" and "relatives" referrals?

   Do you give equal consideration for jobs to friends and relatives of minority and female employees?

   Do you encourage minority and female employees to refer relatives and friends?

7. **Walk-ins**

   For what jobs do you accept applications from walk-ins?

   How effective is this approach in receiving applications from minorities and women?

   How long do you keep applications?

8. **Special Minority/Female Sources**

   What organizations do you use for what jobs?

   Do you notify them in writing?

   What is the effectiveness of these sources?

9. **Sources of Handicapped Applicants**

   Have you made contacts to handicap organizations for referrals?

   Are your managers alert that there may be a request for "accommodation" to a handicap?

10. **Veterans**

    Have you made contacts to veterans' organizations for referrals?

    Are your managers alert that there may be a request for "accommodation" to a veteran?

11. **Write-ins**

    For what jobs do you accept resumes?

    Do you consider these applications?

    Do you send reply letters to write-ins?

    How effective is this source?

12. **Special Problems**

    Is transportation adequate from minority areas to your facility?

    Does the company have a policy on nepotism?

    Does the company provide daycare facilities for employees?

13. **Applicant Flow Data on Applicant Log**

    Is the date of application indicated?

    Is the applicant's name, apparent race, and sex indicated?

Is there an area to indicate the position applied for?

Is the source of referral indicated?

Is there an area to indicate if the job was offered?

Is there an area to indicated the disposition?

Are individual minority groups applying in proportion to their availability in the recruitment area?

Are minorities and women applying for positions in jobs where they are underutilized?

Are you offering minorities and women jobs in job groups that are underutilizing them?

What are your principal reasons for rejecting applicants?

Who makes the final decision to hire and on what basis?

Has any part of the advertisement, recruitment, or selection process been challenged?

14. Hiring

Is the employment office clearly designated and easily located and accessible from the street?

Is the office "wheelchair accessible"?

Do you post required EEO information?

Have you trained the people who first see the applicant in the employment office in affirmative action policies and procedures?

How do you issue application forms?

Do you interview applicants prior to completing an application form?

Do you provide assistance in completing a form?

Do you keep applicant flow statistics and records?

15. Application Forms

Do they conform with federal, state, and local laws?

What is the retention period?

Is your real reason for nonhire listed on the form?

Do you have application forms for minorities and women available for easy retrieval at the time of subsequent job openings?

Is the information on the application form entirely job-related?

What are your rejection ratios for minorities and for women?

Do you respond to rejected applicants in writing?

16. Job Descriptions

Do you have written job descriptions or job specifications?

Do you review all job descriptions periodically to ensure consistency with actual job requirements?

17. Job Interviews

Are your interviews standardized? Are applicants for the same job asked the same questions?

Do you keep adequate and accurate records of the interview?

How do you rate interviews?

Has the hiring or interview process ever been challenged?

18. Testing

Do you use any tests as a hiring criterion in the selection process?

Do these tests conform with the federal Uniform Selection Guidelines?

Is the person who administers the test trained in correct testing procedures?

Do you give the same test to minorities and women as you give to nonminorities or men for the same job?

What is your pass/fail rate for minorities, women, nonminorities, and men applying for the same job?

What weight do you give to these tests in the hiring decision?

Do you notify applicants of their scores on the tests?

19. Placement

Do you employ as interviewers minorities and women, or handicapped, or disabled veterans?

Who conducts the hiring interviews?

Do you involve the EEO coordinator?

Who has the final decision-making authority?

Who reviews these decisions?

Are these selectors aware of AAP goals and timetables?

Do you keep written interview guidelines?

Do you keep evaluation forms and records?

20. Job Offers

Have you kept data and done an analysis for the last 12 months?

21. Analysis of New Hires

What are your sources of new hires?

Do you retain application forms?

For how long?

Do you assign women and minorities to specific kinds of jobs where there are high rates of termination?

22. Advancement

Do you have a formal appraisal system?

Does the employee participate in the appraisal discussion?

Do you provide counseling or career guidance?

What is your history of mobility for minorities and women?

How do you communicate job vacancies?

Do you have pre-supervisory and supervisory training?

Do you have a tuition refund program?

Have you identified training needs for minorities and women in the workforce?

Do you have a formal orientation program?

23. Termination

Do you conduct exit interviews?

What are your procedures for discharge?

Do you keep records?

What was your record of minorities and of women in termination ratios?

What are your reasons for termination?

Do you give out references for terminated employees?

Do you have a complaint or termination procedure for employees who have been disciplined or terminated?

24. **Layoff and Recall Procedures**

    Do you have controls to ensure uniformity of application?

    If seniority is controlling, was plantwide seniority used as a key factor?

25. **Auditing Personnel Activities**

    What follow-up do you have for corrective action when practices are in violation of established policy or government regulations?

Appendix B

How to Avoid Violating the Privacy Rights of Applicants and Employees

Getting adequate information about job applicants in order to make an informed decision about their employment suitability has been a thorny problem for all employers, and the legal conditions that accompany employer restrictions are making this task increasingly more difficult. Consequently, the issue of applicant and employee privacy rights is often characterized as a delicate balancing act. On the one hand, employers need to supplement preemployment tests and other formal kinds of evaluation with personal information about unknown job applicants. Applicants who are entirely unknown to the employer concerning their behavioral traits, habits, inclinations, and any patterned modes of conducting themselves give employers a legitimate concern about the trustworthiness and other characteristics of people hired to perform such tasks as handling monetary transactions, operating equipment, serving customers, and the like.

On the other hand, each person has the right to a certain amount of privacy concerning their personal life and events that take shape in the course of normal living, including that portion spent in employment. Such fundamental protections are afforded each of us in the United States Constitution, state constitutions, and federal and state laws. The intent of laws that protect individual privacy rights are, of course, to prevent abuse by those who may cross the line of relevant purpose and use of private information, thereby exposing the person to inappropriate harm. Therein lies the balance that must be stricken by employers—to recognize and safeguard the reasonable privacy rights of applicants; to determine the kind of information that is both necessary and relevant to make a determination of suitability for the job in question; and to handle all information in a highly discreet manner.

This discussion will help you become more familiar with the legal and managerial boundaries that define unlawful or marginally improper privacy rights violations that tend to occur during hiring and employment, and how you can prevent the assortment of violations. After reading this chapter, you may wish to refer to Chapter 7 to learn more about how to obtain the right kind of information about applicants seeking jobs with specific responsibilities only measured by gathering investigatory information.

B.1 Federal and State Laws on Employment Privacy Rights

There are three sources of law that define and determine individual privacy rights, and they are: federal and state constitutional law, federal and state statutory law, and general tort law that has been shaped by the courts in their dealings with specific cases. In these cases, the courts have observed the apparent need to begin formulating at least some guiding principles that would serve as the foundation for adjudicary public policy concerning the intrepidation of individual rights compared to the interest of those who seek infringement upon those rights. In the absence of very specific statutory law protecting a vast assortment of individual privacy rights, the courts have had to rely on legal doctrines such as those contained in the Constitution's First, Third, Fourth, Fifth, Ninth, and Fourteenth Amendments to justify necessary decisions of wrongdoing. For example, one of the first privacy right cases to reach the U.S. Supreme Court was in 1965 *(Griswold v. Connecticut)* wherein the court gave recognition to a "penumbra" (a lessor issue in the shadow of a major provision) of Constitutional rights in reaching its decision, and again the penumbra was used by the high court in its 1973 abortion rights case of *Roe v. Wade*.

The evolution and clarity of national policies concerning the privacy rights of employers and employees has been slow and obscured. Most of the principles now attached to employment condition privacy rights have emanated from the courts on a case-by-case basis over a considerable period of time, and then the focus has been on ensuring the protection of *employee* rights. The obscurity of reasonable guidelines by which employers and employees alike might achieve balance is due largely to the absence of a single administrative compliance agency to prepare regulations, standards, and procedural controls as in the case of other types of employment law. Rather, since privacy rights violations are presently a matter of tort law, the guidelines defining the boundaries of wrongful conduct and remedies are left largely to the courts.

What should be remembered by employers is that, unlike discrimination and other "make whole" employment laws, privacy right violations are actionable under tort law and are adjudicated by jury trial whose decisions carry broad authority over the setting of monetary damages. Jury trials are also a considerably more expensive forum for employers to plead their defense than are administrative hearings. A brief review of those federal and state laws that protect certain privacy rights should help you distinguish the kinds of hiring practices that are likely to result in violations.

Crime Control Act of 1968

The law relates to employment in the primary context of unlawful interception of private conversations—even between employees—and the employer's use of such information to the unreasonable disadvantage (such as, discipline or termination) of the employee. The law prohibits deliberate interception of private telephone (wiretapping) and other forms of conversation, and carries civil or criminal penalties for violations, depending on circumstances. As this law might apply to the initial training of a new hire, it prohibits supervisors from listening in on the telephone conversations of employees under a *pretext* of (sales) training or performance monitoring. However, if an employee is informed in advance that the supervisor will be conducting telephone training or monitoring their conversational performance in dealing with others, and that this is the customary practice of this supervisor who has a legitimate reason to do so, then no privacy violation should occur so long as the supervisor disregards (and promptly hangs up the telephone) if a private conversation is being conducted at the time of monitoring—see *Watkins v. L. M. Berry & Co. (Eleventh Cir., 1983)*.

One approach for employers to avoid this type of privacy right violation is to adopt policies allowing supervisors to monitor the conversational performance of their subordinates *with advance notice*, and limiting or even prohibiting employees from making or receiving personal telephone calls during work periods, except under emergency circumstances.

Privacy Protection Act of 1974

Due to the public notoriety brought about by the two aforementioned Supreme Court cases, Congress saw the need to develop statutory law relating to the protection of various individual privacy rights. In 1974 the Privacy Protection Act was adopted to establish strict controls over the collection, control, and disclosure of employment related information on applicants and employees. For reasons of political expediency, the Act did not require compliance by private sector employers except those doing business with the federal government (i.e., contractors, subcontractors, and grant/financial assistance recipients). Instead, the Act was amended to take an indirect approach to compliance by private employers by establishing a Privacy Protection Study Commission to determine if private employers should be covered by the Act. Not surprisingly the Commission's 1977 report conclusion was to exempt private employers, but several [proposed guideline] recommendations were given for private employers to follow in handling employment transactions, and they are:

1. Review personnel information practices to determine how and for what purpose information is collected.
2. Limit information collected only to what would be relevant to employment decision making.
3. Inform employees about the type of information kept on file and how it is used.
4. Allow employees to inspect their files and, if necessary and appropriate, correct inaccurate information.
5. Keep sensitive material such as medical records and investigations apart from the primary personnel file.
6. Limit the internal use and exposure of personal information to only those that have a need to know.
7. Limit external disclosure of employee information in the absence of the employee's authorization.
8. Keep records current to ensure their accuracy.

Fair Credit Act of 1978

This law is intended to protect people from the unreasonable acquisition, interpretation, and decision making use of their credit history in matters like employment. The Act contains notice requirement to applicants and other types of safeguards in the handling of credit, character, and related kinds of information obtained by an employer through its use of third party agencies who conduct information research and interviews (from credit bureaus, law enforcement agencies, and public records). Additionally, other types of character information about applicants—such as through employment agencies, executive search firms, and psychological testing—that is obtained by personal interviews are subject to notice-and-use limitations prescribed by the Act. Notice and disclosure requirements by the user of credit, character, and related personal information obtained by employers necessitates:

1. The employer mail or deliver a written notice to the applicant that an investigative report "possibly concerning their character, general reputation, personal characteristics and mode of living" will be made; and,
2. The employer must provide a complete disclosure of the nature and scope of the investigation to the applicant upon request.

Employee Polygraph Protection Act of 1988

This law ended an eighteen-year effort on the part of Congress to find a suitable compromise bill that would set some restrictions on private sector employers in acquiring and using inappropriate personal information obtained through polygraph (lie detector) examinations. Due largely to the rather speculative accuracy of different polygraph testing devices, these tests have been found to be unreliable in some instances of measuring the applicants, and were unreasonably intrusive into the personal habits of job applicants. The resultant weaknesses of their use led Congress to disfavor/prohibit using polygraph tests for employment matters, excluding security-related governmental agencies, security firm employers, public health and safety employers, and manufacturers or distributors of controlled substances where an employee would have direct access to the substance.

The law thus prohibits applicable private employers from requiring or requesting an applicant or employee to submit to a polygraph test; or from discharging, discriminating against, or denying employment or promotion to an applicant or employee for their refusal to submit to testing. As defined by the Act, "lie detector" consists of such devices as a polygraph, deceptograph, or any other method of rendering diagnostic opinions about an individual's honesty. Theoretically then, attaching these devices to an individual without their consent could be legally considered an act of assault upon the individual, while the questioning of an individual under nonconsensual circumstances could be an act of unlawful invasion of privacy. There are, however, a few conditions permitted under the Act by which employers can test applicants and employees, but even these conditions have strict limitations on how tests are administered. Conditions considered legal for polygraph testing are:

1. The test is part of an ongoing investigation of losses suffered by the employer;
2. The person being tested had access to the property in question;
3. The employer has reasonable suspicion of the involvement of the employee being tested; and,
4. The employer provides a statement of the bases of the above conditions.

State Constitutional and Statutory Protections

As alluded to in previous chapters, the separate states frequently exercise their sovereign powers of "home rule" when it comes to legal matters that define the obligations and rights of state residents, including employers. Whenever significant federal laws are adopted, some states will predictably adopt their own version of the same legal issue—but with more strict controls on employers in employment law matters—while some other states take pride in adopting laws to deal with certain issues even before Congress has adopted a national policy on the issue. Privacy rights, discrimination, and wage and hour laws are good examples of the kinds of employment issues that have created this sort of "double jeopardy" legal environment for employers.

Twelve states (Alaska, Arizona, California, Florida, Hawaii, Illinois, Louisiana, Massachusetts, Montana, Rhode Island, South Carolina, and Washington) have elected to embody provisions in their state constitutions to protect the privacy and other individual rights of residents much the same as various amendments of the U.S. Constitution. Other employment condition privacy rights law adopted by the separate states tends to focus on the transgressions and misuse by a few employers of information about applicants and employees pertaining to their credit, personal habits and lifestyles, and encounters with law enforcement. State laws governing personnel records tend to seek a means of creating balance between the rights of employers to collect and create personal information on applicants and employees, and the rights of employees to know what information is being kept and to deny release of certain information by not providing the employer with a written authorization to release it.

Some states adopted specific privacy right laws prior to the enactment of federal law, such as those relating to credit (and character) reporting and polygraph testing. Where state and federal law differs in at least some respect, employers must comply with the provisions of both state and federal law. If, however, the more recent enactment of federal law creates more stringent compliance requirements than that contained in state law, the state law may well be negated—thus requiring employers in those states to abide by the more stringent federal law. This latter event is exemplified by the 1988 enactment of the Employee Polygraph Protection Act which may have nullified weaker laws in several states. Employers doing business in separate states, and in particular those employers doing business in multiple states, should become familiar with specific state laws concerning these types of employment privacy rights or controls in order to determine what compliance measures need to be taken where duplication or difference with federal law occurs.

B.2 Legal Causes of Action for Violating Privacy Rights

Rejected applicants and disgruntled employees who feel they have been wronged by an employer are quickly prone to sue—sometimes because their principles of fairness have been breached, and sometimes to seek a recovery of the damage that has been done. In either case, the present legal environment of applicant and employee protectionism almost encourages the filing of legal actions against employers, while the abundance of attorneys willing to accept even marginal cases makes litigation easy. Nor are these conditions likely to lessen much in the future. Conversely, those cases tried in court or defined in law have served to establish legal theory by which privacy right violations occur during various hiring and employment circumstances. Regrettably, this educational process has been at the expense of several unknowing or misguided employers, but we can learn from their costly lessons.

When constitutional and tort laws are violated, the victim can recover compensatory, liquidated, and punitive damages set by the court, and these costs can be substantial where some demonstrated loss occurred by an applicant or employee as the result of an employer's mishandling of the individual's privacy rights. The most common violations, and therefore causes of legal action, are defamation, invasion of privacy, false impression, false imprisonment, and assault and battery. Here are some basic elements of these causes of action.

Defamation

The defaming of a person occurs when one person communicates false, injurious information about another person. The most well-publicized accounts of defamation have been that of employers providing false, biased, or distorted information about a former employee to a prospective employer, who uses it as the basis to reject the applicant from further employment consideration. Most cases won by plaintiff applicants were well deserved due to the indefensible statements made by supervisors and managers that were second-hand, (*Sigal Construction Corp. v. Stanbury*, 1991), unsubstantiated, seriously distorted, subjectively biased, or just plain false; the result of which was to cost the plaintiff an opportunity to continue employment with a reputation free from any shadow of uncertainty about character and/or performance.

Most employers have overreacted to the fear of litigation concerning the defamation potential inherent in providing other employers with reference information about former employees. The most common practice now is to provide only the former employee's job title and dates of employment. However, in recent legal reviews, some courts have found no objection to the giving of additional performance related information about the caller's applicant so long as the information is stated in factual and objective content. Further, there have been court cases wherein the former employer was determined to be falsely withholding reasonable and legitimate employment information from another employer by refusing to give any (or excessively limited) information about former employees.

Yet another common way defamation can arise is during and after internal investigations, including inquiries into employee conduct, physical condition, sexual harassment, drug abuse, and AIDS. These types of defamation violations can equally occur with applicants during preemployment investigations and medical examinations. Special effort must be made in these situations to handle the investigation and related documents in a highly discreet, confidential manner. Only those company representatives who have a legitimate interest and *need to know* should be privy to the conduct and results of such inquiries, and employment decisions must be carefully weighed for relevance to the job and to the nature of the employer's business.

There is one notable exception to the handling of information that might otherwise have defamation potential, and that exception is the doctrine of "privileged" communications. A privilege is said to exist when the communication pertains to delicate personal matters involving applicants and employees. In order to be privileged communications, the information must be: 1) carefully guarded (handled and transmitted); 2) restricted to only those who need to know in order to render decisions; and, 3) sufficiently valuable to the interests of the employer, factual, obtained by reliable authority, and shared in a discreet fashion. Derogatory but factual information about an applicant or employee that is shared between select (usually internal) individuals is generally considered to be a "qualified privilege" exemption, meaning the employer will generally not be held liable. This is the type of common communication that occurs between supervisors, managers, human resource professionals, union representatives, and company agents concerning particularly delicate employment matters. Despite these types of exemptions, you are cautioned that any privilege will be lost when the communication is found to violate a person's privacy rights where the information is knowingly false, communicated with a reckless disregard of truth (from not gathering all the facts), spiteful, excessively shared as in the case of *Dillard Department Stores v. Felton,* 1982, or in other respects the privilege is abused.

Invasion of Privacy, Intrusion, and False Impression

There are four types of invasion of an individual's privacy that can easily occur for the unsuspecting employer trying to gather personal background information about applicants and in dealing with new hires. Violations that can give rise to a legal cause of action are:

1. Misappropriation of a person's name or likeness.
2. Placing an individual in a false light (false impression) in the public eye.
3. Public disclosure of private acts.
4. Unreasonable intrusion upon the seclusion of an individual.

Some of the more frequent employment events that intrude upon the legal principles of invasion of privacy, intrusion, and false impression have to do with applicant background investigations, medical examinations, fingerprinting, polygraph testing, and the collection and processing (confidential handling) of hiring and employment documents. It is the invasion of privacy principle that prevents or restricts employers from conducting surveillance, search, and seizure of applicants and employees in the absence of a good reason or highly sensitive business purpose for intruding on their personal right to privacy or seclusion. Consequently, it is the invasion of privacy theory that has generally barred employers from requiring random drug and alcohol testing of employees (unreasonable search and seizure); from having an investigator observe the personal behavior of applicants and employees (unreasonable surveillance); and from inspecting the personal property of employees, including their assigned desk, locker, files, and the like. Furthermore, with regard to the creation and handling of documents (performance and disciplinary reports), there exists the common law theory that employers have an obligation to exercise a duty to use reasonable care, the failure of which is actionable.

Generally, it is not a misappropriation of an applicant's likeness to photograph them for purposes of identification badges or personnel file attachments, but it would be to use their photo without consent in a company newsletter or to allow the posting/distribution of a caricature of an employee. Placing another in false light is referred to as false impression and is a serious misrepresentation of their privacy interests. Examples of false impression include distortions about an applicant's test scores, background, or interview results, or requiring that a terminated employee inform future employers that the reason they were let go was something other than what actually happened.

Intrusion into an individual's right of privacy and seclusion is one of the more frequently cited causes of action in cases when an employer went too far in their actions to obtain personal living habits information about an applicant, conducted unwarranted surveillance, or required the individual to undergo either a polygraph or psychological examination, the inquiries of which went beyond the bounds of relevance to the job or employer's business interests as in the case of *Phillips v. Smalley Maintenance Service*, 1983. Likewise, intrusion is associated with entering a place held or entitled to be private such as an employee's office, desk drawer, file cabinet, locker, or personal mail (*Venors v. Young*, 1976), as well as the acquisition of personnel information about an applicant or employee by those who do not have a right to know.

False Imprisonment

This deprivation of an individual's privacy right has to do mostly with the unreasonable restraint of an employee. Moreover, to be a libelous cause of action, false imprisonment requires proof that the person was deprived of the reasonable ability to move freely such as prolonged interrogation of an employee (or interview of a job applicant) following their objection to the confinement and request to leave. The most common employer actions that give rise to legal action based on false imprisonment are

- Requiring an employee to work overtime in one location without a meal or rest break during which the employee would be free to move about.
- Refusing to allow an employee to leave a work location after they have expressed a legitimate need and desire to do so.
- Not allowing an employee to leave the work location for the normal consumption of a meal or for bodily functions.

Assault and Battery

Assault and battery may strike you as a far-fetched notion of a deliberate employment-related action, but it does happen—more frequently with employees than with applicants, but it is worth mentioning here because some applicants become employees, and if the action occurs during their initial employment period, they are still applicants. Assault and battery occurs when an individual has been deprived of their physical or emotional (sense of safety) well being by the act or actions of another. While most of us might tend to think of assault and/or battery upon another person to be a brutal act, it need not be so for one's physical or emotional privacy to be violated. Assault by legal definition is any act that places another person in fear of battery such as by voice (yelling at them), language (using provoking or hostile terminology), and body gestures (clenched fist, finger shaking, or moving within an arm's distance).

Battery is defined as the nonconsensual touching, pushing, grabbing, hitting, or offensive body contact by another person. While assault and/or battery privacy right violations are not normally associated with job applicants, they are rather frequent charges made against employers in cases involving the misconduct actions of supervisors. This can occur when supervisors treat employees in an abusive physical or emotional fashion, and in cases of sexual harassment where threats or bodily contact of any type was made with an employee by an agent of the employer.

Assault and battery is just one more reason employers should exercise additional caution when selecting, training, and evaluating supervisory and managerial staff. The degree and manner of the actions of supervisors and managers, as well as the rather fluid perception employees have of these individual's actions, can mean the difference between a mild misunderstanding and a formal complaint or law suit alleging assault and/or battery. When such events become formal it is usually too late for the company to correct the misbegotten behavior of its agent, and the best the company can expect is an out-of-court settlement.

B.3 Preventing Violations of the Most Vulnerable Hiring and Employment Practices

As you have probably discovered by now, preventing legal violations associated with the deprivation of various employment related privacy rights is no easy task. Given the breadth of employer actions that are considered to be infringements on an applicant's or employee's right to certain types of privacy, it becomes very difficult for employers to exercise even reasonable forms of inquiry into an applicant's suitability for the job in question, or to protect their interests by assuring that they have hired a reliable employee. Clearly, the degree of employee protectionism that has occurred through legal prohibitions is the direct result of abuse by some employers, and now all employers must suffer the consequences. In the case of employment related privacy rights, consequences means either the inability to conduct certain types of inquiries, or the narrow constraints in doing so where prohibitions do not (yet) exist.

The hiring of employees is perhaps *the* most critical decision you will make in behalf of your company. Because each employer relies on the skills, abilities, honesty, integrity, and loyalty of its employees to produce successful business transactions, it follows that every employer must do everything within its power to assure that *each* hiring and promotional decision is based on tests and other information that is *in all respects* predictive of the individual's success in the job. For this reason alone, it becomes imperative for employers to gather as much reasonable job and business related information about applicants as the law will allow. Such information should be gathered and used for employment decision making *only* in the context of "whole picture" evaluations of each applicant's suitability to the job and/or nature of the employer's business—not on the basis of subjectively biased, arbitrary, or capricious judgments of the applicant's character, lifestyle, or worthiness. In order to gather this information in a reliable and lawful way, and thereby prevent violations of vulnerable hiring practices, you are encouraged to consider the conditions and approaches to the following practices used by most employers to supplement applicant information in the hiring decision.

Polygraph (Lie Detector) Examinations

As it was pointed out earlier, only certain employers are allowed by law to conduct preemployment polygraph tests to job applicants, and then only to those applicants whose jobs would pertain directly to the nature of exempt types of jobs or employers. All other employers must refrain from using polygraph, deceptograph, or similar measurement devices to assess the honesty, personal habits or proclivities, and character of applicants as a matter of preemployment inquiry. For those employers having a legitimate business or job related reason to ascertain the prospects of an applicant's honesty (primarily related to the person's access to financial transactions, money, vital records, and the like), other tests will have to be used. These other sources consist of validated psychological evaluations or written honesty tests, both of which should be approached with a great deal of caution since these tests are highly subject to undue invasion of privacy and lack of pretest validity for types of jobs in your employ.

Public Record Searches

Under authority of the Public Information Act of 1974, various public agencies may use their discretion in releasing information they have gathered from employers and other sources, including information collected on the basis of an individual's name and/or other identifying data (such as social security number, date of birth, address, etc.). Those agencies most called upon to provide information concerning individuals relate to claims of discrimination, occupational accidents (worker compensable injuries), and law enforcement violations (particularly criminal prosecutions). While these agencies are in general reluctant to release information that, in their opinion, may be misused or is not appropriate to the nature of the inquiry, they may be persuaded to release some or all information they have on a particular person (applicant) if you send them a written explanation of your inquiry purpose, the confidential manner in which your company will treat the information, and a reasonable justification as to why the job in question is reliant on the information being requested.

CAUTION

While these types of public records may be requested, and information received, without the applicant's knowledge, it is not the most prudent approach. To prevent unintentional invasion or discriminatory decision making resulting from the undisclosed receipt of personal information, you should provide applicants with advance notice that background investigations may be required, and that employment is conditional on acceptable results. Then, at the time you are considering the hiring of a particular applicant, have that person sign an authorization and release form such as the one provided in Appendix D. In this way, you're acquiring the applicant's written consent to seek the information and use the results in your employment decision making with their advance knowledge. Additionally, the form itself can be a useful attachment to letters of inquiry to those agencies and individuals having personal information on your applicant with respect to overcoming their reluctance to release such information because of their disclosure liability fear.

A good source for information concerning what information may be obtained from public records, and the names and addresses of where to send your requests is *The Guide To Background Investigations* (Source Publications, 1994). However, with regard to the often desired arrest records of applicants, you should know that the following states prohibit employer inquiries into, or use of, *arrest* (not conviction) records for hiring decisions:

• California	• Maryland	• Oregon
• Colorado	• Massachusetts	• Pennsylvania
• Connecticut	• Michigan	• Rhode Island
• Georgia	• Minnesota	• Texas
• Hawaii	• New York	• Virginia
• Illinois	• Ohio	• Wisconsin
• Iowa		

Those states having laws that allow employer use of *conviction* records information in employment decision making on either an unlimited or limited basis are:

• Alabama	• Iowa	• Nebraska
• Arizona	• Kentucky	• Nevada
• California	• Louisiana	• No. Carolina
• Connecticut	• Maine	• Oregon
• Florida	• Maryland	• Pennsylvania
• Georgia	• Minnesota	• Rhode Island
• Hawaii	• Montana	• Vermont

Credit and Character Reports

These reports are usually sought by employers because the job being considered has direct responsibilities dealing with cash or monetary transaction, bonding insurance requirements, or there exists some sensitive element of the job relating to the company's reputation. Where these conditions exist, there may be sufficient (and advisable) justification to investigate the financial and personal integrity of an otherwise desirable applicant. To prevent violations of federal and state laws concerning both privacy and discrimination, you must have a sound, defensible reason for needing credit or character information during preemployment investigations.

The only defensible reason is that the job requires handling financial transactions pertinent to credit trustworthiness (BFOQ justification), or that the job carries a strong influence on the company's business reputation (business necessity justification). To prevent discriminatory violations, you must be able to demonstrate that the company requires and has performed similar investigations on *all* former applicants for this job who were under serious and final consideration—not just minority applicants because your company felt these applicants may have a more tarnished credit record and wanted a report to verify or refute such a preconceived notion.

If your company feels the need to conduct credit and character investigations on job applicants, and there is justifiable reason to do so on the basis of the job and/or nature of the business, you should consider using these simple prevention measures:

1. Place a notice and acknowledgement at the end of your employment application form that the company may require a satisfactory credit and/or character report on applicants as a condition of their employment, and employees as a condition of their continued employment. If such reports are required for the job being applied for, the applicant will have to provide the company with a written authorization to obtain this information and releasing any party who possesses such information from liability for providing it. It should be further stated that adverse information will not necessarily disqualify applicants, and that the contents of such reports are handled by the company in a highly confidential manner.

2. Be very thorough about your selection of a reputable credit reporting agency or investigative firm to be used by your company as the source for credit and/or character information. Check with at least three of their clients for reference information, and get to know the background credentials of those conducting these inquiries. Also, ask a few questions concerning privacy rights to determine their knowledge of laws, and to ensure that they exercise safeguards.

3. Adopt a personnel policy similar to that provided in this book that reserves the company's right to require credit and/or character investigations on applicants and employees whose

jobs rely on the individual's trustworthiness, character, reputation, and other factors that bear on the person's suitability for employment.

4. Use a form like the Authorization to Require Credit Report found in Appendix D. You should require that the applicant read the contents to assure they understand what type of information is being requested (specifically credit, character, general reputation, and mode of living), from what sources, methods used to gather the information, and that the applicant is releasing these sources from liability in the disclosure of this information. Only after the applicant has acknowledged these understandings should you ask that the form be signed by the applicant.

5. Share information received only with those company officials who have a legitimate interest and need to know, to maintain a high degree of confidentiality. In fact, it is advisable that the affected supervisor only be told that the results are acceptable or unacceptable—not the specific details leading to that conclusion.

6. File credit and character reports in lockable cabinets located in a secure area such as the personnel office, and apart from employee personnel files. In many states having privacy rights laws concerning employees' rights to access and review their personnel files, sensitive records like credit, reference, character, and medical reports are exempted from the employee's access.

7. Comply with the request of an applicant or employee being subjected to a credit and/or character investigation that they receive a copy of the resultant report, and be prepared to inform him or her about how adverse or erroneous information can be corrected.

When you receive results of these kinds of reports, it is suggested that you carefully weigh the appropriateness and gravity of seemingly adverse information. Some of the more important factors you should consider before rendering a decision are the date of an incident's occurrence (lapse of time since last negative incident), severity of the incident, repetitiousness of a particular incident, patterns and relationship of negative incidents, and which kinds of incidents are job or business related as opposed to those that legal sources would probably consider insufficiently related.

Drug and Alcohol Testing

Just about every employer, small and large alike, has developed a keen interest in having a program of testing both applicants and employees for drug and/or alcohol use since the scope of this workplace problem came to widespread public attention during the 1980s. For example, in 1980 a government study estimated that drug use alone was costing American business $25.7 billion related to the illness, absence, health care premium increases, reduced work quality, decreased productivity, and theft. Other similar studies performed during the mid-1980s estimated the actual employer cost to be closer to $75 billion per year. Yet other concerns raised by employers about the effects of drug and alcohol use are the employer's (vicarious) liability for employees working under diminished capacities (judgment and safety hazards), loss or damage to the company's reputation and image, and loss of business from damaged customer relationships.

Given the variety of employment conditions in which serious problems have occurred, employers have determined the need to establish comprehensive control programs to deal with the drug and alcohol issue that is estimated to involve one in every ten workers. Initially, employer controls meant testing job applicants. Later, testing was expanded to include existing employees by random selection at which time employer rights were curtailed by the courts due to the imbalance between employer interests and the arbitrary invasion of employee privacy rights. Now, employer control programs typically consist of policies to address testing, the prohibition of employee use, manufacture, sale, or distribution of controlled substances, and how abuse (addictive attachment to drugs or alcohol) will be treated. The latter issue of abuse often takes a proactive approach by the employer's provision of an Employee Assistance Program and/or policies that allow a leave of absence for mandatory rehabilitative treatment.

By 1987, it was estimated from a study of 2,000 representative companies that half of them were conducting drug and alcohol testing, and that twice as many tests were being given to applicants as existing employees. One reason applicants are more frequently tested than employees is because many courts have held that employees possess a greater (vested) right to protection from adverse employment decisions than those not yet hired, and who therefore have less to lose. Further, the courts have made some important distinctions between applicants and employees in terms of defining the primary privacy right issues that should be considered and protected with each group.

The courts seem to be telling employers that you cannot test any or all applicants merely because they are not yet vested in the job. Rather, the job being applied for must possess some reasonable conditions that would classify the work as sensitive, hazardous, or impacting *significantly* on the welfare and reputation of the business. Employees, on the other hand, should generally be subject to testing only where the employer has reasonable suspicion of the employee's use or abuse of controlled substances. In the few cases heard by the U.S. Supreme Court where some employers have been allowed to continue their random or scheduled mandatory testing of employees, the jobs subject to these liberal testing allowances had direct bearing on the interests of public safety as in the case of airline pilots, train engineers, bus drivers, and the like.

Perhaps the first ray of hope for employers seeking legal approval for the preemployment testing of job applicants was the 1989 California Appellate Court's decision in *Wilkinson v. Times Mirror Corporation*. While this and similar cases like it in other states are subject to supreme court appeals, the case represents a good example of how many courts are giving greater consideration to the employer's approach to preemployment drug and alcohol testing, and the reasonableness of interests the employer is trying to protect as opposed to the applicant's (state constitutional) privacy rights. The case involved a class action suit by applicants for legal writer positions with Matthew Bender & Company (book publishing), a subsidiary of the Times Mirror Corporation (news media). The Appellate Court's reversal of the lower court's finding in behalf of plaintiff applicants was based in large part on the employer's drug and alcohol testing program, which attempted to minimize the intrusiveness into an applicant's expectation of privacy. The employer's program included these elements:

1. Applicants were given advance notice that offers of employment were contingent on the applicant's consent to drug and alcohol testing, and satisfactory results thereof.

2. The employer's policies reflected a sincere interest in establishing and maintaining a drug-free workplace.

3. Applicants were required to undergo a routine physical examination including a urinalysis (the court determined it to be only slightly more intrusive to supply a sufficient sample to perform drug and alcohol tests).

4. Urine samples were collected in a medical environment by persons unrelated to the employer, and applicants were not observed by others during the furnishing of samples.

5. Results of the test were kept confidential inasmuch as the applicant's medical history and specific test results were not disclosed to the employer; only whether or not the applicant passed the entire physician exam standards.

6. The applicant was notified by the examining authority of the portion of the test that caused failure.

7. The employer provided an opportunity for rejected applicants to question and challenge test results.

8. The employer allowed rejected applicants to reapply for employment after a six-month period from the date of their physical examination failure.

Once again, these program conditions were accepted by one court as reasonable for the purpose of conducting preemployment drug and alcohol tests. However, this program profile is not conclusive for all other employers, nor is this intended to be a complete list of all of the balancing principles used by all courts in all privacy rights matters. It does, nevertheless, demonstrate some important precautionary steps for employers to take in establishing policy and program controls to ensure optimal protection for both the employer and applicants.

Another employer program of drug and alcohol testing implemented in 1987 by Miami Valley Hospital (Dayton, Ohio), which was considered acceptable to 98 percent of the 1,076 employees surveyed, had these program elements:

1. No random chemical testing of employees would be conducted. Rather, testing would only occur under the employer's policy which provided that an employee may be asked to agree to a fitness-for-duty evaluation based on observable behaviors, including chemical screening, a physical examination, and a session with an employee assistance manager.

2. Preemployment chemical testing of applicants as a condition of employment would take effect on the implementation date of the program.

3. Employees would only be tested on a finding of probable cause (reasonable suspicion) according to policy.

4. First-time offenders identified through the testing and evaluation procedure had to be offered treatment rather than termination.

5. Initial tests to be used by the employer were to be the Immunoassay-First Level Screen (EMIT) and Thin Layer Chromatography (TLC) tests, and for confirmation of positive results under these tests the employer would use the Gas Chromatography/Mass Spectrometry (GC/MS) test.

6. All managers were to receive training on the program, policies, detection, and handling of workplace drug and alcohol matters.

7. All employees were required to participate in drug awareness training sessions.

As you can see from these two program approaches to both applicant and employee testing, considerable emphasis has been placed on the development of control standards that would likely satisfy legal and individual privacy interests. Therefore, it is reasonable to conclude that prevention of privacy rights and discrimination violations in matters of drug and alcohol testing equates to the employer's development of the following measures:

1. Develop personnel policies that state a sincere company interest in establishing and maintaining a workplace free from the effects of controlled substance use or abuse. Be explicit about the ways in which it affects company costs and operations, damage to employee lives, relationships and work abilities, and the nature of the company's business.

    Develop, publish, and distribute policies concerning the drug and alcohol testing of some applicants as part of the company's preemployment physical examination, and that employees may be subject to testing, surveillance, or property searches whenever there exists reasonable evidence that they are engaged in the use, possession, sale, or distribution of illegal substances.

    Develop policies and a program of employee referral to an Employee Assistance Program for counseling; to rehabilitative services and opportunities for a leave of absence to undergo treatment; and for termination of employees who refuse testing or mandatory completion (job conditional) of treatment participation.

2. Place a notice and acknowledgement on your applicant form that informs job applicants of your company's policy on preemployment drug and alcohol testing; particularly that their consent, compliance, and satisfactory results are required as a condition of employment, and continuation thereafter.

3. Develop a list of all job titles in your company's employ that the company regards as having work conditions containing one or more of the elements of safety risk, hazardous conditions risk, customer relations risk, crucial business or financial information risk, or significant operations risk. Beside each job title, define the job responsibility that gives rise to one or more of these risk factors, or any other risk factor your company regards as a defensible purpose to justify conducting preemployment drug and alcohol tests on applicants on these jobs. When your list is finished, have it reviewed by a qualified *labor* law attorney and make any recommended changes. Thereafter, test only applicants for those jobs identified on this list.

4. Develop some quality controls in your testing program. For example, you should consider the use of an industrial medical group (or consult your workers' compensation claims adjuster for other reliable medical examiners) to conduct your preemployment physicals, who will work with reliable independent labs to get rapid test results. Further, you should insist that proper clinical procedures be used in the collection, identification, transportation (if necessary), and testing methods of samples. If available within a reasonable geographic location to your business, you should use a lab that has state-of-the-art computer analysis of the EMIT and TLC tests, and if initial results are positive you should immediately request a confirming analysis using the GC/MS test as the most legally defensible testing methods available. A list of those labs certified by the National Institute on Drug Abuse as having met strict standards imposed by the Mandatory Guidelines for Federal Workplace Drug Testing Programs is provided at the end of this chapter for your reference.

5. Develop tightly controlled internal information handling procedures to assure the highest possible degree of confidentiality over drug and alcohol testing details. Only one company official should be responsible for dealing with applicants, medical examiners, and lab representatives. This management level staff person should confine disclosure of acceptable or unacceptable results only to those in the company who have a direct interest in the applicant's qualifying for the job. Written reports received by the company concerning physical examination results should be placed in a confidential, locking file cabinet where other sensitive and nonaccessible personnel records are kept.

6. Applicants should be notified promptly as to whether their test results were satisfactory or not. If not, and the cause was due to a positive drug or alcohol result, they should be informed of the company's interest in having a confirming test performed. Given the average rejection rate of 10 to 40 percent of all applicants tested for drug and alcohol presence, it is likely that many applicants who are tested positive initially will decline confirming tests, but you should at least offer the opportunity as a matter of preventative defense.

AIDS, Hepatitis B, and Other Communicable Disease Testing

Here is yet another vital hiring issue where the separate interests of applicant and employer collide. Applicants are concerned with the deprivation of their privacy rights and discriminatory effect that testing for communicable diseases may have on their employability, while employers usually have both an interest and legal obligation to protect their workplaces from undue health and safety risks. The testing of job applicants for such communicable diseases as Acquired Immune Deficiency Syndrome (AIDS), Hepatitis B, Tuberculosis, and other communicable diseases may have some kinship to drug and alcohol testing inasmuch as it requires the analysis of body fluids, but communicable disease testing is considered far more intrusive.

Testing for communicable diseases requires the extraction of blood—the more tests being performed, the more blood is required—that would not otherwise be necessary for a routine preemployment physical examination. According to most courts who have rendered case decisions where applicants have been rejected from employment due to the presence of a *potentially* communicable condition, this form of health testing and the resultant rejection decision is unlawful under most employment conditions. Those employment conditions, say the courts, must present a clear, imminent, if not irrefutable danger to the applicant or others in the workplace in order to be considered reasonable and therefore lawful testing.

The legal issues raised by testing applicants for AIDS, hepatitis B, and similar communicable diseases are the following privacy rights and discrimination protections that are vulnerable to violation:

1. ***U.S. Constitution, First Amendment;*** right to free association with other individuals and groups (rejection for AIDS presence implies rejection for association with homosexuals and/or drug users when, in fact, other means of acquisition are possible).

2. ***U.S. Constitution, Fourth Amendment;*** protection against unreasonable searches (the mandatory extraction of blood to determine the presence of communicable diseases is generally held as an unwarranted search unless the employer can show reasonable cause).

3. ***U.S. Constitution, Fifth Amendment;*** protection from an individual's having to provide self-incriminating information to others (being compelled to participate in testing by threat of automatic rejection where the tests results are known by the applicant to self-incriminate their condition).

4. ***State Constitutional Provisions;*** protecting the above and perhaps even more specific privacy rights as they relate to the intrusiveness of communicable disease testing or the false impression stigmatization of an applicant that may follow from disclosure of such health conditions.

5. ***Federal and State Discrimination Statutes;*** providing protection from unwarranted—meaning without sufficient job or business justification—physical disability discrimination (applicants who are otherwise "qualified" to perform the job, but who are rejected because of the *potential* hazards associated with their condition is often found to be a form of discrimination, and most communicable diseases are generally protected forms of a disability).

By 1987, six states had rendered legal opinions that AIDS and ARC were within the definition of protected handicap discrimination; and they include California, Florida, Oregon, Massachusetts, New York, and Wisconsin. Likewise, the Ninth Circuit Court of Appeals has determined that AIDS is a physical handicap under the 1973 Vocational Rehabilitation Act in the case of *Chalk v. U.S. District Court* (1988), thereby federalizing AIDS-related discrimination. Given the latitude of statutory provisions contained in the 1990 Americans with Disabilities Act, it is also likely that communicable diseases will be a protected handicap within the meaning of this law for private sector employers.

The two key issues pertaining to an employer's testing for communicable diseases are: 1) does there exist a high risk factor inherent in the job or employment environment that *will* (not potentially) cause infection to others, and 2) is the applicant able to perform the essential tasks of the job with no more than reasonable accommodation? If the answer to the first issue is yes, then you may have sufficient reason to require communicable disease tests only on those applicants for the specific jobs that create the risk. If the answer to the second issue is yes, and this applicant is clearly the most qualified for the job in terms of such factors as skill, training, experience, and so forth, then this applicant should be hired. To do otherwise would be begging for legal backlash.

Of all the communicable diseases, AIDS presents the greatest threat and fear for employers: threat in terms of legal violations, risk to others, and the higher than usual probability of temporary employment; and fear associated with the cost impact on the company's liability, the reaction of other employees who are likely to learn about the new employee's condition sooner or later, and the prospect of the employee's ultimate death as a result of the condition. AIDS therefore represents the proverbial placing of employers between the "rock and a hard place" when it comes to the question of whether or not to test applicants. If you don't test, your company is forced to operate under the assumption that all applicants are free from communicable diseases and, as employees, will remain healthy until a particular condition arises at which time you will deal with the situation as needed. If you do test for communicable diseases, and AIDS in particular, you run the risk of violating any one or all of the legal rights cited earlier. Before deciding, here are a few additional points you may wish to know about.

Information and research concerning AIDS is relatively new. Medical information only emerged publicly since the early 1980s, yet some sources in the medical community have already classified the virus as an epidemic due in large part to the rapid growth in the number of infected persons diagnosed as having or dying from the disease. Alarm by the employment community rose equally fast, and in particular with those organizations employing people who were considered high risk contractors of the disease and those who employed people having contact with (potentially) infected persons such as hospital workers, ambulance attendants, and law enforcement personnel. By 1987, it was estimated that between five and ten million of the world's population were infected with the Human Immuno-deficiency Virus (HIV), with the greatest concentration in Africa.

Within the United States, the Center For Disease Control estimated in 1988 that the total HIV infected population was approximately 1.5 million people. Of this population, there are believed to be 41,000 cases of reported AIDS (with a ratio of 15 males to one female), the balance being persons with AIDS Related Complex (ARC). ARC is a nonsymptomatic carrier of the virus believed to have (there is no method of accounting for ARC individuals) an incidence rate five to ten times greater than that of AIDS. To make matters more difficult, not all ARC individuals will become fully symptomatic with AIDS, yet both conditions can be and often are fatal. It is further estimated by the United States Public Health Service that the number of diagnosed AIDS cases will rise to 270,000 by the early 1990s, of which about 179,000 will have already died from the inability of their immune systems to counter the effects of life threatening infections.

The incubation period between the presence of HIV antibodies in the blood and the occurrence of death can vary from three months to as much as five or more years. Once the individual becomes fully symptomatic, the deterioration of physical ability to function normally, and eventually death, progress rather rapidly. This individual, according to the courts, must be accommodated by employers until the person can no longer perform or physically endure his or her job duties. The most common methods of transmitting the disease by those considered to be in the highest risk group of people are:

Method of Transmission	High Risk Group
1. Sexual contact such as by infectious semen to vaginal or anal canal (absorbed into bloodstream).	1. Homosexuals
	2. Intravenous Drug Users
2. Direct blood receipt of infected blood.	3. Females having sex with the above and/or hemophiliacs
3. Fetal infection of a new-born by infection prior to or during pregnancy.	4. Prostitutes and those having sex with them
	5. Sexually active, non-monogamous heterosexuals

You should be further aware that there is no singular test to diagnose AIDS with full accuracy. The most reliable test currently available is referred to as the ELISA test, but this test merely measures the presence or absence of HIV antibodies in an individual's blood supply. However, positive test results do not necessarily indicate the presence of AIDS; only that there is a high probability for the individual to develop AIDS or ARC sometime during the incubation period. A second ELISA test should be performed to confirm the first positive results, followed by either the Western blot or Immunofluorescence tests to determine if the individual is "true positive" infected with AIDS. Naturally, any information relating to HIV testing of applicants or employees—providing there exists adequate justification or conditions to conduct such tests—is to be guarded with the strictest confidence as a matter of the individual's privacy rights protection. To ensure that applicants are not discriminated against, nor have their privacy rights deprived in the hiring process, it is suggested that you follow these preventative measures:

1. Do not establish personnel policies on the issue of dealing with AIDS or ARC employees. Doing so only creates an obvious differentiation that singles out this individual or group as being treated differently. AIDS or ARC employees should be treated the same as any other employee having a medical condition or disability that will require flexible working arrangements.

2. Do not test applicants for AIDS or any other communicable diseases without exceedingly good reason, meaning a very real and present set of conditions that would endanger the health of others. The only way that you may become aware of an applicant who has (or believes they may have, or had) a communicable disease is if your examining physician uses a medical history form where various respiratory, circulatory, and other body disorders are listed for the individual's identification of past or present conditions.

   Should an applicant's response be affirmative to any such *present* disorders, and the job being applied for has significant relatedness to this existing medical condition, then your testing of the applicant for confirmation of *that* condition to determine suitability should be reasonably justified. However, under no circumstances should an employer provide an applicant with a medical history form or request that an applicant complete one for the employer's file.

3. Consult with experienced legal, medical, or human resource professionals to ascertain the justification for requiring preemployment communicable disease testing of applicants for particular jobs, the presence of work conditions that present an unusual risk of transmission or contraction, and what measures should be taken in the way of confidential procedures should an employee become afflicted with AIDS.

Smokers' Versus Nonsmokers' Rights

Smoking is both a personal and an addictive habit carried over from a more socially accepting period of time which is no longer socially acceptable in our current health-conscious society. As a personal habit, smoking can be construed as a privacy right but it tends to infringe on the rights of nonsmokers with a greater health interest (physical intrusion by the effects of secondary smoke) shared by a larger group of people. Therefore, smoking will generally not withstand the test of an inalienable right, at least in such settings as the workplace. As a personal addiction, smoking could reasonably be defined as a physical handicap within the meaning of federal and state discrimination laws, and handled like any other addictive trait of an employee. You should remember, however, that it is not a discriminatory act for an employer to refuse employment to an individual having a present addiction that would adversely influence their work or workplace conditions. Accommodation is only required when the addiction would not interfere with employment and the person is not engaging in the addictive behavior.

The issue of smokers' versus nonsmokers' personal rights and individual proclivities has long been a difficult subject of employment decision making for numerous employers. In the absence of state or local laws establishing specific prohibitions, such as a ban on smoking in public facilities, each employer must decide how to deal with the issue as a matter of workplace conditions. Some of the employment interests that should be weighed are:

1. Should the company establish a total ban on workplace smoking (Smoke-Free Workplace Policy)?
   - How will we handle the "grandfathering" of current employees who smoke?
   - What health codes or related laws can we cite if needed to defend this policy?
   - What work, workplace, or industry related conditions can we cite as a business necessity reason for the policy?
   - How many and which current employees are we likely to lose if we impose the policy on them?
   - Are we willing to hire a possible second choice nonsmoker because our first choice is a smoker?

2. Should the company establish a restricted smoking policy?
   - Do we have an isolated area or location that can be used as a designated smoking area?
   - Are there other locations such as private offices where smoking could/should be at the option of the individual employee?
   - Are allowable smoking locations compatible with the ventilation system to prevent secondary smoke and odor from being carried elsewhere?
   - How should we deal with employees who violate the policy?

To avoid the potential effect of violating an applicant's privacy right concerning unwarranted intrusion into their personal habits, it is advisable to disregard whether or not the applicant is a smoker. That information can be learned and dealt with during a medical examination or asked (based on the company's policy) of a pending new hire before a job offer is made. Providing you can cite company policy and a sound basis of the policy, then your rejection of smoking applicants will likely not pose a threat of legal violation for privacy or discrimination rights. An even better preventative method in cases where the company prohibits or restricts smoking is to let that fact be known to applicants either in your recruitment advertising or at the time application is made.

Dress and Grooming Standards

The personal appearance of employees is another sensitive interest of almost every employer. It is also one of those personal characteristics of people that carries the implication of privacy right and discriminatory violations with respect to hiring processes as well as employment practices. For example, privacy rights can be infringed upon when employers go too far into investigating the personal proclivities of applicants regarding hygiene and clothing. It can be a further psychological intrusion to require an employee to wear revealing attire or to wear less revealing attire.

In terms of potential discrimination effects of making hiring decisions on the basis of subjective dress and grooming standards, a few employers have been surprised to learn that transvestisms (cross-sex dressing) and transsexualism (sex change) can be considered a protected handicap under federal law. Another dress related consideration of employment that can be established as a discriminatory hiring practice is requiring employees to wear costly attire, and rejecting those applicants who do not wear such attire on appearance for interviews. While it is reasonable to reject an applicant for "improper" attire (reasonably inappropriate to the nature of the job), and appearance that might be observed at the time of application or during interviews, the rejection of an applicant for not meeting specific dress standards and/or expectations can easily be construed as discrimination against economically disadvantaged applicants.

To prevent the violation of an applicant's privacy rights and discrimination on the basis of an employer's dress and grooming standards, you should take at least these steps:

1. Base any company dress policies on the job and/or business related needs specific to those jobs in which a particular mode of dress is required (e.g., shop coats in the lab, professional attire for office and customer contact personnel, or business apparel for sales personnel). All but a very few employers will want to include in their dress policies a prohibition against the wearing of revealing attire. Policies that address the proper grooming of employees should apply to all employees since hygiene is generally considered a function of grooming, and hygiene can be defended as noninvasive and nondiscriminatory if applied to all employees on the basis of the company's interest and obligation to maintain a healthy, unoffensive work environment.

2. Do not mention or comment on an applicant's dress or grooming during an interview. If the applicant emerges as the best qualified person for the job in all other respects, you can address the issue of your dress and/or grooming expectations through the medical examination (hygiene can often be a medically related matter that might be correctable, but it thereby becomes a potential for handicap discrimination) or prior to a job offer. Conversely, if an applicant's dress or grooming is very inconsistent with the nature of the job or the company's business, then the applicant may be considered not qualified for the job on this basis alone.

3. Refrain from making hiring decisions or establishing employment practices that tend to be intrusive into the private lives of applicants or employees, or that tend to be oriented to just females or males.

Outside Employment Restrictions

Some employers are interested in restricting employees from engaging in outside, additional employment. The reason might be a good one—usually having to do with noninterference in the employee's availability or quality of performance in his or her primary job—but not necessarily a legitimate one in terms of a legal view of unreasonable control over the private lives of employees. Consequently, policies that serve to restrict or forbid the outside employment of employees are frequently rejected by the courts, and the employer held liable for violating the employee's privacy rights. Such policies need not be written to create a violation. A company representative merely needs to ask an applicant during an interview if they have, are now, or would work at more than one job (in order to satisfy their personal financial needs), or pose a similar question to one of the applicant's reference sources. Whether or not a written policy exists, a violation can occur merely by asking questions related to the subject of outside employment.

The conditions under which an employer can establish reasonable restrictions on outside employment or job specific or based on the reasonable and genuine interests of the employer's business. To be job specific there must be a particular set of employment related conditions that are attached to the job itself based on the nature of the employer's business. For example, if the *business* has to do with providing service to customers 24 hours a day (hospitals, public utilities, towing services, etc.), and the *job* under consideration is one of the positions designated for stand-by or call-back duty, then applicants for such jobs should be informed in advance of these conditions (policies). Consequently, the applicant's acceptance or rejection from employment may be based on their availability for such assignments and adherence to the company's policies. Even in these kinds of businesses the company should avoid blanket policies on outside employment restrictions. Likewise, an employer may restrict or limit outside employment for those jobs where a conflict of interest could easily arise. In these cases, an employer may be well justified in controlling outside employment in jobs that conflict with the company's interests (such as working for a competitor) or the objectivity of the employee in their company job (for example, working as a tax accountant for a customer).

Notwithstanding the above, employers are not prevented from adopting and enforcing policies concerning how employees will be treated if they require an absence—usually disability related—from work in connection with other employment. Here, it is reasonable for an employer to seek protection from unwarranted liability over such matters as fraudulent workers' compensation claims, continuation of health care benefit payments, continued accrual of sick and vacation leave benefits, and implied job return rights that might otherwise guarantee employees the ability to return to the same job after an extended period of absence. In fact, it may be in the best interest of employers to establish policies that define restrictions on employment benefits when employees are disabled due to outside employment rather than policies that restrict participation in outside employment, excluding those jobs where there exists legitimate business reasons for the restriction.

To prevent the unintentional deprivation of applicants' rights to control their private lives, you should consider these actions:

1. Do not adopt blanket policies, or unwritten practices, that prohibit or restrict employees from engaging in outside employment. Policy restrictions may be adopted that are job-specific to the conditions surrounding the requirement that particular jobs are subject to being available for on-call or stand-by response if warranted by the nature of the employer's business. If the job(s) subject to such a policy are represented by a union, the policy will then be subject to collective bargaining agreement, as are other employment condition policies.

2. Do not make preemployment inquiries into an applicant's participation in outside employment. If your company has a legitimate reason to restrict outside employment for the job in question, announce the restriction as a BFOQ during recruitment, in job ads, and attach a notice to the application forms of individuals applying for this particular job to establish advance notice and self-screening.

3. At the time of making a job offer to an applicant, have the applicant sign a form that confirms knowledge of the conditional nature of employment based on an outside employment restriction/limitation. By signing the form, the applicant agrees to abide by the policy or be terminated for its violation.

Nepotism and Spousal Employment Restrictions

Excluding relatives of employees from employment, or establishing excessively harsh restrictions on the employment of relatives and spouses, is very similar to the privacy rights and discriminatory principles that accompany outside employment practices. That is, using restrictive and conditional employment policies based on the private lives and relationships of people for unwarranted reasons has the effect of discriminating on the basis of sex, marital status, or family ties. Several courts have examined the inherent discriminatory effect that nepotism and spousal employment policy prohibitions have on employment decision making. Additionally, such policies and hiring practices raise an intrusive element of disclosure about the private lives and relationships of applicants to existing employees, and doing so creates a potential violation of an applicant's right to privacy—at least until you're ready to extend a job offer.

The general rule-of-thumb concerning nepotism and spousal employment policies is that blanket policies are unnecessary since restrictions are most likely to be justified on the basis of particular employment, operational, and job conditions where there is a need to establish control. For this reason, most policies that aim to establish controls over the hiring of applicants who are relatives or spouses of employees do so by use of flexible, case-by-case determinations based on the four elements of *safety, security, supervision,* and *morale.* For example, most people (including the courts) would not deny that hiring a spouse or the offspring of an employee who would supervise their work or be required to exercise managerial authority over their employment is not a good practice. It raises personal and family problems, coworker morale problems, potential breaches of security, and a host of other difficult situations that should be avoided in the workplace setting. On the other hand, it is not a justifiable practice to unilaterally exclude such individuals from employment consideration merely because of their spousal or blood relationship with an employee who would have no direct job or work environment ties with the spouse or relative. Thus, blanket policies that prohibit the employment of spouses and/or relatives are frowned on by legal sources.

To prevent the violation of an applicant's privacy right or discriminatory effect of prohibitive policies on the hiring of spouses and/or relatives, you should consider taking these courses of action:

1. If you establish such policies and practices, they should be based on the presence of a direct relationship or working contact between the job being applied for by the applicant and the job of their spouse or relative. The factors to use as the basis of acceptance or rejection of the applicant should be the effect of their relationship on safety, security, supervision, and morale.

    Further, you may wish to have your policy address the condition of spousal or relative job changes, the nature of which creates a policy conflict, including how marriages between employees will be handled by the company in the event their working relationship conflicts with one or more of the conditional factors.

2. Do not place an inquiry on your employment application form, or ask interview questions that solicit information about the applicant's personal relationship with any of your existing employees. This information can and probably should be ascertained before a job offer is made, but not before you have identified the applicant as the person you wish to hire. If the applicant is related by marriage or blood to an existing employee, then you can consider the effect of the four factors before making your hiring decision.

3. Do not transfer or terminate an employee who marries, or becomes related to another employee through marriage, until you have given full consideration of the effect the four factors are most likely to have on their jobs, work relationships, coworkers, and the like. If your conclusion results in an adverse employment decision for one of them, be prepared to provide documented justification for each factor used in your decision.

Employment References

Obtaining previous employment reference information remains one of the most sensitive and vulnerable of all employment practices for both the inquiring employer and the responding employer. This sensitivity is born in large part from the well publicized notoriety given to exorbitant damages paid to employees by their former employers who said or publicized defaming, dishonest, or other libelous information. Regrettably, the effect of these frequent and costly legal actions has been the placing of "gag orders" on the release of any, or extremely limited and thereby useless, information concerning the work history of former employees.

To complicate matters, some courts are now saying that the unreasonable withholding of work history information about a former employee from inquiring prospective employers may be unlawful, particularly when the former employee has expressly requested and authorized the release of employment information. The question thus becomes, what information should you release (certainly not all), and whether the proper authorizations have been received and verified. With respect to making former employment references, you need to obtain and use an authorization form such as that provided in Appendix D to have your finalist applicant complete for each separate inquiry to be made.

Generally, making reference telephone calls to prior employers will only result in very guarded conversation that provides little of the useful or insightful kind of information for which you made the call. However, telephone attempts are better than no attempts. If you use telephone calls rather than authorization forms—presumably because your decision time is limited—here are a few suggestions to help you get the most useful and detailed information from reluctant managers and supervisors.

1. Ask to speak to the person (by name) who directly supervised your applicant. Identify yourself by name, title, and company. State the nature of your call—to seek their help in identifying and verifying employment characteristics related to the job under consideration. Offer the supervisor the opportunity to call you back if they would like to verify the authenticity of your call.

2. Let the supervisor know that you are knowledgeable about the sensitive nature of a former employee's privacy rights. Then, assure him/her that your company regards this conversation as confidential and that the details of your conversation (your notes) will not be made known or available to the applicant; providing the law in your state allows the nonaccessible filing of reference information.

3. Begin your questions by asking the supervisor to verify the applicant's stated dates of employment, last salary/wage rate, and if there were any other positions held other than the stated position at the conclusion of employment.

4. Then, ask about other aspects of the applicant's work history and relationship with the supervisor, but stick to questions that are pertinent to the job being applied for, the nature of your company's business, and particular working conditions associated with the job. This is the point at which you may wish to delve into such areas as the applicant's

   - Attendance record including any extended durations of absence and, if so, for what causes.

   - Compliance with company policies, work rules and procedures, and instructions from the supervisor.

   - Speed, accuracy, and quality with which work was carried out. How many errors were made and did work have to be returned to the applicant for correction? Were repetitive instructions necessary to accomplish learning routine tasks?

   - Quality of relationships with coworkers, superiors, and other contacts required in the course of employment. Were there any behavioral or interpersonal problems encountered with particular types of people or situations such as dealing in group settings or getting along with women, men, particular minorities, etc.

   - Ability to read, comprehend, interpret, and write information at least at the level required for the job in question.

   - Honesty and trustworthiness based on the kinds of conditions present in the prospective job and work environment exposure. This is where the conversation may get cold, and you should not dwell on this issue since all responses are likely to be entirely subjective and merely speculative.

- History of disciplinary actions and disability leaves associated with either on- or off-duty activities. Again, this information is not normally given out even if it exists because this type of information is more prone to liability for defamation, false impression, and discrimination charges than are the other more objective and work skills related question areas previously mentioned. If the supervisor declines comment on this area of the applicant's employment, then merely express your appreciation for their cooperation in providing answers to your other questions and end the conversation.

5. If the supervisor refuses to give you no more than a verification of the applicant's employment dates and job titles held, or is obstinate, you should persist in your attempt to get more thorough and job relevant information by taking any of the following courses of action you feel most appropriate to the situation:

    - Inform the supervisor that some courts have found companies legally liable for the unnecessary withholding of reasonable job related information because potential employers (such as yourself) cannot hire people in the absence of this kind of information. Then ask the supervisor to cooperate by helping you with your questions.

    - Ask the supervisor for the name of his/her superior, and to connect you with that person so that you can explain the reason for your questions and the potential legal liability their company could face should the applicant not be hired and wish to pursue a legal discovery of the reason.

    - Ask either of these prior employment representatives if they would be more comfortable responding to a form inquiry containing the applicant's authorization to disclose requested information with a waiver of liability.

6. Document each question you asked and the answer given. Quote the supervisor's exact words where possible, but at least paraphrase his or her remarks for future reference if the need arises.

7. Treat your notes as a highly confidential document source. Do not disclose this document to the applicant or others who do not have a need to see it. If allowed by state law, store your documented notes in a separate, nonaccessible file where other sensitive personnel records are kept. The person who would be supervising this applicant should merely be told whether the applicant was acceptable or unacceptable with respect to the entire preemployment check.

Again, you are likely to experience limited success with telephone reference inquiries. However, since employers are increasingly being held liable for the negligent acts of employees they hire, as you will learn more about in the next chapter, telephone attempts to obtain potentially vital prior employment history on *every* applicant under serious consideration can provide some defense should your company find itself involved in a negligent hiring suit.

Privacy Control System Checklist

Personnel Policies

❑   Have a written and well disseminated policy on preparing, handling, use, and access of confidential employment information.

❑   Have a preemployment medical testing policy that assures only job valid testing will be conducted, including the reserved right of management to require medical testing when circumstances warrant (e.g., return to work, contagious condition absence, and workers' compensation disability).

❑   Have a drug/alcohol testing policy for new hires related only to sensitive, hazardous, or other legitimate business interest jobs, and based on the presence of a reasonable suspicion for all other employees.

❑   Have a policy on the obtaining and giving of employment references, including letters of recommendation and requiring written authorizations to obtain/give references.

Personnel Files

❑   Have a designated "records custodian" who is the ultimate authority on control, access, and use of file documents.

❑   Have a list of designated staff whose jobs necessitate access and use of file documents.

❑   Have a procedure for the access and review of file documents by employees and authorized supervisory and management staff.

❑   Highly personal and sensitive documents are kept in a second or sealed file (if allowed by state law).

Applicant/Employee Authorizations

❑   Have an authorization form for the applicant's authorization to obtain any desired prior employment information and release of liability for the former employer.

❑   Have an authorization form for employee's written release of pertinent work history information and release of liability.

Application Form and Interviews

❑   No inquiries are listed on the employment application form that solicit information concerning the applicant's identification of protected privacy right details.

❑   Questions are not asked during preemployment interviews concerning an applicant's relationship with existing employees, mode of living, addictive habits, law enforcement violations, or other types of protected privacy right information.

Employment References

❑   Provided only by well trained human resource or management personnel.

❑   Confined only to factual and objective work history about the applicant's (if acquiring) or employee's (if giving) job performance characteristics, job scope, behavior and relationships, adherence to policies and instructions, and attendance.

❑   Incoming calls are verified that the requestor is duly authorized, and the former employee's written release has been obtained and verified.

Performance Appraisals and Discipline Notices

- ❑ Information is factual, objectively stated, honest, and reviewed by departmental management before discussion/copies to the employee.

- ❑ Documents are reviewed by a human resource professional prior to deposit in personnel files.

- ❑ Employees are given an opportunity to write their own comments or rebuttal to statements or ratings that are disagreeable.

- ❑ Employees are informed—preferably in writing—of their right to appeal adverse actions (denial of pay increase, suspension, demotion, etc.); providing the company has an established appeal mechanism.

Supervisory Training

- ❑ *All* supervisory and management personnel receive frequent and in-depth training on all pertinent aspects of applicant/employee privacy rights, including the limits of their authorities.

Appendix C

A New Threat: Employer Liability for Negligent Hiring

As if the myriad of previously discussed employment laws affecting an employer's hiring decision are not more than sufficient to constrain choices within a "free" business economy, now comes forth the resurrection of old common law principles packaged in new legal theories that is costing American employers billions for negligence liability—this time due to negligence in the hiring process. Suing employers has not only become a fashionable practice among applicants and employees, but now it has reached profitable proportions among third parties who have sustained some injurious damage as a result of the improper acts of a company's employees.

The society as a whole, and the courts in particular, are decidedly more prone than in years past to place the economic burden of injury squarely on the shoulders of employers. Until suitable relief is found through legislation that recognizes at least some limitations on an employer's liability for such matters as their hiring decisions, you are stuck with the need to take extra precautions so that this liability does not occur as a result of the employees you choose to hire.

In the previous appendix, you learned that violating an applicant's or employee's privacy rights could create a legal cause of action under tort law which represents a civil wrongdoing that can result in the awarding of compensatory, liquidated, and punitive damages set by the court, as well as attorney and court costs. Likewise, negligence is a tortuous cause of action and it can take many forms. In the case of negligent hiring, the tort is typically associated with an act or omission on the part of the employer—specifically the person responsible for handling the hiring process—whereby the person hired injures another person in the course of their employment and the employer *should have known* about the employee's propensity, established adequate controls, or not hired the individual.

The dilemma for employers should be obvious. In order to gain reasonable confidence in the totality of skills, knowledge, behavior, and personal characteristics of applicants before hiring them, an employer has to obtain a considerable amount of information about these traits. Yet to do so would subject the employer to violating other legal limitations in order to protect their negligent hiring liability. For example, to ascertain an applicant's personal character, you would have to risk invasion of privacy; to test an applicant's honesty, you risk not only violation of privacy, but also discrimination on the basis of the test not being job valid; to determine the applicant's past employment history, you need cooperation from past employers who are fearful of defamation suits so they won't provide insightful information; and to learn about an applicant's prospective criminal or other law enforcement records, you again risk invasion of privacy and even possible discrimination charges.

This discussion, then, is intended to help you maneuver through the proverbial minefield of these risks, while at the same time avoiding major cost and operational destruction associated with the trip wires of negligent hiring. But, we must face one hard fact at the out-set—hiring relatively unknown people to represent the interests of your company and to carry out the responsibilities and authorities inherent in each job is risky in and of itself. There is no avoiding risk, only minimizing the potential for adverse outcomes. The greater the potential for serious risk associated with each employer's business and the nature of jobs being employed, the more precise should the precautions be that are taken to assure success in every hiring decision. Clearly, hiring new people presents a set of conditions that requires the weighing and balancing of risks.

So, on occasion, you may find that some of the suggestions contained in this discussion have the appearance of risking the potential violation of some employment laws mentioned in earlier chapters and appendices as a condition that should be avoided. You're free to accept or reject any such risk that is suggested here, because ultimately it is you who must weigh and determine which risks are worth taking, to protect your company's interests. The underlying assumption being taken throughout this discussion is that most employers cannot afford to hire those who are disreputable for the job in question, and to hire them without knowing these traits is too great a risk to bear the consequences. Naturally, this assumption is tempered by the realization that not every applicant need be approached with grave suspicion; the trick is to discover which ones can cause your company grave harm.

C.1 What Is the Legal Basis of Negligent Hiring?

You're no doubt aware that when one of your employees is involved in an auto accident during work hours and in the course of their employment, your company's business insurance will cover any damages. If the employee is injured, benefits are provided through workers' compensation insurance, their vehicle repaired through their own or the company's insurance on autos, and the other party taken care of through the company's general liability insurance. The same holds true if one of your employees enters a customer's home and breaks a treasured vase or mars furniture. But, have you ever wondered what the company's liability might be if one of your employees was suspected of alcohol abuse, had a history of driving under the influence of alcohol unbeknownst to your company, and sped through a traffic light killing the occupants of another vehicle?

Or, instead of your employee breaking a vase, suppose the police showed up at your company to take the employee into custody for sexual assault and rape of a customer while in the customer's home? Is your company liable? Can you be held personally liable as a codefendant when the company is sued? Will ordinary business insurance cover the cost of litigation and damages, and will the company provide representation of your defense as a codefendant? These are not very pleasant thoughts, but they do represent questions that every company official who is responsible for hiring processes should carefully consider.

Regrettably, these and other seriously injurious events occur with some frequency, and they happen to an employee who acts on his or her own source of motivation and personal propensities. The fact that such acts are predicated on the personal characteristics of employees does not necessarily exonerate the employer from liability, particularly if it can be shown that the employer should have known about the employee's propensities but failed to obtain the information, was aware of the propensity but chose to do nothing about it, or merely failed to establish safeguards to protect others from known sources of possible injury.

Generally, the common law doctrine of negligent hiring operates only when an employee performs an injurious act within the scope of his or her employment, and it can be shown that the employer could and should have prevented the injury to another person by exercising due care. Due care usually means that

1. The employer should have been more thorough about checking the employee's background prior to hiring, and if the employer had done so, the individual probably would not have been hired due to the nature of the job or work conditions that provided the opportunity to create the injurious situation.

2. The employer would have recognized the potential liabilities of each job and taken adequate control measures to ensure that people were properly matched to jobs, rules were followed, and that supervisors regularly monitored the actions of employees.

3. The employer recognizes that when an employee is found to be insufficiently skilled, capable, or possesses harmful tendencies, the employee (including supervisors) should be removed from that job or work setting and either given a job with lesser risk attached or terminated.

Course and Scope of Employment

The fundamental reason an employer may be held negligently liable for injurious acts to third parties by an employee is that the employer is regarded as having "implied control" over what each employee does in carrying out their duties. That is, the employer delegates duties to its employees and is thus responsible for their actions in the course and scope of those duties. Since the employer is also free to frame reasonable policies, procedures, and rules to control the employee's performance of assigned duties, the employer can be held liable for inadequate control and/or supervision when employees conduct themselves beyond the desired or intended scope of their jobs.

However, not all injurious or criminal actions of employees need to be performed during working hours for employers to be liable. Some courts have held that, under certain circumstances where an employee represents himself as an agent or as being associated with the employer (i.e., wearing a uniform or driving a company vehicle), the employee can possibly be held as being in the *course* and/or *scope* of his or her employment. This legal expansion of the notion of an employer's ability to exercise control over the actions of its employees forms the justification and need for employers to establish policies concerning the off-duty conduct of employees, such as prohibiting representation of their employment to others.

The allegation in most negligent hiring, training, retention, or supervision suits is that the employer acted wrongly by employing a person having some characteristic that made the individual incompetent or unfit for the job. The wrongful act on the part of the employer is usually that the employer knew or should have known—through adequate precautions during the hiring process or subsequent employment experience—that the person would be prone to create harmful injury to another person. Common examples of information that employers should act on, and are held liable for by omission, are a person's criminal record, prior employment or other history of violent acts, drug or alcohol addiction, reckless behavior including driving or operating equipment, assault and battery, theft, and emotional disorders, to name a few. Consequently, a plaintiff's attorneys will attempt to demonstrate the employer's negligent hiring of an individual who has injured their client by trying to prove that your employee is

- unfit because of habitual carelessness or possesses some physical infirmity such as epilepsy;
- lacking the requisite mental, emotional, or educational capacity to understand and perform the job in a responsible manner;
- lacking adequate experience or was not provided proper training for the responsibilities associated with the job;

- addicted to the use of intoxicants or other controlled substances; and/or,
- a person having a reckless or vicious disposition toward others.

Therefore, at least part of the determination as to the employer's liability lies in determining whether the employee was acting within the scope of employment when the injurious act occurred. An employee acts within the authority of employment when performing services for which they are being employed or anything reasonably incidental to their employment. The determination does not, however, rest on whether the employee's specific conduct was expressly authorized or prohibited by the employer, but whether the conduct was reasonably foreseeable by the employer. If the employee's conduct was precipitated entirely by personal reasons, bore no interests to the employer's business, and could not have been reasonably foreseen by the employer, then the employer is not likely to be regarded as liable. It is more likely that employers will be held liable for the reckless, intentional, willful, or malicious acts of its employees, including their disobedient and careless acts when performed in the course of employment.

In order to demonstrate the employee's incompetence or unfitness, the plaintiff's attorney must be able to show a strong correlation between the employee's personal characteristic(s) and specific traits and conditions of the person's job that are necessary to perform such work with a reasonable degree of skill and safety. It should be apparent that the goal of a plaintiff's attorney is to show convincing evidence that a serious injury occurred to their client; that the injury was propagated by your incompetent or unfit employee; and that your company was negligent in that employee's hiring, training, retention, or supervision inasmuch as your company knew or should have known about the employee's propensities if the company had exercised reasonable care during the hiring or subsequent employment process.

Legal Elements of a Negligent Hiring Claim

For an employer's act or omission during the hiring of an employee to constitute negligence, four elements must be present. First, there must be a legal duty of care that is owed to an injured party. Second, a breach of that duty must have occurred. Third, there must be evidence of injury to another person, their property, or legal rights. Fourth, there must be a close cause and effect relationship between the breach of duty and the injury. A closer examination of these elements may prove instructive for purposes of your constructing prevention and control measures in your company's hiring and employment practices.

Duty of Reasonable Care

This duty is said to be formed when an employment relationship is made between an employer and employee. The duty rests with the employer to ensure that the person being hired is *competent* and will not likely act in a *foreseeable* manner that would or could cause injury to another person. In carrying out such a duty, the employer is responsible for taking reasonable steps to measure each employee's competence and provide controls over their performance, as well as establishing safeguards for the protection of others with whom the employee may have contact.

Breach of Duty

Employers may thus be held liable for breach of duty by virtue of their acts or omissions in measuring employee competence, establishing controls, or providing reasonable safeguards where an employee, acting in the course or scope of employment, causes injury to another beyond mere circumstantial accident (that is, is incompetent or unfit). Additionally, negligence in the breach of this duty occurs when the employer knew, should have known by some available information or observation of personal traits, or could foresee the potential for harm but failed to act in a diligent manner—through such efforts as individualized training and supervision, job redesign or reassignment, transfer, or termination.

Cause-in-Fact and Employer's Proximate Cause

A cause-in-fact occurs when the employer's negligence gives rise to, or is directly associated with, the employee's injury to another person when the injury was produced by a characteristic determined to be a source of incompetence of the employee. The employer's conduct may also be said to have a proximate cause to the injury to another person at the hand of an employee, therefore constituting negligence when

1. The injury could have been reasonably foreseeable if the employer used adequate screening, testing, job matching, placement, training, and supervision practices;
2. The employer's failure to investigate the employee, or otherwise to establish controls and safeguards, in itself created a risk, and the injured person's situation fell within this risk; or,
3. The person's injury was the direct result of the employer's negligence in exercising reasonable and adequate controls over the obligation inherent in the employment relationship.

Damage

For there to be a cause of legal action, there must be some substantive damage or injury that has been caused to another person by an employee's incompetence or unfitness and attributable to the employer's negligence. The more visible, apparent, or conjective the injury, the higher the compensatory award is likely to be. The more apparent and inexcusable the employer's hiring or employment practices that gave rise to their negligence, the higher the punitive award is likely to be. And finally, the more complex a legal action is to prove *both* employee incompetence and employer negligence (neither of which are easy), the more costly are the attorney fees and court costs likely to be.

In evaluating these legal elements and circumstantial conditions, the courts often measure the employer's actions (or omissions) against the "reasonable person" test. That is, what would or should a reasonable person do who possessed this type of liability and knowledge of the risks associated with employment events like the situation at hand in order to prevent it from happening, knowing of the likelihood of it happening, and in the taking of precautions to control the likelihood of it ever occurring.

Legal Theories Used to Establish Employer Liability

There are two primary legal theories taken from common law that apply to the creation of a legal duty for companies to take precautions against a negligence liability. A third theory, although connected to the first two, applies to the individual actions of supervisors and managers.

Respondeat Superior Theory

This common law doctrine holds that an organization who establishes an employment relationship and has the authority to exercise control over what activities its people perform, and how they conduct themselves, is equally liable for the torts and criminal acts of its employees. Respondeat superior means "the master must answer." The rationale in law is that the master (employer) should be held accountable for the tasks and conduct of each servant (employee) during their performance of duties assigned by and under the control of the master, even if the task unforeseeably results in harm to a third person. The master is regarded as having the relative freedom to take whatever precautions it deems necessary and suitable to the hiring of each servant, and to establish or not establish whatever controls are appropriate to job assignments and how work is to be performed or not performed. When the lack of precautions and controls used by an employer are contributing factors to the harm brought to a third party, the employer is more apparently liable for negligence.

Fellow Servant Rule

At first glance, the fellow servant rule can be deceiving because it generally bars an employee from suing the employer for an injury caused by a coworker. This common law theory was adopted and used regularly by the courts after workers' compensation laws provided economic relief for job related injury and disability of employees who were sometimes injured as a result of the acts of a coworker. Prior to workers' compensation laws, most plaintiffs in respondeat superior cases were other employees who were injured by a coworker, principally because there was no other form of economic relief available. After workers' compensation laws provided such relief, at least in part, most litigants in respondeat superior cases became third parties injured by an employee in the course of their employment.

The exception to the follow servant rule has thus become injury to a coworker that could have been reasonably foreseen or avoided had the employer properly exercised its duty to use reasonable care in the hiring, training, or supervision of the employee who caused the injury. In other words, a plaintiff's (injured employee) attorney may be able to influence the court to set aside the follow servant rule if it can be shown that your company was negligent in hiring the employee causing the injury based on such factors as the individual's past employment history, repeated horseplay or similar safety hazards, or the company's failure to release the employee following disobedience of safety rules or warnings. Additionally, employer liability can also be established on the basis of such contributing negligent management practices as requiring the use of improper tools, unsafe equipment, and insufficient numbers or training of workers to perform a job.

Vicarious Liability

This legal principle as it applies to torts has the purpose of holding individuals separately liable for their actions that result in injury to others, or their acts or omissions that materially contributed to the injury. Vicarious liability is typically applied to those individuals who have particular responsibility and authority inherent in their job function that entrusts them with control over decisions and actions to be taken by others. With respect to negligent hiring, vicarious liability is frequently being placed on the shoulders of the human resources manager, but occasionally it may rest with the employee's supervisor or the manager responsible for a decision or oversight that was in some respect connected to the employee's causing injury to a third party.

Generally, common law recognizes that supervisors, managers, and similar employed agents of an employer are immune from being held individually liable for their actions because they are regarded as instruments of the employer's decision-making structure. However, under certain circumstances, these corporate agents can perform in such a way as to go beyond the boundaries of reasonable decisions and actions, the nature of which contributes significantly to an employee's injuring another person. Therefore, vicarious liability has the effect of removing the corporate agent's immunity, and thus renders them separately liable for negligence as a contributing factor to the injury. For this reason, supervisors and managers are fair game for plaintiff attorneys to name as a codefendant in negligence suits, but doing so is more of a psychological tactic than purposeful goal. After all, it is the corporate assets that the plaintiff's attorney is after, not the more limited assets of an individual corporate agent. If, however, the supervisor or manager who was "in charge" of the wrongful acting employee is sufficiently fearful of the outcome of a legal action, that fear factor alone may play into the hands of the plaintiff attorney in showing that the company was *materially* at fault—which was the attorney's goal in the first place!

C.2 Employer Liability for Negligent Hiring, Training, Retention, and Supervision

The legal basis for negligent employment actions is contained in the Restatement of Torts, Second Section 307, which states that it is considered negligence to use an instrumentality, whether a human being or a thing, that the actor knows or should have known, to be incompetent, inappropriate or defective, and that its use involves an unreasonable risk of harm to others. Thus, when an employee (instrumentality) performs an injurious act against another person, and the employer knew or should have known about the employee's propensity to act in this manner, or creates working conditions conducive to such acts, the employer is said to have liability for negligence in connection with the employee's act. The issue of an employee's incompetence can be established not only by demonstrating an absence of skills or knowledge about performing various aspects of the job itself, but may include such personal characteristics as the employee's previous criminal activities, employment misconduct, and such psychological characteristics as quick temper, anxiety, violence and personality disorders (e.g., schizophrenia).

The courts are an insightful place to look for answers concerning the types of employment situations that have given rise to judgments of employer negligence in the hiring, retention, training, and supervision of employees. The focus of negligent employment litigation tends to be on particular employment practices, decisions, and conditions established by or allowed to exist by the employer, as well as the physical and/or psychological characteristics of the acting employee, that subsequently led to another person's injury—be they another employee or a third party such as a customer, contractor, or simply a person in the public domain.

First, it must be established that an injury occurred to another person. Second, it must be shown that the injury was brought about by the employee. Third, it must be shown that the employee's act was in some respect a form of incompetence in the performance of their job, and that there was a reasonable connection between the injurious act and the performance of their job (acting in the course and/or scope of employment). Fourth, it must be shown that the injury could and should have been prevented by the employer (who knew or should have known about the employee's form of incompetence). Negligence is thus established when it can be shown that the employer's employment practices (hiring and training in particular), decisions (retention after becoming aware of an employee's propensities), or failure to establish suitable working conditions (responsible supervision) contributed to the injury of another person.

Auto Accident by Intoxicated Employee

The case of *Otis Engineering Corp. v. Clark* (1983) decided by the Texas Supreme Court reaffirmed for employers the improper employment practice of sending an intoxicated employee home by use of their own vehicle, when in the course of such travel the employee injures other persons. In the case at hand, the intoxicated employee was released from work early due to his condition and allowed to use his own vehicle during which he caused injury to plaintiff in an automobile accident. The court, recognizing that an employer does not normally have an obligation over the acts of its employees during the conduct of their personal lives, held the employer negligently liable for plaintiff's injury inasmuch as the employer should have reasonably foreseen the prospect of an automobile accident resulting from the employee's diminished capacity. The majority opinion of the court was to hold the employer liable for malfeasance, while the (more accurate) minority opinion was that the employer's liability arose from an act of omission created by the custodial duty to use reasonable care in dealing with the condition of its employees.

Employee Theft of Another's Property

Generally, most courts have recognized that an employer owes special duty to its customers and others it serves in the conduct of its business, including any injury or damage that may arise in connection with the acts of the employer's agents—its employees. The greater the risk of damage or injury to others, the greater the duty owed and liability that can result from improper employment practices or omissions by the employer. Such was the finding of a Rhode Island court in the case of *Welsh Manufacturing Division of Textron, Inc. v. Pinkerton's Inc.* (1984) wherein an employee of the defendant's security guard company was assigned to the plaintiff's premises as a guard. Unbeknownst to the security company, the employee had preplanned a robbery of large amounts of gold from the assigned company. Despite the employee's preplanning the robbery, during trial it was established that the employee had been working for the security company for only six months before being given such a responsible assignment, that the employee had been suspected of dishonesty by his supervisor in a previous assignment, and that the employee was not sufficiently supervised. In essence then, the court found the employer liable on the basis of contributory negligence.

Similar rationale has been applied by several courts hearing cases concerning damage, injury, or death incurred by another party resulting from the act or omission of an employee whose job or working conditions impose an abnormally high risk. Common examples are where employees are required to carry weapons, transport dangerous substances, provide public safety or transportation services, enter private property (as the next case illustrates), or where the nature of the employer's business invites the public to be on the employer's premises.

Customer's Murder by Employee on Own Premises

Tragically, there are a number of negligent hiring cases where an employer failed to perform a sufficient background investigation on a new employee—or worse yet—none at all, and the employee subsequently murdered or caused the death of another person while performing work in behalf of the employer. This situation is well illustrated in the case of *Kendall v. Gore Properties, Inc.* (1956) decided by the District of Columbia Court of Appeals. While there are more recent cases like *Kendall* (such as *Henley v. Prince George's County, 1986*), this case serves as a succinct example of the essential conditions for employer liability.

This employer hired an employee to work on the interiors of apartments that were occupied by tenants. The employer never took steps to perform a background check of the employee's reputation, personal character, or criminal record. Rather, the employee was merely told what work needed to be done, and given keys to those apartments needing attention. The employee later entered an apartment occupied by a young woman and thereupon murdered her. The court concluded that work requiring the entering of private, occupied property was an obvious employment risk that should have been accounted for through effort on the part of the employer to acquire background information beyond what can be expected from a mere interview with the prospective employee, and the employer's failure to do so amounted to its assumption of liability for any associated results. The employer was thus found guilty of negligent hiring of the young woman's murderer. Similarly, an apartment manager's rape of a tenant created employer liability in the case of *Ponticas v. K.M.S. Investments* (Minn., 1983).

Coworker Injured by Employee Due to Employer's Perpetuation of Unsafe Working Conditions

Another example of employer liability for negligence (hiring and retention in this case) can be brought about by the employer's knowledge of an unsafe working condition or as a result of its own management practices. In these kinds of situations, it is normally the employer's preexisting knowledge and acts or omissions concerning internal controls to assure the safety of employees—even against each other—that become the focal issues of the employer's liability for injury to others. In the case of *McBride v. Hershey's Chocolate Corp.* (1963), one employee intentionally scalded a coworker with steam from a hot water pipe. Despite the employer's knowledge that considerable animosity existed between these two employees, and that threats had been made in the past by the assailant to the injured coworker, the employer made an active decision to assign the two men to work together.

The court determined that the employer's prior knowledge of the employees' combative relationship was sufficient to warrant that they exercise more controlling judgment over their work assignments, and assigning them to the same proximity was equivalent to perpetuating a known unsafe working condition, thus placing liability for the injury sustained by one employee as the responsibility of the employer.

Woman Beaten by Laundromat Employee

While some courts may find the aberrational violent tendencies of juveniles lacking intentional substance, a California appellate court disagreed in *Nigg v. Patterson (1990)*. Here, a plaintiff brought suit for damages against the Laundromat employing a youth who beat the plaintiff with his fists and hit her with a hammer. The employee was a resident of a juvenile rehabilitation program, on probation for committing a burglary, and had been previously charged with molesting a child. The only defense the employer could muster was that it relied on the rehabilitation program's screening process rather than conduct its own investigation about the employee's criminal conduct and/or behavioral tendencies.

Restaurant Employee Molests Customer's Child

Here's a classic example of an employer who was attempting to demonstrate moral, social and legal consciousness toward the use of developmentally disabled employees, but got stung due to a lack of definitive prescreening and adequate supervision. The employee in this case of *R.M. v. McDonald's Corporation (1991)* was an employee in the McJobs program—employment and training for mentally and physically disabled persons. The employer failed to investigate all the reference sources provided by the employee, in violation of their own screening procedures, including the state agency counselor who referred the employee to McDonald's. Had the employer questioned the referring counselor, they would have discovered this employee's prior conviction for child molestation. Given the outcome of this case, both the employer and State of Colorado were found guilty of negligent hiring, and the counselor was fired for not advising the employer of this individual's known conviction history.

Employer Liable for Negligence of Independent Contractor

While it is generally true that an employer's liability for negligent acts of a bona fide independent contractor may be limited, the conditions under which contractors perform work can often maintain liability for the employer. This situation is clearly illustrated in *Leith v. Hughes Aircraft (1987)* where the defendant employer hired an independent trucking company to haul mud to a dump site under authority of a permit that required the activity to be performed in a manner that would "safeguard life, health, property, and the public welfare."

Enroute to the dump site with a fully loaded truck, an employee of the trucking company fell asleep at the wheel. The truck crossed the center line and struck two passenger vans occupied by Boy Scouts and their troop leaders. Five people were killed and six others sustained serious and permanent injuries. In assigning liability to the contracting employer, the California Court of Appeal determined that the employer's duty to ensure that the work performed was done in a safe manner was non-delegable to the trucking company.

The cases cited in this section are only a few of the kinds of employment situations that tend to arise in the context of employer liability for negligent hiring, training, retention, and supervision. Clearly, there are many more circumstances under which employers can, and have been, found liable for the acts of unfit employees based on the employer's own hiring and subsequent employment practices. The courts have made it profoundly apparent that the responsibility for thorough preemployment evaluation of prospective employees, and well managed employment practices thereafter, are the obligation of every employer.

C.3 Where Is Your Company Most Vulnerable?

In order to prevent the risks associated with hiring incompetent and otherwise unfit employees, as well as those risks that emanate from poorly conceived management practices, it is advisable for you to begin an examination of the manner in which your company operates. Periodic audits of company operations and employment practices can be very helpful in early identification and correction of acts and omissions that tend to produce a foreseeable risk of harm to third parties, and therefore are vulnerable to liability for the employer. For those employers who take the position that you only fix that which is broken, you might want to remember that an ounce of prevention is worth a pound of cure.

To assist you in your evaluation of operational conditions within your company, the following issues have been prepared so that you can examine them within the context of how your company operates its business to determine the type and level of potential risk. If you find that any of the following exist in a reasonably foreseeable way, it should be considered a potential negligence vulnerability and corrected immediately.

Personnel Actions Vulnerable to Employer Negligence

There are seven types of personnel activities and practices that tend to render employers vulnerable to allegations of negligence. These activities and practices consist of hiring, training, promotion, retention, supervision, work assignments, and personnel policies and work procedures.

Hiring

This is, of course, the greatest source of liability for employers since, if the person wasn't hired, the injury would not have occurred to another person. Most negligence cases require a showing that the responsible employee was incompetent or unfit in some respect, and that the employer knew or should have known about the employee's deficiency had the employer done a proper job of determining qualifications prior to hiring. Consequently, it is important for employers to require that each prospective new hire is thoroughly tested for their adequacy of skills, knowledge, and other job-related characteristics to establish competence. These "tests" should be documented accounts of what was required and results achieved.

The weakest practice among most employers held liable for negligent hiring was their failure to conduct a reasonably diligent background investigation of an applicant—and the documentation (written evidence) to support any findings when an effort was made. Minimally, employers should *attempt* to acquire prior employment information concerning the applicant's skills, limitations, emotional and behavioral tendencies, and any information relating to acts of misconduct. Where the nature of the company's business or the job to be performed is itself a source of risk, then further testing and/or investigative checking may be appropriate to protect the employer's potential liability. Such actions might include checks of the applicant's criminal record, driving record, character references, and psychological examination by qualified professionals rather than merely written tests that have prepared interpretive answers.

Training

Once an employee is hired, and presumably qualified by the employer to perform a job whether or not such decision was the result of adequate testing, the employer continues to possess a liability for the actions of each employee when acting in the scope and course of his or her employment. If an employee commits an injurious act, and the cause of the act can be established as a deficiency in the employee's job skills or knowledge, then the employer is often held accountable for inadequately training the employee to perform the job in a safe or proper manner.

This condition should obviate the need for each employer to not only give an appropriate battery of job-related preemployment tests to measure the acceptability of requisite skills, knowledge, and demonstration of aptitudes, but to also provide the operational counterparts of intense one-on-one training of new and promoted employees, close supervision until complete competence is demonstrated, and routine monitoring of the employee's activities thereafter. Each of these employment practices should be fully documented in the same way that other business transactions are documented—in brief but succinctly descriptive detail.

Retention

When an employer learns that an employee presents some foreseeable risk to others—such as an annual driving report on employees, an employee's temporary incarceration, or behavioral misconduct (violent tendencies) on the job—the employer is said to have constructive knowledge of the employee's character that can give rise to some job-related risk. If the nature of the employee's risk is not dealt with by the employer in the form of reassignment, demotion, or termination, then the employer becomes vulnerable to liability due to its implied acquiescence to the risk of continuing to retain the employee in an unmodified employment manner. Since it is the employment and its related conditions that provided the employee an opportunity to injure another person, then the employer is likely to carry the burden of liability for any resulting damage when no action is taken once the risk became known (or the employer should have known due to evidence available to the employer).

These conditions make it imperative that employers act quickly to investigate and gather sufficient facts to draw a conclusion when information comes forward on employees that presents a risk of foreseeable harm to others. Then, it is incumbent on employers to take action fitting the risk and facts in its possession. Both the facts and *reasonable* risks should support the employer's decision to reassign, demote (and possibly transfer), provide additional training and supervision, terminate, or take no action but at least document the reasons for this decision (e.g., the nature of the risk is minimal, it occurred many years ago, the employee has not demonstrated any signs of propensity toward such behavior, and the employee has been made aware of the company's knowledge of the past events).

Promotion

This personnel action carries the inherent risk of potential incompetence and it customarily arises in negligence cases involving senior level workers, supervisors, and managers who were promoted into more responsible jobs without adequate testing to measure their abilities, or they were not adequately monitored by higher level personnel to assure their proper exercise of authority and decision making. The objective of plaintiff attorneys in negligent injury cases is usually to show that the employer used the "Peter Principle" in promoting a perhaps otherwise competent employee into a position beyond their competent ability, and the employer did so without adequate testing, training, and supervisorial monitoring.

Promotions should therefore be dealt with like any other new hire; after all, it is a new job for the employee, and merely because the employee is a known person doesn't mean that the employee is a known performer in the new job. Each promotional applicant should be thoroughly and precisely tested on at least the more important conditions of the higher job. Because many higher jobs require new and different skills—particularly jobs involving supervision and management where such aptitudes as judgment, decision making, and leadership are involved—each applicant should be measured on the associated job skills required for success in the position, then provided additional training and close monitoring until full competence is demonstrated.

Supervision

Hiring and assigning highly skilled workers the task of supervising the work of subordinate employees is a necessary function in most any business. In carrying out the tasks associated with the job of supervisor, there is a considerable amount of authority inherent in ordinary activities that has been underestimated by most employers. Supervisors must exercise frequent judgment, independent decision making, assigning work and assuring the smooth flow of work, and provide routine monitoring of employee activities, all of which is to be done concurrently with accomplishing their own work. The two supervisory functions most vulnerable to charges of negligence are 1) the inadequacy of training provided by a supervisor to a subordinate employee, and 2) inadequate monitoring by the supervisor of each employee's performance.

To lessen the kinds of negligence vulnerability associated with supervision, employers should

1. Strengthen hiring criteria and testing;
2. Assure that each supervisor is adequately trained in all essential principles and skills associated with the job;
3. Provide "train-the-trainer" educational programs for supervisors; and,
4. Assure that supervisors have sufficient time and instructions to regularly monitor the performance activities of their employees.

Work Assignments

Some employers have been found guilty of employment negligence on the basis of differing management practices and decisions. A frequently cited form of employment practice negligence has been where an employer was aware of an employee's situational hostility or violence, yet the employer continued to place the employee in a position of exercising his or her situational temperament as in the aforementioned case of *McBride v. Hershey Chocolate Corp.* So, there are two elements present in these situations; 1) the employer's knowledge of a risky behavioral characteristic of a particular employee, and 2) the work conditions that provide an opportunity (or trigger) for the employee to act out the risk. When these two elements exist together, and the employer takes no action on either element, then the courts are likely to determine that the employer failed to exercise due control and is thus negligently liable.

Employers must take more affirmative actions when it becomes known that an employee is demonstrating a propensity toward such risks as violence, hostility, threats against any other person, delusional behavior, or even "horseplay" and pranks. When such behavioral or performance risks become apparent, they should be brought to the attention of upper management for decision making and action. The actions that would be appropriate are, of course, contingent on numerous factors on a case-by-case basis, but may include such measures as offering the employee professional services through an Employee Assistance Program, counseling the employee on their behavior followed by close supervision, reassignment to another job or work location that sufficiently alters the condition of their risk tendency, or termination. Naturally, all events associated with and leading up to the employer's action should be fully documented.

Policies and Work Procedures

Management has at its discretion considerable latitude in the development of numerous operational policies, work procedures, and decisions that determine the conditions under which employees are to perform. If such policies, procedures, or decisions create a condition that bring about injury to another person at the hand of an employee, then the employer's conduct will probably be found to be a proximate cause of the injury.

Employers should take great care in the framing and application of operational policies and work procedures, whether written or verbally assigned by supervisors. In particular, employers should be cautious about decisions concerning working conditions, work assignments, company equipment, or anything within the employer's control that might create a foreseeable risk of harm to others.

Injurious Causes of Action Associated with Employer Negligence

When an attorney representing a third party who has been injured as a result of the actions of an employee decides to evaluate the merits of a potential negligence case, the attorney usually starts with acquiring certain employment records and gathering circumstantial facts through deposition statements. By subpoenaing records pertaining to the propagating employee, evidence might be found to support the contention that 1) the employee is in some respect incompetent or unfit to perform; 2) the employer had knowledge of detrimental information upon which it did not act; and/or, 3) the employer failed to adequately investigate the background of the applicant/employee.

Further information to either support or refute the employer's liability for negligence is obtained by the attorney through interviews and depositions from those persons involved in, or having any part of, the circumstances relating to the injury. The process is time consuming, costly, and intense for those individuals involved. Moreover, it should be apparent that the plaintiff attorney is gathering and searching for detailed facts that will support litigation against the employer for direct or contributory negligence that had a causal relationship to the injury of the client. The more common types of injury sustained by third parties from acts of employees where the employer may have a negligence liability to defend are such causes of legal action as:

- Theft
- Sexual Assault
- Rape
- Murder
- Disfiguration/Dismemberment

- Assault and Battery
- Sexual Harassment
- Emotional Distress
- Wrongful Death
- False Imprisonment

Some of the kinds of evidence that will be sought by plaintiff attorneys to establish possible employer negligence include: 1) the absence of preemployment test results with regard to the employee's skills, knowledge, work methods, character, and past reputation; 2) the nature of training provided by the employer to the employee; 3) the qualifications and routine activities of the employee's supervisor; 4) prior conduct accounts of the employee known by the present employer; and, 5) the policies, work procedures, and management decisions relating to assignments of the employee. Armed with this kind of information, the plaintiff attorney may then be well prepared to launch a difficult-to-defend case against your company for major damages.

To further aid you in your evaluation of measures that can help prevent this event, you may wish to know what types of jobs and working conditions tend to be the most vulnerable to employment negligence litigation. By increasing your awareness of these jobs and working conditions, you might begin to see a few employment practices within your company that should be altered—particularly in the areas of preemployment testing, dealing with disciplinary behavior, job assignments, and the adequacy of supervision.

The Jobs and Working Conditions Most Vulnerable to Negligent Employment

There are two focal points concerning the types of jobs most likely to give rise to injury to another person; 1) those jobs where workers are more likely to function from maladjusted behaviors or other psychological problems, and 2) those jobs which provide environmental opportunity to injure other persons if poor judgment or improper behavioral proclivities are used by the worker. Based on a collection of case law decisions where the employer was found liable for negligent employment, the types of workers most commonly found to create injury to another person are:

1. Unskilled and semiskilled trade workers
2. Maintenance workers
3. Apartment managers
4. Drivers (cab, delivery, truck, and heavy equipment)
5. Ambulance attendants
6. Public transportation operators (trains, buses, and airplanes)
7. Law enforcement officers
8. Security guards
9. Domestic workers (maids, housecleaning, janitors)
10. Traveling businesspeople
11. Any worker known to use or abuse controlled substances
12. Any worker with a recent history of violent behavior
13. Workers engaged in the handling of money or financial records

It should not be surprising, then, to know that the working conditions commonly associated with negligent employment litigation relates in most cases to the nature of the environment in which the employee performs their job. Some of the working conditions that contribute to high risk opportunities for the injury to others are:

1. Work involving direct contact with members of the public or individuals in their private domain.
2. Work involving the performance of independent job functions where observation by supervision is minimal, infrequent, or unavailable.
3. Work performed on private property.
4. Work involving the operation of inherently dangerous equipment or the operation of equipment that, if performed improperly, creates a serious hazard.

5. Work involving the access to, or use of, weapons such as guns, batons, knives, and harmful chemicals.

6. Work involving discretionary judgment by employees whose jobs and resultant decisions directly affect other people.

7. Work involving employee access and responsibility in connection with business or private financial transactions.

Given the antecedent conditions addressed in this section that tend to contribute to an employer's liability for negligent employment, you should now be in a much better position of performing periodic audits of your company's operations in an effort to identify and take corrective action on various vulnerabilities. Additionally, the final section that follows should further assist you in activating preventative measures concerning the specific liability for negligent *hiring* concerns.

C.4 How Employers Can Lessen Their Negligent Hiring Liability

One of the more discomforting realities for employers seeking profitable business ventures in a litigious society is the fact that nothing completely shields an employer from being sued. However, in order to protect a company's assets and operational objectives, it becomes imperative to establish safeguards that will *lessen* the likelihood of legal wrongdoing and provide for a quick, positive defense of allegations when called upon to do so. Maximizing prevention is of course the best way to deal with avoidance of such employment liabilities as negligent hiring, but if the challenge should arise every employer must be positioned properly to make an expedient and affirmative defense for its actions.

Another simple fact inherent in hiring people to carry out work for our business operations is that we cannot possibly learn all there is to know about each person's temperament, sources of motivation, and conditions that are antecedent to the vast complexities of human behavior at all times. Yet, because these characteristics are functions of how people perform their work, it is important to do more than cursory testing of the people we hire, and to use prudent management practices thereafter to assure that work is being performed in the most advantageous way possible. If negligent hiring, training, retention, and supervising legal doctrines have brought anything to our attention, it is the fact that the courts hold employers responsible for more careful, precise, and well thought out selection and monitoring practices of those hired to carry out their missions.

For employers to act in a more responsible way, and to alleviate the prospects of negligent employment litigation, it is suggested that you use as many of the following measures as you determine are needed or appropriate to the nature of your business and its operations. Every effort should be made to increase the consistency of your hiring process (i.e., procedural steps). Further, it is advisable for employers to develop their own checklist of steps to be taken during each phase of the hiring process to ensure that vital details like investigative backgrounds are performed on all finalist applicants whose jobs carry certain types of liability for the employer. Because each employer differs so greatly, hiring checklists should be custom designed to fit the unique conditions of each employer. However, the following areas of suggestions may help you construct just such a checklist for your company.

Prehire Administrative Practices

Before embarking on the task of selecting a set of procedures to follow during the hiring process of each new employee, step back and evaluate the need for any additions or changes in your existing personnel and management practices. These include the administrative details that either support or weaken the existence of a hiring *program*, and consist of the following kinds of practices.

1. Avoid making job offers until all preemployment screening, testing, and other investigations relating to the individual's suitability are completed. Granted, doing so takes a little longer but it will eliminate the problem of *terminating* a new hire that then raises questions by the employee and coworkers, and the need for unnecessary turnover.

2. Review your company's personnel policies to ensure that they contain adequate language and coverage of such topics as:

    *   At-will employment statements that reinforce the concept that employment may be terminated by either the company or employee at any time, with or without notice, and for any reason.

    *   Prohibitions against, and disciplinary action for, such misconduct as sexual and other forms of harassment, assault and battery, acts of dishonesty, creating disharmony, provoking physical altercations, carrying or concealing weapons, theft, unnecessary absenteeism, improper use of authority, neglect of duty, and misrepresentation.

    *   Probationary (initial on-the-job testing period) periods for all initial hires and promotional employees.

    *   Preemployment testing of all applicants to entry or promotional jobs, and ongoing performance evaluation, on the basis of job related factors and conditions.

    *   Drug and alcohol testing of all new hires, and mandatory compliance with testing requests of any employee where there exists reasonable suspicion or just cause.

    *   Reference and background checks may be made on any new hire, and that periodic similar checks may be made on employees to ensure their continued suitability for employment (annual reports on employee driving records by the company's insurance carrier is a common one).

    *   Postemployment reference: what information will be given to verified employers; requirement that employee sign a release and waiver form giving consent for the information; and disallowing letters of reference unless approved by a manager of high authority (Personnel Manager).

3. Establish an Employee Assistance Program for self-referral of any employee having personal problems or exhibiting deviant behavior at work. Supervisors should likewise document their advice to any employee to seek the services of the EAP based on the existence of personal or behavioral problems having a job performance manifestation. If your company cannot afford a complete EAP, or there are a small number of employees in your company, then you may wish to minimally set up an anonymous referral program directly to a local clinical psychologist.

4. Prepare a "hiring matrix" in which you identify each job by its title down the vertical column and each type of preemployment screening process down the horizontal column. The latter processes might include such items as:

    *   Initial Screening; applications and resumes, job related written and/or performance tests, personal interviews, and other ability tests.

    *   Medical Exams; based only on job related factors, but including drug and alcohol testing with advance notice of this requirement to all applicants.

    *   Driving Record Checks; if the job requires driving as a condition or requirement of employment based on actual responsibilities.

    *   Credit and Character Reports; if the job carries a sensitive responsibility for such matters as dealing with assets, financial records, care or custody of individuals, access to private property, and similar conditions that would render the job "sensitive."

- Criminal Records Check; if the job has those conditions of being classified as "sensitive."
- Prior Employment and Character References; should perform on all new hires, and other employees as the appropriate need arises based on skill or conduct problems being encountered.

5. Conduct regular (at least annual) performance evaluations on all employees by means of predefined, objective, and job related performance dimension standards. Train performance evaluators to be specific and honest about the nature of work deficiencies, and to monitor progress closely.

6. Conduct immediate investigations of observed or reported employee misconduct, marked behavioral change, performance effectiveness, safety infractions, tension between employees, and similar types of potential injury risk to others arising out of the employee's incompetence, habits, or emotional health. Verify all uncertain information and give the applicant/employee an opportunity to give explanation without making accusations before you have all the facts. Act on investigations and resultant information promptly, and if appropriate, terminate employment.

7. Provide regular training to supervisory and management staff on such topics as the fundamentals of employment laws, advanced interviewing skills, how to train employees, human behavior in the workplace, conducting performance reviews and monitoring results, and how to handle disciplinary problems.

8. Do not give serious misconduct employees the option of resigning in exchange for a concealed reference should another employer inquire. Doing so can make your company a party to the liability of this employee's future act based on falsely withholding information. You may be better off if the misconduct investigation is completed sufficiently to establish firm guilt and terminate the employee for just cause.

9. Treat all preemployment documents and information as a highly confidential record— store this information in a well secured file among other sensitive and private personnel files; do not allow employee access unless state law requires otherwise; and do not allow access by others who do not have a right and do not need to know the contents of such records.

10. Advise applicants who are being rejected based on reference or investigatory results simply that they have not been selected for the job, rather than stating what eliminated them. A common practice is to inform rejected applicants that, "our decisions have favored the hiring of another applicant whose qualifications are considered more suitable to the needs of the position and the company's operations."

Preemployment Hiring Procedures

Each of the following procedures should be used as a function of the preemployment hiring process with virtually *every* applicant who is under serious consideration for employment. While it is true that doing so will cause a delay in getting new hires on board, the extra time and effort to assure their suitability should be viewed as a cost-saving measure rather than a mere administrative delay to check records. If not done properly, thoroughly, and prior to an employment offer, you will find yourself in the position of dealing with unnecessary turnover during the first six months of employment.

Further, appearances can be extremely deceiving in this era of enlightened job applicants. Job seekers at all levels can present a very convincing appearance and thereby lead the unsuspecting interviewer or hiring authority to believe that scrutinizing their qualifications and background is an "obvious" waste of important time. Taking such an approach will certainly prove to be a trap for the unwary one day, and the consequences of that failure in completing the hiring process could cost your company greatly.

A final point to be made is that each phase in the preemployment testing and qualifications review process should be carefully *documented*. For reason of potential litigation defense, it may serve little purpose to conduct thorough hiring procedures if you have not documented events, findings, and conclusions. Litigation and other forms of necessary recall demand that employers keep some type of documentation on employment events *as they occur* rather than to attempt reconstruction of the facts well after an event.

So, here now are the areas and procedures that employers should follow in conducting preemployment reviews to enhance the hiring of only suitable applicants, and to lessen the likelihood of negligent hiring.

Application and Resume Review

1. Require that all job applicants complete the company's employment application form, even applicants for management positions who expect that their resume will suffice in lieu of an application. The reason for this requirement is that the application form contains predetermined questions and topics in which information is sought by the employer which is often not answered by those who submit resumes. Also, applications require more specific information such as dates, references, reasons for leaving past employment, convictions, and the applicant's acknowledgement of the employer's notices (such as at-will employment, consent to verify information, truth of statement, etc.) at the end of the application form.

   Industry surveys have revealed that as many as one-half of all employment applications and resumes submitted to employers are fraudulent in some respect. This fact alone should serve as notice to those conducting prescreening to review them with an eye toward false and/or misleading statements and information.

2. Gaps in education, work history, and residence should be marked, questioned, and later verified for reasons if the individual becomes a final contender for the job. Even when gaps are not shown (many applicants will conceal gaps that they don't want questioned by falsely connecting dates), dates should be verified when conducting the background and reference reviews.

3. Verify the dates of graduation and schools attended beginning with high school—many applicants lie outright about their educational qualifications, and in particular college degrees.

4. Read the applicant's description of prior employment responsibilities (and accomplishments on resumes) for misleading statements about the type and level of skills the applicant claims to possess. These should be verified by reference contacts and carefully measured by your own skills and knowledge testing process.

5. Be sure that your application form contains a section at the end of the form for the applicant to sign acknowledgement of such conditions as mentioned in item 1 above, and that the applicant has in fact signed and dated the application.

Skill and Knowledge Testing

1. Critical to the avoidance of liability for negligent employment is the verification that each new hire possesses at least minimum skill and knowledge qualifications established by the employer for successful performance, and thereby determined to be competent at the time of hire. Therefore, preemployment testing to verify the applicant's possession of various abilities is tantamount to competence, and such testing should be based on the more essential and difficult aspects of actual job conditions.

2. When preparing abilities tests, make sure that each part of the test is directly related to the job being applied for, that it measures the proper level of ability, and that none of the test components become known to any of the applicants before taking the test.

3. When scoring test results, pay attention to the importance of test areas answered incorrectly, even if the applicant passed the test overall. Wrong answers and incorrect methods can be a source of demonstrated weakness (or incompetence when taken to the extreme) that may be used against you if overlooked by you and later discovered by a plaintiff attorney.

Employment and Character References

1. Another major condition associated with an employee's incompetence is unsuitable behavior, background, or reputation for creating harmful effects. According to most courts deciding negligent employment cases, it is either an employee's lack of abilities or their personal characteristics that give rise to some injurious act, and the burden for knowing about the history of such characteristics is on the employer.

2. Employment application forms should request information on both prior employment and personal character references. Prior employment should include the applicant's duration, jobs held, responsibilities, name and address of employer, name and phone number of last supervisor, and the specific reason for leaving. Personal character references should be the names of at least three people not related to, but known to the applicant, for more than five years, and include occupation (reputability), address, and phone number. Each of these sources should be contacted directly and asked questions specific to the job being applied for with respect to the applicant's abilities and personal characteristics.

3. You may wish to use the form provided in Appendix D for your employment reference form to send to prior employers, along with the applicant's consent statement and signature at the end of your employment application form (sample also provided in this book). Most employers are leery of replying to past employment reference, so when your telephone requests for information fail to provide you with the details you desire, you should follow up with a written request form. This form also serves as a record of your attempt, and limits information being requested to only that needed for employment decision making.

   You may also need to be insistent enough to tell the prior employer that some courts have held prior employers liable for unreasonably withholding pertinent job history information, and that their refusal to give you performance related information is contrary to the written request and consent of their former employee. Then document the fact that you forewarned the prior employer of these facts.

4. After receiving returned employment reference forms, check them for completeness and detail. It's always a good idea to follow up by calling the supervisor or person completing the form to thank them and then clarify any vague or incomplete information. You may also wish to conclude your conversation with them by asking if there is anything else that they were reluctant to write down on the form that you should know before making a hiring offer to the applicant. In particular, you should inquire about such matters as threats made to others, drug and/or alcohol use, improper safety acts, fraud and misrepresentation, theft, lying, altercations, relations with other people, or anything similar that comes to the supervisor's mind that had, or could have had, a detrimental effect.

5. When talking with character references, make sure that you write down your questions and the answers given. Your questions should focus on the applicant's personal characteristics relating to their reliability, responsibility, honesty, trustworthiness,

carefulness, personal habits related to the job or working conditions, and the existence of any acute behaviors or beliefs.

Driving Records

1. Request that your company's insurance carrier do a driving record search on any applicant who will or might be required to operate a company-owned or personally-owned vehicle. The search should include a continuous record of a minimum of five and maximum of ten years of driving, meaning that some searches will have to include the acquisition of out-of-state records.

2. The more responsibility the applicant will have for driving, the more scrutinizing should be your evaluation of results of the applicant's driving record. Violations during the prior five years for (anything more than a forgiving) moving violation or parking ticket should be taken very seriously. There can be consequential problems associated with hiring a person who has had incidents of driving under the influence of controlled substances, repetitive moving violations, speeding or reckless driving citations, or suspended driving privileges.

Credit and Character Reports

1. These can be useful investigations into an applicant's credit history, financial stability and reliability, and personal character as viewed by neighbors, friends, and other associates. However, two conditions must be present to conduct such an investigation. First, you must have a job or business related purpose for acquiring such information, and show consistency in performing this type of investigation on this and similar jobs—rather than on particular applicants based on your suspicions. Second, you must abide by the information and disclosure requirements of the 1978 Fair Credit Reporting Act. This means that you must inform these applicants in advance that employment may be conditioned on acceptable results of an investigation concerning their credit, character, mode of living, and general reputation, and that they must be given adverse information if requested.

2. It is advisable for employers to use a reputable consumer credit agency to perform these investigations and prepare reports. Internal security or investigatory sources may also be used, but their findings should be the result of their independent effort.

3. Results should be evaluated on a case-by-case basis in light of the job and working conditions. As a general rule, adverse information beyond the last five years may be worth obtaining but is normally not seen as consequential. Conversely, a more recent history of bad debts and late or partial payments may reasonably suggest that the person is dealing with financial difficulty, and possibly prone to theft or "get rich quick" opportunities. These are decisions in which caution should be balanced with compassion—at least in some cases.

Law Enforcement Records

1. To avoid the extremes of potential theft, violence, and similar kinds of injury to other persons by employees, it is advisable for employers to obtain information relating to (finalist) applicant encounters with law enforcement agencies; particularly convictions resulting in imprisonment. These record investigations—through local, state, and national law enforcement agencies—should be made on all pending hires who would be occupying "sensitive" jobs, and those involving perhaps other kinds of working conditions in which the employer feels legitimately vulnerable to a person with a history of such violations.

2. To assure proper access and interpretation of law enforcement records, you should use an external investigatory agency or legal counsel to perform the search. The investigation should include local, state, and federal law enforcement agencies with emphasis on convictions, or pleas of *nolo contendere* (no contest), of offenses that bear a reasonable relationship to the applicant's job function, working conditions, and/or nature of the employer's business.

3. Reports of this type are highly confidential and should not be made accessible to either the job applicant (unless otherwise required by state law) or others in the organization. Supervisors and other interested management personnel should be advised that "the applicant was not deemed suitable" if adverse information supports such a decision.

From the purely legal perspective, employers must come to terms with the fact that the courts require that employers *know* or *should know* about the performance and personal characteristics of people hired to carry out work as agents of the employer's business. It therefore becomes essential that *every* employer begin to conduct thorough evaluations of prospective new hires in order to accumulate sufficient information to make a well-informed decision. To do otherwise, the courts are telling us, creates reason to believe the employer is acting in a negligent fashion by not obtaining proper and relevant information. Additionally, when an employer learns about some potentially injurious condition of an employee, and then fails to act in a manner that controls the opportunity for injury to occur (acquiesces), the employer may likewise become a party to the act of the employee that resulted in injury to another person.

The most reliable approach to lessening your company's potential liability for negligent employment, and improving the assurance that your new employees are in all respects suitable, is to incorporate the suggested steps provided in this section as a programmed portion of your overall selection process. This will require support from upper management, understanding and cooperation from operational managers and supervisors, a checklist of internal procedures to be followed, use of forms to document findings, drafting a few personnel policies, setting up a personnel file drawer for sensitive records, and use of external investigation sources. If performed properly, a good preemployment screening program can save your company thousands of dollars in theft, turnover, injuries, and damages. If performed improperly, it leaves your company vulnerable and at risk of a potentially serious liability.

Checklist for the Prevention of Negligent Hiring Liability*

All records should be kept in such a manner as to demonstrate that the employer has taken reasonable steps to assure the competence of the employee or employees in question. It is probably a good idea to place certain information on a cover sheet, including:

1. Name of employee and social security number
2. Date of initial hiring
3. Application form used, if any
4. For each position held:
   a. Title
   b. Description of duties (from a standardized list, if this proves convenient and accurate) [Author's note: this should be a full job description as discussed in Chapter 2, and is further testimony for the need of employers to prepare accurate job descriptions]
   c. Period of time for which the position was held
   d. Supervisor(s).

In addition, the employment record should contain information regarding:

1. The circumstances surrounding the formation of the employment relationship, and
2. Information concerning the employee's performance for each position held within the company.

The following outline is similar to the ones provided for attorneys representing either the plaintiff or the defendant employer in a negligent employment suit. The reader should bear in mind that not all of the steps listed below are necessary in order to discharge the employer's obligations. The steps that should be undertaken will depend on the risks inherent in a particular employment position. The employer will adapt and change the outline presented to fit with its organizational and operational needs. For example, in a small company, it may be unnecessary to specify the names of supervisors or the person(s) involved in making the hiring decision, and so forth.

Formation of the Employment Relationship

_____ 1. Date of hiring
_____ 2. Position for which employee was hired
_____ 3. Interview(s), if any
_____ 4. Background check, if any
_____   a. Contacts made
_____   b. Information obtained
_____   c. Action taken
_____ 5. Position and authority of persons performing activities listed above
_____   a. Name
_____   b. Position and duties at time of hiring

*SOURCE: James R. Branch Jr., *Negligent Hiring Practice Manual*, John Wiley & Sons, 1988. Copyright John Wiley & Sons, 1988. Reprinted by permission of John Wiley & Sons, Inc.

_____   c. Qualifications to perform activity

_____   d. Present position and duties

_____   e. Nature of each individual's involvement

_____   f. Means by which each individual listed above can be reached

_____ 6. Records, if any, of the hiring process

_____ 7. Other person with knowledge of or involvement with the decision to hire the employee.

Notice of Incompetence Prior to Hiring

_____ 1. Police record

_____   a. Nature, date, and circumstances of each prior arrest or conviction of the employee

_____   b. Persons and organizations contacted regarding prior arrest(s) or conviction(s), if any

_____ 2. Reputation in the community (personal references)

_____   a. Nature of reputation

_____   b. Persons and organizations contacted

_____   c. Steps taken

_____ 3. Other pre-employment incidents indicating incompetence

_____   a. Nature, date, and circumstances of each previous incident

_____   b. Persons and organizations contacted regarding these incidents

_____   c. Steps taken

_____ 4. Physical or mental characteristics indicating incompetence

_____   a. Nature of characteristics

_____   b. Persons and organizations contacted regarding characteristic

_____   c. Steps taken

Job Performance

_____ 1. Positions held with company

_____   a. Title of position

_____   b. Duties

_____   c. Date on which position was undertaken

_____   d. Steps taken to evaluate fitness for each position

_____   e. Training received from company

_____   f. Persons making the decision to assign the employee to each position

_____ 2. Ongoing employer supervision and evaluation

_____   a. Names of supervisor(s) and period of time in which each was responsible for supervising the employee

_____   b. Frequency and manner of supervision

_____   c. Persons previously lodging complaints against the employee and the nature of their complaints

_____   d. Steps taken to investigate and rectify situation.

Appendix D

What Forms Are Required to Support a Smooth and Orderly Hiring Process

The use of proper forms in the hiring process is important for a number of reasons. First, they will help you to plan and organize each activity and sequential step in the hiring process. Second, forms enable you to structure information in a way that ensures accuracy, completeness, and consistency during this rather vital stage of handling employment operations. Third, some forms are essential for carrying out particular personnel functions and transactions, such as conducting job analyses or compiling a composite record on each new employee hired. Fourth, forms provide an easy source of reference when the need arises to check records, process information about employees, and in other ways use the information that is normally gathered during the hiring process. Last, some forms are legally required records that must be kept by employers based on compelling federal law. Likewise, there may also be various state laws that compel employers to keep certain types of written hiring records on employees, and you should consult with applicable sources of state law recordkeeping requirements.

The forms in this appendix are intended for your ready use, or use after minor modification to suit any difference that may exist in your type of business operations. These are not just "textbook" forms. Rather, they were originally the product of several hours of forms research; redesign to capture the best of several similar forms; and actual use in various employment settings. The original design of some forms appearing in this appendix were prepared for, and taken from, *Manual of Personnel Policies, Procedures and Operations* (Prentice-Hall, 1993). They reappear here not only because of the author's experience in their use, but because of the numerous comments from users of that book as to the helpfulness of these forms in countless different organizations.

Finally, to aid you in following a sequential use of hiring forms, they have been placed in order of their application according to chapter arrangement. Thus, these forms are divided into the three major stages of the hiring process: administrative support, hiring activities, and initial employment. Each of the three forms sections begin with a brief explanation or instruction about the use of each form that appears in the section. This is intended to provide you with a source of easy reference, and to keep each form arranged in an orderly fashion for reproduction convenience.

D.1 Forms for Supporting the Administrative Needs of the Hiring Process

Administrative forms are those used by the employment office or human resources department to prepare documents in support of the hiring process. The two most common types of forms used by employers for this purpose are job analysis forms to aid the development of job descriptions, and a personnel requisition form to process the request to fill a vacancy or recruit for a newly created job.

Explanations and Instructions on the Use of Administrative Forms

Job Analysis Questionnaire Form (Set 1): This 16-page form should be completed by incumbent employees in those jobs where existing job descriptions are obsolete, inaccurate, deficient in detail, or where there is no description and your goal is to create a suitable one. Although the form is self-instructive, it is recommended that you conduct two-hour training sessions for participating employees in accordance with instructions provided in Chapter 2, to familiarize them with the contents of the form, instructions and samples on how to complete it, and selling them on the notion that the more information they provide, the better the company will be able to ascertain such decisions as pay setting, promotion, training, and the like. The supplemental two-page form on Performance Accountabilities is optional, but has the advantage of providing you with specific performance appraisal measures that have been determined to be job-related to each different job.

Supervisor's Job Analysis Review Form: This two-page form should be attached as the last page (copy back-to-back) of the Job Analysis Questionnaire Form when given to incumbent employees. Copy this form on a different color paper so that it stands out as being separate from the pages to be completed by employees. The intent of this form is to allow the employee's supervisor to review and comment on any aspect of the employee's tasks, responsibilities, requirements, and conditions with which the supervisor disagrees.

Job Analysis Interview Form: This form should be used by the Job Analyst, or employment office representative, who will prepare a job description from the information provided by incumbent employees and reviewing supervisors. Once the Job Analyst has carefully reviewed completed Job Analysis Questionnaire and Supervisor Review forms, the Job Analyst should conduct interviews with incumbent employees to ensure that all pertinent aspects of the job are identified and described in sufficient detail. Interviewing incumbent employees (and where necessary, the supervisor) often results in new information, a clearer understanding of the importance or detail of some job responsibility, and provides employees with greater confidence in the thoroughness of the process to create their job descriptions.

Personnel Requisition Form: The primary functions of this form are to document internal approvals to fill jobs, to create a record of vacancies and new jobs, to give advance notice to your employment office that an employee is leaving the company, and to provide a mechanism by which operating managers must justify the creation of new positions. The form used for these purposes should contain all four elements, so if your preference is to modify this form for your company's use, be sure to include each of these elements. The use of Personnel Requisition forms also has the advantage of taking the surprise out of job vacancies and miscommunications between operating departments and the employment/human resources office. It also provides those in the company's decision-making chain an opportunity to consider any desired alternative decisions with each vacancy or new job.

JOB ANALYSIS QUESTIONNAIRE

General Instructions

(Please read all instructions carefully before completing this form)

This form is used to obtain information about your job duties and requirements, and to determine your job classification.

Complete the form in your own words. Please be clear, accurate, detailed, and thorough in the information you provide. You may answer "N/A"—not applicable, to any question which does not apply to your position. For additional space, attach extra pages identified with your name, department, and the question and/or page number being continued on the additional page.

Please read the complete instructions for each page before attempting to complete corresponding questions. Then go back and review the instructions for each item on the page as you complete the item.

It is recommended that you first prepare your answers on scratch paper. When you believe your answers are accurate and complete, neatly print or type your statements on this form, and give it to your supervisor by the prescribed date.

Your immediate supervisor and department manager will review your form to ensure completeness and accuracy. They will complete a review form providing additional information and/or explanations concerning the duties and responsibilities associated with your job—not your individual performance in the job. However, under no circumstances should any supervisor change the answers given and certified by you.

Thank You For Your Help And Participation

GENERAL INFORMATION	
Name:	Position Title:
Work Unit (Dept./Divis.)	Work Location:
Supervisor's Name:	Title:
Time in Present Job:	In Occupation:

SUPERVISION: Routine supervisory activities performed on a regular basis:

❑ Interviews/Hiring recommendations	❑ Assigning and reviewing work
❑ Pay increase recommendations	❑ Coaching and counseling
❑ Disciplinary recommendations	❑ Training subordinate employees
❑ Termination recommendations	❑ Evaluating employee performance

EMPLOYEES YOU SUPERVISE: D=Directly   I=Indirectly

Name	Title	D or I
_____	_____	_____
_____	_____	_____
_____	_____	_____
_____	_____	_____
_____	_____	_____
_____	_____	_____
_____	_____	_____
_____	_____	_____

MAJOR DOMAINS OF JOB RESPONSIBILITIES

List below the four (4) to eight (8) major domains of your job. Domains are the general areas in which you have major and significant duties, responsibilities, authorities, and which are carried out by performing a variety of specific tasks. Examples of domains are:

Processing Billing/Insurance Data	Filing
Repairing Electrical Tools	Scheduling Conferences
Preparing Technical Reports	Building Finished Cabinets
Designing & Teaching Training Programs	

	Percentage Weight
DOMAIN A:	
DOMAIN B:	
DOMAIN C:	
DOMAIN D:	
DOMAIN E:	
DOMAIN F:	
DOMAIN G:	
DOMAIN H:	
Total:	100%

WRITING TASK STATEMENTS

On the following pages you will be asked to write the more essential tasks associated with each major job domain. Emphasize those tasks that are the most frequent, important, and difficult to perform in terms of WHAT is done and HOW it is done when performed properly.

You should describe your "whole job" based on year-round activities, not just those performed during rush or peak periods of work, or when you are substituting for another person.

WORDS TO AVOID: Please try to avoid the use of words like assist, help, handle, communicate, maintain, and similar words that do not describe what you actually do when performing the task. Be very specific and detailed about each task.

HINT: It's easiest to start writing a task statement with your most frequent and important duties in each domain.

Poor Task Statements	**Good Task Statements**
Assist in handling correspondence.	Receive, open, time stamp, and route incoming mail.
Our unit is responsible for keeping all purchase records.	Compare invoices with purchases on all purchasing record orders. Review requisitions submitted by different departments for accuracy. Give requisitions to the Purchasing Agent for approval.
Do quality assurance.	Check machine calibrations using ICS & DCS instruments daily, log data on weekly averages, and prepare analytical reports monthly.
Supervise clerical staff.	Organize work activities and schedules for eight secretaries and two file clerks. Assign and review the work of staff. Guide employees to solve problems and set priorities. Evaluate performance and initiate recommendations on hiring, transfers, promotions, and discipline.
Process claim forms.	Check computer-generated forms for accuracy and completeness; research, correct, and add data as necessary; sign and separate forms, and forward copies to appropriate people for filing or information.

DOMAIN A: _____ **WEIGHT:** _____ %

Provide task statements that are descriptive of what and how significant duties and responsibilities are performed when work is done effectively and efficiently.

	R/L	F	I	D
1.				
2.				
3.				
4.				
5.				
6.				
7.				
8.				

DOMAIN B: _____ **WEIGHT:** _____ %

Provide task statements that are descriptive of what and how significant duties and responsibilities are performed when work is done effectively and efficiently.

	R/L	F	I	D
1.				
2.				
3.				
4.				
5.				
6.				
7.				
8.				

DOMAIN C: _____ **WEIGHT:** _____ %

Provide task statements that are descriptive of what and how significant duties and responsibilities are performed when work is done effectively and efficiently.

	R/L	F	I	D
1.				
2.				
3.				
4.				
5.				
6.				
7.				
8.				

DOMAIN D: _____ **WEIGHT:** _____ %

Provide task statements that are descriptive of what and how significant duties and responsibilities are performed when work is done effectively and efficiently.

	R/L	F	I	D
1.				
2.				
3.				
4.				
5.				
6.				
7.				
8.				

DOMAIN E: _____ **WEIGHT:** _____ %

Provide task statements that are descriptive of what and how significant duties and responsibilities are performed when work is done effectively and efficiently.

	R/L	F	I	D
1.				
2.				
3.				
4.				
5.				
6.				
7.				
8.				

DOMAIN F: _____ **WEIGHT:** _____ %

Provide task statements that are descriptive of what and how significant duties and responsibilities are performed when work is done effectively and efficiently.

	R/L	F	I	D
1.				
2.				
3.				
4.				
5.				
6.				
7.				
8.				

DOMAIN G: _____ **WEIGHT:** _____ %

Provide task statements that are descriptive of what and how significant duties and responsibilities are performed when work is done effectively and efficiently.

	R/L	F	I	D
1.				
2.				
3.				
4.				
5.				
6.				
7.				
8.				

DOMAIN H: _____ **WEIGHT:** _____ %

Provide task statements that are descriptive of what and how significant duties and responsibilities are performed when work is done effectively and efficiently.

	R/L	F	I	D
1.				
2.				
3.				
4.				
5.				
6.				
7.				
8.				

RATING TASK STATEMENTS

After writing the task statements which fully represent each job domain, go back to each domain sheet and enter the letter or number which most accurately represents the entry level required to perform the work and the frequency, importance, and difficulty of each task relative to all other tasks of the job.

Definitions	Scales
Entry requirements: The knowledge and skills needed to do the tasks or functions absolutely required of the applicant prior to employment, or that can be learned on the job in a reasonably short period of time.	R = Required L = Learned
Frequency: How often is this task or function performed under normal conditions?	1 = Semi-annual/Annual 2 = Quarterly 3 = Monthly 4 = Weekly 5 = Daily
Importance: Compared to other tasks or functions you perform, how important is this task on the success of your work and/or impact on your work unit?	1 = Routine/minor importance 2 = Important 3 = Very important 4 = Essential 5 = Critical
Difficulty: Compared to other tasks or functions you perform, how difficult is this task to either learn or carry out in a way that yields the best possible results?	1 = Repetitious 2 = Moderately easy 3 = Moderately difficult 4 = Difficult 5 = Complex

DO NOT CONTINUE UNTIL ALL TASK STATEMENTS HAVE BEEN WRITTEN AND RATED

MINIMUM REQUIREMENTS

In order to successfully perform the position you occupy, what entry-level skills, knowledge, and abilities must a minimally qualified person possess? NOTE: Also indicate any courses, training programs, and previous experience that have been particularly important to the successful performance of your position.

Education: What do you feel is the minimal level of formal education, or its equivalent, to perform your job satisfactorily?

- ❑ No formal education required
- ❑ Eighth grade education
- ❑ High school diploma
- ❑ 2-year college degree (or equivalent)
- ❑ 4-year college degree (or equivalent)
- ❑ Graduate work and/or advanced degree (specify): _____
- ❑ Professional license (specify): _____

Experience:

Amount   Kind: _____

- ❑ None   _____
- ❑ Less than 6 months   _____
- ❑ 6 months to one year   _____
- ❑ 2–4 years   _____
- ❑ 5–7 years   _____
- ❑ 8–10 years   _____
- ❑ 10+ years   _____

Skills/Abilities: State the skills and abilities needed to adequately perform the more essential aspects of your work. Example: type accurately at 60 wpm; ability to read blueprints; perform mathematical calculations accurately; administer and interpret vocational tests; ability to analyze situations accurately and pursue an effective course of action.

1. _____

   _____

2. _____

   _____

3. _____

   _____

4. _____

   _____

Knowledge: Indicate whether a qualified person would need general, working, or technical knowledge, followed by a description of the area of knowledge that should be possessed by the individual. Example: General knowledge of local hiring trends: working knowledge of standard office procedures; technical knowledge of the laws, rules, and regulations governing employment law.

1. _____

2. _____

3. _____

4. _____

5. _____

PHYSICAL CHARACTERISTICS

Physical characteristics are the physical demands and requirements placed on you by the nature of your work activities. Think about how often, or for how long, various physical activities must be performed in your job. For example, a job requiring prolonged standing requires more physical effort than a job requiring periodic standing.

1. Physical strength and mobility is needed in my job to _____

_____

Examples: lift and carry heavy (or large) objects; move furniture; crawl in confined spaces; stoop to lower file drawers; frequently climb three flights of stairs; climb extension ladders.

2. My job requires that I have the stamina to _____
_____ for a considerable number of my work hours.

Examples: stand for 8 consecutive hours, except for breaks and lunch; walk rapidly for prolonged periods of time; concentrate on precise and critical information for repetitive 2-hour intervals.

3. The environmental exposures connected to my job are _____

_____

Examples: high-level noise; fumes; obnoxious odors; dust; extremes of temperature; rain; confined working space; poor lighting.

4. Other (list): _____ _____

_____

OTHER PERFORMANCE CHARACTERISTICS

People are required to perform a variety of other functions and activities related to their jobs, and are often evaluated, rewarded, or disciplined based on how they handle these situations or comply with conditions. Please complete the statements that apply to your job, or enter N/A for not applicable.

1. **Judgment/Decision Making:** What tasks do you perform that require you to take action on your own, or to make recommendations? _____

   _____

   For what type of work do you make final decisions on? _____

   _____

2. **Independent Solutions:** Describe those parts of your job that require you to interpret and think through in order to develop a solution to a problem. _____

   _____

3. **Special Requirements:** These include such conditions as the necessary possession of technical/trade certificates, driver's licenses, being available for 24-hour on-call duty or overtime/weekend work, travel within a prescribed distance, speak effectively before large groups, attend evening meetings; fluently speak and read a particular foreign language.

   A. _____

   _____

   B. _____

   _____

   C. _____

   _____

   D. _____

   _____

4. I routinely have to deal with people who are _____

   _____

   Example: assertive; complaining about problems; rude; fearful; uneducated.

5. I work under such adverse conditions as _____

   _____

   _____

   Examples: changing priorities; short deadlines; more than one supervisor; conflicting expectations and standards; uncooperative co-workers.

JOB ANALYSIS SUPPLEMENT
ADA ESSENTIAL PHYSICAL, MENTAL, AND
ENVIRONMENTAL JOB REQUIREMENTS

Job Title: _____ Code: _____

Department: _____ Location: _____

To comply with the Americans with Disabilities Act (ADA), all essential physical, mental and other requirements or qualifications must be job-related in order to be valid. Therefore, the following characteristics of the job must be stated in specific rather than general terms linked to the successful performance of actual job tasks.

Activity Codes
Place an activity code beside each of the following activities that apply to this position, then briefly describe the activity or condition under which the job is performed.

O—Occasionally: Activity or condition exists less than one-third of work time.

F—Frequently: Activity or condition exists between one-third and two-thirds of work time.

C—Constant: Activity or condition exists more than two-thirds of work time.

Physical Requirements

_____ 1. SITTING:

_____ 2. STANDING/WALKING:

_____ 3. CROUCHING (bend at knees):

_____ 4. KNEELING/CRAWLING:

_____ 5. STOOPING:

_____ 6. TWISTING (knees, waist, neck):

_____ 7. REACHING (overhead):

_____ 8. PUSHING/PULLING (lbs./size):

_____ 9. LIFTING/CARRYING (lbs./size):

_____ 10. HANDLING/COORDINATION:

Use of Senses

_____ 1. TALKING IN PERSON:

_____ 2. TALKING ON TELEPHONE:

_____ 3. HEARING:

_____ 4. VISION (near/far/color/depth):

_____ 5. SMELL:

Mental Requirements

_____ 1. UNDERSTAND & CARRY OUT ORAL INSTRUCTIONS:

_____ 2. READ & CARRY OUT WRITTEN INSTRUCTIONS:

_____ 3. DEADLINES/MULTIPLE PRIORITIES:

_____ 4. FLEXIBILITY & PACE:

_____ 5. PLAN & SCHEDULE:

_____ 6. ATTENTION TO DETAIL:

_____ 7. COMPLEXITY:

_____ 8. ANALYZE/INTERPRET TECHNICAL INFORMATION

Environmental Setting

_____ 1. SAFETY REQUIREMENTS:

_____ 2. EXPOSURES:

_____ 3. OPERATION OF EQUIPMENT:

_____ 4. OPERATION OF VEHICLES:

_____ 5. STOOPING:

_____ 6. TWISTING (knees, waist, neck):

_____ 7. WORK INSIDE:

_____ 8. WORK OUTSIDE (conditions):

List any other physical, mental or environmental requirements of this job that have not already been covered.

Is there any other information about this job or the conditions under which work is performed which would be helpful in understanding the physical, mental or environmental requirements, conditions or qualifications?

Reviewed by _____ Date _____

Approved by _____ Date _____

SUPERVISORY REVIEW FORM
(Please Print or Type)

Supervisor's Name _____ Title _____

Employee Being Reviewed _____ Title _____

Dept. _____ Divis./Unit _____ Location _____

1. How long have you provided direct supervision of the review position? _____

2. After a thorough review of this employee's job analysis questionnaire, please identify the domain, task statement number, and specific comments or concerns you have with statements made. Please pay particular attention to the accuracy of reported statements made, domain titles and weights, and the ratings on task statement scales.

Domain	Task #	Comments

3. Please list any additional tasks and related rating scales that may have been overlooked by the employee, but are important enough to be listed.

Domain	Task Statement	R/L	F	I	D

4. Please provide any other comments or amplifications concerning the characteristics or qualifications of this position that you feel would be helpful in describing and/or classifying the job.

Certification: I have reviewed the referenced employee's job analysis questionnaire and find it to be an accurate representation of the position to the best of my knowledge, except as otherwise noted by my comments herein.

Supervisor's Signature	Date

❑ I would like to discuss this employee's position in greater detail with the Job Analyst.

PERFORMANCE ACCOUNTABILITIES

Enter the name of each job domain applicable to your job. After reviewing the task statement you filled out in each domain, place a check mark (✓) on the Performance Index line that corresponds to the task(s) in each domain.

Performance Index	Domain A	Domain B	Domain C	Domain D
Work Quantity				
Amount	____	____	____	____
Promptness	____	____	____	____
Complete/Thorough	____	____	____	____
Efficiency	____	____	____	____
Work Quality				
Skills/Accuracy	____	____	____	____
Knowledge	____	____	____	____
Effectiveness	____	____	____	____
Judgment	____	____	____	____
Problem Solving	____	____	____	____
Decision Making	____	____	____	____
Creativity	____	____	____	____
Work Traits & Conditions				
Punctuality/Attendance	____	____	____	____
Communications	____	____	____	____
Cooperation	____	____	____	____
Initiative	____	____	____	____
Demeanor/Appearance	____	____	____	____
Personal Relations				
Co-workers	____	____	____	____
Supervisors/Managers	____	____	____	____
General Public	____	____	____	____
Behavior/Conduct	____	____	____	____
Adaptability				
Job Progress	____	____	____	____
New/Unusual Situations	____	____	____	____
Changing Conditions and Priorities	____	____	____	____
Compliance	____	____	____	____

Comments: _____

_____

_____

_____

_____

_____

> **Your business
> name/logo
> here**

Job Analysis
Interview Form*

Position Title: _____　　Department: _____

Incumbent: _____　　Time in Job: _____

Interviewer: _____　　Date: _____

1. Describe briefly *what* you do and, if possible, *how* you do it. Include duties in the following categories:

    a. daily duties (those performed on a regular basis every day or almost every day)

    b. periodic duties (those performed weekly, monthly, quarterly, or at other regular intervals)

    c. duties performed at irregular intervals

2. Describe the successful completion and/or end results of the job.

3. What do you feel is the most important part of your job? Why?

4. What do you feel is the most difficult or complicated part of your job? Why?

5. Has your job changed since you were hired? How?

continued

---

*SOURCE: Joseph D. Levesque, *Manual of Personnel Policies, Procedures and Operations* 2/E, (Englewood Cliffs, NJ: Prentice-Hall, Inc., 1993) pp. 253–258.

6. Are you performing duties you consider *unnecessary?* If so, describe.

7. Are you performing duties not presently included in the job description? Describe?

8. Describe your repetitive job tasks. Are you frequently bored on the job?

9. Are there any exceptional problems you encounter in performing the job under normal conditions? If so, describe.

   a. What is *the degree* of independent action you are allowed to take?

   b. What decisions are you permitted to make?

10. What kinds of problems or questions would you ordinarily refer to your supervisor?

11. Are you responsible for any confidential data? State the type of confidential data handled (personnel files, salary information, business secrets, etc.).

12. Are you responsible for money or things of monetary value? State the type of responsibility and the approximate amount you must safeguard.

13. What kinds of contacts do you have with others? Describe.

    a. Internal

    b. External

14. To what extent is your work supervised?

    a. How do you receive instruction?

    b. How often does your supervisor check your work?

    c. What written material do you have to read in the course of your job?

15. How many employees do *you* supervise directly? _____ indirectly? _____

16. What do you feel is necessary in terms of formal education or its equivalent to perform this job satisfactorily?

_____ No formal education required	_____ 4-year college degree (or equivalent)
_____ Eighth grade education	_____ Graduate work or advanced degree (specify: _____)
_____ High school diploma (or equivalent)	
_____ 2-year college degree (or equivalent)	_____ Professional license (specify: _____)

continued

17.   Can you specify the training *time* needed on the job to arrive at a level of competence?

18.   What job duty took the longest time to learn? The shortest?

19.   How much job experience (in terms of **weeks, months, or years**) is needed to perform the job satisfactorily? **Where** can this type of experience be obtained (inside the organization or elsewhere)?

_____ None   _____ One to three years

_____ Less than one month   _____ Three to five years

_____ One to six months   _____ Five to ten years

_____ Six months to one year   _____ More than ten years

Check the location of one job

_____ Outdoor   _____ Underground

_____ Indoor   _____ Other _____

20.   Check any objectionable conditions found on the job and note afterward how frequently each is encountered (rarely, occasionally, constantly, etc.).

_____ Dirt   _____   _____ Wetness/humidity   _____

_____ Dust   _____   _____ Vibration   _____

_____ Heat   _____   _____ Sudden temperature changes   _____

_____ Cold   _____   _____ Darkness or poor lighting   _____

_____ Noise   _____   _____ Other (specify)   _____

_____ Fumes   _____   _____

_____ Odors   _____   _____

21.   Check any undesirable health and safety conditions under which you must perform and note how often they are encountered.

_____ Elevated work place _____   _____ Fire hazards   _____

_____ Mechanical hazards _____   _____ Radiation   _____

_____ Explosives   _____   _____ Other (specify) _____

_____ Electrical hazards   _____   _____

22. Describe briefly what machines, tools, equipment, or work aids you work with on a regular basis.

23. Are there any personal attributes (special aptitudes, physical characteristics, personality traits, etc.) required by the job?

24. Describe those activities that are part of your supervisory duties.

    Work assignments

    Instruction/training/coaching

    Hiring/placement

    Performance appraisal

    Discipline

    Grievance handling

    Work or material flow

    Follow-up/follow-through

    Cost reduction

continued

Quality control/improvement

Developing new products or patterns

Troubleshooting

Incentives

Methods

Reports

Other

25. If you think there are other relevant facts we should know about your job, please describe them.

PERSONNEL REQUISITION FORM

POSITION TITLE _____

DEPARTMENT _____ WORK LOCATION _____

_____ New Position _____ Replacement for _____

_____ Full-time _____ Part-time _____ Regular _____ Temporary/On-Call

Work hours and Days: _____

REASON NEEDED (If replacement, state why employee being replaced. If new position, attach separate justification.) _____

_____

PLEASE ATTACH <u>CURRENT</u> JOB DESCRIPTION.

SPECIAL REQUIREMENTS (i.e., special training/experience, drivers license, etc.):

_____

_____

Requested By: _____   Date _____
               Signature

Approvals: _____   Date _____
               Department Head

               _____   Date _____
               Personnel Director

Personnel Department Use

Disposition:

Person Hired:
Offer Date: Budget Code:
Start Date: Range:

GUIDELINES FOR REQUESTING
APPROVAL OF NEW POSITIONS

1. A Personnel Requisition Form must be completed.

2. In addition to a job description, submit the following information:
   A. Estimated salary and benefits costs.
   B. Economic factors to be considered:
      (1) Number of overtime hours to be reduced weekly.
      (2) Increase in revenue to be generated annually.
      (3) Other cost savings.
   C. Consideration for the quality of services rendered and customer satisfaction.
   D. The effect on operations should this position not be filled.
   E. The anticipated date that the new position must be filled.

3. The Human Resources Director should be notified at the earliest possible time if salary or benefits surveys will be required.

4. When the above outlined justification items are satisfactorily completed, the request will be forwarded by the Human Resources Director to the Personnel Committee for review at the next regularly scheduled meeting.

D.2 Forms for Ensuring a Proper Hiring Process

These forms constitute the documents you will need, or legally require, to carry out each phase of hiring activities—particularly the recruitment and selection testing processes. They will aid you in gathering the type of information you need to evaluate applicants, record legally required information (or ensure that potentially discriminatory information is omitted), and allow the separation of information that is only permissible once you have made a hiring decision.

Explanations and Instructions on the Use of Hiring Activity Forms

Employment Application Form: This form has been developed to omit potentially discriminatory information about job applicants while at the same time capturing essential information about the applicant's employment-related background and characteristics. You will also notice that the applicant's certification at the bottom of the last page contains a waiver of liability for reference information and at-will employment statement. You may also wish to add that employment will/may be subject to a satisfactory preemployment physical examination including drug and alcohol testing.

EEO Identification (Voluntary Information for Government Monitoring Purposes) Form: This form should be used by employers with fifty or more employees, federal contractors or subcontractors, and recipients of federal grants in order to maintain affirmative action data on applicants and employees. The form should be attached to each Employment Application form, and completed forms removed by someone who is not responsible for selection or screening of applications. This form should then be placed in a separate file as a source of data to compile information of the Applicant Flow Data form.

Job Interest Form: This form can be used as an alternative to the Employment Application form by those employers who do not want to take full applications when vacancies do not exist. When job openings occur, this form provides you with a pool of interested and potentially qualified applicants which can be reviewed for preliminary qualifications, then mailed a job announcement and Employment Application form. Forms such as this, along with unsolicited resumes, should be periodically removed from your files in order to maintain a relatively current pool of potential applicants.

Employee Transfer Request Form: This form is a source of internal applicants for various jobs for those employers who have a sufficient number of jobs to make transfers possible. Although some employers deliberately avoid handling transfers because they tend to delay an ultimate hiring process, allowing transfers before external recruiting begins can in some cases improve employee relations in an operational unit where an employee would be more satisfied if relocated. Normally, transfer requests are only considered when vacancies to the same or substantially similar position exists, and where both the existing and receiving supervisors agree to the transfer.

Applicant Flow Data Form: This form is essential for those employers who desire (voluntary affirmative action efforts), or are legally required, to maintain composite data on the characteristics of applicants for each hiring process. This form is usually requested for review by fair employment compliance agency representatives during the investigation of discrimination complaints, or during audits by these agencies.

Employment Interview Rating Form: There are virtually thousands of interview rating forms in use, and nearly all of them vary to some degree in format, rating categories, and rating scales used to evaluate and rank applicants. The form provided should prove useful for a large number and variety of jobs since evaluation categories are defined in general terms, apply to a large range of jobs, and use a weighted rating scale that can be adjusted for different jobs. The most important thing is that you use a form to evaluate applicants on predetermined, objective categories and standards as a matter of record. These forms are also helpful sources of reference when hiring decisions are delayed, or additional applicants from the same interview process are considered at a later date.

Telephone Reference Check Form: This form should be used for informal, yet documented, conversations with former employers concerning reference information on applicants under final hiring consideration. You should follow the information on this form when talking to former employers, and write in responses during your conversation. The form itself should be placed in either: 1) a confidential folder with other employment reference documents (if permitted by state law); 2) placed in a personnel file folder on the employee but not accessible for the employee's review (if permitted by state law); or, 3) placed in a sealed envelope marked "To Be Opened Only By *(name of company officers)* before deposit into the employee's personnel file."

Authorization for Employment Reference Form: This form is very similar to the Telephone Reference Check form, but it is used to mail to former employers and has the advantage of explaining how you use this information, its confidentiality, and the former employee's signed authorization to release this type of employment related information. By including information concerning the individual's performance, strengths and weaknesses, and functional abilities, it provides you with much needed information about the person's competence or training/supervision needs relative to the job for which they are being considered. The completed form should be handled in the same way as the Telephone Reference Check form, inasmuch as they contain very similar confidential information that should not be accessible to persons who do not have a need and right to know its contents.

Authorization to Acquire Credit Report Form: This form should be used by those employers whose business necessitates an evaluation of an applicant's credit and/or character worthiness. Even then, it should be used only for those applicants whose job responsibilities provide them with access to, handling of, or use of monetary transactions related to the employer's business or its customers. As the form indicates, applicants who request copies of the report are entitled to obtain them when such reports are conducted by a consumer credit reporting agency.

Employment Eligibility Verification (I-9) Form: This is the form required by the U.S. Immigration and Naturalization Service (INS) to be completed by *all* employers on *all* employees hired after November 6, 1986 as a condition of the Immigration Reform and Control Act of 1986. Completed and verified forms should be placed in a single (I-9 Forms) file where you store other general confidential employee records. Failure to use this form, or failure to obtain verifying proof of legal presence and employment in the United States as specified on the form, can result in severe fines and penalties.

Instructions For Completing Form I-9: These are the essence of the instructions provided by INS for employer's guidance on how the I-9 form is to be filled out and what types of documents can be used for verifying proof. You should note that proof documents are to be photocopied and attached to each I-9 form. If you wish to obtain the entire instructional booklet or request a small supply of forms, contact your nearest INS field office as listed on their "Need Help" brochure included herein.

**PLEASE PRINT
IN INK OR TYPE**

EMPLOYMENT APPLICATION *

	YOUR BUSINESS NAME AND/OR LOGO HERE

EQUAL OPPORTUNITY EMPLOYER: It is our policy to abide by all Federal and State laws prohibiting employment discrimination solely on the basis of a person's race, color, creed, national origin, religion, age (over 40), sex, marital status, or physical handicap, except where a reasonable, bona fide occupational qualification exists.

━━ PERSONAL ━━

NAME (LAST)	(FIRST)	(MIDDLE)	TELEPHONE (AREA CODE AND NO.)
ADDRESS (STREET)	(CITY)	(STATE)	(ZIP CODE)

PREVIOUS ADDRESSES DURING THE LAST FIVE YEARS

STREET ADDRESS	CITY	STATE	ZIP	FROM	TO
STREET ADDRESS	CITY	STATE	ZIP	FROM	TO

OTHER EMPLOYMENT-RELATED INFORMATION

CHECK THE FOLLOWING OPTIONS WHICH YOU WOULD CONSIDER:

☐ Full-Time   ☐ Part-Time   ☐ Temporary

IF MINOR, AGE

LIST ANY RELATIVES WORKING FOR THIS ORGANIZATION
Name   Department

CAN YOU, AFTER EMPLOYMENT, SUBMIT A BIRTH CERTIFICATE OR OTHER PROOF OF U.S. CITIZENSHIP?   Yes ☐   No ☐

IF NOT A U.S. CITIZEN, CAN YOU, AFTER EMPLOYMENT, SUBMIT VERIFICATION OF YOUR LEGAL RIGHT TO WORK PERMANENTLY IN THE U.S.?   Yes ☐   No ☐

WERE YOU PREVIOUSLY EMPLOYED BY THIS ORGANIZATION?   Yes ☐   No ☐

Date(s)

HAVE YOU EVER BEEN CONVICTED OF A FELONY, OR PLEADED NO CONTEST IN A FELONY, OR BEEN CONVICTED OF A MISDEMEANOR RESULTING IN IMPRISONMENT OR A FINE OVER $500 DURING THE LAST TEN YEARS? (Conviction will not necessarily disqualify an applicant.)   Yes ☐   No ☐

If yes, explain

DO YOU HAVE ANY PHYSICAL LIMITATIONS TO PERFORM THE JOB APPLIED FOR? (IF YES, EXPLAIN THE TYPE OF ACCOMMODATION REQUIRED.)   Yes ☐   No ☐

ACCOMMODATION

━━ EDUCATION & TRAINING ━━

HIGH SCHOOL	COMPLETE ADDRESS		Graduated: Yes ☐ No ☐
COLLEGE OR UNIVERSITY	COMPLETE ADDRESS	MAJOR	DEGREE/YEAR
COLLEGE OR UNIVERSITY	COMPLETE ADDRESS	MAJOR	DEGREE/YEAR
TRADE SCHOOL	COMPLETE ADDRESS	SUBJECTS	Completed: Yes ☐ No ☐ YEAR
APPRENTICE SCHOOL	COMPLETE ADDRESS	SUBJECTS	Completed: Yes ☐ No ☐ YEAR

LIST ANY OTHER EDUCATION, TRAINING, SPECIAL SKILLS, OR CERTIFICATES/LICENSES THAT YOU POSSESS RELATED TO THIS JOB.

LIST ANY MACHINES OR EQUIPMENT THAT YOU ARE QUALIFIED AND EXPERIENCED AT OPERATING.

LIST ANY LANGUAGES THAT YOU FLUENTLY:

SPEAK: READ: WRITE:

━━ REFERENCES ━━

LIST BUSINESS PERSONS KNOWN, BUT NOT RELATED, TO YOU FOR AT LEAST THREE YEARS

	NAME	TITLE	BUSINESS	PHONE	YEARS KNOWN
1.					
2.					
3.					

POSITION APPLIED FOR: **DATE:**   **LAST NAME:**   **FIRST NAME:**   **INITIAL:**

continued

* SOURCE: Joseph D. Levesque, *Manual of Personnel Policies, Procedures and Operations* 2/E, (Englewood Cliffs, NJ: Prentice-Hall, Inc., 1993) pp. 166–167.

EXPERIENCE

List the last 10 years' work experience beginning with most recent.

NAME OF EMPLOYER	TYPE OF BUSINESS		
ADDRESS	CITY	STATE ZIP	PHONE ( ) —
DATES EMPLOYED FROM TO	STARTING TITLE	LAST TITLE	
NAME AND TITLE OF SUPERVISOR	MAY WE CONTACT? YES ☐ NO ☐	WAS EMPLOYMENT FULL-TIME ☐ PART-TIME ☐	REASON FOR LEAVING
BRIEF DESCRIPTION OF DUTIES			

NAME OF EMPLOYER	TYPE OF BUSINESS		
ADDRESS	CITY	STATE ZIP	PHONE ( ) —
DATES EMPLOYED FROM TO	STARTING TITLE	LAST TITLE	
NAME AND TITLE OF SUPERVISOR	MAY WE CONTACT? YES ☐ NO ☐	WAS EMPLOYMENT FULL-TIME ☐ PART-TIME ☐	REASON FOR LEAVING
BRIEF DESCRIPTION OF DUTIES			

NAME OF EMPLOYER	TYPE OF BUSINESS		
ADDRESS	CITY	STATE ZIP	PHONE ( ) —
DATES EMPLOYED FROM TO	STARTING TITLE	LAST TITLE	
NAME AND TITLE OF SUPERVISOR	MAY WE CONTACT? YES ☐ NO ☐	WAS EMPLOYMENT FULL-TIME ☐ PART-TIME ☐	REASON FOR LEAVING
BRIEF DESCRIPTION OF DUTIES			

DRIVERS

DO YOU HAVE A VALID DRIVER'S LICENSE IN THIS STATE?   YES ☐   NO ☐

IF YES, LICENSE NO:

_____

LIST ANY MOVING VIOLATIONS DURING THE LAST FIVE YEARS UNDER "COMMENTS."

COMMENTS

LIST ANY COMMENTS OR QUALIFYING STATEMENTS YOU CARE TO MAKE.

_____
_____
_____
_____
_____
_____

APPLICANT'S CERTIFICATION

Please read carefully before signing. If you have any questions regarding the following statements, please ask for assistance.

I certify that, to the best of my knowledge and belief, the answers given by me to the foregoing questions and the statements made by me in this application are correct and complete. I understand that any false information contained in this application may result in my discharge.

I authorize you to communicate with all my former employers, school officials and persons named as references. I hereby release all employers, schools and individuals from any liability for any damage whatsoever resulting from giving such information.

I understand that as this organization deems necessary, I may be required to work overtime hours or hours outside a normally defined work day or work week. If employed, I understand and agree that such employment may be terminated at any time and without any liability to me for any continuation of salary, wages, or employment related benefits.

Date_____   Signature_____

> Your business
> name/logo
> here

Voluntary Information
for Government Monitoring Purposes*

This organization is an Equal Opportunity/Affirmative Action employer.

The information below is needed to measure the effectiveness of our recruitment efforts and is in conformity with federal government guidelines which require us to compile statistical information about applicants for employment. You are not required to furnish this information, but are encouraged to do so. The law provides that an employer may neither discriminate on the basis of this information, nor on whether you choose to furnish it. However, if you choose not to furnish it, under federal regulations, this employer is required to note race and sex on the basis of visual observation or surname.

This Voluntary Information Sheet will be kept in a confidential file separate from the Application for Employment.

Position Applied For: _____

I wish to furnish this information _____ (please print name) _____
I do not wish to furnish this information _____ (please print name) _____

Please check the appropriate box: ☐ Male   ☐ Female

ETHNIC CATEGORY (Check One)

_____ WHITE (Not of Hispanic origin)—All persons having origins in any of the original peoples of Europe, North Africa, or the Middle East.

_____ BLACK (Not of Hispanic origin)—All persons having origins in any of the Black racial groups of Africa.

_____ ASIAN OR PACIFIC ISLANDER—All persons having origins in any of the original peoples of the Far East, Southeast Asia and Indian Subcontinent, or the Pacific Islands. This area includes, for example, China, Japan, Korea, the Philippine Islands, and Samoa.

_____ AMERICAN INDIAN OR ALASKA NATIVE—All persons having origins in any of the original peoples of North America, and who maintain cultural identification through tribal affiliations or community recognition.

_____ HISPANIC—All persons of Mexican, Puerto Rican, Cuban, Central or South American, or other Spanish culture or origin, regardless of race.

Please check if the following categories are applicable:

_____ HANDICAPPED INDIVIDUAL—Any person who (1) has a physical or mental impairment that substantially limits one or more of his or her major life activities; (2) has a record of such impairment, or (3) is regarded as having such an impairment. A handicap is "substantially limiting" if it is likely to cause difficulty in securing, retaining, or advancing in employment.

_____ VETERAN ELIGIBILITY—Served in armed forces between August 5, 1964 and May 7, 1975.

_____ DISABLED VETERAN ELIGIBILITY—A veteran with a disability, service connected or otherwise.

*SOURCE: Joseph D. Levesque, *Manual of Personnel Policies, Procedures and Operations* 2/E, (Englewood Cliffs, NJ: Prentice-Hall, Inc., 1993) p. 169.

Job Interest Form[*]

To help _____ understand your job interests, please indicate what type of jobs interest you. Checking "Yes" or "No" will not exclude you from being considered for any job for which you are qualified.

Your business name/logo here

PLEASE INDICATE YOUR INTEREST:

Check (✓) your interest for each item below:

	Yes	No

1. Are you interested in overtime work?   1.

2. Are you interested in performing routine tasks daily?   2.

3. Are you interested in jobs having rotating days off including week-ends and holidays?   3.

4. Are you interested in the following types of work?

    (a) Office work?   4a.

    (b) Out of doors?   4b.

    (c) Shop or plant?   4c.

5. Are you interested in one or more kinds of work having the following physical demands?

    (a.) **Sedentary Work (very light):** 5a.
Lifting 10 lbs. maximum and occasionally lifting and/or carrying such articles as dockets, ledgers and small tools. Although a sedentary job is defined as one which involves sitting, a certain amount of walking and standing is often necessary in carrying out job duties. Jobs are sedentary if walking and standing are required only occationally and other sedentary criteria are met.

    (b.) **Light Work:** 5b.
Lifting 20 lbs. maximum with frequent lifting and/or carrying of objects weighing up top 10 lbs. Even though the weight lifted may be only a negligible amount, a job is in this category when it requires walking or standing to a significant degree, or when it involves sitting most of the time with a degree of pushing and pulling of arm and/or leg controls.

    (c.) **Medium Work:** 5c.
Lifting 50 lbs. maximum with frequent lifting and/or carrying of objects weighing up to 25 lbs.

    (d.) **Heavy Work:** 5d.
Lifting 100 lbs. maximum with frequent lifting and/or carrying of objects weighing up to 50 lbs.

    (e.) **Very Heavy Work:** 5e.
Lifting objects in excess of 100 lbs. with frequent lifting and/or carrying of objects weighing 50 lbs. or more.

List below titles of jobs in which you're most interested:

1. _____   4. _____

2. _____   5. _____

3. _____   6. _____

Name (last)

Address (street)

(city)

(first)

(state)

(initial)

(zip code)

Day telephone (area code and no.)

Date filed

[*]SOURCE: Joseph D. Levesque, *Manual of Personnel Policies, Procedures and Operations* 2/E, (Englewood Cliffs, NJ: Prentice-Hall, Inc., 1993) pp. 179–180.

Job Interest Form—continued

CERTIFICATION:

I understand that the purpose of this form is to advise _____ of my interest in employment in the jobs I have listed, and that _____ will make every effort to notify me of job vacancies for the listed jobs for a period of one year from the date of filing of this form. I further understand that this form does not constitute a job application, that I must file a job application to be considered for any vacancy, and that _____ does not accept job applications except for current vacancies.

Signed: _____ Date: _____

FOR OFFICE USE ONLY:

Dates contacted applicant	Position	Application received?
1. _____	_____	_____
2. _____	_____	_____
3. _____	_____	_____
4. _____	_____	_____
5. _____	_____	_____

_____is an Equal Opportunity Employer, and does not discriminate on the basis of a person's race, color, creed, national origins, religion, age (40-70)), sex, marital status or physical handicap. Thus, every job applicant considered is for employment into jobs for which they are qualified.

Your business
name/logo
here

Employee Transfer Request[*]

Date: _____

Employee's Name: _____

Position Title: _____

Hire Date: _____

SSN or Employee
Payroll Number: _____

Current Pay Rate: _____

The following transfer is requested:

	FROM (current job)	TO
Position		
Location		
Department		
Hourly Status	Full-Time _____ or Part-Time _____	Full-Time _____ or Part-Time _____ (hrs. per) (week)

Employee Qualifications: _____

_____

_____

Reason's for Request: _____

_____

Employee Signature: _____

Note: Separate forms must be filed for each separate request of transfer to other positions, locations, or departments.

*SOURCE: Joseph D. Levesque, *Manual of Personnel Policies, Procedures and Operations* 2/E, (Englewood Cliffs, NJ: Prentice-Hall, Inc., 1993) p. 259.

APPLICANT FLOW DATA *
(Print All Information)

Position Title: _____   Process Period: _____

EEO-1 Category*: _____   Prepared By: _____

Name of Applicant	Sex		Age 40+	EEO Identification*									Disposition*	Complete this Section if Hired		
	M	F		W	B	HP	API	AI	HCI	VE	DVE			Hire Date	Position Title	Pay Rate
Total																

CODES*

EEO-1 Categories

1. Officials and Managers
2. Professionals
3. Technicians
4. Sales Workers
5. Office and Clerical
6. Crafts — Skilled
7. Operatives — Semiskilled
8. Laborers — Unskilled
9. Service Workers

EEO Identification

W — WHITE (Not of Hispanic origin) — All persons having origins in any of the original peoples of Europe, North Africa, or the Middle East.

B — BLACK (Not of Hispanic origin) — All persons having origins in any of the Black racial groups of Africa.

HP — HISPANIC — All persons of Mexican, Puerto Rican, Cuban, Central or South American, or other Spanish culture or origin, regardless of race.

API — ASIAN OR PACIFIC ISLANDER — All persons having origins in any of the original peoples of the Far East, Southeast Asia and Indian Subcontinent, or the Pacific Islands. This area includes, for example, China, Japan, Korea, the Philippine Islands and Samoa.

AI — AMERICAN INDIAN OR ALASKA NATIVE — All persons having origins in any of the original peoples of North America, and who maintain cultural identification through tribal affiliations or community recognition.

HCI — HANDICAPPED INDIVIDUAL — Any person who (1) has a physical or mental impairment that substantially limits one or more of his or her major life activities; (2) has a record of such impairment, or (3) is regarded as having such impairment. A handicap is "substantially limiting" if it is likely to cause difficulty in securing, retaining or advancing in employment.

VE — VETERAN ELIGIBILITY — Served in armed forces between August 5, 1964 and May 7, 1975.

DVE — DISABLED VETERAN ELIGIBILITY — A veteran with a disability, service connected or otherwise.

Disposition

A — Hired

B — Applicant rejected offer of employment

C — Qualified applicant, but no vacancy

D — Failed to complete application

E — Insufficient educational background or equivalent experience

F — Unsatisfactory work history

G — Unfavorable interview

H — Unfavorable reference check

I — Inadequate transportation

J — Did not meet other job requisites

K — Under consideration

*SOURCE: Joseph D. Levesque, *Manual of Personnel Policies, Procedures and Operations* 2/E, (Englewood Cliffs, NJ: Prentice-Hall, Inc., 1993) p. 193.

| Your business name/logo here |

Employment Interview Rating Form[*]

INSTRUCTIONS: Assign a number from __ to __ for each scale below. In rating each scale, check the area above a phrase if you feel the phrase adequately summarizes your evaluation of the applicant. If, on the other hand, you feel that your evaluation of the applicant falls between two of the phrases along the scale, check the area between the phrases.

Please write relevant comments in the space provided above each scale. Try to give a rating for the applicant on each dimension. If you feel that you do not have sufficient information to make a rating on a certain dimension, write "Cannot Rate" in the comment space.

Applicant's Name:	Date:
Position Title:	Time:
Interviewer's Name:	Interviewer's Title:

I. *Relevant Knowledge and Skills:*
Demonstrates possession of required technical competencies and expertise acquired through past experience, education, and record of achievement to date. Ability to successfully apply knowledge.

Weight (Points)

Low (_____|_____|_____|_____) High

| Lacking in scope and grasp of technical knowledge. Some areas severely deficient or out-of-date. | Generally good grasp of job technical knowledge requirements. Some gaps in information and currency of knowledge. | Has thorough, complete and up-to-date knowledge of technical skills and abilities needed by the job. |

II. *Oral Communication Skills:*
Speaks in a clear and understandable manner so listener grasps message. Is able to persuade verbally, summarize, and justify effectively. Elicits feedback and is able to draw others into conversation. Listens attentively to others.

Weight (Points)

Low (_____|_____|_____|_____) High

| Articulation poor, mumbled a great deal, extremely difficult to understand. | Articulation good, used appropriate language. Listened attentively but some | States ideas very clearly. Speaks in complete, organized sentences. Uses |

continued

[*]SOURCE: Joseph D. Levesque, *Manual of Personnel Policies, Procedures and Operations* 2/E, (Englewood Cliffs, NJ: Prentice-Hall, Inc., 1993) pp. 182–184.

Poor listener— numerous questions had to be repeated.	questions needed to be repeated. Responded appropriately.	adequate and/or job-related vocabulary. Good listener— no repeated questions. Quick and appropriate responses.

III. *Interpersonal Sensitivity Skills:*
Ability to interact with individuals without eliciting negative or hurt feelings. Awareness of the needs and feelings of other individuals. Ability to make appropriate statements or actions in order to pacify hostile persons or situations. Answers questions diplomatically and avoids excessive argumentation. Maintains open and approachable manner.

Weight (Points)

Low (_____|_____|_____|_____) High

Would be insensitive and uncooperative. Would antagonize and alienate co-workers and employees.	Would get along well with most people. Would provide support and enthusiasm to co-workers and employees. Would be liked and respected.	Very sensitive, good listener. Very effective in conflict/ awkward interpersonal situations. Provides excellent support and enthusiasm to co-workers and staff.

IV. *Planning and Organization:*
Ability to set priorities, and to coordinate and schedule tasks or events in a logical manner to maximize staff and material resources, increase efficiency, and anticipate problems. Ability to meet a predefined goal with a prescribed timetable. Anticipates problems and is proactive rather than reactive to problems. Takes steps to alleviate problems.

Weight (Points)

Low (_____|_____|_____|_____) High

Unable to set priorities in an efficient manner. Lacks time-management skills. Would be poor decision maker, indecisive and missing critical elements. Would use old solutions for new and different problems. Little initiative and poor work under pressure.	Sets priorities most of the time. Would generally make good decisions using relevant information. Adapts well to new problems. Shows initiative and flexibility. Works well in organization, even under pressure.	Always plans work and sets priorities in accordance with reasonable time schedules. Would use all pertinent information to make excellent decisions. Good common sense. Adapts quickly and efficiently to new situations. Copes efficiently with pressure.

continued

V. *Management Control Skills:*

Coordinates and delegates work within office. Able to assess capabilities and skills in order to optimize utilization of staff personnel. Able to train and develop staff members. Keeps staff members informed on new developments, and handles/prevents personnel problems.

Weight (Points)

Low (_____|_____|_____|_____) High

Unable to delegate work in an efficient manner. No follow-through. Cannot explain requirements clearly.	Delegates work most of the time. Follows up and provides training assistance when required. Effective evaluator.	Always assigns work to appropriate person and provides training. Excellent and fair evaluator. Always follows up.

VI. *Summary and Recommendations:*

Add Ratings: I ( )   II ( )   III ( )   IV ( )   V ( ) = TOTAL (   )

( )   I do not feel this applicant is suited for this kind of work. I would definitely not recommend hiring.

( )   The applicant might do well in this kind of work, but I would have some reservations about hiring.

( )   I would endorse this applicant. I feel the individual should do well in this type of work.

( )   I would endorse this applicant with confidence. Applicant is a high-level performer and would do very well in this kind of work.

Notes/Comments:

_____
(Date)

_____
(Interviewer's Signature)

> Your business
> name/logo
> here

Telephone Reference Check [*]

By: _____ Date: _____

Name of
Applicant: _____ S.S. No. _____
     (Last)   (First)   (Middle Initial)

Position
Applied For: _____

Name of Person Title and
Being Contacted: _____ Department: _____

                                                Telephone
Company: _____ Number: _____

INFORMATION STATED

Employment
Dates: From _____ To _____

Leaving
Salary: $ _____ Per _____

Leaving
Position: _____

Reason(s)
for Leaving: _____
_____

REFERENCE CHECK

From _____ To _____

$ _____ Per _____

Started
Position: _____

Leaving
Position: _____

Reason(s)
for Leaving: _____
_____

PERFORMANCE FACTORS

Major
Duties: _____
                                             How
_____ Long: _____

Application of Quality of
Skills and Knowledge: _____ Work: _____

Ability to Plan Supervision:
and Follow Through: _____ How much required: _____

Comparison to Other Employees
in the Same Classification: _____

continued

* SOURCE: Joseph D. Levesque, *Manual of Personnel Policies, Procedures and Operations* 2/E, (Englewood Cliffs, NJ: Prentice-Hall, Inc., 1993) pp. 186–187.

SUPERVISORY ABILITY/POTENTIAL

No. of People   How   Ability to Select,
Supervised: _____ Long _____ Motivate, Discipline _____

Evaluation of
Supervisory Potential: _____

_____

PERSONAL FACTORS

Ability to Work   Work
with Others: _____ Habits: _____

Strength or
Strong Points: Technical _____ General _____

Negative or   (Note: Probe
Weak Points: suspected fault)_____

Attendance: Good_____ Average_____ Poor(state reason)_____
Were There Any Personal Reasons
that Affected Job Performance: _____

OVERALL EVALUATION

Eligible
for Rehire: Yes _____ No(state reason)_____
(Note: Describe position under
consideration and its requirements) _____

_____

Would You Consider
Applicant Suitable: Yes_____ No(state reason)_____
Any Additional
Comments: _____

_____

(ATTACH TO EMPLOYMENT APPLICATION AFTER COMPLETION)

AUTHORIZATION FOR EMPLOYMENT REFERENCE INFORMATION

TO:
Reference Name _____ Title _____
Organization _____ Phone (_____) _____-_____
Address _____
City _____ State _____ Zip _____

FROM:
(Name and title of person form to be returned to)
(Company name)
(Company address)
(City, state, zip code)

The person whose signature appears below has applied to this company for employment as a _____. In order to complete our determination of this person's overall suitability for employment in this position and with this company, it is important to us to obtain prior employment, education, and other related information about prospective employees.

While we recognize that prior employers and others having confidential information on their people are reluctant to divulge such information to "outsiders" due to privacy rights laws, we would like to assure you that the contents of this document is treated by us as confidential, is stored separately from an employee's normal personnel file in accordance with (state name) law, and is not allowed to be reviewed by applicable employees under routine access policy established by (state name) law. In addition, to assure your further comfort in supplying us with the information requested below, we have obtained the reference person's written authorization allowing you to release the information requested.

Thank you in advance for your help and cooperation in this matter, and please use the confidential envelope enclosed for the return of your response.

APPLICANT IDENTIFICATION DATA

Applicant's Name _____   Position _____

Date of Birth _____   Social Security No. _____-_____-_____

Current Address _____   City/State _____

Prior Address _____   City/State _____

Home Phone (_____) _____-_____   Drivers Lic. No. _____ State _____

PRIOR EMPLOYMENT INFORMATION

Date of Hire _____   Position Title _____

Pay Rate $ _____/_____

Previous Positions Held _____   Date _____   Rate$_____/_____

Last Position Held _____   Date _____   Rate$_____/_____

Reason for leaving _____

_____

_____   Last Work Date _____

What was this person's most noteworthy job responsibilities? _____

_____

_____

(continued)

Performance Strengths Were? _____

_____

_____

Performance Weaknesses Were? _____

_____

Date and Nature of Disciplinary Problems (prior 3 years) _____

_____

Notable Recognitions, Awards, or Achievements _____

_____

_____

BASED ON OVERALL EMPLOYMENT HOW WOULD YOU RATE THIS PERSON'S PERFORMANCE?	Superior	Good	Fair	Poor
Job Knowledge and Use of Skills				
Attention to Detail and Memory				
Use of Time/Efficiency				
Relations with Coworkers				
Relations with Superiors				
Customer Relations				
Compliance with Rules and Policies				
Tardiness				
Honesty and Trustworthiness				
Personal Grooming				
Absenteeism				
____ hours absence during last 12 months of employment				

Disclosure Authorization and Release

I hereby authorize *(name of former employer or school)* and its employees and representatives to provide any and all information they deem appropriate regarding my employment and job performance to *(name of your company)* and any of its employees, representatives, and agents. This information may be provided either verbally or in writing. In addition to authorizing the release of any information regarding my employment, I hereby fully waive any rights or claims I have or may have against *(name of your company)* and its employees, representatives, and agents; and I release *(name of your company)* and its employees, representatives, and agents from any and all liability, claims, or damages that may directly or indirectly result from the use, disclosure, or release of any such information by any person or party, whether such information is favorable or unfavorable to me.

Signature _____ Date _____

Typed or Printed Full Name _____

APPLICANT AUTHORIZATION TO ACQUIRE CREDIT REPORT

Personal Identification Information

Applicant Name _____	Birthdate _____
Current Address _____	How Long? _____
City _____	State ____ Zip _____
Previous Address _____	How Long? _____
City _____	State ____ Zip _____
Social Security # _____	Driver's Lic. # _____

Financial And Credit References

BANK AND SAVINGS ACCOUNTS	CREDIT ACCOUNTS
Name _____	Company _____
Branch _____	Address _____
Account # _____	Account # _____
Account Type _____	Account Type _____
Name _____	Company _____
Branch _____	Address _____
Account # _____	Account # _____
Account Type _____	Account Type _____
Name _____	Company _____
Branch _____	Address _____
Account # _____	Account # _____
Account Type _____	Account Type _____

(Company Name) has determined that the job for which you are being considered requires that an investigation be made about your credit history, personal character, and general reputation prior to confirming your employment. This notice is given to you in compliance with Public Law 91-508, otherwise known as the Fair Credit Reporting Act, to inform you that a routine inquiry may be made concerning your credit, character, general reputation, personal characteristics or mode of living, and we expect to receive a report thereon. Further information on the nature and scope of such report, if one is made, will be available to you upon your written request that we, or the reporting agency, provide you with a copy.

I HEREBY AUTHORIZE (Company Name) TO ACQUIRE INFORMATION FROM THE SOURCES PROVIDED ABOVE, AND OTHER APPLICABLE SOURCES DEEMED SUITABLE, CONCERNING MY CREDIT, CHARACTER, REPUTATION, AND MODE OF LIVING.

Signature _____   Date _____

IMMIGRATION

NEED HELP?
HAVE QUESTIONS?

The answers to your immigration questions may be as close as your telephone.

Inside you will find a listing of the information services provided by the Immigration and Naturalization Service (INS) to meet the public's needs.

U. S. Department of Justice
Immigration and Naturalization Service
Western Region

"Ask Immigration" and Forms by Phone

"Ask Immigration" provides 24-hour a day recorded information on a wide range of immigration benefits and procedures. INS forms may also be ordered at this number. Live assistance is available during normal working hours, once you have listened to at least one taped message. Call the number in your area:

Anchorage, AK	(907) 271-4953
Fresno, CA	(209) 487-5091
Honolulu, HI	(808) 541-1379
Las Vegas, NV	(702) 451-3597
Los Angeles, CA	(213) 526-7647
Portland, OR	(503) 326-3006
Phoenix, AZ	(602) 379-3122
Reno, NV	(702) 784-5427
Sacramento, CA	(916) 551-2785
San Diego, CA	(619) 557-5570
San Francisco, CA	(415) 705-4411
San Jose, CA	(408) 291-7876
Seattle, WA	(206) 553-5956
Spokane, WA	(509) 353-2129
Tucson, AZ	(602) 670-4624
For the hearing impaired:	1-800-767-1TDD

National Hotline

Use this national "800" number to receive the latest information about new immigration initiatives, such as the recent "green card" replacement program.

1-800-755-0777

Western Service Center Assistance

You may check the status of any petition or application you have filed with the Western Service Center by calling the number below and entering the letters WAC and the 10 digit number from the upper left-hand corner of your I-797 receipt notice. Live assistance is available during normal working hours. Assistance by mail is also available. Write: Western Service Center, P.O. Box 30111, Laguna Niguel, CA 92607-0111.

(714) 643-4880

Asylum Assistance

Recorded information about the requirements and procedures to apply for asylum may be obtained by calling the two numbers below. Live assistance is available during normal working hours.

Los Angeles	(714) 635-0126
San Francisco	(415) 744-8411

Job Discrimination

If you believe you have been discriminated against in the hiring or referral process because of national origin or citizenship, you may call the Justice Department, Office of Special Counsel.

1-800-255-7688

For the hearing impaired: TDD 1-800-237-2515

If you are unable to obtain the information you need from the sources listed in this guide, you may visit one of the INS offices listed below.

Alaska

620 East 10 Ave.
Anchorage, AK 99513-7581

Arizona

300 W. Congress
Tucson, AZ 85701-1386

2035 N. Central Ave.
Phoenix, AZ 85004

California

300 N. Los Angeles St.
Los Angeles, CA 90012

880 Front St.
San Diego, CA 92101-8834

14560 Magnolia Blvd.
Westminster, CA 92683

630 Sansome St.
San Francisco, CA 94111

280 South First St.
San Jose, CA 95113

3403 E. Plaza Blvd.
National City, CA 91950-4140

711 J St.
Sacramento, CA 95814

865 Fulton Mall
Fresno, CA 93721

Hawaii
Guam

595 Ala Moana Blvd.
Honolulu, HI 96813

238 Archbishop Flores
Agana, Guam 96910

Nevada

3373 Pepper Lane
Las Vegas, NV 89120

1351 Corporate Blvd.
Reno, NV 89502

Oregon

511 N.W. Broadway
Portland, OR 97249

Washington

815 Airport Way, South
Seattle, WA 98134

West 920 Riverside
Spokane, WA 99201

417 Chestnut St.
Yakima, WA 98907

Naturalize Now!

Form WR-730 3231
Rev. 07/01/94Y

U.S. Department of Justice
Immigration and Naturalization Service

OMB No. 1115-0136
Employment Eligibility Verification

INSTRUCTIONS
PLEASE READ ALL INSTRUCTIONS CAREFULLY BEFORE COMPLETING THIS FORM.

Anti-Discrimination Notice. It is illegal to discriminate against any individual (other than an alien not authorized to work in the U.S.) in hiring, discharging, or recruiting or referring for a fee because of that individual's national origin or citizenship status. It is illegal to discriminate against work eligible individuals. Employers **CANNOT** specify which document(s) they will accept from an employee. The refusal to hire an individual because of a future expiration date may also constitute illegal discrimination.

Section 1 - Employee. All employees, citizens and noncitizens, hired after November 6, 1986, must complete Section 1 of this form at the time of hire, which is the actual beginning of employment. **The employer is responsible for ensuring that Section 1 is timely and properly completed.**

Preparer/Translator Certification. The Preparer/Translator Certification must be completed if Section 1 is prepared by a person other than the employee. A preparer/translator may be used only when the employee is unable to complete Section 1 on his/her own. However, the employee must still sign Section 1 personally.

Section 2 - Employer. For the purpose of completing this form, the term "employer" includes those recruiters and referrers for a fee who are agricultural associations, agricultural employers, or farm labor contractors.

Employers must complete Section 2 by examining evidence of identity and employment eligibility within three (3) business days of the date employment begins. If employees are authorized to work, but are unable to present the required document(s) within three business days, they must present a receipt for the application of the document(s) within three business days and the actual document(s) within ninety (90) days. However, if employers hire individuals for a duration of less than three business days, Section 2 must be completed at the time employment begins. **Employers must record:** **1)** document title; **2)** issuing authority; **3)** document number, **4)** expiration date, if any; and **5)** the date employment begins. Employers must sign and date the certification. Employees must present original documents. Employers may, but are not required to, photocopy the document(s) presented. These photocopies may only be used for the verification process and must be retained with the I-9. **However, employers are still responsible for completing the I-9.**

Section 3 - Updating and Reverification. Employers must complete Section 3 when updating and/or reverifying the I-9. Employers must reverify employment eligibility of their employees on or before the expiration date recorded in Section 1. Employers **CANNOT** specify which document(s) they will accept from an employee.

- If an employee's name has changed at the time this form is being updated/ reverified, complete Block A.

- If an employee is rehired within three (3) years of the date this form was originally completed and the employee is still eligible to be employed on the same basis as previously indicated on this form (updating), complete Block B and the signature block.

- If an employee is rehired within three (3) years of the date this form was originally completed and the employee's work authorization has expired **or** if a current employee's work authorization is about to expire (reverification), complete Block B and:
  - examine any document that reflects that the employee is authorized to work in the U.S. (see List A **or** C),
  - record the document title, document number and expiration date (if any) in Block C, and
  - complete the signature block.

Photocopying and Retaining Form I-9. A blank I-9 may be reproduced provided both sides are copied. The Instructions must be available to all employees completing this form. Employers must retain completed I-9s for three (3) years after the date of hire **or** one (1) year after the date employment ends, whichever is later.

For more detailed information, you may refer to the INS Handbook for Employers, (Form M-274). You may obtain the handbook at your local INS office.

Privacy Act Notice. The authority for collecting this information is the Immigration Reform and Control Act of 1986, Pub. L. 99-603 (8 U.S.C. 1324a).

This information is for employers to verify the eligibility of individuals for employment to preclude the unlawful hiring, or recruiting or referring for a fee, of aliens who are not authorized to work in the United States.

This information will be used by employers as a record of their basis for determining eligibility of an employee to work in the United States. The form will be kept by the employer and made available for inspection by officials of the U.S. Immigration and Naturalization Service, the Department of Labor, and the Office of Special Counsel for Immigration Related Unfair Employment Practices.

Submission of the information required in this form is voluntary. However, an individual may not begin employment unless this form is completed since employers are subject to civil or criminal penalties if they do not comply with the Immigration Reform and Control Act of 1986.

Reporting Burden. We try to create forms and instructions that are accurate, can be easily understood, and which impose the least possible burden on you to provide us with information. Often this is difficult because some immigration laws are very complex. Accordingly, the reporting burden for this collection of information is computed as follows: **1)** learning about this form, 5 minutes; **2)** completing the form, 5 minutes; and **3)** assembling and filing (recordkeeping) the form, 5 minutes, for an average of 15 minutes per response. If you have comments regarding the accuracy of this burden estimate, or suggestions for making this form simpler, you can write to both the Immigration and Naturalization Service, 425 I Street, N.W., Room 5304, Washington, D. C. 20536; and the Office of Management and Budget, Paperwork Reduction Project, OMB No. 1115-0136, Washington, D.C. 20503.

Form I-9 (Rev. 11-21-91) N

EMPLOYERS MUST RETAIN COMPLETED I-9
PLEASE DO NOT MAIL COMPLETED I-9 TO INS

U.S. Department of Justice
Immigration and Naturalization Service

OMB No. 1115-0136
Employment Eligibility Verification

Please read instructions carefully before completing this form. The instructions must be available during completion of this form. **ANTI-DISCRIMINATION NOTICE.** It is illegal to discriminate against work eligible individuals. Employers **CANNOT** specify which document(s) they will accept from an employee. The refusal to hire an individual because of a future expiration date may also constitute illegal discrimination.

Section 1. Employee Information and Verification. To be completed and signed by employee at the time employment begins

Print Name: Last	First	Middle Initial	Maiden Name

Address *(Street Name and Number)*	Apt. #	Date of Birth *(month/day/year)*

City	State	Zip Code	Social Security #

I am aware that federal law provides for imprisonment and/or fines for false statements or use of false documents in connection with the completion of this form.

I attest, under penalty of perjury, that I am (check one of the following):
- ☐ A citizen or national of the United States
- ☐ A Lawful Permanent Resident (Alien # A_____)
- ☐ An alien authorized to work until____/____/____
  (Alien # or Admission #_____)

Employee's Signature	Date *(month/day/year)*

Preparer and/or Translator Certification. *(To be completed and signed if Section 1 is prepared by a person other than the employee.)* I attest, under penalty of perjury, that I have assisted in the completion of this form and that to the best of my knowledge the information is true and correct.

Preparer's/Translator's Signature	Print Name

Address (Street Name and Number, City, State, Zip Code)	Date *(month/day/year)*

Section 2. Employer Review and Verification. To be completed and signed by employer. **Examine one document from List A OR examine one document from List B and one from List C** as listed on the reverse of this form and record the title, number and expiration date, if any, of the document(s)

List A	OR	List B	AND	List C
Document title: _____		_____		_____
Issuing authority: _____		_____		_____
Document #: _____		_____		_____
Expiration Date *(if any):* ___/___/___		___/___/___		___/___/___
Document #: _____				
Expiration Date *(if any):* ___/___/___				

CERTIFICATION - I attest, under penalty of perjury, that I have examined the document(s) presented by the above-named employee, that the above-listed document(s) appear to be genuine and to relate to the employee named, that the employee began employment on *(month/day/year)* ____/____/____and that to the best of my knowledge the employee is eligible to work in the United States. **(State employment agencies may omit the date the employee began employment).**

Signature of Employer or Authorized Representative	Print Name	Title

Business or Organization Name	Address *(Street Name and Number, City, State, Zip Code)*	Date *(month/day/year)*

Section 3. Updating and Reverification. To be completed and signed by employer

A. New Name *(if applicable)*	B. Date of rehire *(month/day/year)* *(if applicable)*

C. If employee's previous grant of work authorization has expired, provide the information below for the document that establishes current employment eligibility.

Document Title:_____ Document #:_____ Expiration Date (if any):___/___/___

I attest, under penalty of perjury, that to the best of my knowledge, this employee is eligible to work in the United States, and if the employee presented document(s), the document(s) I have examined appear to be genuine and to relate to the individual.

Signature of Employer or Authorized Representative	Date *(month/day/year)*

Form I-9 (Rev. 11-21-91) N

LISTS OF ACCEPTABLE DOCUMENTS

LIST A		LIST B		LIST C
Documents that Establish Both Identity and Employment Eligibility	**OR**	**Documents that Establish Identity**	**AND**	**Documents that Establish Employment Eligibility**

LIST A — Documents that Establish Both Identity and Employment Eligibility

1. U.S. Passport (unexpired or expired)

2. Certificate of U.S. Citizenship *(INS Form N-560 or N-561)*

3. Certificate of Naturalization *(INS Form N-550 or N-570)*

4. Unexpired foreign passport, with *I-551 stamp or* attached *INS Form I-94* indicating unexpired employment authorization

5. Alien Registration Receipt Card with photograph *(INS Form I-151 or I-551)*

6. Unexpired Temporary Resident Card *(INS Form I-688)*

7. Unexpired Employment Authorization Card *(INS Form I-688A)*

8. Unexpired Reentry Permit *(INS Form I-327)*

9. Unexpired Refugee Travel Document *(INS Form I-571)*

10. Unexpired Employment Authorization Document issued by the INS which contains a photograph *(INS Form I-688B)*

LIST B — Documents that Establish Identity

1. Driver's license or ID card issued by a state or outlying possession of the United States provided it contains a photograph or information such as name, date of birth, sex, height, eye color, and address

2. ID card issued by federal, state, or local government agencies or entities provided it contains a photograph or information such as name, date of birth, sex, height, eye color, and address

3. School ID card with a photograph

4. Voter's registration card

5. U.S. Military card or draft record

6. Military dependent's ID card

7. U.S. Coast Guard Merchant Mariner Card

8. Native American tribal document

9. Driver's license issued by a Canadian government authority

For persons under age 18 who are unable to present a document listed above:

10. School record or report card

11. Clinic, doctor, or hospital record

12. Day-care or nursery school record

LIST C — Documents that Establish Employment Eligibility

1. U.S. social security card issued by the Social Security Administration *(other than a card stating it is not valid for employment)*

2. Certification of Birth Abroad issued by the Department of State *(Form FS-545 or Form DS-1350)*

3. Original or certified copy of a birth certificate issued by a state, county, municipal authority or outlying possession of the United States bearing an official seal

4. Native American tribal document

5. U.S. Citizen ID Card *(INS Form I-197)*

6. ID Card for use of Resident Citizen in the United States *(INS Form I-179)*

7. Unexpired employment authorization document issued by the INS *(other than those listed under List A)*

Illustrations of many of these documents appear in Part 8 of the Handbook for Employers (M-274)

D.3 Forms for Achieving Successful Initial Employment Results

These are the forms that will enable you to handle in-processing transactions of new employees along with planning for their successful transition into your employment setting. The form that has the greatest legal implication is the Employee Information Log where much of the basic employee information is required by the Fair Labor Standards Act (FLSA).

The remainder of the forms in this section also have legal implications making their use prudent but not legally compelling. Moreover, the use of these noncompelling forms become an instrumental part of planning, organizing, monitoring, and evaluating the successful adaptation of each new employee. That is, after all, our goal in hiring new employees, so it only makes sense to document each successive step in the effort to ensure their proper adjustment.

Explanations and Instructions on the Use of Initial Employment Forms

Employee Information Log Form: Every employer is required to record and maintain basic information on each of their employees. This form captures basic and supplemental data on new employees that is helpful to most employers for the compilation of this type of information. Typically, many employers end up gathering information of this type and variety on several forms rather than as a composite form. The form provided here should enable you to gather both initial employment and ongoing data relevant to employment decision making. It is suggested that you have employees complete applicable parts of this form at the time of hire, place it in a fixed place in their personnel file jacket, and enter data on training, pay changes, performance results, and the like as these events occur in order to create an easy to read and research composite record.

New Employee Orientation Checklist Form: This form enables you and other supervisors/managers in your organization to conduct consistent and thorough orientations on each new employee. It also provides you with a potentially important source of documented evidence that a particular issue, policy, benefit, or condition of employment was explained to the employee should there arise a future claim of the employee not being informed (pleading ignorance and therefore nonresponsibility). You should keep in mind that orientations are the beginning of a new employee's integration process. It is therefore important to develop a structured method, such as provided by an orientation checklist form, to start that process on the basis of providing all new employees with equally general information considered essential for their initial adjustment to internal conditions.

Employee Handbook Acknowledgement Form: The use of this form is an unfortunate result of some employees who have sued their employers and successfully alleged they were not told about, nor provided a copy of, some relevant policy or condition of their employment bearing on the nature of their lawsuit. As a consequence of an employer's vulnerability to these types of allegations, the use of this form is suggested. The form requires employees to sign their acknowledgement of receipt and responsibility to familiarize themselves with the contents of employee handbooks (or personnel policy manuals).

Initial Employment Training Plan Form: This form, as simple as it may appear, is instrumental in helping you and each new employee's supervisor plot out the specific type of training the employee should receive during this critical period of their integration into company operations. It should be developed by you and the new employee's supervisor as a planning and monitoring tool so that there exists some guidance as to what the new employee is to learn, by what methods, and what results, and the manner of determining results. The form is designed to allow you to enter briefly concise statements of what training topics are to be provided to the employee, and what the learning objectives are that will be evaluated. You and the supervisor should keep in mind that learned skills are best evaluated by work sample demonstrations, learned knowledge by written tests, and learned interactive abilities by the supervisor's documented accounts of actual work situations.

Employee Information Log*

Date prepared

Attach
Photograph
Here

EMPLOYEE

Print Last First Middle				Sex
Name				

Number Street City State Zip	Telephone No.
Address	( )

Social Security number	Driver license (state/no.)	Marital Status	Fingerprints Taken	Record
— —			

Date of Birth	Date Verified	Place of Birth	U.S. Citizen

Handicap (nature)

DEPENDENTS

No. of dependents Spouse Children Parents Other			
Name	Relationship	Sex	Age
1.			
2.			
3.			
4.			
5.			

Test	Range	Range	Init.
Clerical			
Mechanical			
Verbal			
Nonverbal			
Dexterity			
Electricity			
Language			
Typing	Speed	Errors	
Dictation	Speed	Errors	
Others (list)			

EMERGENCY

In case of emergency notify	Relationship
Name	
Address	Day Phone No. ( )
	Evening Phone No. ( )

DATA

Date Hired	Position	Location/Department/Office

Full-time/Part-time (No. of Hours)	Exempt/Non-Exempt	Starting salary	Employee (payroll) Number	EEO No.

REFERENCES	DATE VERIFIED	INITIALS

EMPLOYMENT

Education Record	Years	Graduated	Date Verified	Vocational or special training
Elementary School				
High School				
College		Years Completed		
Major Subject		Graduated?		
Degree		Date Left		
Hobbies or avocational skills				
Relative employed in this company				

COMMENTS

INITIAL

Military Record	Rank of Rating	Branch of Service	Period of Service	Date of Transfer or Discharge
Active Service				
Reserve Status				Until

continued

*SOURCE: Joseph D. Levesque, *Manual of Personnel Policies, Procedures and Operations* 2/E, (Englewood Cliffs, NJ: Prentice-Hall, Inc., 1993) pp. 197–199.

Employee Information Log— continued
Checklist of Required Forms

FORMS	DATE GIVEN TO EMPLOYEE OR SENT	DATE RETURNED	MISSING INFORMATION	DATE SENT BACK TO EMPLOYEE	FOLLOW-UP	FINAL RETENTION DATE	COMMENTS
Application							
Application Supplement							
Preemployment Medical History							
Payroll Authorization Form							
W-4 Form							
Acknowledgment of Employee Handbook							
Security Form							
Insurance Enrollment Form							Effective Date
Reference Verification							
Others (list)							

Company Service Record

Date Effective	Job Title	Exempt Nonexempt	Hours	Rate	Location	Nature of Change

Employee Educational Record

Date	Title of Class or Course	Remarks

Performance Evaluation Reports

Date	Date	Date	Date	Date	Date

Employee Leave Record

Date	Code	Days	Date	Code	Days

CODE:
DF = Death in Family
J = Jury Duty
S = Sick Leave
V = Vacation
FH = Floating Holiday
X-1 = Excused Absence-
     Other (with pay)
X-2 = Excused Absence-
     Other (without pay)
U = Unexcused Absence
     (without pay)
M = Military Leave

continued

452   *WHAT FORMS ARE REQUIRED TO SUPPORT A SMOOTH AND ORDERLY HIRING PROCESS*

Employee Information Log—continued
Pre-Employment Medical History
(to be completed by applicant)

Date Prepared _____

Name	Last	First	Initial	Social Security Number __ __

Have you had or do you now have any of the following: (Check yes or no)

YES	NO		YES	NO		YES	NO	
		Abdominal Pain			Gall Bladder Trouble or Gall Stones			Rupture
		Alcoholism			Goiter			Serum Reaction
		Allergy			Hearing Impairment			Severe Eye, Ear, Nose, or Throat Trouble
		Arthritis			Hernia			Shortness of Breath
		Asthma			High or Low Blood Pressure			Sinusitis
		Back Injury			Jaundice			Skin Disorders
		Bone, Joint, or Other Deformity			Kidney Disease, Nephritis			Sleeplessness
		Chest or Lung Disease			Kidney Stone or Blood in Urine			Spitting of Blood
		Chronic Back Trouble			Loss of Memory			Stomach, Liver, or Intestinal Trouble
		Chronic Cough			Marked Fatigue			TB
		Constipation			Marked Increase or Decrease in Weight			Tumor, Growth, Cyst, or Cancer
		Depression			Menstrual Difficulty			Undue Worry or Fear
		Diabetes			Nervous or Mental Trouble			Veneral Disease
		Discharging Ear			Pain or Pressure in Chest			HAVE YOU EVER:
		Dizziness or Unconsciousness			Painful or Trick Shoulder, Elbow, or Knee			Worn Glasses
		Drug or Narcotic Addiction			Palpitation or Heart Disease			Worn an Artificial Eye
		Epilepsy or Convulsions			Paralysis (Including Infantile)			Worn Hearing Aids
		Family History Diabetes			Piles or Rectal Disease			Worn a Brace or Support
		Female Disorders			Pleurisy			Had Foot Trouble
		Fracture			Pneumonia			Lived with Anyone Who Had TB
		Frequent Headaches			Pregnancy			Had a Heart Murmur
		Frequent or Painful Urination			Rheumatic Fever			

1. Have you had illness other than those listed above?_____ No _____Yes if yes, describe and indicate dates below:

   Illness_____ Date _____

   Illness_____ Date _____

2. Have you been under a doctor's care within the past 5 years?_____No _____ Yes if yes, give details:_____

   _____

3. Have you ever had an injury at work elsewhere covered by Workers' Compensation Insurance? _____No _____Yes if yes, describe below

   Injury_____Date_____Employer_____

4. Was permanent disability awarded?_____No _____Yes if yes, give percent_____

5. Are you allergic to any drugs? _____No _____Yes if yes, what?_____

6. Are you currently taking medication? _____No _____Yes if yes, what?_____

7. Is vision good in both eyes? _____Yes _____No if no, explain below:
   Corrected by Glasses_____Contact Lenses_____Other_____

8. Is hearing good in both ears? _____Yes _____No if no, explain:_____

9. Do you have any physical limitations/restrictions? _____No _____Yes if yes, explain below:

   _____

   _____

I certify that information given above is accurate to the best of my knowledge. I understand that any misstatement of fact is grounds for dismissal.

SIGNATURE _____   DATE _____

**Your business
name/logo
here**

NEW EMPLOYEE ORIENTATION CHECKLIST*

NOTE: All appropriate information must be discussed with each new employee.

Employee's Name: _____   Social Security Number: _____

Job Title: _____   Date: _____

PERSONNEL DEPARTMENT: In order to avoid duplication of instructions, the information checked (✓) below has been given or explained to the employee by the Personnel Department.

I. *Compensation and Benefits*
- Time sheet/card ( )
- Payroll procedures ( )
- Insurance Program Booklet ( )
- Pension Plan Booklet ( )
- Educational Assistance ( )
- Credit Union ( )
- Stock Purchase Plan ( )
- Savings Bond Plan ( )
- Sick Benefits, A&S, Limitations, etc. ( )

II. *Leaves, Promotions, and Transfers*
- Probationary Period ( )
- Performance Evaluations ( )
- Promotions ( )
- Transfers ( )
- Vacations ( )
- Holidays ( )
- Absences or Tardiness ( )
- Jury Duty ( )
- Leaves of Absence—Maternity/ Medical, etc. ( )

III. *General*
- Employee Handbook/Labor Agreement/Rules Booklet ( )
- Disciplinary Procedures ( )
- Difficulties, Complaints, Discrimination, and Grievance Procedures ( )
- Patient Agreement ( )
- ID Card ( )
- Introduction to Guards ( )
- Transportation ( )
- Parking Facilities ( )
- Safety Booklet ( )
- First Aid and Requirements of Reporting Injury ( )
- Bulletin Boards/Company Newsletters ( )
- Voluntary Resignation Notice ( )
- (Others)

SUPERVISOR: The following is a checklist of information necessary to orient the new employee to the job in your department. Please check off each point as you discuss it with the employee and return to the _____ within _____ days following employee placement in the job.

(continued)

*SOURCE: Joseph D. Levesque, *Manual of Personnel Policies, Procedures and Operations* 2/E, (Englewood Cliffs, NJ: Prentice-Hall, Inc., 1993) pp. 201–203.

I. *Receive the New Employee*
- Review copy of employee's application. Be familiar with employee's experience, training, and education. ( )
- Review job description with employee, including the duties, responsibilities, and working relationships. ( )
- Discuss with the employee the unit organization and the department division organization. Explain the function of your department/division as related to the total organization and how the employee fits in. ( )
- Discover the employee's career goals and objectives. Relate them to the goals and objectives of the department. ( )
- Confirm that employee has a copy of employee handbook. Set aside one hour in first week for employee to read employee handbook and to understand it. ( )

II. *Welcome the New Employee*

Introduce Employee to Co-workers:
- Indicate to each co-worker the new employee's position. ( )
- Explain the functions of each person as you introduce the new employee. ( )

Show New Employee Around:
- Tour the department, plant, or company. ( )
- Explain where lavatories, coffee areas, and parking facilities are located. ( )
- Explain the various departments within the organization. ( )

III. *Introduce the New Employee to Job*
- Ensure that new employee's working area, equipment, tools, and supplies are prepared and available. ( )
- Explain the levels of supervision within the department. ( )
- Provide new employee with necessary and required training. ( )
- Explain use of: Telephones (personal/company calls) ( )
  - Copy machines ( )
  - Company vehicles ( )
  - Mail procedures ( )
  - Supply procedures ( )
- Explain hours of work, overtime, call-in procedures. ( )
- Give new employee department telephone number. ( )
- Review location of department's first aid equipment. ( )
- Explain housekeeping responsibilities. ( )

IV. *Follow-Up:*
- Set date and time within one week to cover any questions or concerns of the new employee. ( )
- Inform employee of date for first probationary review. ( )

_____   _____
Supervisor's Signature   Employee's Signature

_____   _____
Supervisor's Title   Date

_____
Department

_____
Date

**UPON COMPLETION, FILE ORIGINAL IN EMPLOYEE'S
PERSONNEL FOLDER, WITH A COPY TO THE EMPLOYEE**

PERSONNEL MANUAL/EMPLOYEE HANDBOOK
ACKNOWLEDGMENT FORM*

This will acknowledge my receipt of *(Company)* personnel handbook and my responsibility to become familiar with its contents. I further understand and agree to the following:

- This handbook represents a brief summary of some of the more important *(Company)* policies relative to employment, but not intended to be all inclusive of company policies or practices.

- The *(Company)* retains the sole right in its business judgment to modify, suspend, interpret, or cancel in whole or part at any time, and with or without notice, any of the published or unpublished personnel policies or practices.

- This *(Company)* does not recognize verbal or implied contracts for employment. Only the *(President)* of the *(Company)* has the authority to enter into any agreement of employment for specified durations. Such employment agreements will only be valid and binding on the *(Company)* when the agreement is set forth in a written document signed by the employee and *(President)*, or other authorized agent, of the *(Company)*.

- The contents of this handbook does not constitute an expressed or implied contract of employment.

- I have the right to end my employment relationship with the *(Company)*, with or without advance notice or cause, and I acknowledge that the *(Company)* has the same right.

Employee's Name (Print or type): ————————————————————

Employee's Signature: ————————————————————————

Date: —————————————— Witness: ————————————————

Title: —————————————— Date: ————————————————

---

*SOURCE: Joseph D. Levesque, *Manual of Personnel Policies, Procedures and Operations* 2/E, (Englewood Cliffs, NJ: Prentice-Hall, Inc., 1993) p. 205.

INITIAL EMPLOYMENT TRAINING PLAN FORM

Employee's Name _____ Job Title _____

Hire Date: _____ Supervisor: _____ Job Title _____

KNOWLEDGE LEARNING OBJECTIVES

1.		
2.		
3.		
4.		
5.		
6.		
7.		
8.		
9.		
10.		

SKILLS & ABILITIES LEARNING OBJECTIVES

1.		
2.		
3.		
4.		
5.		
6.		
7.		
8.		
9.		
10.		

References

Chapter 1: Prehire Issues You Should Consider Before Getting Started

Joseph D. Levesque, *People in Organizations: A Guide to Solving Critical Human Resource Problems*, (Sacramento, CA: American Chamber of Commerce Publishers, 1989).

George Munchus, "Employee Leasing: Benefits and Threats," *Personnel Practice Ideas* (June 1988).

J. L. Simonetti and others, "Temporary Employees: A Permanent Boon?" *Personnel* (August 1988).

Guy W. Millner, "Professional 'Temps' in Today's Workforce," *Personnel* (October 1989).

Marvin R. Selter, "On the Plus Side of Employee Leasing," *Personnel Journal* (April 1986).

Paul C. Driskell, "A Manager's Checklist for Labor Leasing," *Personnel Journal* (October 1986).

William G. Kuchta, "Part-Year vs. Part-Time Employment," *Personnel Administrator* (May 1988).

Lennie Copeland, "Valuing Diversity, Part 2: Pioneers and Champions of Change," *Personnel* (July 1988).

Jeff Hallett, "New Patterns in Working," *Personnel Administrator* (December 1988).

Wayne Wending, "Response to a Changing Work Force," *Personnel Administrator* (November 1988).

Dan Kleinman, "What to Look for in Tomorrow's Employee," *Personnel Journal* (October 1987).

Edward D. Bewayo, "What Employees Look for in First and Subsequent Employers," *Personnel* (April 1986).

Lynne F. McGee, "Innovative Labor Shortage Solutions," *Personnel Administrator* (December 1989).

Jane Easter Bahls, "Getting Full-Time Work from Part-Time Employees," *Management Review* (February 1990).

Elizabeth Ehrlich, "The Mommy Track: Juggling Kids and Careers in Corporate America Takes a Controversial Turn," *Business Week* (March 20, 1989).

Gloria Glickstein and Donald C. Z. Ramer, "The Alternative Employment Marketplace," *Personnel Administrator* (February 1988).

Nancy Howe, "Match Temp Services to Your Needs," *Personnel Journal* (March 1989).

Charles Ford Harding, "How to Analyze a Labor Market," *Proceeding From The 41st ASPA Conference, Boston, MA* (June 1989).

Barbara Mandell and Susan Kohler-Gray, "Management Development That Values Diversity," *Personnel* (March 1990).

Steve Bergsman, "Part-Time Professionals Make the Choice," *Personnel Administrator* (July 1990).

Hermine Zagat Levine, "Alternative Work Schedules: Do They Meet Workforce Needs? Part 1," *Personnel* (February 1987).

Arlene Martin, "There's No Place Like Home . . . To Work," *Human Resource Executive* (July 1989).

"Some Facts About Employee Leasing," *Personnel Practice Ideas* (June 1988).

Sally McKinney, "Interim Managers: Stop-Gap Staffing," *Personnel Journal* (February 1992).

William M. Lewis and Nancy Molloy, *How to Choose and Use Temporary Services*, (Washington, DC: AMACOM Books, 1991).

Jeffery E. Struve, "Making the Most of Temporary Workers," *Personnel Journal* (November 1991).

Linda Thornburg, "The Age Wave Hits: What Older Workers Want and Need," *HR Magazine* (February 1995).

Kim Macalister, "The X Generation," *HR Magazine* (May 1994).

Chapter 2: How to Develop and Use Job Descriptions to Achieve Quality Hiring Results

Joseph D. Levesque, *Manual of Personnel Policies, Procedures and Operations* 2/E, (Englewood Cliffs, NJ: Prentice-Hall, Inc., 1993).

Maryellen Lo Bosco, "Job Analysis, Job Evaluation, and Job Classification," *Personnel* (May 1985).

P. M. Wright and K. N. Wexley, "How to Choose the Kind of Job Analysis You Really Need," *Personnel* (May 1985).

Roger J. Plachy, "Writing Job Descriptions That Get Results," *Personnel* (October 1987).

Philip C. Grant, "Why Job Descriptions Don't Work," *Personnel Journal* (January 1988).

Philip C. Grant, "What Use Is a Job Description?" *Personnel Journal* (February 1988).

Edward Levine, "Evaluation of Job Analysis Methods by Experienced Job Analysts," *Academy of Management Journal* (June 1983).

Leonard N. Persson, *The Handbook of Job Evaluations & Job Pricing*, Bureau of Law & Business, Inc. (1982).

"How to Analyze Jobs: A Step-by-Step Approach," *Bureau of Business & Law, Inc.* (1982).

Chapter 3: Using Personnel Policies to Shape Effective Hiring Practices

Joseph D. Levesque, *People in Organizations: A Guide to Solving Critical Human Resource Problems*, (Sacramento, CA: American Chamber of Commerce Publishers, 1989).

Joseph D. Levesque, *Manual of Personnel Policies, Procedures and Operations* 2/E, (Englewood Cliffs, NJ: Prentice-Hall, Inc., 1993).

David A. Copus (Ed.), *Model Human Resource Policies.* (Alexandria, VA: American Society for Personnel Administration, 1989).

Robert J. Nobile, "Putting Out Fires With a No Smoking Policy," *Personnel* (March 1990).

J. Carroll Swart, "Corporate Smoking Policies: Today and Tomorrow," *Personnel* (August 1988).

Robert Ford and Frank McLaughlin, "Nepotism," *Personnel Journal* (September 1985).

Rosen, Benson, and Schwoerer, "Balanced Protection Policies," *HR Magazine* (February 1990).

Hermine Zagat Levine, "Job Posting Practices," *Personnel* (November-December 1984).

Milan Moravec, "Effective Job Posting Fills Dual Needs," *HR Magazine* (September 1990).

"Promotion From Within: A Method of Developing Tomorrow's Managers," *Small Business Report* (January 1987).

Horace E. Johns and H. Ronald Moser, "Where Has EEO Taken Personnel Policies?" *Personnel* (September 1989).

Chapter 4: Maintaining Proper Hiring and Employment Records

Joseph D. Levesque, *Manual of Personnel Policies, Procedures and Operations* 2/E, (Englewood Cliffs, NJ: Prentice-Hall, Inc., 1993).

Joseph D. Levesque, *People in Organizations: A Guide to Solving Critical Human Resource Problems*, (Sacramento, CA: American Chamber of Commerce Publishers, 1989).

Margaret Magnus and David J. Thomsen, "Microcomputer Software Guide," *Personnel Journal* (February 1990).

"Personnel Records May Not Be as Confidential as You Think," *Personnel Practice Ideas*, Warren, Gorham & Lamont, Inc. (September 1988).

"Many Control and Limit Access to Personnel Files, Survey Finds," *Resource*, American Society for Personnel Administration (June 1989).

"Guide to Record Retention Requirements (CFR)," *U.S. Government Printing Office* (1989).

Chester Delaney, "Integrated Powerhouses," *HR Magazine* (March 1990).

D. E. Kirrane and P. R. Kirrane, "Managing by Experts Systems," *HR Magazine* (March 1990).

Barbara A. Bland-Acosta, "Developing an HRIS Privacy Policy," *Personnel Administrator* (July 1988).

Chapter 5: Planning and Sourcing Your Recruiting Efforts and

Chapter 6: Selecting the Best Recruiting Methods, and Designing Your Own Advertising Material to Attract the Attention of Quality Applicants

Diane Authur, *Recruiting, Interviewing, Selecting & Orienting New Employees*, (New York, NY: AMACOM, 1986).

Wayne F. Cascio (Ed.), *Human Resource Planning Employment & Placement*, (Washington, DC: The Bureau of National Affairs, ASPA-BNA Series 2, 1989).

Erica Klein, *Write Great Ads: A Step-by-Step Approach*. New York, NY: John Wiley & Sons, Inc., 1990.

Recruiting and Hiring Handbook, Bureau of Business Practices, (Prentice-Hall, Inc., 1990).

Andrew Bargerstock, "Low-Cost Recruiting for Quality," *HR Magazine* (August 1990).

Allan Halcrow, "Anatomy of a Recruitment Ad," *Personnel Journal* (August 1985).

Allan Halcrow, "Employees Are Your Best Recruiters," *Personnel Journal* (November 1988).

Thomas Bergmann and M. Susan Taylor, "College Recruitment: What Attracts Students to Organizations," *Personnel* (May-June 1984).

Eileen Kaplan, "College Recruitment: The View from Both Sides," *Personnel* (November 1985).

Laura M. Graves, "College Recruitment: Removing Personal Bias from Selection Decisions," *Personnel* (March 1989).

Donald A. Levenson, "Needed: Revamped Recruiting Services," *Personnel* (July 1988).

Thomas J. Hutton, "Increasing the Odds for Successful Searches," *Personnel Journal* (September 1987).

John J. Herring, "Establishing an Integrated Employee Recruiting System," *Personnel* (July 1986).

Margaret Magnus, "Recruitment Ads at Work," *Personnel Journal* (August 1985).

Margaret Magnus, "Is Your Recruitment All It Can Be?" *Personnel Journal* (February 1987).

R. Wayne Mondy and others, "Successful Recruitment: Matching Sources and Methods," *Personnel* (September 1987).

Bruce S. Algar, "How to Hire in a Hurry: Meet Increased Demands for Personnel," *Personnel Journal* (September 1986).

Cathy Edwards, "Aggressive Recruitment: The Lessons of High-Tech Hiring," *Personnel Journal* (January 1986).

Albert H. McCarthy, "Research Provides Advertising Focus," *Personnel Journal* (August 1989).

Melissa A. Rogge, "Locate and Hire Technical Employees," *Personnel Journal* (November 1989).

Liz Amante, "Help Wanted: Creative Recruitment Tactics," *Personnel* (October 1989).

Elizabeth Blacharczyk, "Recruiters Challenged by Economy, Shortages, Unskilled," *HR News* (February 1990).

Chuck Cosentino and others, "Choosing the Right People," *HR Magazine* (March 1990).

Milton N. Dossin and Nancie L. Merritt, "Sign-On Bonuses Score for Recruiters," *HR Magazine* (March 1990).

Ronal G. Borgman, "Winning the Recruiting Battle in Small Business," *Journal of Small Business Management* (July 1973).

Sara L. Rynes and Alison E. Barber, "Applicant Attraction Strategies: An Organizational Perspective," *Academy of Management Review*, Vol. 15, No. 2 (1990).

Bob Martin, "Recruitment Ad Ventures," *Personnel Journal* (August 1987).

Barbara Hunger, "How to Choose a Recruitment Advertising Agency," *Personnel Journal* (December 1985).

Jennifer Koch, "Recruitment Ads With Flair," *Personnel Journal* (October 1989).

Jennifer Koch, "Beyond Nuts & Bolts," *Personnel Journal* (February 1990).

John P. Kohl and David B. Stephens, "Wanted: Recruitment Advertising That Doesn't Discriminate," *Personnel* (February 1989).

"Recruitment Advertising: Ten of the Finest," *Human Resource Executive* (August 1989).

Andy Bargerstock and Hank Engel, "Six Ways to Boost Employee Referral," *HR Magazine* (December 1994).

Lizabeth A. Barclary and Alan R. Bass, "Get the Most from Recruitment Efforts," *HR Magazine* (June 1994).

William C. Delone, "Telephone Job Posting Cuts Costs," *Personnel Journal* (April 1993).

Ben V. Luden, "HR vs. Executive Search," *Personnel Journal* (May 1992).

Catherine D. Fyock, "19 Ways to Recruit Top Talent," *HR Magazine* (July 1991).

Anthony M. Micolo, "High-Tech Recruiting at Low Cost," *HR Magazine* (August 1991).

Maury Hanigan, "Key Campus Strategies," *HR Magazine* (July 1991).

Chapter 7: Using Preemployment Selection Tests to Evaluate Applicants and Make the Right Hiring Choice

Wayne F. Casio (Ed.), *Human Resource Planning Employment & Placement*, (Washington, DC: Bureau of National Affairs, ASPA-BNA Series 2, 1989).

James A. Douglas and others, *Employment Testing Manual*, (Boston, MA: Warren, Gorham & Lamont, 1989).

The Guide to Background Investigations, (Tulsa, OK: National Employment Screening Services, Source Publications, 1989).

Jeffrey G. Allen, *The Perfect Job Reference*, (New York, NY: John Wiley & Sons, Inc., 1990).

Raymond M. Berger, "How to Evaluate a Selection Test," *Personnel Journal* (February 1987).

Karen M. Evans and Randall Brown, "Reducing Recruitment Risk Through Preemployment Testing," *Personnel* (September 1988).

Laurence V. Moore, "Maps to a Good Match," *Personnel Administrator* (May 1988).

K. Dow Scott and others, "Selecting the Right Employee," *Personnel Administrator* (December 1988).

John Aberth, "Pre-Employment Testing Is Loosing Favor," *Personnel Journal* (September 1986).

Jim Castelli, "Finding the Right Fit," *HR Magazine* (September 1990).

C. Cosentino and others, "Choosing the Right People," *HR Magazine* (March 1990).

Linda Stockman Vines, "Unmasking the Work Force," *Human Resources Executive* (October 1989).

Sylvia Levine, "Written Honesty Exams: Panacea or Pandora's Box?" *EEO Review* (August 1987).

Robin Inwald, "How to Evaluate Psychological/Honesty Tests," *Personnel Journal* (May 1988).

Robin Inwald, "Those 'Little White Lies' of Honesty Test Vendors," *Personnel* (June 1990).

Hermine Zagat Levine, "Supervisory Selection Systems," *Personnel* (October 1986).

Rosemary M. Collyer, "Pre-Employment Medical Testing: An Overview," *ASPA Legal Report* (Summer 1989).

David Stier, "Many Ask But Don't Give References," *HR News* (February 1990).

Kenneth L. Soveriegn, "Pitfalls of Withholding Reference Information," *Personnel Journal* (March 1990).

Thomas J. Von der Embse and Rodney E. Wyse, "Those Reference Letters: How Useful Are They?" *Personnel* (January 1985).

Robert Half, "Tactics for Aggressive Reference Checking," *Personnel Journal* (September 1985).

Erwin S. Stanton, "Fast-and-Easy Reference Checking by Telephone," *Personnel Journal* (November 1988).

Michael G. Aamodt and Deoborah L. Peggans, "Rejecting Applicants With Tact," *Personnel Journal* (April 1988).

Linda Palmarozza, "Preemployment Testing: Truth and Consequences," *Human Resource Executive* (April 1990).

Eric Rolfe Greenberg, "Workplace Testing: The 1990 AMA Survey, Part 1 & 2," *Personnel* (June-July 1990).

"Assessment Centers: Identifying Leadership Through Testing," *Small Business Report* (June 1987).

"Reference Checks: The Sticky Area of Getting and Giving Information," *Personnel Practice Ideas* (November 1987).

"Arrests and Convictions: Can You Investigate When Records Are Sealed?" *Personnel Manager's Legal Reporter* (August 1989).

"How to Use Public Records in the Hiring Process," *Personnel Practice Ideas* (September 1989).

"Psychometric Testing: Facts and Fallacies," *Human Resource Executive* (July 1990).

Bill Leonard, "The Tough Decision to Use Confidential Information," *HR Magazine* (July 1993).

Mark Thomas and Harry Brull, "Tests Improve Hiring Decisions at Franciscan," *Personnel Journal* (November 1993).

Charlene Marmer Solomon, "Testing Is Not at Odds with Diversity Efforts," *Personnel Journal* (March 1993).

Scott L. Martin and Loren P. Lehnen, "Select the Right Employees Through Testing," *Personnel Journal* (June 1992).

Rob Brookler, "Industry Standards in Workplace Drug Testing," *Personnel Journal* (April 1992).

"Adjusted Scoring Now Illegal," *HR Magazine Legal Reporter* (March 1992).

Chapter 8: Screening Applicants and Conducting Interviews

Joseph D. Levesque, *Manual of Personnel Policies, Procedures and Operations* 2/E, (Englewood Cliffs, NJ: Prentice-Hall, Inc., 1993).

Neil Yeager and Lee Hough, *Power Interviews: Job-Winning Tactics from Fortune 500 Recruiters*, (New York, NY: John Wiley & Sons, Inc., 1990).

Jeffrey G. Allen, *The Complete Q & A Job Interview Book*, (New York, NY: John Wiley & Sons, Inc., 1988).

Diane Arthur, *Recruiting, Interviewing, Selecting, and Orienting New Employees*, (New York, NY: AMACOM Books, 1986).

Stephen D. Bruce, *Face-to-Face: Every Manager's Guide to Better Interviewing*, (Madison, CT: Bureau of Law & Business, Inc., 1984).

Thomas F. Casey, "Making the Most of a Selection Interview," *Personnel* (September 1990).

William H. Holley and others, "Resumes and Cover Letters: What Do HR Managers Really Want?" *Personnel* (December 1988).

Robert P. Vecchio, "The Problem of Phony Resumes: How to Spot a Ringer Among the Applicants," *Personnel* (March-April 1984).

Jo Ann L. Compton, "Interview to Determine Potential Success, Fit," *Personnel Administrator* (April 1988).

M. Ronald Buckley and Robert W. Eder, "The First Impression," *HR News* (February 1990).

C. Thomas Dortch, "Job-Person Match," *Personnel Journal* (June 1989).

Dan Kleinman, "What to Look for in Tomorrow's Employee," *Personnel Journal* (October 1987).

Barry M. Farrell, "The Art and Science of Employment Interviews," *Personnel Journal* (May 1986).

David J. Weston and Dennis L. Warmke, "Dispelling the Myths About Panel Interviews," *Personnel Administrator* (May 1988).

Vincent Loretto, "Effective Interviewing Is Based on More Than Intuition," *Personnel Journal* (December 1986).

Diane Arthur, "Preparing for the Interview," *Personnel* (February 1986).

Michael W. Mercer and John J. Seres, "Using Scorable Interview 'Tests' in Hiring," *Personnel* (June 1987).

Susan Harwood and Dennis R. Briscoe, "Improving the Interview Process," *Personnel* (September 1987).

Ronald J. Karren and Stella M. Nkomo, "So, You Want to Work For Us . . . ," *Personnel Administrator* (April 1988).

John J. Coleman, "Age-Conscious Remarks: What You Say Can Be Used Against You," *Personnel* (September 1985).

Books Mitchell, "Interviewing Face-to-Interface," *Personnel* (January 1990).

Lester L. Tobias, "Selecting for Excellence: How to Hire the Best," *Nonprofit World* (March-April 1990).

Elvis C. Stephens, "How Resume Fraud Works as a Defense in EEO Cases," *HR Magazine* (February 1994).

Larry Stevens, "Resume Scanning Simplifies Tracking," *Personnel Journal* (April 1993).

Sandy Sillup, "Applicant Screening Cuts Turnover Costs," *Personnel Journal* (May 1992).

Dennis L. Warmke and David J. Weston, "Success Dispels Myths About Panel Interviews," *Personnel Journal* (April 1992).

Chapter 9: Making Employment Offers and Negotiating Employment Agreements

Joseph D. Levesque, *Manual of Personnel Policies, Procedures and Operations* 2/E, (Englewood Cliffs, NJ: Prentice-Hall, Inc., 1993).

Joseph D. Levesque, *People in Organizations: A Guide to Solving Critical Human Resource Problems,* (Sacramento, CA: American Chamber of Commerce Publishers, 1989).

Deborah J. Launer, *Modern Personnel Forms* (Rev. Ed.), (Boston, MA: Warren, Gorham & Lamont, Inc., 1983).

Milton N. Dossin and Nancie L. Merritt, "Sign-On Bonuses Score Big For Recruiters," *HR Magazine* (March 1990).

Walter W. Tornow, "Contract Redesign," *Personnel Administrator* (October 1988).

Robert Goddard and others, "The Job-Hire Sale," *Personnel Administrator* (June 1989).

Morton E. Grossman, "Relocation Is on the Rise," *Personnel Journal* (December 1988).

Colette A. Frayne and Phillip L. Hunsaker, "Strategies for Successful Interpersonal Negotiating," *Personnel* (May-June 1984).

Chapter 10: Assuring Successful Employment Adjustment Through Orientation and Integration

Joseph D. Levesque, *Manual of Personnel Policies, Procedures and Operations* 2/E, (Englewood Cliffs, NJ: Prentice-Hall, Inc., 1993).

Joseph D. Levesque, *People in Organizations: A Guide to Solving Critical Human Resource Problems*, (Sacramento, CA: American Chamber of Commerce Publishers, 1989).

Diane Arthur, *Recruiting, Interviewing, Selecting & Orienting New Employees*, (New York, NY: AMACOM Books, 1986).

Edmund J. McGarrel Jr., "An Orientation System That Builds Productivity," *Personnel* (November-December 1983).

Marcia Manter and Janice Y. Benjamin, "How to Hold on to First Careerists," *Personnel Administrator* (September 1989).

Milan Moravec and Kevin Wheeler, "Speed New Hires Into Success," *Personnel Journal* (March 1989).

Milan Moravec and others, "Getting College Hires on Track Fast," *Personnel* (May 1989).

Kenneth Oldfield, "Survival of the Newest," *Personnel Journal* (March 1989).

Jeffrey P. Davidson, "Starting the New Hire on the Right Foot," *Personnel* (August 1986).

William H. Wagel, "Making New Hires Part of the Company," *Personnel* (May 1986).

Susan Berger, "Ongoing Orientation at Metropolitan Life," *Personnel Journal* (December 1989).

Muhammad Jamal, "Shift Work Creates Unusual Problems," *Personnel Journal* (May 1989).

H. Lon Addams, "Up to Speed in 90 Days: An Orientation Plan," *Personnel Journal* (December 1985).

Brian Bolton and Richard Roessler, "After the Interview: How Employers Rate Handicapped Employees," *Personnel* (July 1985).

Margo Murray, *Beyond the Myths and Majic of Mentoring: How to Facilitate an Effective Mentoring Program*, (San Francisco, CA: Jossey Bass, 1991).

Richard F. Federico, "Six Ways to Solve the Orientation Blues," *HR Magazine* (May 1991).

Chapter 11: Training New Employees to Meet Job Demands and Monitoring Their Performance and

Chapter 12: Reducing Costly Turnover of Quality Employees Through Retention Efforts

Joseph D. Levesque, *People in Organizations: A Guide to Solving Critical Human Resource Problems*, (Sacramento, CA: American Chamber of Commerce Publishers, 1989).

Robert L. Craig (Ed.), *Training & Development Handbook: A Guide to Human Resource Development*, 2nd Ed., (New York, NY: McGraw-Hill, Inc., 1976).

How to Develop and Conduct Successful In-Company Training Programs, (Chicago, IL: Dartnell Publishing Co., 1974).

Eric Rolfe Greenberg, "Some Pointers on Basic Training Techniques," *Personnel* (September 1989).

Isiah Turner, "Training and Retraining: Preparing for the Year 2000 and Beyond," *Proceedings From The 41st ASPA Conference, Boston, MA* (June 1989).

George Albert Ford, "Training Trends and Techniques for the 1990s," *Proceedings From The 41st ASPA Conference, Boston, MA* (June 1989).

Martin Levy, "Almost-Perfect Performance Appraisals," *Personnel Journal* (April 1989).

Anthony J. Vaccaro, "Personality Clash," *Personnel Administrator* (September 1988).

Beverly L. Kaye, "Performance Appraisal and Career Development: A Shotgun Marriage," *Personnel* (March-April 1984).

Kenneth R. Phillips, "Red Flags in Performance Appraisal," *Training & Development Journal* (March 1987).

Frank L. Schmidt and others, "Impact of Job Experience and Ability on Job Knowledge, Work Sample Performance, and Supervisory Ratings of Job Performance," *Journal of Applied Psychology*, Vol. 71, No. 3 (1986).

William Wertzel, "How to Improve Performance Through Successful Performance Appraisals," *Personnel* (October 1987).

L. R. Watts and H. C. White, "Assessing Employee Turnover," *Personnel Administrator* (April 1988).

G. S. Bladeslee and others, "How Much Is Turnover Costing You?" *Personnel Journal* (November 1985).

Philip J. Harkins, "Manage Turnover," *Personnel Journal* (May 1989).

E. F. Jackofsky and others, "Reducing Turnover Among Part Time Employees," *Personnel* (May 1986).

Jac Fitz-enz, "Getting—and Keeping—Good Employees," *Personnel* (August 1990).

"Employee Turnover: Management and Control," *Small Business Report* (February 1987).

"BNA's Quarterly Report on Job Absence and Turnover," *Bulletin To Management*, Bureau of National Affairs (September 1990).

Appendix A: What Employers Should Know About Employment Laws and How to Avoid Hiring Process Violations

Joseph D. Levesque, *People in Organizations: A Guide to Solving Critical Human Resource Problems*, (Sacramento, CA: American Chamber of Commerce Publishers, 1989).

Steven C. Kahn and others, *Personnel Director's Legal Guide*, 2nd Ed., (New York, NY: Warren, Gorham & Lamont, Inc., 1990).

How to Write an Affirmative Action Plan, (Madison, CT: Bureau of Law & Business, Inc., 1989).

William J. Connelly, "How to Navigate the River of Legal Liability When Hiring," *Personnel Journal* (March 1986).

Sandra Baley, "The Legalities of Hiring in the 1980s," *Personnel Journal* (March 1985).

David E. Terpstra, "Who Gets Sexually Harassed?: Knowing How to Educate and Control Your Work Environment," *Personnel Administrator* (March 1989).

David E. Terpstra and S. E. Cook, "Complaint Characteristics and Reported Behaviors and Consequences Associated With Formal Sexual Harassment Charges," *Personnel Psychology*, Vol. 38 (1985).

Charlene M. Solomon, "The Corporate Response to Work Force Diversity," *Personnel Journal* (August 1989).

Diane Feldman, "Employing Physically and Mentally Impaired Employees," *Personnel* (January 1988).

Alfred Klein, "Employees Under the Influence—Outside the Law," *Personnel Journal* (September 1986).

James E. Peters, "How to Bridge the Hiring Gap: Linking People With Disabilities With Employers Who Need Qualified Workers," *Personnel Administrator* (October 1989).

James G. Frierson, "Religion in the Workplace: Dealing in Good Faith?" *Personnel Journal* (July 1988).

Charles Burgess and Guangli Zhu, "Should All Mentally Challenged People Work?" *Personnel* (January 1990).

Eric Rolfe Greenberg, "Workplace Testing: Who's Testing Whom?" *Personnel* (May 1989).

Robert J. Nobile, "The Drug-Free Workplace: Act On It!" *Personnel* (February 1990).

George E. Stevens, "Exploding the Myths About Hiring the Handicapped," *Personnel* (December 1986).

William R. Tracey, "Auditing ADA Compliance," *HR Magazine* (October 1994).

Appendix B: How to Avoid Violating the Privacy Rights of Applicants and Employees

Joseph D. Levesque, *People in Organizations: A Guide to Solving Critical Human Resource Problems,* (Sacramento, CA: American Chamber of Commerce Publishers, 1989).

Kurt H. Decker, *A Manager's Guide to Employee Privacy,* (New York, NY: John Wiley & Sons, Inc., 1989).

Alan M. Koral, *Employee Privacy Rights,* (New York, NY: Executive Enterprises, Inc., 1988).

Privacy Rights in the Workplace: When Employer-Employee Rights Collide, (New York, NY: Modern Business Reports, Alexander Hamilton Institute, 1987).

Joseph D. Levesque, "Controlling the Preservation of Employee Privacy Rights," *Proceedings From The 41st ASPA Conference, Boston, MA* (June 1989).

Ted W. Hunter, "Understanding and Managing the Drug Abuse Revolution," *Proceedings From The 41st ASPA Conference, Boston, MA* (June 1989).

Christopher J. Bachler, "Walking the Privacy Tightrope," *Human Resource Executive* (July 1990).

S. R. Mendelson and K. K. Morrison, "The Right to Privacy at the Workplace, Part 2: Testing Applicants for Alcohol and Drug Abuse," *Personnel* (August 1988).

S. R. Mendelson and A. E. Libbin, "The Right to Privacy at the Workplace, Part 3: Employee Alcohol-and-Drug Testing Programs," *Personnel* (September 1988).

A. E. Libbin and J. C. Stevens, "The Right to Privacy at the Workplace, Part 4: Employee Personal Relationships," *Personnel* (October 1988).

Peter A. Veglahn, "Drug Testing That Clears the Arbitration Hurdle," *Personnel Administrator* (February 1989).

Barbara Smith, "Employee-Supported Drug Testing," *Personnel Journal* (October 1988).

David W. Hoyt and others, "Drug Testing in the Workplace—Are Methods Legally Defensible?" *Journal of the American Medical Association*, Vol. 258, No. 4 (1987).

Gary Tidwell, "Searching a Worker on the Job: The Caution Light Is Flashing," *Business Forum* (Summer 1989).

Lawrence E. Dube Jr., "Employment References and the Law," *Personnel Journal* (February 1986).

Donald Harris, "A Matter of Privacy: Managing Personal Data in Company Computers," *Personnel* (February 1987).

George Munchus, "An Update on Smoking: Employee Rights and Employer's Responsibilities," *Personnel* (August 1987).

Gerald P. Panaro, "Minimizing the Danger of Giving References," *Personnel Journal* (August 1988).

Stephen J. Vodanovich and Milano Reyna, "Alternatives to Workplace Testing," *Personnel Administrator* (May 1988).

Robert Stambaugh, "Protecting Employee Data Privacy: The System Challenges for the '90s," *Computers in HR Management* (February 1990).

Allan Hanson, "What Employees Say About Drug Testing," *Personnel* (July 1990).

Janet Deming, "Drug-Free Workplace Is Good Business," *HR Magazine* (April 1990).

"References Are Getting Harder to Get—And Give," *EEO Review* (August 1987).

"Do Employees Have the Right to Smoke?" *Personnel Journal* (April 1988).

Appendix C: A New Threat: Employer Liability for Negligent Hiring

Joseph D. Levesque, *People in Organizations: A Guide to Solving Critical Human Resource Problems*, (Sacramento, CA: American Chamber of Commerce Publisher, 1989).

James A. Branch Jr., *Negligent Hiring Practice Manual*, (New York, NY: John Wiley & Sons, Inc., 1988).

The Guide to Background Investigations, (Tulsa, OK: Source Publications, 1989).

William Connelly, "How to Navigate the River of Legal Liability When Hiring," *Personnel Journal* (March 1986).

Sandra Baley, "The Legalities of Hiring in the 80s," *Personnel Journal* (November 1985).

L. M. Franze and R. M. Gaswirth, "The Manager's Individual Liability in Workplace Litigation and Employment Law Update," *Legal Report*, SHRM (Winter 1989).

George Odiorne and Patrick Henry, "Hiring Ex-Offenders," *Personnel Administrator* (September 1988).

Suzanne H. Cook, "Playing It Safe: How to Avoid Liability for Negligent Hiring," *Personnel* (November 1988).

Tim Chauran, "The Nightmare of Negligent Hiring," *Recruitment Today*, Vol. 2, No. 1 (1989).

Diane Stanton, "Negligent Hiring—The Big New Legal Trap," *Boardroom Reports* (1989).

H. Aubrey Ford and Deborah Holloman, "Employer's Increasing Exposure for Negligent Hiring," *Employment Outlook*, Vol. 1, No. 10 (1989).

Pat Vaccaro, "Negligent Hiring: Precautions," *Human Resource Executive* (March 1988).

John Morehouse, "Negligent Hiring," *ERM Journal*, Vol. 4, No. 1 (Spring 1989).

Mitchell S. Novit, "Employer Liability for Employee Misconduct: Two Common Law Doctrines," *Personnel* (January-February 1982).

J. A. Glover and Roger King, "Traps for the Unwary Employer: How to Avoid Exposure to Negligent Hiring Liability," *Personnel Administrator* (July 1989).

James W. Fenton Jr., "Negligent Hiring/Retention Adds to Human Resource Woes," *Personnel Journal* (April 1990).

"How Employee Selection Devices Can Be Used in a Negligent Hiring Suit," *Personnel Practice Ideas* (September 1987).

"You May Pay for Workers' Crimes," *Nation's Business* (October 1988).

"Employers Can Reduce Risk of Negligent Hiring Liability," *Labor and Employment Law and Preventative Strategies* (November 1988).

Caleb S. Atwood & James M. Neel, "New Lawsuits Expand Employer Liability," *HR Magazine* (October 1990).

Appendix D: What Forms Are Required to Support a Smooth and Orderly Hiring Process

Joseph D. Levesque, *Manual of Personnel Policies, Procedures and Operations* 2/E, (Englewood Cliffs, NJ: Prentice-Hall, Inc., 1993).

Deborah J. Launer, *Modern Personnel Forms*, Rev. Ed., (New York, NY: Warren, Gorham & Lamont, Inc., 1983).

Robert D. Carlson and James F. McHuge, *Handbook of Personnel Administration Forms and Formats*, (Englewood Cliffs, NJ: Prentice-Hall, Inc., 1978).

Joseph Famularo, *Handbook of Personnel Forms, Records and Reports*, (New York, NY: McGraw-Hill, Inc., 1982).

Loretta D. Foxman and Walter L. Polsky, "Select the Right Application Form," *Personnel Journal* (October 1989).

James P. Jolly and James G. Frierson, "Playing It Safe," *Personnel Administrator* (June 1989).

INDEX